Language
Network

Grammar • Writing • Communication

McDougal Littell
A HOUGHTON MIFFLIN COMPANY

ISBN 0-395-96744-9

Acknowledgments: page 682

1 2 3 4 5 6 7 8 9 – WMW – 05 04 03 02 01 00

Language Network

Grammar • Writing • Communication

Grades 6-12

Easy to Use...
even easier to understand.

Language Network's handy format helps teachers and students quickly access key topics and readily find the answers to questions. The result is a language arts text that is remarkably easy to use and lessons that are even easier to understand.

LANGUAGE ARTS MADE EASY

An efficient organization divides the text into four sections that address

- Grammar, Usage, and Mechanics
- Essential Writing Skills
- Writing Workshops
- Communicating in the Information Age

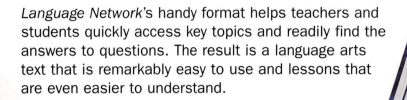

NO INFORMATION OVERLOAD

Concise lessons cover most topics in two or three pages. Concepts are explained clearly in an appealing, relevant style.

LESSON 5 — Elaborating to Visualize

❶ Images

One of the most effective means of elaborating is with **images**, such as sketches, drawings, photographs, maps, and paintings.

Uses of Images You can use images to demonstrate a process, set a mood, tell a story, or present all kinds of visual information such as color, size, proportion, angles, and physical relationships. Images can add a note of humor to your writing.

Sources of Images Look for images in magazines, newspapers, dictionaries, encyclopedias, multimedia resources, and the Internet. Even better, create your own drawings based on any of these sources, or take your own photographs.

❷ Diagrams

Use **diagrams**—such as time lines, flow charts, and labeled drawings—to elaborate informative writing. The diagram below shows the layout of a regulation basketball court.

Restraining circle   Center circle   Free-throw line

LESSON 5 — Subjects in Unusual Positions

❶ Here's the Idea

In most sentences, the subject is placed before the verb. In some sentences, however, the subject appears after the verb, while in others it is not stated at all.

Inverted Sentences

▶ In an inverted sentence, the subject appears after the verb or between the words that make up the verb phrase. An inverted sentence can be used for variety or emphasis. What effect does the inverted order have on the following sentences?

Usual Order:	An 800-pound pumpkin grew in his garden.
Inverted:	In his garden grew an 800-pound pumpkin.
Usual Order:	The neighbors had never seen such a squash!
Inverted:	Never had the neighbors seen such a squash!

Sentences Beginning with *Here* or *There*

... sentence begins with *here* or *there*, the subject ... ws the verb. *Here* and *there* are almost never the ... sentence.

... re and there almost always function as adverbs of ... Expletives. **Adverbs of place** modify verbs by answering ... where? **Expletives** do not have meaning in and of ... These "subject delayers" introduce and draw attention ...

... he World Pumpkin Confederation's official Web page.

... the Web page? The Web page is **here**.

... adverb.

... re growers ... f giant vegetables all over the world.

There does not tell where. It is an expletive.

Questions

▶ In most questions, the subject appears after the verb or between the words that make up the verb phrase.

Subject After Verb:
Was the cabbage large?

Subject Inside Verb Phrase:
Did you see it?

In many questions that begin with whom, what, or how many, the subject falls between the parts of the verb.

How many pounds did the cabbage weigh?

In some questions, however, the interrogative pronoun functions as the subject and comes before the verb.

Who won the contest?

Imperative Sentences

▶ The subject of an imperative sentence is always *you*. Even when not directly stated, you is understood to be the subject.

Request: (You) Please eat your vegetables.
Command: (You) Don't complain!

❷ Why It Matters in Writing

You can vary the tone and emphasis of your sentences with inverted sentences and commands. This is especially useful in creating realistic dialogue and dialects, as in the following example.

LITERARY MODEL

"Quit that," said the woman. "Can't you see you're raising ashes?"

"What harm is ashes?"

"I'll show you what harm," she said, taking down a plate of cabbage and potato from the shelf over the fire. "There's your dinner destroyed with them."

—Mary Lavin, "Brigid"

CHAPTER 2

SENTENCE PARTS

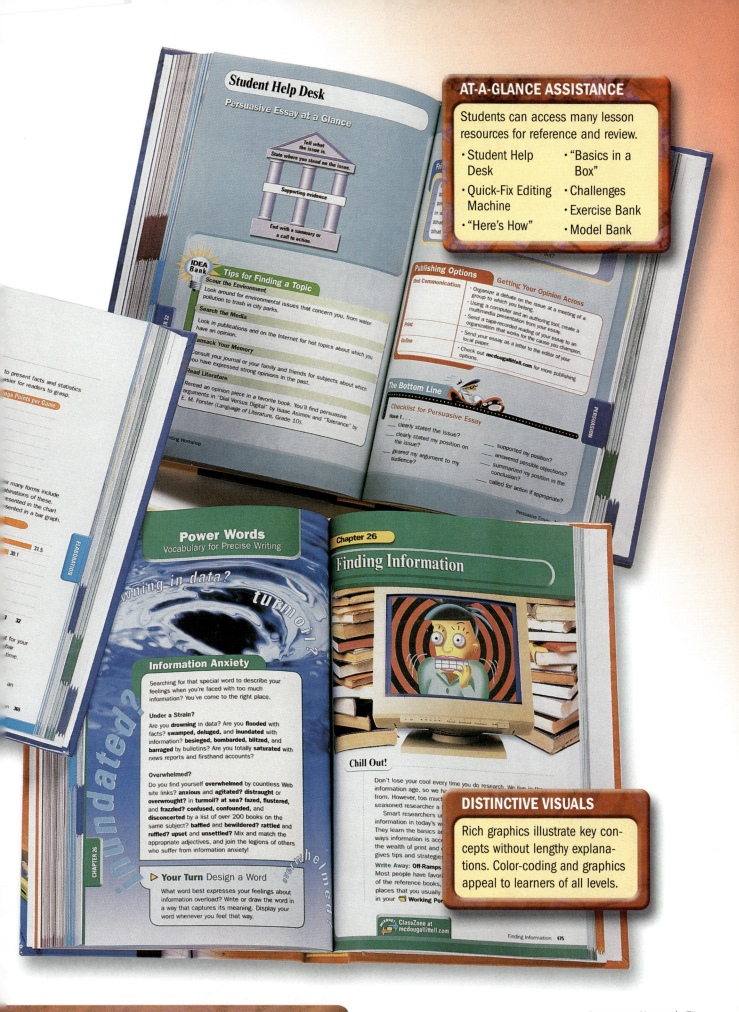

Student Help Desk

Persuasive Essay at a Glance

Tell what the issue is.

State where you stand on the issue.

Supporting evidence

End with a summary or a call to action.

IDEA Bank · Tips for Finding a Topic

Scour the Environment
Look around for environmental issues that concern you, from water pollution to trash in city parks.

Search the Media
Look in publications and on the Internet for hot topics about which you have an opinion.

Ransack Your Memory
Consult your journal or your family and friends for subjects about which you have expressed strong opinions in the past.

Read Literature
Reread an opinion piece in a favorite book. You'll find persuasive arguments in "Dial Versus Digital" by Isaac Asimov and "Tolerance" by E. M. Forster (Language of Literature, Grade 10).

Publishing Options

Getting Your Opinion Across

Oral Communication
· Organize a debate on the issue at a meeting of a group to which you belong.
· Using a computer and an authoring tool, create a multimedia presentation from your essay.

Print
· Send a tape-recorded reading of your essay to an organization that works for the cause you champion.

Online
· Send your essay as a letter to the editor of your local paper.
· Check out mcdougallittell.com for more publishing options.

The Bottom Line

Checklist for Persuasive Essay

Have I . . .
— clearly stated the issue?
— clearly stated my position on the issue?
— geared my argument to my audience?
— supported my position?
— answered possible objections?
— summarized my position in the conclusion?
— called for action if appropriate?

Persuasive Essay

Power Words
Vocabulary for Precise Writing

writing in data? turmoil?

Information Anxiety

Searching for that special word to describe your feelings when you're faced with too much information? You've come to the right place.

Under a Strain?

Are you **drowning** in data? Are you **flooded** with facts? **swamped, deluged,** and **inundated** with information? **besieged, bombarded, blitzed,** and **barraged** by bulletins? Are you totally **saturated** with news reports and firsthand accounts?

Overwhelmed?

Do you find yourself **overwhelmed** by countless Web site links? **anxious** and **agitated**? **distraught** or **overwrought**? in **turmoil**? **at sea**? **fazed, flustered,** and **frazzled**? **confused, confounded,** and **disconcerted** by a list of over 200 books on the same subject? **baffled** and **bewildered**? **rattled** and **ruffled**? **upset** and **unsettled**? Mix and match the appropriate adjectives, and join the legions of others who suffer from information anxiety!

▷ **Your Turn** Design a Word
What word best expresses your feelings about information overload? Write or draw the word in a way that captures its meaning. Display your word whenever you feel that way.

inundated? overwhelmed?

CHAPTER 26

Chapter 26

Finding Information

Chill Out!

Don't lose your cool every time you do research. We live in the information age, so we ha... from. However, too much... seasoned researcher a ...

Smart researchers u... information in today's w... They learn the basics an... ways information is acce... the wealth of print and ... gives tips and strategies...

Write Away: Off-Ramps
Most people have favori... of the reference books,... places that you usually... in your **Working Por...**

INTERNET **ClassZone at** mcdougallittell.com

Finding Information 475

AT-A-GLANCE ASSISTANCE

Students can access many lesson resources for reference and review.

· Student Help Desk
· Quick-Fix Editing Machine
· "Here's How"
· "Basics in a Box"
· Challenges
· Exercise Bank
· Model Bank

DISTINCTIVE VISUALS

Rich graphics illustrate key concepts without lengthy explanations. Color-coding and graphics appeal to learners of all levels.

Designed to help students succeed...

- *with skill development*
- *on assessments*
- *beyond the classroom*

Teaches students information-age skills...

- *analyzing and creating media*
- *communication in a tech-based world*
- *researching electronically and intelligently*

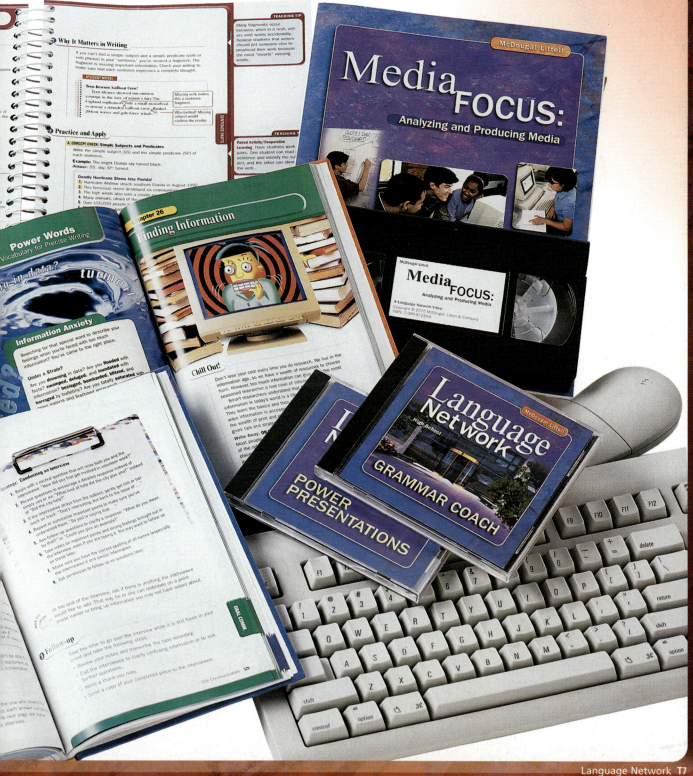

Grammar Lessons...
that connect with students.

Students have a chance to take a look at language from their own point of view, at how grammar fits into their world and why it is important.

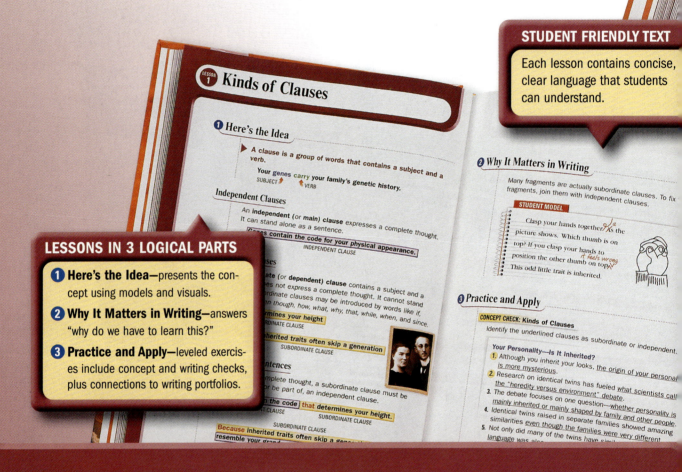

STUDENT FRIENDLY TEXT

Each lesson contains concise, clear language that students can understand.

LESSONS IN 3 LOGICAL PARTS

1 **Here's the Idea**—presents the concept using models and visuals.

2 **Why It Matters in Writing**—answers "why do we have to learn this?"

3 **Practice and Apply**—leveled exercises include concept and writing checks, plus connections to writing portfolios.

Visual Grammar™
Put grammar concepts into action! Color-coded models in the student book are reinforced with grammar tiles for the overhead projector.

Grammar Coach
This interactive and engaging set of diagnostic activities and tutorials teaches students essential grammar concepts as they "work" at a media center or TV studio.

Additional Teaching Resources

- **Grammar, Usage, and Mechanics Workbook**
- **Students Acquiring English/ESL English Grammar Survival Kit**
- **Quick-Fix Grammar and Style Charts (transparencies)**
- **Power Presentations for Grammar**
- **ClassZone: Grammar Quiz**

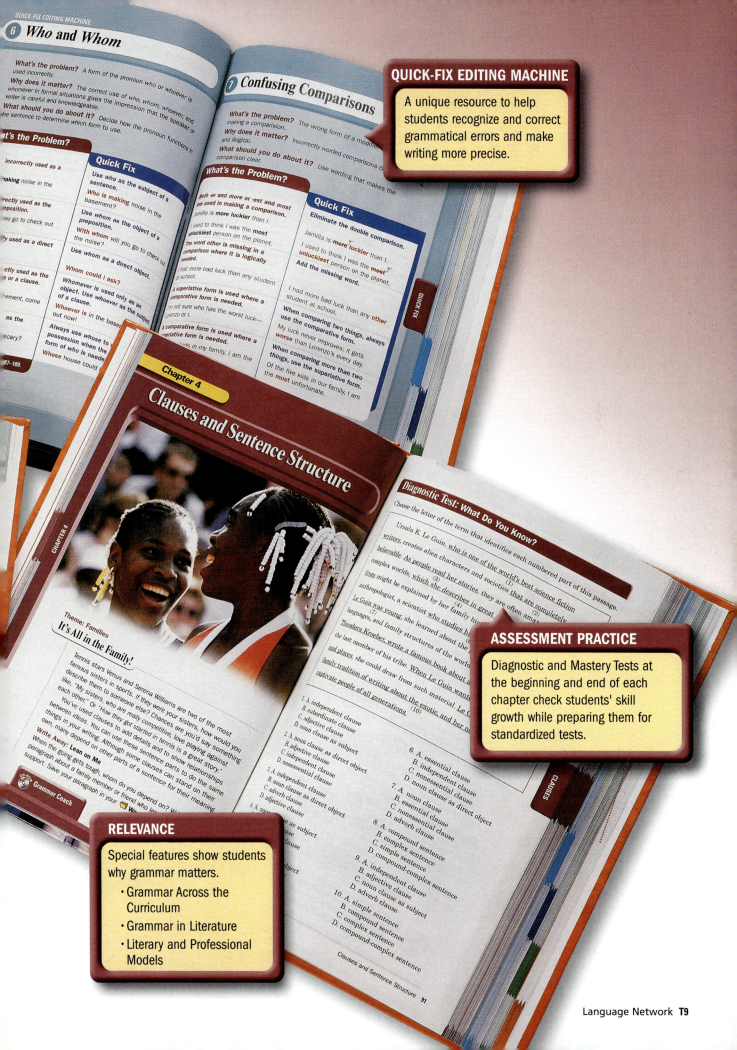

QUICK-FIX EDITING MACHINE

6 Who and Whom

What's the problem? A form of the pronoun who or whoever is used incorrectly.

Why does it matter? The correct use of who, whom, whoever, and whomever in formal situations gives the impression that the speaker or writer is careful and knowledgeable.

What should you do about it? Decide how the pronoun functions in the sentence to determine which form to use.

What's the Problem?

incorrectly used as a

making noise in the

rectly used as the preposition.

you go to check out

ly used as a direct

ctly used as the e or a clause.

ement, come

as the

scary?

87–189.

Quick Fix

Use who as the subject of a sentence.

Who is making noise in the basement?

Use whom as the object of a preposition.

With whom will you go to check out the noise?

Use whom as a direct object.

Whom could I ask?

Whomever is used only as an object. Use whoever as the subject of a clause.

Whoever is in the basement, come out now!

Always use whose to show possession when the form of who is needed.

Whose house could

7 Confusing Comparisons

What's the problem? The wrong form of a modifier making a comparison.

Why does it matter? Incorrectly worded comparisons can and illogical.

What should you do about it? Use wording that makes the comparison clear.

What's the Problem?

Both -er and more or -est and most are used in making a comparison.

Jamilla is more luckier than I.

I used to think I was the most unluckiest person on the planet.

The word other is missing in a comparison where it is logically needed.

I had more bad luck than any student at school.

A superlative form is used where a comparative form is needed.

I'm not sure who has the worst luck— Lorenzo or I.

A comparative form is used where a superlative form is needed.

kids in my family, I am the

Quick Fix

Eliminate the double comparison.

Jamilla is more luckier than I.

I used to think I was the most unluckiest person on the planet.

Add the missing word.

I had more bad luck than any other student at school.

When comparing two things, always use the comparative form.

My luck never improves; it gets worse than Lorenzo's every day.

When comparing more than two things, use the superlative form.

Of the five kids in our family, I am the most unfortunate.

QUICK FIX

QUICK-FIX EDITING MACHINE

A unique resource to help students recognize and correct grammatical errors and make writing more precise.

Chapter 4

CHAPTER 4

Clauses and Sentence Structure

Theme: Families
It's All in the Family!

Tennis stars Venus and Serena Williams are two of the most famous sisters in sports. If they were your sisters, how would you describe them to someone else? Chances are you'd say something like, "My sisters, who are really competitive, love playing against each other." Or "How they got started in tennis is a great story."

You've used clauses to add details and to show relationships between ideas. You can use these sentence parts to do the same things in your writing. Although some clauses can stand on their own, many depend on other parts of a sentence for their meaning.

Write Away: Lean on Me
When the going gets tough, whom do you depend on? W paragraph about a family member or friend who in support. Save your paragraph in your

Grammar Coach

Diagnostic Test: What Do You Know?

Choose the letter of the term that identifies each numbered part of this passage.

Ursula K. Le Guin, who is one of the world's best science fiction writers, creates alien characters and societies that are completely believable. As people read her stories, they are often ama complex worlds, which she describes in great from might be explained by her family hi Le Guin was young, she learned about the languages, and family structures of the worlds anthropologist, a scientist who studies h Theodora Kroeber wrote a famous book about a the last member of his tribe. When Le Guin wante and places, she could draw from such material. Le family tradition of writing about the exotic, and her n captivate people of all generations.

1. A. independent clause
   B. subordinate clause
   C. adjective clause
   D. noun clause as subject

2. A. noun clause as direct object
   B. adjective clause
   C. independent clause
   D. nonessential clause

3. A. independent clause
   B. noun clause as direct object
   C. adverb clause
   D. adjective clause

4. A. noun   e as subject
                   use
          clause

        bject

6. A. essential clause
   B. independent clause
   C. nonessential clause
   D. noun clause as subject

7. A. noun clause as direct object
   B. essential clause
   C. nonessential clause
   D. adverb clause

8. A. compound sentence
   B. complex sentence
   C. simple sentence
   D. compound-complex sentence

9. A. independent clause
   B. adjective clause
   C. noun clause as subject
   D. adverb clause

10. A. simple sentence
    B. compound sentence
    C. complex sentence
    D. compound-complex sentence

Clauses and Sentence Structure 91

ASSESSMENT PRACTICE

Diagnostic and Mastery Tests at the beginning and end of each chapter check students' skill growth while preparing them for standardized tests.

RELEVANCE

Special features show students why grammar matters.
- Grammar Across the Curriculum
- Grammar in Literature
- Literary and Professional Models

The Writing Process...
made simple.

Two entire sections in *Language Network* are devoted to the writing process and to developing and enhancing students' writing skills.

Essential Writing Skills chapters provide students with all the tools they need to grow as writers.

Writing Workshops give them the opportunity to apply what they learn.

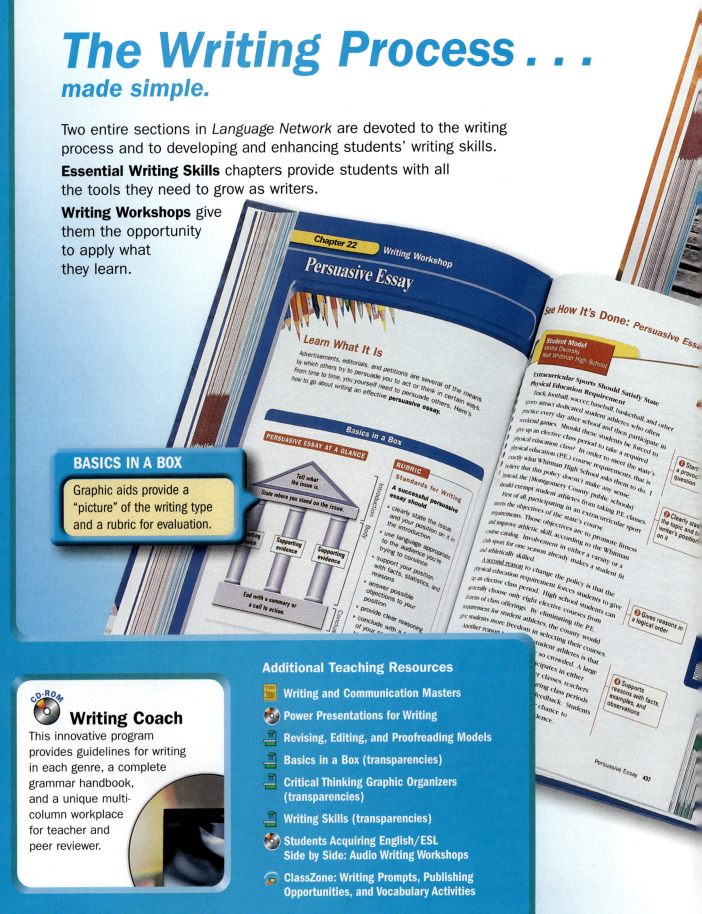

BASICS IN A BOX

Graphic aids provide a "picture" of the writing type and a rubric for evaluation.

Writing Coach

This innovative program provides guidelines for writing in each genre, a complete grammar handbook, and a unique multi-column workplace for teacher and peer reviewer.

Additional Teaching Resources

- **Writing and Communication Masters**
- **Power Presentations for Writing**
- **Revising, Editing, and Proofreading Models**
- **Basics in a Box (transparencies)**
- **Critical Thinking Graphic Organizers (transparencies)**
- **Writing Skills (transparencies)**
- **Students Acquiring English/ESL Side by Side: Audio Writing Workshops**
- **ClassZone: Writing Prompts, Publishing Opportunities, and Vocabulary Activities**

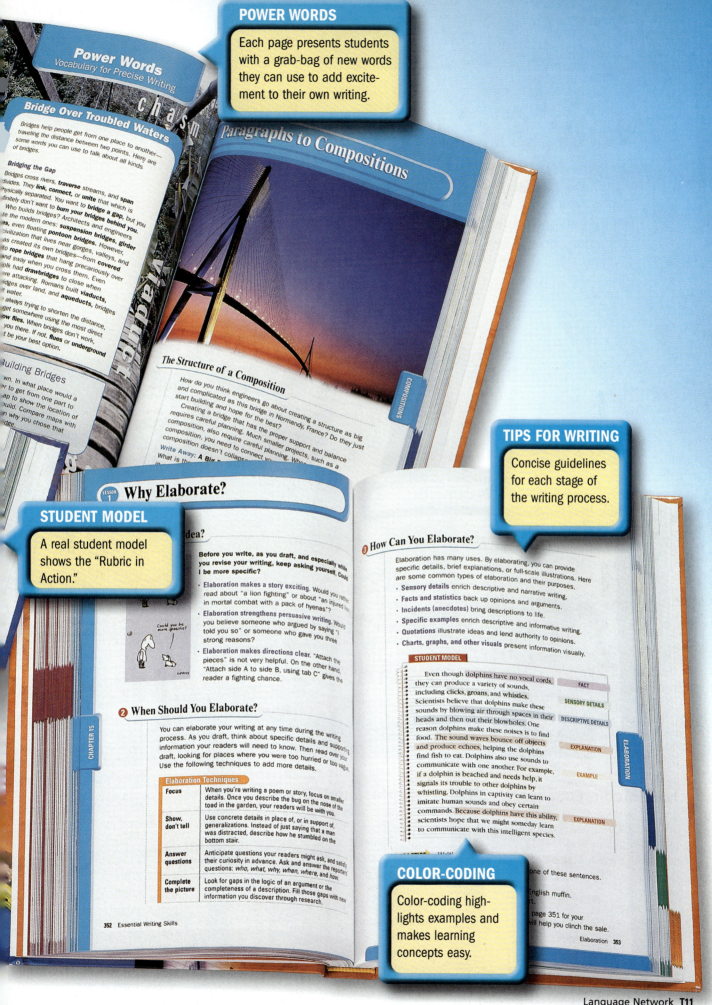

Power Words
Vocabulary for Precise Writing

chasm

Bridge Over Troubled Waters

Bridges help people get from one place to another—traversing the distance between two points. Here are some words you can use to talk about all kinds of bridges.

Bridging the Gap

Bridges cross rivers, **traverse** streams, and **span** divides. They **link**, **connect**, or **unite** that which is physically separated. You want to **bridge a gap**, but you definitely don't want to **burn your bridges behind you.** Who builds bridges? Architects and engineers create the modern ones: **suspension bridges**, **girder** bridges, even floating **pontoon bridges.** However, every civilization that lives near gorges, valleys, and created its own bridges—from covered bridges to **rope bridges** that hang precariously over and sway when you cross them. Even folk had **drawbridges** to close when attacking. Romans built **viaducts**, bridges over land, and **aqueducts**, bridges water.

always trying to shorten the distance, get somewhere using the most direct flies. When bridges don't work, you there. If not, **flues** or **underground** the best option.

Building Bridges

In what place would a to get from one part to to show the location of Compare maps with why you chose that

Paragraphs to Compositions

COMPOSITIONS

The Structure of a Composition

How do you think engineers go about creating a structure as big and complicated as this bridge in Normandy, France? Do they just start building and hope for the best?

Creating a bridge that has the proper support and balance requires careful planning. Much smaller projects, such as a composition, also require careful planning. When composition, you need to connect your composition doesn't collapse

Write Away: A Big
What is the

LESSON 1

Why Elaborate?

idea?

Before you write, as you draft, and especially while you revise your writing, keep asking yourself, Could I be more specific?

- Elaboration makes a story exciting. Would you rather read about "a lion fighting" or about "an injured lion in mortal combat with a pack of hyenas"?
- Elaboration strengthens persuasive writing. Would you believe someone who argued by saying "I told you so" or someone who gave you three strong reasons?
- Elaboration makes directions clear. "Attach the pieces" is not very helpful. On the other hand, "Attach side A to side B, using tab C" gives the reader a fighting chance.

Could you be more specific?

2 When Should You Elaborate?

You can elaborate your writing at any time during the writing process. As you draft, think about specific details and supporting information your readers will need to know. Then read over your draft, looking for places where you were too hurried or too vague. Use the following techniques to add more details.

Elaboration Techniques

Focus	When you're writing a poem or story, focus on smaller details. Once you describe the bug on the nose of the toad in the garden, your readers will be with you.
Show, don't tell	Use concrete details in place of, or in support of, generalizations. Instead of just saying that a man was distracted, describe how he stumbled on the bottom stair.
Answer questions	Anticipate questions your readers might ask, and satisfy their curiosity in advance. Ask and answer the reporters' questions: who, what, why, when, where, and how.
Complete the picture	Look for gaps in the logic of an argument or the completeness of a description. Fill those gaps with new information you discover through research.

CHAPTER 15

352 Essential Writing Skills

3 How Can You Elaborate?

Elaboration has many uses. By elaborating, you can provide specific details, brief explanations, or full-scale illustrations. Here are some common types of elaboration and their purposes.

- **Sensory details** enrich descriptive and narrative writing.
- **Facts and statistics** back up opinions and arguments.
- **Incidents (anecdotes)** bring descriptions to life.
- **Specific examples** enrich descriptive and informative writing.
- **Quotations** illustrate ideas and lend authority to opinions.
- **Charts, graphs, and other visuals** present information visually.

STUDENT MODEL

Even though dolphins have no vocal cords, they can produce a variety of sounds, including clicks, groans, and whistles. Scientists believe that dolphins make these sounds by blowing air through spaces in their heads and then out their blowholes. One reason dolphins make these noises is to find food. The sound waves bounce off objects and produce echoes, helping the dolphins find fish to eat. Dolphins also use sounds to communicate with one another. For example, if a dolphin is beached and needs help, it signals its trouble to other dolphins by whistling. Dolphins in captivity can learn to imitate human sounds and obey certain commands. Because dolphins have this ability, scientists hope that we might someday learn to communicate with this intelligent species.

FACT

SENSORY DETAILS

DESCRIPTIVE DETAILS

EXPLANATION

EXAMPLE

EXPLANATION

ELABORATION

one of these sentences.

English muffin.

page 351 for your
will help you clinch the sale.

Elaboration 353

New Skills. . .
for the Information Age.

Exciting, informative lessons ensure that students will be equipped to work with the challenges of a technology driven, media-centered world.

FINDING INFORMATION

Focused instruction on finding and evaluating information with an emphasis on the internet and electronic sources.

Media Focus

A video, with accompanying sourcebook, teaches students to analyze media and provide them with step-by-step models for creating media products of their own.

Research Zone

Found within ClassZone, this on-line component builds on the research lessons provided in the book and ensures that students have the most up-to-date instruction possible.

Additional Teaching Resources

- **Writing and Communication Masters**
- **Weekly Vocabulary and Spelling**
- **Communications Skills (transparencies)**
- **Media Focus SourceBook**
- **Writing Research Papers Booklet**

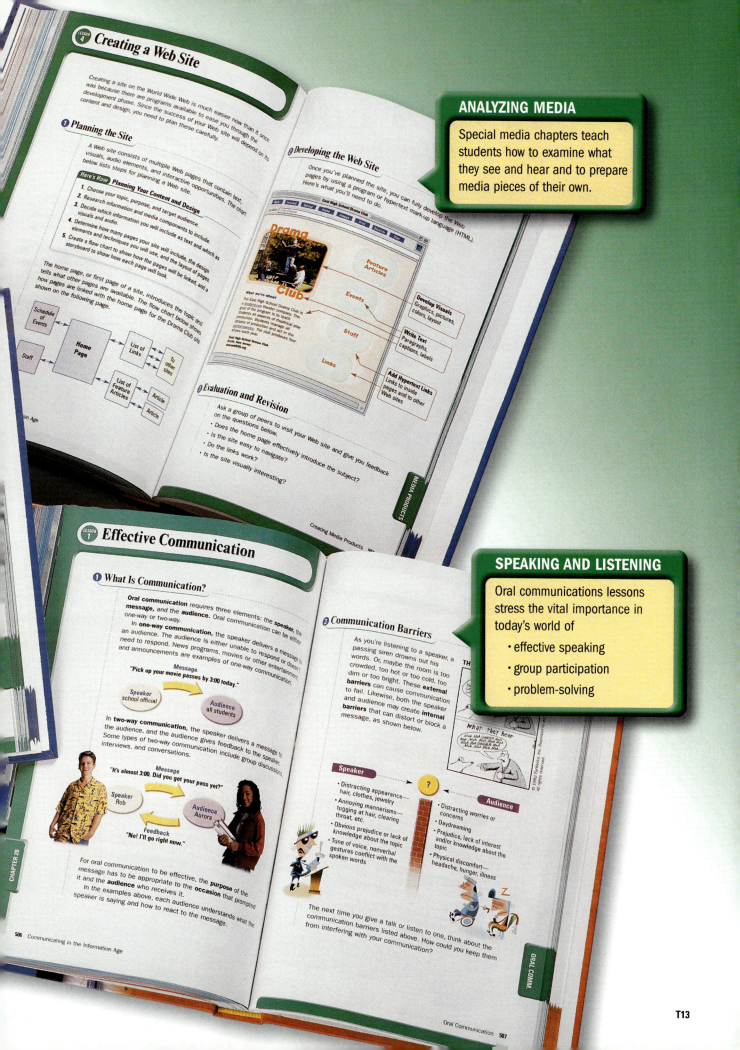

Creating a Web Site

Creating a site on the World Wide Web is much easier now than it once was because there are programs available to ease you through the development phase. Since the success of your Web site will depend on its content and design, you need to plan these carefully.

❶ Planning the Site

A Web site consists of multiple Web pages that contain text, visuals, audio elements, and interactive opportunities. The chart below lists steps for planning a Web site.

Here's How **Planning Your Content and Design**

1. Choose your topic, purpose, and target audience.
2. Research information and media components to include.
3. Decide which information and media components to include as text, visuals and audio.
4. Determine how many pages your site will include and which as elements and techniques you will use, and the layout of pages.
5. Create a flow chart to show how the pages will be linked and a storyboard to show how each page will look.

The home page, or first page of a site, introduces the topic and tells what other pages are available. The flow chart below shows how pages are linked with the home page for the Drama Club site, shown on the following page.

❷ Developing the Web Site

Once you've planned the site, you can fully develop the Web pages by using a program or hypertext mark-up language (HTML). Here's what you'll need to do.

Develop Visuals
Graphics, pictures, colors, layout

Write Text
Paragraphs, captions, labels

Add Hypertext Links
Links to inside pages and to other Web sites

❸ Evaluation and Revision

Ask a group of peers to visit your Web site and give you feedback on the questions below.
- Does the home page effectively introduce the subject?
- Is the site easy to navigate?
- Do the links work?
- Is the site visually interesting?

MEDIA PRODUCTS

Special media chapters teach students how to examine what they see and hear and to prepare media pieces of their own.

Effective Communication

❶ What Is Communication?

Oral communication requires three elements: the **speaker**, the **message**, and the **audience**. Oral communication can be either one-way or two-way.

In **one-way communication**, the speaker delivers a message to an audience. The audience is either unable to respond or doesn't need to respond. News programs, movies or other entertainment, and announcements are examples of one-way communication.

Message
"Pick up your movie passes by 3:00 today."

Speaker
school official

Audience
all students

In **two-way communication**, the speaker delivers a message to the audience, and the audience gives feedback to the speaker. Some types of two-way communication include group discussions, interviews, and conversations.

Message
"It's almost 3:00. Did you get your pass yet?"

Speaker
Rob

Audience
Aurora

Feedback
"No! I'll go right now."

For oral communication to be effective, the **purpose** of the message has to be appropriate to the **occasion** that prompted it and the **audience** who receives it.

In the examples above, each audience understands what the speaker is saying and how to react to the message.

❷ Communication Barriers

As you're listening to a speaker, a passing siren drowns out his words. Or, maybe the room is too crowded, too hot or too cold, too dim or too bright. These **external barriers** can cause communication to fail. Likewise, both the speaker and audience may create **internal barriers** that can distort or block a message, as shown below.

Speaker
- Distracting appearance— hair, clothes, jewelry
- Annoying mannerisms— tugging at hair, clearing throat, etc.
- Obvious prejudice or lack of knowledge about the topic
- Tone of voice, nonverbal gestures conflict with the spoken words

Audience
- Distracting worries or concerns
- Daydreaming
- Prejudice, lack of interest and/or knowledge about the topic
- Physical discomfort— headache, hunger, illness

The next time you give a talk or listen to one, think about the communication barriers listed above. How could you keep them from interfering with your communication?

Oral communications lessons stress the vital importance in today's world of
- effective speaking
- group participation
- problem-solving

CHAPTER 28

ORAL COMM.

A Teacher's Edition...
that gives just enough support at just the right places.

Exciting, informative lessons ensure that students will be equipped to work with the challenges of a technology driven, media-centered world.

DAILY TEST PREPARATION

Test items are provided in the formats of standardized tests. **Teaching Points** provide strategies for arriving at the correct answer.

TEACHING TIPS

Provide information at point-of-use for enhancing instruction.

CUSTOMIZING TIPS

Help you address instructional needs of specific populations.

CHAPTER 2

LESSON OBJECTIVES

To recognize the two parts of a sentence—subject and predicate—and to apply this information in writing

DAILY TEST PREPARATION

Analogies: Vocabulary Write the following item on the board or use ☐ **Daily Test Preparation Transparency** p. DT5.

Choose the lettered pair that *best* expresses a relationship similar to the pair in capital letters.

LAMB : SHEEP ::

A. baby : infant

B. hen : rooster

C. calf : cow

D. gaggle : goose

Teaching Point: For analogies, determine the relationship expressed by the original pair of words (a *LAMB* is a baby *SHEEP*). The correct answer must express the same relationship (a *calf* is a baby *cow*).

TEACHING TIP

Color Coding A color code is used throughout the grammar section to help students understand sentence parts and how they function. In this lesson, blue represents the subject; green indicates the predicate.

CUSTOMIZING TIP

Colorblind Students
Check to see whether students who are colorblind can distinguish between the green and the blue type. Work with them to establish a code they can perceive. For most students, the blue will appear darker than the green.

CHAPTER 2

LESSON 1

Simple Subjects and Pre

❶ Here's the Idea

▸ Every sentence has two basic par a predicate.

The **subject** tells whom or what the The **predicate** tells what the subject to the subject.

Huge cresting waves	pound
SUBJECT	

Hurricane-force winds tear the
The **fragile sailboat is thrown o**

WATCH OUT

Both parts are usually necessary t words to be clear. When a subject group of words is a **sentence frag**

For more on fragments, see p. 116–119.

▸ The basic elements of a senter and the simple predicate.

The **simple subject** is the key wo The **simple predicate** is the verb something about the subject.

Here's How Finding Simple Subj

The violent storm battered th

Simple subjects and simple predi words, phrases, or clauses.

Simple subject Ask who or what is or does something.

What battered the sailboat? **stor**

The violent storm battered

38 Grammar, Usage, and Mechanics

TEACHING RESOURCES

☐ Time-Saver Transparencies Binder:
  • Daily Test Preparation p. DT5
☐ Grammar, Usage, and Mechanics
  Workbook p. 25

SKIL

② Why It Matters in Writing

If you can't find a simple subject and a simple predicate (verb or verb phrase) in your "sentence," you've created a fragment. The fragment is missing important information. Check your writing to make sure that each sentence expresses a complete thought.

STUDENT MODEL

Teen Rescues Sailboat Crew!

Terri Alvarez showed uncommon courage in the face of nature's fury. The Capland sophomore *had* only a small motorboat to rescue a stranded sailboat crew. *He* Battled 20-foot waves and gale-force winds. . . .

> The missing verb makes this a sentence fragment.

> Who battled? The missing subject would confuse the reader.

③ Practice and Apply

A. CONCEPT CHECK: Simple Subjects and Predicates

Write the simple subject and the simple predicate of each sentence.

Example: The bright Florida sky turned black.
Answer: sky; turned.

Deadly Hurricane Slams into Florida!

1. Hurricane Andrew struck southern Florida in August 1992.
2. This ferocious storm destroyed six communities.
3. The high winds also tore a county zoo apart.
4. Many animals, afraid of the wind, cowered in their cages.
5. Over 150,000 people lost their homes or businesses.
6. Many residents had no water, electricity, or shelter.
7. Relief workers distributed food, clothing, and medicine.
8. Midwesterners sent bottled water to the area.
9. Many Florida residents will remember this storm for the rest of their lives!
10. It was the most costly natural disaster in U.S. history.

→ **For a SELF-CHECK and more practice, see the EXERCISE BANK, p. 588.**

ts Parts **39**

SENTENCE PARTS

SENTEN

Coo
Hav
One
ten
and
the

Answers

Print-Out Option You may create worksheets of exercise A for your students by using the ⚡ **Electronic Teacher Tools CD-ROM.**

A. CONCEPT CHECK

Self-Check For a self-check of simple subjects and predicates, direct students to p. 588 of the Pupil's Edition for the answers to the items circled in yellow.

Answers shown on page. Simple subjects are underlined. Simple predicates are double underlined.

THE LANGUAGE OF LITERATURE

The exercises on the student page relate to *The Perfect Storm* in *The Language of Literature,* Level 9.

The Sentence and Its Parts **39**

Teaching with Technology

The Language Network truly is a network! Each tech component ensures that you have the right tool for each aspect of your teaching. And each component, from pupil book to video to CD-ROM, is designed to enhance or complement the others.

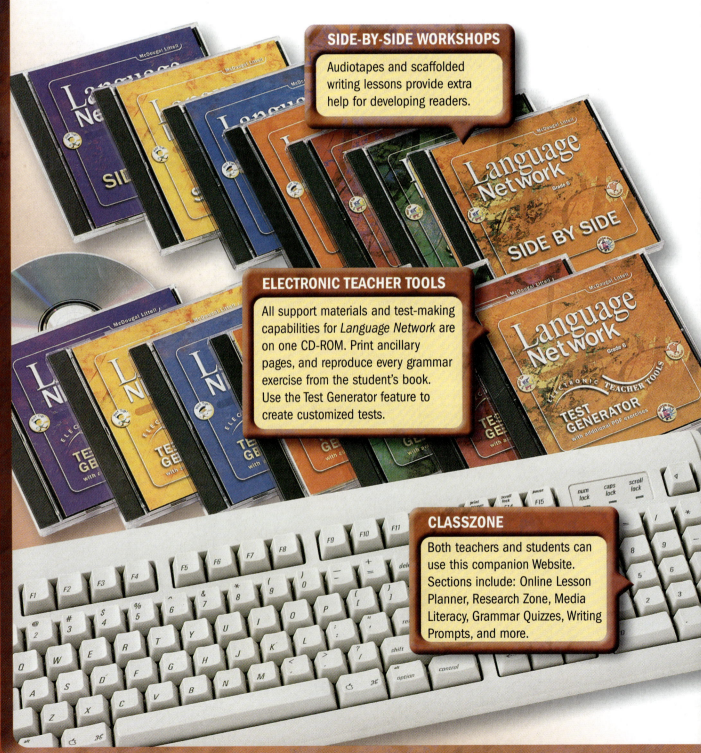

SIDE-BY-SIDE WORKSHOPS

Audiotapes and scaffolded writing lessons provide extra help for developing readers.

ELECTRONIC TEACHER TOOLS

All support materials and test-making capabilities for *Language Network* are on one CD-ROM. Print ancillary pages, and reproduce every grammar exercise from the student's book. Use the Test Generator feature to create customized tests.

CLASSZONE

Both teachers and students can use this companion Website. Sections include: Online Lesson Planner, Research Zone, Media Literacy, Grammar Quizzes, Writing Prompts, and more.

POWER PRESENTATIONS

The printed page comes to life in these animated lecture aids that allow you to present concepts that literally race across the screen!

MEDIA FOCUS

Analyzing and Producing Media
This instructional videotape, with accompanying resource book, helps students evaluate today's media and learn to create their own.

GRAMMAR COACH CD-ROM

This interactive CD-ROM pretests, prescribes, tutors, and post-tests students' mastery of grammar and usage concepts in a very engaging TV studio atmosphere.

WRITING COACH CD-ROM

This interactive, multimedia CD-ROM supports students' writing skills with a unique multi-column workspace.

Ancillary Package

	Print	**Transparencies Binder**
Grammar Support	STUDENT WORKBOOK **Grammar, Usage, and Mechanics Workbook** 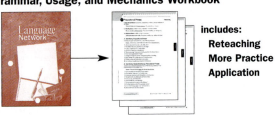 includes: Reteaching More Practice Application	TRANSPARENCIES **Quick-Fix Grammar and Style Charts**  **Visual Grammar™ Instruction Book** 
Writing and Communication Support (Includes Speaking and Listening Support)	COPYMASTERS **Writing and Communication Masters**  includes: Essential Writing Skills Writing Workshops Student Models Communication Skills **Weekly Vocabulary and Spelling** **Writing Research Reports**	TRANSPARENCIES **Quick-Fix Grammar and Style Charts** **Revising, Editing, and Proofreading Models** **Writing and Communication Skills** **Vocabulary and Spelling** **Critical Thinking Graphic Organizers** **Basics in a box**
Test Preparation	COPYMASTERS **Test Preparation** 	TRANSPARENCIES **Daily Test Preparation** 
Teacher Management Tools	COPYMASTERS **Lesson Plans** **Teacher's Edition**  	

Students Acquiring English/ESL

Testing Tools

Technology

COPYMASTERS	**COPYMASTERS**	**TECHNOLOGY TOOLS**

COPYMASTERS

Students Acquiring English/ESL
English Grammar Survival Kit
for grades 6 – 12

Good for Low-Level Readers

COPYMASTERS

Assessment Masters

includes:
Chapter Pretests
Chapter Mid-point Tests
Chapter Mastery Tests

Grammar, Usage, and Mechanics Mastery Tests

TECHNOLOGY TOOLS

Grammar Coach CD-ROM

ClassZone at
mcdougallittell.com
Grammar Quiz

COPYMASTERS

Students Acquiring English/ESL
Side by Side: Audio Writing Workshops

Good for Low-Level Readers

includes:
Writing Prompts
Writing Workshops
  Student Models
Rubrics

TECHNOLOGY TOOLS

 Writing Coach CD-ROM

 ClassZone at
mcdougallittell.com
Writing Prompts
Research Zone
Vocabulary Activities

 Media Focus:
Analyzing and Producing Media

COPYMASTERS

Students Acquiring English/ESL
Test Preparation

Good for Low-Level Readers

TECHNOLOGY TOOLS

 ClassZone at
mcdougallittell.com
Test Practice

PROFESSIONAL RESOURCES

Students Acquiring English/ESL
Teacher's SourceBook for Language Development

COPYMASTERS

Teacher's Guide to Assessment and Portfolio Use

Test Generator CD-ROM

TECHNOLOGY TOOLS

 Power Presentations CD-ROM

 Electronic Teacher Tools CD-ROM

 ClassZone at
mcdougallittell.com
Online Lesson Planner
Professional Articles

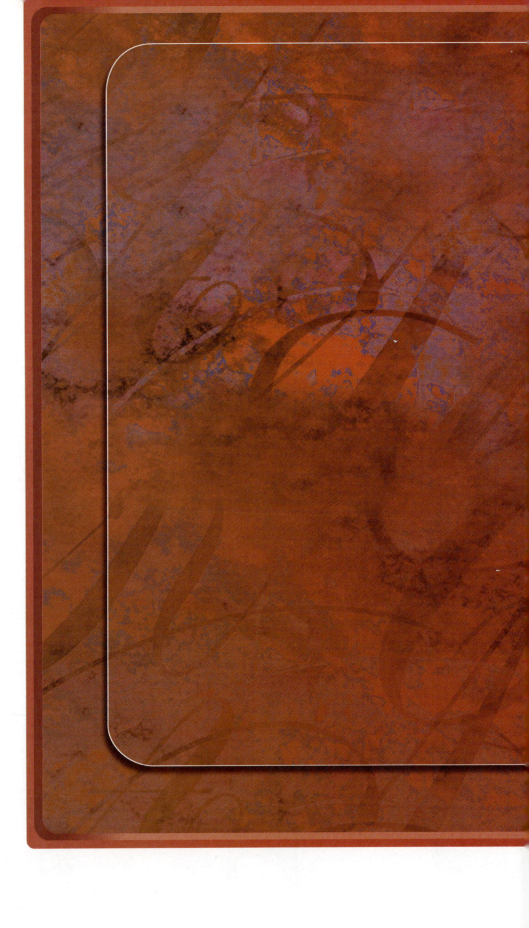

Language
Network

- Grammar, Usage, and Mechanics
- Essential Writing Skills
- Writing Workshops
- Communicating in the Information Age

McDougal Littell
A HOUGHTON MIFFLIN COMPANY

ISBN 0-395-96737-6

Acknowledgments begin on page 682.

1 2 3 4 5 6 7 8 9 – VJM – 05 04 03 02 01 00 99

Teacher Panels

The teacher panels helped guide the conceptual development of *Language Network*. They participated actively in shaping and reviewing prototype materials for the pupil edition, determining ancillary and technology components, and guiding the development of the scope and sequence for the program.

Gloria Anderson, Campbell Junior HIgh School, Houston, TX
Luke Atwood, Park Junior HIgh School, LaGrange, IL
Donna Blackall, Thomas Middle School, Arlington Heights, IL
Karen Bostwick, McLean Middle School, Fort Worth, TX
Rebecca Hadavi, Parkland Middle School, El Paso, TX
Sandi Heffelfinger, Parkland Junior High School, McHenry, IL
Diane Hinojosa, Alamo Middle School, Pharr, TX
Patricia Jackson, Pearce Middle School, Austin, TX
Sue Kazlusky, Lundahl Middle School, Crystal Lake, IL
Tom Kiefer, Cary Junior High School, Cary, IL
Keith Lustig, Hill Middle School, Naperville, IL
Joanna Martin, Haines Middle School, St. Charles, IL
Sandy Mattox, Coppell Middle School, Lewisville, TX
Susan Mortensen, Deer Path Junior High School, Lake Forest, IL
Adrienne Myers, Foster Middle School, Longview, TX
Kathy Powers, Welch Middle School, Houston, TX
Patricia Smith, Tefft Middle School, Streamwood, IL
Frank Westerman, Jackson Middle School, San Antonio, TX
Bessie Wilson, Greiner Middle School, Dallas, TX
Kimberly Zeman, Hauser Junior High School, Riverside, IL

Content Specialists

Dr. Mary Newton Bruder, former Professor of Linguistics at University of Pittsburgh; (creator of the Grammar Hotline Web site)
Rebekah Caplan, High School and Middle Grades English/Language Arts Specialist for the New Standards Project, National Center on Education and the Economy, Washington, D.C.
Dr. Sharon Sicinski Skeans, Assistant Professor, University of Houston–Clear Lake
Richard Vinson, Retired Teacher, Provine High School, Jackson, Mississippi

Technology Consultants

Dr. David Considine, Media Studies Coordinator, Appalachian State University, Boone, NC (author of *Visual Messages: Integrating Imagery into Instruction*)

Heidi Whitus, Teacher, Communication Arts High School, San Antonio, Tex.

Anne Clark, Riverside-Brookfield High School, Riverside, Ill.

Pat Jurgens, Riverside-Brookfield High School, Riverside, Ill.

Ralph Amelio, Former teacher, Willowbrook High School, Villa Park, Ill.

Cindy Lucia, Horace Greeley High School, New York, N.Y.

Aaron Barnhart, Television writer for the *Kansas City Star* and columnist for *Electronic Media,* Kansas City, Mo.

ESL Consultants

Dr. Andrea B. Bermúdez, Professor of Studies in Language and Culture; Director, Research Center for Language and Culture; Chair, Foundations and Professional Studies, University of Houston-Clear Lake, Clear Lake, Tex.

Inara Bundza, ESL Director, Kelvyn Park High School, Chicago, Ill.

Danette Erickson Meyer, Consultant, Illinois Resource Center, Des Plaines, Ill.

John Hilliard, Consultant, Illinois Resource Center, Des Plaines, Ill.

John Kibler, Consultant, Illinois Resource Center, Des Plaines, Ill.

Barbara Kuhns, Camino Real Middle School, Las Cruces, N.M.

Teacher Reviewers

Gloria Anderson, Campbell Junior High School, Houston, TX

Patricia Jackson, Pearce Middle School, Austin, TX

Sandy Mattox, Coppell Middle School, Lewisville, TX

Adrienne Myers, Foster Middle School, Longview, TX

Frank Westerman, Jackson Middle School, San Antonio, TX

Bessie Wilson, Greiner Middle School, Dallas, TX

Student Reviewers

Saba Abraham, Chelsea High School

Julie Allred, Southwest High School

Nabiha Azam, East Kentwood High School

Dana Baccino, Downington High School

Christianne Balsamo, Nottingham High School

Luke Bohline, Lakeville High School

Nathan Buechel, Providence Senior High School

Melissa Cummings, Highline High School

Megan Dawson, Southview Senior High School

Michelle DeBruce, Jurupa High School

Brian Deeds, Arvada West High School

Ranika Fizer, Jones High School

Ashleigh Goldberg, Parkdale High School

Jacqueline Grullon, Christopher Columbus High School

Dimmy Herard, Hialeah High School

Sean Horan, Round Rock High School

Bob Howard, Jr., Robert E. Lee High School

Rebecca Iden, Willowbrook High School
Agha's Igbinovia, Florin High School
Megan Jones, Dobson High School
Ed Kampelman, Parkway West High School
David Knapp, Delmar High School
Eva Lima, Westmoor High School
Ashley Miers, Ouachita High School
Raul Morffi, Shawnee Mission West High School
Sakenia Mosley, Sandalwood High School
Sergio Perez, Sunset High School
Jackie Peters, Westerville South High School
Kevin Robischaud, Waltham High School
Orlando Sanchez, West Mesa High School
Selene Sanchez, San Diego High School
Sharon Schaefer, East Aurora High School
Mica Semrick, Hoover High School
Julio Sequeira, Belmont High School
Camille Singleton, Cerritos High School
Solomon Stevenson, Ozen High School
Tim Villegas, Dos Pueblos High School
Shane Wagner, Waukesha West High School
Swenikqua Walker, San Bernardino High School
Douglas Weakly, Ray High School
Lauren Zoric, Norwin High School

Student Writers

Elizabeth Albertson, Chute Middle School
Britney Chilcote, Fort Morgan Middle School
Joe Clark, Springfield Junior High
Kate Frasca, John Jay Middle School
Rachel Smith, King Philip Middle School
Andy Sturgeon, Thomas Middle School
Aaron Vinson, Northbrook Junior HIgh
Dan Walsh, Hauser Junior High
Caroline Watkins, Lake Forest Country Day School

Contents Overview

Grammar, Usage, and Mechanics

Essential Writing Skills

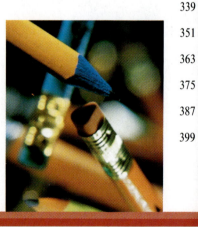

Writing Workshops: Writing for Different Purposes

Communicating in the Information Age

Student Resources

Grammar, Usage, and Mechanics

The Sentence at a Glance

    Subjects and Predicates *Bricks and Mortar*

    Complements *Finishing the Job*

    Kinds of Sentences *Adding Interest*

    The Bottom Line *Checklist for Editing Sentences*

xiii

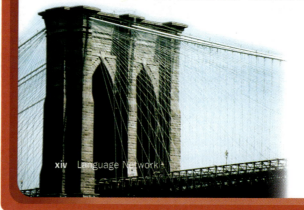

Seat 1379
July 30   2:30 P.M.
Congress Center
The Opening Ceremonies

xv

Quick-Fix Editing Machine

Essential Writing Skills

14 Building Paragraphs

Table of Contents **xxi**

Writing Workshops

Communicating in the Information Age

Special Features

Grammar Across the Curriculum

Grammar in Literature

Power Words: Vocabulary for Precise Writing

Quick-Fix Editing Machine

Student Resources

Table of Contents   **1**

Grammar, Usage, and Mechanics

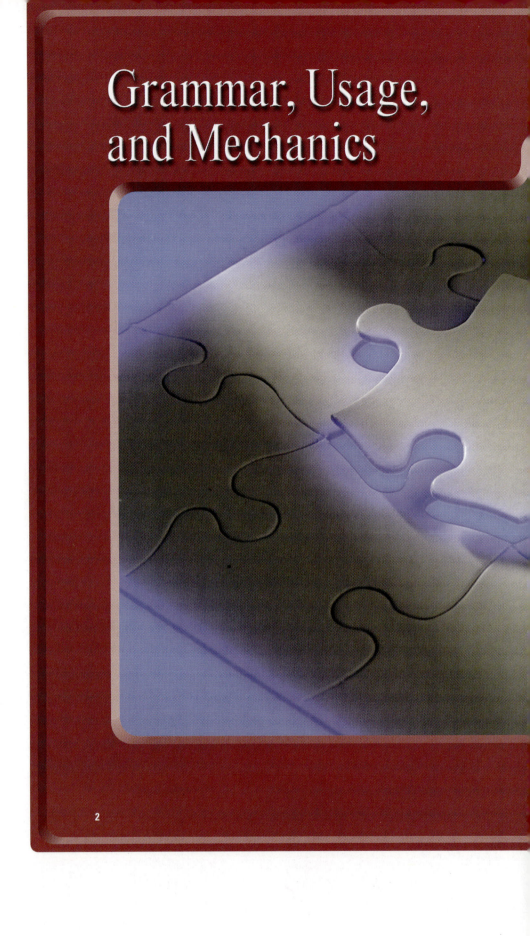

2

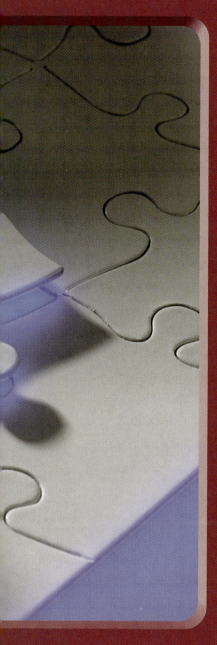

Putting the Pieces Together

When the pieces of a puzzle come together correctly, they form a clear picture. When words come together correctly, they form a clear message. By following the rules of grammar, you can be sure you've put it all together the right way.

3

Chapter 1 The Sentence and Its Parts

Use the online lesson planner at mcdougallittell.com to customize instruction.

Pupil's Edition

Pupil's Edition	Print Resources — Grammar, Usage, and Mechanics Workbook	Time-Saver Transparencies Binder — Daily Test Preparation	Quick-Fix Grammar and Style Chart	Visual Grammar Tiles	Integrated Technology and Media — Electronic Teacher Tools	Power Presentations	Grammar Coach CD ROM	Students Acquiring English/ESL — English Grammar Survival Kit
LESSON 1 Complete Subjects and Predicates pp. 6-7 **Exercise Bank** p. 584	pp. 1-3	p. DT 1			Concept Check			
LESSON 2 Simple Subjects pp. 8-9 **Exercise Bank** p. 584	pp. 4-6	p. DT 1			A. Concept Check		Lesson 1	
LESSON 3 Simple Predicates, or Verbs pp. 10-11 **Exercise Bank** p. 585	pp. 7-9	p. DT 2			A. Concept Check		Lesson 1	
LESSON 4 Verb Phrases pp. 12-13 **Exercise Bank** p. 585	pp. 10-12	p. DT 2			Concept Check		Lesson 1	pp. 25-28
LESSON 5 Compound Sentence Parts pp. 14-15 **Exercise Bank** p. 586	pp. 13-15	p. DT 3		Lessons 1-2	A. Concept Check B. Revising			
LESSON 6 Kinds of Sentences pp. 16-17 **Exercise Bank** p. 586	pp. 16-18	p. DT 3			A. Concept Check			
LESSON 7 Subjects in Unusual Order pp. 18-20 **Exercise Bank** p. 586	pp. 19-21	p. DT 4		Lessons 3-5	A. Concept Check B. Revising			pp. 39-40
LESSON 8 Complements: Subject Complements pp. 21-22 **Exercise Bank** p. 587	pp. 22-24	p. DT 4		Lesson 6	A.Concept Check B. Revising			
LESSON 9 Complements: Objects of Verbs p. 23-24 **Exercise Bank** p. 587	pp. 25-27	p. DT 5			Concept Check			
LESSON 10 Fragments and Run-ons pp. 25-27 **Exercise Bank** p. 588	pp. 28-30	p. DT 5	pp. QF 1-2		A. Concept Check B. Revising	Lesson 1		

ASSESSMENT

Pupil's Edition	Assessment Masters	Test Generator CD-ROM	mcdougallittell.com
Diagnostic Test p. 5 Mastery Test p. 31	Chapter Pretest pp. 2-3 Chapter Mid-Point Test p. 24 Chapter Mastery Tests pp.35-42	Test Generator Chapter 1	Grammar Chapter Quiz

INTEGRATING WRITING AND LITERATURE

Writing Activities

Paragraph about home p. 4

Sentences about young animals p. 9

Sentences that describe soil p. 11

Combining sentences p. 15

Dialogue based on a cartoon p. 17

Rewrite sentences for variety p. 20

Revise to correct fragments and run-ons p. 27

Description of ideal room or home p. 29

Literary Models

*"A Christmas Carol" p. 16

*"Thank you M'am" p. 24

*"Homeless" p. 28

* from *McDougal Littell Language of Literature*

RESOURCE MANAGEMENT GUIDE

Chapter 2 Nouns

INTERNET Use the online lesson planner at mcdougallittell.com to customize instruction.

Pupil's Edition	Print Resources — Grammar, Usage, and Mechanics Workbook	Time-Saver Transparencies Binder — Daily Test Preparation	Integrated Technology and Media — Electronic Teacher Tools	Students Acquiring English/ESL — English Grammar Survival Kit
LESSON 1 Kinds of Nouns pp. 36-38 **Exercise Bank** p. 588	pp. 31-33	p. DT 6	A. Concept Check	pp. 1-2
LESSON 2 Singular and Plural Nouns pp. 39-41 **Exercise Bank** p. 589	pp. 34-36	p. DT 6	A. Concept Check B. Proofreading	
LESSON 3 Possessive Nouns pp. 42-43 **Exercise Bank** p. 589	pp. 37-39	p. DT 7	A. Concept Check B. Revising	
LESSON 4 Compound Nouns pp. 45-46 **Exercise Bank** p. 590	pp. 40-42	p. DT 7	A. Concept Check B. Revising	
LESSON 5 Nouns and Their Jobs pp. 47-49 **Exercise Bank** p. 591	pp. 43-45	p. DT 8	A. Concept Check B. Revising	

ASSESSMENT

Pupil's Edition	Assessment Masters	Test Generator CD-ROM	mcdougallittell.com
Diagnostic Test p. 35 Mastery Test p. 53	Chapter Pretest pp. 4-5 Chapter Mid-Point Test p. 25 Chapter Mastery Tests pp. 43-46	Test Generator Chapter 2	Grammar Chapter Quiz

INTEGRATING WRITING AND LITERATURE

Writing Activities

Design a landmark p. 34

A humorous dialogue p. 38

Use data to compare bridges p. 41

Directions for a tour p. 49

Draw a map and use nouns for labels p. 51

Literary Model

Immigrant Kids p. 40

* from *McDougal Littell Language of Literature*

Chapter 3 Pronouns

Use the online lesson planner at mcdougallittell.com to customize instruction.

Pupil's Edition	Grammar, Usage, and Mechanics Workbook	Daily Test Preparation	Quick-Fix Grammar and Style Charts	Visual Grammar Tiles	Electronic Teacher Tools	Grammar Coach CD-ROM	Power Presentations	English Grammar Survival Kit
LESSON 1 **What Is a Pronoun?** pp. 58-60 **Exercise Bank** p. 591	pp. 46-48	p. DT 8			A. Concept Check B. Revising	Lesson 8	Lesson 4	
LESSON 2 **Subject Pronouns** pp. 61-62 **Exercise Bank** p. 592	pp. 49-51	p. DT 9	p. QF 6		A. Concept Check	Lesson 9		pp. 5-6
LESSON 3 **Object Pronouns** pp. 63-64 **Exercise Bank** p. 592	pp. 52-54	p. DT 9	p. QF 10		Mixed Review	Lesson 9		pp. 7-8
LESSON 4 **Possessive Pronouns** pp. 65-67 **Exercise Bank** p. 593	pp. 55-57	p. DT 10			A. Concept Check B. Proofreading	Lesson 10		
LESSON 5 **Reflexive and Intensive Pronouns** pp. 68-69 **Exercise Bank** p. 593	pp. 58-60	p. DT 10			Concept Check			
LESSON 6 **Interrogatives and Demonstratives** pp. 70-72 **Exercise Bank** p. 594	pp. 61-63	p. DT 11	p. QF 7	Lesson 7	A. Concept Check	Lesson 10		
LESSON 7 **Pronoun Agreement** pp. 73-75 **Exercise Bank** p. 594	pp. 64-66	p. DT 11	p. QF 5		Concept Check	Lessons 7-8	Lesson 4	
LESSON 8 **Indefinite-Pronoun Agreement** pp. 76-78 **Exercise Bank** p. 595	pp. 67-69	p. DT 12	p. QF 5		A. Concept Check B. Proofreading			
LESSON 9 **Pronoun Problems** pp. 79-80 **Exercise Bank** p. 596	pp. 70-72	p. DT 12	pp. QF 5, 6		A. Concept Check B. Revising	Lesson 8		
LESSON 10 **More Pronoun Problems** pp. 81-83 **Exercise Bank** p. 596	pp. 73-75	p. DT 13	pp. QF 5, 6		A. Concept Check B. Proofreading	Lessons 7-8		

ASSESSMENT

Pupil's Edition	Assessment Masters	Test Generator CD-ROM	mcdougallittell.com
Diagnostic Test p. 57 Mastery Test p. 87	Chapter Pretest pp. 6-7 Chapter Mid-Point Test p. 26 Chapter Mastery Tests pp. 47-54	Test Generator Chapter 3	Grammar Chapter Quiz

INTEGRATING WRITING AND LITERATURE

Writing Activities

Description of a mystery p. 56

Write a dialogue p. 60

Use demonstrative pronouns to write sentences p. 72

Use a map to write an explanatory paragraph p. 83

Write a dialogue p. 85

Literary Models

*"The Scholarship Jacket" p. 59

*"A Retrieved Reformation" p. 84

*"Waiting" p. 86

* from McDougal Littell *Language of Literature*

Chapter 4 Verbs

Use the online lesson planner at mcdougallittell.com to customize instruction.

Pupil's Edition

	Print Resources	Time-Saver Transparencies Binder			Integrated Technology and Media			Students Acquiring English/ESL
	Grammar, Usage, and Mechanics Workbook	Daily Test Preparation	Quick-Fix Grammar and Style Charts	Visual Grammar Tiles	Electronic Teacher Tools	Grammar Coach CD-ROM	Power Presentations	English Grammar Survival Kit
LESSON 1 What Is a Verb? pp. 92-94 **Exercise Bank** p. 597	pp. 76-78	p. DT 13	p. QF 9		A. Concept Check B. Writing			
LESSON 2 Action Verbs and Objects pp. 95-97 **Exercise Bank** p. 597	pp. 79-81	p. DT 14			A. Concept Check B. Revising			
LESSON 3 Linking Verbs and Predicate Words pp. 98-99 **Exercise Bank** p. 598	pp. 82-84	p. DT 14			Concept Check			
LESSON 4 Principal Parts of Verbs pp. 100-101 **Exercise Bank** p. 598	pp. 85-87	p. DT 15			Concept Check	Lesson 6	Lesson 2	
LESSON 5 Irregular Verbs pp. 102-104 **Exercise Bank** p. 599	pp. 88-90	p. DT 15			Concept Check	Lesson 6		pp. 33-34, 51-53
LESSON 6 Simple Tenses pp. 105-107 **Exercise Bank** p. 599	pp. 91-93	p. DT 16			A. Concept Check B. Revising	Lesson 6	Lesson 2	pp. 23-24, 25-26, 29-30, 31-32, 35-36, 54-55
LESSON 7 Perfect Tenses pp. 108-110 **Exercise Bank** p. 600	pp. 94-96	p. DT 16	p. QF 9		A. Concept Check B. Writing	Lesson 6	Lesson 2	pp. 27-28, 35-36, 54-55
LESSON 8 Using Verb Tenses pp. 111-114 **Exercise Bank** p. 600	pp. 97-99	p. DT 17	p. QF 9	Lesson 8	A. Concept Check B. Editing	Lesson 6	Lesson 2	
LESSON 9 Troublesome Verb Pairs pp. 115-117 **Exercise Bank** p. 601	pp. 100-102	p. DT 17			A. Concept Check B. Proofreading			

ASSESSMENT

Pupil's Edition	Assessment Masters	Test Generator CD-ROM	mcdougallittell.com
Diagnostic Test p. 91 Mastery Test p. 111	Chapter Pretest pp. 8-9 Chapter Mid-Point Test p. 27 Chapter Mastery Tests pp. 55-60	Test Generator Chapter 4	Grammar Chapter Quiz

INTEGRATING WRITING AND LITERATURE

Writing Activities

Use more specific verbs p. 94

Revise a paragraph to correct tense use p. 107

Rewrite a paragraph to correct tense use p. 110

Use tense as clue to reorganize a paragraph p. 114

Write a scene for a drama p. 119

Use a picture to write sentences p. 120

Literary Model

*"Talking with Ray Bradbury" p. 96

* from McDougal Littell Language of Literature

RESOURCE MANAGEMENT GUIDE

Chapter 5 Adjectives and Adverbs

Use the online lesson planner at mcdougallittell.com to customize instruction.

Pupil's Edition	Print Resources — Grammar, Usage, and Mechanics Workbook	Time-Saver Transparencies Binder — Daily Test Preparation	Time-Saver Transparencies Binder — Quick-Fix Grammar and Style Charts	Integrated Technology and Media — Electronic Teacher Tools	Integrated Technology and Media — Grammar Coach CD-ROM	Students Acquiring English/ESL — English Grammar Survival Kit
LESSON 1 — **What Is an Adjective?** pp. 126-127 **Exercise Bank** p. 602	pp. 103-105	p. DT 18		Concept Check		pp. 3-4, 9-10
LESSON 2 — **Predicate Adjectives** pp. 129-130 **Exercise Bank** p. 602	pp. 106-108	p. DT 18		A. Concept Check		
LESSON 3 — **Other Words Used as Adjectives** pp. 131-133 **Exercise Bank** p. 603	pp. 109-111	p. DT 19		A. Concept Check B. Revising		
LESSON 4 — **What is an Adverb?** pp. 134-136 **Exercise Bank** p. 603	pp. 112-114	p. DT 19		A. Concept Check B. Writing		
LESSON 5 — **Making Comparisons** pp. 137-139 **Exercise Bank** p. 604	pp. 115-117	p. DT 20	p. QF 8	A. Concept Check	Lesson 11	pp. 13-14, 15-16
LESSON 6 — **Adjective or Adverb?** pp. 140-141 **Exercise Bank** p. 604	pp. 118-120	p. DT 20		Concept Check		pp. 11-12
LESSON 7 — **Avoiding Double Negatives** pp. 142-143 **Exercise Bank** p. 605	pp. 121-123	p. DT 21		A. Concept Check B. Proofreading		

ASSESSMENT

Pupil's Edition	Assessment Masters	Test Generator CD-ROM	mcdougallittell.com
Diagnostic Test p. 125 Mastery Test p. 147	Chapter Pretest pp. 10-11 Chapter Mid-Point Test p. 28 Chapter Mastery Tests pp. 61-66	Test Generator Chapter 5	Grammar Chapter Quiz

INTEGRATING WRITING AND LITERATURE

Writing Activities

Description of aircraft in picture p. 124

Write riddles using predicate adjectives p. 130

Use nouns as adjectives p. 133

Revise a paragraph to add adverbs p. 136

Use comparative and superlative forms p. 139

Write a scene with two people in the rain p. 145

Literary Models

*Dragonwings p. 129

*"The Eternal Frontier" p. 132

*"The White Umbrella" p. 144

* from *McDougal Littell Language of Literature*

RESOURCE MANAGEMENT GUIDE

Chapter 6 Prepositions, Conjunctions, Interjections

Use the online lesson planner at **mcdougallittell.com** to customize instruction.

Pupil's Edition	Print Resources — Grammar, Usage, and Mechanics Workbook	Time-Saver Transparencies Binder — Daily Test Preparation	Time-Saver Transparencies Binder — Visual Grammar Tiles	Integrated Technology and Media — Electronic Teacher Tools	Integrated Technology and Media — Grammar Coach CD-ROM	Students Acquiring English/ESL — English Grammar Survival Kit
LESSON 1 — **What Is a Preposition?** pp. 152-154 **Exercise Bank** p. 606	pp. 124-126	p. DT 21		Concept Check		pp. 17-18
LESSON 2 — **Using Prepositional Phrases** pp. 155-157 **Exercise Bank** p. 606	pp. 127-129	p. DT 22	Lessons 9-10	A. Concept Check	Lesson 12	pp. 19-20, 21-22
LESSON 3 — **Conjunctions** pp. 158-160 **Exercise Bank** p. 606	pp. 130-132	p. DT 22		A. Concept Check B. Revising		
LESSON 4 — **Interjections** pp. 161	pp. 133-135	p. DT 23				

ASSESSMENT

Pupil's Edition	Assessment Masters	Test Generator CD-ROM	mcdougallittell.com
Diagnostic Test p. 151	Chapter Pretest pp. 12-13	Test Generator Chapter 6	Grammar Chapter Quiz
Mastery Test p. 165	Chapter Mid-Point Test p. 29		
	Chapter Mastery Tests pp. 67-70		

INTEGRATING WRITING AND LITERATURE

Writing Activities

Paragraph about bugs p. 150

Detailed description of a spider p. 157

Revise a paragraph p. 160

Write a caption p. 161

Summary of observations p. 163

Literary Model

* "Ant and Grasshopper" p. 154

* from *McDougal Littell Language of Literature*

Chapter 7 Verbs and Verbal Phrases

Use the online lesson planner at **mcdougallittell.com** to customize instruction.

Pupil's Edition	Print Resources — Grammar, Usage, and Mechanics Workbook	Time-Saver Transparencies Binder — Daily Test Preparation	Integrated Technology and Media — Electronic Teacher Tools	Grammar Coach CD-ROM
LESSON 1 Gerunds pp. 170-171 Exercise Bank p. 607	pp. 136-138	p. DT 23	A. Concept Check	
LESSON 2 Participles pp. 172-173 Exercise Bank p. 607	pp. 139-141	p. DT 24	Concept Check	Lesson 12
LESSON 3 Infinitives pp. 174-175 Exercise Bank p. 608	pp. 142-144	p. DT 24	A. Concept Check B. Revising	
LESSON 4 Verbal Phrases pp. 176-177 Exercise Bank p. 608	pp. 145-147	p. DT 25	A. Concept Check	

Pupil's Edition	Assessment Masters	Test Generator CD-ROM	mcdougallittell.com
Diagnostic Test p. 169	Chapter Pretest pp. 14-15	Test Generator Chapter 7	Grammar Chapter Quiz
Mastery Test p. 181	Chapter Mid-Point Test p. 30		
	Chapter Mastery Tests pp. 71-74		

INTEGRATING WRITING AND LITERATURE

Writing Activities

A paragraph about an animal p. 168

Use gerunds to list daily activities p. 170

Use infinitives to revise a paragraph p. 174

An action story about animals p. 179

Literary Models

*"Dirk the Protector" p. 173

*"Rikki-Tikki-Tavi" p. 178

* from *McDougal Littell Language of Literature*

RESOURCE MANAGEMENT GUIDE

Chapter 8 Sentence Structure

Use the online lesson planner at **mcdougallittell.com** to customize instruction.

Pupil's Edition	Print Resources Grammar, Usage, and Mechanics Workbook	Time-Saver Transparencies Binder Visual Grammar Tiles	Time-Saver Transparencies Binder Daily Test Preparation	Integrated Technology and Media Electronic Teacher Tools
LESSON 1 **What is a Clause?** p. 186-188 **Exercise Bank** p. 609	pp. 148-150		p. DT 25	A. Concept Check B. Editing
LESSON 2 **Simple and Compound Sentences** pp. 189-191 **Exercise Bank** p. 610	pp. 151-153	Lesson 11	p. DT 26	A. Concept Check B. Revising
LESSON 3 **Complex Sentences** pp. 192-193 **Exercise Bank** p. 610	pp. 154-156	Lesson 11	p. DT 26	A. Concept Check B. Revising
LESSON 4 **Kinds of Dependent Clauses** pp. 194-197 **Exercise Bank** p. 611	pp. 157-159	Lessons 12-13	p. DT 27	A. Concept Check B. Writing
LESSON 5 **Compound-Complex Sentences** pp. 198-199 **Exercise Bank** p. 611	pp. 160-162	Lesson 11	p. DT 27	A. Concept Check B. Writing

ASSESSMENT

Pupil's Edition	Assessment Masters	Test Generator CD-ROM	mcdougallittell.com
Diagnostic Test p. 185	Chapter Pretest pp. 16-17	Test Generator Chapter 8	Grammar Chapter Quiz
Mastery Test p. 203	Chapter Mid-Point Test p. 31		
	Chapter Mastery Tests pp. 75-78		

INTEGRATING WRITING AND LITERATURE

Writing Activities

Write about someone that helped p. 184

Write a caption describing volunteers p. 188

Expand sentences by adding clauses p. 197

Combine sentences p. 199

Combine clauses to eliminate fragments p. 202

Literary Models

*"A Crush" p. 196

*"The Serial Garden" p. 198

*"Eleanor Roosevelt" p. 200

from McDougal Littell Language of Literature

RESOURCE MANAGEMENT GUIDE

Chapter 9 Subject-Verb Agreement

Use the online lesson planner at **mcdougallittell.com** to customize instruction.

Pupil's Edition	Print Resources — Grammar, Usage, and Mechanics Workbook	Time-Saver Transparencies Binder — Daily Test Preparation	Time-Saver Transparencies Binder — Quick-Fix Grammar and Style Charts	Time-Saver Transparencies Binder — Visual Grammar Tiles	Integrated Technology and Media — Electronic Teacher Tools	Integrated Technology and Media — Grammar Coach CD-ROM	Integrated Technology and Media — Power Presentations
LESSON 1 **Agreement in Number** pp. 208-210 **Exercise Bank** p. 612	pp. 163-165	p. DT 28	p. QF 3		A. Concept Check B. Writing	Lesson 5	Lesson 3
LESSON 2 **Compound Subjects** pp. 211-212 **Exercise Bank** p. 613	pp. 166-168	p. DT 28	p. QF 3	Lesson 14	A. Concept Check B. Revising	Lesson 4	
LESSON 3 **Agreement Problems in Sentences** pp. 213-215 **Exercise Bank** p. 613	pp. 169-171	p. DT 29	p. QF 4	Lesson 15	A. Concept Check B. Proofreading and Editing	Lessons 4-5	Lesson 3
LESSON 4 **Indefinite Pronouns as Subjects** pp. 216-218 **Exercise Bank** p. 614	pp. 172-174	p. DT 29	p. QF 3	Lesson 16	A. Concept Check B. Writing	Lesson 4	
LESSON 5 **Problem Subjects** pp. 219-221 **Exercise Bank** p. 614	pp. 175-177	p. DT 30	p. QF 4		A. Concept Check B. Writing	Lesson 5	Lesson 3

ASSESSMENT

Pupil's Edition	Assessment Masters	Test Generator CD-ROM	mcdougallittell.com
Diagnostic Test p. 207	Chapter Pretest pp. 18-19	Test Generator Chapter 9	Grammar Chapter Quiz
Mastery Test p. 225	Chapter Mid-Point Test p. 32		
	Chapter Mastery Tests pp. 79-82		

INTEGRATING WRITING AND LITERATURE

Writing Activities

Description of public work of art p. 206

Caption for a photograph p. 210

Rewrite newspaper article for agreement p. 212

Write sentences describing data in bar graph p. 221

Write and solve a math word problem p. 223

Literary Model

*"Zebra" p. 214

* from *McDougal Littell Language of Literature*

Chapter 10 Capitalization

Use the online lesson planner at **mcdougallittell.com** to customize instruction.

Pupil's Edition	Print Resources Grammar, Usage, and Mechanics Workbook	Time-Saver Transparencies Binder Daily Test Preparation	Integrated Technology and Media Electronic Teacher Tools
LESSON 1 People and Cultures pp. 230-232 **Exercise Bank** p. 615	pp. 178-180	p. DT 30	Concept Check
LESSON 2 First Words and Titles pp. 233-235 **Exercise Bank** p. 615	pp. 181-183	p. DT 31	A. Concept Check
LESSON 3 Places and Transportation pp. 237-239 **Exercise Bank** p. 616	pp. 184-186	p. DT 31	A. Concept Check
LESSON 4 Organizations and Other Subjects pp. 240-241 **Exercise Bank** p. 617	pp. 187-189	p. DT 32	Concept Check

ASSESSMENT

Pupil Edition	Assessment Masters	Test Generator CD-ROM	mcdougallittell.com
Diagnostic Test p. 228	Chapter Pretest pp. 20-21	Test Generator Chapter 10	Grammar Chapter Quiz
Mastery Test p. 245	Chapter Mid-Point Test p. 33		
	Chapter Mastery Tests pp. 83-86		

INTEGRATING WRITING AND LITERATURE

Writing Activities

Description of Olympic event p. 228

Sentences naming favorite media p. 235

Correct capitalization errors on map p. 235

Correct capitalization errors on school calendar p. 241

Write an article based on a diagram p. 243

Literary Model

*"Casey at the Bat" p. 233

* from *McDougal Littell Language of Literature*

Chapter 11 Punctuation

Use the online lesson planner at mcdougallittell.com to customize instruction.

Pupil's Edition

	Print Resources Grammar, Usage, and Mechanics Workbook	Time-Saver Transparencies Binder Daily Test Preparation	Time-Saver Transparencies Binder Quick-Fix Grammar and Style Charts	Integrated Technology and Media Electronic Teacher Tools	Integrated Technology and Media Grammar Coach CD-ROM
LESSON 1 Periods and Other End Marks pp. 250-252 Exercise Bank p. 617	pp. 190-192	p. DT 32		A. Concept Check B. Writing	
LESSON 2 Commas in Sentences pp. 253-255 Exercise Bank p. 618	pp. 193-195	p. DT 33	p. QF 10	Concept Check	Lesson 3
LESSON 3 Commas: Dates, Addresses, and Letters pp. 256-257 Exercise Bank p. 618	pp. 196-198	p. DT 33		A. Concept Check B. Writing	Lesson 3
LESSON 4 Punctuating Quotations pp. 258-261 Exercise Bank p. 619	pp. 199-201	p. DT 34	p. QF 10	A. Concept Check B. Editing	Lesson 3
LESSON 5 Semicolons and Colons pp. 262-263 Exercise Bank p. 619	pp. 202-204	p. DT 34		A. Concept Check	
LESSON 6 Hyphens, Dashes, and Parentheses pp. 264-265 Exercise Bank p. 620	pp. 205-207	p. DT 35		Concept Check	
LESSON 7 Apostrophes pp. 266-267 Exercise Bank p. 620	pp. 208-210	p. DT 35		A. Concept Check B. Writing	
LESSON 8 Punctuating Titles pp. 268-269 Exercise Bank p. 621	pp. 211-213	p. DT 36			

ASSESSMENT

Pupil's Edition	Assessment Masters	Test Generator CD-ROM	mcdougallittell.com
Diagnostic Test p. 248	Chapter Pretest pp. 22-23	Test Generator Chapter 11	Grammar Chapter Quiz
Mastery Test p. 273	Chapter Mid-Point Test p. 34		
	Chapter Mastery Tests pp. 87-92		

INTEGRATING WRITING AND LITERATURE

Writing Activities

Message in code p. 248

Correctly punctuate notes p. 252

A letter p. 257

Change direct quotations to indirect quotations p. 261

A business letter p. 263

Use possessives to rewrite phrases p. 267

Write titles of favorite media p. 269

Literary Models

*"The Serial Garden" p. 260

*"Mooses" p. 270

* from *McDougal Littell Language of Literature*

WHAT IS VISUAL GRAMMAR™?

Have you ever found it challenging to teach difficult grammar and writing concepts because the words in your textbooks are trapped on the printed page? Visual Grammar™ provides the solution to this problem. These color-coded "tiles," which are designed to support specific lessons in the Pupil's Edition, are actually pre-printed transparency strips that represent different parts of a sentence. They help students understand sentence structure, sophisticated grammar concepts, and sentence combining by enabling them to physically rearrange sentence parts on an overhead projector and then analyze the results. With Visual Grammar™, abstract concepts become visually concrete.

In addition to the pre-printed tiles, blank tiles are provided to allow you to create Visual Grammar™ activities that contain the content and skills of your choosing. These tiles may also be used with the additional sentences provided in the back of this Teacher's Edition to provide more examples for corresponding grammar lessons in the Pupil's Edition. Visual Grammar™ Tiles work effectively as whole group instruction, or they can be used by students in small groups or as an independent study aid.

WHAT ARE THE COMPONENTS OF VISUAL GRAMMAR™?

Your Visual Grammar™ kit consists of:

- Color-coded sentence tiles corresponding to specific lessons in the Pupil's Edition.

- A detailed, full-color instruction book that shows you how to manipulate sentences and sentence parts to teach specific grammar and writing skills.

- Blank sentence tiles for creating additional Visual Grammar™ examples or activities.

- Storage sleeves to help you store your Visual Grammar™ tiles .

WHEN DO I USE THE VISUAL GRAMMAR™ TILES?

On the corresponding Teacher's Edition page of selected lessons in the Pupil's Edition, you will see a box marked Visual Grammar™. This box will show you which sentence tile set to use with the lesson. Detailed instruction for presenting the activity are found in the instruction book.

HOW DO I USE THE ADDITIONAL SENTENCES?

To use the additional sentences located at the end of the Teacher's Edition, you will follow the instructional steps as presented in the instruction book. Following is an example of what is provided at the end of the Teacher's Edition.

- Each sentence is identified by lesson number and sentence letter. For example,

LESSON 1
Sentence A

- Step 1 shows the initial sentence or sentences you will use to begin the lesson. For example,

Step 1

- In Step 2 arrows and X's show you which words to move, add, delete, or change. For example,

Step 2 *Move:*

- Finally, the finished product is shown for your convenience. For example,

Result:

Additional Visual Grammar™ sentences continue on p.689.

CHAPTER OVERVIEW

CHAPTER RESOURCES

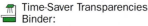 Time-Saver Transparencies
Binder:
- Daily Test Preparation
  pp. DT1–5
- Quick-Fix Grammar and
  Style Charts pp. QF1–2
- Visual Grammar™ Tiles
  Lessons 1–6

Grammar, Usage, and
Mechanics Workbook
pp. 1–30

Integrated Technology and Media

Electronic Teacher Tools
CD-ROM

Grammar Coach CD-ROM
Lessons 1–2

Power Presentations
CD-ROM Lesson 1

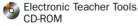 mcdougallittell.com

Assessment

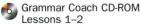 Assessment Masters:
- Chapter Pretest pp. 2–3
- Chapter Mid-point Test
  p. 24
- Chapter Mastery Tests
  pp. 35–42

Test Generator CD-ROM

 mcdougallittell.com
Grammar Chapter Quiz

Students Acquiring English/ESL

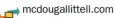 English Grammar
Survival Kit pp. 25–28, 39-40

 Side by Side p. 30

Chapter 1

The Sentence and Its Parts

Theme: There's No Place Like Home

If You Build It . . .

A pile of bricks is not a home. To be a home, the bricks must
be assembled and combined with doors and windows to make
a building that will house a family.

In the same way, the pair of words "*Home is*" is not a
sentence. To be a sentence, the words must be combined with
other words to make a complete thought.

Write Away: Home Is . . . ?

Where do you feel most at home? Why? Write a paragraph
answering these questions and place it in your **Working
Portfolio.**

4

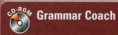 **Grammar Coach**

Diagnostic Test: What Do You Know?

Choose the letter that correctly identifies each underlined item.

> <u>What is a home?</u> That depends on the home. <u>Skyscrapers, space</u>
> <u>(1)</u>   <u>(2)</u>
> <u>stations, burrows, and nests</u> are all homes to living things. People
> and animals <u>build</u> <u>homes</u> from many different materials. However,
>   <u>(3)</u>   <u>(4)</u>
> for human beings a <u>home</u> is more than a building. For some people
>   <u>(5)</u>
> home <u>may be</u> the place where they were born. For others home is
>   <u>(6)</u>
> the <u>place</u> where they feel most comfortable. We use the <u>word</u> in
>   <u>(7)</u>   <u>(8)</u>
> many ways. <u>Expressions like *home team, home plate, home page.*</u>
>   <u>(9)</u>
> You <u>will</u> learn a lot about people by discussing their idea of home.
>   <u>(10)</u>

1. A. declarative sentence
   B. interrogative sentence
   C. exclamatory sentence
   D. imperative sentence

2. A. compound subject
   B. main verb
   C. helping verb
   D. indirect object

3. A. compound subject
   B. main verb
   C. helping verb
   D. object

4. A. simple subject
   B. direct object
   C. compound verb
   D. compound subject

5. A. simple subject
   B. simple predicate
   C. compound verb
   D. compound subject

6. A. indirect object
   B. subject
   C. direct object
   D. verb phrase

7. A. compound subject
   B. compound verb
   C. predicate noun
   D. verb phrase

8. A. subject
   B. predicate
   C. direct object
   D. indirect object

9. A. run-on sentence
   B. interrogative sentence
   C. sentence fragment
   D. exclamatory sentence

10. A. main verb
    B. helping verb
    C. complement
    D. subject

SENTENCE PARTS

SENTENCE PARTS

The Sentence and Its Parts **5**

LESSON OBJECTIVES

To identify and use complete subjects and complete predicates in writing

DAILY TEST PREPARATION

Error Identification:

Capitalization Write the following item on the board or use **Daily Test Preparation Transparency** p. DT1. Decide which type of error, if any, appears in the underlined section.

> After going to the store with my Uncle, we decided to see a movie.

A. Spelling error

B. Capitalization error

C. Punctuation error

D. No error

Teaching Point: Error identification questions often test your knowledge of basic capitalization rules. This item tests whether you know that words referring to family relationships, such as *uncle,* are not capitalized unless they are a part of someone's name *(Uncle Robert).*

TEACHING RESOURCES

 Time-Saver Transparencies Binder:
  • Daily Test Preparation p. DT1
  Grammar, Usage, and Mechanics Workbook p. 1

SKILLS PRACTICE RESOURCES

  Grammar, Usage, and Mechanics Workbook pp. 2–3
  Pupil's Edition Exercise Bank p. 584

LESSON 1 Complete Subjects and Predicates

❶ Here's the Idea

In order to share ideas and information successfully, you need to use complete sentences.

▶ **A sentence is a group of words that expresses a complete thought.**

Here is a group of words.

surprise can us architects

These words are good building blocks, but to get a message across, they need a structure. Here is a sentence built from the words. Notice that the sentence communicates a complete idea.

Architects can surprise us

▶ **Every complete sentence has two basic parts: a subject and a predicate.**

1. The **complete subject** includes all the words that tell whom or what the sentence is about.

COMPLETE SUBJECT

Some architects bring nature indoors.

2. The **complete predicate** includes the verb and all the words that modify the verb.

COMPLETE PREDICATE

Some architects bring nature indoors.

Here's How Finding Complete Subjects and Predicates

Some architects bring nature indoors.

1. **To find the complete subject, ask who or what does something (or is something).**
   Who brings nature indoors? **Some architects**

2. **To find the complete predicate, ask what the subject does (or is).**
   What do some architects do? **bring nature indoors**

② Why It Matters in Writing

Jotting down ideas is a good way to prepare to write. For example, you might write down *Frank Lloyd Wright, didn't copy,* and *unique buildings* as you take notes or brainstorm. To share these ideas with others, though, you need both subjects and predicates. Notice what the writer has added in the paragraph below.

PROFESSIONAL MODEL

> **Frank Lloyd Wright was different from other architects. This dreamer from the prairie states didn't copy other people's designs. He created his own unique buildings instead.**
>
> —M. Carton

③ Practice and Apply

CONCEPT CHECK: Complete Subjects and Predicates

In separate columns on a sheet of paper, write the complete subjects and complete predicates of these sentences.

Amazing Designs
1. Frank Lloyd Wright designed an unusual home in the Pennsylvania woods.
2. The owners called the house Fallingwater.
3. Sections of the house jut over a waterfall.
4. Its stone walls blend in with the natural surroundings.
5. More than 130,000 people visit the site each year.
6. Tourists can see a very different house near Spring Green, Wisconsin.
7. The architect Alex Jordan built House on the Rock on a column of sandstone.
8. Its many rooms contain unique furnishings.
9. An automated band plays music all day for the tourists.
10. This odd house attracts half a million visitors a year.

➡ **For a SELF-CHECK and more practice, see the EXERCISE BANK, p. 584.**

The Sentence and Its Parts **7**

Fallingwater

SENTENCE PARTS

TEACHING TIP

A color code is used throughout the grammar section to help students understand sentence parts and how they function. In this lesson, blue represents the subject; green indicates the predicate.

TEACHING TIP

Explain to students that the complete subject and complete predicate often contain prepositional phrases. Prepositional phrases that come before the verb usually are part of the complete subject. Prepositional phrases that come after the verb usually are part of the complete predicate.

Answers

Print-Out Option You may create worksheets of this exercise for your students by using the 💿 **Electronic Teacher Tools CD–ROM.**

CONCEPT CHECK

Self-Check For a self-check of complete subjects and predicates, direct students to p. 584 in the Pupil's Edition for the answers to the items circled in yellow.

Answers shown on page.

Complete subjects are underlined. Complete predicates are double underlined.

Spice It Up!

Have students divide into small groups. Each member of a group takes turns writing a noun and a verb on a card and holding up the card. The other members of the group compete to make up sentences by using the two words. The group member who completes a sentence first wins.

LESSON 2 Simple Subjects

❶ Here's the Idea

You have learned that one basic part of a sentence is the complete subject. Now you will learn about the key part of the complete subject.

▶ **The simple subject is the main word or words in the complete subject.** Descriptive words are not part of the simple subject.

COMPLETE SUBJECT

| An expectant seal | builds a shelter in a snowdrift. |

SIMPLE SUBJECT

The cozy **shelter** hides her newborn pup.

SIMPLE SUBJECT

When a proper name is used as a subject, all parts of the name make up the simple subject.

Robert Peary explored the North Pole.

SIMPLE SUBJECT

❷ Why It Matters in Writing

The simple subject tells the reader whom or what the sentence is about. Be sure to choose as accurate a word as possible for this key part.

STUDENT MODEL

Polar bears' ^noses^ stand out against the white snow. When bears lie in wait for a seal, their white ~~fur~~ paws serves as a mask. Then their ~~enemy~~ prey cannot see them.

8 Grammar, Usage, and Mechanics

A. CONCEPT CHECK: Simple Subjects

Write the simple subject of each sentence. Remember, descriptive words are not part of the simple subject.

Example: The river beavers built a new lodge.
Simple subject: beavers

Winter Lodges

1. Many <u>animals</u> need shelter from cold and predators.
2. <u>Lodges</u> on islands often give beavers the best protection.
3. These <u>homes</u> are built up from the bottom of the pond.
4. Strong <u>saplings</u> are anchored into the mud.
5. The sturdy <u>rodents</u> then pile debris into a mound.
6. <u>Branches</u> buried in the mud are food for the winter.
7. The whole <u>family</u> lives together in the snug burrow.
8. Their warm <u>bodies</u> keep the temperature comfortable.
9. <u>Predators</u> can claw at the frozen lodge.
10. The crafty <u>beavers</u> stay safe and warm inside.

➡ **For a SELF-CHECK and more practice, see the EXERCISE BANK, p. 584.**

B. WRITING: Synthesizing Information in Science Answers in column.

A classmate did research on how long young animals stay with their parents. Write one sentence about each animal described below. Underline the simple subject.

Example: An arctic seal <u>pup</u> spends two weeks in a shelter with its mother.

Leaving Home

Animal	Name of Young	Length of Time Spent with Parents
Arctic seal	pup	2 weeks in shelter with mother
Penguin	chick	23 days with parents
Kangaroo	joey	7 to10 months in mother's pouch
Beaver	kitten	more than a year with parents
Human	child	usually 18 years at home

The Sentence and Its Parts **9**

Answers

Print-Out Option You may create worksheets of this exercise for your students by using the 💿 **Electronic Teacher Tools CD–ROM.**

A. CONCEPT CHECK

Answers on page.

Self-Check For a self-check of simple subjects, direct students to p. 584 in the Pupil's Edition for the answers to the items circled in yellow.

B. WRITING

Answers will vary. Sample answers follow. Simple subject is underlined.

1. An arctic seal <u>pup</u> stays for two weeks in a shelter with its mother.
2. A penguin <u>chick</u> spends 23 days with its parents.
3. A kangaroo <u>joey</u> stays for 7–10 months in its mother's pouch.
4. A beaver <u>kitten</u> remains more than a year with its parents.
5. A human <u>child</u> usually lives at home for 18 years.

Spice It Up!

Prepare a stack of cards with nouns of varying difficulty on them. Put prices on the cards. The easy words will be worth $1. The moderately difficult words will be worth $5, and the most difficult words will be worth $10 in play money. Divide the class into groups and give each group four cards. Have students take turns holding up a card. The first group member to come up with a sentence using that word as a simple subject wins the card. The student who ends up with the most play money wins the game.

LESSON 3 # Simple Predicates, or Verbs

❶ Here's the Idea

You have learned about the simple subject of a sentence. You also need to know about the simple predicate.

▶ **The simple predicate, or verb, is the main word or words in the complete predicate.**

COMPLETE PREDICATE

Prairie pioneers | **lived in sod houses.**

SIMPLE PREDICATE

Few trees **grow** in the prairie grasslands.
SIMPLE PREDICATE

▶ **A verb is a word used to express an action, a condition, or a state of being.** A **linking verb** tells what the subject *is.* An **action verb** tells what the subject *does,* even when the action cannot be seen.

Pioneers **made** sod bricks. (action you can see)

They **wanted** a sturdy home. (action you cannot see)

Sod houses **stayed** cool in hot weather. (linking)

❷ Why It Matters in Writing

You can make your writing more interesting by substituting strong verbs for weaker ones. Strong verbs can add important information about the subject.

STUDENT MODEL

A prairie fire ~~burned~~ *destroyed* almost everything in its path. The fire ~~was~~ *grew* enormous. It ~~went~~ *stretched* from one end of the horizon to the other.

❸ Practice and Apply

A. CONCEPT CHECK: Simple Predicates, or Verbs

Write the simple predicate, or verb, in each sentence.

On the Lone Prairie

1. My great-grandparents <u>lived</u> in a sod house, or "soddy," on the Kansas prairie.
2. They <u>traveled</u> west from their home in Tennessee.
3. The men <u>used</u> nearly an acre of sod for the house.
4. The home <u>had</u> only two windows and one door.
5. My family <u>built</u> their soddy in the side of a hill.
6. Sometimes the cows <u>ate</u> the grass on the roof.
7. Once, a cow <u>fell</u> through the roof into the house!
8. Heavy rains at times <u>soaked</u> through the sod.
9. The dirt floor <u>turned</u> into a giant mud puddle.
10. Still, sod houses <u>protected</u> my family from harsh winters.

➡ **For a SELF-CHECK and more practice, see the EXERCISE BANK, p. 585.**

B. WRITING: Preparing a Science Report   Answers in column.

A science student drew this diagram and took notes about the soil in her neighborhood. Use a different verb with each note to create three sentences that describe the soil.

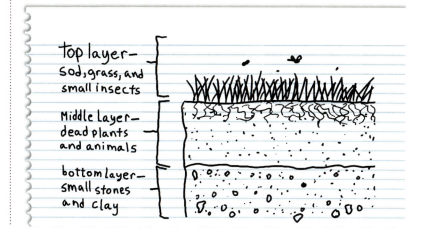

Answers

Print-Out Option You may create worksheets of exercise A for your students by using the 💿 **Electronic Teacher Tools CD–ROM.**

A. CONCEPT CHECK

Answers will vary. Sample answers follow.

1. The top layer contains sod, grass, and small insects.
2. The middle layer is made up of dead plants and animals.
3. The bottom layer consists of small stones and clay.

B. WRITING

Answers underlined on page.

Self-Check For a self-check of simple predicates, direct students to p. 585 in the Pupil's Edition for the answers to the items circled in yellow.

SENTENCE PARTS

SENTENCE PARTS

LESSON OBJECTIVES

To recognize verb phrases and use them in writing

TEACHING TIP

Explain to students that *be*, *have*, and *do* can function as main verbs or helping verbs. Examples:

They <u>are going</u> home.

They <u>are</u> home now.

He <u>has finished</u> the book.

He <u>has</u> another one to read.

<u>Did</u> you <u>practice</u> this morning?

I <u>did</u> it!

LESSON 4

Verb Phrases

❶ Here's the Idea

The simple predicate, or verb, may consist of two or more words. These words are called a verb phrase.

▶ **A verb phrase is made up of a main verb and one or more helping verbs.**

>   VERB PHRASE
> A "smart house" **may cook** your food for you.
>   HELPING VERB   MAIN VERB

Main Verbs and Helping Verbs

A **main verb** can stand by itself as the simple predicate of a sentence.

> Computer networks **run** smart houses. (action)
>   MAIN VERB

> The network **is** the brain of the house. (linking)
>   MAIN VERB

One or more **helping verbs** help main verbs express action or show time.

>   VERB PHRASE
> Computer networks **will run** smart houses.
>   HELPING VERB   MAIN VERB

> The network **has been** turning the lights on and off.

> It **will have been** programmed for all seasons.

Sometimes the main verb changes form when used with a helping verb. For more on these changes, see pages 108–110.

Common Helping Verbs	
Forms of *be*	is, am, are, was, were, be, been
Forms of *do*	do, does, did
Forms of *have*	has, have, had
Others	may, might, can, should, could, would, shall, will

---

12   Grammar, Usage, and Mechanics

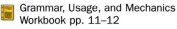
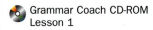

② Why It Matters in Writing

Writers often use verb phrases to help show time. Notice how the verb phrases in the paragraph below show past, present, and future time.

PROFESSIONAL MODEL

Long before scientists or architects had considered the possibility, the author Ray Bradbury wrote about a smart house. In a 1950 story, he described a kind of super-automated house that technologists now are hoping they will make a reality.

PAST

PRESENT

FUTURE

—J. Timothy Bagwell

③ Practice and Apply

CONCEPT CHECK: Verb Phrases

Write the verb phrase in each sentence below. Be sure to include all the helping verbs.

Smart Houses
1. The first "smart house" was developed in the early 1980s.
2. Its appliances could communicate with each other.
3. Suppose you were running the vacuum cleaner.
4. The noise might keep you from hearing the phone.
5. In that situation the house would stop the vacuum cleaner automatically.
6. Those with disabilities may benefit the most from a smart house.
7. The house will perform some of the tasks beyond their capability.
8. For example, meals could be brought to a person's bed.
9. The food will have been prepared by a smart kitchen.
10. Surely you can imagine other uses for a smart house.

➡ **For a SELF-CHECK and more practice, see the EXERCISE BANK, p. 585.**

The Sentence and Its Parts **13**

TEACHING TIP

Ask students to answer the questions below in one sentence. Have students identify helping verbs in their answers and state whether the actions take place in the past, present, or future. This exercise gives students practice in using the present, past, and future tenses appropriately and consistently.

1. Where are you living now? **Possible answer:** *I am living at home.*—present
2. Where were you living two years ago? **Possible answer:** *I was living at home.*—past
3. What will you do when you get home? **Possible answer:** *I will call my friends.*—future

SENTENCE PARTS

SENTENCE PARTS

CUSTOMIZING TIP

Students Acquiring English/ESL
Because some languages, including Spanish and French, do not have present progressive verb forms, students might have difficulty choosing between the present and present progressive tenses in their writing. For instruction and practice with the present and present progressive forms, see **English Grammar Survival Kit** pp. 25–28.

Answers

Print-Out Option You may create worksheets of this exercise for your students by using the ⊙ **Electronic Teacher Tools CD–ROM.**

CONCEPT CHECK

Self-Check For a self-check of verb phrases, direct students to p. 585 in the Pupil's Edition for the answers to the items circled in yellow.

Answers underlined on page.

LESSON OBJECTIVES

To identify and use compound subjects and compound verbs in writing.

DAILY TEST PREPARATION

Definition: Vocabulary Write the following item on the board or use **Daily Test Preparation Transparency** p. DT3.

Decide which of the four answers has most nearly the same meaning as the underlined word.

> Water that is <u>tepid</u> is

A. lukewarm

B. scalding

C. frigid

D. calm

Teaching Point: For definitions, rule out any answer options that are related to the underlined word but that do not have the same meaning. *Scalding* and *frigid* both describe extreme water temperatures; *lukewarm,* however, is the closest in meaning to *tepid.*

CUSTOMIZING TIP

Less Proficient Learners Offer students additional practice in recognizing compound verbs by having students rewrite the model sentences as separate sentences.

The skylab crew worked in close quarters. The skylab crew slept in close quarters. They worked hard. They slept little.

LESSON 5 # Compound Sentence Parts

❶ Here's the Idea

Sentences can have **compound subjects** and **compound verbs**.

▶ **A compound subject is made up of two or more subjects that share the same verb.** The subjects are joined by a conjunction, or connecting word, such as *and, or,* or *but.*

COMPOUND SUBJECT

Salyut 1 and *Skylab* were the first space stations.
SUBJECT   SUBJECT

American astronauts or Russian cosmonauts lived aboard the stations.

▶ **A compound verb is made up of two or more verbs that have the same subject.** The verbs are joined by a conjunction such as *and, or,* or *but.*

COMPOUND VERB

The *Skylab* crew worked and slept in close quarters.
VERB   VERB

They worked hard but slept little.

❷ Why It Matters in Writing

You can use compound subjects and verbs to combine sentences and avoid repetition in your writing.

> **STUDENT MODEL**
>
> Weightlessness is fun. ~~Weightlessness can have serious side effects.~~ *but is dangerous* In zero gravity, your muscles do less work. ~~Your bones do less work, too.~~ *and bones* Without exercise, they lose strength quickly.

TEACHING RESOURCES

Time-Saver Transparencies Binder:
- Daily Test Preparation p. DT3
- Visual Grammar™ Tiles Lessons 1–2

Grammar, Usage, and Mechanics Workbook p. 13

SKILLS PRACTICE RESOURCES

Grammar, Usage, and Mechanics Workbook pp. 14–15

Pupil's Edition Exercise Bank p. 586

❸ Practice and Apply

A. CONCEPT CHECK: Compound Sentence Parts

Write the compound subject or the compound verb in each sentence.

Home Away from Home

1. Space stations and orbiting platforms are our first step away from Earth.
2. In the future, we may design and build outer-space cities.
3. Several nations or international groups could pool their resources.
4. They could create and manage a colony on the moon.
5. Minerals and other raw materials would be shipped to colonies in space.
6. We already design and plan model cities.
7. In one design, two huge cylinders and their solar panels form the main body of the space city.
8. The cylinders rotate and create an artificial gravity.
9. Special greenhouses shelter and sustain the city's food.
10. These cities or other space colonies could bring us closer to the stars!

➡ **For a SELF-CHECK and more practice, see the EXERCISE BANK, p. 586.**

B. REVISING: Using Compound Subjects and Verbs   Answers in column.

Combine each pair of sentences, following the instructions in parentheses.

1. A group of nations is building an international space station. They are supplying it too. (Use a compound verb.)
2. Astronauts will be carried up on the space shuttle. Their supplies also will be carried on the shuttle. (Use a compound subject.)
3. Scientists will grow plants in zero gravity. They will study plants in zero gravity as well. (Use a compound verb.)

Skylab

Answers

Print-Out Option You may create worksheets of exercises A and B for your students by using the **Electronic Teacher Tools CD–ROM.**

A. CONCEPT CHECK

Self-Check For a self-check of compound sentence parts, direct students to p. 586 in the Pupil's Edition for the answers to the items circled in yellow.

Answers shown on page. Compound subjects are underlined. Compound verbs are underlined twice.

B. REVISING

1. A group of nations is building and supplying an international space station.
2. Astronauts and their supplies will be carried up on the space shuttle.
3. Scientists will grow and study plants in zero gravity.

ASSESSMENT

📖 Assessment Masters:
• Chapter Mid-point Test p. 24

📖 Visual Grammar™

Use **Visual Grammar™ Tiles Lessons 1–2** and **Sentence A** to show how to make compound subjects and verbs. Here is part of Lesson 1.

Combine sentences.

| JAGUARS | ARE ENDANGERED ANIMALS | . |

| GRAY WOLVES | ARE ENDANGERED ANIMALS | . |

Result:

| JAGUARS | AND | GRAY WOLVES |

| ARE ENDANGERED ANIMALS | . |

LESSON OBJECTIVES

To identify and use different kinds of sentences in writing

THE LANGUAGE OF LITERATURE

The passage on the student page is from *A Christmas Carol* in *The Language of Literature,* Level 7.

LESSON 6 Kinds of Sentences

❶ Here's the Idea

▶ **A sentence can be used to make a statement, to ask a question, to make a request or give a command, or to show strong feelings.**

Four Kinds of Sentences		
	What It Does	**Examples**
Declarative .	Makes a statement; always ends with a period.	I see something weird in that tree. It looks like a gray basketball.
Interrogative ?	Asks a question; always ends with a question mark.	What do you think it is? Is it a hornet's nest?
Imperative . or !	Tells or asks someone to do something; usually ends with a period but may end with an exclamation point.	Please don't get too close to it. Be careful!
Exclamatory !	Shows strong feeling; always ends with an exclamation point.	I see hornets flying out! I'm getting out of here!

❷ Why It Matters in Writing

You can use different kinds of sentences to imitate the way people really talk. Notice how three kinds of sentences are used in this conversation between Ebenezer Scrooge and his nephew, Fred.

LITERARY MODEL

Scrooge . . . . Come, come, what is it you want? Don't waste all day, Nephew.
    Fred. I only want to wish you a Merry Christmas, Uncle. Don't be cross.

— Charles Dickens, *A Christmas Carol*, dramatized by Frederick Gaines

INTERROGATIVE
IMPERATIVE
DECLARATIVE

16   Grammar, Usage, and Mechanics

---

❸ Practice and Apply

A. CONCEPT CHECK: Kinds of Sentences

Identify each of the following sentences as declarative (D), interrogative (INT), exclamatory (E), or imperative (IMP).

Dangerous Nests

1. Did you know that some wasps build round, gray nests that can be as big as beach balls? **INT**
2. The nests are made from cellulose and are very strong. **D**
3. Stay away from wasps. **IMP**
4. Their sting is very painful! **E**
5. Yellow jackets are really yellow and black. **D**
6. Do they eat many insect pests? **INT**
7. They live in colonies and build papery nests in spaces underground or in walls and attics. **D**
8. Did you know that their nests may have from 300 to more than 100,000 cells? **INT**
9. Yellow jackets are dangerous only if you get too close to their nest. **D**
10. Don't ever try to move a nest yourself. **IMP**

➡ **For a SELF-CHECK and more practice, see the EXERCISE BANK, p. 586.**

B. WRITING: Creating Dialogue   Answers in column.

Read the following *Fox Trot* comic strip. Notice the kinds of sentences used in the first two frames. Then, on a sheet of paper, write dialogue for the last two frames. Use complete sentences and as many sentence types as you can.

Fox Trot by Bill Amend

A. CONCEPT CHECK

Self-Check For a self-check of kind of sentences, direct students to p. 586 in the Pupil's Edition for the answers to the items circled in yellow.

Answers shown on page.

B. WRITING

The first frame has a declarative sentence and an interrogative sentence; the second, an imperative sentence. Answers will vary. Students should use more than one sentence type. The following are possible responses:

Frame 3

Jason: Would you also hold my iguana, Quincy? *(Int.)*

Paige: Get that thing away from me! *(Imp.)*

Frame 4

Jason: That sound was just perfect! *(Exc.)*

Paige: It's your turn to hold the microphone. *(Dec.)*

LESSON OBJECTIVES

To identify and use subjects in unusual order in writing

 LESSON 7

Subjects in Unusual Order

❶ Here's the Idea

In most declarative sentences, subjects come before verbs. In some kinds of sentences, however, subjects can come between verb parts, follow verbs, or not appear at all.

Questions

▶ **In a question, the subject usually comes after the verb or between parts of the verb phrase.**

Is she ready?

    ══ VERB PHRASE ══

Does the weather look good for the game?

        ⬆ SUBJECT

To find the subject, turn the question into a statement. Then ask who or what is or does something.

Are you staying home?

You are staying home. (Who is staying? *you*)

Commands

▶ **The subject of a command, or imperative sentence, is usually *you*.** Often, *you* doesn't appear in the sentence because it is implied.

(You) Meet us at the concession stand.

  ⬆ IMPLIED SUBJECT

(You) Bring money for snacks!

Inverted Sentences

In an inverted sentence, the subject comes after the verb. Writers use inverted sentences to emphasize particular words or ideas.

TEACHING RESOURCES

 Time-Saver Transparencies Binder:
- Daily Test Preparation p. DT4
- Visual Grammar™ Tiles Lessons 3–5

 Grammar, Usage, and Mechanics Workbook p. 19

SKILLS PRACTICE RESOURCES

 English Grammar Survival Kit pp. 39–40

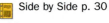 Side by Side p. 30

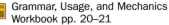 Grammar, Usage, and Mechanics Workbook pp. 20–21

Pupil's Edition Exercise Bank p. 586

Students Acquiring English/ESL
For instruction and practice with inverted word order, see **English Grammar Survival Kit** pp. 39–40, as well as **Side by Side** p. 30

Inverted Subject and Verb	
Normal	The first **batter** **walked** up to the plate.
Inverted	Up to the plate **walked** the first **batter**.
Normal	The **fans** **cheered** loud and long.
Inverted	Loud and long **cheered** the **fans**.

Sentences Beginning with *Here* or *There*

▶ **In some sentences beginning with *here* or *there*, subjects follow verbs. To find the subject in such a sentence, look for the verb and ask the question *who* or *what*.** Find the subject by looking at the words that follow the verb.

WHO COMES?

Here **comes** your all-state championship **team**.
　　VERB　　　　　　　　　　　　　　SUBJECT

WHO GOES?

There **goes** our best **rebounder**.
　　VERB　　　　SUBJECT

② Why It Matters in Writing

You can add variety and interest to your sentences by changing the order of subjects and verbs. Notice how the inverted sentences in the revision below create a more suspenseful tone.

STUDENT MODEL

DRAFT

It was the bottom of the ninth inning, the score was tied, and two men were on base. Then the Yankees' best hitter stepped up to the plate. A deafening roar rolled from the upper decks.

REVISION

It was the bottom of the ninth inning, the score was tied, and two men were on base. **Then up to the plate stepped the Yankees' best hitter. From the upper decks rolled a deafening roar.**

The Sentence and Its Parts **19**

MORE MODEL SENTENCES

Write the following sentences on the board and have students invert the order.

1. The mother stormed into the house. Into the house stormed the mother.

2. His uncle came out to inspect the roof. **Possible answer:** Out came his uncle to inspect the roof.

Discuss with students how inverting the word order changes the emphasis of the sentence.

SENTENCE PARTS

Spice It Up!
Quotable Quote "You may write for the joy of it, but the act of writing is not complete in itself. It has its end in its audience." —Flannery O'Connor

Have students rephrase clauses in the quote as a question, a command, and an inverted sentence.

Answers

Print-Out Option You may create worksheets of exercises A and B for your students by using the ⊙ **Electronic Teacher Tools CD–ROM.**

A. CONCEPT CHECK

Self-Check For a self-check of subjects in unusual order, direct students to p. 586 in the Pupil's Edition for the answers to the items circled in yellow.

Answers shown on page. Subjects are underlined. Verbs and verb phrases are underlined twice. When the subject *you* is implied, *you* is written in the margin.

B. REVISING

1. Did you watch the Women's World Cup soccer games?

2. There are two reasons why women's soccer is becoming more popular.

3. From all over the U.S. come women with different backgrounds.

4. Do their schools have strong soccer programs for all grades?

5. Onto the field ran the undefeated U.S. team.

❸ Practice and Apply

A. CONCEPT CHECK: Subjects in Unusual Order

In separate columns on a sheet of paper, write the subjects and the verbs (or verb phrases) in these sentences.

Home Field Advantage

1. There <u>are</u> some <u>benefits</u> to games at the home stadium.

2. In the bleachers <u>sit</u> all your <u>fans</u>.

3. There <u>are</u> fewer hostile <u>fans</u> from the other team.

4. <u>Is</u> travel <u>time</u> shorter to and from the game?

5. On the field <u>can be seen</u> special <u>landscaping</u>.

6. <u>Will</u> the <u>umpires</u> <u>give</u> the home team a break?

7. <u>Does</u> the <u>team</u> usually <u>play</u> better on its own field?

8. <u>Look</u> at the team's record for the season. **You**

9. There <u>are</u> more <u>wins</u> at home.

10. <u>Plan</u> more home games for next year. **You**

➡ **For a SELF-CHECK and more practice, see the EXERCISE BANK, p. 586.**

B. REVISING: Adding Variety   Answers in column.

Rewrite the following sentences according to the instructions given in parentheses.

1. You watched the Women's World Cup soccer games. (Change the sentence to a question.)

2. Women's soccer is becoming more popular for two reasons. (Begin the sentence with *There are*.)

3. Women with different backgrounds come from all over the United States. (Invert subject and verb, and begin with *From all over the United States*.)

4. Their schools have strong soccer programs for all grades. (Change the sentence to a question.)

5. The undefeated U.S. team ran onto the field. (Invert subject and verb, and begin with *Onto the field*.)

In your 📁 **Working Portfolio,** find the paragraph that you wrote for the **Write Away** on page 4. Add variety to the sentences by changing the position of the subjects in some of them.

📖 Visual Grammar™

Use **Visual Grammar™ Tiles Lessons 3–5** and **Sentences B–C** to show how to find subjects in unusual order. Here is part of Lesson 4.

Rearrange the sentence and identify the subject and the verb.

| BENEATH THE ICE | SWAM | A HUGE FISH | . |

Result:

| A HUGE FISH | SWAM | BENEATH THE ICE | . |

Complements: Subject Complements

❶ Here's the Idea

A complement is a word or a group of words that completes the meaning of a verb. Two kinds of complements are **subject complements** and **objects of verbs**.

▶ **A subject complement is a word or group of words that follows a linking verb and renames or describe the subject.** A linking verb links the subject with a noun or an adjective that tells more about it.

LINKING VERB ↘
Butterflies are fragile.
SUBJECT ↗　　　↖ COMPLEMENT

Common Linking Verbs	
Forms of *be*	am, is, are, was, were, be, been
Other linking verbs	appear, become, feel, look, sound, seem, taste

Predicate Nouns and Predicate Adjectives

Both nouns and adjectives can serve as subject complements.

▶ **A predicate noun follows a linking verb and defines or renames the subject.**

DEFINES
Monarch butterflies are insects.
SUBJECT ↗　　　↖ PREDICATE NOUN

RENAMES
Cocoons become butterfly nurseries.

▶ **A predicate adjective follows a linking verb and describes a quality of the subject.**

DESCRIBES
Monarchs look beautiful.
SUBJECT ↗　　　↖ PREDICATE ADJECTIVE

The Sentence and Its Parts **21**

LESSON OBJECTIVES

To identify and use subject complements in writing

DAILY TEST PREPARATION

Sentence Completion: Subject-Verb Agreement Write the following item on the board or use 🖥 **Daily Test Preparation Transparency** p. DT4. Choose the word that belongs in the space.

> I, along with my classmates, _____ writing a poem for my teacher.

A. want

B. is

C. are

D. am

Teaching Point: For sentence completion questions, the correct answer will always
- fit the meaning of the sentence (*want* does not make sense with *writing*).
- fit grammatically within the sentence (*is* and *are* do not agree with the subject *I*).

TEACHING TIP

Speaking and Listening Have students use predicate nouns and predicate adjectives to describe common items in the classroom. Have the class listen to the clues and guess what the item is. (Example: This item is rectangular. It looks dark brown. It sounds squeaky. Answer: *It is the classroom door.*)

In this exercise, students are expected to monitor their own understanding of the spoken message and evaluate that message in terms of its content. Students are also expected to support their spoken ideas with examples.

TEACHING RESOURCES

 Time-Saver Transparencies Binder:
- Daily Test Preparation p. DT4
- Visual Grammar™ Tiles Lesson 6

Grammar, Usage, and Mechanics Workbook p. 22

SKILLS PRACTICE RESOURCES

 Grammar, Usage, and Mechanics Workbook pp. 23–24
Pupil's Edition Exercise Bank p. 587

CHAPTER 1

MORE MODEL SENTENCES

Write the following sentences on the board. Ask students to identify the predicate nouns and predicate adjectives.

The attic in my house is very <u>*creepy*</u>. **PA**

It always seems <u>*dark*</u>. **PA**

It is a scary <u>*place*</u>. **PN**

Answers

Print-Out Option You may create worksheets of exercises A and B for your students by using the ⊙ **Electronic Teacher Tools CD–ROM.**

A. CONCEPT CHECK

Self-Check For a self-check of subject complements, direct students to p. 587 in the Pupil's Edition for the answers to the items circled in yellow.

Answers shown on page.

B. REVISING

Answers shown on page.

❷ Why It Matters in Writing

Subject complements can provide important information and vivid details about your subjects.

PROFESSIONAL MODEL

Arctic terns **are** <mark>marathoners</mark> of the bird world. They **appear** too <mark>small</mark> and <mark>insignificant</mark> to be great athletes, but every year they fly from the Arctic to the Antarctic and back again.

PREDICATE NOUN

PREDICATE ADJECTIVES

—S. Baugh

❸ Practice and Apply

A. CONCEPT CHECK: Subject Complements

Write the underlined word in each sentence, and identify it as a predicate noun (PN) or a predicate adjective (PA).

Migration Matters

1. Migration routes are <u>highways</u> in the sky for birds. **PN**
2. The migration of songbirds is <u>difficult</u> to track. **PA**
3. The birds are too <u>little</u> to carry radio transmitters. **PA**
4. Identification bands can be <u>useful</u> in tracking migration. **PA**
5. The bands often become <u>loose</u>, however. **PA**
6. Fortunately, the isotope deuterium has been <u>helpful</u>. **PA**
7. Deuterium is a <u>form</u> of hydrogen found in rainwater. **PN**
8. Deuterium becomes <u>part</u> of plants, insects, and birds. **PN**
9. Deuterium levels become <u>higher</u> as you go farther south.
10. Now scientists feel <u>hopeful</u> about tracking migrations. **PA**

➡ **For a SELF-CHECK and more practice, see the EXERCISE BANK, p. 587.**

B. REVISING: Adding Subject Complements

Choose the word *time, residents,* or *remarkable* to fill in each missing subject complement below.

Monarch butterflies are **(1)** (predicate adjective). In the remarkab summer, the adults in the northern United States lay their eggs. Then, it is **(2)** (predicate noun) for them to die. By late summer, the great-grandchildren of the original butterflies migrate. They become **(3)** (predicate noun) of Mexico. residents

 Visual Grammar™

Use **Visual Grammar™ Tiles Lesson 6** and **Sentence D** to show how to identify predicate nouns and adjectives. Here is part of Lesson 6.

Predicate nouns:

[SOCCER] [IS] [A SPORT FOR ALL AGES] [.]

[SOCCER] [IS] [A CHALLENGE] [.]

Predicate adjectives:

[SOCCER] [IS] [VERY POPULAR] [.]

[SOCCER] [IS] [FUN FOR ALL AGES] [.]

Complements: Objects of Verbs

LESSON 9

❶ Here's the Idea

In addition to subject complements, there are objects of verbs. Action verbs often need complements called direct objects and indirect objects to complete their meaning.

Direct Objects

▶ **A direct object is a word or group of words that names the receiver of the action of an action verb.** A direct object answers the question *what* or *whom*.

BORROW WHAT?

Movie producers often borrow real homes.
DIRECT OBJECT

The right house can charm viewers. (can charm whom? *viewers*)

Indirect Objects

▶ **An indirect object is a word or group of words that tells to whom or what (or for whom or what) an action is performed.** An indirect object usually comes between a verb and a direct object.

TO WHOM?

We lent the producer our house.
INDIRECT OBJECT   DIRECT OBJECT

She offered us free movie passes.

Verbs that are often followed by indirect objects include *bring, give, hand, lend, make, offer, send, show, teach, tell, write,* and *ask.*

> **Here's How** Finding Direct and Indirect Objects
>
> **The producer paid us rent money.**
>
> 1. Find the action verb in the sentence. *paid*
> 2. To find the direct object, ask, Paid what? *money*
> 3. To find the indirect object, ask, Paid to or for whom? *us*

The Sentence and Its Parts **23**

SENTENCE PARTS

LESSON OBJECTIVES

To identify and use direct and indirect objects of verbs in writing

 DAILY TEST PREPARATION

Sentence Completion: Vocabulary
Write the following item on the board or use 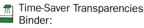 **Daily Test Preparation Transparency** p. DT5.
Choose the word that <u>best</u> fits the meaning of the sentence.

> This cool weather is
> _____; it's often
> steamy this time of year.

A. abnormal

B. alteration

C. accumulative

D. vital

Teaching Point: For sentence completion questions, the correct answer will always

- fit the meaning of the sentence (answers C and D do not).
- fit grammatically within the sentence (answer B does not).

TEACHING RESOURCES

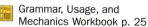 Time-Saver Transparencies Binder:
- Daily Test Preparation p. DT5

 Grammar, Usage, and Mechanics Workbook p. 25

SKILLS PRACTICE RESOURCES

Grammar, Usage, and Mechanics Workbook pp. 26–27
Pupil's Edition Exercise Bank p. 587

SENTENCE PARTS

Spice It Up!

Ask students to imagine that they have prepared a time capsule that will let future generations know what the early years of the 2000s were like. Have students use direct objects to complete the following sentence and describe what they put in the capsule.

I placed _____ in the time capsule.

THE LANGUAGE OF
LITERATURE

The passage on the student page is from "Thank You, Ma'am" in *The Language of Literature,* Level 7.

Answers

Print-Out Option You may create worksheets of this exercise for your students by using the 💿 **Electronic Teacher Tools CD–ROM.**

A. CONCEPT CHECK

Self-Check For a self-check of objects of verbs, direct students to p. 587 in the Pupil's Edition for the answers to the items circled in yellow.

Answers shown on page.

Objects are underlined. They are identified in the margin using these codes:

DO=direct object

IO=indirect object

❷ Why It Matters in Writing

By using both direct and indirect objects, a writer can describe complicated events clearly and simply.

LITERARY MODEL

She **heated** some lima **beans** and **ham** she had in the icebox, **made** the **cocoa,** and **set** the **table.** The woman **did** not **ask** the **boy anything** about where he lived, or his folks, or anything else that **would embarrass him.**

DIRECT OBJECTS

INDIRECT OBJECT

—Langston Hughes, "Thank You, M'am"

❸ Practice and Apply

CONCEPT CHECK: Objects of Verbs

Write the objects in these sentences, identifying each as a direct object (DO) or an indirect object (IO).

One Person's Dream House
1. Bill Gates owns a very technologically advanced <u>house</u>. DO
2. The house gives its <u>inhabitants</u> a high <u>level</u> of comfort IO and convenience.
3. Each visitor to the house carries an electronic <u>identifier</u>. DO
4. The device gives the <u>house</u> <u>information</u>. IO/DO
5. The house can then grant the visitor's <u>wishes</u>. DO
6. Such a house can teach <u>researchers</u> many <u>things</u> IO/DO about homes for people with disabilities.
7. For example, the house can bring <u>you</u> <u>music</u> in IO/DO every room.
8. A similar house could provide <u>aids</u> for the visually DO challenged.
9. Voice instructions could give a visually challenged <u>person</u> <u>information</u> about running appliances. IO/DO
10. Gates's house also has a 32-screen video <u>wall</u>. DO

➡ **For a SELF-CHECK and more practice, see the EXERCISE BANK, p. 587.**

Spice It Up!

List the following subjects, verbs, and objects on the board. Have students use an item from each list to create sentences—no matter how strange the results. Example: *My cousin brushes his bed.*

Subjects	Verbs	Objects
brother	brush	breakfast
sister	eat	bed
cousin	feed	teeth
uncle	make	cat

LESSON 10 # Fragments and Run-Ons

❶ Here's the Idea

Sentence fragments and run-on sentences are writing errors that can make your writing difficult to understand.

Sentence Fragments

▶ **A sentence fragment is a part of a sentence that is written as if it were a complete sentence.** A sentence fragment is missing a subject, a predicate, or both.

FRAGMENTS

The Rungus people in Malaysia. (missing a predicate)

Build traditional homes called longhouses. (missing a subject)

On top of stilts away from floodwaters. (missing both)

To make a complete sentence, add a subject, a predicate, or both.

REVISION

The Rungus people live in Malaysia.

They build traditional homes called longhouses.

These homes often are constructed on top of stilts, away from floodwaters.

SENTENCE PARTS

 DAILY TEST PREPARATION

Sentence Completion: Vocabulary Write the following item on the board or use **Daily Test Preparation Transparency** p. DT5. Choose the word that *best* fits the meaning of the sentence.

> This algebra equation is too _____ for me to grasp.

A. abstract

B. comprehensible

C. ideal

D. complicate

Teaching Point: For sentence completion questions, the correct answer will always

• fit the meaning of the sentence (*comprehensible* and *ideal* do not make sense with *grasp*).

• fit grammatically within the sentence (*complicate* does not).

TEACHING TIP

Point out to students that sentence fragments are incomplete thoughts. Explain that as they read a sentence fragment they may be left with such questions as *What is this about?* or *What happened?* Keeping these questions in mind as they check their own writing will help them correct any sentence fragments they may find.

TEACHING RESOURCES

 Time-Saver Transparencies Binder:
• Daily Test Preparation p. DT5
• Quick-Fix Grammar and Style Charts pp. QF1–2

Grammar, Usage, and Mechanics Workbook p. 28

SKILLS PRACTICE RESOURCES

 Grammar, Usage, and Mechanics Workbook pp. 29–30
Pupil's Edition Exercise Bank p. 588

Grammar Coach CD-ROM Lessons 1–2

CUSTOMIZING TIP

Less Proficient Learners Some students may be uncertain about breaks between sentences. They may have difficulty recognizing where one thought ends and another begins.

Such uncertainties may lead to a higher frequency of run-on sentences in their writing. Have student pairs read aloud the sample sentences. Encourage them to listen for the natural break and falling tone that signals the end of a sentence in English.

Run-On Sentences

▶ **A run-on sentence is two or more sentences written as though they were a single sentence.**

RUN–ON

The longhouse **roof is made** of palm leaves, the **walls are made** of tree bark.

REVISION

The longhouse **roof is made** of palm leaves**.** The **walls are made** of tree bark.

REVISION

The longhouse **roof is made** of palm leaves**, and** the **walls are made** of tree bark.

When combining two sentences with a conjunction, use a comma before the conjunction.

CUSTOMIZING TIP

Gifted and Talented Point out to students that some run-on sentences can be fixed with a semicolon if the two thoughts are closely related.

② Why It Matters in Writing

Fragments and run-on sentences can make your writing confusing and difficult to read. If you fix these problems, your writing will read more clearly.

> **STUDENT MODEL**
>
> **DRAFT**
>
> Each Rungus family has its own apartment the family shares a common living area with other families. Many may live in a longhouse. Twenty to 40 families. In each apartment, a raised sleeping and dining area.
>
> **REVISION**
>
> Each Rungus family has its own apartment, **but** the family shares a common living area with other families. Twenty to 40 families **may live in a longhouse.** In each apartment **there is** a raised sleeping and dining area.

CUSTOMIZING TIP

Less Proficient Learners For students who need more practice identifying complete sentences, write the following sentence fragments on the board and ask students to make complete sentences.

1. Modern homes not always well built. **Possible answer:** *Modern homes are not always well built.*

2. A brand new two-car garage. **Possible answer:** *We built a brand new two-car garage.*

3. To spend hours in the park. **Possible answer:** *My cousins like to spend hours in the park.*

26 Grammar, Usage, and Mechanics

Spice It Up!
Divide the class into groups to play an animal guessing game. Have students take turns supplying a fragment that is missing a subject or predicate. The rest of the group tries to guess the animal's identity by making a complete sentence.

Example: has a long neck

Possible answer: *A giraffe has a long neck.*

③ Practice and Apply

A. CONCEPT CHECK: Sentence Fragments and Run-Ons

Identify each of the following sentences as a fragment (F), a run-on (RO), or a complete sentence (CS).

Mayan Homes
1. The Maya live in Mexico. **CS**
2. Their traditional homes. **F**
3. Have been much the same for centuries. **F**
4. Some were made of stucco or stone. **CS**
5. Today Mayan houses have electricity and telephones **RO** other things haven't changed.
6. Modern building materials. **F**
7. The Maya now use such materials as cinder blocks and **CS** cement for walls.
8. They build roofs from corrugated metal they also use **RO** tarpaper.
9. The tombstones in some Mayan cemeteries. **F**
10. Are shaped like little houses. **F**

➡ For a SELF-CHECK and more practice, see the EXERCISE BANK, p. 588.

B. REVISING: Clearing Up Confusion   Answer in column.

You are out hiking on a beautiful sunny day when suddenly a thunderstorm rolls in. You pull out a friend's notes on building a temporary shelter. Yikes! The notes are hard to understand. Revise them so that the next person to use them won't be frustrated by fragments and run-ons.

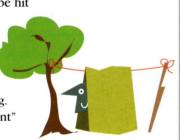

BUILDING A TEMPORARY SHELTER
   First, you need to find a small tree. Away from open areas. Won't be hit by lightning. Second, drive a three-foot stick into the ground nearby take out your rain poncho. Tie a string between the tree and the stick. Drape over the string. Sit underneath the poncho "tent" lie down if you hear thunder.

Answers

Print-Out Option You may create worksheets of exercises A and B for your students by using the 💿 **Electronic Teacher Tools CD–ROM.**

A. CONCEPT CHECK

Self-Check For a self-check of sentence fragments and run-ons, direct students to p. 588 in the Pupil's Edition for the answers to the items circled in yellow.

Answers shown on page.

B. REVISING

Answers will vary. Sentences should be combined using conjunctions to avoid fragments. Run-ons can be corrected by using punctuation. Possible response:

First, you need to find a small tree away from open areas so it won't be hit by lightning. Second, drive a three-foot stick into the ground nearby. Tie a string between the tree and the stick. Next, take out your rain poncho and drape it over the string. Now you can sit underneath the poncho "tent." Lie down if you hear thunder.

ASSESSMENT

 Assessment Masters:
• Chapter Mastery Tests pp. 35–42
 Test Generator CD-ROM

 mcdougallittell.com Grammar Chapter Quiz

LESSON OBJECTIVES

To recognize and use sentence variety in writing

THE LANGUAGE OF LITERATURE

The passage on the student page is from "Homeless" in *The Language of Literature,* Level 7.

Grammar in Literature

Varying Your Sentences

Writers use sentences of different types to keep their writing interesting and to call attention to certain ideas. In the following passage, notice how Anna Quindlen varies her sentences effectively to describe and give readers a feel for her subject.

from Homeless
by Anna Quindlen

Her name was Ann, and we met in the Port Authority Bus terminal several Januarys ago. I was doing a story on homeless people. She said I was wasting my time talking to her; she was just passing through, although she'd been passing through for more than two weeks. To prove to me that this was true, she rummaged through a tote bag... and brought out her photographs...

They were not pictures of family, or friends... They were pictures of a house... The house was yellow. I looked on the back for a date or name, but neither was there. There was no need for discussion. I knew what she was trying to tell me, for it was something I had often felt. She was not adrift, alone, anonymous although her bags and her raincoat with the grime shadowing its creases had made me believe she was. She had a house, or at least once upon a time she had one. Inside were curtains, a couch, a stove, potholders. You are where you live. She was somebody.

SHORT DECLARATIVE SENTENCES

help proclaim these simple statements of fact.

INVERTED SENTENCE

draws the reader into the house.

SHORT SENTENCES

neatly summarize the writer's feelings about Ann.

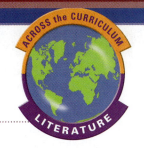

Practice and Apply

A. Using Sentence Variety

Follow the directions below to revise this passage by varying sentences.

> **(1)** The temperature of 17 degrees below zero was dangerous. **(2)** People could die from exposure in only a few hours. **(3)** Volunteers tried to get homeless people into the city shelters. **(4)** The police tried to get them to go, too. **(5)** Homeless people could warm up. **(6)** They could eat hot meals, also. **(7)** A stubborn homeless man was on one street. **(8)** He refused to move, and at first no one knew why. **(9)** His wife was afraid to go to the shelter he wouldn't leave her, home was where she was, he said. **(10)** Volunteers finally got them into a warm shelter.

1. Revise sentences 1 and 2 to express a complete thought.
2. Revise sentences 3 and 4 by using a compound subject.
3. Use a compound predicate to combine sentences 5 and 6.
4. Revise sentence 7 by reversing the subject and the verb and beginning with *On one street*.
5. Revise run-on sentence 9 by creating three shorter sentences.

B. WRITING: Description

Use the ideas from this chapter or your own ideas to write a paragraph describing your ideal room or home. Save your paragraph in your 📁 **Working Portfolio.**

29

Answers

PRACTICE AND APPLY

A. USING SENTENCE VARIETY

Answers will vary. Possible responses:

1. The temperature of 17 degrees below zero was dangerous. People could die from exposure in only a few hours.
2. Volunteers and police tried to get homeless people into the city shelters.
3. Homeless people could warm up and eat hot meals.
4. On one street was a stubborn homeless man.
5. His wife was afraid to go to the shelter. He wouldn't leave her. Home was where she was, he said.

B. WRITING

Answers will vary. The paragraph should provide details that give a clear picture of the room or home students are describing. Students may also wish to include details that reveal how they feel about the place. Make sure students use sentence variety.

Mixed Review

Answers

Print-Out Option You may create worksheets of exercises A and B for your students by using the 🌐 **Electronic Teacher Tools CD–ROM.**

A. SUBJECTS, PREDICATES, AND COMPOUND SENTENCE PARTS

1. skies
2. declarative
3. compound subjects: falcons, hawks
4. has increased
5. like the high ledges of skyscrapers and tall bridges
6. sites
7. the birds' favorite foods
8. interrogative
9. hunter
10. compound verbs: can live, hunt

B. COMPLEMENTS

Answers shown on page using these codes:

PN = predicate noun

PA = predicate adjective

IO = indirect object

DO = direct object

Mixed Review

A. Subjects, Predicates, and Compound Sentence Parts Read the passage, then write the answers to the questions below it. **Answers in**

   (1) The skies over many big cities echo with the cries of peregrine falcons. **(2)** These birds are raptors, or birds of prey. **(3)** Falcons and hawks were once nearly extinct in the eastern United States. **(4)** However, a restoration program has increased their numbers. **(5)** Falcons like the high ledges of skyscrapers and tall bridges. **(6)** There are perfect nesting sites in these places. **(7)** The birds' favorite foods are pigeons and starlings. **(8)** What happens when a soaring falcon spots its prey? **(9)** Down drops the hunter at nearly 200 miles an hour! **(10)** Falcons can live and hunt with ease in major cities.

   1. What is the simple subject of sentence 1?
   2. What kind of sentence is sentence 2?
   3. What is the compound part in sentence 3?
   4. What is the simple predicate of sentence 4?
   5. What is the complete predicate of sentence 5?
   6. What is the simple subject of sentence 6?
   7. What is the complete subject of sentence 7?
   8. What kind of sentence is sentence 8?
   9. What is the simple subject of sentence 9?
   10. What is the compound part in sentence 10?

B. Complements Identify each underlined word as a predicate noun (PN), a predicate adjective (PA), an indirect object (IO), or a direct object (DO).

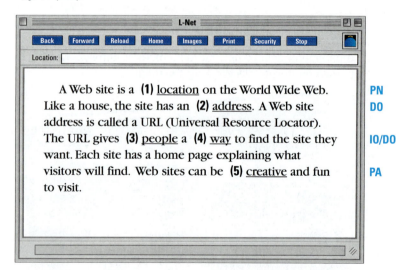

A Web site is a **(1)** location on the World Wide Web. Like a house, the site has an **(2)** address. A Web site address is called a URL (Universal Resource Locator). The URL gives **(3)** people a **(4)** way to find the site they want. Each site has a home page explaining what visitors will find. Web sites can be **(5)** creative and fun to visit.

PN
DO

IO/DO

PA

Mastery Test: What Did You Learn?

Choose the letter of the term that correctly identifies each underlined part of this passage.

> Elevators made skyscrapers and high-rises possible. Why? There
> (1)
> is a simple reason. Few people would want to walk up 30 or 40
> (2)
> flights to their office or home each day. Elevators offer other
> (3)
> benefits too. Their automated cars are actually safer than stairs.
> (4) (5)
> Every three days, elevators collect and transport the equivalent of
> (6)
> the world's population. The fastest elevator ever built is in
> Yokohama, Japan. It carries people up 68 floors in 40 seconds. Don't
> (7)
> think this invention is always a convenience, though. Elevators can
> (8)
> also cause passengers real trouble. A man in England was trapped
> (9) (10)
> in an elevator for 62 hours! He was finally rescued.

1. A. declarative sentence
   B. interrogative sentence
   C. exclamatory sentence
   D. imperative sentence

2. A. main verb
   B. helping verb
   C. complete predicate
   D. verb phrase

3. A. imperative sentence
   B. interrogative sentence
   C. exclamatory sentence
   D. declarative sentence

4. A. subject
   B. predicate
   C. complement
   D. indirect object

5. A. compound subject
   B. predicate noun
   C. simple subject
   D. predicate adjective

6. A. simple subject
   B. complement
   C. compound verb
   D. compound subject

7. A. simple subject
   B. verb phrase
   C. direct object
   D. indirect object

8. A. declarative sentence
   B. interrogative sentence
   C. exclamatory sentence
   D. imperative sentence

9. A. simple predicate
   B. direct object
   C. predicate noun
   D. indirect object

10. A. declarative sentence
    B. interrogative sentence
    C. exclamatory sentence
    D. imperative sentence

Mastery Test

As an option, two other Chapter Mastery Tests appear in 📖 **Assessment Masters** pp. 35–42.

Answers circled on page.

PRESCRIPTION FOR MASTERY	
If students miss item number:	Use **Teaching Resources** and **Skills Practice Resources** for lesson:
1,3,8,10	➏ Kinds of Sentences p. 16
2	➍ Verb Phrases p. 12
4	➋ Simple Subjects p. 8
5	➑ Complements: Subject Complements p. 21
6	➎ Compound Sentence Parts p. 14
7,9	➒ Complements: Objects of Verbs p. 23

Student Help Desk

Students can use the Student Help Desk prior to testing or as a quick review or reference as they revise a piece of writing.

Teacher's Notes

WHAT WORKS:

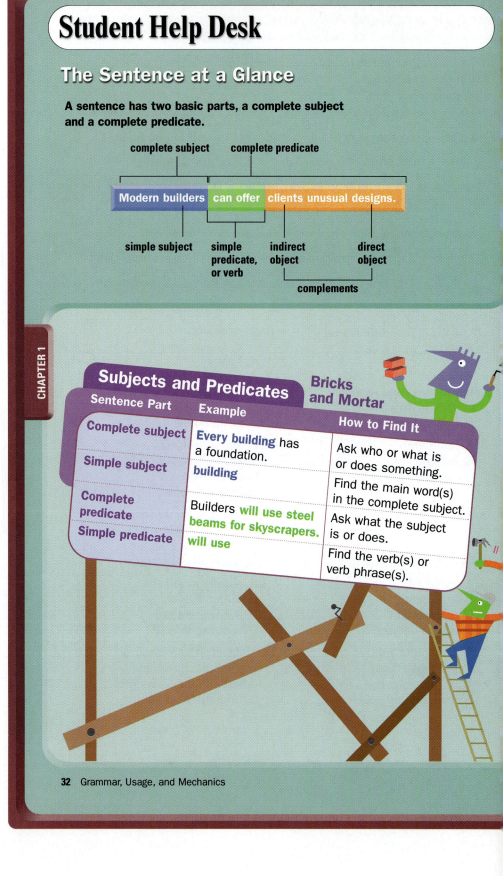

Student Help Desk

The Sentence at a Glance

A sentence has two basic parts, a complete subject and a complete predicate.

complete subject | complete predicate

| Modern builders | can offer | clients unusual designs. |

simple subject | simple predicate, or verb | indirect object | direct object

complements

Subjects and Predicates

Bricks and Mortar

Sentence Part	Example	How to Find It
Complete subject	Every building has a foundation.	Ask who or what is or does something.
Simple subject	building	Find the main word(s) in the complete subject.
Complete predicate	Builders will use steel beams for skyscrapers.	Ask what the subject is or does.
Simple predicate	will use	Find the verb(s) or verb phrase(s).

Complements — Finishing the Job

	Type of Complement	Example	What It Does
Linking verbs	Predicate noun	This building is my **home.**	Renames or defines the subject
Linking verbs	Predicate adjective	It is **gorgeous.**	Describes the subject
Action verbs	Direct object	We painted the **house.**	Completes the action of the verb
Action verbs	Indirect object	A neighbor gave **us** some blue shutters.	Tells to whom/what or for whom/what the action is done

Kinds of Sentences — Adding Interest

Declarative sentence	Someone is coming**.**
Interrogative sentence	Are you the repairman**?**
Imperative sentence	**(You)** Fix our furnace**.**
Exclamatory sentence	We are freezing**!**

The Bottom Line

Checklist for Editing Sentences

Have I . . .

____ made sure that each sentence has a subject and a predicate?

____ corrected any fragments or run-on sentences?

____ combined sentences with similar ideas by using compound subjects or verbs?

____ used different kinds of sentences and different orders of sentence parts for variety?

____ used complements to make the meanings of sentences clear?

Teacher's Notes
WHAT DOESN'T WORK:

A Slice of Life

"Words are all we have."
—Samuel Beckett

Just for Laughs   © Randy Glasbergen, 1996

GLASBERGEN

"It's true, I did jump over the moon.
I had waaaaay too much coffee that day!"

Chapter 2

Nouns

CHAPTER OVERVIEW

CHAPTER 2

CHAPTER RESOURCES

 Time-Saver Transparencies
Binder:
  • Daily Test Preparation
    pp. DT6–8

 Grammar, Usage, and
Mechanics Workbook
pp. 31–45

Integrated Technology and Media

 Electronic Teacher Tools
CD-ROM

 mcdougallittell.com

Assessment

 Assessment Masters:
  • Chapter Pretest pp. 4–5
  • Chapter Mid-point Test
    p. 25
  • Chapter Mastery Tests
    pp. 43–46

 Test Generator CD-ROM

 mcdougallittell.com
Grammar Chapter Quiz

Students Acquiring English/ESL

English Grammar
Survival Kit pp. 1–2

CHAPTER 2

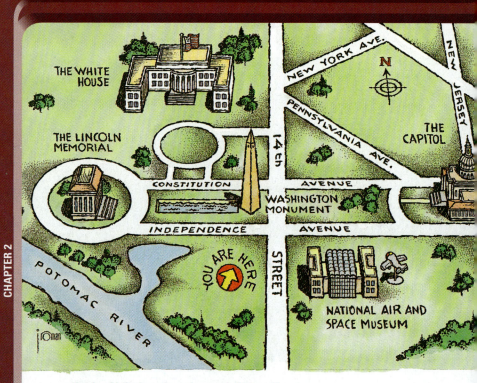

Topic: U.S. Landmarks and Attractions

You Are Here

If you were visiting Washington, D.C., a map like the one above
could help you get to all the important sites. Using the map,
explain how you would get from the White House to the
National Air and Space Museum. What roads would you use?
Which landmarks would you pass?

The labels for the roads and landmarks are nouns—
important words that allow us to name persons, places,
things, and ideas. Without nouns we'd all have trouble finding
our way around.

Write Away: Roll Out the Plans

Write about a landmark you would design. What would it look
like? Whom or what might it honor? Save your work in your
 Working Portfolio.

Grammar Coach

34

Diagnostic Test: What Do You Know?

For each underlined item, choose the letter of the term that correctly identifies it.

Each year, millions of <u>people</u> visit the remarkable <u>National Air and Space Museum</u> in Washington, D.C. Opened in 1976, this museum is part of the Smithsonian Institution. It features more than 20 <u>galleries</u>, a <u>theater</u>, and a planetarium. Among its displays of early aircraft are the Wright <u>brothers'</u> original 1903 <u>airplane</u>, *Flyer,* and <u>Charles Lindbergh's</u> *Spirit of St. Louis.* Other exhibits include <u>spacecraft</u> from various missions, including *Columbia,* the command module of the *Apollo 11* spacecraft that carried astronauts <u>Neil Armstrong,</u> Buzz Aldrin, and Michael Collins to the moon and back. Those who want to learn more about the <u>courage</u> of pilots and the history of flying should really stop in.

(1) people (2) National Air and Space Museum (3) galleries (4) theater (5) brothers' (6) airplane (7) Charles Lindbergh's (8) spacecraft (9) Neil Armstrong, (10) courage

1. A. proper noun
   B. plural noun *(circled)*
   C. possessive noun
   D. compound noun

2. A. noun as subject
   B. noun as direct object *(circled)*
   C. noun as indirect object
   D. noun as predicate noun

3. A. collective noun
   B. plural noun *(circled)*
   C. possessive noun
   D. compound noun

4. A. common noun *(circled)*
   B. abstract noun
   C. proper noun
   D. compound noun

5. A. singular possessive noun
   B. plural possessive noun *(circled)*
   C. compound noun
   D. abstract noun

6. A. singular possessive noun
   B. plural possessive noun
   C. singular compound noun *(circled)*
   D. plural compound noun

7. A. singular common noun
   B. plural proper noun
   C. singular possessive noun *(circled)*
   D. plural possessive noun

8. A. proper noun
   B. abstract noun
   C. possessive noun
   D. compound noun *(circled)*

9. A. common noun
   B. abstract noun
   C. proper noun *(circled)*
   D. possessive noun

10. A. concrete noun
    B. abstract noun *(circled)*
    C. possessive noun
    D. compound noun

Diagnostic Test

As an option, a Chapter Pretest appears in ▣ **Assessment Masters** pp. 4–5.

Answers circled on page.

Use the chart below to determine which lessons students need.

PRESCRIPTION FOR SUCCESS	
If students miss item number:	Work on lessons:
1, 3	❷ Singular and Plural Nouns p. 39
2	❺ Nouns and Their Jobs p. 47
4, 9, 10	❶ Kinds of Nouns p. 36
5, 7	❸ Possessive Nouns p. 42
6, 8	❹ Compound Nouns p. 45

The **Diagnostic Test** parallels the **Mastery Test** on page 53. Have students keep the test in their portfolio to compare with their results on the **Mastery Test**.

NOUNS

NOUNS

BLOCK SCHEDULING

Pressed for Time?
Concentrate on **Lesson 3, Possessive Nouns,** and **Lesson 5, Nouns and Their Jobs.** Have students complete **Here's the Idea** and **Practice and Apply, Concept Check** only, for those lessons.

Time for More?
After all the lessons have been covered, have students draw a map of their neighborhood, labeling roads, buildings, and monuments using the appropriate types of nouns.

To recognize common, proper, concrete, abstract, and collective nouns and to use them in writing

CHAPTER 2

Kinds of Nouns

❶ Here's the Idea

▶ **A noun is a word that names a person, place, thing, or idea.**

PLACES
park
Sierra Nevada

THINGS
sequoia
backpack

IDEAS
curiosity
surprise

PERSONS
guide
Terry

Common and Proper Nouns

A **common noun** is a general name for a person, place, thing, or idea. Common nouns are usually not capitalized. A **proper noun** is the name of a particular person, place, thing, or idea. Proper nouns are always capitalized.

Common	leader	forest	mountain
Proper	Sequoya	Giant Forest	Mount Whitney

Concrete and Abstract Nouns

A **concrete noun** names a thing that can be seen, heard, smelled, touched, or tasted. Examples include *rainbow, thunder, sapling, feather,* and *blueberry.*

On the path we spotted a large, slithery snake.

An **abstract noun** names an idea, feeling, quality, or characteristic. Examples include *happiness, beauty, freedom, humor,* and *greed.*

> **We felt tremendous relief after the snake passed us.**

Every noun is either common or proper and either concrete or abstract. For example, *desert* is common and concrete; *Mohave Desert* is proper and concrete. *Nature* is common and abstract.

Collective Nouns

A **collective noun** is a word that names a group of people or things. Examples include *class, crowd, family, staff, trio,* and *team.*

> **Our family gathered around the campfire for breakfast.**

Some collective nouns name specific groups of animals. Examples include *school, herd, pack,* and *colony.*

> **At night, a pack of wolves howled at the moon.**

② Why It Matters in Writing

Although common nouns can be very specific, the proper nouns in the passage below leave no doubt about exactly what trail or tree the writer means.

PROFESSIONAL MODEL

I began my park explorations on the **Congress Trail**—just up the road from my cabin in **Giant Forest**—for nowhere can you get a quicker grasp of the life cycle of the big trees. I set out early, when the air was bracing and few people stirred. For companions I had fussy Steller's jays and a trio of mule deer. The two-mile paved walkway starts right at the base of the **Sherman Tree.**

—Paul Martin, "California's Wilderness Sisters"

TEACHING TIP

Point out that *nature* is a common abstract noun that is capitalized in the **Hot Tip** because it is the first word in the sentence. An example of an abstract proper noun is *Mother Nature.*

CUSTOMIZING TIP

Gifted and Talented Tell students that a collective noun takes a singular verb if the members of the group act together. A collective noun takes a plural verb if the members of the group act as individuals.

CUSTOMIZING TIP

Students Acquiring English/ESL For instruction and practice with countable and collective nouns, see **English Grammar Survival Kit** pp. 1–2.

Nouns **37**

Spice It Up!
Using a large classroom poster or scenic photograph, have students work in small groups to think of as many nouns as they can to describe items in the picture. Give them three minutes. Have each group record their answers on a large sheet of paper.

Answers

Print-Out Option You may create worksheets of exercise A for your students by using the 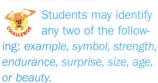 **Electronic Teacher Tools CD–ROM.**

Self-Check For a self-check of kinds of nouns, direct students to p. 588 in the Pupil's Edition for the answers to the items circled in yellow.

Answers shown on page. Common nouns are underlined once. Proper nouns are underlined twice. Collective nouns are circled.

Students may identify any two of the following: *example, symbol, strength, endurance, surprise, size, age, or beauty.*

B. WRITING

Answers will vary, but students should include *school, herd, pack, colony* **or other collective nouns that refer to animals.**

---

❸ Practice and Apply

A. CONCEPT CHECK: Kinds of Nouns

Write the nouns in these sentences, identifying each as common or proper. Then identify the two collective nouns.

California's Living Monuments
1. Among the largest living <u>things</u> on our <u>planet</u> are <u>sequoias</u>.
2. They are named for <u><u>Sequoya</u></u>, a Cherokee <u>scholar</u> and <u>leader</u>.
3. The most impressive <u>example</u> is the <u><u>General Sherman Tree</u></u>.
4. It bears the <u>name</u> of a Northern <u>commander</u> of the <u><u>Civil War</u></u>.
5. This <u>sequoia</u> weighs 12 million <u>pounds</u> and soars 275 feet, a <u>symbol</u> of <u>strength</u> and <u>endurance</u>.
6. The <u>size</u> of its <u>trunk</u>, as wide as a <u>highway</u> with three <u>lanes</u>, comes as a great <u>surprise</u> to many <u>people</u>.
7. A (team) of <u>researchers</u> estimated its <u>age</u> as between 2,200 and 2,500 <u>years</u>.
8. In past <u>centuries</u> <u>sequoias</u> grew across the <u><u>Northern Hemisphere</u></u>.
9. Now they are found chiefly in national <u>reserves</u> in <u><u>California</u></u>.
10. The <u>beauty</u> of these <u>trees</u> amazes (crowds) every <u>day</u>.

Find two abstract nouns in the sentences above.

Answers in column.

➡ **For a SELF-CHECK and more practice, see the EXERCISE BANK, p. 588.**

B. WRITING: Collective Nouns

Flock is a collective noun referring to a group of birds. Of all the collective nouns, those referring to groups of animals may be the most unusual. Write a funny piece of dialogue about or between two members of an animal group. Be sure to use the right collective noun.

Farcus by David Waisglass Gordon Coulthart

© 1993 Farcus Cartoons   WAISGLASS/COULTHART

"Some of the guys in the flock think you're showing off."

Singular and Plural Nouns

LESSON 2

1 Here's the Idea

▶ **A singular noun names one person, place, thing, or idea. A plural noun names more than one person, place, thing, or idea.**

> **One tourist noticed a statue.** (singular nouns)
>
> **Many tourists looked at statues.** (plural nouns)

One of the hardest things about plural nouns is spelling them correctly. Use these rules in the Quick-Fix Spelling Machine.

QUICK–FIX SPELLING MACHINE: PLURALS OF NOUNS

SINGULAR	RULE	PLURAL
① statue dream	Add -*s* to most nouns.	statues dreams
② wish sandwich	Add -*es* to a noun that ends in *s, sh, ch, x,* or *z*.	wishes sandwiches
③ photo	Add -*s* to most nouns that end in *o*.	photos
hero	Add -*es* to a few nouns that end in *o*.	heroes
④ city	For most nouns ending in *y*, change the *y* to an *i* and add -*es*.	cities
valley	When a vowel comes before the *y*, just add -*s*.	valleys
⑤ wolf life	For most nouns ending in *f* or *fe*, change the *f* to *v* and add -*es* or -*s*.	wolves lives
chief	Just add -*s* to a few nouns that end in *f* or *fe*.	chiefs
⑥ deer buffalo	For some nouns, keep the same spelling.	deer buffalo

Nouns **39**

LESSON OBJECTIVES

To recognize singular and plural nouns and to use them correctly in writing

DAILY TEST PREPARATION

Error Correction: Sentence Fragments Write the following item on the board or use 🏛 **Daily Test Preparation Transparency** p. DT6.

> For three days, and then you may return to school.

How is this fragment best written?

A. For three days, but then you may return to school.

B. For three days. Then you may return to school.

C. Rest for three days, and then you may return to school.

D. As it is

Teaching Point: Error correction questions often test your ability to recognize sentence fragments. In this item, you must know to supply a verb to complete the sentence. Note that the imperative phrase *Rest for three days* includes the implied subject *you*.

CUSTOMIZING TIP

Less Proficient Learners Remind students not to confuse plural nouns with verbs that end in -s. Write the following sentences on the board and ask students to identify the underlined words as verbs or plural nouns.

1. He <u>walks</u> verb by the <u>stores</u> plural noun.

2. The <u>vegetables</u> plural noun in small <u>shops</u> plural noun are fresher.

3. He <u>shops</u> verb for fresh fruit in neighborhood <u>markets</u> plural noun.

Also suitable for:

Students Acquiring English/ESL

TEACHING RESOURCES

Time-Saver Transparencies Binder:
• Daily Test Preparation p. DT6

Grammar, Usage, and Mechanics Workbook p. 34

SKILLS PRACTICE RESOURCES

English Grammar Survival Kit pp. 1–2

Grammar, Usage, and Mechanics Workbook pp. 35–36

Pupil's Edition Exercise Bank p. 589

TEACHING TIP

Cross-Curricular Connection
Science Have students use a dictionary to look up the plural forms of the following astronomical terms:

nebula nebulae

spectrum spectra

nova novae

THE LANGUAGE OF
LITERATURE

The passage on the student page is from *Immigrant Kids* in *The Language of Literature*, Level 7.

Answers

Print-Out Option You may create worksheets of exercise A for your students by using the
💿 **Electronic Teacher Tools CD–ROM.**

Self-Check For a self-check of singular and plural nouns, direct students to p. 589 in the Pupil's Edition for answers to items circled in yellow.

A. CONCEPT CHECK

1. engineers
2. coverings; pieces
3. inches
4. rays
5. corporations; individuals; schoolchildren
6. stresses; years
7. leaves

▶ **The plurals of some nouns are formed in irregular ways.**

Singular	man	child	foot	mouse
Plural	men	children	feet	mice

❷ Why It Matters in Writing

Imagine writing without plural nouns! Writers use so many plurals that learning the spelling rules is important.

> **LITERARY MODEL**
>
> **Passengers** all about us were crowding against the rail. Jabbered conversation, sharp **cries, laughs** and **cheers**—a steadily rising din filled the air. **Mothers** and **fathers** lifted up **babies** so that they too could see, off to the left, the Statue of Liberty.
>
> —Russell Freedman, *Immigrant Kids*

❸ Practice and Apply

A. CONCEPT CHECK: Singular and Plural Nouns   Answers in column.

Write the plural forms of the nouns in parentheses.

A Makeover for Lady Liberty

1. When the Statue of Liberty was almost a century old, (engineer) began to worry about her.
2. The copper (covering) had worn down, and (piece) of the torch were falling.
3. Photos showed that the head was 24 (inch) out of line.
4. This caused one of the (ray) in the crown to rub against the copper cover of the right arm.
5. Money for repairs came from (corporation), (individual), and (schoolchild).
6. A major job was repairing the arm and the torch, which had endured many (stress) over the (year).
7. Thin (leaf) of gold were applied to the torch's "flame" so that it would reflect the sun.

40   Grammar, Usage, and Mechanics

Spice It Up!

Play a game to practice spelling plural nouns. Divide the class into two teams and draw two 15-block pyramids on the chalkboard—5 blocks on the bottom row, 4 on the second row, 3 on the third, 2 on the fourth, and 1 at the top. Have teams line up several feet from the board and designate a captain for each team. Give each captain 15 index cards with singular nouns written on them. The captains should read the words to their team players, who take turns writing the plural form in the pyramid blocks.

8. In addition to the anniversary celebration in New York, many (community) around the country held their own (celebration).

9. On July 3, 1986, (speech), (concert), and (party) were held.

10. Lady Liberty began her second century on July 4, 1986, with many (festivity) and fireworks (display).

➜ **For a SELF-CHECK and more practice, see the EXERCISE BANK, p. 589.**

B. PROOFREADING: Spelling Plural Nouns

Ten plural nouns in the following passage are misspelled. Find them and write the correct spellings.

Show Me Your Golden Gate

San Francisco is one of California's largest <u>citys</u>. It has **cities** <u>bunchs</u> of attractions, including cable cars, <u>ferrys</u>, and **bunches/ferries** <u>wharfes</u>. Its most popular sight, however, is the Golden Gate **wharves** Bridge. Completed in 1937, the bridge connects San **communities** Francisco to northern <u>communitys</u>. Its main span stretches more than 4,200 feet across the Golden Gate waterway. The bridge has withstood bad weather, strong winds, and **earthquakes** <u>earthquakies</u>. Its steel structure remains solid, protected by <u>coates</u> of orange rustproof paint. The <u>lifes</u> of residents and **coats** <u>touristes</u> alike seem affected by the bridge's beauty. Few **lives** can resist snapping <u>photoes</u> of it. **tourists/photos**

C. WRITING: Interpreting Data   Answers in column.

Using the table below, write a few sentences comparing two famous suspension bridges—New York City's Brooklyn Bridge and San Francisco's Golden Gate Bridge. Use a variety of plural nouns in your sentences.

Comparing Two Bridges		
	Brooklyn Bridge	**Golden Gate Bridge**
Length of main span	1,595 feet	4,200 feet
Years to complete	14	4
Total cost	$15,000,000	$35,500,000
Construction deaths	21	0

(Answers continued)

8. communities; celebrations

9. speeches; concerts; parties

10. festivities; displays

Print-Out Option You may create worksheets of exercise B for your students by using the ⊙ **Electronic Teacher Tools CD–ROM.**

B. PROOFREADING

Answers shown on page. Misspelled nouns are underlined. Correct spellings are printed on the margin.

C. WRITING

Answers will vary, but students should use plural nouns such as *feet, years, dollars,* and *deaths* in their comparisons.

LESSON OBJECTIVES

To recognize possessive forms of nouns and to use them in writing

LESSON 3 Possessive Nouns

❶ Here's the Idea

▶ **The possessive form of a noun shows ownership or relationship.**

I held **Corey's camera** as she tied her shoe.
OWNERSHIP

Rick's parents met us at the train station.
RELATIONSHIP

You may use possessive nouns in place of longer phrases.

George Washington Carver's home.
We visited ~~the home of George Washington Carver.~~

QUICK–FIX SPELLING MACHINE: POSSESSIVES

NOUN		RULE	POSSESSIVE
Singular	sun Charles	Add an apostrophe and -s.	The sun's heat Charles's souvenirs
Plural ending in -s	states farmers	Add an apostrophe.	states' border farmers' crops
Plural not ending in -s	children geese	Add an apostrophe and -s.	children's toys geese's migrations

❷ Why It Matters in Writing

Possessive nouns can help writers show even the most unusual relationships, as in the model below.

PROFESSIONAL MODEL

In Ashburn, Georgia, stands an unusual monument. Here you will find the **world's** largest sculpture of a peanut, the local **growers'** pride. The **peanut's** length is an amazing ten feet, seven feet greater than that of its rival, **Oklahoma's** "big peanut."

③ Practice and Apply

A. CONCEPT CHECK: Possessive Nouns

Write the possessive form of each noun in parentheses. Then label each possessive form as singular or plural.

George Washington Carver Slept Here

1. In (Missouri) southwestern corner stands a modest frame home. **Missouri's, Sing.**
2. The (farmhouse) appearance is like that of many others. **farmhouse's, Sing.**
3. Visitors may not recognize one of our (country) monuments. **country's, Sing.**
4. Yet, within its walls lived one of (history) finest agricultural scientists, George Washington Carver. **history's**
5. As a young boy he survived most (children) worst nightmare, the loss of both parents. **children's, Pl.**
6. (Neighbors) actions helped him to overcome his greatest difficulties. **Neighbor's, Pl.**
7. At the monument, children can walk through the (area) many woods and fields. **area's, Sing.**
8. Here (Carver) own interest in plants and agriculture began. **Carver's, Sing.**
9. In time his work benefited many (farmers) lives. **farmer's, Pl.**
10. The (home) simplicity reminds visitors of this great (person) humble background. **home's, Sing.; person's, Sing.**

➡ For a SELF-CHECK and more practice, see the EXERCISE BANK, p. 589.

B. REVISING: Using Possessive Nouns *Answers in column.*

Use possessive nouns to make these phrases short enough to fit on signposts.

Example: The Mammoth Caves of Kentucky
Answer: Kentucky's Mammoth Caves

1. the Space Needle in Seattle
2. Preservation Hall in New Orleans
3. the beaches of California
4. the Hermitage of Andrew Jackson
5. the Gateway Arch in St. Louis

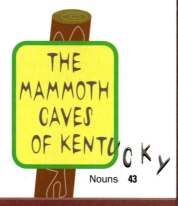

THE MAMMOTH CAVES OF KENTUCKY

Nouns 43

NOUNS

Answers

Print-Out Option You may create worksheets of exercises A and B for your students by using the 💿 **Electronic Teacher Tools CD–ROM.**

A. CONCEPT CHECK

Self-Check For a self-check of possessive nouns, direct students to p. 589 in the Pupil's Edition for the answers to the items circled in yellow.

Answers shown on page. Possessive forms are labeled using these codes:

Sing. = singular

Pl. = plural

B. REVISING

1. Seattle's Space Needle
2. New Orleans's Preservation Hall
3. California's beaches
4. Andrew Jackson's Hermitage
5. St. Louis's Gateway Arch

ASSESSMENT

Assessment Masters:
• Chapter Mid-point Test p. 25

Spice It Up!

Have students rewrite the humorous newspaper headlines below, making at least one of the nouns in each headline possessive. Tell students that they may have to change the form of other words and rearrange words.

• School Lunch Mystifies Pupils

• Pupils' School Lunch a Mystery

• School Uniforms Change Color in Laundry

• School Uniforms' Color Changes in Laundry

• Class Field Trip Cancelled

• Class's Field Trip Cancelled

Print-Out Option You may create worksheets of exercises A and B for your students by using the 💿 **Electronic Teacher Tools CD–ROM.**

Answers shown on page. Common nouns are under- lined once. Proper nouns are underlined twice. Collective nouns are circled. Students may identify two of the three collective nouns: *family,* *team,* and *class.*

Answers shown on page. Correct choices are under- lined. They are identified by these codes:

PL.=plural

Poss.=possessive

CHAPTER 2

CHAPTER 2

Mixed Review

A. Kinds of Nouns Write the 12 nouns that appear in the message on the postcard below. Identify each as common or proper. Then identify two collective nouns.

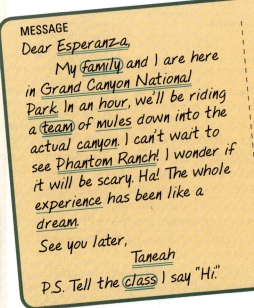

MESSAGE

Dear Esperanza,

My family and I are here in Grand Canyon National Park. In an hour, we'll be riding a team of mules down into the actual canyon. I can't wait to see Phantom Ranch! I wonder if it will be scary. Ha! The whole experience has been like a dream.

See you later,

Taneah

P.S. Tell the class I say "Hi."

ADDRESS

Esperanza Diaz

154 Elm Street

Encinitas, California

91303

B. Plural and Possessive Nouns Choose the correct word in parentheses, and identify it as plural or possessive.

1. An incomplete sculpture of Chief Crazy Horse stands in the (<u>Black Hills</u>, Black Hill's) several (<u>miles</u>, mile's) from Mount Rushmore. **Pl./Pl.**

2. The (<u>Lakotas</u>, Lakota's) chose to celebrate the great (<u>warriors</u>, warrior's) spirit with this sculpture. **Pl./Poss.**

3. Work began over 50 years ago, and many (<u>hands</u>, hand's) continue to help in the process. **Pl.**

4. In 1998 the (statues, <u>statue's</u>) massive face was unveiled. **Poss.**

5. The (monuments, <u>monument's</u>) final form will show the (chiefs, <u>chief's</u>) entire figure seated on a horse. **Poss./Poss.**

In your 📁 **Working Portfolio,** return to the writing you did for the **Write Away** on page 34. Revise it to make the nouns more specific.

Compound Nouns
LESSON 4

1 Here's the Idea

▶ **A compound noun is made of two or more words used together as a single noun.** The parts of a compound noun may be written as

- a single word: **toothbrush, watermelon**
- two or more separate words: **sleeping bag, dining room**
- a hyphenated word: **runner-up, great-aunt**

Plural Compound Nouns

QUICK–FIX SPELLING MACHINE: COMPOUND NOUNS

SINGULAR	RULE	PLURAL
One word rooftop	Add -s to most words.	rooftops
paintbrush	Add -es to a word that ends in s, sh, ch, x, or z.	paintbrushes
Two or more words or hyphenated words compact disc lily of the valley sixteen-year-old sister-in-law	Make the main noun plural. The main noun is the noun that is modified.	compact discs lilies of the valley sixteen-year-olds sisters-in-law

2 Why It Matters in Writing

Compound nouns are very descriptive—they actually describe themselves. They also help writers paint clear pictures.

PROFESSIONAL MODEL

Dreamland Amusement Park is closed for the winter. . . . Taffy stands are shuttered, no **teenagers** screaming on the **roller coaster,** . . . and at the **merry-go-round,** the exquisite carousel which has been right here since 1915, the horses are frozen in their classical posture, waiting for another spring.

—Charles Kuralt, *On the Road with Charles Kuralt*

45

NOUNS

NOUNS

LESSON OBJECTIVES
To recognize compound nouns and to use them in writing

DAILY TEST PREPARATION

Revision-in Context: Punctuation
Write the following item on the board or use 📺 **Daily Test Preparation Transparency** p. DT7.

1 "To study for English is
2 reasonable," attested
3 Tim, "but for gym, it's
4 absurd"!

What is the **BEST** change, if any, to make in the sentence in lines 3–4?

A. Replace the exclamation point with a period

B. Replace *gym* with *Gym*

C. Place the exclamation point inside the quotation marks

D. Make no change

Teaching Point: A common item in revision-in-context questions is punctuation. This item tests whether you know that an end mark, such as an exclamation point, must be placed inside the quotation marks when it is part of the quotation.

TEACHING TIP

Remind students that they can use a dictionary to find out if a compound noun is a single word, two or more separate words, or a hyphenated word.

TEACHING RESOURCES

🖥 Time-Saver Transparencies Binder:
- Daily Test Preparation p. DT7
📒 Grammar, Usage, and Mechanics Workbook p. 40

SKILLS PRACTICE RESOURCES

📒 Grammar, Usage, and Mechanics Workbook pp. 41–42
Pupil's Edition Exercise Bank p. 590

TEACHING TIP

Encourage students to use dictionaries to double check the accuracy of their responses. Some students may find it difficult to identify certain compound nouns. Students should be able to find compound nouns listed in dictionaries.

❸ Practice and Apply

A. CONCEPT CHECK: Compound Nouns

Write each compound noun in the sentences below, indicating whether it is singular or plural.

Not Corny to Farmers

1. The plains produce <u>foodstuffs</u> such as corn, wheat, and rye.
2. The <u>cornstalks</u> stand tall in <u>South Dakota</u>, a state that loves corn. **Pl./Sing.**
3. The <u>Corn Palace</u> is a famous building in Mitchell, a prairie town that welcomes <u>cornhuskers</u>. **Sing./Pl.**
4. Today it is called the agricultural <u>show place</u> of the world.
5. Each spring, the outside of the concrete building is covered with wall designs made of <u>sweet corn</u>, grains, and grasses.
6. Corn is so popular in Mitchell that the local radio station uses the <u>call letters</u> KORN. **Pl.**
7. <u>Sportswriters</u> cover the local <u>high school's</u> teams, which are named the Kernels. **Pl./Sing.**
8. <u>Corn Palace Week</u> celebrates <u>harvest home</u>, the end of the harvest, with themes such as "South Dakota birds."
9. The state produces other products: <u>livestock</u> are fattened in <u>feedlots</u> in eastern <u>South Dakota</u>. **Pl./Pl./Sing.**
10. Even though <u>meatpacking</u> is a major industry in <u>Sioux Falls</u>, <u>corncribs</u> throughout the state remind visitors that corn is king. **Sing./Sing./Pl.**

➡ For a SELF-CHECK and more practice, see the EXERCISE BANK, p. 590.

B. REVISING: Adding Compound Nouns   Answers may vary.

Read the following description. Then choose five compound nouns from the list to replace the words in parentheses.

1. Ferris wheel
2. billy goats
3. racetrack dirtbikes
4. fireworks

During our summer vacation, my family usually visits the annual state fair. **(1)** Mom, Dad, and Cindy like to start off by riding the **(singular compound)**. **(2)** Cindy also enjoys petting animals especially furry ones— sheep, rabbits, and **(plural compound)**. **(3)** My brother Tom and I, however, like to tear up the **(singular compound)** on our **(plural compound)**. **(4)** By evening, we all look forward to the rodeo and loud, sparkling **(plural compound)**.

skateboard
billy goats
thunderstorm
Ferris wheel
dirt bikes
fireworks
barnyard
rattlesnakes
racetrack

46 Grammar, Usage, and Mechanics

Spice It Up!

Play a compound word game. Begin the game with the word *rooftop*. Have a student name a compound word that starts with the word's last letter—in this case, *p*. Continue having students name compound words that begin with the last letter of the previous compound word. For example, if *piggy bank* follows *rooftop*, then the next word must start with *k*. Play until each student has contributed a word.

LESSON 5 — Nouns and Their Jobs

❶ Here's the Idea

Because they name many things, nouns have different jobs in sentences.

Nouns as Subjects

A **subject** tells whom or what a sentence is about. Nouns are often subjects, as this description shows.

> **PROFESSIONAL MODEL**
>
> **Independence Hall** in Philadelphia is one of the nation's most popular landmarks. Here, the **Declaration of Independence** was approved by the 13 colonies on July 4, 1776.

Nouns as Complements

A **complement** is a word that completes the meaning of a verb. Three kinds of complements are predicate nouns, direct objects, and indirect objects.

Nouns as Complements		
Predicate noun	Renames, identifies, or defines the subject after a linking verb.	Benjamin Franklin was a **Founding Father** of our country.
Direct object	Names the receiver of the action after an action verb.	Thomas Jefferson wrote the **Declaration of Independence**.
Indirect object	Tells to whom or what or for whom or what an action is done.	Mom gave my **brother** a miniature replica of the Liberty Bell.

Nouns as Objects of Prepositions

An **object of a preposition** is the noun or pronoun that follows a preposition.

Paul Revere left on his ride.
PREPOSITION 🡕   🡔 OBJECT OF PREPOSITION

You'll learn more about prepositions on pp. 152–157.

Nouns **47**

LESSON OBJECTIVES

To identify and use nouns as subjects, complements, and objects of prepositions

DAILY TEST PREPARATION

Definition: Vocabulary Write the following item on the board or use 🖳 **Daily Test Preparation Transparency** p. DT8. Choose the word that means the same, or about the same, as the underlined word.

> The FBI gathers <u>forensic</u> evidence against criminals

A. judicial

B. secretive

C. genetic

D. legislative

Teaching Point: For definitions, use context clues to determine the meaning of the underlined word. *Forensic* evidence is used in a court of law to prosecute criminals. Therefore, *judicial*, related to the word *judge*, is closest in meaning.

NEED MORE INFORMATION?

For a review of the role of linking verbs, direct students to **Chapter 1, The Sentence and Its Parts.**

TEACHING TIP

Point out to students that *all* of a proper name serves as the subject, complement, or object of a sentence.

The *Statue of Liberty* subject stands proudly in the harbor.

The sculptor was *Auguste Bartholdi* predicate noun.

The statue is located in the harbor of *New York City* object of preposition.

TEACHING RESOURCES

 Time-Saver Transparencies Binder:
• Daily Test Preparation p. DT8

 Grammar, Usage, and Mechanics Workbook p. 43

SKILLS PRACTICE RESOURCES

 Grammar, Usage, and Mechanics Workbook pp. 44–45
Pupil's Edition Exercise Bank p. 591

Answers

A. CONCEPT CHECK

Self-Check For a self-check of nouns and their jobs, direct students to p. 591 in the Pupil's Edition for the answers to the items circled in yellow.

Answers shown on page using these codes:

S = subject

Comp. = complement

OP = object of preposition

1. country: indirect object; sorrow: direct object

4. contest: direct object

5. Washington D.C.; direct object

6. Lin: indirect object; idea: direct object

7. memorial: direct object

8. place: direct object

10. experiences: predicate noun

---

❷ Why It Matters in Writing

Specific complements can help you create a sharp picture. Notice how the complements in this description add specific details.

PROFESSIONAL MODEL

In the nation's capital, the Washington Monument seems a giant arrow, piercing the highest skies. This tremendous column climbs 555 feet into the air. The monument's sparkling beauty still astounds children and adults more than a century after its completion.

PREDICATE NOUN

DIRECT OBJECTS

❸ Practice and Apply

A. CONCEPT CHECK: Nouns and Their Jobs

Identify each underlined noun as a subject, a complement, or an object of a preposition.

Maya Lin and the Vietnam Veterans Memorial

S/Comp./Comp. **1.** The Vietnam War brought our country much sorrow.
2. More than 58,000 Americans died or remained missing in action. **S**
3. Veterans of the war wished to honor those who died. **S/OP**
4. A committee set up a contest to choose someone to design a memorial. **S/Comp.**
5. Maya Lin, a young architect, visited Washington, D.C., to view the memorial site. **S/Comp.**
6. The landscape gave Lin an idea. **S/Comp./Comp.**
S/Comp./OP **7.** The architect designed a memorial of two marble walls.
8. She created a meeting place between earth and sky. **Com**
9. The names of dead and missing Americans appear on the walls. **S/OP/OP**
10. Visits to the memorial have been healing experiences for millions of Americans. **OP/Comp./OP**

➡ For a SELF-CHECK and more practice, see the EXERCISE BANK, p. 591.

Label each complement as a predicate noun, a direct object, or an indirect object. **Answers in column.**

Spice It Up!

Quotable Quote

"What's in a name? That which we call a rose
By any other name would smell as sweet."
—William Shakespeare, *Romeo and Juliet*, Act II, Scene ii.

Read the lines and ask students to identify each noun as a subject, a complement, or an object of a preposition.
name, object of preposition
rose, complement
name, object of preposition

B. REVISING: Identifying Complements

Identify each underlined complement as a predicate noun, a direct object, or an indirect object.

The Cradle of Liberty

1. Boston, Massachusetts, is the <u>city</u> where American **PN** independence began.
2. Today, the Freedom Trail gives <u>tourists</u> a <u>walk</u> through **IO/DO** history.
3. At Faneuil Hall colonists regularly protested the British **DO/DO** <u>king</u> and his <u>taxation</u>.
4. In 1773, at Griffin's Wharf, patriots boarded three <u>ships</u>. **DO**
5. The patriots were active <u>participants</u> in the destruction of **PN** British property—tea.

C. WRITING: Using Nouns in Directions   Answers in column.

A Tour of the White House

Imagine that you have been asked to prepare directions for tour guides at the White House. The tour begins in the Rose Garden and continues clockwise through the first floor. Using the floor plan shown below, write simple directions for the guides. Include nouns used as subjects, complements, and objects of prepositions. Then identify and label each.

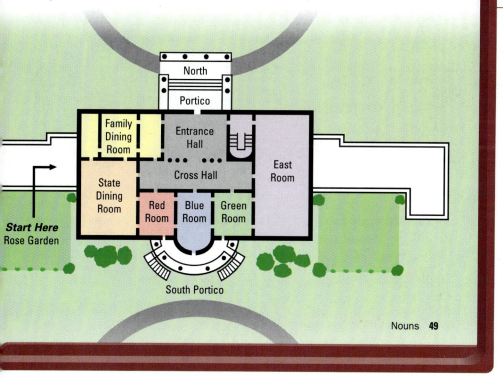

Answers

Print-Out Option You may create worksheets of exercise B for your students by using the
⊙ **Electronic Teacher Tools CD–ROM.**

B. REVISING

Answers shown on page using these codes:

PN = predicate noun

DO = direct object

IO = indirect object

C. WRITING

Answers will vary, but students should use nouns as subjects, complements, and objects of prepositions throughout their descriptions.

ASSESSMENT

 Assessment Masters:
• Chapter Mastery Tests pp. 43–46

 Test Generator CD-ROM

 mcdougallittell.com Grammar Chapter Quiz

LESSON OBJECTIVES

To identify and use nouns in maps, legends, and directions

Grammar in Social Studies

Using Nouns Effectively

In social studies classes you learn about important people, places, and things,—and you use nouns to name them. Creating a map is a good way to show information rather than talking about it. Mapmaking allows you to present clearly where important places are and where important events took place. Notice how common and proper nouns are used on this map of the famous Route 66.

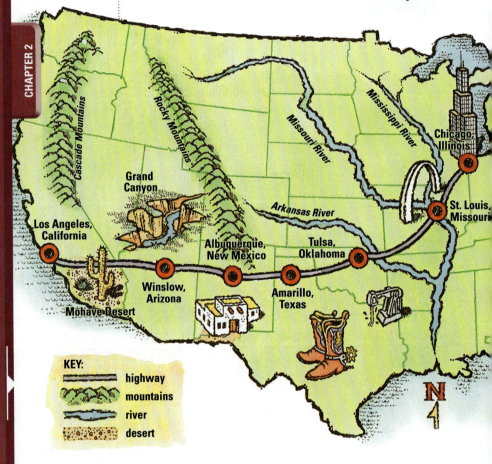

KEY:
- highway
- mountains
- river
- desert

50 Grammar, Usage, and Mechanics

TEACHING TIP

Make sure students know how to use a map key. Point out that a key explains the symbols used in a map and that these symbols can represent geographic features (for example, mountains) or man-made features (for example, highways). Then ask students to identify the kind of nouns used in the key (common).

Practice and Apply

A. REVISING: Using Proper Nouns

The message below is hard to understand because the writer uses many common nouns rather than specific proper ones. On a separate sheet of paper, write proper nouns to replace the underlined common nouns. Use the map to find the proper nouns.

Dear Anya,
    Driving on <u>this road</u> is so cool. We started out at <u>a lake</u> and ended up at <u>the ocean.</u> We went through eight states and crossed <u>two of the country's major rivers.</u> <u>One city</u> on a river had a huge arch sticking up into the sky. Near the end of the trip, we passed by <u>one desert</u> and finally jumped into the surf at our final destination.
    I wish you could have come with us.
    See you soon,
        Winona

Anya Taylor
501 S. Francisco Ave.
Chicago, IL 60601

B. WRITING: Make a map of your own.

Draw a map of your neighborhood, a nearby park, zoo, or any other area. Include the following landmarks:

- natural features such as rivers, lakes, and mountains
- streets
- buildings
- other interesting attractions

Be sure to label each landmark with an appropriate proper noun. Use different colors or symbols for features like streets, rivers, and bike paths. Use common nouns to create a key that explains the symbols.

A colorful strip along Route 66.

Nouns **51**

TEACHING TIP

Speaking and Listening To give students extra practice, read the following sentences aloud. Instruct students to listen for the nouns and then tell if they are common or proper, and if they are possessive:

1. The <u>river</u> (common) roared through the <u>canyon</u> (common).

2. <u>The Colorado River</u> (proper) raced through the <u>Grand Canyon</u> (proper).

3. The <u>Grand Canyon's</u> (proper and possessive) <u>scenery</u> (common) is spectacular.

This exercise satisfies several standard purposes. It requires students:

- to listen critically to evaluate the content of the spoken sentences
- to monitor their own understanding of the types of nouns mentioned in the spoken sentences
- to compare their own perception of the nouns mentioned with the perception of others

Answers

Print-Out Option You may create worksheets of exercise A for your students by using the
🅒 **Electronic Teacher Tools CD–ROM.**

A. REVISING

Answers will vary. Possible responses:

1. Route 66
2. Mississippi and Missouri rivers
3. St. Louis
4. the Mohave Desert

B. WRITING

Maps will vary. Students should label landmarks using appropriate proper nouns. They should use common nouns to create the key.

Mixed Review

Answers

Print-Out Option You may create worksheets of exercises A and B for your students by using the ⊙ **Electronic Teacher Tools CD–ROM.**

A. Plurals, Possessives, and Compounds

1. Fred's: possessive
2. necklace: compound
3. watches: plural
4. grandfather clocks: compound and plural
5. baseball: compound
6. diaries: plural
7. schoolhouse: compound
8. Elvis's: possessive
9. scarves: plural
10. Beatles': possessive and plural

B. Nouns and Their Jobs

Answers shown on page using these codes:

S = subject

PN = predicate noun

DO = direct object

IO = indirect object

OP = object of a preposition

Mixed Review

A. Plurals, Possessives, and Compounds Read the following sign advertising a roadside attraction, and correct ten errors in spelling. Then identify each corrected noun as plural, possessive, or compound. For some of the nouns, you will use more than one label.

Answers in column.

Freds' Famous Fantastic Museum!

★ **Come see our attractions:**

Queen Victoria's neck lace

Antique watchs and grandfatherclocks

★ A base ball autographed by Babe Ruth

Settlers' original diarys

An entire school house from 1900

Elvis' white scarfs

★ The Beatles's bus from their first U.S. tour

B. Nouns and Their Jobs In the following sentences, nouns are used in various ways. Identify each underlined noun as a subject, a predicate noun, a direct object, an indirect object, or an object of a preposition.

1. A favorite site of many tourists is the <u>Everglades.</u> **PN**
2. The <u>Everglades</u> are wetlands in southern Florida. **S**
3. The naturalist Marjory Stoneman Douglas saved the <u>Everglades</u> from <u>destruction</u> several decades ago. **DO/OP**
4. Still, the <u>Everglades</u> continued to be drained, and much of the habitat of <u>alligators</u> and wading birds disappeared. **S/OP**
5. Now a congressional agreement gives the <u>Everglades</u> millions of dollars for preservation. **IO**
6. Every tourist should honor <u>John Muir</u> for his life and work. **DO**
7. <u>Muir</u> was a lifelong tourist himself. **S**
8. His parents brought <u>Muir</u> and his sisters from Scotland to Wisconsin as children. **DO**
9. <u>Muir</u> later traveled the country and was responsible for saving Yosemite as a national park. **S**
10. The conservationist who founded the Sierra Club was <u>John Muir.</u> **PN**

Mastery Test: What Did You Learn?

For each underlined item, choose the letter of the term that correctly identifies it.

> In the East and the <u>Midwest</u>, travelers can visit many <u>sites</u>
> (1)   (2)
> associated with the Underground Railroad. This "railroad" consisted
> of people and places that helped Southern slaves escaping to the
> North and to Canada. Both blacks and whites were <u>"conductors"</u>
> (3)
> and guided the <u>runaways</u>. Some conductors were slaves who had
> (4)
> already escaped and then traveled back south to lead others to
> safety. Over 2,000 slaves passed through <u>Levi Coffin's</u> home in
> (5)
> Newport, Indiana. A <u>light</u> in the <u>window</u> of John Rankin's home in
> (6)   (7)
> Ohio showed slaves that no slave catchers were nearby. Today the
> homes of <u>Levi Coffin</u>, John Rankin, and others are open so that the
> (8)
> <u>public</u> can learn about the "railroad" of <u>courage</u>.
> (9)   (10)

1. A. singular common noun
   B. plural common noun
   C. singular proper noun
   D. plural proper noun

2. A. noun as subject
   B. noun as predicate noun
   C. noun as direct object
   D. nouns as indirect object

3. A. noun as subject
   B. noun as predicate noun
   C. noun as direct object
   D. noun as indirect object

4. A. singular possessive noun
   B. plural possessive noun
   C. singular compound noun
   D. plural compound noun

5. A. singular collective noun
   B. plural collective noun
   C. singular possessive noun
   D. plural possessive noun

6. A. noun as subject
   B. noun as predicate noun
   C. noun as direct object
   D. noun as indirect object

7. A. concrete noun
   B. abstract noun
   C. possessive noun
   D. compound noun

8. A. noun as direct object
   B. noun as subject
   C. noun as predicate noun
   D. noun as object of a preposition

9. A. compound noun
   B. collective noun
   C. proper noun
   D. possessive noun

10. A. compound noun
    B. concrete noun
    C. abstract noun
    D. possessive noun

Mastery Test

As an option, two other Chapter Mastery Tests appear in **Assessment Masters** pp. 43–46.

Answers circled on page.

PRESCRIPTION FOR MASTERY	
If students miss item number:	Use **Teaching Resources** and **Skills Practice Resources** for lesson:
1, 7, 9, 10	❶ Kinds of Nouns p. 36
2, 3, 6, 8	❺ Nouns and Their Jobs p. 47
4	❷ Singular and Plural Nouns p. 39 and ❹ Compound Nouns p. 45
5	❸ Possessive Nouns p. 42

NOUNS

NOUNS

Student Help Desk

Nouns at a Glance

A noun names a person, place, thing, or idea. There are several ways to classify nouns.

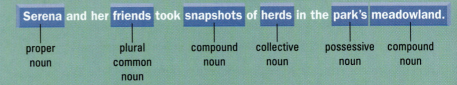

Serena and her friends took snapshots of herds in the park's meadowland.

| proper noun | plural common noun | compound noun | collective noun | possessive noun | compound noun |

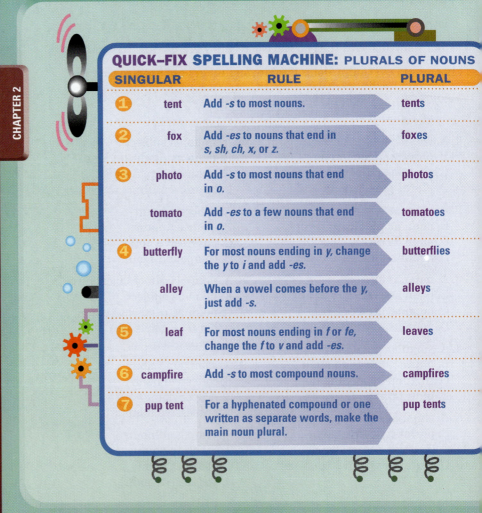

QUICK–FIX SPELLING MACHINE: PLURALS OF NOUNS

	SINGULAR	RULE	PLURAL
1	tent	Add -s to most nouns.	tents
2	fox	Add -es to nouns that end in s, sh, ch, x, or z.	foxes
3	photo	Add -s to most nouns that end in o.	photos
	tomato	Add -es to a few nouns that end in o.	tomatoes
4	butterfly	For most nouns ending in y, change the y to i and add -es.	butterflies
	alley	When a vowel comes before the y, just add -s.	alleys
5	leaf	For most nouns ending in f or fe, change the f to v and add -es.	leaves
6	campfire	Add -s to most compound nouns.	campfires
7	pup tent	For a hyphenated compound or one written as separate words, make the main noun plural.	pup tents

Classifying Nouns — Sorting Your Stuff

Possessives of Nouns

Relationship	Ownership
Douglas's sister	Natalie's marshmallow

Collective Nouns

Collective Noun	Group of Animals
colony	colony of ants, badgers, or frogs
flock	flock of birds or sheep
school	school of fish
herd	herd of cattle, deer, or elephants

More Noun Types

Concrete	Abstract
tent	nature
lake	beauty

Nouns and Their Jobs — What's Happening at Camp?

Use of Noun	Example
Subject	**Mosquitoes** swarmed around Meg's head.
Predicate noun	The bullfrogs were our **entertainers** for the night.
Direct object	Tim tipped his **canoe** over in the icy river.
Indirect object	Kyra just handed **Jordan** a moldy plum.
Object of a preposition	We're hiking down to **Old Faithful** this afternoon.

The Bottom Line

Checklist for Nouns

Have I . . .

____ chosen precise nouns?

____ spelled plural nouns correctly?

____ spelled possessive nouns correctly?

____ used possessive nouns to shorten my sentences?

____ spelled compound nouns correctly?

Teacher's Notes
WHAT DOESN'T WORK:

TEACHER'S LOUNGE

Just for Laughs

Teacher: "Can someone in this class give me three collective nouns?"

Student: "Flypaper, wastebasket, and vacuum cleaner."

Brain Break

Find the word that best completes the following series:

Elephant   Antelope   Operable   _____

1. Bleacher   **2.** Leopard   **3.** Herd   **4.** Pebble

Answer: *Bleacher* because each consecutive word in the series starts with the last three letters of the previous word

CHAPTER 3

CHAPTER RESOURCES

 Time-Saver Transparencies Binder:
- Daily Test Preparation pp. DT8–13
- Quick-Fix Grammar and Style Charts pp. QF5–7
- Visual Grammar™ Tiles Lesson 7

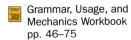 Grammar, Usage, and Mechanics Workbook pp. 46–75

Integrated Technology and Media

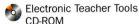 Electronic Teacher Tools CD-ROM

Grammar Coach CD-ROM Lessons 7–10

Power Presentations CD-ROM Lesson 4

 mcdougallittell.com

Assessment

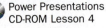 Assessment Masters:
- Chapter Pretest pp. 6–7
- Chapter Mid-point Test p. 26

- Chapter Mastery Tests pp. 47–54

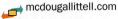 Test Generator CD-ROM

 mcdougallittell.com Grammar Chapter Quiz

Students Acquiring English/ESL

English Grammar Survival Kit pp. 5–8

Chapter 3

Pronouns

CHAPTER 3

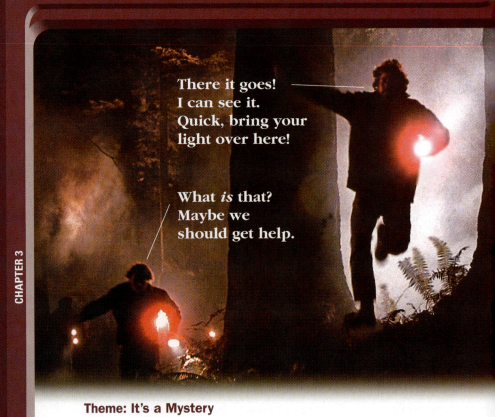

> There it goes! I can see it. Quick, bring your light over here!
>
> What *is* that? Maybe we should get help.

Theme: It's a Mystery

Who Did What?

Imagine this conversation without the words *it, I, your, what, that,* and *we.* These words, called **pronouns,** can streamline your writing by taking the place of nouns or other pronouns. Be careful though. If you don't use pronouns correctly, you may create a mystery for your readers.

Write Away: Real-Life Mysteries

You don't need to be a detective to solve mysteries. In a sense, you solve a mystery whenever you find the answer to a math problem or succeed in locating your new homeroom. Write a paragraph describing a mystery you've solved. Place the paragraph in your 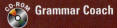 **Working Portfolio.**

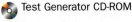 **Grammar Coach**

56

Diagnostic Test: What Do You Know?

Choose the letter that correctly identifies each underlined word.

Ball lightning is one of nature's most baffling mysteries. Small glowing spheres appear during violent thunderstorms. No one knows what causes <u>them</u>. <u>Their</u> behavior is truly weird. One
(1)   (2)
eyewitness said <u>he</u> saw a blue sphere go right through <u>his</u>
(3)   (4)
windowpane, burning a neat hole in the glass. If <u>you</u> are in an
(5)
airplane during a thunderstorm, you <u>yourself</u> might see ball
(6)
lightning rolling down the aisle! <u>This</u> has actually happened on
(7)
some flights. In one city, a multicolored sphere entered a factory, traveled along the metal girders, hit a window, and disappeared. The workers must have argued among <u>themselves</u> about whether
(8)
to tell <u>anyone</u>. <u>Who</u> would believe such a strange story?
(9)   (10)

1. A. subject pronoun
   B. object pronoun
   C. possessive pronoun
   D. demonstrative pronoun

2. A. indefinite pronoun
   B. subject pronoun
   C. demonstrative pronoun
   D. possessive pronoun

3. A. first-person pronoun
   B. second-person pronoun
   C. third-person pronoun
   D. plural pronoun

4. A. plural possessive pronoun
   B. singular possessive pronoun
   C. plural object pronoun
   D. singular object pronoun

5. A. personal pronoun
   B. interrogative pronoun
   C. reflexive pronoun
   D. demonstrative pronoun

6. A. indefinite pronoun
   B. reflexive pronoun
   C. intensive pronoun
   D. interrogative pronoun

7. A. demonstrative pronoun
   B. intensive pronoun
   C. complement pronoun
   D. interrogative pronoun

8. A. personal pronoun
   B. indefinite pronoun
   C. reflexive pronoun
   D. possessive pronoun

9. A. demonstrative pronoun
   B. indefinite pronoun
   C. reflexive pronoun
   D. interrogative pronoun

10. A. demonstrative pronoun
    B. interrogative pronoun
    C. indefinite pronoun
    D. reflexive pronoun

Diagnostic Test

As an option, a Chapter Pretest appears in ▦ **Assessment Masters** pp. 6–7.

Answers circled on page.

Use the chart below to determine which lessons students need.

PRESCRIPTION FOR SUCCESS	
If students miss item number:	**Work on lesson:**
1	❸ Object Pronouns p. 63
2, 4	❹ Possessive Pronouns p. 65
3, 5	❶ What Is a Pronoun? p. 58
6, 8	❺ Reflexive and Intensive Pronouns p. 68
7, 10	❻ Interrogatives and Demonstratives p. 70
9	❽ Indefinite-Pronoun Agreement p. 76

The **Diagnostic Test** parallels the **Mastery Test** on page 87. Have students keep the test in their portfolio to compare with their results on the **Mastery Test.**

BLOCK SCHEDULING

Pressed for Time?
Review the last four lessons in the chapter to cover the material that students typically have the most trouble with. Have them complete **Here's the Idea** and **Practice and Apply, Concept Check** only, for those lessons.

Time for More?
After completing all of the lessons, have students write and then read aloud sentences that use pronouns. Encourage students to use at least two types of pronouns in a sentence: possessive, reflexive, intensive, indefinite, or demonstrative pronouns.

LESSON OBJECTIVES

To recognize personal pronouns and use them in writing

DAILY TEST PREPARATION

Error Identification:
Capitalization Write the following item on the board or use **Daily Test Preparation Transparency** p. DT8.

Look for mistakes in capitalization in the sentence. Decide which line, if any, contains a mistake.

A. Jack and I took a train

B. Downtown to meet Sue,

C. one very large T-rex.

D. No mistakes

Teaching Point: Error identification questions often test your knowledge of basic capitalization rules. Because *downtown* is not a proper noun, it should be lowercase.

CUSTOMIZING TIPS

Gifted and Talented Point out that a pronoun should agree with its antecedent not only in person and number but also in gender. Examples:

Preston took his sister to school. (The masculine pronoun *his* refers to *Preston*, not *sister*.)

Emily plays soccer and Dad coaches her. (The feminine pronoun *her* agrees with *Emily*, not *Dad*.)

That wallet should be returned to its owner, Ms. Contreras. (The neuter pronoun *its* refers to *wallet*, not *Ms. Contreras*.)

LESSON 1 · What Is a Pronoun?

❶ Here's the Idea

▶ **A pronoun is a word that is used in place of a noun or another pronoun.** A pronoun can refer to a person, place, thing, or idea. The word that a pronoun refers to is called its **antecedent**.

REFERS TO

Ramon visited Death Valley, and **he** was impressed.

REFERS TO

Death Valley is mysterious. **It** is silent.

Personal Pronouns

▶ **Pronouns such as *we, I, he, them*, and *it* are called personal pronouns.** Personal pronouns have a variety of forms to indicate different **persons, numbers,** and **cases.**

Person and Number There are first-person, second-person, and third-person personal pronouns, each having both singular and plural forms.

Singular	Plural
I went out.	**We** left early.
You left too.	**You** are leaving.
He came by bus.	**They** came by car.

Case Each personal pronoun forms three cases: subject, object, and possessive. Which form to use depends on the pronoun's function in a sentence.

Subject: **He read about Death Valley.**

Object: **Julie asked him about the rocks.**

Possessive: **Ramon brought his book.**

The chart on the next page shows all the forms of the personal pronouns.

TEACHING RESOURCES

 Time-Saver Transparencies Binder:
• Daily Test Preparation p. DT8

 Grammar, Usage, and Mechanics Workbook p. 46

SKILLS PRACTICE RESOURCES

 English Grammar Survival Kit pp. 5–8

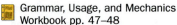 Grammar, Usage, and Mechanics Workbook pp. 47–48

Pupil's Edition Exercise Bank p. 591

 Grammar Coach CD-ROM Lesson 8

Personal Pronouns			
	Subject	**Object**	**Possessive**
Singular			
First person	I	me	my, mine
Second person	you	you	your, yours
Third person	he, she, it	him, her, it	his, her, hers, its
Plural			
First person	we	us	our, ours
Second person	you	you	your, yours
Third person	they	them	their, theirs

❷ Why It Matters in Writing

Pronouns help you talk about people concisely when you're telling a story. Notice how pronouns are used in this passage.

> **LITERARY MODEL**
>
> **I** knew **I** had to be honest with Grandpa; **it** was **my** only chance. **He** saw **my** shadow and looked up. **He** waited for **me** to speak. **I** cleared **my** throat nervously. . . .
>
> —Marta Salinas, "The Scholarship Jacket"

❸ Practice and Apply

A. CONCEPT CHECK: What Is a Pronoun?

Write the personal pronouns in these sentences.

Mystery in Death Valley

1. Death Valley is famous for <u>its</u> strange moving boulders. **Death Valley**
2. <u>They</u> are found in a dry lake bed called Racetrack Playa.
3. The rocks slide on <u>their</u> own, leaving long tracks behind <u>them</u>. **rocks/rocks**
4. Can <u>you</u> think of an explanation for this curious event?
5. Investigators offer two major theories for <u>us</u> to consider.

Pronouns   **59**

6. One geologist thinks that when floodwater freezes, an ice sheet can form under a rock and help <u>it</u> slide. **rock**

7. Other scientists disagree with <u>his</u> theory. **geologist**

8. <u>They</u> believe that the wind alone can move the rocks. **scientists**

9. Some scientists have hedged <u>their</u> bets, telling <u>us</u> that both theories could be true.

10. <u>We</u> still don't know for sure how the rocks move.

Name the antecedents of the personal pronouns in sentences 1, 3, 6, 7, and 8.

➡ For a SELF-CHECK and more practice, see the EXERCISE BANK, p. 591.

B. REVISING: Substituting Pronouns for Nouns

Rewrite this draft of a social studies report by changing each underlined noun to a pronoun.

STUDENT MODEL

It

They

their

his *or* her

they

Death Valley is a land of extremes. <u>Death Valley</u> contains the lowest point in the United States. Temperatures reflect the harsh, arid landscape. <u>Temperatures</u> range from 125° in summer to near freezing in winter.

The valley was named in 1849 by pioneers after <u>the pioneers'</u> long, hard journey. In 1868 a California state geologist mentioned the valley in <u>the geologist's</u> published paper. The valley interested other geologists when <u>the geologists</u> heard about the valuable minerals discovered there.

C. WRITING: Dialogue   Suggestions in column.

Use the information in exercise A to write a short dialogue between two people who are visiting Racetrack Playa. Use personal pronouns to make the dialogue sound natural.

Example:

SPEAKER 1. Did **you** see that boulder move?

SPEAKER 2. No, **I** didn't. Maybe **it** just wobbled a little.

SPEAKER 1. Don't tell **me** that. **You** can see the track!

Death Valley

LESSON 2 · Subject Pronouns

LESSON OBJECTIVES

To recognize subject pronouns and use them correctly in writing

1 Here's the Idea

▶ **A subject pronoun is used as a subject in a sentence or as a predicate pronoun after a linking verb.**

Subject Pronouns	
Singular	**Plural**
I	we
you	you
he, she, it	they

Pronouns as Subjects

Use a subject pronoun when the pronoun is a subject or part of a compound subject.

The Hope diamond has a fascinating history.

It has been bad luck for many owners.
(*It,* referring to *The Hope diamond,* is the subject of the sentence.)

You and he think the diamond is cursed.

Predicate Pronouns

A predicate pronoun follows a linking verb and identifies the verb's subject. Use the subject case for predicate pronouns.

The owner was he.
   SUBJECT   PREDICATE PRONOUN

The buyers are you and she.

The royal jewelers are they.

Remember, the most common linking verbs are forms of the verb *be,* including *is, am, are, was, were, been, has been, have been, can be, will be, could be,* and *should be.*

 DAILY TEST PREPARATION

Error Correction: Spelling Write the following item on the board or use 🖥 **Daily Test Preparation Transparency** p. DT9.

Read the sentence carefully. Decide if one of the words is misspelled or if there is no mistake.

The program is <u>technicaly</u>
                          A

sound, and <u>incorporates</u> many
                   B

good <u>features</u>. <u>No mistake</u>.
       C   **D**

Teaching Point: A common spelling item in error–correction questions is adding suffixes. When adding the suffix *-ly* to a word ending in *l* (*technical*), keep both *ll*'s (*technically, finally, actually,* etc.)

PRONOUNS

TEACHING TIP

Point out that forms of *become, seem, look,* and *appear* can be linking verbs, too. A pronoun that follows those verbs should be written in the subject case.

TEACHING RESOURCES

 Time-Saver Transparencies Binder:
- Daily Test Preparation p. DT9
- Quick-Fix Grammar and Style Charts pp. QF6

Grammar, Usage, and Mechanics Workbook p. 49

SKILLS PRACTICE RESOURCES

 Grammar, Usage, and Mechanics Workbook pp. 50–51
Pupil's Edition Exercise Bank p. 592

Grammar Coach CD-ROM Lesson 9

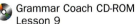

2 Why It Matters in Writing

A subject pronoun may not sound right to you. But as the writer of the passage below discovered, you can't always rely on sound to choose the correct case.

STUDENT MODEL

The huge French Blue diamond, later recut into the Hope diamond, was certainly bad luck for Marie Antoinette. The rulers of France in the years before the French Revolution were ~~her~~ *she* and Louis XVI. Marie Antoinette and ~~him~~ *he* were executed during the revolution.

3 Practice and Apply

CONCEPT CHECK: Subject Pronouns

Write the correct pronoun form to complete each sentence.

Investigating the Hope Diamond Legend
1. The diamond detectives were Carla and (<u>I</u>, me).
2. According to legend the huge blue diamond has had many owners, and (<u>they</u>, them) all came to a bad end.
3. Jean Baptiste Tavernier brought the original blue diamond from India; the first owner to die was (him, <u>he</u>).
4. (<u>He</u>, him) is said to have been killed in India by wild dogs.
5. Marie Antoinette and Louis XVI inherited the diamond; (<u>we</u>, us) know that the next victims were (them, <u>they</u>).
6. Carla and (me, <u>I</u>) learned that a Dutch diamond cutter may have recut the stone to disguise it.
7. His son and (<u>he</u>, him) died tragically soon afterward.
8. In the 1830s Henry Hope bought the recut gem; the person for whom the diamond was named was (<u>he</u>, him).
9. (<u>We</u>, Us) discovered that the Hope diamond is now in the Smithsonian Institution in Washington, D.C.
10. "Hope diamond experts" are (us, <u>we</u>)!

➡ **For a SELF-CHECK and more practice, see the EXERCISE BANK, p. 592.**

Object Pronouns

❶ Here's the Idea

▶ **An object pronoun is used as a direct object, an indirect object, or an object of a preposition.**

Object Pronouns

Singular	Plural
me	us
you	you
him, her, it	them

Direct Object The pronoun receives the action of a verb and answers the question *whom or what.*

FASCINATES WHOM?

The mysterious death of King Tut fascinates me.

DIRECT OBJECT

Did someone murder him? (murder whom? *him*)

Indirect Object The pronoun tells to whom or what or for whom or what an action is performed.

TO WHOM?

Chu lent me a video on the topic.

INDIRECT OBJECT DIRECT OBJECT

I told her the whole story.

Object of a Preposition The pronoun follows a preposition (such as *to, from, for, against, by,* or *about*).

Will you save the video for them?

PREPOSITION

I can tell the story to you and him.

Always use object pronouns after the preposition *between.*

This secret is between you and me. (not *between you and I*)

Pronouns **63**

DAILY TEST PREPARATION

Sentence Completion: Subject-Verb Agreement Write the following item on the board or use 🖥 **Daily Test Preparation Transparency** p. DT9. Choose the word or words that belong in the space.

_____ one's mind imitate the motion of the planets?

A. Do

B. Doing

C. Has Been

D. Does

Teaching Point: Sentence completion questions often test your knowledge of subject-verb agreement. In this case, the item tests your knowledge of agreement within inverted sentences, such as questions. The subject *mind* takes a singular verb *(does imitate).*

TEACHING TIP

Tell students that when two objects follow a preposition or a verb, they can decide whether to use the subject or object form of a pronoun by mentally screening out one object.

Example:

I can tell the story to you and (he, him).

I can tell the story to he. Incorrect

I can tell the story to him. Correct

TEACHING RESOURCES

 Time-Saver Transparencies Binder:
• Daily Test Preparation p. DT9

Grammar, Usage, and Mechanics Workbook p. 52

SKILLS PRACTICE RESOURCES

 Grammar, Usage, and Mechanics Workbook pp. 53–54

Pupil's Edition Exercise Bank p. 592

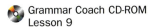 Grammar Coach CD-ROM Lesson 9

Speaking and Listening Write the following prepositions on the board: *of, over, in, above, across, after, with, beside, toward, around,* and *near.* Have students create and read sentences using the prepositions with object pronouns. Ask other students to listen to determine whether the pronouns are in the object case. In this exercise, students are expected to understand the major ideas (use object pronouns after prepositions) and supporting evidence in spoken messages. Students are also expected to demonstrate effective communication skills that reflect such demands as providing information.

Answers

Print-Out Option You may create worksheets of this exercise for your students by using the 💿 **Electronic Teacher Tools CD–ROM.**

MIXED REVIEW

Self-Check For a self-check of subject and object pronouns, direct students to p. 592 in the Pupil's Edition for the answers to the items circled in yellow.

Answers shown on page. Correct pronouns are underlined. Labels appear in the margin.

❷ Why It Matters in Writing

In conversation, people sometimes misuse subject and object pronouns ("Him and me went to the store"). When you write for school, however, you should always use the correct forms.

> **STUDENT MODEL**
>
> The Egyptologist Bob Brier studied King Tut's mummy.
> *him*
> Evidence uncovered by ~~he~~ suggests that Tut was killed by
> a blow to the head. Others say he was poisoned. Brier and
> *they*
> ~~them~~ agree, however, that the king was murdered.

❸ Practice and Apply

MIXED REVIEW: Subject and Object Pronouns

Choose the correct pronoun in these sentences, and identify them as subject or object pronouns.

Who Killed King Tut?

1. King Tutankhamen was only about nine years old when the priests crowned (he, <u>him</u>) as the new pharaoh. **object**

2. (<u>He</u>, Him) and his wife were not in power long before the young pharaoh died. **subject**

3. (<u>I</u>, Me) saw a video showing x-ray pictures of Tut's skull. **subject**

4. (<u>They</u>, Them) revealed that someone had struck Tut on the back of the head. **subject**

5. It occurred to (I, <u>me</u>) that only someone the king knew could get so close to (he, <u>him</u>). **object/object**

6. There are several possible suspects, but two of (<u>them</u>, they) had the best opportunity—the queen and the royal minister, Ay. **object**

7. (<u>She</u>, Her) and Ay married when Ay became pharaoh. **subject**

8. A ring discovered in 1931, however, shows that Ay married another queen after (she, <u>her</u>). **object**

9. Just between you and (<u>me</u>, I), I believe that Ay is the most likely killer. **object**

10. All the suspects may be long dead, but the evidence has outlived (they, <u>them</u>). **object**

➡ **For a SELF-CHECK and more practice, see the EXERCISE BANK, p. 592.**

Possessive Pronouns

1 Here's the Idea

▶ **A possessive pronoun is a personal pronoun used to show ownership or relationship.**

Possessive Pronouns	
Singular	**Plural**
my, mine	our, ours
your, yours	your, yours
her, hers, his, its	their, theirs

The possessive pronouns *my, your, her, his, its, our,* and *their* come before nouns.

> *OWNERSHIP*
> **The Chinese museum kept its amazing secret for years.**

> *OWNERSHIP*
> **No one saw the mummies in their colorful clothes.**

> *RELATIONSHIP*
> **Then Professor Mair and his tour group arrived.**

The possessive pronouns *mine, yours, hers, his, ours* and *theirs* can stand alone in a sentence.

> **The secret was theirs. Now the secret is ours.**

> **Is that book yours? No, mine has a blue cover.**

> **His looks torn. Is hers in better shape?**

Possessive Pronouns and Contractions

Some possessive pronouns sound like contractions (*its/it's, your/you're, their/they're*). Because these pairs sound alike, writers often confuse possessive pronouns with contractions.

Remember, a possessive pronoun *never* has an apostrophe. A contraction, however, *always* has an apostrophe. The apostrophe shows where a letter or letters have been left out after combining two words.

PRONOUNS

PRONOUNS

DAILY TEST PREPARATION

Error Correction: Run-On Sentences Write the following item on the board or use **Daily Test Preparation Transparency** p. DT10.

> We gave Rex a bath last weekend he had fleas.

How is this sentence *best* written?

A. We gave Rex a bath last weekend and he had fleas.

B. We gave Rex a bath last weekend. He had fleas.

C. We gave Rex a bath last weekend, he had fleas.

D. As it is

Teaching Point: Error correction questions often test your ability to recognize and revise run-on sentences. Answer B turns the independent clauses into two separate sentences.

CUSTOMIZING TIP

Students Acquiring English/ESL
Keep in mind that in some languages, possessive pronouns agree with the noun they modify, rather than with the gender of the possessor. For example, in Spanish, *su padre* means "his/her father."

TEACHING RESOURCES

 Time-Saver Transparencies Binder:
  • Daily Test Preparation p. DT10
 Grammar, Usage, and Mechanics
  Workbook p. 55

SKILLS PRACTICE RESOURCES

 Grammar, Usage, and Mechanics
  Workbook pp. 56–57
  Pupil's Edition Exercise Bank p. 593

 Grammar Coach CD-ROM
  Lesson 10

Write the following passage on the board and have students correct the contraction and possessive pronoun mistakes where necessary.

If you think only Egypt and China have mummies, your you're *in for a surprise. About 700 naturally preserved mummies, in they're* their *original clothing, have been found in Danish bogs. Its* It's *assumed that their* they're *the remains of people who lived about 2,400 years ago.*

QUICK–FIX SPELLING MACHINE

Possessive pronouns		Contractions	
its	Its clothes look great.	it's	It's well preserved.
your	Your pictures are great.	you're	You're talented!
their	Their colors are vivid.	they're	They're beautiful.

② Why It Matters in Writing

Proofread your work carefully to be sure you haven't confused possessive pronouns with contractions. The spell-checker on a computer will not catch these mistakes.

The desert, with ~~it's~~ *its* dry air, salt, and sand, is the best preserver of ancient textiles. Once these materials are uncovered, however, ~~their~~ *they're* easily damaged. Even the moisture from ~~you're~~ *your* hands and breath can harm the fibers. For this reason, archaeologists always wear masks when they work with ancient cloth.

Experts use tools in *their* work.

66

❸ Practice and Apply

A. CONCEPT CHECK: Possessive Pronouns

Choose the pronoun or contraction to complete each sentence.

The Amazing Mummies of Ürümqi

1. Imagine (your, <u>you're</u>) visiting a museum in Ürümqi, in the desert of northwest China.

2. In one room, you find remarkable mummies in (<u>their</u>, they're) cases.

3. The leggings, shirts, and cloaks on the mummies look as colorful as (<u>your</u>, you're) clothes today.

4. This experience really happened to Professor Mair and his tour group on (<u>their</u>, they're) trip to China in 1987.

5. The mummies are about 3,000 years old, and (<u>they're</u>, their) European, not Chinese!

6. (<u>It's</u>, Its) a mystery why these Europeans went all the way to China.

7. Mair's astonishing report made (<u>its</u>, it's) way around the world.

8. Some 3,000 years ago, a group of European Celts may have started trading with (<u>their</u>, they're) Chinese neighbors.

9. When one of the Celts was buried, the dry, salty desert preserved the body and (it's, <u>its</u>) clothing perfectly.

10. You can satisfy (<u>your</u>, you're) curiosity about these mummies of Ürürmqi by reading articles about them.

➡ **For a SELF-CHECK and more practice, see the EXERCISE BANK, p. 593.**

B. PROOFREADING: Using Possessive Pronouns

Correct the errors in the use of pronouns and contractions in the paragraph below. If a sentence contains no error, write *Correct*.

(1) <u>Its</u> common for archaeologists to name the mummies **1. It's**
they find. **(2)** Sometimes they're named for the way they look, **2. Correct**
other times for a person or place. **(3)** <u>Your</u> probably not aware **3. You're**
that three mummies in the Smithsonian Institution are named
Indiana Jones, Ancient Annie, and Minister Cox. **(4)** You can
guess how the first two got <u>they're</u> names, but how did   **4. their**
Minister Cox get <u>him</u>? **(5)** The mummy was named after a   **his**
former diplomat, Mr. Cox, who donated the mummy to the
museum for <u>it's</u> Egyptian collection. **5. its**

Answers

Print-Out Option You may create worksheets of exercises A and B for your students by using the 💿 **Electronic Teacher Tools CD–ROM.**

A. CONCEPT CHECK

Self-Check For a self-check of possessive pronouns, direct students to p. 593 in the Pupil's Edition for the answers to the items circled in yellow.

Answers underlined on page.

B. PROOFREADING

Answers shown on page. Pronoun errors are underlined. Correct pronouns appear in margin.

TEACHING TIP

Cooperative Learning Have students get into groups of three to collaborate on composing a second paragraph for the proofreading exercise. The paragraph may be a response to the information in the first paragraph or may provide suggestions for names for mummies that students might discover. Remind students to use possessive pronouns and contractions correctly.

LESSON 5 Reflexive and Intensive Pronouns

❶ Here's the Idea

A pronoun that ends in *self* or *selves* is either a reflexive or an intensive pronoun.

Reflexive and Intensive Pronouns		
myself	yourself	herself, himself, itself
ourselves	yourselves	themselves

Reflexive Pronouns

▶ **A reflexive pronoun refers to the subject and directs the action of the verb back to the subject.** Reflexive pronouns are necessary to the meaning of a sentence.

REFLECTS

Houdini called **himself** a master escape artist.

REFLECTS

Lynne dedicated **herself** to learning Houdini's secrets.

Notice that if you drop a reflexive pronoun, a sentence no longer makes sense ("Lynne dedicated to learning Houdini's secrets").

Intensive Pronouns

▶ **An intensive pronoun emphasizes a noun or another pronoun the same sentence.** Intensive pronouns are not necessary to the meaning of a sentence.

You yourselves have seen magic shows on TV.

I myself like to perform magic tricks.

Notice that when you drop an intensive pronoun, a sentence still makes sense ("I like to perform magic tricks").

Hisself and *theirselves* may look like real words, but they are not. Use *himself* and *themselves* instead.

68 Grammar, Usage, and Mechanics

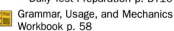

② Why It Matters in Writing

You can use reflexive pronouns to describe a person's actions more clearly.

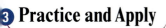

PROFESSIONAL MODEL

In the Water Torture Cell, Houdini doubled **himself** up and picked the lock that held his feet. Then, still holding his breath, he stood and unlocked the top of the tank. He hauled **himself** out.

—L. S. Baugh

③ Practice and Apply

CONCEPT CHECK: Reflexive and Intensive Pronouns

Write the reflexive or intensive pronoun in each sentence. Then label it *reflexive* or *intensive*.

Houdini's Great Escapes

1. During the 1920s, Harry Houdini labeled himself "the most daring escape artist in the world." **reflexive**
2. His name itself makes people think of magic. **intensive**
3. In one famous trick, Houdini freed himself from a tank that was filled to the top with water and securely locked. **reflexive**
4. He also called himself "the handcuff king" and said no handcuffs in the world could hold him. **reflexive**
5. The police officers themselves were amazed at Houdini. **intensive**
6. Some people convinced themselves that Houdini really had mysterious powers. **reflexive**
7. The magician himself said that wasn't true. **intensive**
8. He said people could develop these skills themselves. **intensive**
9. Still, we probably couldn't become Houdinis even if we taught ourselves his secrets. **reflexive**
10. Even today's professional magicians themselves don't try Houdini's dangerous escapes. **intensive**

➡ **For a SELF-CHECK and more practice, see the EXERCISE BANK, p. 593.**

Pronouns **69**

Answers

Print-Out Option You may create worksheets of this exercise for your students by using the **Electronic Teacher Tools CD–ROM.**

A. CONCEPT CHECK

Self-Check For a self-check of reflexive and intensive pronouns, direct students to p. 593 in the Pupil's Edition for the answers to the items circled in yellow.

Answers shown on page. Reflexive and intensive pronouns are underlined. Labels appear in the margin.

ASSESSMENT

Assessment Masters:
- Chapter Mid-point Test p. 26

PRONOUNS

PRONOUNS

LESSON OBJECTIVES

To recognize and use interrogative and demonstrative pronouns in writing

DAILY TEST PREPARATION

Error Identification: Punctuation
Write the following item on the board or use 🏛 **Daily Test Preparation Transparency** p. DT11.
Decide which type of error, if any, appears in the underlined section.

> It took a <u>long time but we managed</u> to cross the river.

A. Spelling error

B. Capitalization error

C. Punctuation error

D. No error

Teaching Point: Error identification questions often test your knowledge of basic punctuation rules. This item tests whether you know to place a comma before a conjunction in a compound sentence (*It took a long time, but . . .*).

TEACHING TIP

To help students decide whether to use *who* or *whom* in a question, have students try answering the question with both a subject and an object pronoun. If the subject pronoun is correct, they should use *who* in the question. If the object pronoun is correct, they should use *whom*.

Who/Whom saw the movie?

She saw the movie

The subject pronoun *who* should be used.

Who/Whom did Jon see?

Jon saw her.

The object pronoun *whom* should be used.

LESSON 6 Interrogatives and Demonstratives

❶ Here's the Idea

Interrogative Pronouns

▶ **An interrogative pronoun is used to introduce a question.**

Who made up this riddle?

Which riddle are you talking about?

Using Interrogative Pronouns	
Interrogative Pronoun	**Use**
who, whom	refers to people
what	refers to things
which	refers to people or things
whose	indicates ownership or relationship

Using *Who* and *Whom*

▶ ***Who* is always used as a subject or a predicate pronoun.**

Subject: **Who** knows the answer to the riddle?

Predicate pronoun: **Your favorite comedian is who?**

▶ ***Whom* is always used as an object.**

Direct object: **Whom did you tell?**

Indirect object: **You gave whom the answer?**

Object of preposition: **To whom did you give my name?**

WATCH OUT

Don't confuse *whose* with *who's*. *Whose* is a pronoun. ("Whose book did you borrow?") *Who's* is a contraction that means *who is* or *who has*. ("Who's missing a book"? "Who's returned my book?")

TEACHING RESOURCES

 Time-Saver Transparencies Binder:
- Daily Test Preparation p. DT11
- Quick-Fix Grammar and Style Charts p. QF7
- Visual Grammar™ Tiles Lesson 7

Grammar, Usage, and Mechanics Workbook p. 61

SKILLS PRACTICE RESOURCES

 Grammar, Usage, and Mechanics Workbook pp. 62–63
Pupil's Edition Exercise Bank p. 594

 Grammar Coach CD-ROM Lesson 10

Demonstrative Pronouns

▶ **A demonstrative pronoun points out a person, place, thing, or idea.**

The demonstrative pronouns—*this, that, these* and *those*—are used alone in a sentence, as shown below.

Singular

This is the game that we created.

That is the spinner.

Plural

These are the rules.

Those are the playing pieces.

Never use *here* or *there* with a demonstrative pronoun. The pronoun already tells which one or ones. *This* and *these* point out people or things that are near, or *here*. *That* and *those* point out people or things that are far away, or *there*.

This ~~here~~ is my playing piece.

That ~~there~~ is your playing piece.

② Why It Matters in Writing

Demonstrative pronouns call readers' attention to the people or things being discussed. In the riddles below, the demonstrative pronouns serve as the subjects of the riddles.

STUDENT MODEL

This has 18 legs and catches flies.
Answer: baseball team

These may fall far, but they never break.
Answer: leaves

Although **this** is small, it fills the house.
Answer: a lamp's light

These are bought by the yard and worn by the foot.
Answer: floor carpets

🖍️ **Visual Grammar™**

Determine whether a prepositional phrase is an adjective or adverb phrase, and identify the word it modifies.

Adverb prepositional phrase:

| MARIA | PUT DECALS | ON HER BICYCLE | . |

Adjective prepositional phrase:

| MARIA | ADJUSTED THE SEAT | ON HER BICYCLE | . |

Write the following sentences on the board. Have students supply the correct pronoun for each.

(Who/<u>Whom</u>) *did you see?*

Jessica gave (who/<u>whom</u>) *the points?*

My game piece is (<u>this</u>/these).

The next player is (<u>who</u>/ whom)?

(These/<u>Those</u>) *over there are my favorite games.*

Answers

Print-Out Option You may create worksheets of exercise A for your students by using the 💿 **Electronic Teacher Tools CD–ROM.**

Self-Check For a self-check of interrogatives and demonstratives, direct students to p. 594 in the Pupil's Edition for the answers to the items circled in yellow.

Answers underlined on page.

Answers will vary. Remind students that the demonstrative pronouns are *this, that, these,* and *those.* Sample answers:

<u>This</u> has two missing pieces, and one of <u>those</u> has three sides.

<u>That</u> has four sides.

<u>That</u> is a long narrow strip with four sides.

<u>This</u> is a triangle.

---

❸ Practice and Apply

Interrogatives and Demonstratives

Write the correct word to complete each sentence.

Inventors' Guide to Creating Board Games

1. To create a great board game, you need to answer some basic questions. First, (<u>what</u>, who) is the goal of the game?

2. If several people make up rules, (who's, <u>whose</u>) will you follow?

3. (Who, <u>What</u>) will you use to represent each player?

4. (<u>Who</u>, Whom) will go first?

5. You have to think up penalties. (That, <u>Those</u>) are important to any game.

6. Also, to (who, <u>whom</u>) will you give extra points or turns?

7. You need to create some kind of trap along the way. (These, <u>This</u>) makes the game more challenging.

8. Be careful (<u>which</u>, what) people you tell about the game before you finish it.

9. (<u>Who</u>, Whom) knows—someone might try to copy it.

10. Once you finish the game, (who, <u>whom</u>) will you invite to play it?

➡ For a SELF-CHECK and more practice, see the EXERCISE BANK, p. 594.

Answers in column.

Geometry is important to quilters. Notice the many geometric pieces in the quilt. Can you find the sections that are missing from this quilt? Write a sentence about each missing section, describing its shape and telling how many sides it has. Then write another sentence to compare the missing sections to each other. Use four demonstrative pronouns in your sentences. Underline the demonstrative pronouns.

Pronoun Agreement

LESSON OBJECTIVES

To understand and write pronouns that agree with their antecedents

① Here's the Idea

▶ **The antecedent is the noun or pronoun that a pronoun replaces or refers to.** The antecedent and the pronoun can be in the same sentence or in difference sentences.

REFERS TO
Louis writes **his** own detective stories.
▲ANTECEDENT ▲PRONOUN

REPLACES
Agatha Christie writes mysteries. Her stories are famous.

Pronouns must agree with their antecedents in number, person, and gender.

Agreement in Number

▶ **Use a singular pronoun to refer to a singular antecedent.**

REFERS TO
One story has its setting in Egypt.

▶ **Use a plural pronoun to refer to a plural antecedent.**

REFERS TO
The characters have their motives for murder.

Agreement in Person

▶ **The pronoun must agree in person with the antecedent.**

3RD PERSON
Louis likes his mysteries to have surprise endings.

2ND PERSON
You want a story to grab your attention.

PRONOUNS

Pronouns **73**

PRONOUNS

DAILY TEST PREPARATION

Error Correction: Subject-Verb Agreement Write the following item on the board or use **Daily Test Preparation Transparency** p, DT11. Choose the <u>best</u> way to write the underlined part of the sentence.

> The books of Walter Dean Myers <u>is included</u> in many classroom libraries.

A. includes

B. are included

C. included

D. No change

Teaching Point: Error correction questions often test your knowledge of subject-verb agreement. In this case, the item tests your ability to distinguish between the simple subject *(books)* and an interrupting phrase *(of Walter Dean Myers)*. The subject takes a plural verb *(are included)*.

TEACHING TIP

Point out that an antecedent can include more than one noun or pronoun. Write the following sample sentence on the board: *Librarians* and *booksellers* say *they* can't stock enough mysteries.

TEACHING RESOURCES

 Time-Saver Transparencies Binder:
- Daily Test Preparation p. DT11
- Quick-Fix Grammar and Style Charts p. QF5

Grammar, Usage, and Mechanics Workbook p. 64

SKILLS PRACTICE RESOURCES

 Grammar, Usage, and Mechanics Workbook pp. 65–66
Pupil's Edition Exercise Bank p. 594

Grammar Coach CD-ROM Lesson 8

Avoid switching from one person to another in the same sentence or paragraph.

INCORRECT:

> **Readers know you shouldn't read the ending first.**
> (*Readers* is third person; *you* is second person.)

CORRECT:

> **Readers know they shouldn't read the ending first.**
> (*Readers* and *they* are both third person.)

Agreement in Gender

▶ **The gender of a pronoun must be the same as the gender of its antecedent.**

Personal pronouns have three gender forms: masculine (*he, his, him*), feminine (*she, her, hers*), and neuter (*it, its*).

> **Agatha Christie sets many of her stories in England.**

> **The hero has to use all his wits to solve the crime.**

Don't use only masculine or only feminine pronouns when you mean to refer to both genders.

DRAFT:

Each **character** has **his** alibi ready.
(character could be masculine or feminine.)

There are two ways to make this sentence gender free.

1. Use the phrase *his or her*.
   Each character has his or her alibi ready.

2. Rewrite the sentence, using a plural antecedent and a plural pronoun. Be careful! Other words may also need to be changed.
   The characters have their alibis ready.

② Why It Matters in Writing

In your writing, you will sometimes refer to several people or groups of people. Correct pronoun-antecedent agreement will help your readers keep track of who is who in your writing.

STUDENT MODEL

Mystery lovers should read novels by Agatha Christie. ~~You~~ *They* will never guess who is the real **killer** in any of these stories. *He or she* ~~They~~ usually turn~~s~~ out to be a surprise.

③ Practice and Apply

CONCEPT CHECK: Pronoun Agreement   Answers in column.

Write the pronouns and their antecedents in these sentences.

Agatha Christie: Amateur Archaeologist

1. Agatha Christie loved real-life mysteries of the past. She helped to investigate them in the Middle East.
2. Max Mallowan was an English archaeologist. He was married to Christie for 45 years.
3. The couple went on many archaeological trips and found them exciting and a real source of inspiration.
4. Christie and Mallowan made important discoveries about Assyria. It was a wealthy country in the ancient world.
5. Pottery pieces revealed their secrets about the powerful Assyrian civilization.
6. Although Christie helped Mallowan at the site, she also kept writing mysteries.
7. A mystery writer may use exotic places as background for his or her stories.
8. Christie started *Murder in Mesopotamia* in the desert, but she finished it in England.
9. The story takes place at an archaeological dig. One of its main characters is Dr. Leidner.
10. When Mrs. Leidner is murdered, the detective Hercule Poirot must catch her killer.

Write the number and gender of each personal pronoun.   **Answers in column.**

➡ **For a SELF-CHECK and more practice, see the EXERCISE BANK, p. 594.**

Pronouns   **75**

Answers

Print-Out Option You may create worksheets of this exercise for your students by using the 🔵 **Electronic Teacher Tools CD–ROM.**

A. CONCEPT CHECK

Self-Check For a self-check of pronoun agreement, direct students to p. 594 in the Pupil's Edition for the answers to the items circled in yellow.

Answers use this order and format: pronoun (antecedent):

1. *She (Agatha Christie); them (mysteries)*
2. *he (Max Mallowan)*
3. *them (trips)*
4. *it (Assyria)*
5. *their (price)*
6. *she (Christie)*
7. *his or her (writer)*
8. *she (Christie); it (Murder in Mesopotamia)*
9. *its (story)*
10. *her (Mrs. Leidner)*

Answers use same format as above and these codes:

Sing. = singular
Pl. = plural
Masc. = masculine
Fem. = feminine
Neut. = neuter

1. *She (Sing., Fem.)*
2. *He (Sing., Masc.)*
3. *them (Pl., Neut.)*
4. *It (Sing., Neut.)*
5. *their (Pl., Neut.)*
6. *she (Sing., Fem.)*
7. *his (Sing., Masc.); her (Sing., Fem.)*
8. *she (Sing., Fem.); it (Sing., Neut.)*
9. *its (Sing., Neut.)*
10. *her (Sing., Fem.)*

LESSON OBJECTIVES

To recognize and use indefinite pronouns in writing

DAILY TEST PREPARATION

Sentence Completion: Vocabulary Write the following item on the board or use **Daily Test Preparation Transparency** p. DT12. Choose the word that *best* fits the meaning of the sentence.

Not knowing which flowers to select for the occasion, I asked the _____.

A. botanist

B. arboretum

C. agronomist

D. florist

Teaching Point: For vocabulary questions, use context clues to determine the best answer. In this case, a *florist* is someone who specializes in flowers. When possible, use the parts of a word to determine its meaning (*florist* contains the Latin root *flor,* meaning "flower").

LESSON 8 Indefinite-Pronoun Agreement

❶ Here's the Idea

▶ **An indefinite pronoun does not refer to a specific person, place, thing, or idea.**

Indefinite pronouns often do not have antecedents.

Something unusual is going on in Loch Ness.

Has **anyone** photographed the Loch Ness monster?

▶ **Some indefinite pronouns are always singular, some are always plural, and some can be either singular or plural.**

Indefinite Pronouns			
Singular		**Plural**	**Singular or Plural**
another	neither	both	all
anybody	nobody	few	any
anyone	no one	many	most
anything	nothing	several	none
each	one		some
either	somebody		
everybody	someone		
everyone	something		
everything			

Any pronoun containing *one, thing,* or *body* is singular.

Singular Indefinite Pronouns

▶ **Use a singular personal pronoun to refer to a singular indefinite pronoun.**

REFERS TO

Everyone took **his or her** camera to the lake.

(*Everyone* could be masculine or feminine.)

REFERS TO

One dropped **his** camera in the water by mistake.

76

TEACHING RESOURCES

 Time-Saver Transparencies Binder:
- Daily Test Preparation p. DT12
- Quick-Fix Grammar and Style Charts p. QF5

 Grammar, Usage, and Mechanics Workbook p. 67

SKILLS PRACTICE RESOURCES

 Grammar, Usage, and Mechanics Workbook pp. 68–69

Pupil's Edition Exercise Bank p. 595

 Grammar Coach CD-ROM Lesson 7

Plural Indefinite Pronouns

▶ **Use a plural personal pronoun to refer to a plural indefinite pronoun.**

REFERS TO

Several reported **their** sightings of the monster.

REFERS TO

Many could not believe **their** own eyes!

Singular or Plural Indefinite Pronouns

▶ **Some indefinite pronouns can be singular or plural.** The phrase that follows the indefinite pronoun will often tell you whether the pronoun is singular or plural.

Most of the monster **story** has **its** origin in fantasy.

 ↑SINGULAR INDEFINITE PRONOUN   ↑SINGULAR PERSONAL PRONOUN

Most of the monster **stories** have **their** origins in fantasy.

 ↑PLURAL INDEFINITE PRONOUN   ↑PLURAL PERSONAL PRONOUN

❷ Why It Matters in Writing

Keep your facts and ideas clear. Make sure that all pronouns agree in number with their indefinite antecedents.

STUDENT MODEL

his or her mind

Not everyone has made up ~~their minds~~

about the existence of the Loch Ness

their   *theories*

monster. A few have ~~his or her~~ own ~~theory~~.

> Use singular pronoun to agree with *everyone*

> Use plural pronoun to agree with *few*

Pronouns **77**

MORE MODEL SENTENCES

Write the following sentences on the board. Have students select the correct indefinite pronouns.

SINGULAR: *Someone* showed us (their, <u>her</u>) telescope.

PLURAL: *Few* had (his, <u>their</u>) cameras ready.

SINGULAR: *All* of the town opens (<u>its</u>, their) doors to tourists.

PLURAL: *All* of the towns in the area open (<u>their</u>, its) doors, too.

PRONOUNS

PRONOUNS

Spice It Up!

Divide students into five groups. Have each group make up a slogan for one of the following new products:

NutsOs (a crunchy, nutty cereal)
Sneeze No More (an allergy medicine)
Mini Mouse Bites (a cat food)
Dippy Chippies (a waffle-shaped potato chip)

Have students use indefinite pronouns in each ad. Examples:
Everyone enjoys the taste of new NutsOs on his or her tongue.
Many say their cats love the meaty taste of Mini Mouse Bites.

Answers

Print-Out Option You may create worksheets of exercises A and B for your students by using the 💿 **Electronic Teacher Tools CD–ROM.**

A. CONCEPT CHECK

Self-Check For a self-check of indefinite-pronoun agreement, direct students to p. 595 in the Pupil's Edition for the answers to the items circled in yellow.

Answers underlined on page.

B. PROOFREADING

Answers shown on page. Incorrect pronouns are underlined. Correct pronouns appear in margin.

CHAPTER 3

CHAPTER 3

❸ Practice and Apply

A. CONCEPT CHECK: Indefinite-Pronoun Agreement

Choose the pronoun that agrees with the indefinite pronoun antecedent.

The Quest for "Nessie"

1. All of the tourists want (his or her, <u>their</u>) own monster stories to tell.
2. None of the tourists have (his or her, <u>their</u>) questions answered.
3. Tourists wonder what the Loch Ness creature is. One said that in (their, <u>her</u>) opinion, it was an ancient reptile.
4. Several claim to have photos of (his or her, <u>their</u>) sightings.
5. Many display (his or her, <u>their</u>) very blurry photographs.
6. No one has proved that (their, <u>his or her</u>) pictures are genuine.
7. Everyone around Loch Ness has a nickname for the monster; (<u>he or she</u>, they) calls it "Nessie."
8. Scientists are curious about the mystery, and several have done (his or her, <u>their</u>) own underwater investigations.
9. Each has presented (<u>his or her</u>, their) theory about Nessie.
10. Most of the evidence has (their, <u>its</u>) problems, however.

➡ For a SELF-CHECK and more practice, see the EXERCISE BANK, p. 595.

B. PROOFREADING: Agreement Errors

Rewrite the paragraph, correcting errors in pronoun-antecedent agreement.

Famous Photo a Fake!

his or her   No one could believe <u>their</u> eyes when this famous photo
their   was published. Most of the people had <u>his or her</u> opinions about the picture. Finally, the photographer, R. Kenneth Wilson, admitted it was a fake!
their   Many were crushed that <u>his or her</u> favorite photo of Nessie was not real.

📁 Return to your **Write Away** and correct any errors in pronoun-antecedent agreement.

LESSON 9 — Pronoun Problems

1 Here's the Idea

We and *Us* with Nouns

The pronouns *we* and *us* are sometimes followed by a noun that identifies the pronoun (*we students*, *us students*).

▶ **Use we when the noun is a subject or a predicate noun. Use us when the noun is an object.**

We owners don't always understand our pets.
↑ SUBJECT

Dogs and cats often surprise **us owners.**
↑ OBJECT OF VERB

> **Here's How** Choosing *We* or *Us*
>
> **Dogs think of (us, we) humans as their leaders.**
> **1.** Drop the identifying noun from the sentence.
>
> **Dogs think of (us, we) as their leaders.**
> **2.** Decide whether the sentence calls for a subject pronoun or an object pronoun. This sentence calls for the pronoun that is the object of the preposition *of.*
> **Dogs think of us as their leaders.**
> **3.** Use the correct pronoun with the noun.
> **Dogs think of us humans as their leaders.**

Unclear Reference

▶ **Be sure that each personal pronoun refers clearly to only one person, place, or thing.** If there is any chance your reader will be confused about whom or what you are talking about, use a noun instead of a pronoun.

Confusing: **Tony and Fred want to become veterinarians. He now works at an animal shelter.** (Who works? Tony or Fred?)

Clear: **Tony and Fred want to become veterinarians. Fred now works at an animal shelter.**

Pronouns **79**

PRONOUNS

LESSON OBJECTIVES

To identify pronoun problems and avoid them in writing

DAILY TEST PREPARATION

Error Correction: Spelling Write the following item on the board or use ▤ **Daily Test Preparation Transparency** p. DT12.
Choose the <u>best</u> way to write the underlined section.

> <u>The heart and sole</u> of the matter is not open for debate.

A. Their heart and sole

B. Its heart and sole

C. The heart and soul

D. Correct as is

Teaching Point: Error correction questions often test your knowledge of homophones (words that sound alike but differ in meaning). A *sole* is "the underside of a foot or shoe," whereas a *soul* is "an animating force or vital part." In this item, *soul* should be used.

CUSTOMIZING TIP

Less Proficient Learners Give students more practice with using *we* or *us* with a noun. Write the following sentences on the board. Encourage students to drop the noun in each case to help them supply the correct pronoun:

(<u>We</u>, Us) *ghosts need exercise, too.*

Take (we, <u>us</u>) ghosts out for a walk more often!

PRONOUNS

TEACHING RESOURCES

▤ Time-Saver Transparencies Binder:
• Daily Test Preparation p. DT12
• Quick-Fix Grammar and Style Charts pp. QF5–6
▤ Grammar, Usage, and Mechanics Workbook p. 70

SKILLS PRACTICE RESOURCES

▤ Grammar, Usage, and Mechanics Workbook pp. 71–72
Pupil's Edition Exercise Bank p. 596

💿 Grammar Coach CD-ROM Lesson 8

Have students rewrite the following sentences to avoid confusion due to unclear reference problems.

The Irish setter and the poodle both began to whimper. It stood up and began to twirl around.

The Irish setter and the poodle both began to whimper. The Irish setter stood up and began to twirl around.

Answers

Print-Out Option You may create worksheets of exercises A and B for your students by using the 💿 **Electronic Teacher Tools CD–ROM.**

A. CONCEPT CHECK

Self-Check For a self-check of pronoun problems, direct students to p. 596 in the Pupil's Edition for the answers to the items circled in yellow.

Answers underlined on page.

B. REVISING

Answers shown on page. Pronoun errors are underlined. Corrections appear in the margin.

❷ Why It Matters in Writing

When you write a paper for school, or when you want to persuade someone in authority, your use of correct pronouns will help the reader take your ideas more seriously.

STUDENT MODEL

Dear Mayor Trimble:

We

~~Us~~ students have some ideas about a special dog park for the city. Sarah Fein and Tanya Roberts have written a report *Tanya* on our ideas. ~~She~~ will send it to you soon.

> Use *we*—*students* is a subject.

> *She* could refer either to Sarah or to Tanya. Name the person to avoid confusion.

❸ Practice and Apply

A. CONCEPT CHECK: Pronoun Problems

Choose the correct word in parentheses.

Mysterious Cat Behavior

1. Cats baffle (<u>us</u>, we) owners by the things they do.
2. They often rub themselves against (we, <u>us</u>) humans.
3. My two cats, Pickles and Bert, do this. Surprisingly, (he, <u>Bert</u>) does this even with strangers.
4. However, (he, <u>Pickles</u>) hides when guests arrive.
5. This rubbing is simple. (<u>We</u>, Us) humans are being marked by the cat as part of its territory.

➡ **For a SELF-CHECK and more practice, see the EXERCISE BANK, p. 596.**

B. REVISING: Correcting Pronoun Errors

Correct the pronoun errors in the following paragraph.

A Cat's Point of View

<u>Us</u> cats have rights, too. A new puppy or pet bird in the house can upset us. <u>It</u> has very poor manners and will eat our food in one gulp. <u>It</u> will sit singing in its cage and drive us crazy. <u>It</u> will chase us through the house for fun. Owners need to consider the needs of <u>we</u> cats. **us**

More Pronoun Problems

LESSON OBJECTIVES

To recognize and correctly use pronouns in compounds and in sentences with interfering phrases.

❶ Here's the Idea

Pronouns in Compounds

Pronouns sometimes cause difficulty when they are parts of compound subjects and compound objects.

▶ **Use the subject pronouns *I, she, he, we,* and *they* in a compound subject or with a predicate noun or pronoun.**

> **Kathy and he** decided to research a mystery.

> The research team was **Jim and I.**

▶ **Use the object pronouns *me, her, him, us,* and *them* in a compound object.**

> Samantha asked **Jim and me** about the Bermuda Triangle.

> Kathy loaned our report to **Mac and her.**

To choose the correct case of a pronoun in a compound part, read the sentence with only the pronoun in the compound part. Mentally screen out the noun. Then choose the correct case.

Intervening Phrases

Sometimes words and phrases come between a subject and a pronoun that refers to it. Don't be confused by those words in between. Mentally cross out the phrase to figure out agreement.

> REFERS TO
>
> **Jim,** ~~like the others,~~ brought **his** map. (*His* agrees with *Jim,* not with *others.*)

> REFERS TO
>
> Five **planes** ~~from a Navy airfield~~ lost **their** way in the Bermuda Triangle. (*Their* agrees with *planes,* not with *airfield.*)

 DAILY TEST PREPARATION

Definition: Vocabulary Write the following item on the board or use 📺 **Daily Test Preparation Transparency** p. DT13.

Decide which of the four answers has most nearly the same meaning as the underlined word.

Do you feel <u>optimistic</u>?

A. content

B. despairing

C. hopeful

D. lively

Teaching Point: For definitions, rule out any words that are opposite in meaning to the underlined word (*despairing*). Answer C is closest in meaning.

TEACHING RESOURCES

 Time-Saver Transparencies Binder:
- Daily Test Preparation p. DT13
- Quick-Fix Grammar and Style Charts pp. QF5–6

 Grammar, Usage, and Mechanics Workbook p. 73

SKILLS PRACTICE RESOURCES

 Grammar, Usage, and Mechanics Workbook pp. 74–75

Pupil's Edition Exercise Bank p. 596

💿 Grammar Coach CD-ROM Lesson 7–8

To check that students are using the correct pronoun case, write the following paragraph on the board and have students correct mistakes:

Her **She** *and I chose a project we both liked. The work was divided between her and I* **me.**

Answers

Print-Out Option You may create worksheets of exercise A for your students by using the 💿 **Electronic Teacher Tools CD–ROM.**

A. CONCEPT CHECK

Self-Check For a self-check of more pronoun problems, direct students to p. 596 in the Pupil's Edition for the answers to the items circled in yellow.

Answers underlined on page.

---

❷ Why It Matters in Writing

Some writers think that *between you and I* sounds more formal than *between you and me* and therefore is correct. Don't make that mistake in your writing—*between you and me* is correct.

> To begin our project, my partner and ~~me~~ *I* did some research. However, between you and ~~I~~ *me,* I found many more sources than she did.

❸ Practice and Apply

A. CONCEPT CHECK: More Pronoun Problems

Choose the correct word to complete each sentence.

The Bermuda Triangle: Mystery or Misinformation?

1. Terry, Kathy, Jim and (**I**, me) led a discussion about the Bermuda Triangle.
2. One student asked Jim and (I, **me**) where the Bermuda Triangle is.
3. Terry and (**I**, me) pointed out Bermuda, Puerto Rico, and the east coast of Florida.
4. The triangle, having three geographic boundaries, is named for (**its**, their) shape.
5. Another student asked Kathy and (we, **us**) about the strange disappearances that give the Bermuda Triangle its spooky reputation.
6. Jim and (**I**, me) explained that some ships and planes have mysteriously vanished in that area.
7. Angela, like several other classmates, had (**her**, their) doubts about the Bermuda Triangle stories.
8. Jim and (**I**, me) explained that many investigators agree with Angela.
9. Experts on the Bermuda Triangle said that in (its, **their**) opinion, many reports had been greatly exaggerated.
10. Between you and (I, **me**), I'm not sure how seriously to take this legend either.

➡ **For a SELF-CHECK and more practice, see the EXERCISE BANK, p. 596.**

Spice It Up!

Identify three corners of the classroom as the boundaries of the Bermuda Triangle. Have students take turns completing the sentences in the **Concept Check.** Students who answer correctly move from corner 1 to corner 2. When the next student answers the question correctly, the first student goes to corner 2. Students who move all the way around the triangle, back to corner 1, are safe. However, if a student answers incorrectly, all players on the corners fall into the triangle and "disappear" by returning to their seats.

B. PROOFREADING: Correct Use of Pronouns

Rewrite the passage below, correcting the pronoun errors.

Flight 19: The Mystery Is Solved!

I

Claire and <u>me</u> read about the mysterious disappearance of Flight 19 in the Bermuda

We Triangle. <u>Us</u> students discovered that Flight 19 consisted of five Avenger bombers led

their by Lt. Charles Taylor. Hours after <u>they're</u> take-off from Fort Lauderdale, Florida, they vanished in the Atlantic Ocean.

Who <u>Whom</u> is responsible for the bizarre disappearance of Flight 19? Interestingly, some think that UFOs may have been

What responsible. <u>Which</u> actually happened is less dramatic.

Lt. Taylor thought he was flying southwest when he really was flying east. Taylor, unlike two other crew members, did

his not recognize <u>their</u> mistake. It's clear Taylor led the team farther out into the Atlantic. His men and he finally crashed in the ocean.

me The facts about Flight 19 taught Claire and <u>I</u> not to believe in the myth of the Bermuda Triangle.

C. WRITING: Interpreting a Map   Answers in column.

This map illustrates what may have happened to Flight 19. Working with a partner, use the map and the information in exercise B to write a paragraph, explaining in your own words what probably happened to Flight 19.

Underline the pronouns you use. Proofread your work to be sure you have used the pronouns correctly.

Flight 19's Path

Example: The planes of Flight 19 left *their* base at the Naval Air Station in Fort Lauderdale, Florida.

·········· **Taylor's planned flight path, heading southwest**

·········· **Taylor's actual flight path**

★ **Starting point**   ✗ **Probable crash site**

LESSON OBJECTIVES

To recognize and use pronouns in dialogue

THE LANGUAGE OF
LITERATURE

The passage on the student page is from "A Retrieved Reformation" in *The Language of Literature,* Level 7.

Grammar in Literature

Using Pronouns in Dialogue

Look at the following sentences. Then, compare them with the dialogue in the following passage. How do pronouns change the effect of the words?

"The guard told Jimmy to go out in the morning, brace up, and make a man of himself. The guard told Jimmy he wasn't a bad fellow at heart."

from: ## A Retrieved Reformation

by **O.** Henry

"Now, Valentine," said the warden, "**you**'ll go out in the morning. Brace up and make a man of **yourself.** **You**'re not a bad fellow at heart. Stop cracking safes, and live straight.

"**Me**?" said Jimmy, in surprise. "Why, **I** never cracked a safe in **my** life."

"Oh, no," laughed the warden. "Of course not, Let's see now. How was it **you** happened to get sent up on that Springfield job? Was it because you wouldn't prove an alibi for fear of compromising **somebody** in extremely high-toned society? Or was it simply a case of a mean old jury that had it in for **you**? It's always one or the other with **you** innocent victims."

"**Me**?" said Jimmy, still blankly virtuous. "Why, warden, **I** never was in Springfield in **my** life."

Portrait of Prince Eristoff (1925) Tamara de Lempicka. Private collection, New York. Copyright © 1996 Artists Rights Society (ARS), New York/SPADEM, Paris.

84

Practice and Apply

The following passage from "A Retrieved Reformation" does not include dialogue. Read the passage and follow the steps to create a dialogue for a skit about the passage.

The Elmore Bank had just put in a new safe and vault. Mr. Adams was very proud of it, and insisted on an inspection by everyone. The vault was a small one, but it had a new patented door. It fastened with three solid steel bolts thrown simultaneously with a single handle, and had a time lock. . . . The two children, May and Agatha, were delighted by the shining metal and funny clock and knobs.

Suddenly there was a scream or two from the women, and a commotion. Unperceived by the elders, May, the nine-year-old girl, in a spirit of play, had shut Agatha in the vault. She had then shot the bolts and turned the knob of the combination as she had seen Mr. Adams do.

The old banker sprang to the handle and tugged at it for a moment. "The door can't be opened," he groaned. "The clock hasn't been wound nor the combination set."

Writing About Literature

1. Identify the characters who will speak in your skit. You should include Mr. Adams, Agatha, and May. You might choose to add other visitors to the bank.
2. Write one or two lines of dialogue for each character you choose. Try reading your dialogue aloud to see if it sounds like a real conversation. Check to see if using pronouns instead of nouns will make your dialogue more natural.

Save your dialogue in your 📁 **Working Portfolio.**

PRACTICE AND APPLY

Writing About Literature

1. Answers will vary but will probably include Mr. Adams, Agatha, and May. Students may also add other visitors to the bank.

2. Dialogues will vary but should include information from the passage in the story. In the following example, the pronouns are underlined:

Mr. Adams: Listen everyone! I want you to take a closer look at our new vault. Can you see how the door is fastened with three solid steel bolts? And it operates with a special time clock!

Agatha: Oooh! Look at that funny time clock.

May: Let me see.

Agatha: I want to turn the knobs.

May: Let me try first. (May playfully shuts Agatha in the vault, shoots the bolts, and turns the knobs of the combination.)

Woman: (Screaming!) Wait! Don't close that door! There's a girl inside the vault!

Mr. Adams: Oh no! I can't open that door. No one can. The clock hasn't been wound nor the combination set.

TEACHING TIP

Cooperative Learning Have students work together on the skit. After they have finished writing the dialogue, groups should take turns performing the skit.

Mixed Review

Mixed Review

Answers

Print-Out Option You may create worksheets of exercises A and B for your students by using the ⊙ **Electronic Teacher Tools CD–ROM.**

A. PRONOUNS

1. object pronoun
2. possessive pronoun
3. subject pronoun
4. contraction
5. object pronoun
6. object pronoun
7. object pronoun
8. contraction
9. possessive pronoun
10. subject pronoun

B. PRONOUN USE

Answers shown on page. Pronoun errors are underlined. Correct pronouns appear in the margin.

THE LANGUAGE OF LITERATURE

The passage on the student page is from "Waiting" in *The Language of Literature, 7.*

A. Pronouns Read this passage from "Waiting" by Budge Wilson. Then identify each underlined word as a subject pronoun, object pronoun, possessive pronoun, or contraction. **Answers in column.**

LITERARY MODEL

When the spring came, a gang of **(1)** <u>us</u> would always start going out to The Grove on weekends to start practicing for **(2)** <u>our</u> summer play. Year after year **(3)** <u>we</u> did this, and it had nothing to do with those school plays in which I made such a hit. **(4)** <u>We'd</u> all talk about what stories we liked, and then we'd pick one of **(5)** <u>them</u> and make a play out of **(6)** <u>it</u>. I would usually select the play because I was always the one who directed **(7)** <u>it</u>, so it was only fair that I'd get to do the choosing. If there was a king or a queen, I'd usually be the queen. If **(8)** <u>you're</u> the director, you can't be something like a page or a minor fairy, because then you don't seem important enough to be giving out instructions and bossing people around, and the kids maybe won't pay attention to all the orders. Besides, as **(9)** <u>my</u> mother pointed out, **(10)** <u>I</u> was smart and I could learn my lines fast. . . .

—Budge Wilson, "Waiting"

B. Pronoun Use This passage about theater superstitions contains ten errors in pronoun usage. Rewrite the paragraph, correcting the errors.

his or her   When an actor goes on stage, <u>their</u> fellow actors don't say "Good luck." They say "Break a leg." <u>Whom</u> would wish **Who** someone a broken leg? What does this expression mean? To find out, my friend Kevin and <u>me</u> interviewed Ms. Kay Gilbert, an **I** expert on theater traditions.

me/We   She told him and <u>I</u>, "<u>Us</u> theater people are more superstitious than people in most other fields. I think it's because plays are **they're/** so unpredictable. If <u>their</u> a hit, everything is fine. If not, <u>your</u> out **you're** of work.

"We try to give <u>ourself</u> any advantage we can. All of the actors tell <u>his or her</u> fellow actors something insulting in order **their** to confuse the forces of bad luck. Acting, like other jobs, has <u>their</u> own traditions to uphold." **it's**

So the next time you go on stage, don't worry if someone tells you to "break a leg"!

Mastery Test: What Did You Learn?

Choose the correct replacement for each underlined word, or indicate that the word is correct as is.

> Think of all the information that you have collected and saved over time. <u>Who</u> was the first president of the United States? Name
> (1)
> a favorite CD and picture <u>their</u> cover. Recall for a moment what
> (2)
> <u>you're</u> elementary school looked like. You might say that <u>we</u>
> (3)   (4)
> humans are a little bit like computers; everyone stores countless
> memories in <u>their</u> brain. If you wonder exactly how we store these
> (5)
> memories in <u>my</u> brains, you are not alone. <u>These</u> is a question that
> (6)   (7)
> scientists have asked <u>theirselves</u> for years. Will <u>themselves</u> find
> (8)   (9)
> the explanation in the brain's physical structure, its complex
> chemistry, or both? <u>It's</u> one more mystery that modern science has
> (10)
> yet to solve.

1. A. Whom
   B. Whose
   C. Which
   D. Correct as is ⟵

2. A. his
   B. her
   C. its ⟵
   D. Correct as is

3. A. you
   B. your ⟵
   C. your are
   D. Correct as is

4. A. us
   B. they
   C. them
   D. Correct as is ⟵

5. **A. his or her** ⟵
   B. his
   C. her
   D. Correct as is

6. **A. our** ⟵
   B. their
   C. your
   D. Correct as is

7. A. What
   B. This ⟵
   C. Them
   D. Correct as is

8. A. theirs
   B. yourselves
   C. themselves ⟵
   D. Correct as is

9. A. them
   B. they ⟵
   C. he
   D. Correct as is

10. A. It
    B. Its
    C. Itself
    D. Correct as is ⟵

Mastery Test

As an option, two other Chapter Mastery Tests appear in ▦ **Assessment Masters** pp. 47–54.

Answers circled on page.

PRESCRIPTION FOR MASTERY	
If students miss item number:	**Use Teaching Resources and Skills Practice Resources for lesson:**
1, 7	❻ Interrogatives and Demonstratives p. 70
2, 3, 6, 10	❹ Possessive Pronouns p. 65
4	❾ Pronoun Problems p. 79
5	❽ Indefinite-Pronoun Agreement p. 76
8, 9	❺ Reflexive and Intensive Pronouns p. 68

PRONOUNS

PRONOUNS

Student Help Desk

Pronouns at a Glance

Subject Case	
I	it
you	we
he	you
she	they

Use this case when
- the pronoun is a **subject**
- the pronoun is a **predicate pronoun**

Object Case	
me	it
you	us
him	you
her	them

Use this case when
- the pronoun is a **direct object**
- the pronoun is an **indirect object**
- the pronoun is the **object of a preposition**

Possessive Case	
my/mine	its
your/yours	our/ours
his	your/yours
her/hers	their/theirs

Use this case for
- pronouns that show **ownership or relationship**

Types of Pronouns   Who Did It?

Reflexive & Intensive	Interrogative	Demonstrative	Indefinite
myself	who	this	someone
herself	whom	that	anyone
himself	what	these	each
itself	which	those	several
yourself	whose		many
themselves			all
ourselves			most
yourselves			none

For a full list of indefinite pronouns, see page 76.

Pronoun-Antecedent Agreement

They Lost Their Marbles

A pronoun should agree with its antecedent in number, person, and gender.

A singular antecedent takes a singular pronoun.

Jewell is always writing **her** mystery stories. **(singular)**

A plural antecedent takes a plural pronoun.

The **plots** have **their** twists and turns. **(plural)**

Make sure you use the correct gender.

Each has **his or her** special skill.
They have **their** special skills.

Pronoun Problems

Solving the Case

We: Subject/predicate pronoun	**We** students saw Nessie.
Us: Object	No one believed **us** students.
Who: Subject/predicate pronoun	**Who** wants our story?
Whom: Object	To **whom** shall we write?

The Bottom Line

Checklist for Pronouns

Have I . . .

____ used the subject case for pronouns that are subjects and predicate pronouns?

____ used the object case for pronouns that are objects?

____ used the possessive case to show ownership or relationship?

____ made sure that pronouns agree with their antecedents in number, person, and gender?

____ used *who* and *whom* correctly?

A Slice of Life

The next time you have the chance to correct someone . . . resist the temptation. Instead, ask yourself, "What do I really want out of this interaction?" Chances are, what you want is a peaceful interaction in which all parties leave feeling good. Each time you resist "being right" and instead choose kindness, you'll notice a peaceful feeling within.

TEACHER'S LOUNGE

A Slice of Life

How did "hangout" come to mean a gathering place?

"Hangout" originally meant a place of business—for at one time almost all professional men, artisans, and tradespeople hung out signs to indicate their occupation and place of business. The term had its origin in the phrase, "Where do you hang out your sign?"

Verbs

CHAPTER OVERVIEW

CHAPTER 4

CHAPTER RESOURCES

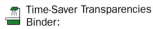 Time-Saver Transparencies
Binder:
- Daily Test Preparation
  pp. DT13–17
- Quick-Fix Grammar and
  Style Charts p. QF9
- Visual Grammar™ Tiles
  Lesson 8

Grammar, Usage, and
Mechanics Workbook
pp. 76–102

Integrated Technology and Media

Electronic Teacher Tools
CD-ROM

Grammar Coach CD-ROM
Lesson 6

Power Presentations
CD-ROM Lesson 2

mcdougallittell.com

Assessment

Assessment Masters:
- Chapter Pretest pp. 8–9
- Chapter Mid-point Test
  p. 27
- Chapter Mastery Tests
  pp. 55–60

Test Generator CD-ROM

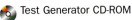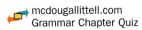 mcdougallittell.com
Grammar Chapter Quiz

Theme: Lights, Camera, Action

A Giant Ape Did What?

Think about going with friends to see a really great movie.
Talking about the movie afterward is almost as much fun as
seeing it for the first time. You'll have to use plenty of verbs to
recreate what you saw. In fact, whenever you speak or write,
you use verbs to let people know exactly what is happening
and how things look, feel, smell, sound, and taste.

Write Away: Tell Me a Movie
Write a paragraph describing an action scene from your
favorite movie or one describing the scene from *King Kong*
shown above. Put the paragraph in your ▭ **Working Portfolio.**

Grammar Coach
CD-ROM

90

Students Acquiring English/ESL

English Grammar
Survival Kit pp. 23–46,
54–55

Diagnostic Test: What Do You Know?

Choose the best way to rewrite each underlined word or group of words.

Spending on entertainment <u>will increase</u> sharply over the last
(1)
several decades. In 1997 the average American household <u>spends</u>
(2)
almost as much on entertainment as it did on health care. Families
now <u>choose</u> from a wide selection of entertainment options. These
(3)
<u>included</u> books, TV, movies, games, CDs, and theme parks, to name
(4)
a few. Think about how prices <u>have rised</u> over the years. In 1939 a
(5)
movie ticket to *Gone With The Wind* <u>costed</u> 75 cents. When a major
(6)
theme park first opened in 1955, visitors <u>paid</u> only $1 to enter
(7)
the park. Although people <u>earned</u> more money today, many
(8)
<u>are spending</u> more of that money on entertainment. Can you
(9)
predict how much prices <u>raise</u> in the future?
(10)

1. A. increases
   B. has increased
   C. does increase
   D. Correct as is

2. A. spending
   B. spent
   C. will spend
   D. Correct as is

3. A. chose
   B. have chosen
   C. chosed
   D. Correct as is

4. A. will include
   B. include
   C. had included
   D. Correct as is

5. A. have rose
   B. raised
   C. have risen
   D. Correct as is

6. **A. cost**
   B. has cost
   C. will cost
   D. Correct as is

7. A. pay
   B. payed
   C. are paying
   D. Correct as is

8. A. will earn
   B. earn
   C. have earned
   D. Correct as is

9. A. spent
   B. have spent
   C. spended
   D. Correct as is

10. **A. will rise**
    B. will raise
    C. rise
    D. Correct as is

Diagnostic Test

As an option, a Chapter Pretest appears in
📘 **Assessment Masters** pp. 8–9.

Answers circled on page.

Use the chart below to determine which lessons students need.

PRESCRIPTION FOR SUCCESS	
If students miss item number:	**Work on lesson:**
1	❼ Perfect Tenses p. 108
2, 4	❻ Simple Tenses p. 105
3, 8, 9	❽ Using Verb Tenses p. 111
5, 10	❾ Troublesome Verb Pairs p. 115
6, 7	❺ Irregular Verbs p. 102

The **Diagnostic Test** parallels the **Mastery Test** on page 121. Have students keep the test in their portfolio to compare with their results on the **Mastery Test**.

BLOCK SCHEDULING

Pressed for Time?
Use the Prescription for Success chart to determine which lessons students need to study. Have them complete **Here's the Idea** and **Practice and Apply, Concept Check** only, for those lessons.

Time for More?
After completing all of the lessons in the chapter, have pairs of students quiz each other on irregular verb forms. In addition to the charts in Lesson 5, students can visit 🔗 **mcdougallittell.com** for possible links to grammar Web sites.

LESSON 1

What Is a Verb?

❶ Here's the Idea

▶ **A verb is a word used to express an action, a condition, or a state of being.** The two main types of verbs are **action verbs** and **linking verbs.** Both kinds can be accompanied by helping verbs.

Action Verbs

An **action verb** tells what its subject does. The action it expresses can be either **physical** or **mental.**

> **King Kong stomps through the streets of New York.**
> (physical action)
>
> **He climbs the Empire State Building.** (physical action)
>
> **Everyone fears Kong.** (mental action)
>
> **Kong loves a woman.** (mental action)

Linking Verbs

A **linking verb** links its subject to a word in the predicate. The most common linking verbs are forms of the verb *be.*

Linking Verbs	
Forms of *be*	is, am, are, was, were, been, being
Verbs that express condition	appear, become, feel, grow, look, remain, seem, smell, sound, taste

LINKS

King Kong is a huge gorilla.
LINKING VERB

He seems angry.

Some verbs can serve as either action or linking verbs.

LINKS

Kong looks at Ann Darrow. She looks frightened.
↑ ACTION VERB   ↑ LINKING VERB

LINKS

He feels sad. She feels his hot breath.
↑ LINKING VERB   ↑ ACTION VERB

Helping Verbs and Verb Phrases

Helping verbs help main verbs express precise shades of meaning. The combination of one or more helping verbs with a main verb is called a **verb phrase**.

VERB PHRASE

We have watched the movie *King Kong* four times.
HELPING ↗   ↖ MAIN

I can rent it any time.

Some verbs can serve both as main verbs and as helping verbs. For example, *has* stands alone in the first sentence below but is a helping verb in the second sentence.

King Kong has no chance of survival.
↑ MAIN VERB

He has angered too many people.
↑ HELPING VERB

Common Helping Verbs	
Forms of *be*	be, am, is, are, was, were, been, being
Forms of *do*	do, does, did
Forms of *have*	have, has, had
Others	could, should, would, may, might, must, can, shall, will

Kong has terrorized New Yorkers.

Verbs **93**

MORE MODEL SENTENCES

Write the following pairs of sentences on the board. Have students identify the verbs as action or linking verbs.

Something smells funny.
linking

I smelled the film burning.
action

The director grew quiet.
linking

I grew tomatoes for the film crew.
action

② Why It Matters in Writing

Strong verbs can make your writing powerful. Try to use verbs that are as specific as possible. Notice the difference that a change to a more precise verb makes in the sentence below.

grabbed
The movie ~~had~~ my attention.

③ Practice and Apply

A. CONCEPT CHECK: What Is a Verb?

Write the verb or verb phrase in each of the following sentences.

The King of the Monster Movies
1. *King Kong* <u>may be</u> the most famous monster movie ever.
2. At the start of the film, a producer <u>is planning</u> a movie. **A**
3. He and a film crew <u>sail</u> to Skull Island. **A**
4. There they <u>find</u> a giant ape, Kong. **A**
5. Kong <u>falls</u> in love with Ann, the movie's star. **A**
6. The producer <u>takes</u> Kong to New York in chains. **A**
7. Kong <u>escapes</u> from his chains. **A**
8. He <u>climbs</u> to the top of the Empire State Building. **A**
9. There, he <u>must struggle</u> against fighter planes. **A**
10. Kong's enemies <u>win</u> in the end. **A**

CHALLENGE

Identify as action or linking each of the verbs you wrote.

➔ **For a SELF-CHECK and more practice, see the EXERCISE BANK, p. 597.**

B. WRITING: Using Specific Verbs

Special Effects
Write a more specific verb to replace each underlined verb in the paragraph below.

created
fashioned
glued

appeared/labored

   Willis O'Brien <u>did</u> the special effects for the *King Kong* movie of 1933. O'Brien <u>made</u> miniature models, including an 18-inch-tall Kong. To make Kong's muscles, he carefully <u>put</u> latex strips under the model's skin. Then he added air bladders in its chest. Now the model <u>was</u> real. O'Brien <u>took</u> many long hours at his task.

Action Verbs and Objects

① Here's the Idea

Action verbs are often accompanied by words that complete their meaning. These complements are **direct objects** and **indirect objects**.

Direct Objects

▶ **A direct object is a noun or pronoun that names the receiver of action.** The direct object answers the question *what* or *whom*.

BEGINS WHAT?

The scriptwriter begins the process.
ACTION VERB · DIRECT OBJECT

The scriptwriter develops a story idea.

Indirect Objects

▶ **An indirect object tells *to what* or *whom* or *for what* or *whom* an action is done.** Verbs that often take indirect objects include *bring, give, hand, lend, make, send, show, teach, tell,* and *write.*

The scriptwriter sends a script. (sends to whom?)

TO WHOM?

The scriptwriter sends the director a script.
INDIRECT OBJECT · DIRECT OBJECT

The director gives the scriptwriter some advice.

WATCH OUT

If the preposition *to* or *for* appears in a sentence, the word that follows it is *not* an indirect object. It is the object of the preposition.

Tell the movie ending to us.
OBJECT OF PREPOSITION

Tell us the movie ending.
INDIRECT OBJECT

Verbs **95**

LESSON OBJECTIVES

To identify and correctly use action verbs with direct and indirect objects

DAILY TEST PREPARATION

Error Correction: Spelling Write the following item on the board or use 🖳 **Daily Test Preparation Transparency** p. DT14.

Read the sentence carefully. Decide if one of the words is misspelled or if there is no mistake.

A. Ms. Sparks <u>compelled</u> me

B. to <u>conceed</u> that I did not

C. study <u>sufficiently</u> for the test.

D. No mistake.

Teaching Point: Error correction questions often test your knowledge of commonly misspelled words such as *concede*.

TEACHING RESOURCES

Time-Saver Transparencies Binder:
• Daily Test Preparation p. DT14
Grammar, Usage, and Mechanics Workbook p. 79

SKILLS PRACTICE RESOURCES

Grammar, Usage, and Mechanics Workbook pp. 80–81
Pupil's Edition Exercise Bank p. 597

THE LANGUAGE OF
LITERATURE

The passage on the student page is from "Talking with Ray Bradbury" in *The Language of Literature,* Level 7.

Transitive and Intransitive Verbs

An action verb that has a direct object is called a **transitive verb.** A verb that does not have a direct object is called an **intransitive verb.**

> **Scriptwriters set the pace of their movies.**
> TRANSITIVE VERB   DIRECT OBJECT

> **The action moves quickly or slowly.**
> INTRANSITIVE VERB (NO OBJECT)

Sometimes an intransitive verb is followed by a word that looks like a direct object but is really an adverb. An adverb tells where, when, how, or to what extent; a direct object tells who or what.

CHOOSE WHAT?

> **Directors choose camera angles.**
> TRANSITIVE VERB   DIRECT OBJECT

CHOOSE HOW?

> **The good ones choose wisely.**
> INTRANSITIVE VERB   ADVERB

❷ Why It Matters in Writing

The correct use of direct objects can help you give clear directions or specific advice. Notice how in the model below, Bradbury uses direct objects to show what he wants you to read and see.

LITERARY MODEL

> Read all the great **books.** Read all the great **poetry.** See all the great **films.** Fill your **life** with metaphors.
>
> —Ray Bradbury, "Talking with Ray Bradbury"

❸ Practice and Apply

A. CONCEPT CHECK: Action Verbs and Objects

Write the 15 complements in these sentences, identifying each as a direct object or an indirect object.

A Crew of Dozens

1. A movie crew includes many people.
2. The director usually tells crew members their assignments.
3. The director of photography gives the director the film footage.
4. The sound crew includes a boom operator.
5. The director tells the composer the mood of the movie.
6. Members of the art department have an important function.
7. They show the director of photography the special effects.
8. The crew also includes wardrobe assistants.
9. Makeup artists give the actors the right look.
10. A movie set provides many creative jobs.

➡ **For a SELF-CHECK and more practice, see the EXERCISE BANK, p. 597.**

B. REVISING: Adding Direct Objects

Read the movie proposal below. From the list at the top, select a direct object to fill in each blank.

world, powers, legs, evil, weights

Proposal for New Film

   The movie begins as a sequel to *The Little Mermaid*. Ariel has changed, however. No longer a fragile little **1. legs** mermaid, she has two strong ___1___. She lifts ___2___ as **2. weights** a hobby. Now she has amazing ___3___. She can switch **3. powers** back and forth from a mermaid to a human. She travels the **4. world** ___4___. She fights ___5___ everywhere. **5. evil**

Verbs **97**

Answers

Print-Out Option You may create worksheets of exercises A and B for your students by using the 💿 **Electronic Teacher Tools CD–ROM.**

A.CONCEPT CHECK

Self-Check For a self-check of action verbs and objects, direct students to p. 597 in the Pupil's Edition for the answers to the items circled in yellow.

Answers shown on page. Direct objects are underlined once. Indirect objects are underlined twice.

B. REVISING

Answers shown on page.

VERBS

VERBS

LESSON OBJECTIVES

To identify linking verbs and correctly use subject complements in writing

DAILY TEST PREPARATION

Sentence Completion: Using Who/Whom Write the following item on the board or use **Daily Test Preparation Transparency** p. DT14. Choose the word or words that belong in the space.

> When, where, and _____ was the ticket given?

A. to who

B. whom

C. to whom

D. whose

Teaching Point: Sentence completion questions often test your knowledge of commonly confused words, such as *who* (a subject pronoun) and *whom* (an object pronoun). In this case, the phrase *to whom* serves as the indirect object of the question.

CUSTOMIZING TIP

Addressing Learning Styles
Visual Write the following sentences on the board to help students understand how a linking verb functions. Have students draw an arrow from the predicate noun or predicate adjective to the subject it identifies or modifies.

They are the editors of the school newspaper arrow from *editors* to *they*.

The school newspaper looks professional arrow from *professional* to *newspaper*.

LESSON 3 Linking Verbs and Predicate Words

❶ Here's the Idea

The word that a linking verb connects its subject to is called a **subject complement.** The subject complement identifies or describes the subject. Some common linking verbs are *is, feel, seem,* and *look.*

> IDENTIFIES
>
> A **movie** **is** a complicated **project.**
> SUBJECT   VERB   SUBJECT COMPLEMENT

> DESCRIBES
>
> A **movie** **must seem** **real.**
> SUBJECT   VERB   SUBJECT COMPLEMENT

Predicate Nouns and Predicate Adjectives

A subject complement can be a **predicate noun** or a **predicate adjective.**

▶ **A predicate noun is a noun that follows a linking verb and identifies, renames, or defines the subject.**

> IDENTIFIES
>
> *Star Wars* **is** a science fiction **film.**
> SUBJECT   VERB   PREDICATE NOUN

> I **am** a science fiction **fan.**

▶ **A predicate adjective is an adjective that follows a linking verb and modifies the subject.**

> MODIFIES
>
> Science fiction **films** **are** **popular.**
> SUBJECT   VERB   PREDICATE ADJECTIVE

> They **look** so **futuristic.**

98   Grammar, Usage, and Mechanics

TEACHING RESOURCES

Time-Saver Transparencies Binder:
• Daily Test Preparation p. DT14
Grammar, Usage, and Mechanics Workbook p. 82

SKILLS PRACTICE RESOURCES

Grammar, Usage, and Mechanics Workbook pp. 83–84
Pupil's Edition Exercise Bank p. 598

② Why It Matters in Writing

Predicate adjectives let you describe subjects with just a word or two. They can help you create vivid descriptions. Notice how predicate adjectives are used in the model below to contrast the characters and briefly convey the situation.

STUDENT MODEL

Look at the characters in *Star Wars*. Princess Leia is **brave.** Luke Skywalker is **tough.** And Han Solo is basically **honest.** Throughout the movie their situation seems **hopeless.** But their cause is **just.** In the end, they triumph.

> Predicate adjectives describe the subjects.

③ Practice and Apply

CONCEPT CHECK: Linking Verbs and Predicate Words

Identify each linking verb, predicate noun, and predicate adjective in the sentences below.

Creature Features

1. Not all creatures in science fiction movies (are) scary.
2. Some (seem) downright friendly.
3. For example, *E.T. the Extra-Terrestrial* (was) a hit.
4. The movie's alien creature (appeared) lovable.
5. E.T. (seemed) afraid of the children at first.
6. In *Close Encounters of the Third Kind* the aliens (were) a mystery for most of the movie.
7. In the end the inhabitants of the giant UFO (were) friendly to humans.
8. In *The Empire Strikes Back* one alien (was) very wise.
9. Yoda (was) a 900-year-old Jedi sage.
10. With Yoda's help Luke Skywalker (became) a Jedi too.

➡ **For a SELF-CHECK and more practice, see the EXERCISE BANK, p. 598.**

STUDENT MODEL

Write the following paragraph on the board. Have students identify the predicate adjectives.

I really don't like adventure films. The types of characters are so flat. Nobody seems that real. The plot seems dull. A lot of the endings are just plain corny.

Answers

Print-Out Option You may create worksheets of this exercise for your students by using the 💿 **Electronic Teacher Tools CD–ROM.**

CONCEPT CHECK

Self-Check For a self-check of linking verbs and predicate words, direct students to p. 598 in the Pupil's Edition for the answers to the items circled in yellow.

Answers shown on page. Predicate nouns are underlined once. Predicate adjectives are underlined twice. Linking verbs are circled.

Spice It Up!

Have students get together in groups and take turns pantomiming common emotions or states of minds. Tell students to solve the charades by using sentences with linking verbs to describe what is being mimed. Example: *Lester is feeling sleepy; Christina is brave.*

To identify and correctly use the four principal parts of verbs

 DAILY TEST PREPARATION

Revision-in-Context: Subject-Verb Agreement Write the following item on the board or use **Daily Test Preparation Transparency** p. DT15.

1 Breakfast, as well as lunch
2 and dinner, are nutritious.

What is the **best** change, if any, to make in the sentence in line 2?

A. Delete the comma after *dinner*

B. Change *are* to *were*

C. Change *are* to *is*

D. Make no change

Teaching Point: A common item in revision-in-context questions is subject-verb agreement. This item tests whether you recognize that the nouns *lunch* and *meal* are part of an interrupting phrase. The verb must agree with the subject *breakfast*.

TEACHING RESOURCES

 Time-Saver Transparencies Binder:
• Daily Test Preparation p. DT15
 Grammar, Usage, and Mechanics Workbook p. 85

SKILLS PRACTICE RESOURCES

Grammar, Usage, and Mechanics Workbook pp. 86–87

Pupil's Edition Exercise Bank p. 598

Grammar Coach CD-ROM Lesson 6

 Principal Parts of Verbs

LESSON 4

❶ Here's the Idea

▶ **Every verb has four basic forms, called its principal parts the present, the present participle, the past, and the past participle.** These principal parts are used to make all of the forms and tenses of the verb. Here are some examples.

Stunt people **take** risks on screen.
PRESENT

Stunt people **are doing** dangerous things all the time.
PRESENT PARTICIPLE

Polly Berson **performed** stunts for 27 years.
PAST

Most stunt people **have trained** for many years.
PAST PARTICIPLE

The Four Principal Parts of a Verb			
Present	**Present Participle**	**Past**	**Past Participle**
jump	(is) jump**ing**	jump**ed**	(has) jump**ed**
crash	(is) crash**ing**	crash**ed**	(has) crash**ed**

Notice that helping verbs are used with the present participle and the past participles.

Regular Verbs

There are two kinds of verbs: regular and irregular.

▶ **A regular verb is a verb whose past and past participle are formed by adding -ed or -d to the present.** The present participle is formed by adding *-ing* to the present.

Present	Present Participle	Past	Past Participle
look	(is) look + **-ing**	look + **-ed**	(has) look + **-ed**

You will learn about irregular verbs in the next lesson.

❷ Why It Matters in Writing

The principal parts of verbs let you express changes in time in your writing. In the model below, notice how the writer uses the past and the present to show a shift in time.

PROFESSIONAL MODEL

An accident paralyzed stuntwoman Heidi von Beltz during a car stunt for the movie *The Cannonball Run*. Still, she works out daily with a special trainer.

PAST

PRESENT

—S. Atlas

❸ Practice and Apply

CONCEPT CHECK: Principal Parts of Verbs

Identify each underlined principal part as the present, the present participle, the past, or the past participle.

Stunt Stand-ins

Stunt people **(1)** <u>perform</u> the dangerous scenes in 1. Pres.
movies and TV shows. Many are athletes who have
(2) <u>decided</u> to pursue careers in show business. When the 2. PA
hero of a movie is **(3)** <u>leaping</u> from a galloping horse or the 3. PR
villain is **(4)** <u>jumping</u> out of a burning helicopter, the person 4. PR
you see is probably a stunt person. Most stunts **(5)** <u>belong</u> 5. Pres.
to five categories: falls, fights, fires, car stunts, and horse
stunts. A safety crew **(6)** <u>stays</u> on hand in case of 6. Pres.
problems. Some stunt people have **(7)** <u>injured</u> themselves. 7. PA
For example, Vic Rivers once **(8)** <u>jumped</u> a truck into a lake 8. Past
and **(9)** <u>drowned</u>. Despite the dangers, most stunters 9. Past
(10) <u>love</u> their exciting jobs. 10. Pres.

➡ **For a SELF-CHECK and more practice, see the EXERCISE BANK, p. 598.**

Verbs **101**

Speaking and Listening Ask each student to use the past tense to form a sentence that tells about something he or she did last night. Another student should recast the sentence, using the present form. The third student should use a present participle, and the fourth, a past participle. Ask students to listen and explain how the different forms change the meaning of the sentences.

Answers

Print-Out Option You may create worksheets of this exercise for your students by using the ⬤ **Electronic Teacher Tools CD–ROM.**

CONCEPT CHECK

Self-Check For a self-check of linking verbs and predicate words, direct students to p. 598 in the Pupil's Edition for the answers to the items circled in yellow.

Answers shown on page using these codes:

Pres. = present

PR = present participle

Past = past

PA = past participle

LESSON OBJECTIVES

To identify and correctly use irregular verb forms

DAILY TEST PREPARATION

Sentence Completion:
Vocabulary Write the following item on the board or use **Daily Test Preparation Transparency** p. DT15. Choose the word that *best* fits the meaning of the sentence.

> Her assignment was to ____ the document from Latin into English.

A. translate

B. transplant

C. transfers

D. transform

Teaching Point: For sentence completion questions, the correct answer will always

- fit the meaning of the sentence (answers B and D do not make sense with from *Latin to English*).

- fit grammatically within the sentence (answer C uses the wrong verb form).

TEACHING RESOURCES

 Time-Saver Transparencies Binder:

- Daily Test Preparation p. DT15

Grammar, Usage, and Mechanics Workbook p. 88

SKILLS PRACTICE RESOURCES

 English Grammar Survival Kit pp. 54–55

Grammar, Usage, and Mechanics Workbook pp. 89–90

Pupil's Edition Exercise Bank p. 599

Grammar Coach CD-ROM Lesson 6

LESSON 5 | Irregular Verbs

1 Here's the Idea

> ▶ **Irregular verbs are verbs whose past and past participle forms are not made by adding *-ed* or *-d* to the present.**

The following chart shows you how to form the past and past-participle forms of many irregular verbs.

Common Irregular Verbs

	Present	Past	Past Participle
Group 1 The forms of the present, the past, and the past participle are all the same.	**burst**	**burst**	**(has) burst**
	cost	cost	(has) cost
	cut	cut	(has) cut
	hit	hit	(has) hit
	hurt	hurt	(has) hurt
	let	let	(has) let
	put	put	(has) put
	set	set	(has) set
	shut	shut	(has) shut
Group 2 The forms of the past and the past participle are the same.	**bring**	**brought**	**(has) brought**
	build	built	(has) built
	buy	bought	(has) bought
	catch	caught	(has) caught
	feel	felt	(has) felt
	have	had	(has) had
	keep	kept	(has) kept
	lay	laid	(has) laid
	leave	left	(has) left
	lose	lost	(has) lost
	make	made	(has) made
	pay	paid	(has) paid
	say	said	(has) said
	sell	sold	(has) sold
	shine	shone	(has) shone
	sit	sat	(has) sat
	sleep	slept	(has) slept
	teach	taught	(has) taught
	think	thought	(has) thought
	win	won	(has) won
	wind	wound	(has) wound

Common Irregular Verbs (continued)

	Present	Past	Past Participle
Group 3 The past participle is formed by adding *-n* or *-en* to the past.	**bite** break choose freeze get lie speak steal tear wear	**bit** broke chose froze got lay spoke stole tore wore	**(has) bitten** (has) broken (has) chosen (has) frozen (has) gotten (has) lain (has) spoken (has) stolen (has) torn (has) worn
Group 4 The past participle is formed from the present, usually by adding *-n* or *-en*.	**blow** do draw drive eat fall give go grow know rise run see take throw write	**blew** did drew drove ate fell gave went grew knew rose ran saw took threw wrote	**(has) blown** (has) done (has) drawn (has) driven (has) eaten (has) fallen (has) given (has) gone (has) grown (has) known (has) risen (has) run (has) seen (has) taken (has) thrown (has) written
Group 5 A vowel in the verb changes from *i* in the present to *a* in the past and to *u* in the past participle.	**begin** drink ring shrink sing sink spring swim	**began** drank rang shrank sang sank sprang swam	**(has) begun** (has) drunk (has) rung (has) shrunk (has) sung (has) sunk (has) sprung (has) swum

The Irregular Verb *Be*

	Present	Past	Past Participle
The past and past participle do not follow any pattern.	**am, are, is**	**was, were**	**(has) been**

Verbs **103**

CUSTOMIZING TIP

Students Acquiring English/ESL Students acquiring English often stumble over irregular verbs. Suggest that students memorize these irregular verbs. For a list of additional irregular verbs, see **English Grammar Survival Kit** pp. 54–55.

CUSTOMIZING TIP

Less Proficient Learners Some students may confuse the past and past participle forms. They can distinguish between the two forms by remembering that only the past participle can follow the helping verb *have.*

TEACHING TIP

Cooperative Learning Have a group of students create charts that expand on the list of irregular verbs presented on the page. (Example: *fly, flew, flown.*) Compile the lists into a master chart that can be posted for classroom use or photocopied for distribution.

Spice It Up!

Divide the class into teams of two students. Have each member of a team select two irregular verbs. Then have two sets of teams compete and take turns providing one-word clues to help their partners guess the verb. Then have each partner name the verb's present, past, and past participle forms.

MORE MODEL SENTENCES

Write the following sentences on the board. Ask students to correct any verb form errors:

In the last scene of the movie, she weared **wore** a yellow ribbon on her hat as a signal.

After the sun had rised **risen,** she throwed **threw** on her hat and rided **rode** to the ranch.

Answers

Print-Out Option You may create worksheets of this exercise A for your students by using the **Electronic Teacher Tools CD–ROM.**

CONCEPT CHECK

Self-Check For a self-check of irregular verbs, direct students to p. 599 in the Pupil's Edition for the answers to the items circled in yellow.

Answers are underlined on page.

ASSESSMENT

Assessment Masters:
- Chapter Mid-point Test p. 27

---

② Why It Matters in Writing

To be a skilled writer, you need to use irregular verb forms correctly. They can be tricky, though. The best way to avoid mistakes is to memorize the principal parts of the most common irregular verbs.

STUDENT MODEL

Special effects ~~maked~~ *made* a skyscraper fall in an instant. Then a gigantic tornado ~~blowed~~ *blew* away the rubble.

③ Practice and Apply

CONCEPT CHECK: Irregular Verbs

In the sentences below, choose the correct forms of the verbs in parentheses.

Movie Magic

1. Movies can convince us that we have (saw, seen) real events on screen.
2. Special effects have (let, letted) filmmakers fool us.
3. They have (bringed, brought) to the screen cloud cities, giant apes, and telephones with teeth.
4. Even in the early days of movies, directors (made, maked) impossible scenes look real.
5. A famous story shows that the Lumière brothers (knowed, knew) how to create a special effect in 1896.
6. A pile of rubble quickly (built, builded) itself into a wall.
7. The brothers had filmed as workers (teared, tore) down a wall.
8. Then they (runned, ran) the film backward.
9. Often filmmakers have (shrank, shrunk) huge monsters to miniature size for filming.
10. In the 1990s filmmakers (beginned, began) using computer-generated effects.

➡ **For a SELF-CHECK and more practice, see the EXERCISE BANK, p. 599.**

Simple Tenses

LESSON OBJECTIVES

To identify and correctly form the simple present, past, and future tenses

❶ Here's the Idea

▶ **A tense is a verb form that shows the time of an action or condition.** Verbs have three **simple tenses:** the present, the past, and the future.

Understanding Simple Tenses

Simple Tenses

The water **rushes** swiftly by the raft.	The **present tense** shows that an action or condition occurs now.
The raft **passed** the point of no return earlier.	The **past tense** shows that an action or condition was completed in the past.
Soon someone **will fall** into the water.	The **future tense** shows that an action or condition will occur in the future

A **progressive** form of a tense expresses an action or condition in progress. The progressive forms of the three simple tenses are used to show that actions or conditions are, were, or will be in progress.

Progressive Forms

People on shore **are calling** for help.	Present Progressive
They **were fishing** before.	Past Progressive
They **will be watching** for the rescue boat.	Future Progressive

Verbs **105**

DAILY TEST PREPARATION

Error Identification: Capitalization Write the following item on the board or use 🏛 **Daily Test Preparation Transparency** p. DT16. Decide which type of error, if any, appears in the underlined section.

> Hadrian's Wall <u>was completed in a.d. 127</u>.

A. Spelling error

B. Capitalization error

C. Punctuation error

D. No error

Teaching Point: Error identification questions often test your knowledge of basic capitalization rules. This item tests whether you know to capitalize the abbreviation *A.D.,* which stands for *Anno Domini,* meaning "in the year of the Lord."

CUSTOMIZING TIP

Students Acquiring English/ESL Some students may have difficulty understanding the progressive form because their language may not use that form. For example, in French, "I watch the film," and "I am watching the film," are said in exactly the same way. For instruction and practice with the simple present and the present progressive, have students use the **English Grammar Survival Kit** pp. 23–26.

TEACHING RESOURCES

 Time-Saver Transparencies Binder:
  • Daily Test Preparation p. DT16

 Grammar, Usage, and Mechanics Workbook p. 91

SKILLS PRACTICE RESOURCES

 English Grammar Survival Kit pp. 23–26

 Grammar, Usage, and Mechanics Workbook pp. 92–93
  Pupil's Edition Exercise Bank p. 599

 Grammar Coach CD-ROM Lesson 6

Forming Simple Tenses

The present tense of a verb is the present principal part. The past tense is the past principal part. To form the future tense, add *will* to the present principal part.

Forming Simple Tenses	Singular	Plural
Present (present principal part)	I direct you direct he, she, it directs	we direct you direct they direct
Past (past principal part)	I directed you directed he, she, it directed	we directed you directed they directed
Future (*will* + present principal part)	I will direct you will direct he, she, it will direct	we will direct you will direct they will direct

To make the progressive form of one of these tenses, add the present, past, or future form of *be* to the present participle.

Present progressive: **I am directing.**

Past progressive: **I was directing.**

Future progressive: **I will be directing.**

❷ Why It Matters in Writing

Changing tenses allows you to be clear about the order in which things happen. Notice how the writer uses the past, the present, and the future tense in the sentence below.

PROFESSIONAL MODEL

Until recently, people considered digital films inferior. Now better cameras produce good, clear images. Soon many filmmakers will produce their movies digitally.

PAST
PRESENT
FUTURE

—Eliza Blackburn

TEACHING TIP

Speaking and Listening Read aloud the following instructions and sentences. Have students listen to the sentences and rephrase accordingly.

Change to the present: *I went to the movies a lot when I was a kid.* **Possible answer:** *I go to the movies all the time.*

Change to the future: *I saw that film twice already.* **Possible answer:** *I will see that film this weekend.*

Change to the past: *I like that movie.* **Possible answer:** *I liked the director's last movie better.*

CUSTOMIZING TIP

Students Acquiring English/ESL English has many verb tenses that are absent or used differently in other languages. If students have difficulties using verbs appropriately, see **English Grammar Survival Kit** pp. 23–26, for explanations and practice with various verb tenses.

❸ Practice and Apply

A. CONCEPT CHECK: Simple Tenses

Identify each underlined verb as present, past, future, present progressive, past progressive, or future progressive.

The Digital Revolution Arrives

1. Digital videodiscs (DVDs) <u>will be</u> standard someday. **Fut.**

2. These shiny platters <u>will transform</u> movie distribution. **Fut.**

3. A digital videodisc <u>holds</u> up to 25 times as much information as a CD. **Pres.**

4. It <u>provides</u> high-quality video images, interactive multimedia features, and surround sound. **Pres.**

5. The movie *Ghostbusters* <u>came</u> out in 1984. **Past**

6. It <u>did</u> well at the box office. **Past**

7. Now it <u>is</u> available in DVD format. **Pres.**

8. Besides the movie, the DVD <u>contains</u> commentary by the director, production notes, and a photo gallery. **Pres.**

9. It also <u>includes</u> a complete script and ten scenes that were cut from the movie. **Pres.**

10. In the next few years, companies <u>will be releasing</u> nearly 100,000 movies on DVD. **Fut. Prog.**

➜ For a SELF-CHECK and more practice, see the EXERCISE BANK, p. 599.

📁 **Working Portfolio:** Find the paragraph you wrote for the **Write Away** on page 91 or a sample of your most recent work. Identify any errors in the use of simple tenses and correct them.

B. REVISING: Correcting Simple Tenses

Rewrite the following paragraph, correcting the tenses of the underlined verbs.

The Cost of DVD

Today, movie distributors **(1)** <u>will spend</u> hundreds of   **1.** spend
millions of dollars on copies of films for theaters. In the
next few years, most of them **(2)** <u>began</u> sending the movies   **2.** will begin
digitally by satellite. When they do so, sending a movie out
(3) <u>costs</u> them only about $150,000. Stefan Avalos and   **3.** will cost
Lance Weiler **(4)** <u>release</u> an all-digital movie by satellite in   **4.** released
1999. They **(5)** <u>will shoot</u> the all-digital movie on borrowed   **5.** shot
digital cameras.

Answers

Print-Out Option You may create worksheets of exercises A and B for your students by using the 💿 **Electronic Teacher Tools CD–ROM.**

A. CONCEPT CHECK

Self-Check For a self-check of simple tenses, direct students to p. 599 in the Pupil's Edition for the answers to the items circled in yellow.

Answers shown on page using these codes:

Pres. = present tense

Past = past tense

Fut. = future tense

Fut. Prog. = future progressive tense

B. REVISING

Answers shown on page.

VERBS

VERBS

LESSON OBJECTIVES

To identify and correctly use the present perfect, past perfect, and future perfect tenses

DAILY TEST PREPARATION

Error Correction: Combining Sentences Write the following item on the board or use **Daily Test Preparation Transparency** p. DT16.

> During an eclipse, it's bad to gaze at the sun. Gazing at the sun can damage your vision.

How are these sentences best written?

A. Gazing at the sun can damage your vision during an eclipse.

B. Gazing during an eclipse at the sun can damage your vision.

C. Gazing at the sun during an eclipse can damage your vision.

D. As they are

Teaching Point: For questions that involve combining sentences, the correct answer will state the information as clearly and consisely as possible (answers A and B contain misplaced phrases and answer D is wordy).

LESSON 7 Perfect Tenses

❶ Here's the Idea

Understanding Perfect Tenses

The **present perfect tense** places an action or condition in a stretch of time leading up to the present.

> **The scientist has created a monster.**

> He created the monster at some indefinite time before the present.

The **past perfect tense** places a past action or condition before another past action or condition.

> **When the scientist had tinkered with him, the monster awakened.**

> The tinkering occurred before the awakening.

The **future perfect tense** places a future action or condition before another future action or condition.

> **The monster will have escaped before the scientist notices.**

> The escaping will occur before the scientist's noticing.

The monster **has walked** here.

The monster **will have walked** here.

TEACHING RESOURCES

 Time-Saver Transparencies Binder:
- Daily Test Preparation p. DT16
- Quick-Fix Grammar and Style Charts p. QF9

Grammar, Usage, and Mechanics Workbook p. 94

SKILLS PRACTICE RESOURCES

 Grammar, Usage, and Mechanics Workbook pp. 95–96

Pupil's Edition Exercise Bank p. 600

 Grammar Coach CD-ROM Lesson 6

Forming Perfect Tenses

To form the present perfect, past perfect, or future perfect tense of a verb, add the present, past, or future form of *have* to the past participle.

Forming Perfect Tenses		
	Singular	**Plural**
Present perfect (*has* or *have* + past participle)	I have screamed you have screamed he, she, it has screamed	we have screamed you have screamed they have screamed
Past perfect (*had* + past participle)	I had screamed you had screamed he, she, i t had screamed	we had screamed you had screamed they had screamed
Future perfect (*will* + *have* + past participle)	I will have screamed you will have screamed he, she, it will have screamed	we will have screamed you will have screamed they will have screamed

In perfect forms of verbs, the tense of the helping verb *have* shows the verb's tense.

❷ Why It Matters in Writing

By using perfect tenses, you can help your readers understand when events occur in relation to other events. Notice the effective use of the past perfect and present perfect tenses in the model.

> **PROFESSIONAL MODEL**
>
> Within a year the brute **had returned** in *Godzilla's Counterattack* and over the years he **has battled** The Thing.
> —Jeremy Pascall, *The King Kong Story*

This action occurred before other events in the past.

This action occurred sometime between the previous action and the present.

VERBS

VERBS

Verbs **109**

❸ Practice and Apply

A. CONCEPT CHECK: Perfect Tenses

Identify the verb in each sentence, and indicate whether its tense is present perfect, past perfect, or future perfect.

Horrors!

Past Perf. 1. For years we <u>had looked</u> for a funny werewolf movie.

Pres. Perf. 2. Now we <u>have found</u> *An American Werewolf in London.*

Fut. Perf. 3. By tomorrow morning we <u>will have watched</u> it four times.

4. *Young Frankenstein* <u>has amused</u> us too. **Pres. Perf.**

5. Many serious Frankenstein movies <u>had appeared</u> before that comedy. **Past Perf.**

6. Film makers <u>had</u> created the first such horror films not long after the invention of movies. **Past Perf.**

7. Even before the 1931 *Frankenstein* there <u>had been</u> a silent version of the Frankenstein story. **Past Perf.**

8. All Frankenstein movies <u>have drawn</u> on Mary Shelley's 1818 novel. **Pres. Perf.**

9. Filmmakers <u>have produced</u> at least eight versions of *Dr. Jekyll and Mr. Hyde*. **Pres. Perf.**

10. What new versions of horror classics <u>will have come</u> out by next year? **Fut. Perf.**

➡ **For a SELF-CHECK and more practice, see the EXERCISE BANK, p. 600.**

B. WRITING: Using Perfect Tenses

The scene described below could happen in a horror movie. Rewrite each underlined verb in the tense named in parentheses.

Horror Scene: Take One

have cut
had thought
have been
has appeared
will have discovered

Three girls <u>cut</u> (present perfect) through a cemetery. They <u>thought</u> (past perfect) it would be a good shortcut, but they <u>were</u> (present perfect) sorry ever since. Suddenly they see a strange light that <u>appeared</u> (present perfect) ahead of them. By the time they round the next tombstone, they <u>discovered</u> (future perfect) the light's source—a mummy!

LESSON 8 · Using Verb Tenses

1 Here's the Idea

A good writer uses different verb tenses to indicate that events occur at different times. If you do not need to indicate a change of time, do not switch from one tense to another.

Writing About the Present

You can write about the present using the present tense, the present perfect tense, and the present progressive form.

> **Motion pictures work** because of our vision.
>
> The brain **sees** a series of still pictures as moving.

The **present tense** places the actions in the present.

> **Filmmakers have created** fantastic special effects.
>
> They **have brought** dinosaurs and alien beings to life.

The **present perfect tense** places the actions in the period of time leading up to the present.

> **Directors are learning** the use of computer effects.
>
> They **are becoming** extremely skilled artists.

The **present progressive forms** show the actions are in progress now.

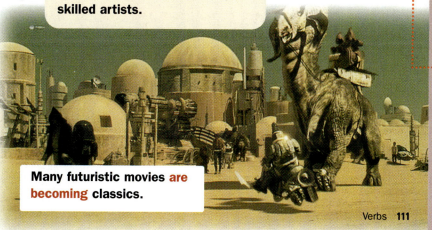

Many futuristic movies are becoming classics.

Verbs **111**

VERBS

VERBS

LESSON OBJECTIVES

To understand and correctly use verb tenses to express sequences of events or states of being

 DAILY TEST PREPARATION

Sentence Completion: Subject-Verb Agreement Write the following item on the board or use 📖 **Daily Test Preparation Transparency** p. DT17. Choose the word or words that belong in the space.

> My dad and Uncle Mario _____ fishing for the weekend.

A. has gone

B. have gone

C. gone

D. is going

Teaching Point: Sentence completion questions often test your knowledge of subject-verb agreement. In this case, the compound subject *My dad and Uncle Mario* takes a plural verb (*have gone*).

TEACHING TIP

Speaking and Listening Ask students to close their books. Read aloud the sample sentences on the student page and have students listen for and identify the verb tenses.

TEACHING RESOURCES

 Time-Saver Transparencies Binder:
- Daily Test Preparation p. DT17
- Quick-Fix Grammar and Style Charts p. QF9
- Visual Grammar™ Tiles Lesson 8

Grammar, Usage, and Mechanics Workbook p. 97

SKILLS PRACTICE RESOURCES

 Grammar, Usage, and Mechanics Workbook pp. 98–99

Pupil's Edition Exercise Bank p. 600

 Grammar Coach CD-ROM Lesson 6

TEACHING TIP

Cross-Curricular Connection Literature Tell students that, while they should use past tense verbs when writing about something that happened long ago, there are exceptions. For instance, students should use the present tense to comment on a literary work, even when the story takes place in another historical time period. For example: *In* Great Expectations, *Dickens* creates *a sympathetic character in Pip.*

Writing About the Past

▶ **The past tense conveys actions and conditions that came to an end in the past.** When you write about the past, you can use past verb forms to indicate the order in which events occurred. Using these forms correctly will make it easier for readers to follow the events.

Thomas Edison's company **launched** the motion-picture industry.

His employee William Dickson **devised** a way of moving film through a camera.

> The **past tense** shows action that began and was completed in the past.

Other inventors **had put** sound with pictures before Edison did.

After the Lumière brothers **had developed** a projector, Edison began projecting his films.

> The **past perfect tense** places the actions before other past actions.

Filmmakers **were inventing** new technologies for years before they began using computers.

They **were trying** to make unreal events look real.

> The **past progressive forms** show that the actions in the past were in progress.

TEACHING TIP

Have students write another caption for the photograph on the page, using a past perfect verb tense.

More than 30 years ago, filmmakers **were creating** realistic space scenes.

112

Spice It Up!

Have pairs of students create mixed-up paragraphs to read to the rest of the class. Have one partner write a brief active scene, leaving blanks where the verbs should go. The student should identify the verb that is needed in each blank. The second student, without reading the scene or story, can then compose a list of verbs that match these tenses. Which team's story makes the most sense? Which team has created the most ridiculous or illogical paragraph?

Writing About the Future

▶ **The future tenses convey actions and conditions that are yet to come.** By using the different future verb forms, you can show how future events are related in time.

Maybe everyone **will make** movies someday.

The line between home movies and professional ones **will blur**.

> The **future tense** shows that the actions have not yet occurred.

Before they can read, children already **will have learned** to use a camera.

Studio films will be less important because the Internet **will have increased** people's access to one another's films.

> The **future perfect tense** places the actions before other future actions.

People **will be making** movies ever more cheaply.

Everyone **will be watching** everyone else's movies.

> The **future progressive forms** show that the actions in the future will be continuing.

TEACHING TIP

To further assist students in writing about the future, ask them to give three predictions about life in the future. Have students use the future tense, the future perfect tense, and the future progressive tense in their predictions.

CUSTOMIZING TIP

Less Proficient Learners If students have difficulty understanding future tenses, have them identify the tenses in the following sentences.

She <u>will have finished</u> that scene by the time the writer arrives. (future perfect tense)

Hollywood <u>will</u> always <u>be having</u> its ups and downs. (future progressive form)

I <u>will be</u> a movie star. (future tense)

Have students write their own sentences, using these examples as a model. They can use both groups of sentences as a reference for their writing.

VERBS

❷ Why It Matters in Writing

When you use the right tenses, you help your readers keep sequences of events straight.

1850
No movies existed.

1900
Few people owned cameras and projectors.

Today
Big studios make movies for profit.

2050
Anyone will be able to make movies.

Verbs **113**

📖 Visual Grammar

Use **Visual Grammar™ Tiles Lesson 8** and **Sentence F** to demonstrate when to use different verb tenses. Here is part of Lesson 8.

Present tense:

| THE CAT | HUNTS | THE MOUSE | . |

Past tense:

| THE CAT | HUNTED | THE MOUSE | . |

Past perfect tense:

| THE CAT | HAD HUNTED | BEFORE |

| THE DOG SCARED IT | . |

CHAPTER 4

Answers

Print-Out Option You may create worksheets of exercises A and B for your students by using the ⊚ **Electronic Teacher Tools CD–ROM.**

A. CONCEPT CHECK

Self-Check For a self-check of using verb tenses, direct students to p. 600 in the Pupil's Edition for the answers to the items circled in yellow.

Answers underlined on page.

1. Past progressive tense
2. Past tense
3. Present perfect tense
4. Past progressive tense
5. Past tense
6. Present progressive tense
7. Present progressive tense
8. Present tense
9. Future tense
10. Future tense

B. EDITING

Answers shown on page. The numbers indicate the correct order of the sentences.

---

③ Practice and Apply

CHAPTER 4

A. CONCEPT CHECK: Using Verb Tenses

In each sentence, choose the correct verb form in parentheses.

Hollywood Goes High-Tech

1. In the 1930s, makers of monster movies (<u>were using</u>, will be using) laughably bad special effects.
2. They (<u>lacked</u>, have lacked) the technology to create realistic monsters.
3. Recently filmmakers (<u>have improved</u>, improved) special effects technology considerably.
4. As early as the 1980s, filmmakers (will be using, <u>were using</u>) computer-generated, or CG, graphics.
5. They (<u>added</u>, will have added) effects on a background.
6. Now they (<u>are refining</u>, were refining) CG technology further.
7. They (will build, <u>are building</u>) characters on a computer.
8. They already (<u>create</u>, will create) everything from aliens to giant gorillas.
9. Soon they (had shown, <u>will show</u>) realistic animated human figures.
10. Yet the story (<u>will remain</u>, remained) the most important element.

Name the tense or form of each verb you chose in the sentences above. **Answers in column.**

➡ **For a SELF-CHECK and more practice, see the EXERCISE BANK, p. 600.**

B. EDITING: Arranging Verb Tenses

Pretend you are a film director. List the numbers of the following directions in a logical order, so that the tenses of the verbs make sense. (Hint: Read all the sentences before you begin.) **2, 4, 3, 5, 1**

1. Now that you know what the scene is about, we will begin.
2. This scene starts just after an alien has made video contact with the reporter Colleen McKay.
3. Colleen is surprised because she expected the alien to look like a bug.
4. First, Colleen sees the alien, who looks like a cat.
5. The alien will tell Colleen his name, Rxxd.

Troublesome Verb Pairs

1 Here's the Idea

Some pairs of verbs seem similar but are actually different words with different meanings. Troublesome verb pairs include *lie* and *lay, sit* and *set, rise* and *raise,* and *may* and *can.*

Lie and *Lay*

Lie means "to recline." It does not take an object.
Lay means "to put or place." It does take an object.

> **The tigers lie at the trainer's feet.**

> **The trainer lays the tiger treats on a tray.**

Lie and *Lay*		
Present	**Past**	**Past Participle**
lie Fido **lies** down.	**lay** Fido **lay** down.	**lain** Fido has **lain** down.
lay Fido **lays** the toy down.	**laid** Fido **laid** the toy down.	**laid** Fido has **laid** the toy down.

Lie and lay are confusing because the present principal part of *lay* is spelled the same as the past principal part of *lie.*

Sit and *Set*

Sit means "to be seated." It does not take an object.
Set means "to put or place." It does take an object.

> **My cat, Luna, sits on the couch.**

> **I set the flea powder down somewhere.**

Sit and *Set*		
Present	**Past**	**Past Participle**
sit We **sit** on the floor.	**sat** We **sat** on the floor.	**sat** I had **sat** for hours.
set Tiff **sets** down the bug.	**set** Tiff **set** down the bug.	**set** Tiff had **set** down the bug.

Verbs **115**

LESSON OBJECTIVES

To distinguish between and correctly use some commonly confused verb pairs

DAILY TEST PREPARATION

Error Correction: Using Precise Words Write the following item on the board or use **Daily Test Preparation Transparency** p. DT17.
Choose the <u>best</u> way to write the underlined part of the sentence.

> Among many compliments, Mr. Peters wrote on John's report card, "John is a <u>good</u> student."

A. nice

B. bullheaded

C. conscientious

D. No change

Teaching Point: Error correction questions often test your ability to use precise words. In this case, the correct answer must be precise (answers A and D are not) and fit the meaning of the sentence (answer B does not).

TEACHING RESOURCES

 Time-Saver Transparencies Binder:
• Daily Test Preparation p. DT17
  Grammar, Usage, and Mechanics Workbook p. 100

SKILLS PRACTICE RESOURCES

  Grammar, Usage, and Mechanics Workbook pp. 101–102
  Pupil's Edition Exercise Bank p. 601

Rise *and* Raise

Rise means "to move upward" or "to get out of bed." It does not take an object. *Raise* means "to lift" or "to care for or bring up." It does take an object.

The sun rises every morning.

King Kong raises a car easily.

Rise *and* Raise		
Present	**Past**	**Past Participle**
rise The water **rises.**	**rose** The water **rose.**	**risen** The water had **risen** earlier.
raise Kong **raises** the car.	**raised** Kong **raised** the car.	**raised** Kong had **raised** the car earlier.

May *and* Can

May means "to be allowed to" or "to be likely to." *Can* means "to be able to." *Might* and *could* serve as the past tense forms of *may* and *can*.

May I pet your dog?

Can he do any tricks?

Can and *may* do not have past participles. They are usually used as helping verbs.

❷ Practice and Apply

A. CONCEPT CHECK: Troublesome Verb Pairs

Choose the correct word in parentheses in each of the following sentences.

The Gentle Jungle

1. With love, patience, understanding, and respect, you (<u>can</u>, may) teach an animal almost anything.

2. The animal trainer Ralph Helfer teaches his animals what they (can, <u>may</u>) do with a system called affection training.

3. To show affection, Helfer (<u>lies</u>, lays) down with a lion.

4. Helfer (lies, <u>lays</u>) his hands on his animals carefully.

5. When Helfer's daughter Tana was little, she often (<u>sat</u>, set) on the trunk of Margie the elephant.

6. Margie the elephant (rose, <u>raised</u>) her trunk.

7. Tana would (<u>rise</u>, raise) in the air.

8. Then Margie would (sit, <u>set</u>) the child on her back.

9. Helfer (rose, <u>raised</u>) the orangutan who costarred with Clint Eastwood in two movies.

10. He even taught a sick chimp to (<u>lie</u>, lay) down and give itself a shot.

➡ **For a SELF-CHECK and more practice, see the EXERCISE BANK, p. 601.**

B. PROOFREADING: What Do They Mean?

List the five verbs that are used incorrectly in the following paragraph. Then change them to the correct verb forms.

Elvis and the Chimp

<u>May</u> you believe this story about Elvis Presley? Elvis used to <u>set</u> on Helfer's floor and play with baby tigers. One day when Elvis arrived, a chimp named Coffee jumped off the roof and knocked him down. Elvis <u>laid</u> on the ground while Coffee jumped up and down on him. After Helfer helped <u>rise</u> Elvis to his feet, Coffee apologized by brushing the dust off the singer. Coffee learned that he should not <u>sit</u> his feet on Elvis Presley!

(margin answers:) **Can** · **sat** · **lay** · **raise** · **set**

Answers

Print-Out Option You may create worksheets of exercises A and B for your students by using the **Electronic Teacher Tools CD–ROM.**

A. CONCEPT CHECK

Self-Check For a self-check of using verb tenses, direct students to p. 601 in the Pupil's Edition for the answers to the items circled in yellow.

Answers underlined on page.

B. PROOFREADING

Answers shown on page. Incorrect verbs are underlined. Correct verb forms appear in the margin.

ASSESSMENT

 Assessment Masters:
* Chapter Mastery Tests pp. 55–60

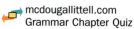 Test Generator CD-ROM

mcdougallittell.com Grammar Chapter Quiz

LESSON OBJECTIVES

To identify and use precise action verbs to write about a dramatic scene

TEACHING TIP

Speaking and Listening Read aloud the stage directions on the student page. Have students listen for and identify the verb tense used in the directions. Ask: Why are all the verbs in the present tense? Verbs describe action that the actors should perform.

Grammar in Fine Arts

Using Verbs in Drama

When you present a dramatic scene, you perform actions. When you write a dramatic scene, you use verbs to indicate those actions. Stage directions are very important because they tell the actors exactly what to do. The verbs in stage directions must clearly describe the desired movements. Notice the verbs in these scenes from *A Christmas Carol*.

(The spirit motions for Scrooge to turn. Scrooge trembles and shakes his head.)

(Dancers whirl around the stage. Fezziwig's wife applauds.)

Spice It Up!

Quotable Quote "All the world's a stage,/ And all the men and women merely players:/They have their exits and their entrances;/And one man in his time plays many parts . . ." —Shakespeare, *As You Like It*

Ask students what Shakespeare means by "one man in his time plays many parts"? Have students discuss the roles—such as child, parent, student, worker, and citizen—that they may perform in their lifetimes.

Practice and Apply

A. WRITING: Describing a Scene

Use your own ideas and the actions shown on page 118 to write a one-minute scene. Include interesting, scary, or funny actions in your scene. Write clear stage directions for your actors. You may use some of the sentences beside the characters to get started.

B. Creating a Blocking Diagram

A director's plans for how actors should move on stage are called blocking. When you are working on a dramatic performance, you may need to write plans for blocking the action. The picture shows a blocking diagram for another scene in the play.

Make your own diagram showing the blocking for your scene. In your diagram, include each of the actors who will be on stage. Indicate who should move. Use arrows to indicate directions. Add verbs on labels that give additional information about how actors should move.

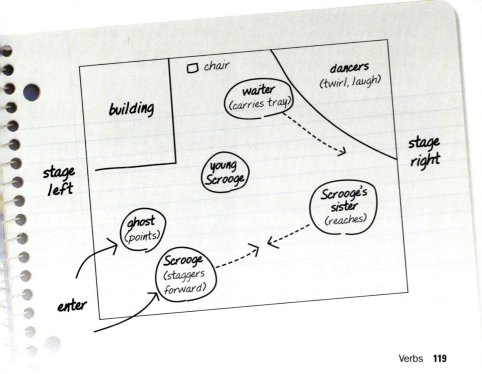

Verbs **119**

VERBS

Answers

PRACTICE AND APPLY

A. Writing

Scenes will vary, but students should use verbs in the stage directions that clearly tell the actors what to do.

Spirit: *(He motions for Scrooge to turn and takes Scrooge's arm).* Open your eyes, Scrooge, and look at the dancers.

Scrooge: *(Scrooge trembles and shakes his head.)* No! I don't want to look!

Spirit: *(He urges Scrooge to look)* Yes, you do.

Scrooge: *(He slowly uncovers his eyes).* There's Fezziwhig! Those people must be having a party!

B. Creating a Blocking Diagram

Blocking diagrams will vary, but plans should look similar to the model on the student page. Diagrams should indicate the positions of all the actors who need to be on stage. Make sure that the verbs indicate precisely how the actors should move.

VERBS

Cooperative Learning/Paired Activity Have student pairs work together on exercise A. This activity will help students use verb tenses, such as the present, past, future, perfect, and progressive forms, appropriately and consistently.

Mixed Review

Answers

Print-Out Option You may create worksheets of exercise A for your students by using the ⦿ **Electronic Teacher Tools CD–ROM.**

A. Revising Incorrect Verbs

Answers shown on page. Incorrect verb forms are crossed out. Correct verb forms appear in the margin.

B. Using Tenses

Students should use verbs correctly as they compose their sentences. Answers will vary. Possible responses:

The clock in the building has not been working properly.

One of the office workers steps out a window and reaches for the clock hand.

Maybe he will jump onto the ledge.

Then he will climb up a rope to the flagpole.

He will fix the clock from there.

Mixed Review

A. Revising Incorrect Verbs Find and correct the incorrect verb in each of the following sentences. Watch out for irregular verbs, troublesome verbs, and incorrect verb tenses.

Preserving Our Past in Movies

1. Today, some movie fans currently ~~have worried~~ about the rate at which movie prints are deteriorating. **worry**
2. They ~~rose~~ the alarm when they found that many early movies ~~have disappeared~~ forever. **raised/had disappeared**
3. Already, time ~~will be destroying~~ nine-tenths of all the movies from the 1920s. **has destroyed**
4. The world has lost half of all the movies that ~~were maked~~ before 1950. **were made**
5. **being lost** Thousands of movies are ~~being losed~~ in studios' vaults right now.
6. The biggest problem ~~had been~~ the decay of the film that moviemakers ~~use~~. **has been/used**
7. **will film** Most directors in the future ~~filmed~~ digitally, without celluloid.
8. Yet electronic ways of recording movies ~~were becoming~~ out of date very fast. **are becoming**
9. Because equipment has changed, most TV stations today ~~were~~ unable to broadcast from the movie tape of 20 years ago. **are**
10. Film restorers work hard now so that people ~~have enjoyed~~ today's movies in the future. **will enjoy**

B. Using Tenses Using the ideas in the phrases listed below, write five sentences about the picture. Tell what happened before the scene shown in the picture, what is happening in it, and what might happen next.
Answers in column.
steps out the window

reaches for the clock hands

fixes the clock

jumps onto the ledge

climbs up a rope to the flagpole

Mastery Test: What Did You Learn?

Choose the best way to rewrite each underlined word or group of words.

Money <u>has been</u> an issue in movies since the beginning. In fact,
(1)
before movies became popular, Thomas Edison <u>vows</u> never to invent
(2)
anything he couldn't sell. He <u>seen</u> the movie camera as a product
(3)
that would make money. As technology improved, some costs
decreased. Other costs <u>rised</u>. For example, in 1959 it <u>costed</u> about
(4)   (5)
$70,000 to film a minute of the epic movie *Ben-Hur.* In 1998 the
filming of *Titanic* cost $1 million per minute. However, soon the cost
of special effects <u>will come</u> down as computer-generated graphics
(6)
are used more widely. In the next 25 years the cost of effects
<u>had dropped</u> by half. Today, all the studios together <u>spent</u> $400
(7)   (8)
million each year on prints of their movies. Soon filmmakers <u>sent</u>
(9)
their movies worldwide by satellite, and the cost <u>sinks</u>.
(10)

1. A. had been
   B. will be
   C. was
   D. Correct as is

2. A. will vow
   B. has vowed
   C. had vowed
   D. Correct as is

3. A. saw
   B. has seen
   C. had saw
   D. Correct as is

4. A. rise
   B. rose
   C. raised
   D. Correct as is

5. A. cost
   B. will cost
   C. is costing
   D. Correct as is

6. A. came
   B. are coming
   C. have come
   D. Correct as is

7. A. drop
   B. have dropped
   C. will drop
   D. Correct as is

8. A. spend
   B. spended
   C. will spend
   D. Correct as is

9. A. send
   B. have sent
   C. will send
   D. Correct as is

10. A. sank
    B. have sunk
    C. will sink
    D. Correct as is

Answers

Mastery Test

As an option, two other Chapter Mastery Tests appear in 🗔 **Assessment Masters** pp. 55–60.

Answers circled on page.

PRESCRIPTION FOR MASTERY	
If students miss item number:	**Use Teaching Resources** and **Skills Practice Resources** for lesson:
1, 2	❼ Perfect Tenses p. 108
3, 5	❺ Irregular Verbs p. 102
4	❾ Troublesome Verb Pairs p. 115
6, 7, 8, 9, 10	❻ Simple Tenses p. 105

VERBS

VERBS

Student Help Desk

Verbs at a Glance

A verb expresses action, condition, or state of being.

People **eat** popcorn at the movies.
ACTION VERB

Popcorn **is** a noisy treat.
LINKING VERB

They **have eaten** too much popcorn.
HELPING VERB   MAIN VERB

Principal Parts of Regular Verbs

Present	Present Participle	Past	Past Participle
present	present + *-ing*	present + *-ed* or *-d*	present + *-ed* or *-d*
act	(is) acting	acted	(has) acted
bellow	(is) bellowing	bellowed	(has) bellowed
cry	(is) crying	cried	(has) cried
drag	(is) dragging	dragged	(has) dragged
emote	(is) emoting	emoted	(has) emoted
film	(is) filming	filmed	(has) filmed
gesture	(is) gesturing	gestured	(has) gestured
help	(is) helping	helped	(has) helped
imitate	(is) imitating	imitated	(has) imitated
join	(is) joining	joined	(has) joined

122 Grammar, Usage, and Mechanics

Keeping Tenses Straight

....It's about Time!

Tense	What It Conveys	Example
Present	Action or condition occurring in the present	I **watch** movies.
Past	Action or condition occurring in the past	I **watched** a movie.
Future	Action or condition occurring in the future	I **will watch** a movie.
Present perfect	Action or condition occurring in the period leading up to the present	I **have watched** movies.
Past perfect	Past action or condition preceding another past action or condition	I **had watched** the movie before I went to bed.
Future perfect	Future action or condition preceding another future action or condition	I **will have watched** five movies by next Tuesday.

The Bottom Line

Checklist for Verbs

Have I . . .

____ used action verbs to express actions?

____ used linking verbs with predicate nouns and predicate adjectives?

____ used direct objects and indirect objects to answer the questions *whom*, *what*, and *to whom* or *to what*?

____ used the correct principal parts of irregular verbs?

____ used tenses correctly to express the times of actions and conditions?

____ used *sit* and *set*, *lie* and *lay*, *rise* and *raise*, and *may* and *can* correctly?

Verbs **123**

Teacher's Notes
WHAT DOESN'T WORK:

VERBS

VERBS

TEACHER'S LOUNGE

Just for Laughs

Teacher: "Tell me, Jimmy, what it means when I say 'I love, you love, he loves.'"

Jimmy: "It means the movie ain't going to be a cowboy story."

Verbs **123**

CHAPTER OVERVIEW

CHAPTER 5

CHAPTER RESOURCES

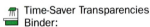 Time-Saver Transparencies
Binder:
- Daily Test Preparation
pp. DT18–21
- Quick-Fix Grammar and
Style Charts p. QF8

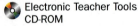 Grammar, Usage, and
Mechanics Workbook
pp. 103–123

Integrated Technology and Media

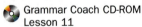 Electronic Teacher Tools
CD-ROM

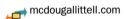 Grammar Coach CD-ROM
Lesson 11

 mcdougallittell.com

Assessment

Assessment Masters:
- Chapter Pretest pp. 10–11
- Chapter Mid-point Test
p. 28
- Chapter Mastery Tests
pp. 61–66

Test Generator CD-ROM

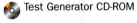 mcdougallittell.com
Grammar Chapter Quiz

Students Acquiring English/ESL

English Grammar
Survival Kit pp. 3–4, 11–14,
41–42

Adjectives and Adverbs

CHAPTER 5

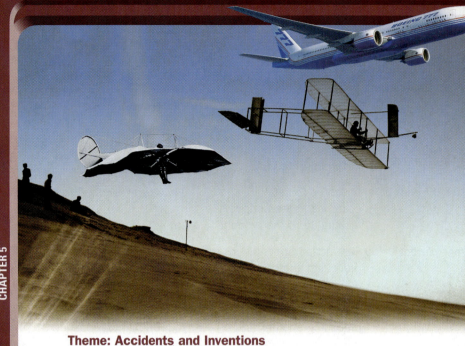

Theme: Accidents and Inventions

Back to the Drawing Board

How did inventors bring us from a primitive glider that barely carried one person to the incredibly sophisticated Boeing 777 that easily carries 300 passengers? It took a long time—and many modifications, or changes. Otto Lilienthal, who invented the first piloted glider (on the left above) in 1891, died after crashing one of his gliders. But other eager inventors continued to fine-tune their vehicles until they created the huge, fast, sleek jets of today.

Writers, like inventors, are fine-tuners. They use adjectives and adverbs to modify, or make more specific, their words. What words would you use to describe the three aircraft above?

Write Away: Moving into the Future
Imagine a transportation invention of the future. Freewrite a paragraph that describes what it does and how it looks. Save the paragraph in your 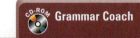 **Working Portfolio.**

Grammar Coach

124

Diagnostic Test: What Do You Know?

For each underlined item, choose the letter of the term that correctly identifies it.

In the late 1700s two <u>French</u> brothers, Jacques and Joseph
(1)
Montgolfier, began experiments that led to the invention of the
<u>modern</u> hot-air balloon. <u>The</u> brothers started <u>really</u> simply, using
(2)   (3)   (4)
small paper bags and wood fires. In <u>these</u> tests the Montgolfiers
(5)
saw that a bag would rise when <u>completely</u> filled with hot air. The
(6)
brothers conducted a <u>more important</u> experiment when they filled
(7)
a large cloth balloon with hot air and launched it. The flight was
<u>successful</u>! Today's balloonists <u>couldn't hardly fly</u> without the
(8)   (9)
methods perfected by the Montgolfiers. Today, by using modern
technologies, modern balloonists fly even <u>farther</u> than the
(10)
Montgolfiers flew.

1. A. adverb
   B. comparative adjective
   C. proper adjective
   D. predicate adjective

2. **A.** adjective
   B. comparative adjective
   C. proper adjective
   D. predicate adjective

3. A. proper adjective
   B. definite article
   C. predicate adjective
   D. indefinite article

4. **A.** adverb describing *simply*
   B. adverb describing *started*
   C. adverb describing *brothers*
   D. adverb describing *bags*

5. **A.** pronoun used as adjective
   B. noun used as adjective
   C. pronoun used as adverb
   D. noun used as adverb

6. A. adverb telling how
   B. adverb telling when
   C. adverb telling where
   D. adverb telling to what extent

7. **A.** comparative adjective
   B. superlative adjective
   C. comparative adverb
   D. superlative adverb

8. A. adverb
   B. comparative adjective
   C. proper adjective
   D. predicate adjective

9. A. adjective
   B. double negative
   C. statement
   D. question

10. **A.** comparative adverb
    B. superlative adverb
    C. comparative adjective
    D. superlative adjective

Adjectives and Adverbs **125**

ADJ. & ADV.

ADJECTIVES AND ADVERBS

LESSON OBJECTIVES

To identify and correctly use adjectives in sentences

LESSON 1

What Is an Adjective?

❶ Here's the Idea

▶ **An adjective is a word that modifies, or describes, a noun or a pronoun.**

MODIFIES

The noisy crowd cheered for Daria.
ADJECTIVE   NOUN

Adjectives help you see, feel, taste, hear, and smell all the things you read about. Notice how adjectives make the second sentence in the following pair more descriptive.

She sped along the track on her bicycle.

She sped along the narrow track on her sleek bicycle.

Adjectives answer the questions *what kind, which one, how many,* and *how much.*

Adjectives			
What kind?	**fast** riders	**crowded** stadium	**steamy** afternoon
Which one or ones?	**first** lap	**inner** lanes	**final** race
How many or how much?	**five** teams	**many** fans	**more** applause

What kind?
green bicycle
sturdy frame

Which one or ones?
second tire
any seat

How many?
21 speeds
several
reflectors

126 Grammar, Usage, and Mechanics

TEACHING RESOURCES

 Time-Saver Transparencies Binder:
• Daily Test Preparation p. DT18
 Grammar, Usage, and Mechanics Workbook p. 103

SKILLS PRACTICE RESOURCES

English Grammar
Survival Kit pp. 3–4
 Grammar, Usage, and Mechanics Workbook pp. 104–105
 Pupil's Edition Exercise Bank p. 602

Articles

The most commonly used adjectives are the **articles** *a, an,* and *the. A* and *an* are forms of the **indefinite article.** The indefinite article is used before a noun that names a nonspecific person, place, thing, or idea.

A sudden turn can cause an accident.
   ↑ INDEFINITE ARTICLE   ↑ INDEFINITE ARTICLE

Use *a* before a word beginning with a consonant sound ("a ball"); use *an* before a word beginning with a vowel sound ("an egg").

The is the **definite article.** It points to a particular person, place, thing, or idea.

The competition continued through the afternoon.
   ↑ DEFINITE ARTICLE   ↑ DEFINITE ARTICLE

Forming Adjectives

Many adjectives are formed from common nouns.

Nouns and Adjectives

Noun	Adjective
storm	stormy
child	childish
music	musical
beauty	beautiful

A **proper adjective** is formed from a proper noun. Proper adjectives are always capitalized.

Proper Nouns and Proper Adjectives

Proper Noun	Proper Adjective
Shakespeare	Shakespearean
Asia	Asian
Spain	Spanish
Islam	Islamic

Adjectives and Adverbs **127**

ADJ. & ADV.

ADJECTIVES
AND ADVERBS

TEACHING TIP

Explain to students that *an* is not used before the long *u* sound (*an* umbrella, *a* uniform). Point out that *an* is sometimes used before words beginning with a silent *h.* Examples: *an hour, an heiress,* and *an herb.*

CUSTOMIZING TIP

Students Acquiring English/ESL Because rules regarding article use vary from language to language, students might be tempted either to use articles where they are not required or omit them when they are required in English. For instruction and practice with article use, have students use **English Grammar Survival Kit** pp. 3–4.

TEACHING TIP

Speaking and Listening Read aloud the following adjectives. Have students listen for and identify the common or proper noun each one is formed from: *cloudy* (cloud); *Chinese* (China); *dramatic* (drama); *Texan* (Texas); *brutish* (brute).

Spice It Up!

Ask students to imagine being so famous that their first or last name has been made into a proper adjective—for example, Dickensian or Johnsonian. Have students create proper adjectives from their names and use the adjective to modify something they are famous for (a Changish joke or a Washingtonian riddle, for instance).

CONCEPT CHECK

Self-Check For a self-check of what an adjective is, direct students to p. 602 in the Pupil's Edition for the answers to the items circled in yellow.

Answers shown on page. Adjectives are underlined once. The words they modify are underlined twice.

Sentence 3: *Northeastern* is a proper adjective formed from *Northeast.*

Sentence 10: *American* is a proper adjective formed from *America.*

❷ Why It Matters in Writing

Adjectives can provide important details. Imagine this description without adjectives.

> **PROFESSIONAL MODEL**
>
> The **first** bicycle was made of wood. This model was **hard** on shoes. Riders moved the bike in an **awkward** way. They pushed their feet backward against the ground. Later, a **Scottish** blacksmith made a **better** model, one with **two** pedals. This **new** bicycle was **easier** to ride and **easier** on shoes.
>
> —L.C. Chaveriat

❸ Practice and Apply

CONCEPT CHECK: What Is an Adjective?

Write each adjective in these sentences, along with the noun or pronoun it modifies. Do not include articles.

Cold Ears, Warm Invention

1. Some successful inventors are mature scientists.
2. Chester Greenwood, however, was a creative teenager when he made the first pair of earmuffs.
3. Chester's cold, red ears bothered him during the harsh Northeastern winters.
4. He didn't like itchy woolen mufflers.
5. One day, Chester had a brilliant idea.
6. He took a piece of flexible wire.
7. His grandmother sewed soft fur to the wire.
8. Charles then put on this strange contraption.
9. Earmuffs made Chester a rich man.
10. Chester received an American patent for the earmuffs at the age of 18.

➡ **For a SELF-CHECK and more practice, see the EXERCISE BANK, p. 602.**

Identify the proper adjectives in the sentences above. For each, write the proper noun from which it is formed.
Answers in column.

Spice It Up!

Have students form pairs to play a word-association game. One student in each pair should start the game by naming a common noun. Partners should respond with whatever adjective comes to mind. Play continues as students take turns naming more adjectives that modify the noun.

Predicate Adjectives

LESSON 2

1 Here's the Idea

▶ **A predicate adjective is an adjective that follows a linking verb and describes the verb's subject.** The linking verb connects the predicate adjective with the subject.

DESCRIBES

The airplanes were strange.
SUBJECT   LINKING VERB

DESCRIBE

They were large, heavy, and often dangerous.

Predicate adjectives can follow linking verbs other than forms of *be.* Forms of *taste, smell, feel, look, become,* and *seem* are often used as linking verbs.

DESCRIBES

Sam felt anxious about the airplane flight.
LINKING VERB   PREDICATE ADJECTIVE

DESCRIBES

The airplane's compartments felt warm.

For more about linking verbs, see page 98.

2 Why It Matters in Writing

Predicate adjectives help you paint pictures with words. Notice how the adjectives in this passage help you visualize the wings.

LITERARY MODEL

The wings themselves were **finer** than the finest rice paper, and yet they were **strong**. . . .

Right then I spread my wings and saw the glory of them! They had been **gold** at first, but now I saw how they shone iridescently—like the rainbow colors you see on a soap bubble. . . .

—Laurence Yep, *Dragonwings*

Adjectives and Adverbs **129**

ADJ. & ADV.

ADJECTIVES AND ADVERBS

LESSON OBJECTIVES

To identify and correctly use predicate adjectives in writing

 DAILY TEST PREPARATION

Error Correction: Punctuation
Write the following item on the board or use **Daily Test Preparation Transparency** p. DT18. Look for mistakes in punctuation in the sentence. Decide which line, if any, contains a mistake.

A. "Jason, theres no way

B. I can take you to the

C. grocery store this morning!"

D. *(No mistakes)*

Teaching Point: Error identification questions often test your knowledge of basic punctuation rules. In this case, the item tests whether you know to use an apostrophe with the contraction *there's.*

TEACHING RESOURCES

 Time-Saver Transparencies Binder:
• Daily Test Preparation p. DT18
 Grammar, Usage, and Mechanics Workbook p. 106

SKILLS PRACTICE RESOURCES

 Grammar, Usage, and Mechanics Workbook pp. 107–108
Pupil's Edition Exercise Bank p. 602

Adjectives and Adverbs **129**

Answers

Print-Out Option You may create worksheets of exercise A for your students by using the **Electronic Teacher Tools CD–ROM.**

A. CONCEPT CHECK

Self-Check For a self-check of predicate adjectives, direct students to p. 602 in the Pupil's Edition for the answers to the items circled in yellow.

Answers shown on page. Predicate adjectives are underlined once. The nouns and pronouns they modify are underlined twice.

1. are
2. seemed
3. were
4. looked
5. became
6. was
7. was
8. was
9. are
10. became

B. WRITING

Answers will vary. Students can imitate the model by beginning with the phrase "What is" followed by a predicate adjective or adjectives.

❸ **Practice and Apply**

A. CONCEPT CHECK: Predicate Adjectives

Write each predicate adjective in these sentences, along with the noun or pronoun it modifies. There may be more than one predicate adjective in a sentence.

Clear and Safe

1. Because of a trolley rider's fear, windshield wipers are common today.
2. To Mary Anderson electric trolleys seemed dangerous.
3. The drivers were alert.
4. The windshields, however, looked blurry and cloudy.
5. The windshields became clean when drivers rubbed them with damp tobacco and onions.
6. Anderson was creative, so she invented a windshield wiper.
7. Her first wiper was clumsy.
8. It was manual, and the driver had to crank a handle.
9. Today's wipers are automatic.
10. Because of Mary Anderson's invention, transportation became safer than it had been.

→ **For a SELF-CHECK and more practice, see the EXERCISE BANK, p. 602.**

Write the linking verb in each sentence above. **Answers in column.**

B. WRITING: Creating Riddles   **Answers in column.**

Choose three of the common inventions in the list below. For each, write a riddle containing one or more predicate adjectives. Then exchange riddles with a partner. Solve your partner's riddles, and underline the predicate adjectives in them.

Example: What is shiny and twisted and keeps papers together? (a paper clip)

television set	toaster
portable radio	doorbell
pencil	bubble gum
computer	cereal
in-line skates	wristwatch

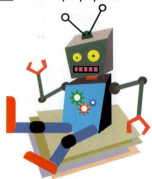

Other Words Used as Adjectives

❶ Here's the Idea

In addition to their usual uses, many nouns and pronouns can be used as adjectives. They can modify nouns to make their meanings more specific.

Pronouns as Adjectives

Demonstrative Pronouns *This, that, these,* and *those* are demonstrative pronouns that can be used as adjectives.

MODIFIES
This phone has a dial.

MODIFIES
That phone has a keypad.

This phone has a cord.

That phone has a battery.

Possessive Pronouns *My, our, your, her, his, its,* and *their* are possessive pronouns that are used as adjectives.

MODIFIES   MODIFIES
Your phone is lighter. **My** phone has better reception.

Indefinite Pronouns Indefinite pronouns such as *all, each, both, few, most,* and *some* can be used as adjectives.

MODIFIES
Originally, **few** people believed in the idea of the telephone.

MODIFIES
Today, **most** households have at least two phones.

ADJ. & ADV.

ADJECTIVES AND ADVERBS

To identify and use pronouns and nouns as adjectives

 DAILY TEST PREPARATION

Error Correction: Capitalization
Write the following item on the board or use 🏛 **Daily Test Preparation Transparency** p. DT19.

> The history of the *oxford english dictionary* is fascinating.

How is this sentence best written?

A. The History of the *oxford english dictionary* is fascinating.

B. The history of the *Oxford English Dictionary* is fascinating.

C. The history of the *Oxford English dictionary* is fascinating.

D. As it is

Teaching Point: Error correction questions often test your knowledge of basic capitalization rules. In this case, the item tests whether you know to capitalize the important words in titles of books, magazines, movies, and other works.

TEACHING TIP

Remind students that possessive pronouns used as adjectives—for example, *yours, theirs,* and *its*—do not have apostrophes.

NEED MORE INFORMATION?
For additional practice with recognizing different types of pronouns and understanding their usage, see **Chapter 3, Pronouns.**

TEACHING RESOURCES

 Time-Saver Transparencies Binder:
• Daily Test Preparation p. DT19

 Grammar, Usage, and Mechanics Workbook p. 109

SKILLS PRACTICE RESOURCES

 Grammar, Usage, and Mechanics Workbook pp. 110–111
Pupil's Edition Exercise Bank p. 603

Nouns as Adjectives

Like pronouns, nouns can be used as adjectives. In the expression "computer keyboard," for example, the word *computer* (normally a noun) is used to modify *keyboard*. Notice the following examples of nouns used as adjectives.

Renata's family just opened up an **Internet** account.

This account should help her complete **school** projects.

❷ Why It Matters in Writing

You can't gesture in writing the way you can in a face-to-face conversation. But you can use demonstrative pronouns as adjectives to "point to" people, and possessive pronouns in order to make relationships clear.

> **LITERARY MODEL**
>
> Transistors, chips, integrated circuits, Teflon, new medicines, new ways of treating diseases, new ways of performing operations, . . . are linked to the space effort. Most of these developments have been so incorporated into our day-to-day life that they are taken for granted, their origin not considered.
>
> —Louis L'Amour, "The Eternal Frontier"

DEMONSTRATIVE PRONOUN

POSSESSIVE PRONOUNS

❸ Practice and Apply

A. CONCEPT CHECK: Other Words Used as Adjectives

Write each noun or pronoun that is used as an adjective in these sentences.

Inventions from Nature
1. Most inventions are made by human beings.
2. But beavers may have inspired those huge dams that we build across rivers.

THE LANGUAGE OF
LITERATURE

The passage on the student page is from "The Eternal Frontier" in *The Language of Literature,* Level 7.

Answers

Print-Out Option You may create worksheets of exercises A and B for your students by using the ● **Electronic Teacher Tools CD–ROM.**

A. CONCEPT CHECK

Self-Check For a self-check of other words used as adjectives, direct students to p. 603 in the Pupil's Edition for the answers to the items circled in yellow.

Answers shown on page. Nouns and pronouns used as adjectives are underlined.

Spice It Up!

Write the following two lists of nouns on the board. Have students select a word from each list and use one to modify the other. Example: marshmallow heart.

List 1	List 2
marshmallow	legs
trampoline	heart
flamingo	storm
balloon	attitude
symbol	paste

3. <u>Our</u> inventions often imitate the contrivances of nature.
4. To escape <u>their</u> enemies, insects mimic flowers and <u>tree</u> limbs.
5. A <u>human</u> army uses camouflage to hide <u>its</u> tanks.
6. Birds adjust <u>their</u> wings to the airflow as they fly.
7. <u>Most</u> airplanes have adjustable <u>wing</u> surfaces, too.
8. Bats use <u>sound</u> waves to locate <u>their</u> prey.
9. With sonar, we use <u>sound</u> waves to map the <u>ocean</u> floor.
10. I'm watching <u>my</u> cat for new ideas!

➡ **For a SELF-CHECK and more practice, see the EXERCISE BANK, p. 603.**

B. REVISING: Adding Pronouns Used as Adjectives

Write a demonstrative, possessive, or indefinite pronoun that can be used as an adjective to fill in each blank in this paragraph.

Young Inventors

Some late-night talk shows feature child inventors. __1__ **These** children use __2__ imaginations to solve everyday problems. **their** Many of __3__ inventions have to do with pets. For example, **their** one girl who didn't like putting __4__ hand on cat food **her** invented a device that feeds __5__ cat automatically. Another **her** invented a doggie entertainment center for times when a dog's owners are away from __6__ home. A boy created a **their** device for petting __7__ dog. __8__ children have used **his/Some** ordinary household items to create __9__ unusual inventions. **their** For __10__ clever ideas, they have sometimes won prizes. **their**

C. WRITING: Using Nouns as Adjectives   Answers in column.

Many nouns used as adjectives name the materials used to make something. Write a different noun used as an adjective for each of the following phrases.

Example   stone   wall
             brick   wall

glass door   gravel road
paper bag   plastic tube
marble statue   leather jacket

TEACHING TIP

Cooperative Learning Have students work in groups of three to identify the **Revising** answers as demonstrative, possessive, or indefinite pronouns. Answers:

1 demonstrative

2, 3, 4, 5, 6, 7, 9, 10 possessive

8 indefinite

Answers

B. REVISING

Answers may vary. Possible responses shown on page.

C. WRITING

Answers may vary. Possible responses:

wood door

plastic bag

bronze statue

dirt road

glass tube

denim jacket

CHAPTER 5

LESSON OBJECTIVES

To identify and correctly use adverbs in writing

DAILY TEST PREPARATION

Sentence Completion:
Vocabulary Write the following item on the board or use **Daily Test Preparation Transparency** p. DT19.

Choose the word that *best* fits the meaning of the sentence.

> Sarah must see a(n) _____, someone who is skilled in treating these problems.

A. novice

B. imbecile

C. specialist

D. doctors

Teaching Point: For sentence completion questions, the correct answer will always

- fit the meaning of the sentence (answers A and B do not make sense with *skilled*).

- fit grammatically within the sentence (answer D uses the plural form instead of the singular).

LESSON 4 What Is an Adverb?

1 Here's the Idea

▶ **An adverb is a word that modifies a verb, an adjective, or another adverb.**

MODIFIES
Historians **strongly** believe that the Chinese invented rockets. ↑ADVERB ↑VERB

MODIFIES
Ancient Chinese warriors fired **very** powerful rockets.
ADVERB↑ ↑ADJECTIVE

MODIFIES
Today, rockets **almost** always power missiles and spacecraft. ↑ADVERB ↑ADVERB

Adverbs answer the questions *how, when, where,* and *to what extent*.

Adverbs	
How?	patiently, loudly, carefully
When?	sometimes, daily, always
Where?	inside, there, everywhere
To what extent?	extremely, nearly, almost

The position of adverbs can vary. An adverb that modifies an adjective or another adverb is generally placed just before the word it modifies. An adverb that modifies a verb can be placed after the verb, before the verb, or at the beginning of the sentence.

The rocket ascended suddenly. (after verb)

The rocket suddenly ascended. (before verb)

Suddenly, the rocket ascended. (at beginning of sentence)

Intensifiers are adverbs that modify adjectives or other adverbs. They are usually placed directly before the words they modify. Intensifiers usually answer the question *to what extent.*

134 Grammar, Usage, and Mechanics

TEACHING RESOURCES

 Time-Saver Transparencies Binder:
- Daily Test Preparation p. DT19

 Grammar, Usage, and Mechanics Workbook p. 112

SKILLS PRACTICE RESOURCES

 Grammar, Usage, and Mechanics Workbook pp. 113–114

Pupil's Edition Exercise Bank p. 603

We covered our ears very quickly at the shuttle launch.

Intensifiers				
almost	extremely	quite	so	usually
especially	nearly	really	too	very

Forming Adverbs

Many adverbs are formed by adding the suffix *-ly* to adjectives. Sometimes a base word's spelling changes when *-ly* is added.

QUICK-FIX SPELLING MACHINE: ADVERBS

ADJECTIVE	RULE	ADVERB
sudden	Add *-ly.*	suddenly
true	Drop the *e* and add *-ly.*	truly
heavy	Change the *y* to *i* add *-ly.*	heavily

❷ Why It Matters in Writing

You will find adverbs helpful when you're writing about historical events. The adverbs in this model help tell readers when and how blue jeans were invented.

PROFESSIONAL MODEL

During the California gold rush, a tailor named Levi Strauss saw miners daily. Their pants were often extremely worn. Strauss worked very carefully to fashion stiff canvas into overalls. These tough pants ultimately became today's blue jeans.

> TELLS WHEN
> TELLS TO WHAT EXTENT
> TELLS HOW

Adjectives and Adverbs **135**

A. CONCEPT CHECK

Self-Check For a self-check of what an adverb is, direct students to p. 603 in the Pupil's Edition for the answers to the items circled in yellow.

1. *experimentally* modifies the verb *were flying*

2. *yet* and *successfully* modify the verb *had flown*

3. *expertly* modifies the verb *repaired*

4. *quite* modifies the verb *popular*

5. *enthusiastically* modifies the verb *bicycled* and the verb *studied; there* also modifies the verb *studied*

6. *fanatically* modifies the verb *worked*

7. *quite* modifies the adjective *crude*

8. *very* modifies the adverb *carefully; carefully* modifies the verb *added; together* modifies the verb *hitched*

9. *quite* modifies the adverb *successfully; successfully* modifies the verbs *flew* and *landed*

10. *twice* modifies the verb *flew*

B. WRITING

Answers may vary. Make sure that students choose adverbs that match what is asked for in the parentheses. Possible responses shown on page.

ASSESSMENT

Assessment Masters:
• Chapter Mid-point Test p. 28

CHAPTER 5

CHAPTER 5

③ **Practice and Apply**

A. CONCEPT CHECK: What Is an Adverb? Answers in column.

Write each adverb and the word it modifies. Identify the modified word as a verb, an adjective, or an adverb. There may be more than one adverb in a sentence.

Like the Birds
1. People were flying gliders experimentally in the early 1900s.
2. No one had yet flown a powered aircraft successfully.
3. In Dayton, Ohio, Orville and Wilbur Wright expertly repaired bicycles.
4. They were quite popular members of the community.
5. They bicycled enthusiastically and also studied gliders there.
6. The brothers worked fanatically to invent a powered aircraft.
7. Their first plane, which was quite crude, was made from wood, wire, and cotton sheets.
8. They very carefully added two propellers and hitched them together with bicycle chains.
9. In 1903 the Wright brothers' flew and landed their *Flyer* quite successfully.
10. Each brother flew the plane twice.

➡ **For a SELF-CHECK and more practice, see the EXERCISE BANK, p. 603.**

B. WRITING: Adding Adverbs

Read the paragraph below. Choose five adverbs from the following list to replace the words in parentheses.

| thoughtfully | cruelly | there | almost | soon |
| energetically | tiredly | very | daily | |

Shopping-Cart Convenience
(1) Sylvan Goldman lived in Oklahoma City and owned a grocery store (answers *where*). **(2)** He watched shoppers there (answers *how*) carry items from aisle to aisle. **(3)** To help his customers, Goldman (answers *how*) set out wheeled carts th for them to use. **(4)** He (answers *to what extent*) sadly noted that no one wanted the carts. Goldman outsmarted them, however. He hired phony shoppers to push around the carts. **(5)** The real shoppers (answers *when*) began to use the carts throughout the store.

Making Comparisons

① Here's the Idea

Adjectives and adverbs can be used to compare people or things. Special forms of these words are used to make comparisons.

▶ **Use the comparative form of an adjective or adverb when you compare a person or thing with one other person or thing.**

> The *Titanic* was **larger** than the *Olympic.*

> It traveled **faster** than the other ship.

▶ **Use the superlative form of an adjective or adverb when you compare someone or something with more than one other thing.**

> In fact, the *Titanic* was the **largest** ship of all.

> Of the fleet's ships, the *Titanic* raced the **fastest.**

Regular Forms of Comparison

For most one-syllable modifiers, add *-er* to form the comparative and *-est* to form the superlative.

One-Syllable Modifiers	Base Form	Comparative	Superlative
Adjectives	tall shiny	tall**er** shini**er**	tall**est** shini**est**
Adverbs	close soon	clos**er** soon**er**	clos**est** soon**est**

You can also add *-er* and *-est* to some two-syllable adjectives. With others, and with two-syllable adverbs, use the words *more* and *most.*

Two-Syllable Modifiers	Base Form	Comparative	Superlative
Adjectives	easy cheerful	easi**er** **more** cheerful	easi**est** **most** cheerful
Adverbs	brightly swiftly	**more** brightly **more** swiftly	**most** brightly **most** swiftly

Adjectives and Adverbs **137**

ADJ. & ADV.

ADJECTIVES AND ADVERBS

LESSON OBJECTIVES

To identlfy and use the comparative and superlative forms of adjectives and adverbs

DAILY TEST PREPARATION

Error Identification: Spelling
Write the following item on the board or use
🏛 **Daily Test Preparation Transparency** p. DT20.
Look for mistakes in spelling. Decide which word, if any, contains a mistake.

A. terrible

B. amazeing

C. rough

D. placement

E. *(No mistakes)*

Teaching Point: Error identification questions often test your knowledge of basic spelling rules. In this case, the items tests whether you know to drop the silent *e* before adding a suffix (as in *amazing*).

TEACHING TIP

Cross-Curricular Connection
Math Point out that the symbols, < (less than) and > (greater than), represent comparative forms in math because two numbers are being compared. Examples:
$10 > 4$ (10 is greater than 4)
$3.59 < 3.7$ (3.59 is less than 3.7)

TEACHING RESOURCES

 Time-Saver Transparencies Binder:
• Daily Test Preparation p. DT20
• Quick-Fix Grammar and Style Charts pp. QF8
 Grammar, Usage, and Mechanics Workbook p. 115

SKILLS PRACTICE RESOURCES

 English Grammar Survival Kit pp. 13–14
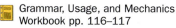 Grammar, Usage, and Mechanics Workbook pp. 116–117
Pupil's Edition Exercise Bank p. 604
 Grammar Coach CD-ROM Lesson 11

With adjectives and adverbs having three or more syllables, use *more* and *most.*

Modifiers with More Than Two Syllables			
	Base Form	**Comparative**	**Superlative**
Adjectives	powerful energetic	**more** powerful **more** energetic	**most** powerful **most** energetic
Adverbs	peacefully comfortably	**more** peacefully **more** comfortably	**most** peacefully **most** comfortably

Use only one sign of comparison at a time. Don't use more and *-er* together or most and *-est* together.

INCORRECT: **The *Titanic* was the most greatest ship.**

CORRECT: **The Titanic was the greatest ship.**

Irregular Forms of Comparison

The comparatives and superlatives of some adjectives and adverbs are formed in irregular ways.

Irregular Modifiers			
	Base Form	**Comparative**	**Superlative**
Adjectives	good bad	better worse	best worst
Adverbs	well much little	better more less	best most least

❷ Why It Matters in Writing

Use comparative and superlative forms of modifiers when you need to compare or contrast things in history or science class.

STUDENT MODEL

Although the *Californian* was the ship **nearest** the *Titanic,* it was the *Carpathia* that rescued the survivors. Those in the life boats were **most likely** to survive.

Spice It Up!
Have students form groups of three to perform pantomimes using the comparative and superlative forms of adjectives. Write the following adjectives on slips of paper and mix them in a box: *thirsty, nervous, shy,* and *chilly.* The first member of a group picks an adjective (e.g., *thirsty*) from the box and pantomimes it. The second member pantomimes the comparative form of the adjective (e.g., *thirstier*). The third member performs the superlative form (e.g., *thirstiest*). After the group has finished, the class guesses what adjectives were pantomimed.

③ Practice and Apply

A. CONCEPT CHECK: Making Comparisons

Choose the correct comparative or superlative form to complete each sentence.

Stronger Than Steel

1. Stephanie Kwolek invented one of the (more original, <u>most original</u>) materials ever developed.
2. She believed that creativity was (<u>more important</u>, most important) for an inventor than technical knowledge.
3. Kwolek planned to study medicine, but she found chemistry (<u>more interesting</u>, most interesting).
4. She was intrigued by all the (most new, <u>newest</u>) chemical processes.
5. She studied the (<u>best</u>, most best) ways of making artificial materials.
6. When Kwolek was working with chemicals, petroleum was the (more, <u>most</u>) common source of plastic.
7. Kwolek invented a chemical fiber called Kevlar, which is five times (more strong, <u>stronger</u>) than steel.
8. Kevlar was one of the (more, <u>most</u>) influential inventions of the 20th century.
9. Kevlar vests are (<u>most</u>, more) famous as police vests.
10. Kwolek's work inventing Kevlar and other materials made her one of the (better-known, <u>best-known</u>) chemists in the United States.

➡ **For a SELF-CHECK and more practice, see the EXERCISE BANK, p. 604.**

B. WRITING: Creating Comparisons   Answers in column.

Examine the three photographs of different kinds of boats. Write five sentences comparing them in terms of appearance, speed, power, or capacity. Use comparative and superlative forms in your writing.

Adjectives and Adverbs **139**

ADJ. & ADV.

ADJECTIVES AND ADVERBS

LESSON OBJECTIVES

To identify and correctly use commonly confused adjectives and adverbs

DAILY TEST PREPARATION

Definition: Vocabulary Write the following item on the board or use ⬚ **Daily Test Preparation Transparency** p. DT20. Decide which of the four answers has most nearly the same meaning as the under-lined word.

To <u>alter</u> the plan

A. mutilate

B. modify

C. model

D. maintain

Teaching Point: For definitions, use words that are related to the underlined word to deci-pher its meaning. The words *alter, alternative,* and *alternate* involve some type of change.

CUSTOMIZING TIP

Less Proficient Learners Tell stu-dents that *good* may be used as a predicate adjective after such linking verbs *as be, sound, taste, appear, feel, look,* and *smell.* Encourage students to memorize the following sen-tence to help them remember that *good* is an adjective that can be used with linking verbs and *well* is an adverb when it modifies action verbs: The car looks *good,* and it runs *well.*

 LESSON 6 # Adjective or Adverb?

① Here's the Idea

Some pairs of adjectives and adverbs are often a source of confusion and mistakes in speaking and writing.

Good and *Well*

Good is always an adjective; it modifies a noun or pronoun. *Well* is usually an adverb, modifying a verb, an adverb, or an adjective. *Well* is an adjective when it refers to health.

MODIFIES
The ice-cream sundae was a good invention.
ADJECTIVE   NOUN

MODIFIES   MODIFIES
Ice cream sold well.   **He doesn't feel well.**
VERB   ADVERB   PRONOUN   ADJECTIVE

Real and *Really*

Real is always an adjective; it modifies a noun or pronoun. *Really* is always an adverb; it modifies a verb, an adverb, or an adjective.

MODIFIES
Medical inventions can make a real difference.
ADJECTIVE   NOUN

MODIFIES
A few inventions have really changed how we live.
ADVERB   VERB

Bad and *Badly*

Bad is always an adjective; it modifies a noun or pronoun. *Badly* is always an adverb; it modifies a verb, an adverb, or an adjective.

MODIFIES
A bad illness can require medicine.
ADJECTIVE   NOUN

MODIFIES
I did badly on the last science quiz.
VERB   ADVERB

140 Grammar, Usage, and Mechanics

TEACHING RESOURCES

 Time-Saver Transparencies Binder:
• Daily Test Preparation p. DT20
Grammar, Usage, and Mechanics Workbook p. 118

SKILLS PRACTICE RESOURCES

 English Grammar Survival Kit pp. 11–12
 Grammar, Usage, and Mechanics Workbook pp. 119–120
Pupil's Edition Exercise Bank p. 604

Read the following sentences. Ask students to choose the correct modifier.

I'm playing really (<u>well</u>, good) today.

The cast's performance was (well, <u>good</u>).

Her intelligence (real, <u>really</u>) impressed me.

He used to behave (bad, <u>badly</u>).

❷ Why It Matters in Writing

Watch out for these tricky pairs of adjectives and adverbs. Mistakes are so common that you need to double-check your work every time you use a form of good, real, or bad.

STUDENT MODEL

> I want to enter this year's science fair because I think my experiment on lasers will be ~~real~~ *really* interesting. I'm planning on talking about the different uses of lasers in grocery stores, hospitals, and banks. All of the lasers seem to work ~~good~~ *well*.
>
> Sincerely,
>
> Jamie D.

Students Acquiring English/ESL
For instruction and practice with adjectives and adverbs, see **English Grammar Survival Kit** pp. 11–12.

Answers

Print-Out Option You may create worksheets of this exercise for your students by using the 💿 **Electronic Teacher Tools CD–ROM.**

Self-Check For a self-check of adjectives and adverbs, direct students to p. 604 in the Pupil's Edition for the answer to the item circled in yellow.

Answers shown on page. Correct modifiers are underlined. They are labeled using these codes:

Adj. = adjective

Adv. = adverb

❸ Practice and Apply

CONCEPT CHECK: Adjective or Adverb?

For each sentence, choose the correct modifier from those given in parentheses. Identify each word you choose as an adjective or an adverb.

Medicine's History—Good or Bad?

1. Today we take (real, <u>really</u>) good medical care for granted, **Adv.** but history is full of examples of ineffective medicine.
2. Many early treatments were (badly, <u>bad</u>). **Adj.**
3. Unsuccessful treatments were (<u>bad</u>, badly) for both patients and doctors. **Adj.**
4. But if they got well, patients thought their doctors were (<u>good</u>, well). **Adj.**
5. The ancient Greek physician Hippocrates helped rid medicine of magic, superstition, and other (real, <u>really</u>) bad elements. **Adv.**

➡ **For a SELF-CHECK and more practice, see the EXERCISE BANK, p. 604.**

Adjectives and Adverbs **141**

ADJ. & ADV.

ADJECTIVES AND ADVERBS

LESSON OBJECTIVES

To recognize double negatives and avoid using them

Error Identification: Spelling
Write the following item on the board or use **Daily Test Preparation Transparency** p. DT21.
Decide which type of error, if any, appears in the underlined section.

> Although my father is an <u>insect specialist, he suffers from arachnofobia.</u>

A. Spelling error

B. Capitalization error

C. Punctuation error

D. No error

Teaching Point: Error identification questions often test your knowledge of basic spelling rules. This item tests whether you know to spell *phobia,* meaning "fear," with *ph* instead of *f.* All words that include *-phobia,* from *arachnophobia* (fear of spiders) to *zoophobia* (fear of animals) are spelled with *ph.*

MORE MODEL SENTENCES

Have students rewrite the following sentences, correcting the double negatives:

Anna felt she wasn't going nowhere. She couldn't hardly wait for the day to be over.

Anna felt she wasn't going anywhere. She could hardly wait for the day to be over.

Avoiding Double Negatives

❶ Here's the Idea

A **negative word** is a word that implies that something does not exist or happen. Some common negative words are listed below.

Common Negative Words				
barely	hardly	never	none	nothing
can't	hasn't	no	no one	nowhere
don't	neither	nobody	not	scarcely

If two negative words are used where only one is needed, the result is a **double negative.** Avoid double negatives in your speaking and writing.

Nonstandard

I **can't hardly** believe someone created pajamas for dogs.

Standard

I **can hardly** believe someone created pajamas for dogs.

I **can't** believe someone created pajamas for dogs.

❷ Why It Matters in Writing

Don't let double negatives creep into your writing when you're trying to make an important point. Double negatives are almost always nonstandard.

> **STUDENT MODEL**
>
> During World War II, pilots flew planes higher than ever before. They didn't have ~~no~~ *enough* air to breathe at very high altitudes. Alice Chatham, a sculptor, designed a mask to supply pilots with oxygen so that they wouldn't ~~never~~ *ever* black out from lack of oxygen.

TEACHING RESOURCES

 Time-Saver Transparencies Binder:
• Daily Test Preparation p. DT21

Grammar, Usage, and Mechanics Workbook p. 121

SKILLS PRACTICE RESOURCES

English Grammar Survival Kit pp. 41–42

Grammar, Usage, and Mechanics Workbook pp. 122–123

Pupil's Edition Exercise Bank p. 605

❸ Practice and Apply

A. CONCEPT CHECK: Avoiding Double Negatives

Write the word in parentheses that correctly completes each sentence.

Sticky Stuff

1. You (<u>can</u>, can't) scarcely imagine a time before sticky notes, can you?

2. You (can't, <u>can</u>) barely put a note in a book without them.

3. Sticky notes (aren't, <u>are</u>) nothing like other bookmarks.

4. They (<u>were</u>, weren't) scarcely Art Fry's first invention.

5. In the 1970s Fry (hadn't, <u>had</u>) nothing but pieces of paper for bookmarks.

6. These scraps of paper (<u>could</u>, couldn't) hardly stay in a book.

7. Fry wanted something that (wouldn't, <u>would</u>) never fall out but wouldn't harm the page.

8. His colleague discovered a glue that (did, <u>didn't</u>) not stick as tightly as other glues.

9. Nobody had (never, <u>ever</u>) made a sticky bookmark that you could pull off a page.

10. Now there (aren't, <u>are</u>) hardly any homes or offices without sticky notes.

➡ For a SELF-CHECK and more practice, see the EXERCISE BANK, p. 605.

B. PROOFREADING: Eliminating Double Negatives

Find and correct the double negatives in the paragraph below.

Cat Feeding for Fun

Suzanna Goodin never wanted to feed her cats. Was she a cat hater? No, she loved her cats. She just didn't want *anything* ~~nothing~~ to do with feeding them. One day Suzanna's teacher *ever* told the class to think of problems they hadn't ~~never~~ been able to solve. Then they should invent solutions. Suzanna invented a cat-feeding spoon that didn't leave *anything* ~~nothing~~ to clean up. The spoon was made from dough baked in the oven.

Students Acquiring English/ESL
In some languages, including Spanish and French, double negative constructions are correct. For example, in Spanish the sentence *No me gusta nada,* literally translated as "I don't like nothing," is grammatically correct. For instruction and practice with negative constructions, see **English Grammar Survival Kit** pp. 41–42.

ADJ. & ADV.

ADJECTIVES AND ADVERBS

Answers

Print-Out Option You may create worksheets of exercises A and B for your students by using the 💿 **Electronic Teacher Tools CD–ROM.**

A. CONCEPT CHECK

Self-Check For a self-check of eliminating double negatives, direct students to p. 605 in the Pupil's Edition for the answers to the items circled in yellow.

Answers underlined on page.

B. PROOFREADING

Answers shown on page. Double negatives are crossed out. Corrections appear in the margin.

ASSESSMENT

📒 Assessment Masters
• Chapter Mastery Tests pp. 61–66

💿 Test Generator CD-ROM

🔗 mcdougallittell.com Grammar Chapter Quiz

LESSON OBJECTIVES

To identify and use adjectives and adverbs in descriptive writing

THE LANGUAGE OF LITERATURE

The passage on the student page is from "The White Umbrella" in *The Language of Literature,* Level 7.

TEACHING TIP

Speaking and Listening Read the passage aloud and ask students to listen for the vivid adjectives and adverbs used by the author. After you have finished reading, ask students to describe the images and mood evoked by the passage. Understanding the power of modifiers will help students use adjectives and adverbs to make their own writing more vivid.

Grammar in Literature

Inventing with Adjectives and Adverbs

One of the gifts an inventor needs is the ability to notice details. Writers use the same gift when they create literature. In your own writing, you can use adjectives and adverbs to help communicate details and convey the tone of your passage.

In the following excerpt, Gish Jen uses adjectives and adverbs to describe an umbrella. Her use of details lets readers sense the speaker's feelings of wonder.

The White Umbrella
by Gish Jen

I stared at the umbrella. I wanted to open it, whirl it around by its slender silver handle...

ADJECTIVE

I could not believe that I was actually holding the umbrella, opening it. It sprang up by itself as if it were alive, as if that were what it wanted to do—as if it belonged in my hands, above my head. I stared at the network of silver spokes and then spun the umbrella around and around and around. It was so clean and white that it seemed to glow, to illuminate everything around it. "It's beautiful," I said.

ADVERB

144 Grammar, Usage, and Mechanics

ACROSS the CURRICULUM
LITERATURE

Practice and Apply

A. DRAFTING: Write a Description

As the speaker and her sister wait for a ride, it begins to rain. Follow the directions to invent two descriptions about rain.

1. First describe two characters waiting for a ride in the rain. Use modifiers that help you create a joyful mood. Think of good descriptive words of your own, or try some of these:

soothing	gently
cool	quietly
clean	briefly
clear	softly
warm	

2. Now use different modifiers to create a depressing mood. Try some of these modifiers:

cold	prickly
soggy	sharply
clammy	steadily
heavy	

B. WRITING: Create a Scene

Put ideas from your two descriptions together to create a scene in which two people are together in the rain and waiting for a ride. One of the people is enjoying the rain. The other is miserable. Save your descriptions in your 🗀 **Working Portfolio.**

ADJ. & ADVERBS

ADJECTIVES AND ADVERBS

PRACTICE AND APPLY

A. DRAFTING

1. Answers will vary. A sample description follows:

A light rain began to fall again as two seventh graders waited for the school bus. They tilted their heads toward the sky, and the rain felt cool and refreshing on their faces. The bus glided to a stop at the corner, its windshield wipers gently brushing clear drops of rain from the windshield.

2. Answers will vary. A sample description follows:

Two seventh graders huddled in the cold waiting for the school bus to appear. Heavy, dark clouds hung above their lowered heads and showered then with icy rain. The school bus screeched to a halt as it approached the corner. its wipers frantically raced across the windshield, unable to clear away the steady, dreary rain.

B. WRITING

Answers will vary. Students will need to change some of the details to incorporate both moods into one scene. A sample follows:

Two seventh graders waited in the rain for the school bus to approach. One of them twirled round and round in the rain. She tilted her head toward the sky to feel the cool rain sprinkle across her face. The other huddled near the buildings, feeling himself grow clammy as the cold rain fell steadily.

Spice It Up!

Quotable Quote "Only where there is language is there world."
—Adrienne Rich
Discuss with students how they can use adjectives and adverbs in writing to create a world. Then ask students to write a paragraph in which they create a fantasy world, using vivid and precise adjectives and adverbs. Have volunteers read their paragraphs aloud.

Mixed Review

Mixed Review

A. Using Modifiers Read this passage and answer the questions below it. **Answers in column.**

(1) Ruth Wakefield, owner of the Toll House Inn, <u>frequently</u> baked a kind of cookie that had melted chocolate in <u>its</u> batter. (2) One day she didn't have <u>enough</u> time to melt the chocolate. (3) So she cut the large slab of chocolate into <u>smaller</u> bits and added them to the batter. (4) She thought they would melt in the oven just as if she had melted the chocolate <u>first</u>. (5) But the <u>chocolate</u> bits didn't melt. (6) They poked up <u>here</u> and <u>there</u> in the cookies' surface. (7) Presto! Wakefield had invented <u>chocolate chip</u> cookies, an invention for which we are all <u>hungrily</u> <u>grateful</u>.

1. In sentence 1, is *frequently* an adjective or an adverb?
2. In sentence 1, what kind of word is *its*? How is it used?
3. In sentence 2, which word does *enough* modify?
4. In sentence 3, what form of adjective is *smaller*?
5. In sentence 4, is *first* an adjective or an adverb? How do you know?
6. In sentence 5, how is *chocolate* used?
7. In sentence 6, what kind of words are *here* and *there,* and what question do they answer?
8. In sentence 7, how is *chocolate chip* used?
9. In sentence 7, which word does *hungrily* modify? What part of speech is *hungrily?*
10. In sentence 7, is *grateful* an adjective or adverb? Which word does it modify?

B. Choosing the Right Modifier Choose the correct words from those given in parentheses.

1. George Crum, a chef, made a (real, <u>really</u>) good discovery in 1853.
2. One guest complained (loud, <u>loudly</u>) that his French fries were too (<u>large</u>, larger).
3. Crum sliced some (<u>thinner</u>, more thin) ones, but the guest (wouldn't say nothing, <u>wouldn't say anything</u>) good about the potatoes.
4. Finally Crum (angerly, <u>angrily</u>) sliced some potatoes (real, <u>really</u>) thin and fried them.
5. The guest loved the dish so (good, <u>well</u>) that potato chips became a specialty of the restaurant.

Mixed Review

Answers

Print-Out Option You may create worksheets of exercises A and B for your students by using the 💿 **Electronic Teacher Tools CD–ROM.**

A. Using Modifiers

1. *Frequently* is an adverb.
2. *Its* is a pronoun. It is used as an adjective.
3. *Enough* modifies *time.*
4. *Smaller* is a comparative adjective.
5. *First* is an adverb because it tells when the chocolate would melt.
6. *Chocolate* is a noun used as an adjective.
7. *Here* and *there* are adverbs that answer *where.*
8. The words *chocolate* and *chip* are nouns used as adjectives.
9. *Hungrily* is an adverb that modifies *are grateful.*
10. *Grateful* is a predicate adjective that modifies *we.*

B. Choosing the Right Modifier

Answers underlined on page.

Mastery Test: What Did You Learn?

For each underlined item, choose the letter of the term that correctly identifies it.

> We <u>don't never</u> run out of discoveries about space. Space is <u>really</u>
> (1)   (2)
> <u>infinite</u>. Recently in *The New York Times Magazine,* James Gleick
> (3)
> stated: "It wasn't until the year 4.5 billion or so . . . that an earthly
> life form managed to hurl <u>some</u> stuff into orbit . . . high enough to
>   (4)
> look <u>down</u> and see our tiny globe for what it is. Counted another way,
>   (5)
> it was Oct. 4, 1957 [when <u>Russian</u> scientists launched the artificial
>   (6)
> satellite *Sputnik.*] . . . Plenty of scientists and rocket buffs were
> listening down below and hatching <u>grander</u> plans. <u>Already</u>, Arthur C.
>   (7)   (8)
> Clarke, the science-fiction writer, had performed one of the
> millennium's <u>most astounding</u> feats of invention. In 1945, he . . .
>   (9)
> published a complete plan for using satellites to relay <u>radio</u> "signals."
>   (10)

1. A. adjective
   B. double negative *(circled)*
   C. statement
   D. question

2. A. adverb *(circled)*
   B. adjective
   C. demonstrative pronoun
   D. predicate adjective

3. A. adverb
   B. predicate adjective *(circled)*
   C. proper adjective
   D. demonstrative pronoun

4. A. pronoun used as adjective *(circled)*
   B. noun used as adjective
   C. pronoun used as adverb
   D. noun used as adverb

5. A. adverb telling when
   B. adverb telling how
   C. adverb telling how much
   D. adverb telling where *(circled)*

6. A. possessive pronoun
   B. adverb
   C. predicate adjective
   D. proper adjective *(circled)*

7. A. comparative adverb
   B. superlative adverb
   C. comparative adjective *(circled)*
   D. superlative adjective

8. A. adverb describing *Clarke*
   B. adverb describing *had performed* *(circled)*
   C. adjective describing *writer*
   D. adjective describing *Clarke*

9. A. comparative adverb
   B. superlative adverb
   C. comparative adjective
   D. superlative adjective *(circled)*

10. A. pronoun used as adjective
    B. noun used as adjective *(circled)*
    C. pronoun used as adverb
    D. noun used as adverb

ADJ. & ADV.

ADJECTIVES AND ADVERBS

Mastery Test

As an option, two other Chapter Mastery Tests appear in ■ **Assessment Masters** pp. 61–66.

Answers circled on page.

PRESCRIPTION FOR MASTERY	
If students miss item number:	**Use Teaching Resources and Skills Practice Resources for lesson:**
1	❼ Avoiding Double Negatives p. 142
2	❻ Adjective or Adverb? p. 140
3	❷ Predicate Adjectives p. 129
4, 10	❸ Other Words Used as Adjectives p. 131
5, 8	❹ What Is an Adverb? p. 134
6	❶ What Is an Adjective? p. 126
7, 9	❺ Making Comparisons p. 137

Students can use the Student Help Desk prior to testing or as a quick review or reference as they revise a piece of writing.

Teacher's Notes

WHAT WORKS:

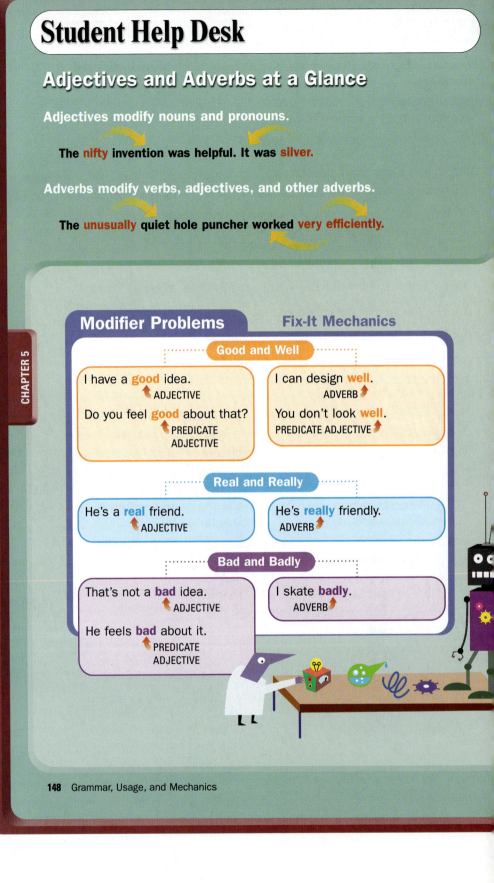

Student Help Desk

Adjectives and Adverbs at a Glance

Adjectives modify nouns and pronouns.

The **nifty** invention was helpful. It was **silver.**

Adverbs modify verbs, adjectives, and other adverbs.

The **unusually** quiet hole puncher worked **very efficiently.**

Modifier Problems — Fix-It Mechanics

Good and Well

I have a **good** idea.
↑ ADJECTIVE

Do you feel **good** about that?
↑ PREDICATE ADJECTIVE

I can design **well.**
ADVERB ↑

You don't look **well.**
PREDICATE ADJECTIVE ↑

Real and Really

He's a **real** friend.
↑ ADJECTIVE

He's **really** friendly.
ADVERB ↑

Bad and Badly

That's not a **bad** idea.
↑ ADJECTIVE

He feels **bad** about it.
↑ PREDICATE ADJECTIVE

I skate **badly.**
ADVERB ↑

Modifiers in Comparisons
Size Adjustments

	Comparative	Superlative
far	farther	farthest
shiny	shinier	shiniest
useful	more useful	most useful
intelligent	more intelligent	most intelligent
happily	more happily	most happily
good	better	best
bad	worse	worst

Avoiding Double Forms
Double Trouble

Double Negative	Fix
we can't never	we can never / we can't
we don't hardly	we hardly / we don't

Double Comparison	Fix
more better	better
most luckiest	luckiest

The Bottom Line

Checklist for Adjectives and Adverbs

Have I remembered to . . .

____ use adjectives to fine-tune my nouns?

____ capitalize proper adjectives?

____ use adverbs to fine-tune descriptions of actions?

____ use correct forms of adverbs and adjectives in comparisons?

____ avoid double negatives?

Teacher's Notes
WHAT DOESN'T WORK:

TEACHER'S LOUNGE

Slice of Life

"Life is a wave, which in no two consecutive moments of its existence is composed of the same particles."—John Tyndall

Brain Booster

Tips for excellent recall:

• Repeat key ideas within 10 minutes after learning them, then 48 hours later, and then seven days later.

• Make a concrete reminder, like an object, token, or artifact.

• Use acrostics (first letter of each key word forms a new word). Example: *My Very Eager Mother Just Sat Upon New Paint* is used to memorize the names of the planets in order.

• Organize your material in groups of seven or less to make each group easy to recall.

Prepositions, Conjunctions, Interjections

Chapter 6

Prepositions, Conjunctions, Interjections

CHAPTER OVERVIEW

CHAPTER 6

CHAPTER RESOURCES

 Time-Saver Transparencies Binder:
- Daily Test Preparation pp. DT21–23
- Visual Grammar™ Tiles Lessons 9–10

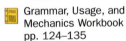 Grammar, Usage, and Mechanics Workbook pp. 124–135

Integrated Technology and Media

 Electronic Teacher Tools CD-ROM

 Grammar Coach CD-ROM Lesson 12

 mcdougallittell.com

Assessment

 Assessment Masters:
- Chapter Pretest pp. 12–13
- Chapter Mid-point Test p. 29
- Chapter Mastery Tests pp. 67–70

 Test Generator CD-ROM

 mcdougallittell.com Grammar Chapter Quiz

Students Acquiring English/ESL

🎧 English Grammar Survival Kit pp. 17–22

CHAPTER 6

Yikes!

Theme: Bugs!

Little Things Mean a Lot

What would you say if you came face to face with this bug? You might express yourself with a small but powerful interjection like the one in the balloon above. Like bugs, interjections, conjunctions, and prepositions are often small but powerful. They not only express emotion but also connect other words and show relationships between words.

Write Away: What Bugs You?
Recall a time when you were up close and personal with a bug. Was the bug disgusting? fascinating? weird? beautiful, perhaps? Write a short paragraph about your bug. Save the paragraph in your 📁 **Working Portfolio.**

 Grammar Coach

150

Choose the letter of the term that correctly identifies each underlined item.

Bugs! Ugh! Do you shriek in horror when you see bugs? Many
(1)   (2)
people are terrified of bugs. Their alien shapes inspire fear, and
(3)   (4)
the way they swarm around their target often causes panic. Bugs
(5)
include both 700,000 known species of insects and more than
(6)   (6)
30,000 known species of spiders. Ecologists are glad that bugs live

among us. Their contributions to the environment are important.
(7)   (8)
For example, bees pollinate flowers. Bugs may seem strange, but
(9)

life as we know it would be impossible without them.
(10)

---

1. A. preposition
   B. interjection
   C. conjunction
   D. adverb

2. A. preposition
   B. object of a preposition
   C. prepositional phrase
   D. interjection

3. A. preposition
   B. object of a preposition
   C. conjunction
   D. interjection

4. A. coordinating conjunction
   B. correlative conjunction
   C. adjective phrase
   D. preposition

5. A. conjunction
   B. interjection
   C. adjective phrase
   D. adverb phrase

6. A. preposition
   B. object of a preposition
   C. coordinating conjunction
   D. correlative conjunction

7. A. preposition
   B. interjection
   C. coordinating conjunction
   D. prepositional phrase

8. A. conjunction
   B. interjection
   C. adjective phrase
   D. adverb phrase

9. A. coordinating conjunction
   B. correlative conjunction
   C. preposition
   D. interjection

10. A. interjection
    B. preposition
    C. object of a preposition
    D. adjective

Diagnostic Test

As an option, a Chapter Pretest appears in 📒 **Assessment Masters** pp. 12–13.

Answers circled on page.

Use the chart below to determine which lessons students need.

PRESCRIPTION FOR SUCCESS	
If students miss item number:	**Work on lesson:**
1	❹ Interjections p. 161
2, 3, 7, 10	❶ What Is a Preposition? p. 152
4, 6, 9	❸ Conjunctions p. 158
2, 5, 8	❷ Using Prepositional Phrases p. 155

The **Diagnostic Test** parallels the **Mastery Test** on page 165. Have students keep the test in their portfolio to compare with their results on the **Mastery Test**.

PREP & CONJ.

PREP. CONJ. INTER.

Pressed for Time?
Teach **Lesson 2, Using Prepositional Phrases,** and **Lesson 3, Conjunctions.** Briefly review interjections. Then have students take the **Mixed Review** and **Mastery Test** and review their answers in class.

Time for More?
After all of the lessons have been covered, have students look for places to add prepositions and conjunctions in their **Write Away** paragraphs. Ask them to insert at least one interjection.

LESSON OBJECTIVES

To identify prepositions and prepositional phrases and to use them to add descriptive details in writing

DAILY TEST PREPARATION

Error Correction: Punctuation
Write the following item on the board or use **Daily Test Preparation Transparency** p. DT21.
Choose the <u>best</u> way to write the underlined part of the sentence.

> <u>Sam do you really think he's</u> from another planet?

A. Sam do you really think his

B. Sam! Do you really think he's

C. Sam, do you really think he's

D. *(No change)*

Teaching Point: Error correction questions often test your knowledge of basic punctuation rules. In this case, the item tests whether you know to place a comma after a direct address.

CUSTOMIZING TIP

Students Acquiring English/ESL
Because the nuances of preposition use vary across languages, students will often interchange *to, at, for, of,* and *in.* For instruction and practice with prepositions and prepositional phrases, have students use **English Grammar Survival Kit** pp. 17–22.

Also suitable for:
Less Proficient Learners

LESSON 1 What Is a Preposition?

❶ Here's the Idea

▶ **A preposition is a word that shows a relationship between a noun or pronoun and some other word in the sentence.** A preposition is always followed by an object, either a noun or a pronoun.

> The article **about** insects is interesting.
> ↑ PREPOSITION

Here, the preposition *about* shows the relationship between the words *article* and *insects.* In the sentences below, notice how each preposition expresses a different relationship between the worm and the apple.

> The worm is **on** the apple.
>
> The worm is **beside** the apple.
>
> The worm is **under** the apple.
>
> The worm is **in** the apple.

Common Prepositions

about	at	despite	like	to
above	before	down	near	toward
across	behind	during	of	under
after	below	except	off	until
against	beneath	for	on	up
along	beside	from	out	with
among	between	in	over	within
around	beyond	inside	past	without
as	by	into	through	

TEACHING RESOURCES

 Time-Saver Transparencies Binder:
• Daily Test Preparation p. DT21

 Grammar, Usage, and Mechanics Workbook p. 124

SKILLS PRACTICE RESOURCES

◯ English Grammar Survival Kit pp. 17–22

 Grammar, Usage, and Mechanics Workbook pp. 125–126

Pupil's Edition Exercise Bank p. 606

This jewelry is inspired by a beetle.

Prepositional Phrases

▶ **A prepositional phrase consists of a preposition, its object, and any modifiers of the object.** The object of the preposition is the noun or pronoun following the preposition.

PREPOSITIONAL PHRASE

Some peoples have depicted insects in art.

PREPOSITION — OBJECT

Beetle images decorate the jewelry of many cultures.

PREPOSITION — MODIFIER — OBJECT

Some believed that dreams come from a butterfly.

Use *between* when the object of the preposition refers to two people or things. Use *among* when speaking of three or more.

Ants share food *between* two nestmates.

Ants share food *among* all the colony members.

Preposition or Adverb?

Sometimes the same word can be used as a preposition or as an adverb. If the word has no object, then it is an adverb.

PREPOSITIONAL PHRASE

The ant scurried out the door.

PREPOSITION — OBJECT

The ant scurried out.

ADVERB

For more on adverbs, see pp. 134–136.

Prepositions, Conjunctions, Interjections **153**

Explain to students that some prepositional phrases may need additional words to clarify meaning. For example, *The giant praying mantis crawled around the house* could refer to an action on the outside or inside of the house. Note that additional words help clarify the sentence: *The giant praying mantis crawled around the outside of the house.* Point out to students the importance of producing coherent written texts by using precise wording.

THE LANGUAGE OF LITERATURE

The passage on the student page is from "Ant and Grasshopper" in *The Language of Literature,* Level 7.

Answers

Print-Out Option You may create worksheets of this exercise for your students by using the ⊙ **Electronic Teacher Tools CD–ROM.**

CONCEPT CHECK

Self-Check For a self-check of what a preposition is, direct students to p. 606 in the Pupil's Edition for the answers to the items circled in yellow.

Answers shown on page.

Prepositions are underlined. Their objects are double underlined.

---

❷ Why It Matters in Writing

Use prepositional phrases in descriptive writing to add detailed information to sentences. For example, a prepositional phrase can tell an exact location. The prepositional phrases in this model tell where the ant found the grain and where she put it.

LITERARY MODEL

... she had taken it from the fields and stowed it away in a hole in the bank, under a hawthorn bush.

PREPOSITIONAL PHRASES

—Aesop, "Ant and Grasshopper,"
retold by James Reeves

❸ Practice and Apply

CONCEPT CHECK: What Is a Preposition?

Write the preposition in each sentence, along with its object.

Smoky the Beetle
1. Some jewel beetles are attracted to forest fires.
2. They can sense a forest fire from 30 miles.
3. Often they fly straight into the flames.
4. Sometimes they swarm around firefighters!
5. With their own infrared detectors, they sense heat.
6. Some scientists now believe that the beetles smell fire through their antennae.
7. Information from the beetles may improve the accuracy of fire alarms.
8. Currently, many fire alarms detect carbon dioxide levels in the air.
9. But the alarms can be fooled by car fumes.
10. Scientists are testing a more accurate alarm that is outfitted with actual insect antennae.

➡ **For a SELF-CHECK and more practice, see the EXERCISE BANK, p. 606.**

Spice It Up!

Write the following sentences on the board. Have students complete the prepositional phrases.

The toad croaked for three hours straight.
The toad croaked in the swampy marsh.
The toad croaked under my window.

LESSON 2 — Using Prepositional Phrases

❶ Here's the Idea

A prepositional phrase is always related to another word in a sentence. It modifies the word in the same way an adjective or adverb would.

Adjective Phrases

▶ **An adjective phrase is a prepositional phrase that modifies a noun or a pronoun.** Like an adjective, a prepositional phrase can tell which one, how many, or what kind.

WHAT KIND?

This spider is a type **of jumping spider.**
NOUN   ADJECTIVE PHRASE

WHICH ONE?

The tiny bug **on the windowsill** is also a jumping spider.

Adverb Phrases

▶ **An adverb phrase is a prepositional phrase that modifies a verb, an adjective, or an adverb.** Like an adverb, a prepositional phrase can tell where, when, how, why, or to what extent.

WHERE?

Jumping spiders live **in many places.**
VERB   ADVERB PHRASE

WHY?

These spiders are famous **for their eight eyes.**
ADJECTIVE

HOW?

They jump far **for their size.**
ADVERB

Several prepositional phrases can work together. Each phrase after the first often modifies the object of the phrase before it.

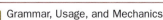
A spider sat **on the tip** **of a twig** **in a tree.**

Prepositions, Conjunctions, Interjections **155**

PREPOSITIONS

PREP. CONJ. INTER.

NEED MORE INFORMATION?

For a review of modifiers, see **Chapter 5, Adjectives and Adverbs.**

Placement of Prepositional Phrases

When you write, try to place each prepositional phrase as close as possible to the word it modifies. Otherwise, you may confuse—or unintentionally amuse—your readers.

Unclear

With eight hairy legs, the bird chased the spider.

(This must be the world's weirdest bird!)

Clear

The bird chased the spider with eight hairy legs.

(Now the reader can tell who has the hairy legs!)

❷ Why It Matters in Writing

When you write about science, use prepositional phrases to answer such questions as *where, how, which one,* and *what kind.* Notice how much information the prepositional phrases supply in the caption of the photograph below.

From one berry and *to another* tell where.

A jumping spider, photographed while jumping **from one berry to another.**

156 Grammar, Usage, and Mechanics

③ Practice and Apply

A. CONCEPT CHECK: Using Prepositional Phrases

Write the prepositional phrase in each sentence, along with the word it modifies. Then indicate whether the phrase is an adjective phrase or an adverb phrase. Warning: One sentence contains two prepositional phrases.

Eight-Legged Heroes

1. Nearly 36,000 known <u>kinds</u> <u>of spiders</u> inhabit the earth. **Adj. P.**
2. Very few spiders are <u>dangerous</u> <u>to people</u>. **Adv. P.**
3. Spiders eat <u>millions</u> <u>of disease-bearing mosquitoes</u>. **Adj. P.**
4. They also control huge <u>populations</u> <u>of garden pests</u>. **Adj. P.**
5. The <u>spider</u>, <u>with its many useful qualities</u>, is often helpful. **Adj. P.**
6. Spiders <u>live</u> <u>in many habitats</u>. **Adv. P.**
7. Some spiders <u>survive</u> <u>in cold climates</u>. **Adv. P.**
8. <u>Spiders</u> <u>with brilliant colors</u> are beautiful. **Adj. P.**
9. <u>Dewdrops</u> <u>on spider webs</u> <u>sparkle</u> <u>in the morning light</u>. **Adj. P./ Adv. P.**
10. The dewdrops usually <u>evaporate</u> <u>by afternoon</u>. **Adv. P.**

→ **For a SELF-CHECK and more practice, see the EXERCISE BANK, p. 606.**

B. WRITING: Using Prepositional Phrases in Science Answers in column.

Suppose that on a field trip you discovered an interesting spider and took this photograph of it. Write a very detailed description of the spider and of the place where you found it. Use adverb phrases to answer questions like *how, when,* and *where.*

PREPOSITIONS

PREP. CONJ. INTER.

Answers

Print-Out Option You may create worksheets of exercise A for your students by using the **◉ Electronic Teacher Tools CD–ROM.**

A. CONCEPT CHECK

Self-Check For a self-check of using prepositional phrases, direct students to p. 606 in the Pupil's Edition for the answers to the items circled in yellow.

Answers shown on page.

Prepositional phrases are underlined. The following codes are used:

Adj. P = adjective phrase

Adv. P = adverb phrase

B. WRITING

Answers will vary. Sample responses:

The spider <u>with the black and yellow coloring</u> sits <u>in the web.</u> The fine silk threads gleam <u>in the sunlight.</u> I found the spider <u>beneath a bush,</u> protected <u>by prickly green leaves.</u>

ASSESSMENT

Assessment Masters:
- Chapter Mid-point Test p. 29

Visual Grammar™

Use **Visual Grammar™ Tiles Lessons 9–10** and **Sentences G–H** to teach prepositional phrases. Here is part of Lesson 9.

Adverb phrase:

| MEGAN | PUT HER AQUARIUM | IN HER ROOM | . |

Adjective phrase:

| MEGAN | PAINTED THE WALLS | IN HER ROOM | . |

DAILY TEST PREPARATION

Revision-in-Context:
Capitalization Write the following item on the board or use **Daily Test Preparation Transparency** p. DT22.

1 Ancient phoenician
2 seafarers used the sun
3 and stars to navigate
4 across the Mediterranean.

What is the best change, if any, to make in the sentence in lines 1–2?

A. Change *sun* to *Sun*

B. Change *used* to *are using*

C. Change *phoenician* to *Phoenician*

D. Make no change

Teaching Point: Revision-in-context questions often test your knowledge of basic capitalization rules. In this case, the item tests whether you know to capitalize proper adjectives, such as *Phoenician*.

TEACHING TIP

Remind students that a conjunction is preceded by a comma when it connects two independent clauses.

LESSON 3 — Conjunctions

❶ Here's the Idea

▶ **A conjunction is a word used to join words or groups of words.** Different kinds of conjunctions are used in different ways.

Coordinating Conjunctions

▶ **A coordinating conjunction connects words used in the same way.** The words joined by a conjunction can be subjects, objects, predicates, or any other kind of sentence parts.

SUBJECTS

Insects and crustaceans have eyes with many lenses.

COORDINATING CONJUNCTION

OBJECTS

Light enters the front or the side of their eyes.

COORDINATING CONJUNCTION

Common Coordinating Conjunctions						
and	but	or	nor	yet	so	for

Use *and* to connect similar ideas. Use *but* to contrast ideas.

Each lens can receive light and form a separate image.
(*And* connects two things each lens can do.)

Insects' eyes are smaller than ours, but their vision is more complex.
(*But* contrasts vision in insects and people.)

A greenbottle fly is small, **but** its eyes contain many lenses.

158

TEACHING RESOURCES

 Time-Saver Transparencies Binder:
• Daily Test Preparation p. DT22
Grammar, Usage, and Mechanics Workbook p. 130

SKILLS PRACTICE RESOURCES

 Grammar, Usage, and Mechanics Workbook pp. 131–132
Pupil's Edition Exercise Bank p. 606

Correlative Conjunctions

▶ **Correlative conjunctions are pairs of words that connect words used in the same way.** Like coordinating conjunctions, correlative conjunctions can join subjects, objects, predicates, and other sentence parts.

SUBJECTS
Both flies **and** mosquitoes have compound eyes.
CORRELATIVE CONJUNCTION

PREDICATE ADJECTIVES
Their eye lenses are **not only** long **but also** cylindrical.
CORRELATIVE CONJUNCTION

Common Correlative Conjunctions		
both . . . and	either . . . or	not only . . . but also
neither . . . nor	whether . . . or	

❷ Why It Matters in Writing

A writer's use of the right conjunction helps readers know which words or ideas are joined together and how they relate to each other. Notice how conjunctions in the model connect similar ideas.

PROFESSIONAL MODEL

Insects **and** spiders have many different kinds of eyes. Some spiders have eight eyes, **so** they can see in several directions at once. Some insects have two compound eyes **and** three simple eyes called ocelli.

—S. Lieb

And connects two subjects in the sentence.

So connects two complete ideas.

And connects the two objects of *have.*

CONJUNCTIONS

CUSTOMIZING TIP

Students Acquiring English/ESL
Some students may have trouble remembering when to use different pairs of correlative conjunctions. Encourage them to compile a list of sentences in which each pair of conjunctions is used. Students can refer to the list as needed.

Also suitable for:
Less Proficient Learners

CUSTOMIZING TIP

Gifted and Talented Point out to students that the construction "not only . . . but also" emphasizes the words that follow "but also." Example: *He was not only handsome but also smart.* (In the sentence *He was handsome and smart,* "handsome" and "smart" are of equal weight.) Encourage students to remember these examples to help them use correlative conjunctions to connect ideas meaningfully.

MORE MODEL SENTENCES

Write the following sentences on the board and have volunteers underline the correlative conjunctions.

Neither cockroaches nor millipedes scare me.

On the other hand, butterflies not only scare me but also give me nightmares.

Spice It Up!
Have pairs of students choose a well-known person (for example, Bill Gates) and describe the person by filling in the following sentences:
Bill Gates is both *intelligent* and *rich.*
Bill Gates is neither *unsuccessful* nor *unhappy.*

TEACHING TIP

Cooperative Learning/Paired Activity Have students work in pairs to complete the **Concept Check.** Have one partner identify the conjunctions and have the other partner identify the words or groups of words that they join.

Answers

Print-Out Option You may create worksheets of exercises A and B for your students by using the ⊙ **Electronic Teacher Tools CD–ROM.**

A. CONCEPT CHECK

Self-Check For a self-check of conjunctions, direct students to p. 606 in the Pupil's Edition for the answers to the items circled in yellow.

Answers shown on page.
Conjunctions are double underlined. The words or groups of words that they join are underlined. For questions 6, 7, and 10, accept answers in which the compound nouns have been underlined.

B. REVISING

Answers shown on page.

---

❸ Practice and Apply

A. CONCEPT CHECK: Conjunctions

Write the conjunction in each sentence, along with the words or groups of words that it joins.

Seeing with Electrons

1. To magnify things, optical microscopes make use of lenses and light waves.

2. Light waves show the details of ordinary objects, but the waves are too long to reveal the smallest structures.

3. Electron microscopes open new worlds, for they show smaller details.

4. They use magnetic "lenses" and electron beams instead of light waves.

5. The beams of electrons have only 1/8,000 the wavelength of visible light, so they can show much more detail.

6. Electron microscopes can be scanning or transmission microscopes.

7. Scanning microscopes and transmission microscopes are much more powerful than optical microscopes.

8. Scanning microscopes not only magnify but also produce a TV picture.

9. They can magnify an object over 100,000 times, but transmission microscopes can magnify up to 1 million times.

10. Bugs can keep no secrets from either scanning or transmission microscopes!

➡ For a SELF-CHECK and more practice, see the EXERCISE BANK, p. 606.

B. REVISING: Changing Conjunctions

The right conjunctions help you say what you mean. Rewrite the conjunctions so that the meaning is clear.

Catch Me If You Can

Flies always see the swatter but flit away from it. Are flies smart and alert? Which characteristic do they have? They are probably alert but sharp-eyed. Their eyes have many parts, or they can see motion even at the edges of their vision. You can hide the swatter, and the fly might still see it. but

LESSON 4 Interjections

1 Here's the Idea

▶ **An interjection is a word or phrase used to express emotion.**

Hey, look at that bug.

It's a cockroach! **Yuck!**

2 Why It Matters in Writing

The Far Side by Gary Larson

"Spiders, scorpions, and insecticides, oh my! . . . Spiders, scorpions, and insecticides, oh my! . . ."

Oh my is an interjection.

Writers often use interjections to express strong emotions, such as concern, terror, anger, and disgust.

3 Practice and Apply

In the cartoon above, the interjection *oh my* shows fear, since spiders, scorpions, and insecticides are all dangerous to insects. Try writing your own caption for the cartoon, using at least one interjection. Add your caption to your **Working Portfolio.**

Prepositions, Conjunctions, Interjections **161**

INTERJECTIONS

PREP. CONJ. INTER.

LESSON OBJECTIVES

To identify and use interjections in writing

 DAILY TEST PREPARATION

Sentence Completion:
Vocabulary Write the following item on the board or use 🏛 **Daily Test Preparation Transparency** p. DT23. Choose the word that *best* fits the meaning of the sentence.

> The lion said to the mouse, "I'm _____ to you for extracting the thorn from my paw."

A. comforted

B. obligation

C. rude

D. grateful

Teaching Point: For sentence completion questions, the correct answer will always

- fit the meaning of the sentence (*rude* does not make sense with the friendly act of *extracting the thorn*.)

- fit grammatically within the sentence (*comforted* and *obligation* do not fit with *to you*).

ASSESSMENT

 Assessment Masters:
  - Chapter Mastery Tests pp. 67–70

 Test Generator CD-ROM

 mcdougallittell.com
Grammar Chapter Quiz

TEACHING RESOURCES

 Time-Saver Transparencies Binder:
  - Daily Test Preparation p. DT23
 Grammar, Usage, and Mechanics Workbook p. 123

SKILLS PRACTICE RESOURCES

Grammar, Usage, and Mechanics Workbook pp. 134–135

Prepositions, Conjunctions, Interjections **161**

Grammar in Science

❶ Using Prepositions to Write about Science

When you write your observations and conclusions in a lab
report, the proper use of prepositions can make a difference.
Prepositions are especially important if you are describing the
physical features of animals or their behavior. In the notebook
below, a student has used arrows on her drawing to show the
location of certain features. For her field notes, she has used
prepositional phrases to express the information
shown in her drawing.

Antennae

eye spots

This butterfly has
antennae **at the top
of its body.** It has
eyespots **on its wings.**

wings

The six legs are
attached **to the middle
section of the body.**
The orange color **on its
wings** suggests it may
be a monarch butterfly.

legs

162 Grammar, Usage, and Mechanics

② Practice and Apply

USING PREPOSITIONS

For a project on insect metamorphosis, your class has observed videos of caterpillars developing into butterflies and moths. You have taken notes on your observations. Write a summary of your observations using your notes as a guide. Use prepositional phrases to explain details about the caterpillar's behavior, the cocoon or pupa stage, and the butterfly or moth. Useful prepositions might include the words *around, inside, before, after, from.* Underline the prepositional phrases in your summary. Save your work in your ▭ **Working Portfolio.**

PREP. & CONJ.

PREP. CONJ. INTER.

Answers

PRACTICE AND APPLY

Answers will vary but should include a variety of prepositional phrases that relate to the photographs and notes. Prepositional phrases are underlined in the example that follows:

The caterpillar, or larva, begins its metamorphosis <u>into a butterfly or moth</u> <u>with the pupa stage.</u> First, the caterpillar becomes stuck <u>to a leaf.</u> <u>Around the caterpillar</u> a film them forms. This film hardens and protects the insect. The caterpillar remains <u>inside its cocoon</u> and reforms itself <u>into a butterfly.</u> Next, the insect begins breaking <u>from the pupa or cocoon.</u> Finally, the butterfly or moth comes <u>outside its cocoon.</u> It then pumps fluid <u>through its wings.</u> <u>After an hour,</u> the butterfly or moth is ready to fly.

Mixed Review

Answers

Print-Out Option You may create worksheets of exercises A and B for your students by using the 🔵 **Electronic Teacher Tools CD–ROM.**

A. PREPOSITIONS, CONJUNCTIONS, AND INTERJECTIONS

Answers shown on page.

Correct words are underlined. The following codes are used:

Prep. = preposition

Conj. = conjunction

Intj. = interjection

B. PREPOSITIONAL PHRASES

Answers shown on page.

Prepositional phrases are underlined. They are identified using the following codes:

Adj. P = adjective phrase

Adv. P = adverb phrase

Mixed Review

A. Prepositions, Conjunctions, Interjections Choose the correct word in parentheses to complete each sentence. Then identify the word as a preposition, a conjunction, or an interjection.

1. New Orleans has many wooden buildings built (<u>on</u>, out) swampland. **Prep.**
2. (<u>For</u>, Off) termites these buildings are like a buffet. **Prep.**
3. The Algiers Public Library (<u>near</u>, up) New Orleans had 79 antitermite treatments. **Prep.**
4. Yet experts examined the ground afterward and found 70 million Formosan termites (<u>beneath</u>, above) the library. **Prep.**
5. (<u>Ugh!</u>, To!) It was the largest known termite colony on earth. **Intj.**
6. Each of the termites was small, (or, <u>yet</u>) together they were like a 500-pound animal eating the building 24 hours a day. **Conj.**
7. A typical Formosan colony is made up of 5 million termites (<u>and</u>, but) eats 1,000 pounds of wood a year. **Conj.**
8. The termites probably traveled (<u>to</u>, until) the United States in wooden crates after World War II. **Prep.**
9. People thought they were relatively harmless, (not, <u>but</u>) by 1965 they had infested a Houston warehouse. **Conj.**
10. (Except, <u>Both</u>) Galveston, Texas (for, <u>and</u>) Charleston, South Carolina are also victims of Formosan termites. **Conj.**

B. Prepositional Phrases Write the prepositional phrases in the paragraph below. Identify each as an adjective or an adverb phrase.

1. Adj. P.
Adj. P./Adj. P.
3. Adv. P.
4. Adv. P.
5. Adv. P.
6. Adj. P.
7. Adj. P.
8. Adv. P.
9. Adv. P.
10. Adv. P.

(1) Butterflies are the darlings <u>of the insect world</u>. **(2)** <u>Like bugs in elaborate costumes</u>, they grace our gardens. **(3)** Yet butterflies work hard <u>despite their delicate appearance</u>. **(4)** Some migrate <u>for 2,000 miles</u>. **(5)** They can soar 7,000 feet <u>above the earth</u>. **(6)** There are more than 20,000 species <u>of butterflies</u>. **(7)** But environmental changes <u>in the modern world</u> have reduced their numbers. **(8)** Industrial and residential development destroys the food and shelter needed <u>by butterflies</u>. **(9)** Pesticides are deadly <u>to them</u>. **(10)** However, "habitat gardening" helps provide butterflies <u>with shelter and food plants</u>.

Mastery Test: What Did You Learn?

Choose the letter of the term that correctly identifies each underlined item.

Jumping spiders are the cats <u>of the spider world</u>. Their quick gait
(1)
<u>and</u> short, sudden jumps help them catch their prey. When they get
(2)
close <u>to</u> an insect, they pounce. A jumping spider can leap 40 times
(3)
its body length. In human terms, it is like a person 6 feet tall who
can jump 240 feet. <u>Wow!</u> The spider is also famous <u>for its excellent</u>
(4)   (5)
<u>vision</u>. <u>With</u> four <u>of</u> its eight eyes very large, it has the best vision of
(6)   (7)
any <u>spider</u> its size. Jumping spiders do not build webs. They spin a
(8)
dragline attached to a wall <u>or</u> a tree. Jumping spiders live in almost
(9)
every environment—you can find them <u>both</u> on your own windowsill
(10)
<u>and</u> 22,000 feet up the slopes of Mount Everest.
(10)

1. (A.) adjective phrase
   B. adverb phrase
   C. coordinating conjunction
   D. correlative conjunction

2. A. preposition
   B. object of a preposition
   (C.) coordinating conjunction
   D. correlative conjunction

3. A. interjection
   (B.) preposition
   C. correlative conjunction
   D. object of a preposition

4. A. object of a preposition
   B. coordinating conjunction
   C. correlative conjunction
   (D.) interjection

5. A. conjunction
   B. interjection
   (C.) adverb phrase
   D. adjective phrase

6. (A.) preposition
   B. conjunction
   C. adverb
   D. interjection

7. A. object of a preposition
   (B.) preposition
   C. correlative conjunction
   D. coordinating conjunction

8. A. interjection
   B. conjunction
   C. prepositional phrase
   (D.) object of a preposition

9. A. preposition
   B. adverb
   (C.) conjunction
   D. interjection

10. A. coordinating conjunction
    (B.) correlative conjunction
    C. preposition
    D. object of a preposition

Mastery Test

As an option, two other Chapter Mastery Tests appear in 📋 **Assessment Masters** pp. 67–70.

Answers circled on page.

PRESCRIPTION FOR MASTERY	
If students miss item number:	Use **Teaching Resources** and **Skills Practice Resources** for lesson:
1, 5	❷ Using Prepositional Phrases p. 155
2, 9, 10	❸ Conjunctions p. 158
3, 6, 7, 8	❶ What is a Preposition? p. 152
4	❹ Interjections p. 161

PREP. & CONJ.

PREP. CONJ. INTER.

CHAPTER 6

Student Help Desk

Prepositions, Conjunctions, Interjections at a Glance

RELATIONSHIP

Ick! The flypaper on the ceiling has caught six flies and an ant.

Interjections show emotion.

Prepositions show relationships.

Conjunctions connect.

CHAPTER 6

Prepositions, Conjunctions, Interjections

Preposition

Shows a relationship. Has an object.

RELATIONSHIP

flypaper on the ceiling
PREPOSITION   OBJECT

Conjunction

Joins words or groups of words.

mosquitoes **or** gnats
Mosquitoes bite, **and** so do gnats.
• Coordinating conjunction: fleas **and** ticks
• Correlative conjunction: **both** fleas **and** ticks

Interjection

Expresses emotion.

Ouch! A mosquito bit me!

166 Grammar, Conjunctions, and Mechanics

Prepositional Phrases — What Do They Do?

Adjective Phrase

Modifies a noun or a pronoun

Tells which one	That little spider **on the wall**
Tells what kind	is a type **of jumping spider.**

Adverb Phrase

Modifies a verb, an adjective, or an adverb

Tells when	**During our recent picnic,**
Tells where	ants came **from everywhere**
Tells why	**for the free food**
Tells how	**in a big rush.**

Interjections! — Splat! Just a Few Ideas . . .

To express concern	oh-oh, oh no, oops
To express disgust	yuck, ick, gross
To express joy	awesome, hooray, yea
To express surprise	wow, what, whoops
To draw attention to	hey

The Bottom Line

Checklist for Prepositions, Conjunctions, Interjections

Have I . . .

____ used prepositions to show relationships between things?

____ placed prepositional phrases close to the words they modify?

____ used coordinating conjunctions to connect words and groups of words?

____ used correlative conjunctions correctly?

____ used interjections to express strong emotion?

Prepositions, Conjunctions, Interjections **167**

Teacher's Notes
WHAT DOESN'T WORK:

TEACHER'S LOUNGE

A Slice of Life

"As I read, my ears are opened to the magic of the spoken word."
—Richard Wright

Brain Break

The millionaire said to his butler, who was blind, "In the top drawer of my bureau are ten pairs of white socks and ten pairs of black socks. Bring me a matching pair of socks. I don't care if they are black or white." "Very good, sir," the butler replied. What is the least number of socks that the butler can pull from the drawer to ensure that his master has at least one pair of the same color?

Answer: There are only two colors of socks—black and white. To be sure of having a matching pair of socks, all the butler has to do is pull out three socks.

Verbals and Verbal Phrases

CHAPTER OVERVIEW

Introduction and Diagnostic Test pp. 168–169

CHAPTER RESOURCES

 Time-Saver Transparencies Binder:
- Daily Test Preparation pp. DT23–25

 Grammar, Usage, and Mechanics Workbook pp. 136–147

Integrated Technology and Media

 Electronic Teacher Tools CD-ROM

 mcdougallittell.com

Assessment

 Assessment Masters:
- Chapter Pretest pp. 14–15
- Chapter Mid-point Test p. 30
- Chapter Mastery Tests pp. 71–74

 Test Generator CD-ROM

 mcdougallittell.com Grammar Chapter Quiz

Fallen Boy Saved by Gorilla!

CHICAGO–
The spectators at the Brookfield Zoo

Theme: Animals to the Rescue

A Surprising Event!

Look at the photograph and newspaper headline above. We can see that the boy is in the gorilla's living area, but how did he get there? How do you know? *Fallen* clearly conveys that he accidentally tumbled in. Although we often use *fallen* as part of a verb, it works here as an adjective, describing the boy. Verb forms that serve as other parts of speech are called verbals. Using them can add excitement and grace to your writing.

Write Away: Caring and Helping

Think about a time when you received help or comfort from an animal. The animal may have been real, a toy, or a character in a book. Write a paragraph that describes the event. Save the paragraph in your 📁 **Working Portfolio.**

 **Grammar Coach**

Diagnostic Test: What Do You Know?

Choose the letter of the answer that correctly identifies each underlined item.

> Brookfield Zoo visitor Eric Allison noticed a small boy climbing the fence at the Tropic World exhibit. Eric watched the boy trying
> (1)
> to lift himself toward the top. He wondered with growing anxiety, is
> (2)   (3)
> he going to go higher? The boy, losing his balance, suddenly
> (4)   (5)
> tumbled into the gorilla enclosure. A terrified crowd watched a
> (6)
> gorilla named Binti approach him. Eric's father, Bob Allison,
> started to photograph the event. Watching in horror was all anyone
> (7)   (8)
> could do. Would Binti hurt the boy? Carrying her own baby, Binti
> (9)
> came near the boy. Her gentle handling of the boy made newspaper
> (10)
> headlines.

1. A. gerund phrase
   B. participial phrase
   C. infinitive phrase
   D. helping verb

2. A. gerund
   B. gerund phrase
   C. infinitive
   D. infinitive phrase

3. A. gerund
   B. present participle
   C. past participle
   D. infinitive

4. A. gerund
   B. gerund phrase
   C. infinitive
   D. infinitive phrase

5. A. gerund
   B. gerund phrase
   C. participle
   D. participial phrase

6. A. gerund
   B. gerund phrase
   C. participle
   D. verb

7. A. gerund
   B. participle
   C. infinitive
   D. helping verb

8. A. infinitive phrase as subject
   B. gerund phrase as subject
   C. participial phrase as adjective
   D. gerund phrase as object of preposition

9. A. gerund
   B. gerund phrase
   C. participial phrase
   D. infinitive phrase

10. A. gerund phrase as subject
    B. gerund phrase as object
    C. participial phrase
    D. infinitive phrase

Diagnostic Test

As an option, a Chapter Pretest appears in

📖 **Assessment Masters,** pp. 14–15.

Answers circled on page.

Use the chart below to determine which lessons students need

PRESCRIPTION FOR SUCCESS	
If students miss item number:	**Work on lesson:**
1, 2, 4, 5, 9	❹ Verbal Phrases p. 176
3, 6	❶ Participles p. 172
7	❶ Infinitives p. 174
8, 10	❸ Gerunds p. 170

The **Diagnostic Test** parallels the **Mastery Test** on page 181. Have students keep the test in their portfolio to compare with their results on the **Mastery Test**.

Pressed for Time?
Use the Prescription for Success chart to determine which lessons students need to study and have them complete **Here's the Idea** and **Practice and Apply, Concept Check** only for those lessons.

Time for More?
After completing all the lessons, have students work in pairs to write brief descriptions of their school for a foreign student interested in visiting. Ask students to include at least one of the three types of verbals in their descriptions.

To identify and use gerunds and gerund phrases in writing

LESSON 1 Gerunds

❶ Here's the Idea

A **verbal** is a word that is formed from a verb and that acts as a noun, an adjective, or an adverb. There are three kinds of verbals: gerunds, participles, and infinitives.

▶ **A gerund is a verbal that ends in *ing* and acts as a noun.** A **gerund phrase** consists of the gerund with its modifiers and complements. Like nouns, gerunds and gerund phrases may be subjects, predicate nouns, direct objects, indirect objects, or objects of prepositions.

GERUND PHRASE

The loud barking of the dogs woke up our neighbors.

GERUND

Using Gerunds	
Subject	**Herding** is something that border collies do well.
Predicate noun	It is their **running** that directs other animals.
Direct object	These dogs like **working**.
Indirect object	They give **herding** their full attention.
Object of a preposition	They are expert at **controlling** sheep and cows.

❷ Why It Matters in Writing

Gerunds are good words for describing activities, because they imply action. Notice how the writer of the sentence below used gerunds and gerund phrases to discuss the many activities of beavers.

PROFESSIONAL MODEL

Felling timber and ornamental or orchard trees, **damming** ditches and culverts, **digging** and **tunneling**, and **eating** food crops make the beaver an unpopular neighbor.

—Peg Boulay, "Beaver!"

170

❸ Practice and Apply

A. CONCEPT CHECK: Gerunds

Write the gerunds in these sentences.

The Horse Therapist

1. Horseback <u>riding</u> has many benefits for people with disabilities. *Horseback riding*

2. People with physical or emotional problems can enjoy <u>moving</u> around. *moving around*

3. One horse, named Silver, was especially good at <u>walking</u> slowly and carefully. *walking slowly and carefully*

4. <u>Waiting</u> took patience, but Silver let the teachers lift a woman named Maria onto his back. *waiting*

5. When Maria started <u>riding</u>, she had never walked in her life.

6. Her activity had been limited to <u>rolling</u> in her wheelchair.

7. From Silver, she learned <u>balancing</u>. *balancing*

8. After <u>building</u> her strength, she could even walk (with a little help). *building her strength*

9. Silver contributed to Maria's <u>healing</u>. *healing*

10. As a result of <u>training</u> with Silver, Maria now lives independently. *training with Silver*

Write the entire gerund phrase in each of the sentences above.

➡ For a SELF-CHECK and more practice, see the EXERCISE BANK, p. 607.

B. WRITING: Understanding Gerunds   *Answers in column.*

Write about your typical day. Make a list, using gerunds to describe your activities at 9:00 A.M., 12:00 noon, 5:00 P.M., and 8:00 P.M.

9:00 A.M. Waking up
12:00 noon Still waking up
5:00 P.M. Falling asleep
8:00 P.M. Staying awake

171

Spice It Up!

Use the **Professional Model** on student page 170 as a way to introduce an animal guessing game. Have students present clues to the class about an animal by using gerunds in the manner of the "Beaver!" passage.

A. CONCEPT CHECK

Self-Check For a self-check of gerunds, direct students to p. 607 in the Pupil's Edition for the answers to the items circled in yellow.

Answers underlined on page. (Gerund phrases in margin are Challenge answers.)

CHALLENGE **Answers shown in margin.**

riding

rolling in her wheelchair

B. WRITING

Answers will vary. Students should use a gerund to describe each activity. Possible answers:

9:00 A.M. Taking notes in history

12 Noon Devouring a pizza

5:00 P.M. Running in a cross-country meet

8:00 P.M. Watching music videos on TV

TEACHING TIP

Cooperative Learning After completing **Practice and Apply,** exercise B, have students work in groups to share and discuss the descriptions of their typical days. Have students compare the ways they used gerunds, and combine their lists to create a list of what an average student does in a day. By carrying out this activity, students will compare their own perception of spoken messages (the way they used gerunds) with the perception of others; connect their own information and ideas with experiences of others through speaking and listening; and, clarify or support their spoken or written ideas with either elaborations or examples.

VERBALS

VERBALS

CHAPTER 7

LESSON OBJECTIVES

To identify and use participles in writing

DAILY TEST PREPARATION

Error Correction: Sentence Fragments Write the following item on the board or use 📗 **Daily Test Preparation Transparency** p. DT24.

> After the invention of the stoplight in Cleveland.

How is the above text best written?

A. After the invention of the stoplight in Cleveland, but I don't know the date.

B. After the invention of the stoplight in Cleveland, there were more traffic jams.

C. After the invention of the stoplight in Cleveland and supported by the iron industry.

D. As it is

Teaching Point: Error correction questions often test your ability to recognize sentence fragments. In answer B, the fragment is connected to an independent clause that logically completes the meaning.

CUSTOMIZING TIP

Less Proficient Learners Some students may need help distinguishing participles from verbs ending in *-ing*. Have students rewrite the following model sentence by placing the participle, *growling,* closer to the noun that it describes:

Growling, the bear rose from his slumber. The growling bear rose from his slumber.

Also suitable for:
Students Acquiring English/ESL

LESSON 2 Participles

❶ Here's the Idea

▶ **A participle is a verb form that acts as an adjective.**

A **participial phrase** consists of a participle along with its modifiers and complements. Like other adjectives, participles and participial phrases can modify nouns and pronouns.

MODIFIES   MODIFIES

A **tired** hiker woke a **sleeping** bear.

PARTICLE   PARTICLE

Present and Past Participles

A **present participle** always ends in *ing.*

MODIFIES

Growling, the bear rose from his slumber.

The **past participle** of a regular verb ends in *ed.* Past participles of irregular verbs, such as *freeze,* are formed in a variety of ways.

MODIFIES

The **terrified** traveler wanted to run.

MODIFIES

Frozen by fear, he was grateful that the bear only licked him.

A word that ends in *ing* may be a gerund, a participle, or part of a verb phrase. Here's how you can tell the difference.

Words That End in *ing*

	Example	Clue
Gerund	We were annoyed by the moth's **fluttering.**	Could be replaced by a noun
Participle	The moth's **fluttering** wings were white.	Could be replaced by an adjective
Present Participle of Verb	The moth was **fluttering** in the breeze.	Always preceded by a helping verb.

Need help in forming past participles of irregular verbs? See page 102–104.

172 Grammar, Usage, and Mechanics

TEACHING RESOURCES

- Time-Saver Transparencies Binder:
  - Daily Test Preparation p. DT24
- Grammar, Usage, and Mechanics Workbook p. 139

SKILLS PRACTICE RESOURCES

- Grammar, Usage, and Mechanics Workbook pp. 140–141
- Pupil's Edition Exercise Bank p. 607

② Why It Matters in Writing

If your descriptive writing seems dull, use participles to liven up your sentences. Notice how strongly the participles in the following sentence convey sounds and actions.

> **LITERARY MODEL**
>
> There was a **snarling** growl that seemed to come from the bowels of the earth, **followed** by the sound of **ripping** cloth, screams, and then the **fading** slap of footsteps **running** away.
>
> —Gary Paulsen, "Dirk the Protector"

③ Practice and Apply

MIXED REVIEW: Gerund or Participle?

Write the verbals in these sentences. Identify each verbal as a gerund or participle.

Animal Actors
1. Many TV commercials feature <u>acting</u> <u>animals</u>. **Pt.**
2. There are bell-ringing <u>turkeys</u> and <u>typing</u> <u>chickens</u>. **Pt./Pt.**
3. <u>Training</u> any type of animal requires patience. **G**
4. Have you seen the dog-food commercial that shows a <u>dog</u> <u>chasing</u> a chuck wagon? **Pt.**
5. The trainer aroused <u>yearning</u> in the dog by <u>hiding</u> a squeaky toy in a closet. **G/G**
6. Then the <u>excited</u> <u>dog</u> was let loose. **Pt.**
7. The dog reacted by <u>racing</u> around the corner, <u>dashing</u> across the kitchen, and <u>skidding</u> to a stop. **G/G/G**
8. <u>Staring</u> at the door, the <u>dog</u> waited for the trainer to open it. **Pt.**
9. In the <u>finished</u> <u>commercial</u>, the chuck wagon disappears right through the cabinet door. **Pt.**
10. <u>Working</u> comes naturally to most animal actors. **G**

For each participle, write the noun it modifies.

 ➡ **For a SELF-CHECK and more practice, see the EXERCISE BANK, p. 607.**

Verbals and Verbal Phrases **173**

VERBALS

VERBALS

TEACHING TIP

Speaking and Listening Have students close their books while you read aloud the **Literary Model.** Have students listen for and identify the participles in each sentence. Then ask them to suggest other participles that could be used to convey sounds and actions in the passage.

THE LANGUAGE OF
LITERATURE

The passage on the student page is from "Dirk the Protector" in *The Language of Literature*, Level 7.

Answers

Print-Out Option You may create worksheets of exercise A for your students by using the
💿 **Electronic Teacher Tools CD–ROM.**

MIXED REVIEW

Self-Check For a self-check of participles, direct students to p. 607 in the Pupil's Edition for the answers to the items circled in yellow.

Answers shown on page. Verbals are underlined once. Gerunds and participles are identified using these codes:

G = gerund

Pt. = participle

 Answers shown on page. Nouns modified by participles are underlined twice.

ASSESSMENT

📋 Assessment Masters:
• Chapter Mid-point Test p. 30

LESSON OBJECTIVES

To identify and use infinitives in writing

DAILY TEST PREPARATION

Sentence Completion: Subject-Verb Agreement Write the following item on the board or use 📺 **Daily Test Preparation Transparency** p. DT24. Choose the word that belongs in the space.

> Buried under a pile of clothes in her room _____ Claire's English assignment.

A. sit

B. is

C. were

D. are

Teaching Point: Sentence completion questions often test your knowledge of subject-verb agreement. In this case, the sentence is inverted: the subject *assignment* appears after the verb. Answer B is the only verb that agrees in number with *assignment*.

TEACHING TIP

Some students may wonder why the text states that infinitives "usually" begin with the word *to*. Tell students that *to* is usually dropped when the infinitive follows such verbs as *see, hear, feel, let, help,* and *need*. Example: *Please help me prepare the meal for the lions.* (Rather than: *Help me to prepare the meal.*)

NEED MORE INFORMATION?

For a review of prepositions and prepositional phrases, see **Chapter 6, Prepositions, Conjunctions, Interjections.**

LESSON 3 Infinitives

❶ Here's the Idea

▶ **An infinitive is a verb form that usually begins with the word *to* and that acts as a noun, an adjective, or an adverb.** An **infinitive phrase** consists of an infinitive along with its modifiers and complements.

INFINITIVE

Sam has always wanted **to work** on his own farm.

Using Infinitives	
Noun	**To run** his farm takes Sam's full energy. (Subject)
	His challenge is **to handle** large animals. (Predicate noun)
	Often, bulls begin **to charge** for no reason. (Direct object)
Adjective	They can be creatures **to fear**.
Adverb	However, the bulls calm down **to receive** food.

How can you tell the difference between an infinitive and a prepositional phrase that begins with *to*? If a verb follows *to*, the words are an infinitive. If a noun or pronoun follows *to*, the words are a prepositional phrase.

INFINITIVE

Sam's dog runs **to distract** the bulls.
⤷ VERB

PREPOSITIONAL PHRASE

The dog runs **to the pen.**
⤷ NOUN

❷ Why It Matters in Writing

Infinitives are often used to talk about goals, dreams, and wishes.

Sam hopes to buy more land and to increase his herd.

174 Grammar, Usage, and Mechanics

 TEACHING RESOURCES

📺 Time-Saver Transparencies Binder:
• Daily Test Preparation p. DT24
📙 Grammar, Usage, and Mechanics Workbook p. 142

 SKILLS PRACTICE RESOURCES

📙 Grammar, Usage, and Mechanics Workbook pp. 143–144
Pupil's Edition Exercise Bank p. 608

❸ Practice and Apply

A. CONCEPT CHECK: Infinitives

Write the infinitives in the following sentences. For sentences without an infinitive, write *none*.

The Cat's Meow

1. Ringo the cat liked <u>to nap</u> indoors every morning. **N**
2. <u>To play</u> outside was for afternoons. **N**
3. Yet one morning he was determined <u>to get</u> out. **Adv.**
4. His owners, Carol and Ray, were too sick <u>to let</u> him out. **Adv.**
5. Carol finally managed <u>to open</u> the door. **N**
6. Meowing, the cat went to the gas meter and began <u>to dig</u>. **N**
7. Carol thought he was trying <u>to tell</u> her about a gas leak. **N**
8. She called the gas company, but the technician didn't find anything—until he checked the hole Ringo had been digging. **none**
9. "Your house is about <u>to blow</u> up!" the technician shouted. **N**
10. Ringo's instinct <u>to warn</u> his owners had saved their lives. **Adj.**

For each infinitive, indicate whether it serves as a noun, an adjective, or an adverb.

➡️ For a SELF-CHECK and more practice, see the EXERCISE BANK, p. 608.

B. REVISING: Using Infinitives

Revise this paragraph by substituting infinitives for the underlined words.

> **(1)** <u>Having</u> a dog or a gerbil was out of the question for **To have**
> Duane Wright. He had trouble breathing whenever he came
> in contact with animal fur. So he found Goliath, a female
> iguana. **(2)** She seemed happy <u>while keeping</u> Duane **to keep**
> company. One night, Duane had stopped breathing.
> **(3)** With her sharp claws Goliath started scratching hard
> <u>with the hope of waking</u> Duane. **(4)** She also began **to wake**
> <u>whipping</u> his face with her scaly tail. Eventually, Duane **to whip**
> began to breathe again. **(5)** Who would believe that an
> iguana would come <u>around rescuing</u> a man? **to rescue**

Verbals and Verbal Phrases **175**

VERBALS

VERBALS

LESSON 4 Verbal Phrases

❶ Here's the Idea

▶ **A verbal phrase includes a verbal and any modifiers or complements it may have.** As you have seen in the preceding lessons, there are three types of verbal phrases: gerund phrases, participial phrases, and infinitive phrases.

A **gerund phrase** consists of a gerund plus its modifiers and complements. Like a gerund itself, the entire phrase is used as a noun.

GERUND PHRASE (subject)

==Sunning== himself is Silas the snake's favorite activity.

GERUND PHRASE (object of a preposition)

He likes it so much he forgets about ==eating== his dinner.

A **participial phrase** consists of a participle plus its modifiers and complements. The entire phrase modifies a noun or pronoun.

PARTICIPIAL PHRASE

==Finishing== his run, the horse walked for a few minutes.

His trainer, ==stunned by his speed==, checked her stopwatch.

An **infinitive phrase** consists of an infinitive plus its modifiers and complements. The entire phrase functions as a noun, an adjective, or an adverb.

INFINITIVE PHRASE (subject)

==To run free in peace and solitude== was Luna's greatest goal.

INFINITIVE PHRASE (adjective)

She took every chance ==to escape== from the house.

❷ Why It Matters in Writing

You can use verbals and verbal phrases to make your descriptions flow. Notice how the revised description at the top of the next page flows better and conveys greater excitement than the draft.

STUDENT MODEL

DRAFT

Noble Cause galloped down 46th Street. He was racing after the criminal, hoping to catch him. The police horse panted and snorted. Finally, he stopped the villain in his tracks.

REVISION

Galloping down 46th Street, Noble Cause raced to catch the criminal. Finally, the police horse, **panting and snorting,** stopped the villain in his tracks.

③ Practice and Apply

A. CONCEPT CHECK: Verbal Phrases

Write the verbal phrase in each sentence, and identify it as a gerund phrase, a participial phrase, or an infinitive phrase.

Priscilla the Piglet

1. Strolling around the neighborhood pleased Priscilla, a three-month-old piglet. **GP**
2. Her owner, Victoria Herberta, would walk the slightly spoiled piglet on a purple leash. **PP**
3. Victoria taught Priscilla to swim with the family dogs. **IP**
4. One day a friend, Carol, took Priscilla to the lake to swim with her son Anthony. **IP**
5. Carol told Anthony to stay in the shallow water. **IP**
6. He decided to follow Carol and the pig into the deep water. **IP**
7. Unfortunately, Anthony felt himself sinking fast. **PP**
8. Rescuing Anthony was now necessary. **GP**
9. Grabbing Priscilla's leash, the boy held on tightly. **PP**
10. The 45-pound piglet began pulling the 90-pound boy back to shore. **GP**

➡ For a SELF-CHECK and more practice, see the EXERCISE BANK, p. 608.

B. REVISING: Understanding Verbal Phrases

Return to the paragraph your wrote for the **Write Away** on page 168. Add three verbal phrases to make your writing more interesting and fluent.

Verbals and Verbal Phrases **177**

VERBALS

STUDENT MODEL

Have students rewrite the following paragraph so that it flows better, using verbals and verbal phrases.

Susan realized that she was about four miles from her house. She decided to return home. At that very moment, her dog was sleeping. He awoke and stood up expectantly.

Possible answer: *Realizing that she was about four miles from her house, Susan decided to return home. At that very moment, her sleeping dog awoke and stood up expectantly.*

Answers

Print-Out Option You may create worksheets of exercise A for your students by using the **Electronic Teacher Tools CD–ROM.**

A. CONCEPT CHECK

Self-Check For a self-check of verbal phrases, direct students to p. 608 in the Pupil's Edition for the answers to the items circled in yellow.

Answers shown on page. Verbal phrases are underlined. They are identified using these codes:

GP = gerund phrase

PP = participial phrase

IP = infinitive phrase

ASSESSMENT

 Assessment Masters:
 • Chapter Mastery Tests pp. 71–74

 Test Generator CD-ROM

mcdougallittell.com Grammar Chapter Quiz

VERBALS

Spice It Up!
Quotable Quote

"Of all the ways of acquiring books, writing them oneself is regarded as the most praiseworthy method . . . ."
—Walter Benjamin

Read the quote aloud. Then have students identify the two verbal phrases in the quote and tell whether each is a gerund phrase, a participial phrase, or an infinitive phrase.

LESSON OBJECTIVES

To identify and use verbals to describe action

TEACHING TIP

Use the annotations alongside the passage and the following as a guide to class discussion.

1. Ask students to make up a sentence beginning with a gerund to explain Rikki's actual action.

Possible response: Jumping up in the air as high as he could go, Rikki saw Nagaina's head whiz by.

2. Have students use gerund or participial phrases to describe Rikki's and Nagaina's behaviors.

Possible responses: Trying to make an end of him, Nagaina crept up behind him as he was talking. Breaking her back with one bite was what Rikki should have done.

3. Ask students to come up with participles that describe the movements of the fighting animals.

Possible responses: attacking, crushing, whipping; thrashing, beating, striking

THE LANGUAGE OF
LITERATURE

The excerpt on the student page is from "Rikki-Tikki-Tavi" in *The Language of Literature*, Level 7.

Grammar in Literature

Using Verbals to Write About Action

Because verbals are formed from verbs, writers often find them especially helpful in writing about action. Notice the way Kipling's use of gerunds, infinitives, and participles adds life to this description. As we enter the story, a tailor bird named Darzee has just warned Rikki-Tikki-Tavi, the story's mongoose hero, that the cobra Nagaina is about to pounce.

Rikki-tikki-tavi
by Rudyard Kipling

Rikki-Tikki knew better than to waste time in staring. He jumped up in the air as high as he could go, and just under him whizzed by the head of Nagaina, Nag's wicked wife. She had crept up behind him as he was talking, to make an end of him; and he heard her savage hiss as the stroke missed. He came down almost across her back, and if he had been an old mongoose, he would have known that then was the time to break her back with one bite; but he was afraid of the terrible lashing return stroke of the cobra. He bit, indeed, but did not bite long enough; and he jumped clear of the whisking tail, leaving Nagaina torn and angry.

"Wicked, wicked Darzee!" said Nag, lashing up as high as he could reach toward the nest in the thorn bush; but Darzee had built it out of reach of snakes, and it only swayed to and fro.

GERUND names an activity. What gerund names the activity Rikki-Tikki actually does?

INFINITIVE PHRASES explain Rikki's and Nagaina's behaviors.

PARTICIPLES describe the rapid movements of the animals as they fight.

Practice and Apply

Using Verbals in Writing

Follow the directions to write your own action story about animals. You can write about the animals in Rikki Tikki Tavi, or you can write about more familiar animals, like cats, dogs, or birds.

1. List four gerunds naming the activities that the animals might do.
2. List four participles you might use as adjectives to describe each of the animals.
3. Briefly explain what would happen. Use at least one infinitive phrase as you describe the action.
4. Evaluate your work. How would your writing be different if you hadn't used participles? Put your writing and your evaluation in your 📁 **Working Portfolio.**

---

1. Gerunds   **2. Participles**

1. hissing   1. fallen
2.   2. defeated
3.   3.
4.   4.

3. The hissing of the cat startled the fallen bird.

Verbals and Verbal Phrases **179**

Answers

Practice and Apply

Using Verbals in Writing

Answers will vary, but should include some of the verbals listed in the students' notes. A sample response follows.

1. gerunds: barking, entertaining, watching, galloping
2. participles: yipping, frustrated, screeching, reclining
3. infinitives: to play, to race

Watching our Shetland sheepdog spy two squirrels on our front lawn is very entertaining. First the screeching squirrels scamper across the fallen leaves and grass in a playful game of tag. Then our dog's herding instinct takes over. Suddenly, she stands, takes a running leap, and jumps up onto the couch. Draping her brown and white paws over the top of the couch, she peers intently out the window.

Answers

A. GERUNDS, PARTICIPLES, AND INFINITIVES

Answers shown on page using these codes:

G = gerund

Pt. = participle

I = infinitive

B. VERBAL PHRASES

Answers will vary. Possible responses:

The hen invited me to floss my teeth after I ate her eggs.

The slithering snake brought us the keys.

Carrying a keg of hot chocolate, the Saint Bernard came to my rescue.

The termite wanted to eat the pencil but gave it to the girl.

Swimming through the sea with a pair of trunks, the dolphin saved the boy from embarrassment.

Mixed Review

A. Gerunds, Participles, and Infinitives Identify each underlined verbal as a gerund, a participle, or an infinitive.

(1) Many animals seem <u>to be able</u> to sense natural disasters 1. I
before they happen. **(2)** There are stories about bears <u>coming</u> out 2. Pt.
of hibernation early, just before an earthquake. **(3)** At other times, 3. Pt.
<u>frightened</u> animals have warned of tornadoes and floods. **(4)** One 4. G
woman told of her cat's <u>stopping</u> a car accident. **(5)** The cat, 5. G
Missey, usually didn't mind <u>riding</u> in the car. **(6)** But one day, she 6. I
refused <u>to go</u>. **(7)** <u>Hiding</u> under the car was his way of avoiding the 7. G
trip. **(8)** As the woman tried to coax Missey out, she saw a car 8. Pt.
<u>coming</u> around the corner. **(9)** <u>Crashing</u> through a row of mailboxes, 9. N
it landed in the lake. **(10)** If the cat hadn't stopped his owner from 10. P
leaving, they would have been in the path of the <u>sinking</u> car.

B. Verbal Phrases   Answers in column.

Look at the cartoon on this page. Then write a sentence describing each of the seven "rescue animals" pictured. You can let your imagination run wild about what the animals are doing or are about to do. Use a variety of verbals and verbal phrases in your sentences.

Examples:
Bringing a pepperoni pizza to the rescue, the rhinoceros rang the doorbell.

The cow delivered a box of cereal *to go with her milk*.

The Far Side by Gary Larson

Some of our more common "rescue" animals

Mastery Test: What Did You Learn?

Choose the letter of the answer that correctly identifies each underlined item.

Bruno was a dog <u>living in Northern Ireland</u>. Having been injured
(1)
by an <u>exploding</u> car bomb, Bruno was frightened of explosives.
(2)
<u>Seeing some thugs with firecrackers near his backyard</u>, Bruno
(3)
barked furiously. One day his owner, Brian McMullan, <u>was working</u>
(4)
on his <u>damaged</u> car in the backyard. McMullan's one-year-old
(5)
daughter, Anne Marie, sat playing nearby. The thugs threw a
firecracker into the yard. When Anne Marie started <u>to reach</u> for it,
(6)
Bruno reacted by <u>jumping</u> in front of her. The firecracker exploded,
(7)
<u>sending Bruno to the ground</u>. Fearing that Bruno was dead,
(8)
McMullan rushed <u>to him</u>. Bruno was scarred, but he survived.
(9)
<u>Saving Anne Marie</u> made Bruno a hero.
(10)

1. A. gerund
   B. gerund phrase
   C. participle
   (D.) participial phrase

2. A. gerund
   (B.) present participle
   C. past participle
   D. infinitive

3. A. gerund
   B. gerund phrase
   C. participle
   (D.) participial phrase

4. A. gerund
   B. participle
   C. infinitive
   (D.) verb

5. A. gerund
   (B.) participle
   C. participial phrase
   D. infinitive

6. (A.) infinitive
   B. participle
   C. gerund
   D. gerund phrase

7. (A.) gerund
   B. participle
   C. infinitive
   D. verb

8. A. infinitive used as adjective
   B. infinitive phrase
   (C.) participial phrase
   D. verb

9. A. infinitive
   B. gerund phrase
   C. participle
   (D.) prepositional phrase

10. (A.) gerund phrase
    B. verb
    C. participial phrase
    D. infinitive phrase

VERBALS

Mastery Test

As an option, two other Chapter Mastery Tests appear in **Assessment Masters,** pp. 71–74.

Answers circled on page.

PRESCRIPTION FOR MASTERY	
If students miss item number:	Use **Teaching Resources** and **Skills Practice** for lesson:
1, 3, 8	❹ Verbal Phrases p. 176
2, 4, 5	❷ Participles p. 172
6, 9	❸ Infinitives p. 174
7, 10	❶ Gerunds p. 170

VERBALS

Student Help Desk

Students can use the Student Help Desk review or prior to testing or as a quick reference as they revise a piece of writing.

Teacher's Notes

WHAT WORKS:

Student Help Desk

Verbals and Verbal Phrases at a Glance

Kind of Verbal	Job	Example
Gerund Phrase	Noun	**Rescuing** hikers is the job of Saint Bernards.
Participial Phrase	Adjective	These dogs, carefully **trained,** brave storms.
Infinitive Phrase	Noun	They have been taught **to search** thoroughly.
	Adjective	They are the dogs **to trust.**
	Adverb	They are always quick **to respond.**

Gerund, Participle, or Verb?   Lending a Hand

	Example	Clue
Gerund	**Swimming** was Sue's only hope for survival.	Could be replaced by a noun
Participle	Her **swimming** movements attracted a sea turtle.	Could be replaced by an adjective
Verb	The turtle that **was swimming** next to her helped her stay afloat.	Always preceded by a helping verb

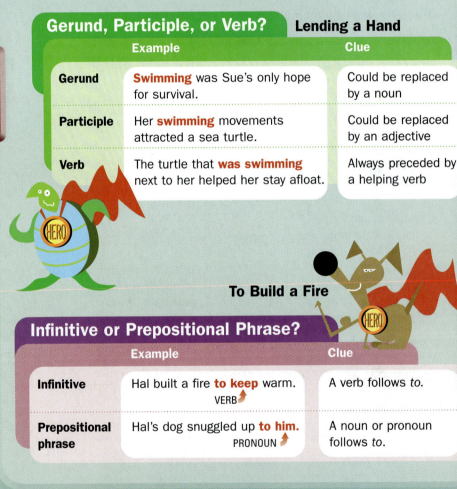

To Build a Fire

Infinitive or Prepositional Phrase?

	Example	Clue
Infinitive	Hal built a fire **to keep** warm. VERB	A verb follows *to.*
Prepositional phrase	Hal's dog snuggled up **to him.** PRONOUN	A noun or pronoun follows *to.*

To Serve and Protect

Infinitive Phrases

Noun

SUBJECT

To own a parrot was Joan's dream.

PREDICATE NOUN

The parrot's favorite activity was **to talk.**

DIRECT OBJECT

Soon, the parrot began **to imitate** voices heard on television.

Adjective

Once, an intruder thought the bird was something **to fear.**

Adverb

For the burglar, the bird's sounds became too strange **to bear.**

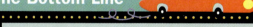

The Bottom Line

Checklist for Verbals and Verbal Phrases

Have I . . .

____ used gerund phrases to express actions?

____ used participial phrases to modify nouns and pronouns?

____ understood the functions of different kinds of words that end in *ing*?

____ understood the difference between infinitives and prepositional phrases beginning with *to*?

____ used infinitive phrases as nouns, adjectives, and adverbs?

____ used verbals and verbal phrases to add fluency and excitement to my writing?

Verbals and Verbal Phrases **183**

Teacher's Notes
WHAT DOESN'T WORK:

TEACHER'S LOUNGE

A Slice of Life

Baked Portobello Mushrooms

portobello mushroom caps
olive oil
balsamic vinegar
garlic powder
salt and pepper

Clean mushroom caps carefully. Place them on a baking tray or dish. Drizzle with olive oil and vinegar. Sprinkle with garlic, salt, and pepper to taste. Bake at 350° for 10 to 12 minutes or until tender.

Brain Break

Most Living Generations in One Family
Augusta Bunge of Wisconsin became a great-great-great-great grandmother on January 21, 1989, when her great-great-great granddaughter gave birth to a son. Augusta was born in 1879.

Sentence Structure

CHAPTER OVERVIEW

CHAPTER 8

CHAPTER RESOURCES

 Time-Saver Transparencies Binder:
- Daily Test Preparation pp. DT25–27
- Visual Grammar™ Tiles Lessons 11–13

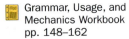 Grammar, Usage, and Mechanics Workbook pp. 148–162

Integrated Technology and Media

 Electronic Teacher Tools CD-ROM

 Grammar Coach CD-ROM Lesson 3

 mcdougallittell.com

Assessment

 Assessment Masters:
- Chapter Pretest pp. 16–17
- Chapter Mid-point Test p. 31
- Chapter Mastery Tests pp. 75–78

 Test Generator CD-ROM

 mcdougallittell.com Grammar Chapter Quiz

Sentence Structure

Mei and Sarah,
Here are your jobs for the Service Club project. Thanks for your help.
✓ Water the shrubs.
Plant flowers.
Also the bulbs.
Paint the jungle gym.
✓ To protect the wood.

Theme: Get Involved

Give It a Try

Have you ever gotten incomplete or confusing directions? Then you might understand why these volunteers were frustrated by their "to do" list. Often you can use compound and complex sentences to communicate clearly. What clear directions can you build from the sentences and fragments in the list?

Write Away: No Big Deal

It's not always a big deal to help other people or improve the environment. However, little things can mean a lot. Write about a time when someone did a small thing that helped you. Put your writing in your 🗂 **Working Portfolio.**

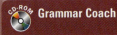 **Grammar Coach**

184

Diagnostic Test: What Do You Know?

Choose the letter that correctly identifies each underlined section.

There are many ways to volunteer, <u>since there are so many</u>
<u>worthy causes</u>. <u>Right now young people are feeding the homeless</u>.
            (1)
They are also working as assistant camp counselors for needy
children, <u>and they are restoring the environment</u>. <u>Although</u> these
                (3)   (4)
ways of volunteering sound very different, <u>each reflects a desire to</u>
                                            (5)
<u>serve others</u>. People <u>who volunteer</u> not only help those in need, but
                        (6)
they help themselves as well. <u>Whatever these people choose to do</u>,
                               (7)
<u>volunteering can make them feel good, and it can change their</u>
                                (8)
<u>outlook on life</u>. It can give them exciting experiences <u>that they</u>
<u>would not have otherwise</u>. <u>Because volunteering can be a lot of</u>
       (9)   (10)
<u>fun</u>, many people work long and hard for their favorite causes.

1. A. independent clause
   (B.) dependent clause
   C. compound sentence
   D. simple sentence

2. (A.) independent clause
   B. dependent clause
   C. compound sentence
   D. complex sentence

3. (A.) part of a compound sentence
   B. sentence fragment
   C. part of a complex sentence
   D. simple sentence

4. A. coordinating conjunction
   (B.) subordinating conjunction
   C. adverb clause
   D. relative pronoun

5. (A.) independent clause
   B. dependent clause
   C. compound sentence
   D. simple sentence

6. A. noun clause
   (B.) adjective clause
   C. adverb clause
   D. independent clause

7. A. coordinating conjunction
   B. subordinating conjunction
   C. relative pronoun
   (D.) independent clause

8. A. simple sentence
   B. compound sentence
   C. complex sentence
   (D.) compound-complex sentence

9. A. noun clause
   (B.) adjective clause
   C. adverb clause
   D. independent clause

10. A. noun clause
    B. adjective clause
    (C.) adverb clause
    D. independent clause

Diagnostic Test

As an option, a Chapter Pretest appears in
▣ **Assessment Masters** pp. 16–17.

Answers circled on page.

Use the chart below to determine which lessons students need

PRESCRIPTION FOR SUCCESS	
If students miss item number:	**Work on lesson:**
1, 2, 5, 7	❶ What Is a Clause? p. 186
3	❷ Simple and Compound Sentences p. 189
4, 6, 9, 10	❹ Kinds of Dependent Clauses p. 194
8	❺ Compound-Complex Sentences p. 198

The **Diagnostic Test** parallels the **Mastery Test** on page 203. Have students keep the test in their portfolio to compare with their results on the **Mastery Test**.

BLOCK SCHEDULING

Pressed for Time?
Review **Lesson 2, 3, and 4.** Have students complete **Here's the Idea** and **Practice and Apply** and **Concept Check** only, for those lessons.

Time for More?
After working through the chapter have students write sentences that could be used as models in the "Sentence Structure at a Glance" chart in the **Student Help Desk.** Ask students to write sentences about a time when they got involved in something.

LESSON OBJECTIVES

To recognize and use independent and dependent clauses in writing

DAILY TEST PREPARATION

Definition: Vocabulary Write the following item on the board or use 📗 **Daily Test Preparation Transparency** p. DT25.
Choose the word that means the same, or about the same, as the underlined word.

> Dad agreed that the next time he borrows your bicycle, he will return it in good <u>repair</u>.

A. appearance

B. figure

C. condition

D. form

Teaching Point: For vocabulary questions, use context clues to decipher the meaning of the underlined word. When used as a noun, *repair* refers to the *condition* of something.

CUSTOMIZING TIP

Less Proficient Learners Some students may assume that the independent clause always precedes the dependent clause. Explain that a dependent clause can come first. Write the following example on the board and have students identify the dependent clause and the independent clause:
Because she was hungry, DC
Anna headed for the kitchen. IC

Also suitable for:

Students Acquiring English/ESL

What Is a Clause?

LESSON 1

❶ Here's the Idea

▶ **A clause is a group of words that contains a subject and a verb.** For example, the following sentence contains two clauses.

SUBJECT↴ ↰VERB
Some students work in the food pantry
because they care about helping hungry people.
SUBJECT↴ ↰VERB

There are two kinds of clauses, independent and dependent.

Independent and Dependent Clauses

▶ **An independent clause expresses a complete thought and can stand alone as a sentence.**

> **Some students work in the food pantry**
> INDEPENDENT CLAUSE

▶ **A dependent clause does not express a complete thought and cannot stand alone as a sentence.** Most dependent clauses are introduced by words like *because, when, if, while,* and *that.*

> **because they care about helping hungry people**
> DEPENDENT CLAUSE

A dependent clause can be joined to an independent clause to add to the complete thought that the independent clauses expresses.

> **Some students work in the food pantry because they care about helping hungry people.**

> **Students also make bag lunches that are distributed at a shelter.**

186 Grammar, Usage, and Mechanics

TEACHING RESOURCES

 Time-Saver Transparencies Binder:
• Daily Test Preparation p. DT25
 Grammar, Usage, and Mechanics Workbook p. 148

SKILLS PRACTICE RESOURCES

 Grammar, Usage, and Mechanics Workbook pp. 149–150
Pupil's Edition Exercise Bank p. 609

Dependent clauses are also known as **subordinate clauses.** These clauses cannot stand alone and are dependent on the main clause.

❷ Why It Matters in Writing

By itself, a dependent clause is a sentence fragment. Notice how connecting the dependent clause to the preceding sentence in the model below makes a sentence that expresses a complete thought.

STUDENT MODEL

Students will organize a coat-and-hat drive this winter. Because homeless people often do not have warm clothes.

> INDEPENDENT CLAUSE
> DEPENDENT CLAUSE

❸ Practice and Apply

A. CONCEPT CHECK: What Is a Clause?

Identify each underlined group of words as an independent clause or a dependent clause.

Helping People Who Are Homeless

1. When Amber Lynn Coffman was only nine years old, she wrote a book report about a biography of Mother Teresa. **DC**

2. The book inspired her to volunteer at a shelter for the homeless when she was ten years old. **DC**

3. Because Amber wanted to do more, she started an organization. **DC**

4. Amber and 14 other student volunteers prepared 600 bag lunches each week. **IC**

5. They did this so that homeless people in their town of Glen Burnie, Maryland, could have a good meal. **IC**

Answers

Print-Out Option You may create worksheets of exercise B for your students by using the 💿 **Electronic Teacher Tools CD–ROM.**

B. EDITING

Answers may vary. Underlining indicates how fragments have been corrected.

My friend Cara had a great idea for her last birthday party. She made it a "wish list" party<u>, so that homeless people could get some of the items they needed</u>. Cara called a shelter to get a wish list. <u>When she sent out her invitations, she</u> sent along copies of the list. Cara asked her friends to bring things from the list instead of gifts. <u>While we had fun at her party, we</u> were also helping others.

C. WRITING

Answers will vary, but each student should write a complete sentence using at least one independent clause and one dependent clause.

---

6. <u>While Amber prepared lunches each week</u>, she thought about doing something special for the holiday season.
7. <u>She organized a huge gift drive</u>, which was very successful.
8. People donated small, useful gifts <u>that were wrapped by volunteers</u>.
9. <u>Amber's work inspired other students around the country</u> because they saw the power of one student to help others.
10. <u>Now Amber's organization exists in about 30 states</u>, and her efforts have been recognized nationally.

➡️ For a SELF-CHECK and more practice, see the EXERCISE BANK, p. 609.

B. EDITING: Fixing Fragments Answers in column.

Read the following first draft of a student's paragraph. Rewrite the paragraph to eliminate sentence fragments. Combine dependent clauses with independent clauses.

STUDENT MODEL

My friend Cara had a great idea for her last birthday party. She made it a "wish list" party. So that homeless people could get some of the items they needed. Cara called a shelter to get a wish list. When she sent out her invitations. She sent along copies of the list. Cara asked her friends to bring things from the list instead of gifts. While we had fun at her party. We were also helping others.

C. WRITING: Creating a Caption Answers in column.

This photograph shows Amber Lynn Coffman and some of her fellow volunteers at work. On a separate sheet of paper, write a caption for the photo, describing what is happening. Use at least one independent clause and one dependent clause.

Simple and Compound Sentences

① Here's the Idea

Simple Sentences

▶ **A simple sentence contains one independent clause and no dependent clauses.** Remember that even a simple sentence can be quite elaborate. Each of the following sentences has only a single independent clause.

> **Shawn tutors.**
> INDEPENDENT CLAUSE

> **Benita teaches young children acrobatics after school.**

Compound Sentences

▶ **A compound sentence contains two or more independent clauses and no dependent clauses.** The clauses in a compound sentence must be closely related in thought.

> **Shawn tutors,** and **he helps students learn math.**
> INDEPENDENT CLAUSE   INDEPENDENT CLAUSE

Independent clauses can be joined by a comma and a coordinating conjunction or by a semicolon.

> **Some children have no books, and volunteers can hold book drives for them.**

> **Some children have no toys; volunteers can collect donated toys for them.**

Coordinating Conjunctions
for   and   nor   or   but   so   yet

Don't mistake a simple sentence with a compound predicate for a compound sentence. No punctuation should separate the parts of a compound predicate.

> **The Newcomers' Club wrote a clever script, and then filmed it.**

189

DAILY TEST PREPARATION

Error Identification: Punctuation
Write the following item on the board or use 📖 **Daily Test Preparation Transparency** p. DT26.
Decide which type of error, if any, appears in the underlined section.

> Philanthropy benefits every-
> one and it stems from a
> universal love of humankind.

A. Spelling error

B. Capitalization error

C. Punctuation error

D. No error

Teaching Point: Error identification questions often test your knowledge of basic punctuation rules. This item tests whether you know to place a comma before a conjunction (such as *and*) that joins two independent clauses in a compound sentence.

CUSTOMIZING TIP

Gifted and Talented Ask students why a writer might want to substitute a semicolon for a comma and coordinating conjunction in a compound sentence. Possible responses: for sentence variety; for an added pause; for dramatic effect; or for added contrast or balance between two similar clauses.

TEACHING RESOURCES

 Time-Saver Transparencies Binder:
• Daily Test Preparation p. DT26
• Visual Grammar™ Tiles Lesson 11
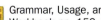 Grammar, Usage, and Mechanics Workbook p. 151

SKILLS PRACTICE RESOURCES

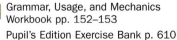 Grammar, Usage, and Mechanics Workbook pp. 152–153
Pupil's Edition Exercise Bank p. 610

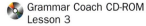 Grammar Coach CD-ROM Lesson 3

② Why It Matters in Writing

You can avoid short, choppy sentences in your writing by using compound sentences. Notice how the writer of the model below combined related ideas to form compound sentences.

STUDENT MODEL

The park in my neighborhood has a lot of garbage all over the place. My friends and I want to clean it up. *so* We wrote to the park district for permission. We just got the OK. *and* We can start this weekend.

Related thoughts combined

③ Practice and Apply

A. CONCEPT CHECK: Simple and Compound Sentences

Identify each sentence as simple or compound.

Help for a Little Girl

1. The vice-principal of Alex Moore's school had a 16-month-old daughter with leukemia.
2. Alex wanted to help; he started making arrangements for a benefit auction to raise money for the girl's treatment.
3. Alex's younger brother, Cameron, and two other friends also became interested in the benefit. **SS**
4. They would charge people for a dinner and hold the auction at the dinner. **SS**
5. The group continued planning the benefit, but not many people would buy the $25 tickets for the dinner. **C**
6. Cameron, a fifth grader, had an idea. **SS**
7. They should get Mark Eaton of the Utah Jazz basketball team at the dinner. **SS**
8. Mark Eaton lived in their hometown—Park City, Utah—and he was happy to help them out. **CD**
9. The boys called 80 sponsors, and all contributed goods. ●

190 Grammar, Usage, and Mechanics

Answers

Print-Out Option You may create worksheets of exercise A for your students by using the ◉ **Electronic Teacher Tools CD–ROM.**

A. CONCEPT CHECK

Self-Check For a self-check of simple and compound sentences, direct students to p. 610 in the Pupil's Edition for the answers to the items circled in yellow.

Answers shown on page using these codes:

SS = simple sentence

CD = compound sentence

Spice it Up!

Write the following sentence on the board: The Martians conquered America and the President and the First Lady managed to survive. Ask students: Did the Martians conquer America and the President? Or did the President and the First Lady manage to survive? Have students place the comma where they think it belongs. Point out how correct comma placement can prevent misunderstanding or confusion.

10. More than 200 people bought tickets to the benefit, so the group raised several thousand dollars. **CD**

→ **For a SELF-CHECK and more practice, see the EXERCISE BANK, p. 610.**

B. REVISING: Combining Sentences   Answers in column.

Combine each pair of sentences to form a compound sentence, using one of the coordinating conjunctions *and, but, for, or, nor, so,* and *yet.* Remember to use a comma before the coordinating conjunction.

Helping Out During a Hurricane

1. Tropical storms often hit Florida. People from this state know how to prepare.
2. Windows are easily broken by fierce winds. The people cover them with plywood.
3. Not only do they board up windows in their own homes. They volunteer to help their neighbors board up too.
4. Volunteers also put sandbags around buildings near the shore. The bags help prevent damage from high waves.
5. Schools are shut down. County and state offices are closed.
6. People on low-lying islands near the shore may need to evacuate. They can go to emergency shelters.
7. Volunteers at the shelters help prepare food. They organize games and other activities for children.
8. After a hurricane there may be a lot of damage to homes. Fallen trees and other debris may be scattered about.
9. Volunteers repair buildings. They also clean up.
10. A hurricane is a great trial for a community. It can awaken the community's volunteer spirit.

📁 **Working Portfolio** Reread what you wrote for the **Write Away** on page 189. Check to see if any short sentences can be combined to form compound sentences.

Sentence Structure **191**

B. REVISING

Answers will vary. Possible responses are given. Added conjunctions are printed in boldface type.

1. Tropical storms often hit Florida, **but** people from this state know how to prepare.

2. Windows are easily broken by fierce winds, **so** the people cover them with plywood.

3. Not only do they board up windows in their own homes, **but** they volunteer to help their neighbors board up too.

4. Volunteers also put sandbags around buildings near the shore, **for** the bags help prevent damage from high waves.

5. Schools are shut down, **and** county and state offices are closed.

6. People on low-lying islands near the shore may need to evacuate, **but** they can go to emergency shelters.

7. Volunteers at the shelters help prepare food, **and** they organize games and other activities for children.

8. After a hurricane there may be a lot of damage to homes, **and** fallen trees and other debris may be scattered about.

9. Volunteers repair buildings, **and** they also clean up.

10. A hurricane is a great trial for a community, **yet** it can awaken the community's volunteer spirit.

Visual Grammar™
Use **Visual Grammar™ Tiles Lesson 11** and **Sentence I** to show how to classify sentences. Continue with this lesson to teach complex and compound-complex sentences. Here is part of Lesson 11.

Simple sentence:

THE CROWD CHEERED .

Compound sentence:

THE CROWD CHEERED ,

AND THE TEAM PUSHED FORWARD .

LESSON OBJECTIVES

To recognize and use complex sentences in writing

DAILY TEST PREPARATION

Error Correction: Subject-Verb Agreement Write the following item on the board or use **Daily Test Preparation Transparency** p. DT26. Choose the best way to write the underlined part of the sentence.

> The suddeness of the discoveries <u>have convinced</u> him to retrace his steps.

A. convincing

B. having convinced

C. has convinced

D. *(No change)*

Teaching Point: A common spelling item in error correction questions is subject-verb agreement. In this case, the subject *suddenness* takes a singular verb (*has convinced*).

STUDENT MODEL

Have students rewrite the following paragraph, forming complex sentences where possible.

Andy was walking down Main Street. A scary thing happened. Mr. Johnson ran into the street. Mr. Johnson is a candy store owner. A fire had started in his store. A faulty wire had caused it.

Possible answer: A scary thing happened as Andy was walking down the street. Mr. Johnson, the candy store owner, ran into the street because a faulty wire had started a fire in his store.

LESSON 3

Complex Sentences

CHAPTER 8

❶ Here's the Idea

▶ **A complex sentence contains one independent clause and one or more dependent clauses.**

Most dependent clauses start with words like *when, until, who, where, because,* and *so that.* Such a clause might tell when something happened, which person was involved, or where the event took place.

DEPENDENT CLAUSE   INDEPENDENT CLAUSE

When we visited, **Mrs. Brodsky shared her memories of working in a shipyard during World War II.**

Mr. Ruiz was a photographer **until he was drafted.**

Mr. Liuzzo, **who is a retired pilot,** **talked to us about his experiences in enemy territory,** **where he was a prisoner of war.**

❷ Why It Matters in Writing

You can use complex sentences to clarify relationships between ideas. First read the passage below without the changes. Then read it as it has been revised. Notice how the revisions clarify why Nick does what he does.

STUDENT MODEL

My friend Nick really enjoys visiting people at the Pines Nursing Home. They *because* have many moving stories of life in our town during World War II. Nick records *so that he can share* their memories. ~~He shares~~ them with his social studies class.

> Tells why Nick enjoys visiting

> Tells why he records memories

TEACHING RESOURCES

 Time-Saver Transparencies Binder:
- Daily Test Preparation p. DT26
- Visual Grammar™ Tiles Lesson 11

Grammar, Usage, and Mechanics Workbook p. 154

SKILLS PRACTICE RESOURCES

 Grammar, Usage, and Mechanics Workbook pp. 155–156

Pupil's Edition Exercise Bank p. 610

③ Practice and Apply

A. CONCEPT CHECK: Complex Sentences

Write these sentences on a sheet of paper. Underline each independent clause once and each dependent clause twice.

Foster Grandparents

1. Although the Foster Grandparent Program is more than 30 years old, many people do not know about it.
2. This program was established so that hospitalized and institutionalized children could get special attention.
3. Anyone can volunteer who is at least 60 years old and meets other requirements.
4. After a volunteer is trained, he or she is assigned two children.
5. Because foster grandparents need to get to know their "grandchildren," they visit the children each day.
6. These daily visits last for two hours so that the children can get careful attention from their foster grandparents.
7. Although foster grandparents are volunteers, they are paid.
8. They also receive travel expenses while they serve.
9. Since this government program was founded in 1965, there have been foster grandparent projects in all 50 states.
10. Because more than 16,000 volunteers have been involved, more than 30,000 children have benefited.

➡ For a SELF-CHECK and more practice, see the EXERCISE BANK, p. 610.

B. REVISING: Varying Sentence Structure   Answers in column.

Rewrite the following paragraph to make the ideas clearer. Combine simple sentences 1 and 2 to make a complex sentence. Do the same with sentences 4 and 5.

STUDENT MODEL

(1) Some retired people enjoy tutoring students in reading or math. (2) Retired people contribute their talents to their community. (3) Volunteers run homework centers after school. (4) They also maintain homework hot lines. (5) Students can get help with questions they have.

Sentence Structure **193**

Answers

Print-Out Option You may create worksheets of exercises A and B for your students by using the 💿 **Electronic Teacher Tools CD–ROM.**

A. CONCEPT CHECK

Self-Check For a self-check of complex sentences, direct students to p. 610 in the Pupil's Edition for the answers to the items circled in yellow.

Answers shown on page. Independent clauses are underlined once. Dependent clauses are underlined twice.

B. REVISING

Answers will vary depending on the conjunction chosen, but a revision might read as follows:

Some retired people enjoy tutoring students in reading or math because they like to contribute their talents to their community. Volunteers run homework centers after school. They also maintain homework hotlines, so students can get help with questions they have.

ASSESSMENT

📒 Assessment Masters:
  • Chapter Mid-point Test p. 31

 Visual Grammar™
Use **Visual Grammar Tiles Lesson 11** and **Sentence I** to show how to classify sentences. Continue with this lesson to teach complex and compound-complex sentences. Here is part of Lesson 11.

Simple sentence:

THE CROWD CHEERED .

Compound sentence:

THE CROWD CHEERED ,

AND THE TEAM PUSHED FORWARD .

DAILY TEST PREPARATION

Error Correction: Punctuation
Write the following item on the board or use **Daily Test Preparation Transparency** p. DT27.

> I didnt expect to win the race, but it feels great!

How is this sentence best written?

A. I didn't expect to win the race; but it feels great!

B. I didn't expect to win the race, but it feels great!

C. I did'nt expect to win the race. But it feels great!

D. As it is

Teaching Point: A common punctuation item in error correction questions is the omission of an apostrophe in a contraction. An apostrophe shows where letters are omitted in a contraction: *didn't=did not.* Answer A can be ruled out because it creates a sentence fragment.

TEACHING TIP

Review with students the correct uses of *who, whom,* and *whose. Who* is used as the subject of a verb or as a predicate pronoun; *whom,* is used as the object of a verb or preposition; and *whose* is used to show possession.

CHAPTER 8

LESSON 4

Kinds of Dependent Clauses

CHAPTER 8

❶ Here's the Idea

Adjective Clauses

▶ **An adjective clause is a dependent clause used as an adjective.** An adjective clause modifies a noun or a pronoun. It tells what kind, which one, how many, or how much.

Student volunteers read stories to the
MODIFIES NOUN
children **who were in the daycare center.**
ADJECTIVE CLAUSE

Adjective clauses are usually introduced by relative pronouns.

Relative Pronouns
who   whom   whose   that   which

The story, **which made them laugh,** is about a monkey.

Notice that a clause that begins with *which* is set off with commas.

Adverb Clauses

▶ **An adverb clause is a dependent clause used as an adverb.** It modifies a verb, an adjective, or an adverb. An adverb clause might tell where, when, how, why, to what extent, or under what conditions.

Adverb clauses are introduced by subordinating conjunctions such as *if, because, even though, than, so that, while, where, when, as if,* and *since.*
MODIFIES ADJECTIVE
They were happy **because they were going to the zoo.**
ADVERB CLAUSE

194   Grammar, Usage, and Mechanics

TEACHING RESOURCES

 Time-Saver Transparencies Binder:
- Daily Test Preparation p. DT27
- Visual Grammar™ Tiles Lessons 12–13

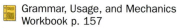 Grammar, Usage, and Mechanics Workbook p. 157

SKILLS PRACTICE RESOURCES

 Grammar, Usage, and Mechanics Workbook pp. 158–159

Pupil's Edition Exercise Bank p. 611

MODIFIES ADVERB

The zoo closed earlier than they expected.

An adverb clause should be followed by a comma when it comes before an independent clause. When an adverb clause comes after an independent clause, a comma may or may not be needed before it.

> **When the field trip ended, the volunteers took the children back to the daycare center.**

> **The volunteers took the children back to the daycare center when the field trip ended.**

For more about adjectives and adverbs, see Chapter 5, pp. 124–149.

Noun Clauses

▶ **A noun clause is a dependent clause used as a noun.**

Like a noun, a noun clause can serve as a subject, a direct object, an indirect object, an object of a preposition, or a predicate noun. In the caption below, the noun clause is the subject of the sentence.

What frustrates many physically challenged people is the problem of getting around.

TEACHING TIP

Cooperative Learning Have students form small groups to discuss the various ways adverb clauses are used in sentences. Group members are expected to monitor their own understanding of the discussion, seek clarification as needed, and compare their own perception of a spoken message with the perception of others in their group. Write the following independent clauses on the board: *We became sleepy.* Ask groups to generate different adverb clauses that could be added to the independent clause to answer *where, when, how, why, to what extent,* and *under what conditions.*

SENTENCES

SENTENCES

 Visual Grammar™
Use **Visual Grammar™ Tiles Lessons 12–13** and **Sentence J** to teach about clauses. Here is part of Lesson 12.

Decide whether this is an independent or dependent clause.

THEY SAW A FOX

Add a dependent clause and determine which word it modifies.

THEY SAW A FOX **WHEN** **THEY WERE HIKING** **.**

CHAPTER 8

THE LANGUAGE OF
LITERATURE

The passage on the student page is from "A Crush" in *The Language of Literature*, Level 7.

Volunteers know <mark>that physically challenged people do not want special treatment.</mark>
NOUN CLAUSE SERVING AS DIRECT OBJECT

NOUN CLAUSE SERVING AS INDIRECT OBJECT
Christopher will tell <mark>whoever</mark> is volunteering the locations of the elevators.

Noun clauses are introduced by words such as those shown the following chart.

Words That Introduce Noun Clauses				
that	how	when	where	whether
why	what	whatever	who	whom
whoever	whomever	which	whichever	

If you can substitute the word *something* or *someone* for a clause in a sentence, it is a noun clause. (Volunteers know *something*. Christopher will tell *someone*.)
For more about nouns, see Chapter 2, pp. 34–55.

② Why It Matters in Writing

You can use dependent clauses to add detail to your writing. They allow you to express important ideas in a few words.

> **LITERARY MODEL**
>
> One of the young men who worked at the group home—a college student named Jack—grew a large garden in the back of the house . . . .
>
> Jack tried to explain to Ernie that the seeds would grow into vegetables, but Ernie could not believe this until he saw it come true.
>
> —Cynthia Rylant, "A Crush"

Adjective claus[e] tells which young men.

Noun clause tells what Jack tried to explain.

Adverb clause tells when Erni[e] could believe.

3 Practice and Apply

A. CONCEPT CHECK: Kinds of Dependent Clauses

Write these sentences on a sheet of paper. Underline each dependent clause, and identify it as an adjective clause, an adverb clause, or a noun clause.

Raising a Guide Dog
1. Some people <u>who are visually challenged</u> have guide dogs. **Adj. C**
2. These dogs are important <u>because they help the people get around in daily life</u>. **Adv. C**
3. A guide dog <u>that completes its training</u> can lead a visually challenged person across busy streets. **Adj. C**
4. In fact, a visually challenged person can handle most traveling situations <u>if a guide dog is with him or her</u>. **Adv. C**
5. There are organizations <u>that raise puppies to be guide dogs</u>. **Adj. C**
6. Each puppy is given to a family who cares for it for a year.
7. They treat the puppy as <u>if it were their own</u>. **Adj. C**
8. <u>When the year is over</u>, they give the dog back for special training. **Adv. C**
9. All family members know <u>why the dog must leave</u>. **NC**
10. They realize <u>that the dog will become a visually challenged person's constant companion</u>. **NC**

➡ For a SELF-CHECK and more practice, see the EXERCISE BANK, p. 611.

B. WRITING: Using Clauses   Answers in column.

Complete the sentence below by adding clauses of the types indicated in parentheses.

> **(1)** Some students (adjective clause) volunteer at animal shelters. **(2)** They help take care of dogs and cats (adverb clause). **(3)** (noun clause) is appreciated by animal lovers everywhere.

Sentence Structure **197**

Answers

Print-Out Option You may create worksheets of exercises A and B for your students by using the 💿 **Electronic Teacher Tools CD–ROM.**

A. CONCEPT CHECK

Self-Check For a self-check of dependent clauses, direct students to p. 611 in the Pupil's Edition for the answers to the items circled in yellow.

Answers shown on page. Dependent clauses are underlined. They are identified using these codes:

Adj. C = adjective clause

Adv. C = adverb clause

NC = noun clause

B. WRITING

Answers will vary, but a completed paragraph with appropriate clauses might read as follows:

Some students **who love animals** volunteer at animal shelters. They help take care of dogs and cats **when the animals first arrive at the shelters. Whatever these student volunteers can do** is appreciated by animal lovers everywhere.

LESSON OBJECTIVES

To recognize and use compound-complex sentences in writing

DAILY TEST PREPARATION

Sentence Completion:
Vocabulary Write the following item on the board or use
📖 **Daily Test Preparation Transparency** p. DT27.
Choose the word that *best* fits the meaning of the sentence.

Dictionaries allow the reader to trace a word's origin by listing its _____.

A. etymology

B. eulogy

C. analogy

D. etymologize

Teaching Point: For sentence completion questions, the correct answers will always

• fit the meaning of the sentence (*eulogy* and *analogy* are not related to *a word's origin*).

• fit grammatically within the sentence (answer D does not).

TEACHING TIP

Cross-Curricular Connection
Science Tell students that they should use compound-complex sentences when they write about complicated scientific events or ideas. Point out this type of sentence structure can help clarify relationships.

THE LANGUAGE OF
LITERATURE
The passage on the student page is from "The Serial Garden" in *The Language of Literature,* Level 7.

LESSON 5

Compound-Complex Sentences

❶ Here's the Idea

▶ **A compound-complex sentence contains two or more independent clauses and one or more dependent clauses.**

DEPENDENT CLAUSE   INDEPENDENT CLAUSE
When our school celebrates Earth Day, we sign up for environmental projects, and we try to complete them all in one day.
                                        INDEPENDENT CLAUSE

Students have cleaned up the beaches, and they have planted flowers in the parks so that the shore looks inviting to visitors.

❷ Why It Matters in Writing

You can use compound-complex sentences in your writing to show complicated relationships between events and ideas. Notice how Joan Aiken used such sentences in a detailed description of what a boy sees in a magical garden.

> **LITERARY MODEL**
>
> The gate grew again above him, and when he opened it and ran across the lawn through the yew arch, he found himself in a flagged garden full of flowers like huge blue cabbages. . . .
>
> The orchard was most wonderful, for instead of mere apples its trees bore oranges, lemons, limes and all sorts of tropical fruits whose names he did not know, and there were melons and pineapples growing, and plantains and avocados.
>
> —Joan Aiken, "The Serial Garden"

INDEPENDENT CLAUSES

DEPENDENT CLAUSES

198 Grammar, Usage, and Mechanics

TEACHING RESOURCES

Time-Saver Transparencies Binder:
• Daily Test Preparation p. DT27
• Visual Grammar™ Tiles Lessons 11

Grammar, Usage, and Mechanics Workbook p. 160

SKILLS PRACTICE RESOURCES

Grammar, Usage, and Mechanics Workbook pp. 161–162
Pupil's Edition Exercise Bank p. 611

❸ Practice and Apply

A. CONCEPT CHECK: Compound-Complex Sentences

Identify each sentence as compound, complex, or compound-complex.

Helping Disaster Victims

1. In 1998 a hurricane swept through Central America, where it hit Honduras and Nicaragua especially hard. **CX**
2. Hurricane Mitch was one of the strongest storms ever in this region; it caused great destruction. **CD**
3. People on the coast tried to flee to higher ground, but flooding and mudslides made escape difficult. **CD**
4. More than 9,000 people were killed, and crops and roads were wiped out. **CD**
5. TV images of homeless and hungry people touched many Americans, who responded generously. **CX**
6. They donated money and supplies, which were flown to the region. **CX**
7. Volunteers helped clear roads so that supplies could get to villages that needed them. **CX**
8. Charity groups distributed food and safe drinking water, and they handed out sleeping bags and mosquito nets, which were needed in the tropical climate. **CC**
9. Medical volunteers treated people who desperately needed care. **CX**
10. Other volunteers rebuilt homes, and they helped restore the farm economy so that people could earn a living again. **CC**

➔ **For a SELF-CHECK and more practice, see the EXERCISE BANK, p. 611.**

B. WRITING: Creating Compound-Complex Sentences   Answers in column.

Combine the following sentences to create a compound-complex sentence. Use *when* and *and* in your new sentence.

It rains. Rivers overflow. Neighborhoods near the rivers flood.

Answers

Print-Out Option You may create worksheets of exercises A and B for your students by using the 💿 **Electronic Teacher Tools CD–ROM.**

A CONCEPT CHECK

Self-Check For a self-check of compound-complex sentences, direct students to p. 611 in the Pupil's Edition for the answers to the items circled in yellow.

Answers shown on page using these codes:

CD = compound sentence

CX = complex sentence

CC = compound-complex sentence

B. WRITING

When it rains, rivers overflow, and neighborhoods near the rivers flood.

ASSESSMENT

📋 Assessment Masters:
   • Chapter Mastery Tests pp. 75–78

💿 Test Generator CD-ROM

↪ mcdougallittell.com Grammar Chapter Quiz

🖼 Visual Grammar™

Continue with **Visual Grammar™ Tiles Lesson 11** and **Sentence I** to show how to classify sentences. Here is the final part of Lesson 11.

Compound-complex sentence:

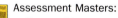

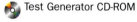

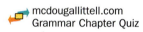

LESSON OBJECTIVES

To recognize and use compound and complex sentences in descriptive writing

TEACHING TIP

Speaking and Listening Have students close their books. Then read aloud the literary model. Have students listen for and identify the compound sentences in the literary model.

TEACHING TIP

Encourage students to search the Internet for more information about Eleanor Roosevelt. Ask volunteers to give brief oral presentations about the results of their research and to share the Internet addresses they visited.

THE LANGUAGE OF
LITERATURE

The passage on the student page is from an excerpt from *Eleanor Roosevelt* in *The Language of Literature*, Level 7.

Grammar in Literature

Using Compound and Complex Sentences

How do you write a description that allows you to create a vivid picture of a person? In the following excerpt, author William Jay Jacobs brings Eleanor Roosevelt to life by using compound and complex sentences. Such sentences allow him to vary the sentence structure and to add important details about Mrs. Roosevelt.

from

Eleanor Roosevelt
by William Jay Jacobs

After becoming interested in the problems of working women, she [Eleanor] gave time to the Women's Trade Union League (WTUL).... It was through the WTUL that she met a group of remarkable women... They awakened her hopes that something could be done to improve the condition the poor. ...

Eleanor helped the Red Cross raise money. She gave blood, sold war bonds. In 1943, for example, she visited barracks and hospitals on islands throughout the South Pacific. When she visited a hospital, she stopped at every bed. Often, after she left, even battle-hardened men had tears in their eyes....

In December 1945 President Harry S. Truman invited her to be one of the American delegates going to London to begin the work of the United Nations. Eleanor hesitated, but the president insisted. He said that the nation needed her; it was her duty.

COMPLEX SENTENCE with adjective clause explaining Eleanor's hopes.

COMPLEX SENTENCE with adverb clauses explains how Eleanor acted and how she was affected by her visits to the hospitals.

COMPOUND SENTENCE with coordinating conjunction explain who Eleanor came to her position at the United Nations.

200 Grammar, Usage, and Mechanics

Practice and Apply

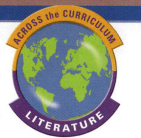

Using Clauses to Create Interesting Sentences

Follow the instructions below to revise this passage by creating compound and complex sentences that add variety and interest to the writing.

> (1) Eleanor Roosevelt had a very unhappy childhood. (2) She did enjoy visits to see her uncle, Theodore Roosevelt. (3) Uncle Ted would read to the children. (4) The children had a day of romping outside and swimming. (5) Hearing his stories was very comforting to Eleanor and the other children. (6) Today volunteers often read to children to comfort them. (7) Who are hospitalized. (8) The volunteers make sure they choose books that each child will understand. (9) They also choose books that are funny. (10) They leave the book with the sick child. Until the next time they come.

1. Combine sentences 1 and 2 to make a compound sentence. Use the conjunction **but** to join the sentences.
2. Combine sentences 3 and 4 into a complex sentence. Begin sentence 4 with the subordinating conjunction *after*.
3. Combine sentence 6 with fragment 7, which is an adjective clause, to make a complex sentence.
4. Combine sentences 8 and 9 to make a compound-complex sentence.
5. Combine sentence 10 with the adverb clause with the sentence to make a complex sentence.

You write it. Explain how your revisions affect the quality of the draft. Which version explains more about Eleanor's actions? Which version is easier to read? Put your paragraph in your 📁 **Working Portfolio.**

Answers

Practice and Apply

Using Clauses to Create Interesting Sentences

Answers will vary. The following is a sample answer:

Eleanor Roosevelt had a very unhappy childhood, but hse did enjoy visits to see her uncle, Theodore Roosevelt. After the children had a day or romping outside and swimming, Uncle Ted would read to them. Hearing his stories was very comforting to Eleanor and the other children. Today volunteers often read to children who are hospitalized to comfort them. The volunteers make sure they choose books that are funny and that each child will understand. They leave the book with the sick child until the next time they come.

You Write It

The revision is easier to read because the sentences are less choppy.

Mixed Review

Mixed Review

Answers

Print-Out Option You may create worksheets of exercises A and B for your students by using the 💿 **Electronic Teacher Tools CD–ROM.**

A. SENTENCE STRUCTURE

1. complex
2. adjective clause
3. simple
4. compound
5. and
6. simple
7. compound-complex
8. She struggled herself; she is thrilled
9. when she was in first grade; that she can help teach someone else
10. one adverb clause; one noun clause

B. COMBINING CLAUSES

Answers will vary, but a revision might read as follows:

Reading is Fundamental is a national organization that promotes literacy. Students who are interested can participate. They can teach adults who may not have had a chance to learn when they were young. After people learn to read, they lead more successful lives.

A. Sentence Structure Read the model about a student volunteer. Then write the answers to the questions below it. **Answers in column.**

> **LITERARY MODEL**
>
> **(1)** Rebecca is a seventh-grader who volunteers in a tutoring program for first-graders at her school. **(2)** The tutors in the program help the younger students with their reading. **(3)** They read stories to the students, and then the younger students read to the tutors. **(4)** Rebecca teaches her student Megan. **(5)** She struggled herself when she was in first grade, and she is thrilled that she can help teach someone else.
>
> —Martin McNamara

1. Is sentence 1 simple or complex?
2. Does sentence 1 have an adjective, adverb, or noun clause?
3. Is sentence 2 simple or complex?
4. Is sentence 3 compound or complex?
5. What is the coordinating conjunction in sentence 3?
6. Is sentence 4 simple or complex?
7. Is sentence 5 compound or compound-complex?
8. Name the independent clauses in sentence 5.
9. Name the dependent clauses in sentence 5.
10. Does sentence 5 have an adjective, adverb, or noun clause?

B. Combining Clauses Rewrite the following paragraph, combining clauses to eliminate sentence fragments and to connect related ideas. **Answers in column.**

Reading Is Fundamental is a national organization. It promotes literacy. Students can participate. Who are interested. They can teach adults. Who may not have had a chance to learn. When they were young. After people learn to read. They lead more successful lives.

Choose the letter of the term that correctly identifies each underlined section.

Do you know <u>that free "volunteer vacations" are available</u>
(1)
<u>through national and state parks</u>? The parks have many types of volunteer positions <u>that need to be filled</u>. <u>Although</u> some of the
(2)   (3)
 positions require experience, others do not, <u>and</u> newcomers are
(4)
 welcomed. <u>Volunteers have the chance to spend time in beautiful</u>
(5)
 <u>natural settings, and they can combine work with pleasure.</u> Their housing, <u>which</u> can be campsites, and their meals are usually
(6)
 provided <u>while they are volunteering</u>. <u>What benefits are available</u>
(7)   (8)
 depends on individual circumstances. <u>There is usually plenty of free</u> <u>time for volunteers to explore the parks on their own,</u> <u>so a volunteer</u>
(9)
 <u>vacation can be quite interesting.</u> Among the most popular parks are those in Alaska and Hawaii, <u>which often have waiting lists</u>.
(10)

1. A. independent clause
   B. dependent clause
   C. compound sentence
   D. simple sentence

2. A. adjective clause
   B. noun clause
   C. simple sentence
   D. adverb clause

3. A. subordinating conjunction
   B. coordinating conjunction
   C. relative pronoun
   D. noun clause

4. A. subordinating conjunction
   B. coordinating conjunction
   C. relative pronoun
   D. noun clause

5. A. simple sentence
   B. compound sentence
   C. complex sentence
   D. compound-complex sentence

6. A. relative pronoun
   B. adjective clause
   C. adverb clause
   D. independent clause

7. A. adjective clause
   B. adverb clause
   C. noun clause
   D. independent clause

8. A. noun clause
   B. adjective clause
   C. adverb clause
   D. independent clause

9. A. simple sentence
   B. compound sentence
   C. complex sentence
   D. sentence fragment

10. A. adjective clause
    B. adverb clause
    C. noun clause
    D. independent clause

SENTENCES

Mastery Test

As an option, two other Chapter Mastery Tests appear in ▦ **Assessment Masters,** pp. 75–78.

Answers circled on page.

PRESCRIPTION FOR MASTERY	
If students miss item number:	Use **Teaching Resources** and **Skills Practice Resources** for lesson:
1	❶ What is a Clause? p. 186
2, 3, 6, 7, 8, 10	❹ Kinds of Dependent Clauses p. 194
4, 5, 9	❷ Simple and Compound Sentence p. 189

SENTENCES

Students can use the Student Help Desk prior to testing or as a quick review or reference as they revise a piece of writing.

Teacher's Notes

WHAT WORKS:

Student Help Desk

Sentence Structure at a Glance

SIMPLE SENTENCE = independent clause
Olivia is running in a 5K race.

COMPOUND SENTENCE = independent clause + independent clause(s)
Nick is also running, but Greg isn't.

COMPLEX SENTENCE = independent clause + dependent clause(s)
Greg can't, because he is officiating.

COMPOUND–COMPLEX SENTENCE =
independent clauses + dependent clauses
Patti will find sponsors, and Jed will collect donations when we are ready.

Punctuating Compound and Complex Sentences

Join Up!

Use commas . . .	Example
to join independent clauses with coordinating conjunctions	She ran to the finish, **but** he dropped out.
after adverb clauses that begin sentences	After the race was over**,** they rested.
to set off adjective clauses that begin with *which*	His injury, **which was painful,** seemed rather severe.
Use semicolons . . .	
to join independent clauses without conjunctions	She was sympathetic**;** he was disappointed.

Help!

Avoiding Clause Confusion

Dependent Clause	Function	Example
Adjective clause	• modifies noun or pronoun • tells what kind, which one, how many, or how much	The **students** who participated enjoyed the race.
Adverb clause	• modifies verb, adjective, or adverb • tells where, when, how, why, to what extent, or under what conditions	They felt **proud** because they had done something worthwhile.
Noun clause	• acts as subject, direct object, indirect object, object of preposition, or predicate noun	What helps others can be rewarding for volunteers too.

The Bottom Line

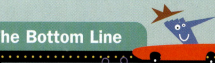

Checklist for Sentence Structure

Can I improve my writing by . . .

____ eliminating sentence fragments?

____ creating compound sentences to link closely related ideas?

____ using dependent clauses to show how ideas are related?

____ using dependent clauses to add details?

____ punctuating compound and complex sentences correctly?

Sentence Structure **205**

Teacher's Notes
WHAT DOESN'T WORK:

TEACHER'S LOUNGE

Just for Laughs

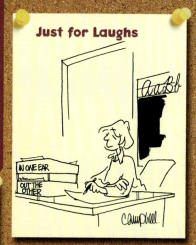

A Slice of Life

"The whole world opened to me when I learned to read."
—Mary McLeod Bethune

CHAPTER OVERVIEW

CHAPTER 9

CHAPTER RESOURCES

 Time-Saver Transparencies Binder:
- Daily Test Preparation pp. DT28–30
- Quick-Fix Grammar and Style Charts pp. QF3–4
- Visual Grammar™ Tiles Lessons 14–16

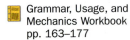 Grammar, Usage, and Mechanics Workbook pp. 163–177

Integrated Technology and Media

 Electronic Teacher Tools CD-ROM

 Grammar Coach CD-ROM Lessons 4–5

 Power Presentations CD-ROM Lessons 3

 mcdougallittell.com

Assessment

 Assessment Masters:
- Chapter Pretest pp. 18–19
- Chapter Mid-point Test p. 32
- Chapter Mastery Tests pp. 79–80

 Test Generator CD-ROM

 mcdougallittell.com Grammar Chapter Quiz

CHAPTER 9

Theme: It's an Art

What's the Message?

What decisions do you think these artists had to make before beginning their mural? When working on a collaborative project, artists must discuss matters such as subject, style, and composition. If they fail to agree, they probably won't succeed in producing a harmonious artwork.

In the art of writing, subject-verb agreement is important for effective communication. Mistakes in agreement may confuse and frustrate readers. This chapter will help you use subjects and verbs correctly.

Write Away: Public Art

Draw a sketch of a public work of art, such as a statue or mural, in your town or neighborhood. Then write a description of the artwork and discuss why someone might have wanted to display it in public. Save your writing in your **Working Portfolio.**

206

 Grammar Coach

Choose the letter of the best revision for each underlined group of words.

Diego Rivera were one of Mexico's greatest artists. His murals
$\overline{\hspace{2cm}(1)\hspace{2cm}}$
and paintings have influenced artists around the world. Many
$\overline{\hspace{4cm}(2)\hspace{0.5cm}}$
portrays historical subjects. For example, *The History of Mexico*
$\overline{(3)}$ $\overline{\hspace{1.5cm}(4)}$
illustrates about 500 years of Mexican history. Within this mural
$\overline{\hspace{3cm}}$
is several groups of images. The first group show life in Mexico
$\overline{(5)}$ $\overline{\hspace{2cm}(6)\hspace{1cm}}$
before the arrival of the Spaniards. Others portrays the Spanish
$\overline{\hspace{3cm}(7)\hspace{1cm}}$
conquest of Mexico and the cruelty of colonialism. The images
$\overline{\hspace{2cm}}$
reflects Rivera's deep concern for the suffering of common people.
$\overline{\hspace{3cm}(8)}$

1. A. Diego Rivera are one of Mexico's greatest artists.
   B. Diego Rivera have been one of Mexico's greatest artists.
   C. Diego Rivera was one of Mexico's greatest artists.
   D. Correct as is

2. A. His murals and paintings has influenced
   B. His murals and paintings has been influencing
   C. His murals and paintings is influencing
   D. Correct as is

3. A. Many portray
   B. Many is portraying
   C. Many has portrayed
   D. Correct as is

4. A. *The History of Mexico* illustrate
   B. *The History of Mexico* do illustrate
   C. *The History of Mexico* have illustrated
   D. Correct as is

5. A. Within this mural was several groups
   B. Within this mural are several groups
   C. Within this mural appears several groups
   D. Correct as is

6. A. The first group shows
   B. The first group are showing
   C. The first group is showing
   D. Correct as is

7. A. Others portray
   B. Others does portray
   C. Others has portrayed
   D. Correct as is

8. A. The images was reflecting Rivera's deep concern
   B. The images reflect Rivera's deep concern
   C. The images has reflected Rivera's deep concern
   D. Correct as is

Diagnostic Test

As an option, a Chapter Pretest appears in
📙 **Assessment Masters** pp. 18–19.

Answers circled on page.

Use the chart below to determine which lessons students need.

PRESCRIPTION FOR SUCCESS	
If students miss item number:	**Work on lesson:**
1, 8	❶ Agreement in Number p. 208
2	❷ Compound Subjects p. 211
3, 7	❹ Indefinite Pronouns as Subjects p. 216
4, 6	❺ Problem Subjects p. 219
5	❸ Agreement Problems in Sentences p. 213

The **Diagnostic Test** parallels the **Mastery Test** on page 225. Have students keep the test in their portfolio to compare with their results on the **Mastery Test**.

S-V AGREEMENT

BLOCK SCHEDULING

Pressed for Time?
Briefly discuss singular and plural subjects and verbs. Then focus on **Lesson 3, Agreement Problems in Sentences, Lesson 4, Indefinite Pronouns as Subjects,** and **Lesson 5, Problem Subjects,** to help students avoid the most common errors in subject-verb agreement.

Time for More?
After completing all of the lessons, have students revise paragraphs from their 📁 **Working Portfolios.** Have students correct any errors in subject-verb agreement and add indefinite pronouns where appropriate.

DAILY TEST PREPARATION

Reading Comprehension: Vocabulary Write the following item on the board or use **Daily Test Preparation Transparency** p. DT28. Neologisms are made every day. A scientist discovers the remains of a strange dinosaur in the Sahara and coins the term *Suchomimus tenerensis*, meaning "crocodile mimic."

Which is another word for neologism?

A. new dinosaur

B. strange idea

C. new logic

D. new word

Teaching Point: For reading comprehension questions, use context clues to determine the best answer. In this case, the author restates the meaning of *neologism* in the phrase *coins the term,* which is an idiom meaning "to make a new word."

CUSTOMIZING TIP

Gifted and Talented Point out to students that not all plural nouns end in –s. Challenge students to think of nouns whose plural forms are spelled the same as their singular forms. Examples: *fish, deer, sheep, tuna, trout, moose.*

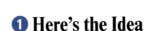 LESSON 1 # Agreement in Number

❶ Here's the Idea

▶ **A verb must agree with its subject in number.**

Number refers to whether a word is singular or plural. A word that refers to one person, place, thing, idea, action, or condition is singular. A word that refers to more than one is plural.

Singular and Plural Subjects

▶ **Singular subjects take singular verbs.**

AGREE

The new **museum** **displays** works by local artists.
SINGULAR SUBJECT   SINGULAR VERB

She **enjoys** the towering sculptures at the art center.

▶ **Plural subjects take plural verbs.**

AGREE

Chicago's art **museums** **display** priceless paintings.
PLURAL SUBJECT   PLURAL VERB

We **enjoy** the peaceful outdoor sculpture garden.

 WATCH OUT

Most nouns that end in *s* or *es* are plural. For example, *artists* and *brushes* are plural nouns. However, most verbs that end in *s* are singular. *Paints* and *draws* are singular verb forms.

Verb Phrases

▶ **In a verb phrase, it is the first helping verb that agrees with the subject.** A verb phrase is made up of a main verb and one or more helping verbs.

AGREE

Theresa **has collected** ceramic figurines.
SINGULAR HELPING VERB

She **is building** a large collection.

208 Grammar, Usage, and Mechanics

TEACHING RESOURCES

 Time-Saver Transparencies Binder:
• Daily Test Preparation p. DT28
• Quick-Fix Grammar and Style Charts p. QF3

 Grammar, Usage, and Mechanics Workbook p. 163

SKILLS PRACTICE RESOURCES

Grammar, Usage, and Mechanics Workbook pp. 164–165
Pupil's Edition Exercise Bank p. 612

Grammar Coach CD-ROM Lesson 5

AGREE

Friends have admired her interesting collection.
↑ PLURAL HELPING VERB

They have been finding new figurines for her collection.

Doesn't and Don't

Two common contractions are *doesn't* and *don't*. Use *doesn't* with all singular subjects except *I* and *you*. Use *don't* with all plural subjects and with the pronouns *I* and *you*.

Samuel doesn't use computer clip art.
SINGULAR VERB: does + not = doesn't

We don't like slick and professional illustrations.
PLURAL VERB: do + not = don't

I don't like these pictures.
WITH PRONOUN I: do + not = don't

❷ Why It Matters in Writing

Errors in subject-verb agreement can occur when you revise your work. If you change a subject from singular to plural or vice versa, be sure to change the verb as well.

STUDENT MODEL

DRAFT

Three statues have been purchased for the park. Residents **want** to beautify the neighborhood.

REVISION

Three statues have been purchased for the park. An important resident **wants** to beautify the neighborhood.

CUSTOMIZING TIP

Students Acquiring English/ESL
One of the most common errors for students acquiring English is interchanging third-person singular and plural verb forms. For example, they might use *she say* instead of *she says*, or *they does* instead of *they do*.

TEACHING TIP

Point out two other common contractions: *wasn't* and *weren't*. Tell students to use *wasn't* with all singular subjects except *you*, and to use *weren't* with all plural subjects and with the pronoun *you*.

Examples:
She wasn't at the gallery opening.
Singular verb: was+not=wasn't

You weren't at the opening either.
Plural verb: were+not=weren't

TEACHING TIP

Discuss with students when it is appropriate and inappropriate to use contractions in their writing. For example contractions are often found in informal writing, but in formal writing it is usually best to avoid them. Discussing when to use contractions will help students select and use a style that is appropriate to their audience and purpose.

CHAPTER 9

Answers

Print-Out Option You may create worksheets of exercises A and B for your students by using the ⊙ **Electronic Teacher Tools CD–ROM.**

A. CONCEPT CHECK

Self-Check For a self-check of agreement in number, direct students to p. 612 in the Pupil's Edition for the answers to the items circled in yellow.

Answers underlined on page.

B. WRITING

Answers underlined on page.

❸ **Practice and Apply**

A. CONCEPT CHECK: Agreement in Number

For each sentence, write the verb form that agrees in number with the subject.

African *Kente* Cloth

1. The Ashanti people of Ghana (has, <u>have</u>) been making *kente* cloth for centuries.
2. *Kente* weavers (creates, <u>create</u>) complex designs with bright colors and geometric patterns.
3. The designs (doesn't, <u>don't</u>) just provide visual pleasure.
4. Each element (<u>has</u>, have) a precise meaning.
5. For example, the color gold (<u>suggests</u>, suggest) mineral wealth.
6. A shield pattern (<u>suggests</u>, suggest) a defense against hostile forces.
7. Weavers often (takes, <u>take</u>) months to complete *kente* garments.
8. The Ashanti people (wears, <u>wear</u>) *kente* cloth on important occasions.
9. Some designs (is, <u>are</u>) reserved for royalty.
10. *Kente* garments (appears, <u>appear</u>) in many museum collections.

➡ **For a SELF-CHECK and more practice, see the EXERCISE BANK, p. 612.**

B. WRITING: Completing a Caption

Choose the correct verb forms to complete the caption for the photograph.

The color gold in this piece of *kente* cloth (<u>symbolizes</u>, symbolize) mineral wealth. These fabrics (is, <u>are</u>) made by the Ashanti people of Ghana.

LESSON 2 Compound Subjects

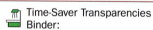

LESSON OBJECTIVES

To identify and correctly use compound subjects that agree with their verbs

❶ Here's the Idea

A **compound subject** is made up of two or more subjects joined by a conjunction such as *and, or,* or *nor.*

Subjects Containing *And*

▶ **A compound subject whose parts are joined by *and* usually takes a plural verb.**

Georgia and Louise paint exceptionally well.

Sometimes a subject containing *and* refers to a single thing or idea, so a singular verb is used.

War and peace is the theme of the mural.

Subjects Containing *Or* or *Nor*

▶ **When the parts of a compound subject are joined by *or* or *nor,* the verb should agree with the part closest to it.**

AGREE

Either ticket stubs or a photo completes your collage.

AGREE

Either a photo or ticket stubs complete your collage.

❷ Why It Matters in Writing

Writers sometimes reverse the order of compound subjects to make them sound more natural. If you do this, you may need to change the verb to make it agree with the new order.

The students or the teacher is attending the show.

The teacher or the students are attending the show.

Subject-Verb Agreement **211**

DAILY TEST PREPARATION

Error Identification: Spelling
Write the following item on the board or use 📽 **Daily Test Preparation Transparency** p. DT28.
Look for mistakes in spelling. Decide which word, if any, contains a mistake.

A. siezed

B. pressed

C. wrinkles

D. treason

E. *(No mistakes)*

Teaching Point: Error identification questions often test your knowledge of basic spelling rules. The word *seized* is an exception to the general rule *i* before *e* except after *c.*

TEACHING RESOURCES

📽 Time-Saver Transparencies Binder:
  • Daily Test Preparation p. DT28
  • Quick-Fix Grammar and Style Charts p. QF3
  • Visual Grammar™ Tiles Lesson 14

📓 Grammar, Usage, and Mechanics Workbook p. 166

SKILLS PRACTICE RESOURCES

📓 Grammar, Usage, and Mechanics Workbook pp. 167–168

Pupil's Edition Exercise Bank p. 613

💿 Grammar Coach CD-ROM Lesson 4

NEED MORE INFORMATION?
Direct students to **Chapter 1, The Sentence and Its Parts,** for more information on compound subjects.

Visual Grammar™
Use **Visual Grammar™ Tiles Lesson 14** and **Sentence K** to teach subject-verb agreement in sentences with compound subjects. Here is part of Lesson 14.

Decide whether a compound subject takes a singular or plural verb.

THE COTTAGES | OR | THE LODGE | IS / ARE

FOR SALE | .

Result:

THE COTTAGES | OR | THE LODGE | IS

FOR SALE | .

CHAPTER 9

❸ **Practice and Apply**

A. CONCEPT CHECK: Compound Subjects

Identify the sentences containing mistakes in subject-verb agreement, and rewrite them correctly. If a sentence contains no error, write *Correct*.

Crafty Arts

1. Arts and crafts are often hard to tell apart. **Correct**
2. A <u>basket</u> or pot <u>serve</u> a practical function, such as food storage. **serves**
3. Yet <u>collectors</u> and museum curators <u>prizes</u> these objects for their beauty. **prize**
4. Many pots and jars display high levels of artistry. **Correct**
5. *appear* Even <u>forks</u> and <u>spoons</u> <u>appears</u> in museum collections.
6. *occupy* <u>Arms</u> and <u>armor</u> <u>occupies</u> special halls in some museums.
7. Neither dirt nor blood stains <u>remains</u> on their shiny surfaces. **remain**
8. *Correct* Adults and children find these tools of warfare appealing.
9. Antique <u>beds</u>, <u>couches</u>, or a <u>rug</u> <u>seem</u> enticing to the weary museum patron. **seems**
10. Fortunately, <u>signs</u> and watchful <u>guards</u> <u>reminds</u> us not to rest on them. **remind**

➡ **For a SELF-CHECK and more practice, see the EXERCISE BANK, p. 613.**

B. REVISING: Making Verbs Agree with Compound Subjects

Rewrite this article for a school newspaper so that verbs agree with compound subjects. There are five errors.

In My Opinion . . .

are Many <u>ideas</u> and <u>opinions</u> <u>is</u> expressed visually in editorial cartoons. Familiar symbols and caricatures communicate the cartoonists' messages. For example, a torn <u>flag</u> or a *suggests* battered <u>Uncle Sam</u> <u>suggest</u> trouble in the nation. Politicians and celebrities are often criticized by exaggerating their physical appearance. Pompous leaders *make* and corrupt <u>people</u> <u>makes</u> good targets. Sometimes neither *brings* <u>caricatures</u> nor a visual <u>symbol</u> <u>bring</u> across a cartoonist's point clearly. In such a case, a speech <u>balloon</u> or a <u>caption</u> <u>help</u> readers understand the cartoon. **helps**

212 Grammar, Usage, and Mechanics

Spice It Up!

Hold a sentence bee. Have students take turns making sentences with the following compound subjects. Allow the rest of the class to correct any errors in agreement.
neither paintings nor drawings
the artists or the art teacher

either oil paint or water colors
video techniques and the computer
either paint brushes or a pen
fifteen photos and one drawing
neither the murals nor the statue

LESSON 3 Agreement Problems in Sentences

❶ Here's the Idea

Some sentences—ones with subjects in unusual positions, ones containing predicate nouns, ones in which prepositional phrases separate subjects and verbs—can be tricky. Here are some tips for choosing the correct verb forms in these situations.

Subjects in Unusual Positions

A subject can follow a verb or part of a verb phrase in a question, a sentence beginning with *here* or *there*, or a sentence in which an adjective, an adverb, or a phrase is placed first.

Subjects in Unusual Positions

Type of Sentence	Example
Question	**Does** this **music video contain** interesting computer graphics?
Sentence beginning with *here* or *there*	Here **is** an on-air **announcer** with an enjoyable play list.
Sentence beginning with adverb, adjective, or phrase	Around the nation is **heard** the **sound.**

The following tips can help you to find the subject in one of these kinds of sentences.

Here's How Choosing a Correct Verb Form

(Is, Are) the visual **effects** better than the song recording?

1. Rephrase the sentence so that the subject precedes the verb.
   The visual **effects** (**is, are**) better than the song recording.

2. Determine whether the subject is singular or plural.
   effects (plural)

3. Choose the verb form that agrees with the subject.
   The visual **effects are** better than the song recording.

4. Add correct verb to the original sentence.
   Are the visual **effects** better than the song recording?

Subject-Verb Agreement **213**

 DAILY TEST PREPARATION

Definition: Vocabulary Write the following item on the board or use 📖 **Daily Test Preparation Transparency** p. DT29.

Decide which of the four answers has most nearly the same meaning as the underlined word.

| <u>Conventional</u> farming practices— |

A. radical
B. ordinary
C. agreeable
D. cooperative

Teaching Point: Definition questions often test your knowledge of different words. *Conventional* farming practices are those that are time-honored and traditional, or, in other words, *ordinary.*

TEACHING TIP

Point out that, no matter how the words in a sentence are positioned, the rules for subject-verb agreement do not change.

TEACHING RESOURCES

 Time-Saver Transparencies Binder:
• Daily Test Preparation p. DT29
• Quick-Fix Grammar and Style Charts p. QF4
• Visual Grammar™ Tiles Lesson 15
Grammar, Usage, and Mechanics Workbook p. 169

SKILLS PRACTICE RESOURCES

 Grammar, Usage, and Mechanics Workbook pp. 170–171
Pupil's Edition Exercise Bank p. 613
 Grammar Coach CD-ROM Lessons 4–5

Predicate Nouns

In a sentence containing a predicate noun, the verb should agree with the subject, not the predicate noun.

AGREE

Nechita's **works** **have been** a **topic** of magazine articles.

Her **inspiration** **is** abstract **paintings** by Pablo Picasso.

Prepositional Phrases

The subject of a verb is never found in a prepositional phrase. Don't be fooled by words that come between a subject and a verb. Mentally block out those words. Then it will be easy to tell whether the subject is singular or plural.

AGREE

The **colors** ~~of a Javanese batik garment~~ **indicate** where it came from.

Traditionally, the **pattern** ~~of symbols~~ **represents** things found in nature.

② Why It Matters in Writing

Writers sometimes place verbs before subjects to make their writing more interesting. When you do this, make sure that the verbs agree with their subjects.

THE LANGUAGE OF
LITERATURE
The passage on the student page is from "Zebra" in *The Language of Literature,* Level 7.

LITERARY MODEL

Between two pieces of cardboard **were** a **letter** and a large color **photograph.**
The photograph showed John Wilson down on his right knee before a glistening black wall.... Leaning against the wall to his right **was** Zebra's **drawing** of the helicopter and the zebra racing together across a facelike landscape.

—Chaim Potok, "Zebra"

❸ Practice and Apply

A. CONCEPT CHECK: Agreement Problems in Sentences

Rewrite these sentences, correcting agreement errors. If a sentence contains no error, write *Correct*.

Poster Power

1. Does your <u>classmates</u> collect posters? **Do**
2. On the walls of many teenagers' rooms hang pictures of favorite singers, actors, and athletes. **Correct**
3. An effective tool for advertising or announcing events is posters. **Correct**
4. Vibrant <u>colors</u> in a poster <u>attracts</u> the public's attention. **attract**
5. Among the greatest of poster artists <u>were</u> <u>Henri de Toulouse-Lautrec</u>. **was**
6. <u>Has</u> <u>you</u> ever <u>seen</u> Toulouse-Lautrec's bold, striking posters? **Have seen**
7. Japanese prints were the source of his inspiration. **Correct**
8. There <u>is</u> few <u>posters</u> more famous than *I Want You!* **are**
9. On that World War I recruitment poster is a portrait of Uncle Sam. **Correct**
10. There <u>is</u> also patriotic <u>posters</u> from World War II. **are**

➡ **For a SELF-CHECK and more practice, see the EXERCISE BANK, p. 613.**

B. MIXED REVIEW: Proofreading and Editing

Find the five errors in subject-verb agreement in this paragraph. In each case, write the correct verb form.

Roll the Videotape

 <u>Does</u> <u>you</u> ever <u>record</u> family celebrations with a video **Do record** camera? Then <u>you</u> probably <u>has</u> the basic skills to create a **have** work of video art. Video artists combine technology with artistic expression. Just as painters apply paint to canvas, video artists record images for television monitors. There <u>is</u> **are** <u>works</u> of video art that tell stories, just like feature films. Others are more like sculptures or paintings. For example, the artist Nam June Paik has created a pyramid out of 40 television sets. On all of the sets <u>play</u> a <u>video</u> of a dancing **plays** man. <u>Paik</u> <u>are</u> one of the most prominent artists working **is** with video.

Subject-Verb Agreement **215**

Answers

Print-Out Option You may create worksheets of exercises A and B for your students by using the 💿 **Electronic Teacher Tools CD–ROM.**

A. CONCEPT CHECK

Self-Check For a self-check of agreement problems in sentences, direct students to p. 613 in the Pupil's Edition for the answers to the items circled in yellow.

Answers shown on page. In sentences in which the subject and verb do not agree, the subject is underlined and the verb is double underlined. Correct verb forms appear in margin.

B. MIXED REVIEW

Answers shown on page. In sentences in which the subject and verb do not agree, the subject is underlined and the verb is double underlined. Correct verb forms appear in margin.

ASSESSMENT

📋 Assessment Masters:
• Chapter Mid-point Test p. 32

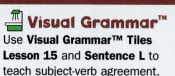

Visual Grammar™
Use **Visual Grammar™ Tiles Lesson 15** and **Sentence L** to teach subject-verb agreement. Here is part of Lesson 15.

Make the verb agree with the subject.

| THE RUNNER | IN THE RED SHOES | IS |
| TAKING A REST | . | ARE |

Result:

| THE RUNNER | IN THE RED SHOES | IS |
| TAKING A REST | . |

LESSON 4 Indefinite Pronouns as Subjects

❶ Here's the Idea

▶ **When used as subjects, some indefinite pronouns are always singular, some are always plural, and some can be singular or plural, depending on how they're used.**
Remember, an indefinite pronoun is a pronoun that does not refer to a specific person, place, thing, or idea.

Indefinite Pronouns

Singular			
	another	everybody	nothing
	anybody	everyone	one
	anyone	everything	somebody
	anything	neither	someone
	each	nobody	something
	either	no one	

Plural				
	both	few	many	several

Singular or Plural					
	all	any	most	none	some

Singular indefinite pronouns take singular verbs.

> **Everyone enjoys Alexander Calder's mobiles.**

> **Something about them reminds people of childhood.**

Plural indefinite pronouns take plural verbs.

> **Few of the mobiles have electric motors.**

> **Many consist of metal, wood, and wire.**

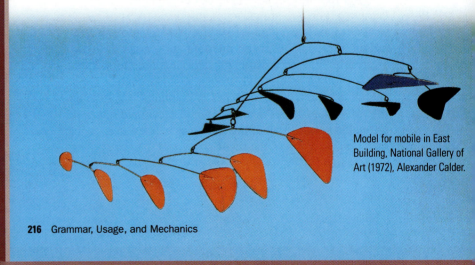

Model for mobile in East Building, National Gallery of Art (1972), Alexander Calder.

216 Grammar, Usage, and Mechanics

Singular or Plural?

The indefinite pronouns *all, any, most, none,* and *some* can be either singular or plural. When you use one of these words as a subject, think about the noun it refers to. If the noun is singular, use a singular verb; if it is plural, use a plural verb.

REFERS TO

All of the mobiles **move** in a breeze.

REFERS TO

Most of the design **is** ingenious.

Sometimes an indefinite pronoun refers to a noun in a previous sentence.

PLURAL NOUN

Many people attended the exhibition. **Most were astonished.**

INDEFINITE PRONOUN   PLURAL VERB

② Why It Matters in Writing

When you write about events for an assignment or a school newspaper, you will probably need to use indefinite pronouns as subjects. To help readers understand your writing, use correct subject-verb agreement.

> **PROFESSIONAL MODEL**
>
> A fascinating art show has opened this weekend in Biloxi. **Each** of the paintings portrays a different blues musician. **Many** are painted in a realistic style. **Some** of the art depicts older musicians who play acoustic instruments.
>
> —Chris Bayard

Less Proficient Learners Caution students against using indefinite pronouns that make the meaning of a sentence unclear. Discuss with students why the following sentence is confusing. Have them identify ways to clarify the sentence.

*We have bananas, strawberries, and bread, but **some** are not ripe.*

We have bananas, strawberries, and bread, but some of the bananas are not ripe.

This activity will help students produce coherent written texts by choosing precise wording.

S-V AGREEMENT

S-V AGREEMENT

Speaking and Listening Read aloud the **Professional Model.** Ask students to listen for and identify the indefinite pronouns and their verbs.

Answers

Print-Out Option You may create worksheets of exercises A and B for your students by using the ⊙ **Electronic Teacher Tools CD–ROM.**

A. CONCEPT CHECK

Self-Check For a self-check of indefinite problems in subjects, direct students to p. 614 in the Pupil's Edition for the answers to the items circled in yellow.

Answers shown on page. In sentences in which the subject and verb do not agree, the subject is underlined and the verb is double underlined. Correct verb forms appear in margin.

B. WRITING

Answers shown on page. Correct forms of the verbs are underlined.

❸ Practice and Apply

A. CONCEPT CHECK: Indefinite Pronouns as Subjects

Rewrite correctly each sentence in which the verb does not agree with the subject. If a sentence is correct, write *Correct.*

In Black and White

1. Many <u>knows</u> the saying "A picture's worth a thousand words." **know**
2. One remembers the fascinating images in photo essays. **Correct**
3. Few merely <u>entertains</u> people. **entertain**
4. Most <u>addresses</u> important real-life issues. **address**
5. For example, both *Let Us Now Praise Famous Men* and *How the Other Half Lives* tell powerful stories. **Correct**
6. <u>Some</u> of the photographs <u>reveals</u> poverty. **reveal**
7. Others <u>portrays</u> nature's fury. **portray**
8. <u>Everyone</u> <u>are</u> touched by pictures that capture human suffering. **is**
9. No one ignores such strong evidence of problems in society. **Correct**
10. <u>All</u> of this photography <u>motivate</u> people to take a stand. **motivates**

Mother and two children on road at Tule Lake City, September 1939. Photo by Dorothea Lange.

➡️ For a SELF-CHECK and more practice, see the EXERCISE BANK, p. 614.

B. WRITING: Agreement with Indefinite Pronouns

For each sentence, choose the verb form that agrees with the subject.

(1) Everybody (<u>enjoys</u>, enjoy) our school's art fairs. **(2)** Most of the artworks (is, <u>are</u>) quite good. **(3)** Something always (<u>makes</u>, make) the students smile because it is so ridiculous. **(4)** Yet one (<u>has</u>, have) no need to fear humiliation. **(5)** None of the artists (gets, <u>get</u>) upset. **(6)** None of the criticism (<u>is</u>, are) mean-spirited. **(7)** Everyone (<u>understands</u>, understand) that artists should be encouraged. **(8)** Some (takes, <u>take</u>) longer to develop their talent. **(9)** Each of us (<u>has</u>, have) the right to express himself or herself in art. **(10)** All of the fairs (is, <u>are</u>) conducted in this spirit.

🖺 **Visual Grammar**™

Use **Visual Grammar**™ **Tiles Lesson 16** and **Sentence M** to teach subject-verb agreement in sentences with indefinite pronouns. Here is part of Lesson 16.

Decide whether an indefinite pronoun takes a singular or plural verb.

| MOST | OF THE APPLES | WAS / WERE | CRISP AND TASTY | . |

Result:

| MOST | OF THE APPLES | WERE | CRISP AND TASTY | . |

Problem Subjects

❶ Here's the Idea

When collective nouns, nouns ending in *s*, titles, and numerical expressions are used as subjects, it can be difficult to tell whether they take singular or plural verbs.

Collective Nouns

Collective nouns name groups of people or things.

Common Collective Nouns					
group	crew	flock	family	class	team
crowd	herd	public	club	faculty	choir

▶ **Many collective nouns can take singular or plural verbs, depending on how they are used.** When a collective noun refers to people or things acting as a group, it takes a singular verb.

The faculty sponsors an art exhibit each year.
(THE FACULTY MEMBERS ARE ACTING AS A GROUP.)

When a collective noun refers to people or things acting as individuals, it takes a plural verb.

The faculty disagree on the rules of the exhibit.
(THE FACULTY MEMBERS ARE ACTING AS INDIVIDUALS.)

Singular Nouns Ending in *S*

▶ **Some nouns that end in *s* or *ics* look plural but actually refer to singular concepts.** When used as subjects, they take singular verbs.

Singular Nouns with Plural Forms			
measles	linguistics	news	pediatrics
politics	forensics	civics	mathematics
genetics	mechanics	physics	economics
ceramics	molasses	mumps	

Subject-Verb Agreement **219**

S-V AGREEMENT

LESSON OBJECTIVES

To identify and use verbs that agree with certain problem subjects.

DAILY TEST PREPARATION

Error Identification: Spelling
Write the following item on the board or use 🖥 **Daily Test Preparation Transparency** p. DT30.
Decide which type of error, if any, appears in the underlined section.

> The document <u>specificaly states the following:</u> "Report this incident to the supervisor immediately."

A. Spelling error

B. Capitalization error

C. Punctuation error

D. No error

Teaching Point: Error identification questions often test your knowledge of commonly misspelled words, such as *specifically*. Spelling questions often include words with double consonants.

TEACHING RESOURCES

🖥 Time-Saver Transparencies Binder:
- Daily Test Preparation p. DT30
- Quick-Fix Grammar and Style Charts p. QF4

📖 Grammar, Usage, and Mechanics Workbook p. 175

SKILLS PRACTICE RESOURCES

📖 Grammar, Usage, and Mechanics Workbook pp. 176–177

Pupil's Edition Exercise Bank p. 614

 Grammar Coach CD-ROM Lesson 5

Spice It Up!

Quotable Quote "The important thing about any word is how you understand it."—Publilius Syrus

Tell students that using a singular or plural verb with a collective noun affects how readers understand the noun. Then have them create two sentences using one of the collective nouns on the student page—one sentence with a singular verb, the other with a plural verb. Ask volunteers to read their sentences aloud. Discuss with students how the different verb forms affect the meaning of the collective nouns.

AGREE
Ceramics is the art of making objects from clay.

AGREE
The news includes information about several exhibits.

Titles

▶ **Titles of works of art, literature, and music are singular.** Even a title consisting of a plural noun takes a singular verb.

   Sunflowers **is a famous painting by Vincent van Gogh.**

Amounts and Time

▶ **Words and phrases that express weights, measures, numbers, and lengths of time are often treated as singular.** They take singular verbs when they refer to amounts rather than numbers of individual items.

Measures and Amounts		
Measures	seven pounds two cups	**Two hundred twenty-five tons is** the weight of the Statue of Liberty.
Amounts	three hours nine dollars	**Four years seems** a long time to work on a single portrait.

A fraction can take a singular or plural verb, depending on whether it refers to a single part or to a number of items.

Five-sixths of the canvas is blank.
   (THE FRACTION REFERS TO ONE PART OF THE CANVAS.)

Two-thirds of the paintings are abstract.
   (THE FRACTION REFERS TO A NUMBER OF PAINTINGS.)

❷ Why It Matters in Writing

When you write about science or math, you need to use numbers, weights, and measures. Show your readers that you know your stuff by using the correct verb forms with them.

Six-tenths of the human body is water.

③ Practice and Apply

A. CONCEPT CHECK: Problem Subjects

Rewrite the underlined words in the following sentences to correct the mistake in subject-verb agreement. If a sentence contains no error, write *Correct*.

Memorial Wall

1. *In Country* <u>describe</u> a girl's effort to learn more about her father, who was killed in Vietnam. **describes**
2. Her family <u>travel</u> to Washington, D.C., to visit the Vietnam Veterans Memorial. **travels**
3. Many <u>spend</u> time at the wall designed by Maya Lin. **Correct**
4. Each of the wall's halves <u>are</u> about 250 feet long. **is**
5. Three days <u>are</u> how long it takes to read all 58,209 **is** names of soldiers killed or missing in the war.
6. Mathematics <u>fails</u> to explain the wall's dramatic effect. **Correct**
7. The public also <u>views</u> other sculptures at the memorial. **Correct**
8. *Three Servicemen* by Frederick Hart <u>stand</u> near the wall. **stands**
9. Our class <u>have</u> looked at an exhibit of objects left at the wall. **has**
10. A group of photos <u>show</u> a young man with family and friends. **shows**

➜ For a SELF-CHECK and more practice, see the EXERCISE BANK, p. 614.

B. WRITING: Using Fractions Correctly

Choose the correct verb form to complete each sentence about the bar graph. Then write a sentence explaining how you chose the correct form.

1. Two-thirds of the class (<u>is</u>, are) gone on the trip to Washington, D.C. **Two-thirds of the class is thought of as a whole.**
2. One-half of the students (has, <u>have</u>) seen the Statue of Liberty. **One-half of the students are thought of as separate units.**

Numbers of Students Who Have Visited Two Sites
(class size = 30)

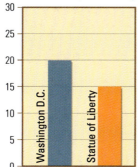

S-V AGREEMENT

Answers

Print-Out Option You may create worksheets of exercises A and B for your students by using the ⊙ **Electronic Teacher Tools CD–ROM.**

A. CONCEPT CHECK

Self-Check For a self-check of agreement problem with problems subjects, direct students to p. 614 in the Pupil's Edition for the answers to the items circled in yellow.

Answers shown on page.

B. WRITING

Correct verb forms are underlined on page. Explanations appear in margin.

ASSESSMENT

 Assessment Masters:
 • Chapter Mastery Tests pp. 79–82

 Test Generator CD-ROM

 mcdougallittell.com
Grammar Chapter Quiz

221

LESSON OBJECTIVES

To identify and use correct subject-verb agreement when solving or writing word problems

TEACHING TIP

Explain to students that recognizing subject-verb agreement will help them better understand word problems. In many cases, recognizing the subject of a question in a word problem will help students identify what information the question is asking for. Knowing this information will help students determine the correct steps to solve the word problem.

Grammar in Math

Word Problems

When you write and solve word problems, you need to pay attention to grammar. Subject-verb agreement can be tricky—especially if you're using fractions. In the following word problem, the subjects and the verbs that agree with them are highlighted.

240 Section 6   Multiplication of Fractions

42 **Theater** Northern Illinois University has a collection of scale models of stage sets. These models show sets that were built for Early American performances of operas. The models are built to a scale of 1/48 of the actual size. The model shown is a set representing a public square in nineteenth century Bohemia, a region of the Czech Republic.

Exploration:

A **door** on one of the buildings in the model **is** 11/16 in. wide and 1 3/4 in. tall. Explain how you would find the actual dimensions of the door on the stage set.

The word *is* agrees with the subject *door,* not with the plural word *buildings.*

EXAMPLE

Describe how you would find the width of the actual door on the stage set.

ANSWER

11/16 in. is multiplied by 48 to find the width of the door on the stage set. (Notice that the singular subject, 11/16 agrees with the singular verb is.)

222 Grammar, Usage, and Mechanics

Spice It Up!

Quotable Quote "Newton's peculiar gift was the power of holding continuously in his mind a purely mental problem until he had seen it through."
—John Maynard Keynes

Discuss with students the advantages of working through a problem mentally. Then ask students to write a paragraph, describing the mental steps they took to solve a problem. Have them exchange papers to check subject-verb agreement.

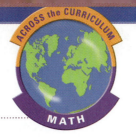

Practice and Apply

A. Use the information on the photograph of the model to write and answer a word problem. Figure out how many poles could be cut from a dowel that is 1 foot long.

$4\frac{5}{8}$ in.

$1\frac{3}{4}$ in.

$\frac{11}{16}$ in.

B. Write and solve a word problem in which you find the size of the pole on the actual stage set. Be sure you explain the proportion of the model to the set. Remember—if you are using fractions as subjects, you should use a singular verb.

Answers

PRACTICE AND APPLY

A. Answers will vary. A sample response follows.
In the photograph of the model public square, a pole is 4 ⅝ in. high. Explain how you would figure out how many poles could be cut from a dowel that is 1 foot long.

Word problem answer: One foot equals 12 in. Divide 12 in. by 4 ⅝ inches to determine the number of poles that can be cut from a 12-in. dowel. Two poles could be cut from a 12-in. dowel, with 2 ¾ in. left on the dowel (12 divided by 4 ⅝ = 2 with a remainder of 2 ¾.).

B. Answers will vary. A sample response follows.
The model in the photograph is built to a scale of 1/48 of the actual size. A pole used in one of the buildings in the model is 4 and ⅝ in. high. Explain how you would find the actual dimensions of the pole on the stage set.

Word problem answer:
Multiply 4 ⅝ in. by 48 to find the actual height of the pole in inches. Next, divide the product (222 in.) by 12 to find the height of the pole in feet. The actual height of the pole is 18 ½ ft.

Mixed Review

Print-Out Option You may create worksheets of exercises A and B for your students by using the 💿 **Electronic Teacher Tools CD–ROM.**

A. Agreement in Number, Compound Subjects, and Indefinite Pronouns

Answers underlined on page.

B. Additional Agreement Problems

Answers shown on page. In sentences in which the subject and verb do not agree, the subject is underlined and the verb is double underlined. Correct verb forms appear in margin.

Mixed Review

A. Agreement in Number, Compound Subjects, and Indefinite Pronouns
Write the verb form that agrees with the subject of each sentence.

1. Curators and conservators (is, <u>are</u>) important employees in museums.
2. Each of these people (<u>has</u>, have) specific responsibilities.
3. A curator (<u>arranges</u>, arrange) artworks in museum galleries.
4. Curators also (looks, <u>look</u>) for artworks to add to museums' collections.
5. Major museums (has, <u>have</u>) a curator for each department.
6. A conservator (<u>cleans</u>, clean) artworks.
7. Conservators also (performs, <u>perform</u>) scientific tests on them.
8. The tests (reveals, <u>reveal</u>) how old the artworks are and how they were made.
9. A conservator or a curator (<u>needs</u>, need) extensive training.
10. Most (has, <u>have</u>) advanced degrees in art history.

B. Additional Agreement Problems Rewrite the following advertisement, correcting six errors in subject-verb agreement.

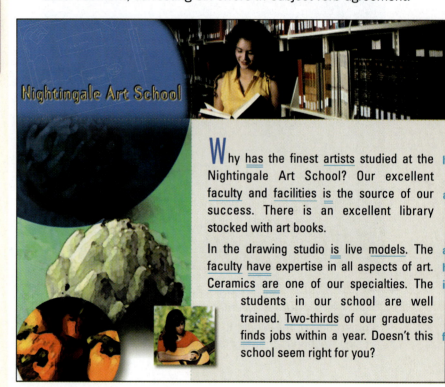

Nightingale Art School

<u>W</u>hy has the finest <u>artists</u> studied at the Nightingale Art School? Our excellent <u>faculty and facilities</u> is the source of our success. There is an excellent library stocked with art books.

In the drawing studio is live <u>models</u>. The <u>faculty</u> have expertise in all aspects of art. <u>Ceramics</u> are one of our specialties. The students in our school are well trained. <u>Two-thirds</u> of our graduates <u>finds</u> jobs within a year. Doesn't this school seem right for you?

Mastery Test: What Did You Learn?

Choose the letter of the best revision for each underlined group of words.

> There are a remarkable example of folk art in Los Angeles,
> (1)
> called the Watts Towers. This group of sculptures were created by
> (2)
> Simon Rodia. The group contain nine sculptures. Some are nearly
> (3)   (4)
> 100 feet tall. Rodia gave them names such as *Ship of Marco Polo*
> and *Santa Maria Tower*. These names remind us of Rodia's Italian
> (5)
> heritage. Each of the sculptures are made of steel rods, wire mesh,
> (6)
> and mortar. Bottle caps, seashells, and other found objects is
> (7)
> imbedded in the mortar for decoration. Tourists from around the
> world comes to view the Watts Towers.
> (8)

1. A. There have been
   B. There is
   C. There were
   D. Correct as is

2. A. group of sculptures are
   B. group of sculpture is
   C. group of sculptures was
   D. Correct as is

3. A. The group contains
   B. The group have contained
   C. The group are containing
   D. Correct as is

4. A. Some is
   B. Some stands
   C. Some was
   D. Correct as is

5. A. names does remind
   B. names has reminded
   C. names is reminding
   D. Correct as is

6. A. Each of the sculptures were made
   B. Each of the sculptures have been made
   C. Each of the sculptures is made
   D. Correct as is

7. A. Bottle caps, seashells, and other found objects was imbedded
   B. Bottle caps, seashells, and other found objects are imbedded
   C. Bottle caps, seashells, and other found objects has been imbedded
   D. Correct as is

8. A. come
   B. has come
   C. is coming
   D. Correct as is

Mastery Test

As an option, two other Chapter Mastery Tests appear in ▣ **Assessment Masters** pp. 79–82.

Answers circled on page.

PRESCRIPTION FOR MASTERY	
If students miss item number:	Use **Teaching Resources** and **Skills Practice Resources** for lesson:
1, 8	❸ Agreement Problems in Sentences p. 213
2, 3	❺ Problem Subjects p. 219
4, 6	❹ Indefinite Pronouns as Subjects p. 216
5	❶ Agreement in Number p. 208
7	❷ Compound Subjects p. 211

Student Help Desk

Students can use the Student Help Desk prior to testing or as a quick review or reference as they revise a piece of writing.

Teacher's Notes
WHAT WORKS:

Student Help Desk

Subject-Verb Agreement at a Glance

A singular subject takes a singular verb.

A plural subject takes a plural verb.

The **artist paints** dancers.

Dancers pose in her studio.

Subjects and Verbs

Tricky Cases

Subjects and Verbs	Tricky Cases
Verb phrase The first helping verb should agree with the subject.	**Folk art is getting** expensive. **Collectors are raising** prices.
Prepositional phrase between subject and verb Block out the phrase when deciding which verb form to use.	The **vases** ~~in this museum~~ **are** priceless.
Compound subject containing *and* Always use a plural verb.	The **artist and** his **work arouse** controversy.
Compound subject containing *or* or *nor* The verb should agree with the part of the subject closest to it.	Neither the **critics nor** the **average citizen likes** this exhibit.
Indefinite pronoun A singular pronouns takes a singular verb; a plural pronoun takes a plural verb. Some pronouns can be singular or plural.	**Everyone admires** this masterpiece. **Few understand** it. **Some** of the paint **is** peeling. **Some** of the critics **want** the museum to restore it.
Collective noun Use a singular verb if it refers to a whole, a plural verb if it refers to individuals.	The **staff selects** the paintings. The **staff are arguing** among themselves.
Singular noun ending in *s* Use a singular verb.	**Politics is** an art.
Title or expression of amount Use a singular verb.	**Three ounces** of gold **was** used in the sculpture.

Other Agreement Problems

Slippery Subjects

Predicate noun Make sure the verb agrees with the subject.	**Animals are** the subject of his photo series. The **subject** of his photo series **is** animals.
Question Change the question to a statement to find the subject.	(**Is, are**) the tapestries on the wall? The **tapestries are** on the wall.
Statement in which subject follows verb Turn the sentence parts around before deciding on a verb form.	Here (**is, are**) the expressionist paintings. The expressionist **paintings are** here. Beneath each painting (**is, are**) a title and a date. A **title** and a **date are** beneath each painting.

The Bottom Line

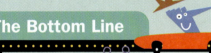

Checklist for Subject-Verb Agreement

Have I . . .

____ used singular verbs with singular subjects?

____ used plural verbs with plural subjects?

____ made the first helping verbs in verb phrases agree with the verbs' subjects?

____ used plural verbs with compound subjects containing *and?*

____ made verbs agree with the closest parts of compound subjects containing *or* or *nor?*

____ used correct verb forms with indefinite-pronoun subjects?

____ used singular verbs to agree with titles and some numerical expressions?

____ used verbs that agree with subjects in unusual positions?

Subject-Verb Agreement **227**

S-V AGREEMENT

SUBJECT-VERB

Teacher's Notes
WHAT DOESN'T WORK:

TEACHER'S LOUNGE

A Slice of Life

"Far better is it to dare mighty things, to win glorious triumphs, even though checkered by failure, than to take rank with those poor spirits who neither enjoy much nor suffer much, because they live in the gray twilight that knows not victory nor defeat."

—Theodore Roosevelt

Just for Laughs

A teacher wrote this sentence on the board and asked her class to correct it: Girls is naturally more beautiful than boys.

One little boy wrote: Girls is artificially more beautiful than boys.

CHAPTER RESOURCES

 Time-Saver Transparencies Binder:
- Daily Test Preparation pp. DT30–32

 Grammar, Usage, and Mechanics Workbook pp. 178–189

Integrated Technology and Media

 Electronic Teacher Tools CD-ROM

 mcdougallittell.com

Assessment

 Assessment Masters:
- Chapter Pretest pp. 20–21
- Chapter Mid-point Test p. 33
- Chapter Mastery Tests pp. 83–86

 Test Generator CD-ROM

 mcdougallittell.com Grammar Chapter Quiz

Chapter 10

Capitalization

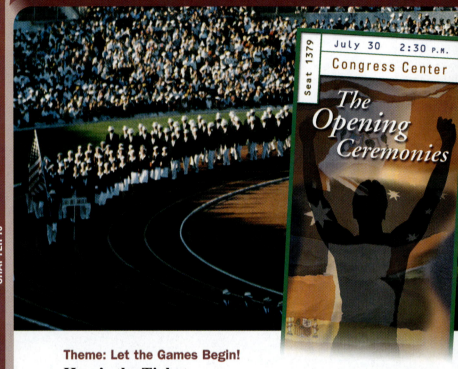

July 30   2:30 P.M.
Congress Center
Seat 1379
The Opening Ceremonies

Theme: Let the Games Begin!

Here's the Ticket

Congratulations! You are one of the lucky spectators who has a ticket to the opening ceremony of the Olympic Games. What is the date and the time of the ceremony? Where is it scheduled to take place? On the ticket above, capitalized words such as *July* and *Congress Center* provide you with the answers. We use capitalization as a way to make certain words—such as names, titles, and dates—stand out from others.

Write Away: Olympic Favorites

Write a paragraph describing your favorite Olympic event or competitor. Save the paragraph in your 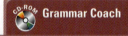 **Working Portfolio.**

Grammar Coach

Diagnostic Test: What Do You Know?

For each underlined passage, choose the letter of the correct revision.

Baron Pierre de coubertin, a french educator, was responsible
_____(1)_____(2)
for creating the modern Olympic Games. He thought that an
_____(3)
International sports competition would promote World peace.
____(4)_____(5)
According to Dave Anderson in *The story of the Olympics,*
_____(6)
Coubertin said, "The revival of the Olympic Games will bring
athletism to a high state of perfection."

The first modern Olympic Games took place in 1896 in athens,
_____(7)
Greece. This site was East of the place where the ancient
_____(8)
Olympics had been held. The track-and-field events were held at
the Panathenaic stadium. The Games were a huge success and set
____(9)_____(10)
the groundwork for many more Olympic competitions.

1. A. baron
   B. pierre
   C. Coubertin ⟵
   D. Correct as is

2. A. French ⟵
   B. Educator
   C. A
   D. Correct as is

3. A. olympic
   B. games
   C. he
   D. Correct as is ⟵

4. A. International Sports
   B. international sports ⟵
   C. international Sports
   D. Correct as is

5. A. World Peace
   B. world Peace
   C. world peace ⟵
   D. Correct as is

6. A. the
   B. Story ⟵
   C. olympics
   D. Correct as is

7. A. athens, greece
   B. Athens, Greece ⟵
   C. Athens, greece
   D. Correct as is

8. A. This site was east ⟵
   B. this site was east
   C. this site was East
   D. Correct as is

9. A. panathenaic stadium
   B. panathenaic Stadium
   C. Panathenaic Stadium ⟵
   D. Correct as is

10. A. the Games
    B. the games
    C. The games ⟵
    D. Correct as is

Capitalization **229**

Diagnostic Test

As an option, a Chapter Pretest appears in
📋 **Assessment Masters** pp. 20–21.

Answers circled on page.

Use the chart below to determine which lessons students need.

PRESCRIPTION FOR SUCCESS	
If students miss item number:	**Work on lesson:**
1, 2	❶ People and Cultures p. 228
3, 4, 5, 10	❹ Organizations and Other Subjects p. 240
6	❷ First Words and Titles p. 233
7, 8, 9	❸ Places and Transportation p. 237

The **Diagnostic Test** parallels the **Mastery Test** on page 245. Have students keep the test in their portfolio to compare with their results on the **Mastery Test**.

BLOCK SCHEDULING

Pressed for Time?
Focus on **Lesson 2, First Words and Titles, and Lesson 3, Places and Transportation,** to help students avoid the most common capitalization errors in their writing.

Time for More?
Have students correct any capitalization errors in paragraphs from their 📁 **Working Portfolios.**

To understand and apply rules for capitalizing words that refer to people and cultures

DAILY TEST PREPARATION

Reading Comprehension: Information vs. Inference Write the following item on the board or use **Daily Test Preparation Transparency** p. DT30.

The *Oxford English Dictionary* was scheduled to be completed in 10 years. Seventy years after its approval date, it was published.

There is enough information in this passage to show that the *Oxford English Dictionary* —

A. is the best dictionary in the world.

B. took 70 years to complete.

C. was not completed by the original editor.

D. was published in 1928.

Teaching Point: Most reading comprehension questions involve either verifying information or making an inference from the details in the passage. In this case, the question asks you to verify information in the passage. Answer B contains the only statement that can be supported by reading the passage.

 LESSON 1

People and Cultures

① Here's the Idea

Names and Initials

▶ **Capitalize people's names and initials.**

    Michelle **K**wan   **J**ackie **J**oyner-**K**ersee

    Robert **D. B**allard   **W. P. K**insella

Personal Titles and Abbreviations

▶ **Capitalize titles and abbreviations of titles that are used before names or in direct address.**

    Mr. Carl Lewis   **D**r. Dot Richardson

    General Colin Powell   **M**s. Jenny Thompson

    Did you write a book about the Olympics, **P**rofessor?

Capitalize abbreviations of some titles when they follow a name.

    Todd Owens, **J**r.   Sylvester Fine, **D.D.S.**

    Mary Mueller, **Ph.D.**

▶ **Capitalize titles of heads of state, royalty, or nobility only when they are used before persons' names or in place of persons' names.**

    Baron Pierre de Coubertin   **D**ame Judi Dench

    Attorney **G**eneral Janet Reno   **E**mperor Hirohito

Do not capitalize these titles when they are used without proper names or after names.

    We saw the **q**ueen sitting in the royal box.

Family Relationships

▶ **Capitalize words indicating family relationships only when they are used as names or before names.**

Aunt Carla **C**ousin Maggie **G**randpa Johnson

Both **D**ad and **U**ncle Ray love to watch the Olympics on TV.

In general, do **not** capitalize a family-relationship word when it follows a person's name or is used without a proper name.

Lisa Fernandez, my **c**ousin, will compete in the next Olympiad.

The Pronoun *I*

▶ **Always capitalize the pronoun *I*.**

Jo and **I** learned how to play softball from my cousin.

Religious Terms

▶ **Capitalize the names of religions, sacred days, sacred writings, and deities.**

Religious Terms	
Religions	**C**hristianity, **B**uddhism, **I**slam
Sacred days	**R**amadan, **E**aster, **Y**om **K**ippur
Sacred writings	**K**oran, **T**orah, **B**ible
Deities	**G**od, **Y**ahweh, **A**llah

Do not capitalize the words *god* and *goddess* when they refer to gods of ancient mythology.

The ancient Olympic Games honored the Greek **g**od Zeus.

Capitalization **231**

CHAPTER 10

CHAPTER 10

Nationalities, Languages, and Races

▶ Capitalize the names of nationalities, languages, races, and most ethnic groups, as well as adjectives formed from these names.

Kurds	**N**ative **A**merican	**F**rench
Hispanic	**A**frican **A**merican	**K**orean

❷ Practice and Apply

CONCEPT CHECK: People and Cultures

Write the 15 words and abbreviations that should be capitalized but are not in the paragraph below. Capitalize each correctly.

An Olympic Legend

(1) When I was in sixth grade, my class studied the history of the ancient Olympic Games. **(2)** My teacher, mr. jones, assigned the books *The Olympic Games* by Theodore knight and *Olympic Games in Ancient Greece* by Shirley glubok and Alfred tamarin. **(3)** Knight tells of a legendary event that is considered the start of the first Olympics. **(4)** According to legend, king oenomaus offered princess hippodamia's hand in matrimony to the man who could find her and escape in a chariot while being pursued by the king. **(5)** After 13 men failed in their attempt to defeat oenomaus, prince pelops determined he would beat the king. **(6)** Somehow while pelops escaped with the princess, the axle in the king's chariot broke. **(7)** Pelops defeated the king and married hippodamia. **(8)** To celebrate his victory, the prince ordered a feast and gave thanks to the god zeus.

➡ For a SELF-CHECK and more practice, see the EXERCISE BANK, p. 615.

First Words and Titles

LESSON OBJECTIVES

To understand and apply rules for capitalizing first words in sentences, lines of poetry, quotations, outlines, and letters and capitalizing titles of works

❶ Here's the Idea

Sentences and Poetry

▶ **Capitalize the first word of every sentence.**

Baseball comes from an English sport called rounders.

▶ **In traditional poetry capitalize the first word of every line.**

LITERARY MODEL

It looked extremely rocky for the Mudville nine that day;
The score stood two to four, with but an inning left to play.
—Ernest Lawrence Thayer, "Casey at the Bat"

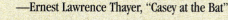

HOT TIP Modern poets sometimes choose not to begin the lines of their poems with capital letters. If you make this choice in your own writing, make sure the meaning of your work is still clear.

Quotations

▶ **Capitalize the first word of a direct quotation presented as a complete sentence.**

Yogi Berra once asked a player, "**H**ow can you think and hit at the same time?"

Babe Ruth once stated that even if a team has "**t**he greatest bunch of individual stars in the world," it won't succeed unless the players play as a team.

▶ **In a divided quotation, do not capitalize the first word of the second part unless it starts a new sentence.**

"Don't worry," said Nina. "**T**here's always next season."

"Yes," said Fred, "**b**ut with us it's always spring training."

Capitalization **233**

DAILY TEST PREPARATION

Error Correction: Subject-Verb Agreement Write the following item on the board or use 🗒 **Daily Test Preparation Transparency** p. DT31. Choose the best way to write the underlined section.

Mom, <u>where's my shoes?</u>

A. where's my shoes!

B. where is my shoes?

C. where are my shoes?

D. Correct as is

Teaching Point: Error correction questions often test your knowledge of subject-verb agreement in inverted sentences. In this case, the subject *shoes* takes a plural verb (*are*). Remember to look for the subject after the verb in questions and other inverted sentences.

THE LANGUAGE OF LITERATURE

The passage on the student page is from "Casey at the Bat" in *The Language of Literature,* Level 7.

CAPITALIZATION

TEACHING RESOURCES

🗒 Time-Saver Transparencies Binder:
• Daily Test Preparation p. DT31
📒 Grammar, Usage, and Mechanics Workbook p. 181

SKILLS PRACTICE RESOURCES

📒 Grammar, Usage, and Mechanics Workbook pp. 182–183
Pupil's Edition Exercise Bank p. 615

MORE MODEL SENTENCES

Write the titles below on the board and ask students to capitalize them correctly.

Book: *how to win friends and influence people*

How to Win Friends and Influence People

Poem: "the rime of the ancient mariner"

"The Rime of the Ancient Mariner"

Song: "i want to hold your hand"

"I Want to Hold Your Hand"

CUSTOMIZING TIP

Students Acquiring English/ESL In many languages, including Spanish, French, and Russian, only the first word in the titles of such literary works as books, plays, poems, stories, and movies, are capitalized. You might want to emphasize to native speakers of these languages the capitalization rules for titles in English.

TEACHING TIP

Point out the correct punctuation of different kinds of titles. Use the chart to show students that titles of books, plays, and so on are italicized; titles of short stories, poems, and songs are placed in quotation marks.

Outlines

▶ **Capitalize the first word of each entry in an outline and the letters that introduce major subsections.**

   I. **T**raditional games
      A. **G**ames played in teams
         1. **B**aseball
         2. **F**ootball
         3. **S**occer
  II. **E**xtreme games
      A. **A**ir games
         1. **S**kydiving
         2. **W**indsurfing

Parts of a Letter

▶ **Capitalize the first word in the greeting and in the closing of a letter.**

Dear Miss Ulasovich:

Yours truly,

Titles of Works

▶ **Capitalize the first word, the last word, and all other important words in a title. Don't capitalize articles, coordinating conjunctions, or prepositions of fewer than five letters.**

Type of Media	Examples
Books	*The Giver, The Call of the Wild*
Plays and musicals	*Bleacher Bums, Les Misérables*
Short stories	"The Noble Experiment," "Thank You, M'am"
Poems	"The Bat," "Ode to an Artichoke"
Periodicals	*Sports Illustrated, Teen People*
Musical compositions	"Take Me Out to the Ball Game," "La Bamba"
Movies	*Hoop Dreams, The Natural*
Television shows	*Weekend Sports, Boy Meets World*
Works of art	*American Gothic, Mona Lisa, The Thinker*

❸ Practice and Apply

A. CONCEPT CHECK: First Words and Titles

Write the words that should be capitalized but are not in these sentences. Capitalize each correctly.

Baseball—America's National Pastime

1. An outline for the game of baseball might begin like this:
   I. how the game is played
     A. equipment
       1. baseball
       2. bat

2. A famous scholar and educator, Jacques Barzun, once wrote, "whoever wants to know the heart and mind of America had better learn baseball."

3. There are many movies about baseball, including *field of dreams*.

4. This movie was based on W. P. Kinsella's book *shoeless joe*.

5. Another enormously popular baseball film is *the natural*.

6. The last line of the poem "casey at the bat" is familiar to many people.

7. It runs, "but there is no joy in Mudville: Mighty Casey has struck out."

8. A letter written by a child to his or her favorite home-run hitter might begin "dear mr. Sosa."

9. The closing of the letter might consist of a phrase such as "sincerely yours."

10. Finally, let us not forget this memorable quote by the New York Mets manager Yogi Berra: "it's never over till it's over."

➡ **For a SELF-CHECK and more practice, see the EXERCISE BANK, p. 615.**

B. WRITING: The Name Game

Identify your favorite short story, magazine, song, movie, and television show. Then for each choice, write a sentence explaining why it's your favorite. Remember to capitalize titles.

235

Answers

Print-Out Option You may create worksheets of exercise A for your students by using the
💿 **Electronic Teacher Tools CD–ROM.**

A. CONCEPT CHECK

Self-Check For a self-check of capitalizing first words and titles, direct students to p. 615 in the Pupil's Edition for the answers to the items circled in yellow.

Answers shown on page. Letters that should be capitalized are underlined three times.

B. WRITING

**Accept all reasonable responses.
Possible responses:**

"Rules of the Game"

Teen People

"Tomorrow"

Titanic

Jeopardy

"Rules of the Game" is my favorite short story because it shows the relationship between a daughter and a mother.

My favorite magazine is *Teen People* because it covers the lives of younger Hollywood stars.

The song "Tomorrow" is my favorite song because it is joyful.

The best movie ever made is *Titanic*; the acting is excellent, and the story line is touching and dramatic.

Jeopardy is my favorite television show because it is challenging.

ASSESSMENT

Assessment Masters:
• Chapter Mid-point Test p. 33

Mixed Review

Answers

Print-Out Option You may create worksheets of exercise A for your students by using the **Electronic Teacher Tools CD–ROM.**

A. Capitalization in Outlining

Answers shown on page. Letters that should be capitalized are underlined three times.

B. Capitalization in a Business Letter

Answers shown on page. Letters that should be capitalized are underlined three times.

CHAPTER 10

TEACHING TIP

Discuss with students the importance of using correct capitalization in a business letter. Ask students to evaluate how well Gabe's letter achieves its purposes.

Mixed Review

A. Capitalization in Outlining Rewrite the following portion of an outline, correcting the nine words that should be capitalized.

I. indoor games
  A. board games
  B. word and picture games
    1. charades
    2. twenty questions
II. outdoor games
  A. ball games
    1. baseball
    2. soccer

B. Capitalization in a Business Letter Rewrite the following business letter, correcting the 15 words that should be capitalized.

1399 Maple Street
Wilmette, Illinois 60091
January 2, 2000

Mr. Dominic d. Domenicas, sr.
The Domino Company
333 Congress Parkway
Highland Heights, Ohio 44143

dear mr. domenicas:
    I am writing about the set of dominoes, made by your company, that i recently purchased. Unfortunately, my set is incomplete, containing only 27 dominoes rather than the usual 28. since your picture is shown on the box, with the words underneath it stating, "your satisfaction is guaranteed or your money will be promptly refunded," i am writing directly to you.
    My uncle david and i are very eager to try out the new dominoes. Please let me know what your company can do to correct this matter.

sincerely yours,
Gabe zaharias
Gabe zaharias

236 Grammar, Usage, and Mechanics

Places and Transportation

1 Here's the Idea

Geographical Names

▶ **In geographical names, capitalize each word except articles and prepositions.**

Geographical Names	
Divisions of the world	Northern Hemisphere, Arctic Circle
Continents	Africa, North America, Australia
Bodies of water	Lake Erie, Pacific Ocean, Nile River
Islands	Oahu, Philippines, Aleutian Islands
Mountains	Rocky Mountains, Mount Hood, Andes
Other landforms	Niagara Falls, Cape Horn, Gobi Desert
Regions	Latin America, Southeast Asia, Gulf of Mexico
Nations	Monaco, Peru, Canada, Czech Republic
States	Texas, California, Florida
Cities and towns	Chicago, Providence, Olympia
Roads and streets	Pennsylvania Avenue, Interstate 55, Main Street

Bodies of the Universe

▶ **Capitalize the names of planets and other specific objects in the universe.**

Milky Way	Halley's Comet	Triton
Venus	Alpha Centauri	Pluto

Two moons of Mars were discovered—Phobos and Deimos.

Capitalization **237**

DAILY TEST PREPARATION

Sentence Completion: Pronoun-Antecedent Agreement Write the following item on the board or use 🖥 **Daily Test Preparation Transparency** p. DT31. Choose the word that belongs in the space.

> Typical teenagers come home after school and seat _____ in front of the television.

A. themselves

B. himself

C. there

D. their

Teaching Point: For sentence completion questions, the correct answer will always

- fit the meaning of the sentence (*there* does not make sense with *seat*).

- fit grammatically within the sentence (*himself* does not agree in number with *teenagers; their* uses the possessive pronoun when the reflexive is needed).

TEACHING TIP

Cross-Curricular Connection

Geography Have students work in pairs to find geographical names that begin with the letters *H, I, K, Y,* and *Z*. Students can use world atlases, maps, and encyclopedias to gather names. Ask volunteers to share their results with the class.

TEACHING RESOURCES

 Time-Saver Transparencies Binder:
- Daily Test Preparation p. DT31

 Grammar, Usage, and Mechanics Workbook p. 184

SKILLS PRACTICE RESOURCES

 Grammar, Usage, and Mechanics Workbook pp. 185–186
Pupil's Edition Exercise Bank p. 616

Regions and Sections

▶ **Capitalize the words *north, south, east,* and *west* when they name particular regions of the United States or the world or are parts of proper names.**

In **S**outh Africa, children use small stones to play a game called *diteko.*

Children who live in the **N**orth might enjoy the snow game known as fox and geese.

Do not capitalize these words when they indicate general directions or locations.

If you go **s**outh on Main Street, you will find Mel's Video Rental.

Buildings, Bridges, and Other Landmarks

▶ **Capitalize the names of specific buildings, bridges, monuments, and other landmarks.**

World **T**rade **C**enter   **S**tatue of **L**iberty

Golden **G**ate **B**ridge   **V**ietnam **M**emorial

Did you know that **F**ort **S**umter is a national monument?

Planes, Trains, and Other Vehicles

▶ **Capitalize the names of specific airplanes, trains, ships, cars, and spacecraft.**

Vehicle Names	
Airplanes	*Air Force One, Spirit of St. Louis*
Trains	*Southwest Chief, Orient Express*
Ships	USS *Arizona, Pinta*
Cars	*Mustang, Prelude, Pathfinder*
Spacecraft	*Challenger, Columbia, Apollo V*

CUSTOMIZING TIP

Less Proficient Learners Have students write the names of places in their neighborhood, city, and state that are capitalized. Students can use this list as a reference for their writing.

TEACHING TIP

Point out that the names Statue of Liberty and Spirit of St. Louis are capitalized like the titles of works. Prepositions with fewer than five letters, such as *of*, are not capitalized. Other examples:

Tower of London

District of Columbia

Spice It Up!

Divide the class into two teams. Read aloud the following sentences and have teams take turns identifying which words should be capitalized.
1. Land is generally flat in the midwest. Midwest
2. I live west of the lake and north of clear springs bridge. Clear Springs Bridge
3. Columbus sailed on the *niña,* the *pinta,* and the *santa maria. Niña,* the *Pinta,* and the *Santa María*
4. The pioneers traveled to the west, searching for new farmland. West

② Practice and Apply

A. CONCEPT CHECK: Places and Transportation

Write the words that should be capitalized but are not in each sentence. Capitalize each correctly.

Just Playing Games

1. Dr. Jane J. Peabody's research for her book took her all over north america.
2. First, she boarded the train called the *cardinal*.
3. In the appalachian mountains she learned about homemade folk games, such as button on a string.
4. Later, in New Orleans, she saw the gulf of mexico for the first time.
5. She rented a Ford taurus for the next leg of her journey.
6. Heading west, she visited at the grand canyon.
7. San luis, a town in northern mexico, provided a wealth of information about Native American games, such as *el coyote*.
8. Driving along the Pacific coastline, Dr. Peabody took some time to see the Redwood National forest.
9. She continued north to vancouver, british Colombia, where she observed Canadian children playing games.
10. Dr. Peabody eventually arrived back home in champaign, illinois, with stacks of information to use for her book.

➡ **For a SELF-CHECK and more practice, see the EXERCISE BANK, p. 616.**

B. REVISING: Correcting Map Titles

Answers in column.

Look at this map of the eastern part of Australia, site of the games of the XXVII Olympiad. Find and correct five capitalization errors.

239

Answers

Print-Out Option You may create worksheets of exercise A for your students by using the
💿 **Electronic Teacher Tools CD–ROM.**

A. CONCEPT CHECK

Self-Check For a self-check of capitalizing names of places and vehicles, direct students to p. 616 in the Pupil's Edition for the answers to the items circled in yellow.

Answers shown on page. Letters that should be capitalized are underlined three times.

B. REVISING

Words that should be capitalized are in boldface type.

1. **Gulf** of Carpentaria
2. Coral **Sea**
3. and 4. Great **Barrier Reef**
5. Flinders **River**

CAPITALIZATION

CAPITALIZATION

LESSON 4 Organizations and Other Subjects

1 Here's the Idea

Organizations and Institutions

▶ **Capitalize all important words in the names of organizations, institutions, stores, and companies.**

Library of Congress   Jefferson Middle School

Harry's Finer Foods   Babe Ruth Baseball League

Historical Events, Periods, and Documents

▶ **Capitalize the names of historical events, periods, and documents.**

Historical Events, Periods, and Documents	
Events	Civil War, Boston Tea Party, French Revolution
Periods	Great Depression, Bronze Age, Middle Ages
Documents	Bill of Rights, Gettysburg Address, Panama Canal Treaty

Do you have any relatives who were in the Gulf War?

Time Abbreviations and Calendar Items

▶ **Capitalize the abbreviations B.C., A.D., A.M., and P.M.**

The first recorded Olympic contest took place in 776 B.C.

The volleyball tryouts are at 5:00 P.M. sharp.

▶ **Capitalize the names of months, days, and holidays, but not the names of seasons (except when they are part of the names of festivals or celebrations).**

April   Saturday   Thanksgiving Day

May   Winter Formal   Fourth of July

This year my birthday, April 7, is on a Sunday.

Memorial Day is the unofficial start of summer.

240 Grammar, Usage, and Mechanics

Special Events, Awards, and Brand Names

▶ **Capitalize the names of special events and awards.**

Heisman **T**rophy   **W**orld **C**up

Pulitzer **P**rize   **P**an-**A**merican **G**ames

The annual **H**arvest **F**estival is scheduled for next weekend.

▶ **Capitalize the brand name of a product but not a common noun that follows a brand name.**

Spiker volleyballs   **E**asy **O**ver hurdles

② Practice and Apply

CONCEPT CHECK: Organizations and Other Subjects Answers in column.

Find and correct ten capitalization errors in the school-calendar page below.

north side junior high

LIONS

Weekly Events

september Events

Sunday, Sept. 1
Monday, Sept. 2:   Labor day
tuesday, Sept. 3:   3:30 P.m. girls' volleyball tryouts

Wednesday, Sept. 4:   Auditions for Thornton Wilder's *Our Town*

Thursday, Sept. 5:   Lions vs. vikings at home football game

Friday, Sept. 6:   District 112 Board of education meeting

Saturday, Sept. 7:   NSJH car wash

241

Spice It Up!
Have groups of students work on posters that announce special events at the school. Make sure students include dates and times, as well as the names of specific people or groups involved. Display the posters in the hallway or on a bulletin board in the class.

LESSON OBJECTIVES

To apply capitalization rules in revising a memo and writing an article

TEACHING TIP

Cooperative Learning Have groups of students work together to write directions to their school from some place in their community: a park, bridge, public building, or other landmark. Ask students to apply the capitalization rules in this chapter as criteria to evaluate their writing.

Grammar in Physical Education

Making the Most of Capitals

Writing is important in everything—even at sports meets. Although athletes may not write while they're throwing the shot put or sprinting the last 50 meters, they do need to share information about rules, schedules, and events.

The team manager for the Mae Jemison Jets has drafted a reminder memo for the members of his team. Because he was in a rush, he made a few errors in capitalization. Luckily, he had a friend proofread his draft.

Instructions for Round-Robin Track Meet

Where:

City is a proper noun.

South Village Recreation Area, Sauk (city)

Less-for-More is a brand name.

Directions for carpool drivers:

Take Onarga Street west to Route 42. Turn left and go three blocks. (You'll pass Martha's Cafe on the right and a (less-for-more) gas station on the left.) Park in the section marked with an orange banner.

When:

Wednesday is a proper noun.

(wednesday)

October 13, 3:00 P.M.

What to bring:

(bring) instruction sheet, track shoes, warm-up suit, and water bottle.

Capitalize the first word in a sentence.

What to do once you get there:

- Go to the area assigned to Mae Jemison (junior high.)

  Proper noun

- Check the schedule.
- (do) your warm-up exercises.
- Be at the track at least 15 minutes before your race.
- *Relax and do your best!*

Michael is a proper noun.

For more information, contact (michael) Warner, 555-3745.

ACROSS the CURRICULUM
PHYSICAL EDUCATION

Practice and Apply

Writing: Reporting the Results Use the results in the diagram to write an article about the Jets for your school newspaper. Include the following information in your article:

• when and where the meet was held

• how each team did

• the name of the winning team (You decide.)

• any particularly exciting or unusual events during the meet

Be sure to check your capitalization. Save your paragraph in your 📁 **Working Portfolio.**

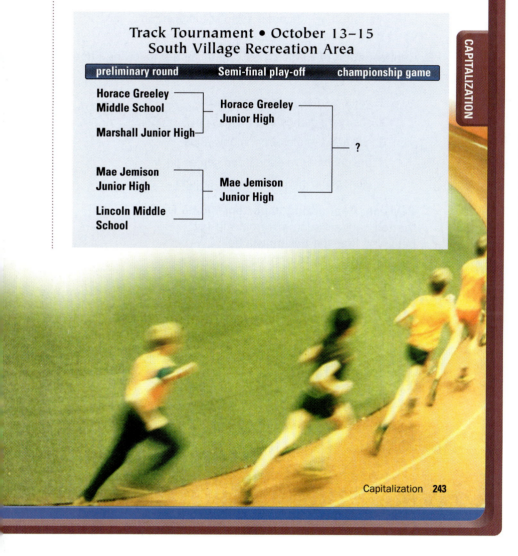

Track Tournament • October 13–15
South Village Recreation Area

preliminary round	Semi-final play-off	championship game

Horace Greeley Middle School
Marshall Junior High
→ Horace Greeley Junior High

Mae Jemison Junior High
Lincoln Middle School
→ Mae Jemison Junior High

?

Capitalization **243**

Answers
PRACTICE AND APPLY

Articles will vary. Students should include information from the chart in their articles. A sample response follows:

Jets Meet the Hornets in Semi-finals

On October 13-15, four schools competed in a Round-Robin Track Tournament at the South Village Recreation Area. In the preliminary round held on October 13, the Horace Greeley Hornets beat the Marshall Magnets. On the next day, the preliminary round continued as the Mae Jemison Jets defeated the Lincoln Cavaliers in an exciting competition.

On October 15, the Jets played against the Hornets in the semi-finals. Though all track events were close, the Hornets crept past the Jets by 1 point and won the championship. Although the Jets came in second overall in the meet, their fans showed their tremendous support by filling the stadium with loud cheers.

Capitalization **243**

Mixed Review

Mixed Review

A. Proofreading: Capitalization Identify and correct the 25 capitalization errors in the following paragraph.

STUDENT MODEL

It takes most people between 10 and 15 minutes to run a mile; only world-class runners can run the mile in less than 4 minutes. On may 6, 1954, in oxford, england, roger bannister broke the 4-minute-mile barrier that many people had failed to surpass. While bannister was a medical student at st. mary's hospital in london, he trained as a runner for britain's amateur athletic association (AAA) team. Bannister's world record of 3 minutes and 59.4 seconds stood for only seven weeks before john landy ran the mile in 3 minutes and 58 seconds in turku, finland. In july 1999 the moroccan runner hicham el guerrouj claimed the world record by running the mile in an astonishing 3 minutes 43:13 seconds in rome, italy.

B. Capitalization of Book Titles Capitalize the following titles of books correctly.

1. board games round the world
2. children's games and rhymes
3. children's games from many lands
4. the cooperative sports and games book
5. games and sports the world around

C. Revision: Capitalizing Important Words Fix the ten capitalization errors in the text below so that the tickets will be correct when they're printed.

wilson basketball tournament
Harrison broncos vs. Lincoln tigers
monday, October 18
4:30 p.m.
washington center

Mastery Test: What Did You Learn?

For each underlined passage, choose the letter of the correct revision.

I received an invitation to a <u>Memorial day party</u> at my friend
(1)
<u>David corny's house</u>. The party was to be on <u>monday, May</u> 27, at
(2)   (3)
<u>12:30 P.m. The</u> invitation stated that we would be going on a
(4)
scavenger hunt. I had never before been on a scavenger hunt.

When I got to David's house, <u>his mom, mrs. Corny</u>, handed each
(5)
of us partygoers a list of items that we needed to find during the
scavenger hunt. About 20 items were listed, including a <u>native
American belt</u>, the book <u>*to Kill a Mockingbird*</u>, a pink sock,
(6)   (7)
<u>Mr. Suds bubble bath</u>, and a roll of candy from <u>the Lions' club</u>.
(8)   (9)
Right then and there I knew that we would all be jumping into

Mrs. Corny's <u>SUV and driving all over Wisconsin</u> for the rest of
(10)
our lives to find all of that stuff.

1. (A) Day
   B. memorial
   C. Party
   D. Correct as is

2. A. House
   B. david
   (C) Corny's
   D. Correct as is

3. (A) Monday, May
   B. monday, may
   C. Monday, may
   D. Correct as is

4. A. the
   B. p.m.
   (C) P.M.
   D. Correct as is

5. A. Mom
   B. corny
   (C) Mrs.
   D. Correct as is

6. A. american
   (B) Native
   C. Belt
   D. Correct as is

7. (A) *To*
   B. *kill*
   C. *mockingbird*
   D. Correct as is

8. A. mr.
   (B) Bubble Bath
   C. suds
   D. Correct as is

9. A. lions'
   (B) Club
   C. The
   D. Correct as is

10. A. wisconsin
    B. Suv
    C. suv
    (D) Correct as is

Mastery Test

As an option, two other Chapter Mastery Tests appear in ▓ **Assessment Masters** pp. 83–86.

Answers circled on page.

PRESCRIPTION FOR MASTERY	
If students miss item number:	Use **Teaching Resources** and **Skills Practice Resources** for lesson:
1, 3, 4, 8, 9	❹ Organizations and Other Subjects p. 240
2, 5, 6	❼ People and Cultures p. 230
7	❷ First Words and Titles p. 233
10	❸ Places and Transportation p. 237

Student Help Desk

Capitalization at a Glance

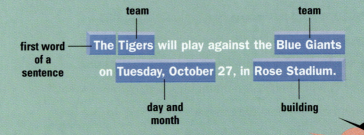

first word of a sentence

team — The **Tigers** will play against the **Blue Giants**

team — **Blue Giants**

on **Tuesday, October** 27, in **Rose Stadium**.

day and month

building

Do Capitalize

 YOU'RE SAFE!

Proper nouns that name particular people, places, or things:
The **F**inn family will visit **S**ydney, **A**ustralia, for the **O**lympic **G**ames.

Family words used with names or in place of names:
Julia watched the hockey game with **U**ncle Tim.

First words of sentences:
Who will win this year's state championship?

First words in lines of traditional poetry:
And somewhere men are laughing, and somewhere children shout,
But there is no joy in Mudville: Mighty Casey has struck out.
—Ernest Lawrence Thayer, "Casey at the Bat"

First words and important words in titles:
The House on Mango Street

Proper nouns that name particular dates, holidays, events, or awards.
On **J**uly 4, **I**ndependence **D**ay, Gus will compete in the **N**ewport **S**ummer **C**ook-**O**ff.

Don't Capitalize

Common nouns referring to people, places, or things:

Our **t**eam is traveling south through the **d**esert for our next meet.

Family words used as common nouns:

My **c**ousin is the fastest sprinter in the entire state.

First words in lines of some contemporary poems:

the world is not a pleasant place

to be without

someone to hold and be held by

    —Nikki Giovanni, "The World Is Not a Pleasant Place to Be"

Articles, conjunctions, and short prepositions in titles:

"Ode **t**o **a**n Artichoke"

Common nouns referring to times, events, or awards:

Jasmine is planning on running the **m**arathon in the spring.

The Bottom Line

Checklist for Capitalization

Have I capitalized . . .

____ people's names and initials?

____ personal titles preceding names?

____ names of races, languages, and nationalities?

____ names of religions and other religious terms?

____ names of bodies of the universe?

____ names of monuments, bridges, and other landmarks?

____ names of particular planes, trains, and other vehicles?

____ names of historical events, eras, and documents?

____ names of special events, awards and brands?

Capitalization **247**

Teacher's Notes
WHAT DOESN'T WORK:

CHAPTER 11

CHAPTER RESOURCES

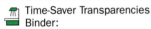 Time-Saver Transparencies
Binder:
- Daily Test Preparation
  pp. DT32–36
- Quick-Fix Grammar and
  Style Charts p. QF10

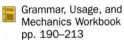 Grammar, Usage, and
Mechanics Workbook
pp. 190–213

Integrated Technology and Media

 Electronic Teacher Tools
CD-ROM

 Grammar Coach CD-ROM
Lessons 2–3

 mcdougallittell.com

Assessment

 Assessment Masters:
- Chapter Pretest pp. 22–23
- Chapter Mid-point Test
  p. 34
- Chapter Mastery Tests
  pp. 87–92

 Test Generator CD-ROM

 mcdougallittell.com
Grammar Chapter Quiz

CHAPTER 11

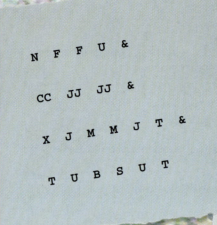

TOP SECRET

SECRET CODE: FOR YOUR EYES ONLY

A=Z	J=I	S=R
B=A	K=J	T=S
C=B	L=K	U=T
D=C	M=L	V=U
E=D	N=M	W=V
F=E	O=N	X=W
G=F	P=O	Y=X
H=G	Q=P	Z=Y
I=H	R=Q	

& = letter space		
AA=1	EE=5	II=9
BB=2	FF=6	JJ=0
CC=3	GG=7	
DD=4	HH=8	

N F F U &

CC JJ JJ &

X J M M J T &

T U B S U T

Theme: Secret Messages

What's It All About?

You may have figured out the words and numbers in the secret
message above, but without punctuation, what do they mean?
Are you to meet at 300 Willis Street? Or are you to meet at
3:00 and go to a movie called *Willis?* Maybe the movie starts
at 3:00, so you'll need to meet earlier. By now, you see how
important punctuation can be!

Write Away: I've Got a Secret

Write a short message to a friend in which you use a simple
code of letters, numbers, or nonsense words. Be sure to use
punctuation in your message. Keep your message and your
code key in your 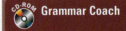 **Working Portfolio.**

Grammar Coach

Diagnostic Test: What Do You Know?

Choose the letter of the best revision of each underlined item.

> Not all secret messages are codes, ciphers are used for secret
> (1)
> communication too. A code is a group of words symbols or numbers
> (2)
> that has meaning to the receiver. For example, in World War II, the
> message It is hot in Suez instructed France's resistance to attack
> (3)   (4)
> railroad lines. In a cipher, by contrast, the letters of a message are
> (5)
> scrambled or replaced by other letters or numbers. You could write
> "I can;t read one half of your cipher" by using a number for each
> (6)   (7)
> alphabet letter. Would it surprise you that *cipher* comes from a
> word meaning "to number" Cryptology, the science of code breaking
> (8)   (9)
> comes from two Greek words meaning "secret wording." To learn
> more, read "The Secret Code Book" by Helen Huckle.
> (10)

1. **A.** codes; ciphers are
   B. codes? Ciphers are
   C. codes! Ciphers are
   D. Correct as is

2. A. words: symbols or numbers
   B. words, symbols or numbers
   C. words, symbols, or numbers
   D. Correct as is

3. A. It is hot in Suez"
   B. "It is hot in Suez"
   C. "It is hot in Suez
   D. Correct as is

4. A. Frances'
   B. Frances
   C. France"s
   D. Correct as is

5. A. In a cipher, by contrast;
   B. In a cipher by contrast,
   C. In a cipher, by contrast
   D. Correct as is

6. A. can,t
   B. can't
   C. cant
   D. Correct as is

7. A. one—half
   B. one-half
   C. one'half
   D. Correct as is

8. A. "to number."
   B. "to number?"
   C. "to number"?
   D. Correct as is

9. **A.** Cryptology, the science of
      code breaking,
   B. Cryptology the science of
      code breaking,
   C. Cryptology; the science of
      code breaking
   D. Correct as is

10. A. The Secret Code Book
    B. *"The Secret Code Book"*
    C. *The Secret Code Book*
    D. Correct as is

Diagnostic Test

As an option, a Grammar Chapter Pretest appears in 📗 **Assessment Masters** pp. 22–23.

Answers circled on page.

Use the chart below to determine which lessons students need.

PRESCRIPTION FOR SUCCESS	
If students miss item number:	Work on lesson:
1	❶ Periods and Other End Marks p. 250
2, 5, 9	❷ Commas in Sentences p. 253
3, 8	❹ Punctuating Quotations p. 258
4, 6	❼ Apostrophes p. 266
7	❻ Hyphens, Dashes, and Parentheses p. 264
10	❽ Punctuating Titles p. 268

The **Diagnostic Test** parallels the **Mastery Test** on page 273. Have students keep the test in their portfolios to compare with their results on the **Mastery Test**.

BLOCK SCHEDULING

Pressed for Time?
Cover the lessons that many students have trouble with: **Lesson 2, Commas in Sentences; Lesson 5, Semicolons and Colons; Lesson 7, Apostrophes.** Have students complete **Here's the Idea** and **Practice and Apply, Concept Check** only, for those lessons.

Time for More?
After covering each lesson, have students revise a paragraph from their 📁 **Working Portfolios.** Students should correct any punctuation errors. Encourage students to find places to use semicolons and colons.

LESSON OBJECTIVES

To recognize and use periods, question marks, and exclamation points correctly

DAILY TEST PREPARATION

Error Identification: Spelling
Write the following item on the board or use 🏛 **Daily Test Preparation Transparency** p. DT32. Decide which type of error, if any, appears in the underlined section.

> The girls were pleased to learn <u>that the chemistry experiment actualy worked</u>.

A. Spelling error

B. Capitalization error

C. Punctuation error

D. No error

Teaching Point: A common spelling item in error identification questions is adding suffixes. When adding the suffix *-ly* to *actual* and other words ending in *l*, keep both *l's*.

TEACHING TIP

Remind students that question marks are used with statement sentences that end with questions. Example: *You're from Iowa, aren't you?*

LESSON 1

Periods and Other End Marks

❶ Here's the Idea

Periods, question marks, and exclamation points are known as **end marks** because they are used to indicate the end of a sentence. Periods have other uses as well.

Periods

▶ **Use a period at the end of a declarative sentence.**

A declarative sentence makes a statement.

> Our team uses a code to make up plays.
>
> The key is a carefully kept secret.

▶ **Use a period at the end of almost every imperative sentence.** An imperative sentence gives a command. Some imperative sentences express excitement or emotion and therefore end with exclamation points.

> Do not ask me to reveal our code.
>
> Stop! Don't tell the other team!

▶ **Use a period at the end of an indirect question.** An indirect question reports what a person asked without using the person's exact words.

INDIRECT QUESTION	The coach asked if our team code had been broken.
DIRECT QUESTION	The coach asked, "Has our team code been broken?"

Question Marks

▶ **Use a question mark at the end of an interrogative sentence.** An interrogative sentence asks a question.

> Did the other team break the code?
>
> Have they figured out all our plays?

250 Grammar, Usage, and Mechanics

TEACHING RESOURCES

 Time-Saver Transparencies Binder:
• Daily Test Preparation p. DT32

 Grammar, Usage, and Mechanics Workbook p. 190

SKILLS PRACTICE RESOURCES

 Grammar, Usage, and Mechanics Workbook pp. 191–192

Pupil's Edition Exercise Bank p. 617

 Grammar Coach CD-ROM Lesson 2

Exclamation Points

▶ **Use an exclamation point to end an exclamatory sentence.** An exclamatory sentence expresses strong feeling.

> What a terrible situation !

▶ **Use an exclamation point after an interjection or any other exclamatory expression.**

> Oh ! I have an idea !
>
> Wow ! Tell us !

Other Uses for Periods

▶ **Use a period at the end of most abbreviations or after an initial.**

Common Abbreviations and Initials			
Abbreviations			
sec. second	**Thurs.** Thursday	**lb.** pound	**gal.** gallon
min. minute	**Pres.** President	**hr.** hour	**mo.** month
St. Street	**Feb.** February	**yr.** year	**in.** inch
Initials			
R.N. registered nurse		**P.M.** *post meridiem* (after noon)	
B.A. bachelor of arts		**M.D.** doctor of medicine	
P.O. post office		**R.K.S.** Rebecca Kate Simmons	
Abbreviations Without Periods			
CIA Central Intelligence Agency		**mph** miles per hour	
VCR videocassette recorder		**cm** centimeter	
CA California		**mm** millimeter	

▶ **Use a period after each number or letter in an outline or a list.**

Outline	List
Uses for Codes	Communication Codes
I. Use in wartime	1. Braille
A. World War I	2. American Sign Language
B. World War II	3. Egyptian hieroglyphics
II. Industrial uses	4. Mayan hieroglyphics
A. To protect new methods	5. Morse code
B. To protect consumers' privacy	6. semaphore

Punctuation **251**

Answers

Print-Out Option You may create worksheets of exercises A and B for your students by using the 💿 **Electronic Teacher Tools CD–ROM.**

A. CONCEPT CHECK

Self-Check For a self-check of periods and other end marks, direct students to p. 617 in the Pupil's Edition for the answers to the items circled in yellow.

Answers shown on page.

B. WRITING

Thurs., Feb. 12

Drive to P.O.

825 Elm St.

Go 25 mph.

Find Dr. Lee.

Get secret VCR tape.

Take tape in a taxi by 8:00 P.M.

Every sec. counts

---

❷ Practice and Apply

A. CONCEPT CHECK: Periods and Other End Marks

Write the proper end mark for each numbered blank below.

Timely Messages

Do you think you are the only one interested in secret writing **1** ? Nonsense **2** ! For hundreds of years, people have used secret messages **3** ⊙ Did you know that the great Roman general Julius Caesar invented a cipher **4** ? He used it to communicate with his staff in Rome **5** ⊙ Consider also Mary Queen of Scots, who smuggled ciphers out of her household in England **6** ⊙ One cipher told of a plot to kill England's queen, Elizabeth I. Poor Mary **7** ! Her note was intercepted and read, and she was put to death. During World War II, what do you think the Allies found in sunken German submarines **8** ? They found German codebooks. They used the books to decode messages about German naval operations **9** ⊙ What do you think happened **10** ?

➡ For a **SELF-CHECK** and more practice, see the **EXERCISE BANK, p. 617.**

B. WRITING: Punctuating Abbreviations   Answers in column.

The notes below were taken by a spy who had forgotten how to punctuate abbreviations. Write the notes, using correct punctuation.

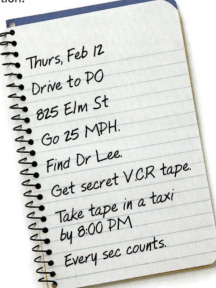

Thurs, Feb 12
Drive to PO
825 Elm St
Go 25 MPH.
Find Dr Lee.
Get secret V.C.R tape.
Take tape in a taxi by 8:00 PM
Every sec counts.

252 Grammar, Usage, and Mechanics

Spice It Up!

Write the following sentence on the board. Have students add periods to the abbreviations where needed. Then have them "decode" the sentence by telling what each abbreviation stands for.

On Tues, Nov 5, MJG, MD, drove to the PO at 35 mph.

On Tues., Nov. 5, M.J.G., M.D., drove to the P.O. at 35 m.p.h.

On Tuesday, November 5, Mary Joe Garcia, Doctor of Medicine, drove to the post office at 35 miles per hour.

Commas in Sentences

1 Here's the Idea

Commas are used to make the meanings of sentences clear by separating certain elements of the sentences.

Commas in Compound Sentences

▶ **Use a comma before a conjunction that joins independent clauses in a compound sentence.**

The ancient Egyptians' written language was called hieroglyphics **,** **and** it was not decoded for many centuries.

In ancient times, scribes could read and write hieroglyphics **,** **but** most other Egyptians could not.

Scribes passed rigorous examinations **,** **or** they were rejected as scribes.

Sometimes a sentence has a two-part compound verb but is not a compound sentence. Do not use a comma in this kind of sentence.

Scribes could **read** and **write** hieroglyphics.

Commas with Items in a Series

▶ **Use a comma after every item in a series except the last one.** A series consists of three or more items.

Symbols of **birds ,** **lions ,** and **snakes** appear in hieroglyphics.

Hieroglyphics could be read **from left to right ,** **from right to left ,** or **from top to bottom.**

Hieroglyphic writing was used for **business contracts ,** **legal documents ,** and other **important records.**

▶ **Use a comma between adjectives of equal rank that modify the same noun.**

Punctuation **253**

TEACHING TIP

Explain to students that, although there is no set limit to the number of items they can list in a series, listing too many items can confuse readers.

TEACHING RESOURCES

 Time-Saver Transparencies Binder:
- Daily Test Preparation p. DT33
- Quick-Fix Grammar and Style Charts p. QF10

 Grammar, Usage, and Mechanics Workbook p. 193

SKILLS PRACTICE RESOURCES

 Grammar, Usage, and Mechanics Workbook pp. 194–195
   Pupil's Edition Exercise Bank p. 618

💿 Grammar Coach CD-ROM Lesson 3

CUSTOMIZING TIP

Gifted and Talented Tell students that sometimes, for sentence variety, a writer will begin a sentence with more than one introductory word or phrase: *Softly, slowly, the cat moved across the room.* Mention that in this case, when a conjunction is not used, commas are needed after each introductory word.

TEACHING TIP

Tell students that the use of commas often depends on the placement of words or phrases in the sentence, not on the words themselves. For example, in the sentence *Closing time, I think, is six o'clock,* the words *I think* are set off with commas. In the sentence *I think the closing time is six o'clock,* the words *I think* are not set off with commas because they don't interrupt the main idea.

TEACHING TIP

Speaking and Listening Tell students that commas often indicate where readers should pause. Read aloud the following sentences. Have students listen for and identify the places where commas should be used.

After a long wait, the dentist could finally see me.

The bakers worked, without stopping once, to finish the cake.

Sara and Keesha, your turn is next.

Here's How **Adding Commas Between Adjectives**

To decide whether a comma is needed between two adjectives modifying the same noun, try one of the following tests.

Hieroglyphics used colorful decorative symbols.

1. Place the word *and* between the adjectives.
   Hieroglyphics used colorful and decorative symbols.

2. If the sentence still makes sense, replace *and* with a comma.
   Hieroglyphics used colorful , decorative symbols.

1. **Or** reverse the order of the adjectives.
   Hieroglyphics used decorative and colorful symbols.

2. If the the sentence still makes sense, replace *and* with a comma.
   Hieroglyphics used decorative , colorful symbols.

WATCH OUT Do not use a comma between adjectives that express a single idea.

The symbols were often painted with brilliant gold paint.

Commas with Introductory Words and Phrases

▶ **Use a comma after an introductory phrase that contains a prepositional phrase. Use a comma after introductory words.**

Even after 2,000 years of study, no one could read hieroglyphics.

Finally, the Rosetta Stone was found in Egypt.

Commas with Interrupters

▶ **Use commas to set off a word or phrase that interrupts the flow of thought in a sentence.**

The stone provided, **at long last,** a key to hieroglyphics.

▶ **Use commas to set off nouns of direct address.** A noun of direct address names the person or group being spoken to.

Alex, your class would be thrilled with this discovery.

Your class, **Alex,** would be thrilled with this discovery.

Commas with Appositives

An **appositive** is a word or phrase that identifies or renames a noun or pronoun that comes right before it. Use commas when the appositive adds extra information; do not use commas when the appositive is needed to make the meaning clear.

Jean Champollion **, a French scholar,** deciphered the Rosetta stone. (The phrase *a French scholar* adds extra information.)

The French scholar **Jean Champollion** deciphered the Rosetta stone. (The phrase *Jean Champollion* tells which French scholar and makes the sentence clear and complete.)

Commas to Avoid Confusion

▶ **Use a comma whenever the reader might otherwise be confused.**

UNCLEAR   Before hieroglyphics records were not kept on stone or paper.

CLEAR   Before hieroglyphics **,** records were not kept on stone or paper.

UNCLEAR   After we studied hieroglyphics were less mysterious.

CLEAR   After we studied **,** hieroglyphics were less mysterious.

❷ Practice and Apply

CONCEPT CHECK: Commas in Sentences

Write the following paragraph, adding commas where they are needed.

A Hairy Story

Think of this readers when you have your next haircut. A Persian king had to get a message to his military leader a Persian general. The king shaved a man's head tattooed a message on his bare scalp and told the man to let the hair grow back. The man then traveled to find the general but no one knew he carried a message. When he reached the general however he delivered his message. Yes as you guessed it he had his head shaved again!

➡ For a SELF-CHECK and more practice, see the EXERCISE BANK, p. 618.

Punctuation   **255**

TEACHING TIP

Explain that the word *appositive* comes from a Latin word meaning "put near." An appositive is placed next to the noun that it explains or renames.

MORE MODEL SENTENCES

Write the following sentences on the board. Have students explain why the sentences are confusing, and then have them add commas to clear up the confusion.

Next door friends and neighbors prepared for the party.

Next door, friends and neighbors prepared for the party.

After we called Joan came over.

After we called, Joan came over.

Answers

Print-Out Option You may create worksheets of this exercise for your students by using the ⊙ **Electronic Teacher Tools CD–ROM.**

A. CONCEPT CHECK

Self-Check For a self-check of commas in sentences, direct students to p. 618 in the Pupil's Edition for the answers to the first two errors in the paragraph.

Answers shown on page.

LESSON OBJECTIVES

To understand and apply rules for using commas in dates, addresses, and letters

DAILY TEST PREPARATION

Error Identification: Punctuation
Write the following item on the board or use ▣ **Daily Test Preparation Transparency** p. DT33. Look for mistakes in punctuation in this sentence. Decide which line, if any, contains a mistake.

A. I continue to return

B. to school, to learn

C. more grammar.

D. *(No mistakes)*

Teaching Point: Error identification questions often test your knowledge of basic punctuation rules. In this item, a comma is not necessary after *school.* The sentence contains only one clause.

TEACHING TIP

Remind students that commas are not inserted in page numbers, addresses, years, and ZIP codes. In general, however, commas are used in numbers of four or more digits.

CHAPTER 11

LESSON 3 # Commas: Dates, Addresses, and Letters

CHAPTER 11

❶ Here's the Idea

See these rules in action in the letter below.

Commas in Dates, Addresses, and Letters	
Commas in dates	In dates, use a comma between the day and the year. (Use a comma after the year if the sentence continues.)
Commas in addresses	Use a comma between the city or town and the state or country. (Use a comma after the state or country if the sentence continues.)
Commas in letters	Use a comma after the greeting of a casual letter and after the closing of a casual or business letter.

1   385 Webster Avenue   **Line 2:** comma between city and state
2   Hanover, MA 02339
3   March 26, 2000   **Line 3:** comma between day and year

4   Dear Alanna,   **Line 4:** comma after greeting
5   Do you remember the code we used
6   to keep secrets from our nosy
7   brothers? Well, some animals have
8   codes too. They understand each
9   other. On February 12, 2000,   **Line 9:** comma after year
10   a scientist from Denver, Colorado,   **Line 10:** comma after state
11   spoke at my school. She told us
12   that bees communicate by the
13   way they move. A bee's dance
14   can tell other bees where to find
15   good flowers for making honey. Isn't
16   that incredible? Come and visit soon.

17   Your friend,   **Line 17:** comma after closing
18   Regina

 Do not use a comma between the state and the ZIP code.

256 Grammar, Usage, and Mechanics

TEACHING RESOURCES

 Time-Saver Transparencies Binder:
• Daily Test Preparation p. DT33
 Grammar, Usage, and Mechanics Workbook p. 196

SKILLS PRACTICE RESOURCES

 Grammar, Usage, and Mechanics Workbook pp. 197–198
Pupil's Edition Exercise Bank p. 618

② Practice and Apply

A. CONCEPT CHECK: Commas in Dates, Addresses, and Letters

Write the following letter, adding any missing commas.

158 W. 23 Street
New York NY 10010
February 20 2000

Dear Hank

Do you know about Katy Payne? Payne studies elephants in countries like Kenya, Africa. She has found out that elephants' voices are below the human level of hearing! Payne proved this with a special tape recorder. Elephants can call to one another over hundreds of miles. What a terrific hidden code! You could call to me in New York City from Albany New York! Today Katy Payne lives in Ithaca New York where she writes and studies her elephant data. She will speak here on March 19 2000 and I can't wait to hear her.

Take care

Sammy

➡ **For a SELF-CHECK and more practice, see the EXERCISE BANK, p. 618.**

B. WRITING: Dear Friend

Put a letter together, using these parts. Don't forget to add commas where they belong.

210 Oak St.

Hinton IA 51104

May 3 2000

Dear Jon

I'm giving a surprise swimming party for Sara next Friday at the public pool in Moville Iowa. Keep it a secret.

Sincerely

Teresa

Punctuation **257**

CUSTOMIZING TIP

Students Acquiring English/ESL
Punctuation of numbers varies across languages. Some languages, for example, use a period to separate thousands and a comma as a decimal point. In these languages, 3,000 is written as 3.000, and 3.25 is written as 3,25. Remind students that this punctuation is reversed in American English.

Answers

Print-Out Option You may create worksheets of exercises A and B for your students by using the 💿 **Electronic Teacher Tools CD–ROM.**

A. CONCEPT CHECK

Self-Check For a self-check of commas in dates, addresses, and letters, direct students to p. 618 in the Pupil's Edition for the answers to the first two errors in the paragraph.

Answers shown on page.

B. WRITING

210 Oak St.
Hinton, IA 51104
May 3, 2000

Dear Jon,

I'm giving a surprise swimming party for Katy next Friday at the public pool in Moville, Iowa. Keep it a secret.

Sincerely,

Teresa

LESSON OBJECTIVES

To understand and apply rules for punctuating quotations

DAILY TEST PREPARATION

Error Identification: Spelling
Write the following item on the board or use **Daily Test Preparation Transparency** p. DT34.
Read the sentence carefully. Decide if one of the words is spelled wrong or if there is no mistake.

My teacher says that I
<u>habitually</u> <u>misspell</u> <u>sufixes</u>.

   A   B   C

No mistake

   D

Teaching Point: Error identification questions that test spelling often include words with double consonants, such as *suffixes*.

TEACHING RESOURCES

 Time-Saver Transparencies Binder:
- Daily Test Preparation p. DT34
- Quick-Fix Grammar and Style Charts p. QF10

 Grammar, Usage, and Mechanics Workbook p. 199

SKILLS PRACTICE RESOURCES

 Grammar, Usage, and Mechanics Workbook pp. 200–201

Pupil's Edition Exercise Bank p. 619

Grammar Coach CD-ROM Lesson 3

LESSON 4 — Punctuating Quotations

❶ Here's the Idea

To punctuate quotations, you need to know where to put quotation marks, commas, and end marks.

Direct Quotations

A direct quotation is a report of a speaker's exact words.

▶ **Use quotation marks at the beginning and the ending of a direct quotation.**

    "Flowers have meaning,**"** said Sophie.

▶ **Use commas to set off explanatory words used with direct quotations (whether they occur at the beginning, in the middle, or at the end of the sentences).**

    Sophie said, "Flowers have meaning."

    "Flowers**," said Sophie,** "have meaning."

    "Flowers have meaning**," said Sophie.**

▶ **If a quotation is a question or an exclamation, place the question mark or exclamation point inside the closing quotation marks.**

    "What do flowers mean**?"** I asked.

▶ **If quoted words are part of a question or exclamation of your own, place the question mark or exclamation point outside the closing quotation marks.**

    Do flowers tell "secret messages**"?**

 Commas and periods always go inside closing quotation marks. They're too little to stay outside.

Indirect Quotations

▶ **Do not use quotation marks to set off an indirect quotation.** An indirect quotation is a restatement, in somewhat different words, of what someone said. An indirect quotation is often introduced by the word *that*. It does not require a comma.

INDIRECT Shakespeare wrote **that** a rose would smell sweet regardless of its name.

DIRECT Shakespeare wrote, "a rose by any other name would smell as sweet."

Divided Quotations

A divided quotation is a direct quotation that is separated into two parts, with explanatory words such as *he said* or *she said* between the parts.

▶ **Use quotation marks to enclose both parts of a divided quotation.**

"A rose," he said, "means love."

▶ **Do not capitalize the first word of the second part of a divided quotation unless it begins a new sentence.**

"A rose," he said, "sometimes means treachery."

"A rose usually means love," he said. "Sometimes it means treachery."

▶ **Use commas to set off the explanatory words used with a divided quotation.**

"A rose," he summed up, "can mean treachery or love."

Students Acquiring English/ESL In some languages, dialogue is indicated by a dash or by marks such as « » or " „. Remind students to use standard American quotation marks to punctuate dialogue.

Gifted and Talented Explain that single quotation marks are used to enclose a title or quotation within a quotation. If the enclosed title or quotation ends the sentence, both the single and double quotation marks should follow the period. Example: *She said, "My favorite song is 'Happy Birthday.'"*

MORE MODEL SENTENCES

Write the following sentences on the board. Have students insert quotation marks where needed.

I love roses, Lisa said, especially red ones.

"I love roses," Lisa said, "especially red ones."

She told me that she hasn't been able to grow any.

No quotation marks needed.

I planted red roses, she said. Unfortunately, though, they didn't live.

"I planted red roses," she said. "Unfortunately, though, they didn't live."

THE LANGUAGE OF LITERATURE

The passage on the student page is from "The Serial Garden" in *The Language of Literature*, Level 7.

Quotation Marks in Dialogue

▶ **In dialogue, a new paragraph and a new set of quotation marks show a change in speakers.**

A dialogue is a conversation between two or more speakers.

LITERARY MODEL

"Indeed. That is most interesting. Did the tune, perhaps, go like this?"

The princess hummed a few bars.

"That's it! How did you know?"

"Why, you foolish boy, it was I who put the spell on the garden, to make it come alive when the tune is played or sung."

—Joan Aiken, "The Serial Garden"

Using Quotation Marks

Use this model to review the punctuation in this lesson.

PROFESSIONAL MODEL

Did you know that some call flowers "secret messages"? Sophie told me that each kind of flower means something different.

"What does a rose mean?" I asked.

"It depends on the color," she explained. "In England, a red rose means true love, but a yellow rose suggests that a person has cheated."

"That's a strong message!" I exclaimed. I asked what a man might do if he received a yellow rose from his girlfriend.

"He might send her white violets," said Sophie, "to proclaim his innocence."

—J. Gallagher

- Question with quoted words
- Indirect quotation
- Dialogue
- Exclamation
- Divided quotation

② Practice and Apply

A. CONCEPT CHECK: Quotation Marks

Write the following passage, correcting errors in the use and placement of quotation marks.

> **The Language of Flowers**
>
> "I want to send Megan flowers," Jay said.
>
> "Are you nuts?" asked Dan. "She'll think you like her."
>
> "I do," said Jay, "and I want her to know it. Now help me look up in this book which flowers mean what."
>
> Dan agreed that he would help.
>
> "Look!" said Jay. "Irises mean faithfulness and courage."
>
> Dan suggested that he send pansies, which mean "I'm thinking of you."
>
> "Good," Jay said. "Geraniums," said Dan, "mean happiness."
>
> Jay decided he had enough ideas.

➡️ **For a SELF-CHECK and more practice, see the EXERCISE BANK, p. 619.**

B. EDITING: Speaking Indirectly   Answers in column.

Write as well as Shakespeare. Make these quotations your own by changing them into indirect quotations.

Example: We asked, "Did Shakespeare study flowers?"

Answer: We asked whether Shakespeare studied flowers.

1. Our teacher said, "Shakespeare knew the language of flowers."
2. In *Hamlet,* he has Ophelia say, "There's rosemary, that's for remembrance."
3. Oberon says "I know a bank where the wild thyme blows."
4. "Thyme meant sweetness," according to *The Book of Flowers and Herbs.*
5. A historian tells us, "Shakespeare's audience knew the meanings of the flowers he mentioned."

Answers

Print-Out Option You may create worksheets of exercises A and B for your students by using the 💿 **Electronic Teacher Tools CD–ROM.**

A. CONCEPT CHECK

Self-Check For a self-check of quotation marks, direct students to p. 619 in the Pupil's Edition for the answers to the first two errors in the paragraph.

Answers shown on page using standard proofreading marks.

B. EDITING

Answers will vary. Possible responses:

1. My teacher said that Shakespeare knew the language of flowers.
2. In *Hamlet,* he has Ophelia say that rosemary is for remembrance.
3. Oberon said that he knew a bank where the wild thyme blew.
4. The *Book of Flowers and Herbs* explains that thyme meant sweetness.
5. A historian tells us that Shakespeare's audience knew the meanings of the flowers he mentioned.

ASSESSMENT

 Assessment Masters:
  • Chapter Mid-point Test p. 34

LESSON 5

Semicolons and Colons

❶ Here's the Idea

A **semicolon** indicates a break in a sentence. It is stronger than a comma but not as strong as a period. A **colon** indicates an abrupt break. A colon indicates that a list follows. Colons are also used after greetings in business letters and in expressions of time.

Semicolons in Compound Sentences

▶ **Use a semicolon to join parts of a compound sentence without a coordinating conjunction.**

Enslaved people sang songs with secret messages**;** the songs told listeners how to escape.

▶ **Use a semicolon between the parts of a compound sentence when the clauses are long and complicated or when they contain commas.**

Runaways navigated by the stars**;** and they lived off the land, slept outdoors, and walked hundreds of miles to freedom.

Semicolons with Items in a Series

▶ **When there are commas within parts of a series, use semicolons to separate the parts.**

The travelers took clues from songs, such as a song about the stars**;** from quilts, which had special coded designs**;** and from other people along the way.

Colons

▶ **Use a colon to introduce a list of items.**

An escapee carried few items**:** a knife, a flint, and a warm cloak.

Avoid using a colon directly after a verb or a preposition.

INCORRECT   The recipients are**:** Joe, Sam, and Rita.
INCORRECT   Send this message to**:** Joe, Sam, and Rita.
CORRECT   Send this message to the following people**:** Joe, Sam, and Rita.

262 Grammar, Usage, and Mechanics

▶ **Use a colon after the formal greeting in a business letter.**

Dear Ms. Smith **:**   Dear Sir **:**

For a model, see the business letter in the Model Bank.

▶ **Use a colon between numerals indicating hours and minutes in expressions of time.**

Meet me at 8 **:** 00 P.M. We'll send the message at 8 **:** 30.

② Practice and Apply

A. CONCEPT CHECK: Semicolons and Colons

Write the following paragraphs, correcting errors in the use of semicolons and colons.

Walking the Underground Railroad

Here are two ways conductors on the Underground Railroad hid messages; in songs and in quilts. "The Drinking Gourd,"   :
for example, sounded like a folk song; however, it was a map   ;
to freedom. The "gourd" was actually the constellation known as the Big Dipper; it points to the North Star. The lyrics of the   ;
song told slaves how to head north; to the free states. The   [no punctuation]
quilts were signal flags; travelers would see them and know   ;
where to go. The following quilt designs carried directions; the   :
Bear's Paw, which told people to follow bear tracks in the mountains; the Crossroads, which said to head to Cleveland,   ;
Ohio; and the Flying Geese; which said to follow geese to   ,
water. Unlike real trains, which might leave at a specific time, say 7:30 P.M., the "freedom trains" left; anytime after dark.   :/[no punctuation]

➡ **For a SELF-CHECK and more practice, see the EXERCISE BANK, p. 619.**

B. WRITING: All Business   Answers in column.

Write a short business letter to the catalog company in this advertisement, ordering a list of items you would need to make a signal quilt. Choose from the items in the ad. Model your letter on the sample business letter in the Model Bank on page 624.

Quilter's Corner
LET US SUPPLY YOUR QUILTING NEEDS!
needles, patterns, fabric, padding, stencils
xxxxxxxxxxxxxxxxxxxxxxxx
2211 N. Lincoln Avenue
Chicago, IL 60614

Punctuation **263**

A. CONCEPT CHECK

Self-Check For a self-check of semicolons and colons, direct students to p. 619 in the Pupil's Edition for the answers to the first two errors in the paragraph.

Answers shown on page using standard proofreading marks. Corrections appear in the margin. Carets indicate where to place corrections.

B. WRITING

Answers will vary. Be sure students use a colon after the greeting and, if they write a list of items they wish to order, a colon to introduce the list. If students use compound sentences or lists that require semicolons, be sure they use this punctuation correctly.

TEACHING TIP

Cooperative Learning Have students work in pairs to write a business letter to your school's principal. Students should suggest a list of improvements for the school. They can also list some things about the school that are going well. Have each pair exchange letters with another pair. Students should review their use of punctuation, especially semicolons and colons. For further review of business letters, refer students to the **Model Bank,** p. 624.

LESSON OBJECTIVES

To recognize and use hyphens, dashes, and parentheses correctly

DAILY TEST PREPARATION

Error Correction: Collective Nouns Write the following item on the board or use 📗 **Daily Test Preparation Transparency** p. DT35. Choose the <u>best</u> way to write the underlined part of the sentence.

> A flock of <u>geese are flying</u> overhead.

A. gooses are flying

B. geese were flying

C. geese is flying

D. *(No change)*

Teaching Point: Error correction questions often test your knowledge of agreement with collective nouns. In this case, *flock,* not *geese* (which is part of a prepositional phrase), is the subject. Because *flock* acts as a single unit, a singular verb (*is flying*) is needed.

TEACHING TIP

Caution students that the overuse of parenthetical statements will weaken their writing. Too many "asides" in parentheses can distract readers and interrupt the main ideas.

LESSON 6 Hyphens, Dashes, and Parentheses

❶ Here's the Idea

Hyphens, dashes, and parentheses help make your writing clear by separating or setting off words or parts of words.

Hyphens

▶ **Use a hyphen if part of a word must be carried over from one line to the next.**

  1. The word must have at least two syllables to be broken.
    RIGHT: num **-** ber   WRONG: co **-** de

  2. Separate the word between syllables.
    RIGHT: let **-** ter   WRONG: lette **-** r

  3. You must leave at least two letters on each line.
    RIGHT: twen **-** ty   WRONG: a **-** cross

▶ **Use hyphens in certain compound words.**

  half **-** dollar   great **-** grandmother

▶ **Use hyphens in compound numbers from twenty-one through ninety-nine.**

  sixty **-** three   twenty **-** six

▶ **Use hyphens in spelled-out fractions.**

  two **-** thirds   three **-** fourths

Dashes

▶ **Use dashes to show an abrupt break in thought.**

  Louis Braille who lost his sight at age three invented an alphabet for blind people.

Parentheses

▶ **Use parentheses to set off material that is loosely related to the rest of a sentence.**

  Each six-dot cell stands for a character **(**a letter of the alphabet, a number, a punctuation mark, or a contraction**)**.

264 Grammar, Usage, and Mechanics

TEACHING RESOURCES

📺 Time-Saver Transparencies Binder:
  • Daily Test Preparation p. DT35
📗 Grammar, Usage, and Mechanics Workbook p. 205

SKILLS PRACTICE RESOURCES

📗 Grammar, Usage, and Mechanics Workbook pp. 206–207
  Pupil's Edition Exercise Bank p. 620

❷ Practice and Apply

CONCEPT CHECK: Hyphens, Dashes, and Parentheses

Read the following paragraph. Then indicate what punctuation mark—hyphen, dash, or parenthesis—is needed in each numbered blank. If no mark is needed, write *None*.

Braille's Brainstorm

Louis Braille was born in a small town in France nearly two hundred years ago. At age three, he was accidentally blinded. He learned to find his way around by tapping with

— a cane ____(1)____ the sound told him where it was safe to

- step. Ten ____(2)____year-old Louis went to the National Institute for Blind Youth in Paris. He had heard the school

[none]/— had a library full of books ____(3)____ he could read ____(4)____ but it had only a few. The letters in the books were

(embossed ____(5)____ so the books were large, bulky, and very expensive to produce).

As a student, Louis met Charles Barbier (a retired army captain

) ____(6)____ Barbier had invented a "night-writing"

— system ____(7)____ involving dots and dashes punched into cardboard—that let soldiers write and read orders in the dark. Louis spent the next several years simplifying Barbier's

[none] system and ____(8)____

- another twenty ____(9)____ seven years fighting to get the Braille alphabet adopted. He

- died at the relatively young age of forty ____(10)____ three.

A person reading braille.

➡ **For a SELF-CHECK and more practice, see the EXERCISE BANK, p. 620.**

TEACHING TIP

Speaking and Listening Complete the **Practice and Apply** exercise in class. Read aloud the paragraph, and ask students to listen for and identify places where punctuation marks may be needed. For example, have them listen for numbers that might require hyphens. Also, have them listen for information that could be set off by dashes or parentheses.

Answers

Print-Out Option You may create worksheets of this exercise for your students by using the 💿 **Electronic Teacher Tools CD–ROM.**

CONCEPT CHECK

Self-Check For a self-check of hyphens, dashes, and parentheses, direct students to p. 620 in the Pupil's Edition for the answers to the first two errors in the paragraph.

Answers shown on page.

PUNCTUATION

CHAPTER 11

LESSON OBJECTIVES

To understand and apply rules for using apostrophes correctly

CHAPTER 11

➊ Here's the Idea

Apostrophes are used in possessive nouns, contractions, and some plurals.

Apostrophes in Possessives

▶ **Use an apostrophe to form the possessive of any noun, whether singular or plural.**

For a singular noun, add 's even if the word ends in s.

Becky**'s** bike   Louis**'s** alphabet

For plural nouns that end in s, add only an apostrophe.

the girl**s'** code   the pioneer**s'** messages

For plural nouns that do not end in s, add 's.

the children**'s** code   the people**'s** plan

Apostrophes in Contractions

▶ **Use apostrophes in contractions.**

In a contraction, words are joined and letters are left out. An apostrophe replaces the letter or letters that are missing.

Commonly Used Contractions		
I am → I'm	you are → you're	you will → you'll
she is → she's	they have → they've	it is → it's
cannot → can't	they are → they're	was not → wasn't

Don't confuse contractions with possessive pronouns, which do not contain apostrophes.

Contractions Versus Possessive Pronouns	
Contraction	**Possessive Pronoun**
it's (*it is* or *it has*)	its (belonging to it – *its tail*)
who's (*who is*)	whose (belonging to whom – *whose coat*)
you're (*you are*)	your (belonging to you – *your book*)
they're (*they are*)	their (belonging to them – *their house*)

266   Grammar, Usage, and Mechanics

Apostrophes in Plurals

▶ **Use an apostrophe and *s* to form the plural of a letter, a numeral, or a word referred to as a word.**

Cross your *t* **'s**.   The speaker used too many *um* **'s**.

How many 5 **'s** are in the answer?

❷ Practice and Apply

A. CONCEPT CHECK: Apostrophes

Write the paragraph, correcting the errors in the use of apostrophes.

> **Give Me an *E***
>
> One person's code is another's challenge. Cryptanalyst's are people who break codes. They're most important clue is ~~Their~~ how often certain letters and word's appear. In English, *e*s and *t*s occur most often, and *the* is the most common word. Code breakers first goal is to identify these frequently occurring letters. Then they'll start to figure out the words the letters appear in. Once they know what the code uses to mean *e* and *t*, they're able to find the word *the*. Then they'll know what the code uses for *h*. Its a hard job, but it's rewards are many.

➡ For a SELF-CHECK and more practice, see the EXERCISE BANK, p. 620.

B. WRITING: Who or What Owns It?

Break the code by writing the correct possessive phrase for each "coded" message below.

Take the car that belongs to you. **Take your car.**

Go to the house owned by Janus. **Go to Janus's house.**

at the end of the day **at the day's end**

for the party that belongs to Marty **for Marty's party**

Bring the gift belonging to the class. **Bring the class's gift.**

Answers

Print-Out Option You may create worksheets of exercises A and B for your students by using the ⊙ **Electronic Teacher Tools CD–ROM.**

A. CONCEPT CHECK

Self-Check For a self-check of apostrophes, direct students to p. 620 in the Pupil's Edition for the answers to the items circled in yellow.

Answers shown on page using standard proofreading marks.

B. WRITING

Answers shown on page.

PUNCTUATION

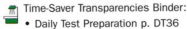

LESSON OBJECTIVES

To understand and apply rules for punctuating titles correctly

Error Identification: Spelling

Write the following item on the board or use ▤ **Daily Test Preparation Transparency** p. DT36. Decide which type of error, if any, appears in the underlined section.

> Sammy appreciated his position in <u>the bating order</u>; cleanup was his specialty.

A. Spelling error

B. Capitalization error

C. Punctuation error

D. No error

Teaching Point: Error identification questions often test your knowledge of basic spelling rules. This item tests whether you know to double the final consonant in a one-syllable word with a short vowel sound (*bat*) before adding the suffix *-ing* (*batting*).

TEACHING TIP

Gifted and Talented Explain to students that italics are also used to emphasize important words in a sentence and to indicate foreign words or phrases.

CHAPTER 11

LESSON 8

Punctuating Titles

❶ Here's the Idea

Use quotation marks and italics correctly in titles to show what kind of work or selection you are writing about.

Quotation Marks

▶ **Use quotation marks to set off the titles of short works.**

Quotation Marks for Titles	
Book chapter	"Dirk the Protector" from *My Life in Dog Years*
Story	"The Richer, the Poorer"
Essay	"Names/ Nombres"
Article	"Primal Compassion"
Song	"Row, Row, Row Your Boat"
Poem	"I Might, I May, I Must"

Italics and Underlining

In handwriting, you show that something should be in italic type by **underlining** it.

▶ **Use italics for titles of longer works and for the names of ships, trains, spacecraft, and airplanes (but not for types of planes).** Show that they should be in italic type by underlining them.

Italics or Underlines for Titles			
Book	*The Phantom Tollbooth*	**Epic poem (book length)**	*Beowulf*
Play	*Rent*	**Painting**	*Mona Lisa*
Magazine	*Spin*	**Ship**	*Titanic*
Movie	*Star Wars*	**Train**	*Broadway Limited*
TV series	*60 Minutes*	**Spacecraft**	*Voyager 1*
Long musical composition or CD	*Surfacing*	**Airplane (specific plane, not type)**	*Spirit of St. Louis* (but not DC-10)

268 Grammar, Usage, and Mechanics

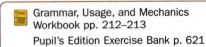

➋ Practice and Apply

A. CONCEPT CHECK: Punctuating Titles

Write the titles in the following paragraph correctly by using quotation marks or underlines.

Surrounded by Codes and Ciphers

The first book on secret writing, or cryptography, was <u>Polygraphia</u>, written in 1499. Today there are several magazines on the subject, including <u>The Journal of Cryptology</u>. An article titled "New Directions in Cryptography" was published not long ago. When Russians captured the German ship <u>Magdeburg</u> during World War I, they found a German naval codebook. To learn how to create and break codes, read the book <u>Codes and Secret Writing</u> by Herbert S. Zim. The hero of Edgar Allan Poe's short story "The Gold Bug" finds a cipher that directs him to pirate treasure. The old TV series <u>The Avengers</u> had plots dealing with secret codes; the recent movie <u>The Avengers</u> did not.

Garden Signs by Paul Klee

Even some songs, such as the 1970 single "Knock Three Times," have referred to codes. Some paintings such as Paul Klee's *Garden Signs* have symbols that may seem to be codes.

➡ **For a SELF-CHECK and more practice, see the EXERCISE BANK, p. 621.**

B. WRITING: Favorite Titles   Answers in column.

Write down the titles of your favorite book, poem, movie, TV show, and song. Then, with a partner, take turns giving clues about each other's favorite titles and write down your guesses. Be sure to use underlines and quotation marks correctly.

Answers

Print-Out Option You may create worksheets of exercise A for your students by using the 💿 **Electronic Teacher Tools CD–ROM.**

A. CONCEPT CHECK

Self-Check For a self-check of punctuating titles, direct students to p. 621 in the Pupil's Edition for the answers to the first two errors in the paragraph.

Answers shown on page. Underlines indicate italics.

B. WRITING

Answers will vary. Encourage students to use a variety of titles, some requiring quotation marks and others underlines.

ASSESSMENT

📋 Assessment Masters:
- Chapter Mastery Tests pp. 87–92

💿 Test Generator CD-ROM

🔗 mcdougallittell.com Grammar Chapter Quiz

PUNCTUATION

PUNCTUATION

Spice It Up!

Ask students the following question: If your life were filmed as a movie, made into a TV sitcom, written as a book, or recorded as a song, what would the titles be? Write students' titles on the board, and ask them to give the correct punctuation for each one.

LESSON OBJECTIVES

To recognize how punctuation helps readers understand poetry and to use punctuation correctly in a poem

TEACHING TIP

Read the poem. Then discuss the annotations alongside it. Ask volunteers how punctuation affects the sound of the poem.

THE LANGUAGE OF
LITERATURE

The poem on the student page, "Mooses," appears in *The Language of Literature,* Level 7.

Grammar in Literature

Punctuation and Poetry

Without punctuation, poetry may seem like it's written in a secret code. The first word of every line is often capitalized and sentences may not end at the end of a line. For these reasons, punctuation marks are especially important in helping you understand and enjoy reading poetry—and writing it too.

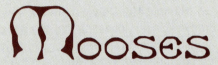

Mooses
by Ted Hughes

The goofy Moose, the walking house-frame
Is lost
In the forest. He bumps, he blunders, he stands.

With massy bony thoughts sticking out near his ears—
Reaching out palm upwards, to catch whatever might be
   falling from heaven—
He tries to think,
Leaning their huge weight
On the lectern of his front legs.

He can't find the world!
Where did it go? What does a world look like?
The Moose
Crashes on, and crashes into a lake, and stares at the
   mountain and cries
"Where do I belong? This is no place!"

He turns and drags half the lake out after him
And charges the cackling underbrush—

He meets another Moose.
He stares, he thinks "It's only a mirror!"

"Where is the world?" he groans, "O my lost world!
And why am I so ugly?
And why am I so far away from my feet?"

He weeps.
Hopeless drops drip from his droopy lips.

The other Moose just stands there doing the same.

Two dopes of the deep woods.

270

> **Missing periods indicate that sentences continue.**

> **Quotation marks indicate the moose's exact thoughts.**

> **A dash tells you that the sentence runs into the next stanza.**

> **Here, the author deliberately uses a sentence fragment.**

Practice and Apply

Write your own poem about one of the strange animals in the pictures. Your poem can stress the humor of the animal's appearance as the model does. It could describe a viewer's response to the animal or the animal's response to the viewer. Even more exciting would be to present two animals reacting to one another. Be sure to use correct punctuation to help readers understand and appreciate your verse. Save your poem in your
Working Portfolio.

Hedgehog

Macaw

Ladybugs

Frog

Chinese Water Dragon

PUNCTUATION

Answers

Practice and Apply

USING PUNCTUATION IN POETRY

Poems will vary. Students may find it helpful to briefly research the animal they choose as the subject of their poem. Poems should be correctly punctuated. The punctuation should indicate where sentences begin and stop. A sample poem follows:

"Ladybug"
Watch out!
Don't crush me
With your big shoes.
I'm bright red
So it's hard to miss me.
You tell me
To fly away home—
But I am home
In your garden.

PUNCTUATION

271

Mixed Review

A. PROOFREADING

Answers shown on page using standard proofreading marks.

B. REVISING

The comma after *Hi* is not specified in Dave Barry's list.

"Hi, Mr. Johnson!" exclaimed Bob. "Where do you want me to put these punctuation marks?"

"Oh, just stick them there at the end of the following sentence," answered Mr. Johnson.

"OK!" said Bob.

Mixed Review

A. Proofreading Rewrite the passage below, adding any missing punctuation.

The Secret of the Navajo Code Talkers

During World War II the United States was looking for ways to ensure that its secret messages could not be decoded by the enemy. Philip Johnston who had grown up on the Navajo Indian Reservation and had become fluent in the Navajo language suggested recruiting Navajo soldiers to speak their native language. The language had no written form or alphabet very few people spoke it.

Navajo code talkers Preston Toledo and Frank Toledo

More than 400 Navajos went to the South Pacific. There they sent and received messages in an unbreakable code, their native tongue. They took part in all the Marines assaults on Pacific islands, from Guadalcanal in 1942 to Okinawa in 1945. Japans surrender occurred on August 14 1945.

"When I was going to boarding school, exclaimed code talker Teddy Draper Sr., "the U.S. government told us not to speak Navajo but during the war, they *wanted* us to speak it!"

In 1969 nearly twenty five years after World War II had ended), the code talkers were nationally recognized. A book called *Warriors: Navajo Code Talkers* tells their story.

B. Revising Read the passage below. Then write the passage, putting the punctuation marks where they belong. Add paragraph breaks. Then see if you can add one mark that is not given.

> **PROFESSIONAL MODEL**
>
> **Punctuation 'R Easy**
>
> Hi Mr Johnson exclaimed Bob Where do you want me to put these punctuation marks Oh just stick them there at the end of the following sentence answered Mr Johnson OK said Bob ".!"."?"",",".."!".
>
> —Dave Barry, *Dave Barry Is Not Making This Up*

Mastery Test: What Did You Learn?

Choose the letter of the best revision of each underlined item.

> People sometimes joke that the initials for the National Security <u>Agency—NSA—</u>stand for Never Say Anything. <u>Its</u> not really a joke, though. The NSA is the <u>largest; most hidden</u> intelligence organization in the United States. Those who work for it must learn to keep quiet about what they <u>do, how they do it and</u> what they learn. The NSA constructs and oversees all the codes used by <u>US</u> intelligence services. <u>Of course—</u>the agency also is involved in decoding other <u>countries</u> messages. I can hear you saying, <u>This is the job for me!</u> But the NSA hires only one of every six people who <u>apply,</u> competition is very tough. However, if you study science or engineering, you could be considered. Do you still want a job as a code maker or a <u>code breaker.</u>
>
> (1) (2) (3) (4) (5) (6) (7) (8) (9) (10)

1. A. Agency, NSA—
   B. Agency—NSA;
   C. Agency NSA—
   D. Correct as is ⟵(circled)

2. A. Its'
   B. It's ⟵(circled)
   C. It(s)
   D. Correct as is

3. A. largest: most hidden
   B. largest most hidden
   C. largest, most hidden ⟵(circled)
   D. Correct as is

4. A. do, how they do it, and ⟵(circled)
   B. do; how they do it; and
   C. do: how they do it, and
   D. Correct as is

5. A. U-S
   B. U,S,
   C. U.S. ⟵(circled)
   D. Correct as is

6. A. Of course;
   B. Of course
   C. Of course, ⟵(circled)
   D. Correct as is

7. A. countries' ⟵(circled)
   B. countrie's
   C. countries's
   D. Correct as is

8. A. This is the job for me!"
   B. "This is the job for me!" ⟵(circled)
   C. This is the job for me!
   D. Correct as is

9. A. apply
   B. apply:
   C. apply; ⟵(circled)
   D. Correct as is

10. A. code breaker!
    B. code breaker? ⟵(circled)
    C. code breaker—
    D. Correct as is

Mastery Test

As an option, two other Chapter Mastery Tests appear in 📄 **Assessment Masters** pp. 87–92.

Answers circled on page.

PRESCRIPTION FOR MASTERY	
If students miss item number:	**Use Teaching Resources and Skills Practice Resources** for lesson:
1	❻ Hyphens, Dashes, and Parentheses p. 264
2, 7	❼ Apostrophes p. 266
3, 4, 6	❷ Commas in Sentences p. 253
5, 10	❶ Periods and Other End Marks p. 250
8	❹ Punctuating Quotations p. 258
9	❺ Semicolons and Colons p. 262

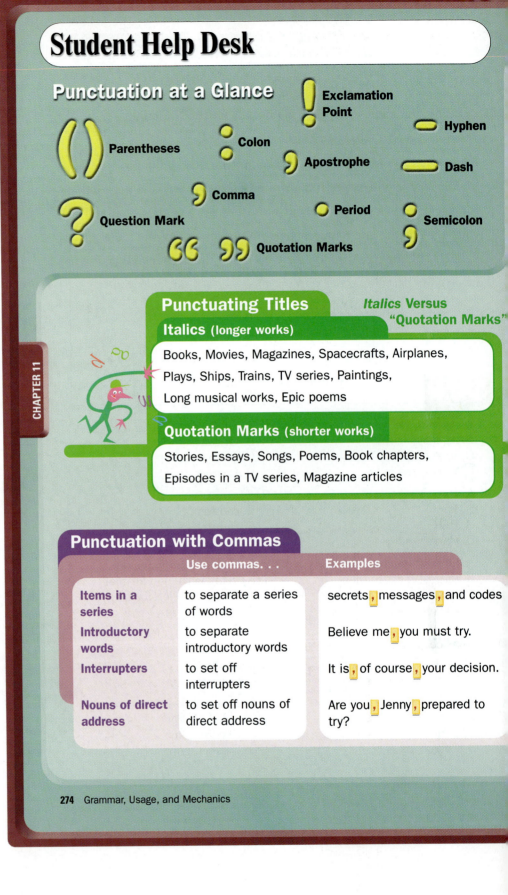

Student Help Desk

Punctuation at a Glance

Parentheses ( )

Colon :

Exclamation Point !

Apostrophe '

Hyphen

Dash

Comma ,

Question Mark ?

Period .

Semicolon ;

Quotation Marks " "

Punctuating Titles

Italics Versus "Quotation Marks"

Italics (longer works)

Books, Movies, Magazines, Spacecrafts, Airplanes, Plays, Ships, Trains, TV series, Paintings, Long musical works, Epic poems

Quotation Marks (shorter works)

Stories, Essays, Songs, Poems, Book chapters, Episodes in a TV series, Magazine articles

Punctuation with Commas

	Use commas. . .	Examples
Items in a series	to separate a series of words	secrets, messages, and codes
Introductory words	to separate introductory words	Believe me, you must try.
Interrupters	to set off interrupters	It is, of course, your decision.
Nouns of direct address	to set off nouns of direct address	Are you, Jenny, prepared to try?

Punctuation with Quotation Marks · The Inside Report

Always Inside (no matter what)

Period	Sly said, "We'll break their code ."
Comma	"We'll learn their secrets," said Guy.

Sometimes Inside (if they punctuate the quoted words)

Question mark	"What's the secret word?" asked Jack.
Exclamation point	"What a horrible shock!" cried the spy.

Sometimes Outside (if they punctuate a sentence containing quoted words)

Question mark	Did you tell Jack to read "The Spy Who Cried"?
Exclamation point	I hated the story "Three Spies and Me"!

The Bottom Line

Checklist for Punctuation

Have I . . .

____ ended every sentence with an appropriate end mark?

____ used commas before the conjunctions in compound sentences?

____ used commas to separate items in a series?

____ used commas correctly in dates, addresses, and letters?

____ used quotation marks before and after a speaker's words?

____ used a semicolon instead of a conjunction in long compound sentences?

____ used apostrophes to form contractions and possessives?

____ used italics and quotation marks correctly for titles?

TEACHER'S LOUNGE

A Slice of Life

"It seems rather incongruous that in a society of supersophisticated communication, we often suffer from a shortage of listeners."
—Erma Bombeck

A Slice of Life

What famous writer regularly omitted the apostrophe in contractions, writing the word *didn't* as "didnt" and *I've* as "Ive?" Answer: George Bernard Shaw, who crusaded for the simplification of spelling and punctuation.

LESSON OBJECTIVES

To understand how parts of a
sentence work within a sentence
and to visually represent them

DIAGRAMMING

Diagramming: Sentence Parts

Mad
Mapper

Here's the Idea

Diagramming is a way of showing the structure
of a sentence. Drawing a diagram can help
you see how the parts of a sentence work
together to form a complete thought.

Watch me for
diagramming tip

Simple Subjects and Verbs

Write the simple subject and verb on one line. Separate them
with a vertical line that crosses the main line.

Campers hiked.

Campers | hiked

Compound Subjects and Verbs

For a compound subject or verb, split the main line. Put the
conjunction on a dotted line connecting the compound parts.

Compound Subject

Campers and counselors hiked.

Campers
and
counselors
hiked

Because
there are
two subjects, the left
side of the main line is
split into two parts.

Compound Verb

Campers hiked and chatted.

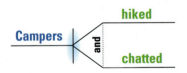

Campers
and
hiked
chatted

Compound Subject and Compound Verb

Campers and counselors hiked and chatted.

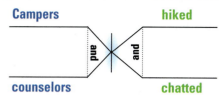

Campers   hiked

and   ×   and

counselors   chatted

Because there are two subjects and two verbs, both sides of the main line are split into two parts.

A. CONCEPT CHECK: Subjects and Verbs

Diagram these sentences, using what you have learned.

1. Bears appeared.
2. Trees creaked and swayed.
3. Bees and butterflies fluttered and swarmed.

Adjectives and Adverbs

Write adjectives and adverbs on slanted lines below the words they modify.

A steep mountain suddenly loomed ahead.

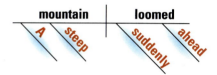

mountain   loomed

A steep   suddenly ahead

B. CONCEPT CHECK: Adjectives and Adverbs

Diagram these sentences, using what you have learned.

1. Dry brown leaves rustled constantly.
2. Gloomy gray clouds floated soundlessly overhead.
3. Sleepy campers rested peacefully.

Answers

A. CONCEPT CHECK

1. Bears | appeared

2. Trees | creaked / and / swayed

3. Bees | fluttered / butterflies | and × and | swarmed

B. CONCEPT CHECK

1. leaves | rustled — Dry, brown, constantly

2. clouds | floated — Gloomy, gray, soundlessly, overhead

3. campers | rested — Sleepy, peacefully

DIAGRAMMING

SENTENCE PARTS

TEACHING TIP

Cooperative Learning/Paired Activity Have students work in pairs to write and then diagram two sentences: one with a predicate noun and one with a predicate adjective. Ask volunteers to draw the diagrams on the board. Then have them explain the diagrams to the class by identifying the role of each word in the sentences.

NEED MORE INFORMATION?

For a review of direct and indirect objects, refer students back to **Chapter 1, The Sentence and Its Parts.**

Subject Complements

- Write a predicate noun or a predicate adjective on the main line after the verb.
- Separate the subject complement from the verb with a slanted line that does not cross the main line.

Predicate Noun

Cave explorers are spelunkers.

Predicate Adjective

Damp, dark caves can be scary.

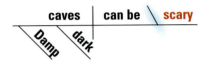

Direct Objects

A direct object follows the verb on the main line.

Brave spelunkers explore mysterious caves.

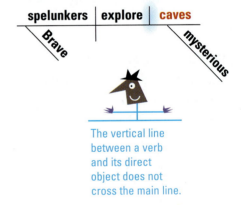

The vertical line between a verb and its direct object does not cross the main line.

Write compound direct objects on parallel lines that branch from the main line.

Cave explorers wear sturdy clothing and hard hats.

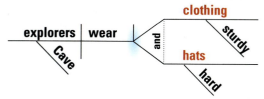

Indirect Objects

Write an indirect object below the verb, on a horizontal line connected to the verb with a slanted line.

Serious explorers give safety their careful consideration.

C. CONCEPT CHECK: Subject Complements and Objects

Diagram these sentences, using what you have learned.

1. Some caves are gigantic.
2. Spelunkers are courageous people.
3. Caves often contain long stalactites and tall stalagmites.

D. MIXED REVIEW: Diagramming

Diagram the following sentences.

1. Jewel Cave is gigantic.
2. It is an unusual underground world.
3. Shiny calcite crystals line the walls.
4. Strange, colorful formations fill the underground rooms.
5. The underground temperature is cool.
6. Visitors wear sturdy shoes and light jackets.
7. Knowledgeable guides give the visitors a lengthy tour.
8. Tourists and guides see shiny crystals and dark pools.
9. Brave visitors can take a candlelight tour.
10. They may encounter many bats!

Diagramming: Sentence Parts   **279**

Answers

C. CONCEPT CHECK

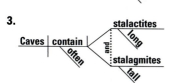

D. MIXED REVIEW

See **Diagramming Answer Key** at the end of the Teacher's Edition.

DIAGRAMMING

SENTENCE PARTS

Spice It Up!

Have rows of students work as a team to diagram a sentence from the **Mixed Review.** Have each team complete their sentence on the chalkboard with colored chalks, on poster board with markers or crayons, or on a bulletin board with construction paper. Assign awards such as the following:

First completed, Most colorful, Easiest to read, Straightest lines, Best teamwork

Diagramming: Phrases and Clauses

Prepositional Phrases

- Write the preposition on a slanted line below the word the prepositional phrase modifies.
- Write the object of the preposition on a horizontal line attached to the slanted line and parallel to the main line.
- Write words that modify the object of the preposition on slanted lines below it.

Adjective Prepositional Phrase

Natural forces may cause cracks in solid rocks.

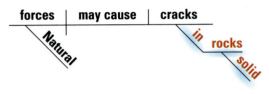

This adjective phrase modifies a noun. Adjective phrases can also modify pronouns and other prepositional phrases.

Adverb Prepositional Phrase

Glaciers move loose rocks down the valley.

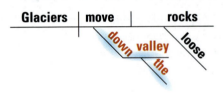

This adverb phrase modifies a verb. Adverb phrases can also modify adjectives and adverbs.

E. CONCEPT CHECK: Prepositional Phrases

Diagram these sentences, using what you have learned.

1. A glacier is a river of ice.
2. The flow of a heavy glacier carves a valley in a mountainside.
3. Inside their houses, people hear the eerie sounds of the ice outside.

Answers

E. CONCEPT CHECK

1.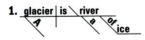

2.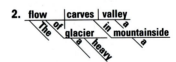

Also accept in a mountainside as an adjective phrase under valley.

3.

Also accept inside their houses as an adverb phrase under hear.

Compound Sentences

- Diagram the independent clauses on parallel horizontal lines.
- Connect the verbs in the two clauses by a dotted line with a step in it.
- Write the coordinating conjunction on the step.

Birds fly naturally, but humans fly in balloons.

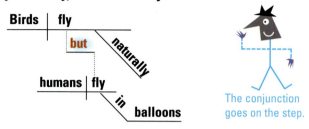

The conjunction goes on the step.

F. CONCEPT CHECK: Compound Sentences

Diagram these sentences, using what you have learned.

1. Balloons travel slowly, and they are blown by the wind.
2. Many have tried around-the-world flights, but few have succeeded.

Complex Sentences

Adjective and Adverb Clauses

- Diagram the main clause first. Diagram the subordinate clause on its own horizontal line below the main line.
- Use a dotted line to connect the word introducing the clause to the word it modifies.

Adjective Clause

The pilot is the person who controls a hot-air balloon.

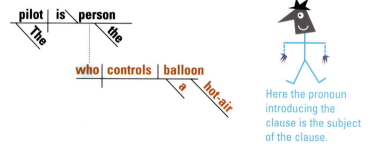

Here the pronoun introducing the clause is the subject of the clause.

Diagramming: Phrases and Clauses **281**

DIAGRAMMING

PHRASES AND CLAUSES

Answers

F. CONCEPT CHECK

1.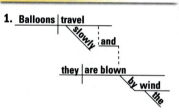

2.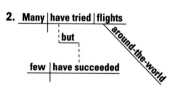

Adverb Clause

After the balloon lands, the pilot releases the air.

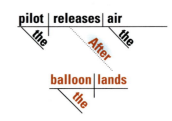

The conjunction goes on the dotted line, which connects the verbs in the two clauses.

Noun Clause

- Diagram the main clause first.
- Figure out what role the subordinate clause plays in the sentence.
- Diagram the subordinate clause on a separate line that is attached to the main line with a vertical forked line.
- Place the forked line in the diagram according to the role of the noun clause in the sentence.
- Diagram the word introducing the noun clause according to its function in the clause.

You may wonder how balloons come down.

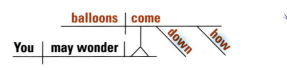

The noun clause functions as direct object in this sentence.

Spice It Up!

Divide the class into small groups to play Diagram Our Sentence. Have each group create a funny sentence or name a famous saying or song lyric. Advise groups to keep the sentences short and uncomplicated; encourage them to use the constructions they have learned. Have groups exchange and then diagram each other's sentences. The first group to correctly diagram a sentence wins.

G. CONCEPT CHECK: Complex Sentences

Diagram these sentences, using what you have learned.

1. Someone who plans trips is a navigator.
2. While the trip continues, the navigator gives directions.
3. The navigator may tell the driver where he should turn.

H. MIXED REVIEW: Diagramming

Diagram the following sentences.

1. The campers planned a canoe trip, and they packed their duffels.
2. They drove for three hours before they put their canoes in the water.
3. When they reached their destination, they were very tired.
4. Some of the campers pitched their tents where they could find shelter.
5. They frowned at the other campers who did not help.
6. They asked why the others had come.
7. The campers who had been resting soon got busy.
8. They unpacked pots and pans, and they searched the duffels for food.
9. Because they could not find the food, they looked for edible plants.
10. What they finally prepared was dandelion greens.

Answers

G. CONCEPT CHECK

1.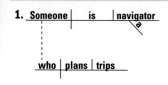

2.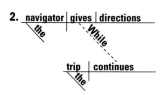

3.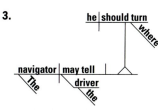

H. MIXED REVIEW

See **Diagramming Answer Key at the end of the Teacher's Edition.**

Quick-Fix Editing Machine

284 Grammar, Usage, and Mechanics

Quick-Fix Editing Machine

You've worked hard on your assignment. Don't let misplaced commas, sentence fragments, and missing details lower your grade. Use this Quick-Fix Editing Guide to help you detect grammatical errors and make your writing more precise.

Fixing Errors

Improving Style

 GRAMMAR COACH CD-ROM TABLE OF CONTENTS

Continued

Lesson 7 Pronoun and Antecedent Agreement I
- agreement with indefinite pronouns
- agreement with compound subjects joined by *or* or *nor*

Lesson 8 Pronoun and Antecedent Agreement II
- no antecedent
- indefinite antecedent
- ambiguous antecedent

Lesson 9 Pronoun Case
- objective case used with predicate pronouns
- nominative case used with object of preposition
- wrong case with comparisons
- wrong case with appositives

Lesson 10 *Who* and *Whom*
- *who/whom* as interrogative pronouns
- *who/whom* as relative pronouns

Lesson 11 Confusing Comparisons
- double comparative forms
- illogical comparisons
- using wrong comparative form

Lesson 12 Misplaced and Dangling Modifiers
- misplaced adjectives or adverbs
- prepositional phrase too far from the word it modifies
- verbal phrase too far from the word it modifies
- verbal phrase does not relate to anything in the sentence

QUICK FIX

QUICK FIX

GRAMMAR COACH CD-ROM

For more on sentence fragments, see **Grammar Coach CD-ROM** Lesson 1.

QUICK-FIX

QUICK-FIX EDITING MACHINE

1 Sentence Fragments

What's the problem? Part of a sentence has been left out.

Why does it matter? A fragment can be confusing because it does not express a complete thought.

What should you do about it? Find out what is missing and add it.

QUICK FIX

What's the Problem?	Quick Fix
A. A subject is missing. Feature four wheels in a row.	**Add a subject.** **In-line skates** feature four wheels in a row.
B. A predicate is missing. In-line skates first in the 1700s.	**Add a predicate.** In-line skates first **appeared** in the 1700s.
C. Both a subject and a predicate are missing. Probably the world's first roller skates.	**Add a subject and a predicate to make an independent clause.** **They were** probably the world's first roller skates.
D. A dependent clause is treated as if it were a sentence. Because they were much faster than traditional roller skates.	**Combine the fragment with an independent clause.** **They became popular** because they were much faster than traditional roller skates. **OR** **Delete the conjunction.** ~~Because~~ they were much faster than traditional roller skates.

For more help, see Chapter 1, pp. 25–27.

GRAMMAR COACH CD-ROM

For more on run-on sentences, see **Grammar Coach CD-ROM** Lesson 2.

2 Run-On Sentences

What's the problem? Two or more sentences have been written as though they were a single sentence.

Why does it matter? A run-on sentence doesn't show where one idea ends and another begins.

What should you do about it? Find the best way to separate the ideas or to show the proper relationship between them.

What's the Problem?

Quick Fix

A. The end mark separating two sentences is missing.

The computer store is a popular spot many kids visit it.

Add an end mark and start a new sentence.

The computer store is a popular spot**.** **M**any kids visit it.

B. Two sentences are separated only by a comma.

My sister wanted an inexpensive game, she rummaged through the sale bins.

Add a coordinating conjunction.

My sister wanted an inexpensive game, **so** she rummaged through the sale bins.

OR

Change the comma to a semicolon.

My sister wanted an inexpensive game**;** she rummaged through the sale bins.

OR

Replace the comma with an end mark and start a new sentence.

My sister wanted an inexpensive game**.** **S**he rummaged through the sale bins.

OR

Change one of the independent clauses to a dependent clause.

Because my sister wanted an inexpensive game, she rummaged through the sale bins.

QUICK FIX

QUICK-FIX

For more help, see Chapter 1, pp. 25–27.

GRAMMAR COACH CD-ROM

For more on subject-verb agreement, see **Grammar Coach CD-ROM** Lessons 4, 5.

QUICK-FIX

QUICK FIX

QUICK-FIX EDITING MACHINE

3 Subject-Verb Agreement

What's the problem? A verb does not agree with its subject in number.

Why does it matter? Readers may think your work is careless.

What should you do about it? Identify the subject and use a verb that matches it in number.

What's the Problem?	Quick Fix
A. The first helping verb in a verb phrase does not agree with the subject. **We has** been practicing our strokes for several weeks.	Decide whether the subject is singular or plural, and make the helping verb agree with it. **We have** been practicing our strokes for several weeks.
B. The contraction doesn't agree with its subject. The other **students doesn't** know how scared I am.	Use a contraction that agrees with the subject. The other **students don't** know how scared I am.
C. A singular verb is used with a compound subject containing *and.* **Reina and the instructor plunges** into the water first.	Use a plural verb with a compound subject joined by *and.* **Reina and the instructor plunge** into the water first.
D. A verb doesn't agree with the nearer part of a compound subject containing *or* or *nor.* Neither the instructor nor the **students uses** the diving board.	Make the verb agree with the nearer part of the compound subject. Neither the instructor nor the **students use** the diving board.
E. A verb doesn't agree with an indefinite-pronoun subject. **Each** of my friends **hope** to pass this class.	Decide whether the pronoun is singular or plural, and make the verb agree with it. **Each** of my friends **hopes** to pass this class.

For more help, see Chapter 9, pp. 206–227.

288 Grammar, Usage, and Mechanics

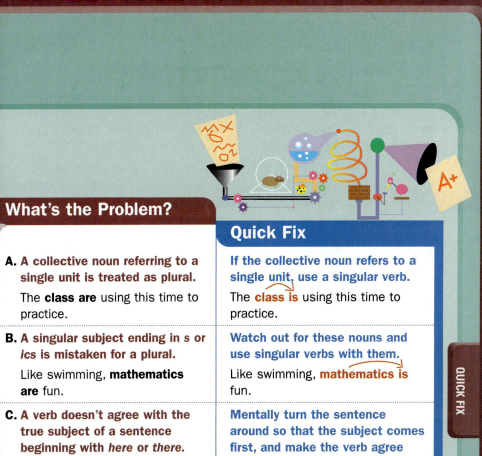

What's the Problem?

Quick Fix

A. A collective noun referring to a single unit is treated as plural.

The **class are** using this time to practice.

> If the collective noun refers to a single unit, use a singular verb.
>
> The **class is** using this time to practice.

B. A singular subject ending in *s* or *ics* is mistaken for a plural.

Like swimming, **mathematics are** fun.

> Watch out for these nouns and use singular verbs with them.
>
> Like swimming, **mathematics is** fun.

C. A verb doesn't agree with the true subject of a sentence beginning with *here* or *there*.

There is encouraging words from my classmates.

> Mentally turn the sentence around so that the subject comes first, and make the verb agree with it.
>
> **There are** encouraging **words** from my classmates.

D. A verb agrees with the object of a preposition rather than with its subject.

The sound of their **voices give** me confidence.

> Mentally block out the prepositional phrase and make the verb agree with the subject.
>
> The **sound** of their voices **gives** me confidence.

E. A plural verb is used with a period of time or an amount.

Four weeks are all it took for me to pass the test!

Thirty dollars are what it cost!

> Use a singular verb.
>
> **Four weeks is** all it took for me to pass the test!
>
> **Thirty dollars is** what it cost.

For more help, see Chapter 9, pp. 206–227.

QUICK-FIX

QUICK-FIX EDITING MACHINE

4 Pronoun Reference Problems

What's the problem? A pronoun does not agree in number, person, or gender with its antecedent, or an antecedent is unclear.

Why does it matter? Lack of agreement or unclear antecedents can confuse your reader.

What should you do about it? Find the antecedent and make the pronoun agree with it, or rewrite the sentence to make the antecedent clear.

What's the Problem?	Quick Fix
A. A pronoun doesn't agree in number with its antecedent. Every **town** has **their** deserted house.	**Make the pronoun agree in number with the antecedent.** Every **town** has **its** deserted house.
B. A pronoun doesn't agree in person or in gender with its antecedent. **Kids** know **you** should stay away from a deserted house.	**Make the pronoun agree with the antecedent.** **Kids** know **they** should stay away from a deserted house.
C. A pronoun doesn't agree with an indefinite-pronoun antecedent. **Anyone** can claim that **they** saw something extraordinary.	**Decide whether the indefinite pronoun is singular or plural, and make the pronoun agree with it.** **Anyone** can claim that **he or she** saw something extraordinary.
D. A pronoun could refer to more than one noun. **Roberto** and **Ishi** went into a deserted house. **He** saw something strange.	**Substitute a noun for the pronoun to make the reference clear.** Roberto and Ishi went into a deserted house. **Ishi** saw something strange.
E. A pronoun agrees with a noun in a phrase rather than with its antecedent. Ishi, like many **people,** let **their** imagination run wild.	**Mentally block out the phrase and make the pronoun agree with its antecedent.** **Ishi,** ~~like many people,~~ let **his** imagination run wild.

For more help, see Chapter 3, pp. 76–83.

290

⊙ **GRAMMAR COACH CD-ROM**

For more on incorrect pronoun case, see ⊙ **Grammar Coach CD-ROM** Lesson 9.

⑤ Incorrect Pronoun Case

What's the problem? A pronoun is in the wrong case.

Why does it matter? Readers may think your work is careless, especially if you are writing a school paper or formal letter.

What should you do about it? Identify how the pronoun is being used, and replace it with the correct form.

What's the Problem?

Quick Fix

A. A pronoun that follows a linking verb is not in the subject case.

The best all-around player **is her**.

> Always use the subject case after a linking verb.
>
> The best all-around player **is she**.

B. A pronoun used as an object is not in the objective case.

Andrea **asked** Inez and **I** to practice.

> A pronoun takes the objective case when it is used as an indirect object, a direct object, or the object of a preposition.
>
> Andrea **asked** Inez and me to practice.

C. A pronoun in a compound subject is in the wrong case.

Ben and me will start the game.

> Always use the subject case when a pronoun is part of a compound subject.
>
> **Ben and I** will start the game.

D. A pronoun followed by an identifying noun is in the wrong case.

Us players are ready to play.

They told **we fans** to yell louder.

> Mentally drop the noun and decide whether the pronoun is a subject or an object.
>
> **We** ~~players~~ are ready to play.
>
> They told **us** ~~fans~~ to yell louder.

E. A contraction is used instead of a possessive pronoun.

You're game has really improved!

> A possessive pronoun never has an apostrophe.
>
> **Your game** has really improved!

For more help, see Chapter 3, pp. 61–64.

QUICK FIX

QUICK-FIX

GRAMMAR COACH CD-ROM

For more on *who* and *whom*, see
Grammar Coach CD-ROM
Lesson 10.

6 *Who* and *Whom*

What's the problem? The pronoun *who* or *whom* is used incorrectly.

Why does it matter? When writers use *who* and *whom* correctly, readers are more likely to take their ideas seriously.

What should you do about it? Decide how the pronoun functions in the sentence, and then choose the correct form.

What's the Problem?	Quick Fix
A. *Whom* **is incorrectly used as the subject pronoun.** **Whom is knocking** at our door?	Use *who* as the subject pronoun. **Who is knocking** at the door?
B. *Whom* **is incorrectly used as a predicate pronoun.** The visitor **is whom?**	Use *who* as the predicate pronoun. The visitor **is who?**
C. *Who* **is incorrectly used as a direct object.** **Who can** we **send** to answer the door?	Use *whom* as a direct object. **Whom can** we **send** to answer the door?
D. *Who* **is incorrectly used as the object of a preposition.** A basket was left **by who?**	Use *whom* as the object of a preposition. A basket was left **by whom?**
E. *Who* **is incorrectly used as an indirect object.** You **gave who** our address?	Use *whom* as an indirect object. You **gave whom** our address?
F. *Who's* **is confused with the possessive pronoun** *whose*. **Who's puppy** is in this basket?	Always use *whose* to show possession. **Whose puppy** is in this basket?

For more help, see Chapter 3, pp. 70–71.

GRAMMAR COACH CD-ROM

For more on confusing comparisons, see **Grammar Coach CD-ROM** Lesson 11.

7 Confusing Comparisons

What's the problem? The wrong form of an adjective or adverb is used when making a comparison.

Why does it matter? Comparisons that are not worded correctly can be confusing.

What should you do about it? Use a form that makes the comparison clear.

What's the Problem?

Quick Fix

A. Both -er and more or -est and most are used in making a comparison.

In the 1920s, cosmetics manufacturers used some of the **most strangest** ingredients in lipstick.

Delete one of the forms from the sentence.

In the 1920s, cosmetics manufacturers used some of the ~~most~~ **strangest** ingredients in lipstick.

B. A comparative form is used where a superlative form is needed.

In fact, dangerous ingredients made lipstick one of the **more** unhealthy cosmetics of that time.

When comparing more than two things, use the superlative form.

In fact, dangerous ingredients made lipstick one of the **most** unhealthy cosmetics of that time.

C. A superlative form is used where a comparative form is needed.

I'm not sure which ingredient was **worst**—spoiled olive oil or dried and crushed insects.

When comparing two things, use the comparative form.

I'm not sure which ingredient was **worse**—spoiled olive oil or dried and crushed insects.

For more help, see Chapter 5, pp. 137–139.

QUICK FIX

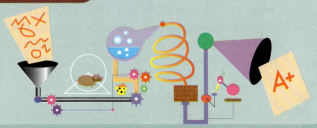

QUICK-FIX

For more on verb forms and tenses, see **Grammar Coach CD-ROM** Lesson 6.

QUICK-FIX EDITING MACHINE

8 Verb Forms and Tenses

What's the problem? The wrong form or tense of a verb is used.

Why does it matter? Readers may regard your work as careless or find it confusing.

What should you do about it? Change the verb to the correct form or tense.

What's the Problem?

Quick Fix

A. The wrong form of a verb is used with a helping verb.

Soft drinks **have rose** in popularity over the past several decades.

Always use a participle form with a helping verb.

Soft drinks **have risen** in popularity over the past several decades.

B. A helping verb is missing.

One consumer group **spoken** out against this trend.

Add a helping verb.

One consumer group **has spoken** out against this trend.

C. A past participle is used incorrectly.

Several decades ago, teens **drunk** twice as much milk as soda pop.

To write about the past, use the past form of a verb.

Several decades ago, teens **drank** twice as much milk as soda pop.

OR

Change the verb to the past perfect form by adding a helping verb.

Several decades ago, teens **had drunk** twice as much milk as soda pop.

D. Different tenses are used in the same sentence even though no change in time has occurred.

Some heavy soda drinkers **drink** as many as five cans a day and **got** one fourth of their calories from these beverages.

Use the same tense throughout the sentence.

Some heavy soda drinkers **drink** as many as five cans a day and **get** one fourth of their calories from these beverages.

For more help, see Chapter 4, pp. 100–114.

QUICK-FIX

QUICK FIX

GRAMMAR COACH CD-ROM

For more on missing or misplaced commas, see **Grammar Coach CD-ROM** Lesson 3.

9 Missing or Misplaced Commas

What's the problem? Commas are missing or are used incorrectly.

Why does it matter? The incorrect use of commas can make sentences hard to follow.

What should you do about it? Figure out where commas are needed, and add them as necessary.

What's the Problem?

	Quick Fix
A. A comma is missing from a compound sentence. Certain plants capture insects and they use them for food.	**Add a comma before the coordinating conjunction.** Certain plants capture insects, and they use them for food.
B. A comma is incorrectly placed after a closing quotation mark. "One such plant is a Venus flytrap", remarked our teacher.	**Always put a comma before a closing quotation mark.** "One such plant is a Venus flytrap," remarked our teacher.
C. A comma is missing before the conjunction in a series. Reggie, Shayna and I hurriedly took notes on the exhibit.	**Add a comma.** Reggie, Shayna, and I hurriedly took notes on the exhibit.
D. A comma is missing after an introductory word, phrase, or clause. After an insect touches the sensitive hairs on a leaf the plant closes like a jaw.	**Add a comma after the introductory word, phrase, or clause.** After an insect touches the sensitive hairs on a leaf, the plant closes like a jaw.
E. Commas are missing around an appositive or a clause that is not essential to the meaning of the sentence. The Venus flytrap which is a fascinating plant takes ten days to digest its prey.	**Add commas to set off the nonessential appositive or clause. Remember that a clause beginning with *which* is preceded by a comma.** The Venus flytrap, which is a fascinating plant, takes ten days to digest its prey.

For more help, see Chapter 11, pp. 253–255.

QUICK FIX

10 Improving Weak Sentences

What's the problem? A sentence repeats ideas or contains too many ideas.

Why does it matter? Repetitive or overloaded sentences can bore readers and weaken the message.

What should you do about it? Make sure that every sentence contains a clearly focused idea.

What's the Problem?

Quick Fix

A. An idea is repeated.

We recently read a news story about bugs **that was in the newspaper.**

Eliminate the repeated idea.

We recently read a news story about bugs~~that was in the newspaper.~~

B. A single sentence contains too many loosely connected ideas.

Radioactive flies and gnats were discovered at a nuclear site in Washington, and officials insisted there was no danger to the public, and one spokesperson said that these insects won't leave the area and they don't fly very far.

Divide the sentence into two or more sentences, using conjunctions such as *and, but, when,* and *because* to show relationships between ideas.

When radioactive flies and gnats were discovered at a nuclear site in Washington, officials insisted there was no danger to the public. **O**ne spokesperson said that these insects won't ever leave the area **because** they don't fly very far.

C. Too much information about a topic is crammed into one sentence.

The nuclear plant is working to get rid of the insects, but authorities insist that the bugs are no threat to people since according to one expert, a person would have to stand on a contaminated spot for an hour to get exposure equal to a dental x-ray.

Divide the sentence into two or more sentences, using conjunctions such as *and, but, when,* and *although* to show relationships between ideas.

Although the nuclear plant is working to get rid of the insects, authorities insist that the bugs are no threat to people. **A**ccording to one expert, a person would have to stand on a contaminated spot for an hour to get exposure equal to a dental x-ray.

For more help, see Chapter 18, pp. 388–391.

11 Avoiding Wordiness

What's the problem? A sentence contains unnecessary words.

Why does it matter? The meaning of wordy sentences can be unclear to readers.

What should you do about it? Use words that are precise and eliminate extra words.

What's the Problem?

Quick Fix

A. A single idea is unnecessarily expressed in two ways.

At 7:30 A.M. **in the morning,** Marissa has to walk two miles to her summer job.

She has a job that doesn't pay well, **and she doesn't make much money.**

Delete the unnecessary words.

At 7:30 A.M. ~~in the morning,~~ Marissa has to walk two miles to her summer job.

She has a job that doesn't pay well. ~~and she doesn't make much money.~~

B. A simple idea is expressed in too many words.

I **am of the opinion** that Marissa needs a bike.

She should ride a bike to work **on account of the fact** she can get there quickly.

Simplify the expression.

I **think** that Marissa needs a bike.

She should ride a bike to work **so** she can get there quickly.

C. A sentence contains words that do not add to its meaning.

What I mean to say is Marissa should save her money to buy a bike.

I have to tell you that Marissa could save the money in just three months.

Delete the unnecessary words.

~~What I mean to say is~~ Marissa should save her money to buy a bike.

~~I have to tell you that~~ Marissa could save the money in just three months.

For more help, see Chapter 18, pp. 388–389.

12 Varying Sentence Structure

What's the problem? Too many sentences begin the same way, or too many sentences of one kind are used.

Why does it matter? Lack of variety in sentences makes writing dull and choppy.

What should you do about it? Rearrange the phrases in some of your sentences, and use different types of sentences for variety and impact.

What's the Problem?

Quick Fix

A. Too many sentences in a paragraph begin the same way.

The fans crowded the sidewalks and waited for the stars to arrive at the premiere. **The fans** screamed and watched their favorite actors enter the theater. The stars waved to their adoring public.

Rearrange words or phrases in some of the sentences.

Crowding the sidewalks, the fans waited for the stars to arrive at the premiere. **As their favorite actors entered the theater,** the fans screamed. The stars waved to their adoring public.

B. Too many declarative sentences are used.

There's the camera crew. My friend waves frantically. The crew hardly notice, because they're searching only for famous faces. They don't find any, since all the stars are already inside the theater.

Add variety by rewriting one sentence as a command, question, or exclamation.

Is that the camera crew? My friend waves frantically. The crew hardly notice, because they're searching only for famous faces. They don't find any, since all the stars are already inside the theater.

For more help, see Chapter 18, pp. 392–393.

13 Varying Sentence Length

What's the problem? A piece of writing contains too many short, repetitive sentences.

Why does it matter? The use of too many short, repetitive sentences makes writing choppy and monotonous.

What should you do about it? Combine or reword sentences to create sentences of varying lengths.

What's the Problem?

Too many short, repetitive sentences are used.

The flea market promised many bargains. The flea market was huge. It was outdoors. Bargain hunters explored every table. They were cheerful. One teen sold used video games. A man sold floral arrangements. One group enjoyed the antics of a clown. At the same time others sampled many different foods. The flea market is held every year. People save their treasures all year long. They can sell them at the market.

Quick Fix

Eliminate repetitive sentences that add only one detail about the subject. Insert those details into other sentences.

The **huge outdoor** flea market promised many bargains. **Cheerful** bargain hunters explored every table.

OR

Use a conjunction such as *or, and,* or *but* to combine related sentences.

One teen sold used video games, **and** a man sold floral arrangements.

OR

Form a complex sentence, using a word such as *because, while,* or *although* to combine ideas.

While one group enjoyed the antics of a clown, others sampled many different foods.

OR

Combine the sentences to form a compound-complex sentence.

The flea market is held every year, **and** people save their treasures all year long **so** they can sell them at the market.

For more help, see Chapter 8, pp. 189–195, and Chapter 18, pp. 394–395.

QUICK FIX

14 Adding Supporting Details

What's the problem? Not enough details are given for readers to fully understand the topic.

Why does it matter? Questions that aren't answered or opinions that aren't supported weaken a piece of writing.

What should you do about it? Add information and details that will make words and statements clear.

What's the Problem?

	Quick Fix
A. An important word is not explained. In 1925, **diphtheria** threatened the town of Nome, Alaska.	**Explain or define the word.** In 1925, diphtheria, **a serious and sometimes fatal disease,** threatened the town of Nome, Alaska.
B. No details are given. Dog-sled teams delivered medical supplies.	**Add details that would help readers understand the significance of an event.** **Twenty** dog-sled teams relayed **almost 700 miles from Anchorage, Alaska, in five days** to deliver **desperately needed** medical supplies.
C. No supporting facts are given. The Iditarod Sled Dog Race is held every year.	**Add supporting facts.** Every year, the Iditarod Sled Dog Race is held **to honor the people and dogs who participated in that rescue mission.**
D. No reason is given for an opinion. There is probably no competitive sport in the world more grueling than this one.	**Add a reason.** There is probably no competitive sport in the world more grueling than this one. **The drivers and dog teams race more than 1,000 miles in high winds and frigid temperatures. They take two to three weeks to reach the finish line.**

For more help, see Chapter 17, pp. 378–381.

15 Avoiding Clichés and Slang

What's the problem? A piece of formal writing contains clichés or slang expressions.

Why does it matter? Clichés do not convey fresh images to readers. Slang is not appropriate in formal writing.

What should you do about it? Reword sentences, replacing the clichés and slang with clear, fresh expressions.

What's the Problem?

Quick Fix

A. A sentence contains a cliché.

The workers were **as busy as bees.**

One person, though, was **as slow as molasses.**

Replace the cliché with a fresh description or explanation.

The workers **bounced from one task to another.**

One person, though, was **as slow as leaves falling from a tree.**

B. A sentence contains inappropriate slang.

The new gymnastics equipment was **the bomb.**

Replace the slang with more appropriate language.

The new gymnastics equipment **would help us prepare for the state meet.**

For more help, see Chapter 19, pp. 402–403 and 408–409.

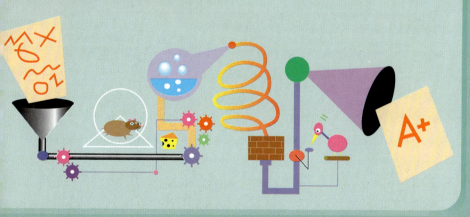

16 Using Precise Words

What's the problem? Nouns, modifiers, and verbs are not precise.

Why does it matter? Writers who use vague or general words don't give readers an accurate picture of their topic.

What should you do about it? Replace vague words with precise and vivid ones.

What's the Problem?

Quick Fix

A. Nouns are too general.

The **people** strapped on their **equipment** and moved into the **street.**

Use specific nouns.

The **anxious skaters** strapped on their **helmets and protective pads** and moved to the **starting line.**

B. Modifiers are too general.

Soon they would be able to show off their **great** skills on **city** streets.

Use vivid adjectives and adverbs.

Immediately, they would show off their **impressive** skills on **winding** city streets.

C. Verbs tell about the action rather than showing it.

The wind **is** against the contestants as they **go** down a steep driveway. The racers **go** around the statue in the park. A barricade forces the skaters to **go** onto the grass.

Use vivid verbs to show the action.

The wind **slaps** the contestants as they **zoom** down a steep driveway. The racers **orbit** the statue in the park. An unexpected barricade forces the skaters to **swerve** onto the grass.

For more help, see Chapter 19, pp. 404–405.

17 Using Figurative Language

What's the problem? A piece of writing is dull or unimaginative.

Why does it matter? Dull writing bores readers because it doesn't help them form mental pictures of what is being described.

What should you do about it? Add figures of speech to make writing lively and to create pictures in readers' minds.

What's the Problem?

A description is dull and lifeless.

Hopelessly bored, we left the house in search of excitement. We trudged down a narrow path toward the park.

All around us the snow was gray.

We stopped at a yard with snow that looked like whipped cream. The gate was half open.

For more help, see Chapter 19, pp. 408–409.

Quick Fix

Add a simile.

Hopelessly bored, we left the house in search of excitement. We trudged down a narrow path toward the park **like an army of defeated soldiers.**

OR

Add a metaphor.

All around us the snow was **a gray carpet in need of a cleaning.**

OR

Use personification.

We stopped at a yard with snow that looked like whipped cream. **The half-open gate invited us to enter.**

QUICK FIX

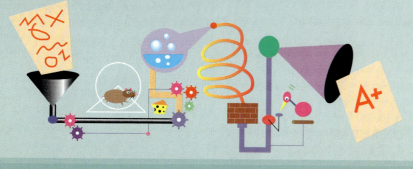

18 Paragraphing

What's the problem? A paragraph contains too many ideas.

Why does it matter? A long paragraph discourages readers from continuing.

What should you do about it? Break the paragraph into smaller paragraphs. Start a new paragraph whenever a new idea is presented or the time, place, or speaker changes.

What's the Problem?

Too many ideas are contained in one paragraph.

Although Aunt Leona isn't known for her cooking ability, she offered to help me bake a birthday cake for my mom's party. I accepted her offer because I'm not known for my cooking ability either. After spending the whole morning in the kitchen, we got something into the oven, but what a mess we had afterward. The kitchen looked like the scene of a science experiment gone awry. Then real disaster struck. The cake broke into chunks when we took it out of the oven. "Oh, Aunt Leona!" I groaned. "How can we fix this mess?" "I have an idea," she said. Later that day we served the cake chunks with strawberries and chocolate sauce. Mom and the guests were quite impressed. Aunt Leona had turned disaster into success.

Quick Fix

Although Aunt Leona isn't known for her cooking ability, she offered to help me bake a birthday cake for my mom's party. I accepted her offer because I'm not known for my cooking ability either.

Start a new paragraph to introduce a new idea.

After spending the whole morning in the kitchen, we got something into the oven, but what a mess we had afterward. The kitchen looked like the scene of a science experiment gone awry. Then real disaster struck. The cake broke into chunks when we took it out of the oven.

Start a new paragraph whenever the speaker changes.

"Oh, Aunt Leona!" I groaned. "How can we fix this mess?"

"I have an idea," she said.

Start a new paragraph when the time or place changes.

Later that day we served the cake chunks with strawberries and chocolate sauce. Mom and the guests were quite impressed. Aunt Leona had turned disaster into success.

For more help, see Chapter 16, pp. 368–370.

What's the Problem?

An essay is treated as one long paragraph.

Scary gigantic beasts are often the subject of today's horror films. However, tales of scary monsters have been told for centuries. One monster that appears in many tales is the fire-breathing dragon. Is it possible that the storytellers were referring to the Komodo dragon? Although it's no monster, the Komodo dragon is the world's largest lizard. It lives on Komodo Island in Indonesia and was discovered in 1912. Before scientists visited the island, rumors about giant dragons persisted. Today we know many facts about this remarkable animal. The Komodo dragon can be as long as 12 feet and weigh as much as 300 pounds. This lizard has strong claws and sharp, sawlike teeth. It eats dead animals as well as live prey. The Komodo dragon does not breathe fire, but it is fearsome. Unlike the dragons in old tales, however, Komodo dragons are protected from hunters, who nearly caused the lizards' extinction.

For more help, see Chapter 16, pp. 368–370.

Quick Fix

Scary gigantic beasts are often the subject of today's horror films. However, tales of scary monsters have been told for centuries.

Start a new paragraph to introduce the first main idea.

One monster that appears in many tales is the fire-breathing dragon. Is it possible that the storytellers were referring to the Komodo dragon? Although it's no monster, the Komodo dragon is the world's largest lizard. It lives on Komodo Island in Indonesia and was discovered in 1912. Before scientists visited the island, rumors about giant dragons persisted.

Start a new paragraph to introduce another main idea.

Today we know many facts about this remarkable animal. The Komodo dragon can be as long as 12 feet and weigh as much as 300 pounds. This lizard has strong claws and sharp, sawlike teeth. It eats dead animals as well as live prey.

Start a new paragraph to give the conclusion.

The Komodo dragon does not breathe fire, but it is fearsome. Unlike the dragons in old tales, however, Komodo dragons are protected from hunters, who nearly caused the lizards' extinction.

QUICK FIX

QUICK-FIX

Essential Writing Skills

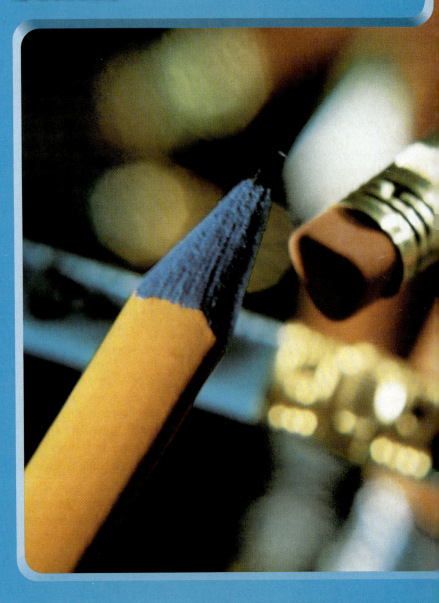

Ready, Set, Write!

Writing doesn't start with a sharpened pencil — it starts with ideas. When you write, you need to choose words carefully, put ideas in order, and include interesting details. Soon you'll be able to express your ideas in a style that's all your own.

307

Chapter 12 Writing Process

Use the online lesson planner at **mcdougallittell.com** to customize instruction.

Pupil's Edition	Print Resources — Writing and Communication Masters	Time-Saver Transparencies Binder — Critical Thinking Graphic Organizers	Time-Saver Transparencies Binder — Daily Test Preparation	Time-Saver Transparencies Binder — Writing and Communication Skills	Students Acquiring English/ESL — Side by Side
LESSON 1 Prewriting: Finding a Topic pp. 310–311	p. 1		p. DT 36		p. 17
LESSON 2 Prewriting: Narrowing and Exploring a Topic pp. 312–314	p. 2	pp. CT 3, 17	p. DT 37	p. WC 1	
LESSON 3 Drafting pp. 315–316	p. 3		p. DT 37		
LESSON 4 Revising pp. 317–318	p. 4		p. DT 38	p. WC 2	
LESSON 5 Editing and Proofreading p. 319	p. 5		p. DT 38	p. WC 3	
LESSON 6 Publishing and Reflecting pp. 320–321			p. DT 39		

ASSESSMENT

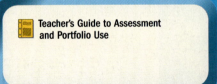

Teacher's Guide to Assessment and Portfolio Use

INTEGRATED TECHNOLOGY AND MEDIA

 mcdougallittell.com

Visit our web site for:
· Student activities
· Links to related resources
· Teaching resources
· Professional articles

 Electronic Teacher Tools

Print-Out Option Exercises in the following components may be printed from the Electronic Teacher Tools as worksheets.

· Writing and Communication Masters
· Test Preparation (Use for levels 6-10)
· College Test Preparation (Use for levels 11 and 12)
· Weekly Vocabulary and Spelling
· Assessment Masters
· Students Acquiring English/ESL
   · English Grammar Survival Kit
   · Side by Side
   · Test Preparation

Chapter 13 Building Sentences

Use the online lesson planner at **mcdougallittell.com** to customize instruction.

Pupil's Edition	Print Resources Writing and Communication Masters	Time-Saver Transparencies Binder Daily Test Preparation	Time-Saver Transparencies Binder Visual Grammar Tiles	Students Acquiring English/ESL Side by Side
LESSON 1 Improving Your Sentences pp. 326-327	p. 6	p. DT 39		pp. 29
LESSON 2 Expanding Sentences pp. 328-329		p. DT 40		
LESSON 3 Combining Complete Sentences pp. 330-331	p. 7	p. DT 40	Lessons 17-18	p. 27
LESSON 4 Combining Sentence Parts pp. 332-333	p. 8	p. DT 41	Lesson 19	
LESSON 5 Using *Who, That,* and *Which* pp. 334-335	p. 9	p. DT 41	Lessons 20-21	

ASSESSMENT

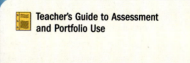

Teacher's Guide to Assessment and Portfolio Use

Chapter 14 Building Paragraphs

Use the online lesson planner at mcdougallittell.com to customize instruction.

Pupil's Edition	Print Resources — Writing and Communication Masters	Time-Saver Transparencies Binder — Critical Thinking Graphic Organizers	Time-Saver Transparencies Binder — Daily Test Preparation	Time-Saver Transparencies Binder — Writing and Communication Skills	Students Acquiring English/ESL — Side by Side
LESSON 1 Qualities of a Good Paragraph pp. 340			p. DT 42		pp. 18-20
LESSON 2 Unity and Coherence pp. 341-343	pp. 10-11	p. CT 3	p. DT 42	p. WC 4	
LESSON 3 Paragraphs: Descriptive and Narrative p. 344-345	p. 12		p. DT 43		
LESSON 3 Paragraphs: Informative and Persuasive p. 346-347		pp. CT 11	p. DT 43		

ASSESSMENT

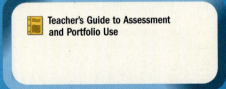

Teacher's Guide to Assessment and Portfolio Use

INTEGRATED TECHNOLOGY AND MEDIA

 mcdougallittell.com

Visit our web site for:
· Student activities
· Links to related resources
· Teaching resources
· Professional articles

 Electronic Teacher Tools

Print-Out Option Exercises in the following components may be printed from the Electronic Teacher Tools as worksheets.

· Writing and Communication Masters
· Test Preparation (Use for levels 6-10)
· College Test Preparation (Use for levels 11 and 12)
· Weekly Vocabulary and Spelling
· Assessment Masters
· Students Acquiring English/ESL
  · English Grammar Survival Kit
  · Side by Side
  · Test Preparation

Chapter 15 Organizing Paragraphs

Use the online lesson planner at **mcdougallittell.com** to customize instruction.

Pupil's Edition	Print Resources	Time-Saver Transparencies Binder			Students Acquiring English/ESL
	Writing and Communication Masters	Critical Thinking Graphic Organizers	Daily Test Preparation	Writing and Communication Skills	Side by Side
LESSON 1 Sequential Order pp. 352-353	p. 13		p. DT 44	p. WC 5	
LESSON 2 Spatial Order pp. 354-355	p. 14		p. DT 44	p. WC 5	
LESSON 3 Cause-and-Effect Order pp. 356-357	p. 15	p. CT 15	p. DT 45	p. WC 5	
LESSON 4 Compare-and-Contrast Order pp. 358-359		p. CT 7	p. DT 45	p. WC 8	pp. 18-20

ASSESSMENT

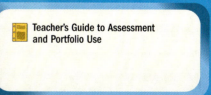

Teacher's Guide to Assessment and Portfolio Use

Chapter 16 Building Compositions

Use the online lesson planner at **mcdougallittell.com** to customize instruction.

Pupil's Edition	Print Resources	Time-Saver Transparencies Binder			Integrated Technology and Media	Students Acquiring English/ESL
	Writing and Communication Masters	Daily Test Preparation	Quick-Fix Grammar and Style Charts	Writing and Communication Skills	Power Presentations	Side by Side
LESSON 1 Structuring a Composition pp. 364-365		p. DT 46		p. WC 6		
LESSON 2 Writing an Introduction pp. 366-367	p. 16	p. DT 46		p. WC 6	Lesson 5	pp. 21-23
LESSON 3 Writing the Body pp. 368-370	p. 17	p. DT 47	pp. QF 19-20	p. WC 7	Lesson 5	
LESSON 4 Writing the Conclusion pp. 371	p. 18	p. DT 47		p. WC 6	Lesson 5	

ASSESSMENT

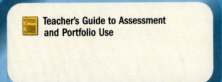 Teacher's Guide to Assessment and Portfolio Use

INTEGRATED TECHNOLOGY AND MEDIA

 mcdougallittell.com

Visit our web site for:
· Student activities
· Links to related resources
· Teaching resources
· Professional articles

 Electronic Teacher Tools

Print-Out Option Exercises in the following components may be printed from the Electronic Teacher Tools as worksheets.

· Writing and Communication Masters
· Test Preparation (Use for levels 6-10)
· College Test Preparation (Use for levels 11 and 12)
· Weekly Vocabulary and Spelling
· Assessment Masters
· Students Acquiring English/ESL
    · English Grammar Survival Kit
    · Side by Side
    · Test Preparation

Chapter 17 Elaboration

Use the online lesson planner at **mcdougallittell.com** to customize instruction.

Pupil's Edition	Print Resources — Writing and Communication Masters	Time-Saver Transparencies Binder — Daily Test Preparation	Time-Saver Transparencies Binder — Quick-Fix Grammar and Style Charts	Time-Saver Transparencies Binder — Writing and Communication Skills	Integrated Technology and Media — Power Presentations	Students Acquiring English/ESL — Side by Side
LESSON 1 Uses of Elaboration pp. 376-377		p. DT 48	p. QF 15			pp. 24-26
LESSON 2 Sensory Details pp. 378-379	p. 19	p. DT 48		pp. WC 8, 9	Lesson 7	
LESSON 3 Facts and Statistics pp. 380-381	p. 20	p. DT 49	p. QF 15	p. WC 8	Lesson 7	
LESSON 4 Visuals pp. 382-383		p. DT 49	pp. QF 18, 20	p. WC 8	Lesson 7	

ASSESSMENT

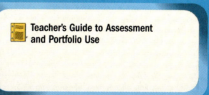

Teacher's Guide to Assessment and Portfolio Use

Chapter 18 Revising Sentences

Use the online lesson planner at **mcdougallittell.com** to customize instruction.

Pupil's Edition	**Print Resources** Writing and Communication Masters	**Time-Saver Transparencies Binder**			**Integrated Technology and Media** Power Presentations
		Daily Test Preparation	Quick-Fix Grammar and Style Charts	Visual Grammar Tiles	
LESSON 1 Padded and Empty Sentences pp. 388-389	p. 21	p. DT 50	pp. QF 11-12		Lesson 7
LESSON 2 Stringy and Over-loaded Sentences pp. 390-391	p. 22	p. DT 50	p. QF 11		Lesson 7
LESSON 3 Varying Sentence Structure pp. 392-393		p. DT 51	p. QF 13	Lesson 22	Lesson 7
LESSON 4 Varying Sentence Length pp. 394-395		p. DT 51	p. QF 14		Lesson 7

ASSESSMENT

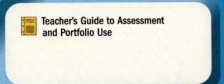

Teacher's Guide to Assessment and Portfolio Use

INTEGRATED TECHNOLOGY AND MEDIA

 mcdougallittell.com

Visit our web site for:
· Student activities
· Links to related resources
· Teaching resources
· Professional articles

 Electronic Teacher Tools

Print-Out Option Exercises in the following components may be printed from the Electronic Teacher Tools as worksheets.

· Writing and Communication Masters
· Test Preparation (Use for levels 6-10)
· College Test Preparation (Use for levels 11 and 12)
· Weekly Vocabulary and Spelling
· Assessment Masters
· Students Acquiring English/ESL
   · English Grammar Survival Kit
   · Side by Side
   · Test Preparation

Chapter 19 Style and Effective Language

Use the online lesson planner at **mcdougallittell.com** to customize instruction.

Pupil's Edition	Print Resources Writing and Communication Masters	Daily Test Preparation	Quick-Fix Grammar and Style Charts
LESSON 1 The Elements of Style pp. 410-411	p. 23	p. DT 52	p. QF 16
LESSON 2 Choosing Language Levels pp. 402-403	p. 23	p. DT 52	p. QF 17
LESSON 3 Choosing Precise Words pp. 404-405	pp. 24	p. DT 53	p. QF 17
LESSON 4 Connotation and Denotation pp. 406-407		p. DT 53	pp. QF 16, 18
LESSON 5 Using Figurative Language pp. 408-409	p. 25	p. DT 54	

Time-Saver Transparencies Binder

ASSESSMENT

 Teacher's Guide to Assessment and Portfolio Use

To increase vocabulary through the recognition and understanding of words that describe how people feel

To use precise words in speaking and in writing that describe how people feel

CHAPTER 12

Power Words
Vocabulary for Precise Writing

Thrilling or Scary?

The next time you face a challenge that scares you a little, use some of these words to express how you feel.

Ready to Go

Aren't you **excited** and **thrilled** when you play your favorite sport? You feel **energized, enthusiastic,** even **exhilarated.** You're **champing at the bit,** which means that you're **eager** to show what you can do. Whether you're playing soccer, baseball, or chess, sports and games can **focus** your mind and make you feel **invigorated.**

Afraid to Take the Plunge?

Some hobbies require a bit more **daring.** Jumping out of an airplane is a **terrifying** thing to do. Even with a parachute, it's **frightening,** maybe even **horrifying** if you don't like **alarming** heights. The plane climbs to a **fearsome** altitude that has you **petrified.** Then you take a deep breath and decide that this **daunting** challenge isn't going to **strike fear into** you any more—and off you go, to a safe, soft landing.

▶ Your Turn A Web of Challenges

With a partner, think of an activity that would excite you and scare you at the same time, such as hang-gliding, climbing Mount Everest, or giving a speech in front of a big audience. Together, make a word web of all the emotions you both would feel.

308 Essential Writing Skills

Writing Process

Taking the Plunge

You've just been assigned to write a paper. You can probably think of 100 things you'd rather do—even organize your sock drawer. The answer may be just to plunge in and start writing. Think of writing as a roller-coaster ride. You may take some unexpected turns, go backwards, or even go in circles sometimes, but in the end you might find yourself saying, "That wasn't so bad after all."

Write Away: Jump Right In

Think of a time you had to do something that frightened you. Maybe you didn't want to try it at first, but you jumped right in anyway. Write a paragraph about one of these experiences that turned out better than you expected. Put your paragraph in your 📁 **Working Portfolio**.

CHAPTER OVERVIEW

CHAPTER RESOURCES

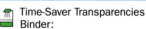 Time-Saver Transparencies Binder:

- Critical Thinking Graphic Organizers pp. CT3, 17
- Daily Test Preparation pp. DT36–39
- Writing and Communication Skills pp. WC1–3

📄 Writing and Communication Masters pp. 1–5

Integrated Technology and Media

 Electronic Teacher Tools CD-ROM

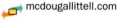 mcdougallittell.com

Assessment

📄 Teacher's Guide to Assessment and Portfolio Use

Students Acquiring English/ESL

 Side by Side p. 17

BLOCK SCHEDULING

Pressed for Time?

Focus on **Lessons 1–3** to emphasize the importance of the prewriting and drafting stages of the writing process. Suggest that students independently study **Lessons 4–6** to familiarize themselves with revising, proofreading, and publishing their work.

Time for More?

After working through the chapter, have students reread the Student Model in **Lesson 4.** Discuss how the six traits work throughout the draft.

LESSON 1   Prewriting: Finding a Topic

In the writing process, two things are certain. You begin with a blank page, and you end up with a final draft. Otherwise, each writer works through the writing process—prewriting, drafting, revising, editing, and publishing—in a different way. You may need to repeat steps or switch the order. But the first step is always finding something to write about. Taking a self-inventory, freewriting, and brainstorming are three helpful ways to begin the writing process and find a topic.

> "Writing is an exploration.
> You start from nothing and learn as you go."
>
> —E.L. Doctorow

❶ Taking a Self-Inventory

Choosing a topic allows you to write about whatever interests you. You probably have a lot of interests, so how do you choose one? One way is to take a self-inventory. Ask yourself the following questions:

- What are some interesting, funny, weird, or annoying things that happened this week?
- What is my favorite way to spend my spare time?
- Who is the most interesting or unusual person I know? What makes that person unique?
- What community issues interest me? Why?
- What fascinates me? confuses me? troubles me? surprises me?
- What do I know a lot about?

Many writers explore ideas in a writer's journal. Throughout the day, try jotting down thoughts and ideas in your journal.

For more on finding ideas, see pg. 322.

TEACHING TIP

Have students freewrite for five to ten minutes about something they did or saw the night before. After they have finished, encourage them to circle ideas they might want to write about.

2 Freewriting

When you freewrite, put pencil to paper and write whatever comes to mind. Write without stopping for at least ten minutes, letting one idea flow into the next. After ten minutes, stop and circle any ideas you like. Then freewrite about one or two of those ideas until you hit on a topic that interests you.

> **STUDENT MODEL**
>
> What a great day! I wish I didn't have to be in (school.) At least I got to ride my (bike)—except for one thing that really bothered me when I rode past the (train station.) The (trash) can was totally gross & overflowing which made me mad because it was full of (newspapers) that could have been (recycled) except that they were all slimy from the garbage thrown on top of them.

CUSTOMIZING TIP

Less Proficient Learners Some students may have difficulty carrying out any kind of writing—even prewriting. Encourage these students to record their ideas using a tape recorder so that they can concentrate on what they have to say instead of on the act of writing.

3 Brainstorming

Brainstorming is a way to come up with ideas in a group. For ten minutes or so, each member of the group offers ideas for topics while one person writes them down. Don't criticize suggestions or try to choose a topic while you brainstorm. When the time is up, read over the list and choose the idea you like best.

sharks
music
outer space
ballet

hot-air balloons
Grand Canyon
baseball
environmental issues

Decide on a topic early so you'll have time to research, draft, and edit your work long before your paper is due.

Writing Process **311**

WRITING PROCESS

WRITING PROCESS

Spice It Up!

Have students get together in pairs to play a free-association word game. One student in each pair should start the game by naming a broad topic, such as movies, sports, television, schools, or books. Partners should respond with whatever word comes to mind. Play continues as students take turns free-associating based on their partners' responses. The game ends when both students in a pair come up with a possible writing topic.

To learn how to narrow and develop a topic and to consider audience and purpose

DAILY TEST PREPARATION

Error Correction: Capitalization
Write the following item on the board or use 📖 **Daily Test Preparation Transparency** p. DT37.
Choose the best way to write the underlined section.

Archaeologists in Northern Ireland uncovered <u>a 4,000-year-old bronze age grave.</u>

A. a four thousand year old bronze age grave.

B. a 4,000-year-old Bronze Age Grave.

C. a 4,000-year-old Bronze Age grave.

D. Correct as is

Teaching Point: Error correction questions often test your knowledge of basic capitalization rules. In this case, the item tests whether you know to capitalize the names of historical periods, such as *the Bronze Age or the Jurassic Period.*

CHAPTER 12

TEACHING TIP

Use **Critical Thinking Graphic Organizer Cluster Diagram** p. CT3, to demonstrate how students can use a cluster diagram to help narrow their focus. Write a general topic in the center oval, and then have students volunteer information to fill in the smaller ovals.

LESSON 2

Prewriting: Narrowing and Exploring a Topic

Once you've decided on a topic, narrow it so that you won't be overwhelmed by information when you start to research it. It's easier to focus on only one aspect of a broad topic. Try narrowing your topic by making a cluster diagram and by considering audience and purpose.

❶ Focusing a Topic

Creating a Cluster Diagram

Suppose you decided to write about environmental issues in your community. You could narrow that topic by making a cluster diagram like the one below. The general topic is in a large oval, while different aspects of that topic are in smaller ovals. You could choose one aspect to focus on in your writing.

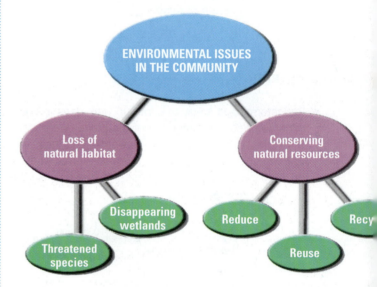

As a way of enlarging your cluster diagram, you can ask yourself questions. For example, ask yourself: What more do I already know about this topic? or What more do I want to know about this topic?

Identifying Audience and Purpose

After you've narrowed your topic, ask yourself two questions: "*Why* am I writing this?" and "To *whom* am I writing?" These questions will identify your purpose and your audience.

1. I want to persuade the student body to recycle.

2. I want to tell a story to my best friend about the day my grandmother and I rode in a hot-air balloon.

3. I want to describe for my classmates the geological formations in the Grand Canyon.

4. I want to explain to the community what happens to forest life when hundreds of trees are cut down.

Once you decide on a topic, think about what you want to say in your writing and who will be reading it. In order to focus your efforts, write your own "I want to . . ." sentence before you begin researching your topic.

❷ Developing a Topic

Asking Specific Questions

You can develop your topic by asking yourself specific questions. Ask **informative** questions to help yourself find out how much you already know and what more you'd like to know. Ask **imaginative** questions to help spark ideas about unusual aspects of your topic.

Informative
- How many households in the community recycle?
- How many different materials can be recycled?

Imaginative
- If every scrap of paper in the country were recycled, how many acres of forests would be saved?
- What would happen if we started fining people for not recycling?

Writing Process **313**

TEACHING TIP

Build off of the audience and purpose discussion and have students choose the correct form for their purpose. Give some examples of reasons to write (purpose) and forms that would be appropriate for each. Ask students to choose a form to match the purpose.

TEACHING TIP

Tell students that the audience they choose to address will affect what they say about their subject and the language they use. Students need to consider how much their audience already knows about the subject and what level of vocabulary is most appropriate. For example, suppose students wanted to write a how-to article about a favorite computer game. What information would they leave out if they wrote for an audience of computer buffs? What language would they use if they wrote for an audience of younger children?

TEACHING TIP

Cooperative Learning/Paired Activity Tell students that they can also ask *who, what, when, where, why,* and *how* questions to find out more about a topic. Have students get together in pairs and take turns interviewing each other about how they spend a special holiday. Students should use *who, what, when, where, why,* and *how* questions to explore the topic.

Researching a Topic

Calvin and Hobbes by Bill Watterson

Calvin may have some trouble writing about bats if he doesn't know much about them. Before you begin writing a draft, do some fact-finding. Check the following sources at the library:

- books
- encyclopedias
- the Internet
- magazines

You could also interview an expert in the field.

Finding information can seem overwhelming. Try to stay focused on what you are looking for instead of getting sidetracked by interesting information that doesn't relate to your topic.

For more on finding information, see p. 493.

❸ Organizing Information

One simple way to organize your information is to list all the things you want to discuss in your report. Once you've made the list, you can experiment with rearranging the order.

STUDENT MODEL

- Why we should recycle
- Strengths and weaknesses of our recycling program
- How our recycling program can be improved
- How kids can get involved in our recycling program

Ways to organize writing include sequential order, spatial order, cause-and-effect order, and compare-and-contrast order.

For more on organizing, see pg. 351.

TEACHING TIP

Tell students that, in general, it is not good to get sidetracked by irrelevant information when researching a topic. However, if their research leads them in a new or related direction, students should feel free to change their topic and write about what really interests them.

CUSTOMIZING TIP

Addressing Learning Styles
Visual Explain to students that a comparison-and-contrast organizer can be useful when they are planning a report that compares and contrasts information. Use ⬛ **Critical Thinking Graphic Organizer Compare/Contrast Chart** p. CT17, to demonstrate. Have students compare two favorite television shows. Ask them how the shows are similar, and write the similarities on the chart. Then ask them to discuss the shows' differences, and add these to the chart. After you have completed the charts, tell students that they could use it to write a compare-contrast essay on the shows.

Drafting

It might surprise you, but there are no set guidelines for writing your first draft. Some writers start in the middle and add the introduction during a later draft. The important thing is to start writing! With each draft, your ideas will change, develop, and come into sharper focus.

"Start by getting something—anything—down on paper. A friend of mine says the first draft is the down draft—you just get it down. The second draft is the up draft—you fix it up. . . . And the third draft is the dental draft, where you check every tooth, to see if it's loose or cramped or even . . . healthy."

—Anne Lamott, *Bird by Bird*

❶ Types of Drafting

You may find that different types of writing call for different types of drafting. To write a report or proposal, you may need to plan out the draft. Personal narratives and short stories may benefit from a discovery draft.

Drafting from a Plan

Suppose that at the organizing stage you made a list of the points you want to cover in your paper. Now you can go back to that list and add more specific details. You may want to think of your paper in terms of an introduction, body, and conclusion and list information that way. Refer to your plan as you write.

Drafting to Discover

Perhaps making an orderly list doesn't appeal to you, and you'd rather just start writing and see what happens. You may find that your discovery draft takes some unexpected twists and turns. These can actually help define the direction of your writing, or you may need to go back and reorganize.

Don't be surprised if, while you draft, you decide to drop some ideas, rearrange other ideas, or even add new ideas.

Writing Process **315**

LESSON OBJECTIVES

To recognize different strategies for beginning a draft and to learn how to offer and receive feedback from others

DAILY TEST PREPARATION

Sentence Completion: Vocabulary Write the following item on the board or use 🏛 **Daily Test Preparation Transparency** p. DT37. Choose the word or words that *best* fit the meaning of the sentence.

> Do you have a(n) _____ amount of information, or is the word problem missing a detail you need to solve it?

A. sufficient

B. treacherous

C. responsible

D. inadequate

Teaching Point: For vocabulary questions, use context clues in the text. In this case, the person solving the word problem either has enough information, or is missing needed information. *Sufficient*, meaning "as much as needed," is the correct choice.

TEACHING TIP

Have students create a draft of a current work in progress on a word processor. Encourage students to follow the writing process through the revising and editing stages, using their word processing program to complete each stage.

TEACHING RESOURCES

 Time-Saver Transparencies Binder:
• Daily Test Preparation p. DT37

SKILLS PRACTICE RESOURCES

 Writing and Communication Masters p. 3

CUSTOMIZING TIP

Students Acquiring English/ESL
Because acceptable methods of criticism and feedback vary across cultures, hold a brief discussion with students about the peer-editing process. Be sure to mention the goal of feedback and the role it plays in the editing process. You might even give examples of appropriate and inappropriate types of criticism.

TEACHING TIP

Speaking and Listening Tell students that they can ask their peer reader just to listen as they read their work aloud. Students can have the reader respond when they finish reading. Or they can ask the reader not to respond at all. Point out that students can tell a great deal about their writing just by reading it aloud. They will be more aware of what they are saying when they have an audience.

TEACHING TIP

Cross-Curricular Connection Science Tell students that when they write science reports they might find it beneficial to receive feedback from a person who is unfamiliar with the subject matter. This way, the reader will be able to pinpoint for the writer which areas are not explained fully or simply enough for a general audience.

CHAPTER 12

---

② Using Peer Response

After you finish a draft, it's often helpful to get some feedback from your peers, or classmates.

As the writer you should . . .	As the reader you should . . .
• ask the reader specific questions	• offer specific feedback
• use only those suggestions that make sense to you	• give positive comments first
• encourage the reader to be honest	• be sensitive to the writer's feelings
• listen politely, and be open-minded	• carefully consider the writer's questions

- **Group Response** With a group response, two or more readers review your work so that you get different points of view and suggestions. If several readers find a certain passage confusing, you may need to rethink that section.

- **One-on-One Response** A one-on-one response gives you and a classmate the chance to analyze your piece together. When you revise, it's important to keep in mind that your classmate's comments are only suggestions. As the writer, you are responsible for the final decisions.

- **E-mail Partner** If you e-mail a draft to a partner, you can include a list of questions or concerns you'd like your partner to think about as he or she reads your work. Your partner could insert comments and suggestions (in another color or typestyle) directly into your draft and e-mail it back to you.

Spice it Up!

Read the following negative peer reader comments. Challenge students to give a more constructive spin to them.

1. This piece is really disorganized. I can't follow your train of thought at all. You have good ideas, but they would be easier to follow if you organized them more carefully. Consider using sequential order, spatial order, cause-and-effect order, or compare-and-contrast order.

2. Your topic is weird! How did you ever come up with something like that? Your topic is really unusual.

3. This example doesn't prove your point at all. Good point, but the example doesn't work. Try to find another that really illustrates what you're trying to say.

Revising

In the revising stage, you start making changes to your draft. As you begin revising, bear in mind the feedback you've gotten from peers. Also remember that revising often involves rewriting entire paragraphs or reorganizing information. You may have to revise several times before you are finished.

❶ Evaluating Your Draft

The following chart shows six traits of good writing. Use these six traits to help evaluate your writing and pinpoint areas that need revision.

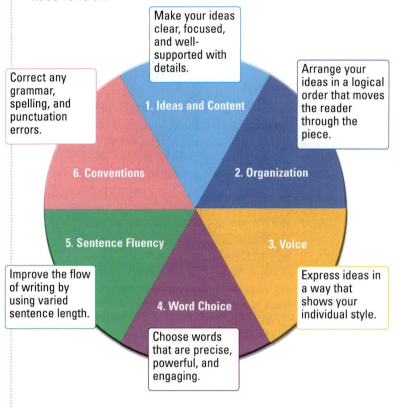

Make your ideas clear, focused, and well-supported with details.

Arrange your ideas in a logical order that moves the reader through the piece.

Correct any grammar, spelling, and punctuation errors.

1. Ideas and Content

2. Organization

6. Conventions

3. Voice

5. Sentence Fluency

4. Word Choice

Express ideas in a way that shows your individual style.

Improve the flow of writing by using varied sentence length.

Choose words that are precise, powerful, and engaging.

HOT TIP
After you've written a draft, let it "cool" for a few hours or days. Don't work on it for a while, and try not to think about it. This will give you a fresh view of your work when you return to revise it again.

Writing Process **317**

WRITING PROCESS

LESSON OBJECTIVES

To recognize and apply the six traits of good writing

DAILY TEST PREPARATION

Revision-in-Context: Using Precise Words Write the following item on the board or use 🖥 **Daily Test Preparation Transparency** p. DT38.

> **1** They had all ready eaten
> **2** the chocolate bars when
> **3** Allen returned from
> **4** gathering wood.

What is the **BEST** change, if any, to make in the sentence in lines 1–2?

A. Change all ready to already

B. Change eaten to ate

C. Insert a comma after bars

D. Make no change

Teaching Point: A common item in revision-in-context questions is using precise words. In this case, this item tests whether you know the difference between *all ready* (the campers are *all ready*) and *already* (I *already* ate the chocolate).

WRITING PROCESS

TEACHING RESOURCES

 Time-Saver Transparencies Binder:
- Daily Test Preparation p. DT38
- Writing and Communication Skills p. WC2

SKILLS PRACTICE RESOURCES

📄 Writing and Communication Masters p. 4

STUDENT MODEL

Write the following paragraph on the board. Then organize students into small groups and have them use the six traits of good writing to revise the paragraph.

A few days ago over 200 students in our school participated in this charity thing that raised a lot of money to inable hospitalized disabled children to go home. There families can't afford to keep them. They say young people dont care. There is supposed to be stuff we do that shows this. Us not caring about other people.

❷ Traits in Action

The following is part of a student's draft. The student's purpose is to persuade members of her community (her audience) to make a stronger commitment to recycling. See how the six traits work throughout this draft.

STUDENT MODEL

Two weeks ago, I was cruising by the train station on my bike. But something just didn't fit in with the beautiful day and the flower-scented breezes I'd been enjoying. The station's trash cans were overflowing with newspapers, foam cups, Sportin' Life Donut bags, soda cans, and even a pair of smelly old running shoes! Bees and flies buzzed in a little cloud above the disgusting container.

Because I am concerned about the destruction of our nation's forests, I was upset that so many newspapers had been contaminated with coffee dregs, flat soda, and stale doughnut crumbs. Those newspapers could have been recycled.

I decided to see what could be done about this problem. First I talked to Ms. Naomi Cohn, the coordinator of the Blue Hill Recycling Center. She told me that recycling a 4-foot stack of newspapers saves a 35-foot tree. Judging by how much newspaper was in the station can, I'd estimate that Blue Hill commuters "throw away" a tree a week. She also told me that placing cans for recyclables next to the trash could solve the problem.

Word Choice:
Writer uses precise words to bring the scene to life.

Sentence Fluency:
Writer uses varied sentence length and structure.

Ideas and Content:
Ideas are clear and supported with details.

Throughout the draft, notice that:

- the writer presents ideas in an **organized** way.
- the writer expresses ideas in her own **voice.**
- the writer has addressed the **conventions** of good writing.

Drive-Through Grammar

Pronoun Reference Remind students that errors in pronoun reference may confuse their readers. Problems can arise whenever more than one word might be a pronoun's antecedent. Write the following sentence on the board: *If cans are left lying around by campers, throw them in trash cans.* Ask: Is the antecedent of *them* the cans or the campers? Then have students revise the sentence and eliminate the pronoun-reference problem.

Cans left lying around by campers should be thrown in trash cans.

Editing and Proofreading

LESSON 5

One way to edit your draft is to check it against the six traits of good writing. Revise your work until you feel it demonstrates those traits.

Proofreading will probably be the final step in your revision process. Read through your work line by line to correct errors in spelling, grammar, and punctuation. Finding errors can be tough!

Use these marks as you proofread.

1 Proofreading Marks

Using Proofreading Marks

Symbol	Explanation	Example
∧	insert letters or words	I've never written a paper before. *research*
⊙	add a period	Writing can be fun⊙ It's better to write about things you like.
∧	add a comma	Outer space, dinosaurs, and sports interest me.
#	add a space	The planet Pluto is farthest from the#sun.
℘	take out letters or words	The T. Rex was one of the largest big dinosaurs.
⌒	close up	I wonder how many points Michael Jordan scored dur ing his career.
¶	begin new paragraph	¶Muhammad Ali was a famous boxer.
≡	capitalize	Researching the origin of boxing in the united states might be interesting.
/	use lowercase	I think I'll do some more freewriting about sports in my Journal.
∼	switch the positions of letters or words	Once I decide which sport to focus no, I'll do a diagram cluster to narrow the topic.

Computer spell check catches spelling mistakes, but it won't alert you to usage errors, such as The slug tracked mud all over there rug. Always proofread your work yourself before presenting it.

Writing Process **319**

LESSON OBJECTIVES

To learn proofreading marks and to use them to edit and correct errors in a draft

 DAILY TEST PREPARATION

Definition: Vocabulary Write the following item on the board or use 🖥 **Daily Test Preparation Transparency** p. DT38.

Choose the word that means the same, or about the same, as the underlined word.

> Convinced of her innocence, Constance made a <u>vigorous</u> defense before her teacher.

A. relaxed

B. daring

C. strong

D. ambiguous

Teaching Point: For definitions, analyze the parts of an unfamiliar word to decipher its meaning. *Vigorous* comes from the Latin word *vigor*, meaning "energy." Since the suffix *-ous* means "full of," *vigorous* means "full of energy."

TEACHING TIP

Teach by example! When you mark students' papers, make spelling, grammar, and punctuation corrections with proofreading marks.

NEED MORE INFORMATION?

For a review of mechanics, refer students to **Chapter 10, Capitalization,** and **Chapter 11, Punctuation.**

To recognize different publishing options and to reflect on the writing process

LESSON 6 · Publishing and Reflecting

Seeing your ideas appear in finished form (in print, on a computer screen, or in performance) will give you a sense of accomplishment. Knowing that others will see your work provides an extra motivation to make sure it is polished and mistake-free.

❶ Exploring Ways to Publish

Print Media

• Enclose a copy of your work in a letter to a friend.

• Get permission to post your work on a classroom bulletin board or in a public place in the school.

• Design and distribute a "zine" containing your writing and original artwork by you or a friend.

• Submit your work to your school or community newspaper.

• Enter a magazine contest.

Electronic Media

• E-mail your work to a friend or relative.

• Post your work on your school's Web site.

• Submit your work to an Internet journal or literary magazine that publishes student writing.

Performance

• Give a dramatic reading of your work to friends or family members.

• Make a radio or television "broadcast" by recording your work on audiotape or videotape.

• Dramatize your piece for an audience you choose. Add music or props to make it lively.

320 Essential Writing Skills

➋ Reflecting on Your Writing

After you've finished, look back and consider how well the writing process worked for you.

Questions for Reflection

- What part(s) of the process were easy or difficult?
- What would I do differently next time?
- What did I learn that will improve my writing skills?

Prewrite ➡ **Draft** ➡ **Revise** ➡ **Edit** ➡ **Publish**

You may need to repeat one or all of these steps to work the final draft into presentation form.

Portfolios

You can save all your writing in folders called portfolios.

📁 Working Portfolio

This portfolio will probably contain the bulk of your work. Even if a piece didn't turn out as well as you had hoped, save it in your working portfolio. You may refer back to work in this portfolio to track your progress as a writer.

📁 Presentation Portfolio

Reserve this portfolio for work that best demonstrates your writing skills. These pieces are ready for publication and may travel with you into next year. If you rework and improve a piece from your **Working Portfolio,** you can place the new version in your Presentation Portfolio.

Writing Process **321**

WRITING PROCESS

WRITING PROCESS

Student Help Desk

Students can use the Student Help Desk as a quick review prior to testing or as a quick reference as they revise a piece of writing.

Teacher's Notes
WHAT WORKS:

CHAPTER 12

Student Help Desk

Writing Process at a Glance

Prewriting   Drafting

Revising and Proofreading

Publishing and Presenting

CHAPTER 12

Finding a Topic   Keep Ideas Flowing

A journal can serve as a valuable writing tool and a source of ideas.

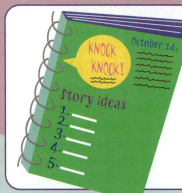

KNOCK KNOCK!

October 14,

Story Ideas
1.
2.
3.
4.
5.

- Carry your journal around with you.
- Jot down things you find funny, weird, sad, annoying, or frustrating.
- Keep a list of short story ideas.
- Write about things you want to do.
- Draw cartoons.
- Write jokes.
- Solve problems.

Editing Hints   Write the Right Words

As you edit, look for these words. Check a dictionary to be sure you have used them correctly.

there, their, or they're?

who's or whose?

than or then?   affect or effect?

principle or principal?   it's or its?

sit or set?   farther or further?

4

Proofreading Tips

Lets Have Some proof

Some tips for spotting writing errors

Read backwards.	Start with the end and read sentence by sentence to the beginning.
Find more eyes.	Ask a peer or family member to review your work after you.
Speak up!	Listen and look for mistakes while you read the piece out loud.
Is there an echo in here? echo echo	Read each sentence twice, out loud or to yourself. Be sure to read slowly.

Getting Published

Submissions, Please!

Whether you are submitting to magazines, books, journals, on-line publications, or radio or TV programs, consider the following:

1. Write the publisher for submission guidelines.
2. Be sure your piece meets the publisher's specifications.
3. Proofread and edit your work one more time before you send it.
4. Include a cover letter and/or a tape of your oral reading, and a SASE (self-addressed stamped envelope).
5. Don't be discouraged if your piece isn't chosen after the first submission. Try, try again!

The Bottom Line

Checklist for Writing

Have I used the six traits of good writing and . . .

____ presented my ideas clearly and used supporting details?

____ logically organized my writing?

____ made my sentences flow smoothly?

____ used precise words?

____ expressed ideas in my own way?

____ spelled every word correctly?

Writing Process **323**

Teacher's Notes
WHAT DOESN'T WORK:

TEACHER'S LOUNGE

A Slice of Life

"Good writing is supposed to evoke sensation in the reader—not the fact that it is raining, but the feel of being rained upon."
— E.L. Doctorow

Just for Laughs The visiting American and his English friend were driving through London when the latter mentioned that his windscreen needed cleaning. "Windshield," the American corrected him.

"Well, over here we call it a windscreen."

"Then you're wrong," argued the American. "After all, we Americans invented the automobile, and we call this a windshield."

"That's all very well, old boy," snapped the Englishman, "but who invented the language?"

OBJECTIVES

To increase vocabulary through the recognition and understanding of words that describe expressions

To use precise words in speaking and in writing that describe how people look

Power Words
Vocabulary for Precise Writing

Face Talk

When you try to describe someone's expression, you will need more than just the words "smile" and "frown."

Smile, Simper, or Smirk?

When you look at the Mona Lisa on the facing page, you may wonder why she is smiling. Then you might ask, Is that really a smile? Perhaps it's her attempt at a smile, and it came out a **smirk** or a **simper.** Could it even be a **sneer?**

A smile can have all kinds of emotions behind it. A **pleased** or **joyous** smile is very different from a **sarcastic, scornful,** or **derisive** smile; a **brave** smile is different from a **self-conscious** smile or a **knowing** one.

A Change of Mood

Imagine that Mona becomes tired of sitting in one position for hours on end. Her smile disappears. She seems **solemn, somber,** even **grave.** As time passes, she might appear increasingly **gloomy, downcast,** and **melancholy.** As the days turn into weeks, her face twists into a **frown, scowl,** or **glower.**

▷ **Your Turn** All Over Your Face

Work in small groups. Each person in the group should choose one of the boldfaced words above and smile or frown in a way that reflects that word. (If you need to, you can look up the words in a dictionary.) Take turns sketching each other's facial expressions. Label each sketch with the word that reflects it.

324

Building Sentences

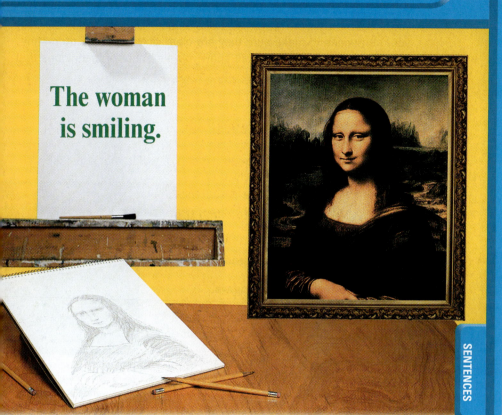

The woman
is smiling.

Making Good Even Better

Any work of art begins with a mere sketch of an idea. Although the sketch is essential, it's not a finished work. The artist adds color and texture to the sketch and improves it.

"The woman is smiling" is a pretty sketchy sentence. Like the sketch above, it needs to be expanded and improved so it will give the reader a clearer picture.

As you write, add details to produce sentences that are richer and clearer—and you may create a masterpiece.

Write Away: *Do Sweat the Small Stuff!*
Write one or more sentences describing the finished painting above to someone who has never seen it. Choose your words carefully to make your writing both accurate and descriptive. Save your work in your ▢ **Working Portfolio.**

Building Sentences **325**

CHAPTER OVERVIEW

SENTENCES

ELABORATION

CHAPTER RESOURCES

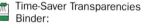 Time-Saver Transparencies Binder:
- Daily Test Preparation pp. DT39–41
- Visual Grammar™ Tiles Lessons 17–21

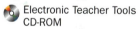 Writing and Communication Masters pp. 6–9

Integrated Technology and Media

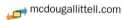 Electronic Teacher Tools CD-ROM

↪ mcdougallittell.com

Assessment

Teacher's Guide to Assessment and Portfolio Use

Students Acquiring English/ESL

Side by Side pp. 27–29

BLOCK SCHEDULING

Pressed for Time?
Focus on **Lesson 1, Improving Your Sentences,** and **Lesson 2, Expanding Sentences,** to give students basic instruction in constructing and expanding sentences.

Time for More?
After you have completed all of the lessons, have students draft a paragraph about shyness when speaking in public. Then have them use the concepts covered in the lessons to improve their sentences.

To identify sentences that are unclear and uninteresting and to write rich, accurate, and detailed sentences

 DAILY TEST PREPARATION

Sentence Completion:
Vocabulary Write the following item on the board or use

📖 **Daily Test Preparation Transparency** p. DT39. Choose the word that *best* fits the meaning of the sentence.

> Teresa made a(n) _____ error when she drove her cousin's car without a dri-ver's license.

A. habits

B. flagrant

C. unimportant

D. excusable

Teaching Point: For sentence completion questions, the correct answer will always

- fit the meaning of the sentence (*unimportant* and *excusable* do not)

- fit grammatically within the sentence (*habits* does not fit with *error*)

TEACHING TIP

Cross-Curricular Connection
History Explain to students that precise words and modifiers serve a very important role in historical texts—the more precise the language is, the more precise the readers' understanding of history will be.

TEACHING TIP

Remind students that impera-tive sentences, although they may seem to lack a subject, are complete sentences because the subject (you) is implied.

CHAPTER 13

LESSON 1 Improving Your Sentences

Have you ever written a sentence that seemed dull to you? Have you written one that your reader had trouble understanding? You can review your sentences to make sure they are clear, accurate, and interesting. The lessons in this chapter will show you a number of techniques that you can use.

❶ Checking for Completeness

A **complete sentence** is a group of words that expresses a complete thought. Which of the following is a complete sentence?

Ingrid prepared to climb the mountain.

Had all the required equipment.

Aware of the dangers.

To express a complete thought, a sentence needs both a **subject** and a **predicate**.

Complete thought

Ingrid prepared to climb the mountain.

COMPLETE SUBJECT   COMPLETE PREDICATE

Complete thought
She had all the required equipment.

Complete thought
The experienced climber was aware of the dangers.

Check your sentences to be sure each one has a subject and a predicate. If you are missing the subject, the predicate, or both, you have created a **sentence fragment.** Sentence fragments are incomplete sentences and can confuse your reader.

For more on fragments, see p. 286.

TEACHING RESOURCES
 Time-Saver Transparencies Binder:
- Daily Test Preparation p. DT39

SKILLS PRACTICE RESOURCES
 Side by Side p. 29
 Writing and Communication Masters p. 6

CUSTOMIZING TIP

Students Acquiring English/ESL
For visual practice with modifier placement, see **Side by Side** p. 29.

❷ Using Precise Words

Your choice of words affects how well your reader understands your sentence. Unclear, general words give your reader a sketchy outline. Accurate, precise words give your reader a clear, detailed picture.

> **The woman breathed.**
>
> **The mountain climber breathed.**
>
> **The mountain climber gasped for air.**

CUSTOMIZING TIP

Students Acquiring English/ESL In many languages, adjectives agree in gender and number with the noun they modify. For example, in Spanish red is *rojo*, but it changes to *rojas* after a feminine plural noun: *las mesas rojas.* Caution students not to add an –s in English to an adjective that modifies a plural noun.

❸ Expanding with Modifiers

Modifiers are words that modify, or make more specific, the meanings of other words. You can use modifiers to add detail to your sentences.

> **The mountain climber gasped for air.**
>
> **The exhausted mountain climber gasped for air.**
>
> **The exhausted mountain climber noisily gasped the thin, cold air.**

 Avoid overused modifiers such as *very, really,* and *totally.* Try using more precise words instead. For example, instead of writing "very cold," try "bitterly cold" or "below freezing." **For more on modifiers, see p. 124.**

PRACTICE ▶ **Make It Clear**

Improve the sentences below by following the directions in parentheses.

1. The view was nice. *(Use precise words.)*
2. The clouds were thick. *(Add modifiers.)*
3. It was windy on the mountain. *(Add modifiers.)*
4. The climber wore layers of clothes. *(Add modifiers.)*
5. The tired climber was happy to reach the top.
   (Use precise words.)

Building Sentences **327**

SENTENCES

ELABORATION

Answers

PRACTICE ▶ **Make It Clear**

Answers will vary. Sample answers:

1. The mountaintop view was breathtakingly clear.
2. The white, puffy clouds were unusually thick.
3. It was extremely windy on the bare mountain.
4. The young climber wore many layers of warm clothes.
5. The worn-out climber was thrilled to reach the top.

CUSTOMIZING TIP

Less Proficient Learners/Paired Activity Have students work in pairs to improve the **PRACTICE** sentences by writing three precise words or modifiers. Then have them choose the best one to read to the class.

Also suitable for:

Students Acquiring English/ESL

Spice It Up!

To reinforce the importance of using precise words, write the following sentence on the board.

The vehicle went by the structure.

Have three volunteers draw pictures that illustrate the sentence. Tape the drawings to the board. Then have the volunteers explain their drawings. Engage students in a discussion about the differences in interpretations. Ask for suggestions on how to make the sentence more precise.

LESSON OBJECTIVES

To identify ways to expand sentences and to write sentences that are informative, accurate, and interesting

DAILY TEST PREPARATION

Error Correction: Irregular Superlatives Write the following item on the board or use **Daily Test Preparation Transparency** p. DT40. Choose the best way to write the underlined section.

> JoAnne is <u>the most best</u> basketball player I know!

A. the bestest

B. the better

C. the best

D. Correct as is

Teaching Point: A common item in error correction questions is double comparisons. In this case, the item tests whether you know that *most* and *best* are not used together. *Best* is the irregular superlative form of the adjective *good*. The comparative *better* (in answer B) cannot be used in this item because more than two players are compared.

TEACHING TIP

Speaking and Listening Read aloud the first three model sentences to emphasize the pleasing rhythm of the sentence openers. After students have listened for enjoyment, ask volunteers to read aloud the last two model sentences, emphasizing the rhythm.

TEACHING RESOURCES

 Time-Saver Transparencies Binder:
- Daily Test Preparation p. DT40

LESSON 2

Expanding Sentences

A sentence becomes more informative, more accurate, and more interesting when it is expanded. Think of everything you want your reader to know about your topic.

❶ Adding Sentence Openers

Introductory words and phrases add information and emphasis. They clarify the message that you want your sentence to deliver.

On the stage, Emil felt extremely nervous.

Shaking and perspiring, he searched the room for an exit.

In the end, Emil was much happier in the audience.

A sentence opener should make the reader want to continue reading. Choose words that will spark your reader's interest.

Although her opponent was tall and strong, Felicia was not afraid.

After four years of training, she was ready to earn her black belt.

> ### PROFESSIONAL MODEL
>
> **With a powerful snap kick,** Felicia sent her opponent crashing to the mat. Felicia is one of thousands of girls who are having fun, staying in shape, and learning to defend themselves through martial arts.
>
> —Elizabeth Gordon

Spice It Up!

Write the following sentence on the board and have students copy it.

[He or she] walked across the room.

Ask volunteers to act out the sentence, adding something creative to their walk. The rest of the class should revise their sentences, using a description of the walk as a sentence opener. (Examples: stoop-shouldered, looking lost, while looking over his shoulder.) Have students read their sentences aloud.

❷ Adding to the Middle

A well-chosen word or phrase in the middle of the sentence will often "spice up" an otherwise ordinary statement. These words and phrases usually go between the subject and the predicate or after the first verb in a compound predicate.

Liz, forgetting her manners, hollered across the table.

The principal, offended, frowned at her.

Liz blushed, completely embarrassed, and quietly apologized.

❸ Adding Sentence Closers

You can also improve your sentences by adding a word or a phrase at the end, after the predicate. A sentence closer can provide more information for your reader.

Stan went to the beach every day last summer.

He swam a lot, becoming stronger and faster.

He plans to be a lifeguard when he turns 18.

> **PRACTICE** Beginning, Middle, and End

Write an imitation of each sentence below. Change the words, but keep the same sentence structure.

1. Juanita planned the party carefully.
2. Some skaters, unhappy with their performance, did not want to see their scores.
3. The smell of pizza came through the air vents, making us hungry.
4. Victorious, the soccer team hurried back to its hotel.
5. Exhausted by two small children, Sandy told herself that she would never baby-sit again.

Building Sentences **329**

SENTENCES

ELABORATION

Combining Complete Sentences

Sometimes a short sentence says all that you need to say. However, a parade of short, choppy sentences is boring to write and boring to read. Combining short, *related* sentences makes your writing flow smoothly.

Combining with Conjunctions

When combining short sentences that have similar or contrasting ideas, use *and, but,* or *or.* This creates a compound sentence.

Draft

> **Nicholas usually dresses smartly. Today his socks did not match.**

Revised

> **Nicholas usually dresses smartly, but today his socks did not match.**

Draft

> **You should hurry. You will be late.**

Revised

> **You should hurry, or you will be late.**

When you join two complete ideas, be sure to add a comma before the conjunction.

> **Spike was looking for the Big Rock Candy Mountain, but it was taking him a long time to find it.**

> **He had been looking all day, and he was feeling tired.**

Peanuts by Charles M. Schulz

PEANUTS reprinted by permission of United Feature Syndicate, Inc.

For more on compound sentences, see p. 184.

Try using *although, because,* or *since* to connect ideas that are related. To connect similar ideas, use *because* or *since.* To connect contrasting ideas, use *although.* When you do this, you create a complex sentence.

Draft

Sheela and Shawna are best friends. They argue quite a bit.

Revised

Although they argue quite a bit, Sheela and Shawna are best friends.

Draft

Dan's lunch will be nothing special. He lost his wallet.

Revised

Dan's lunch will be nothing special because he lost his wallet.

Mix compound and complex sentences with shorter, simpler sentences to lend variety to your writing. Your reader will appreciate it!

For more on complex sentences, see p. 184.

For more on complex sentences, see p. 184.

PRACTICE   **Get It Together**

Combine each set of sentences using the conjunction given in parentheses. Don't forget the comma!

1. A tree fell on the tent. Nobody was hurt. *(although)*
2. Our talent show is Friday. Dell hasn't chosen a song yet. *(but)*
3. Ferrets are goofy creatures. They make terrific pets. *(and)*
4. I fell last winter. I am afraid of icy sidewalks. *(since)*
5. It snowed this morning. Jan was late for school. *(because)*
6. Becky baked a cake for her mother's birthday. She almost forgot to add the eggs. *(but)*
7. Are you going to the mall? Are you staying in the park? *(or)*
8. Marianne had trouble sleeping during the camping trip. She found a beetle in her sleeping bag. *(because)*
9. The bass drum was heavy. I didn't mind carrying it. *(although)*
10. Action movies are my favorites. I always watch them when they are on TV. *(and)*

Building Sentences **331**

Less Proficient Learners
Emphasize that the model sentences are choppy but grammatically correct. Combining them, however, clarifies the relationship between the thoughts contained in the sentences.

Also suitable for:
Students Acquiring English/ESL

Answers
PRACTICE   **Get It Together**

1. Although a tree fell on the tent, nobody was hurt.
2. Our talent show is Friday, but Dell hasn't chosen song yet.
3. Ferrets are goofy creatures, and they make terrific pets.
4. Since I fell last winter, I am afraid of icy sidewalks.
5. Because it snowed this morning, Jan was late for school.
6. Becky baked a cake for her mother's birthday, but she almost forgot to add the eggs.
7. Are you going to the mall, or are you staying in the park?
8. Because she found a beetle in her sleeping bag, Marianne had trouble sleeping during the camping trip.
9. Although the bass drum was heavy, I didn't mind carrying it.
10. Action movies are my favorites, and I always watch them when they are on TV.

 Visual Grammar™
Use **Visual Grammar™ Tiles Lessons 17–18** and **Sentences N–O** to demonstrate how to combine sentences. Here is part of Lesson 17.

Contrasting ideas:

| RACHEL LOVES STRAWBERRIES | . |

| SHE HATES BLUEBERRIES | . |

Result:

 | RACHEL LOVES STRAWBERRIES | , | **BUT** |

| SHE HATES BLUEBERRIES | . |

LESSON OBJECTIVES

To recognize that related sentences can be combined and to add information from one sentence to another

The passage on the student page is from "Thank You, Ma'am" in *The Language of Literature*, Level 7.

LESSON 4 Combining Sentence Parts

Good writers know that they should cut out the fluff. If you write a sentence that offers little new information to the reader, delete that sentence and add the important information to a related sentence. Combining keeps your writing lean and direct.

❶ Creating Compound Parts

Sometimes two or more sentences can be combined by moving part of the second sentence to the first. The new sentence will have a compound part.

> **Norman** was learning to search the Internet. **Gayle** was learning to search the Internet, too.

> **Norman and Gayle** were learning to search the Internet.
> COMPOUND SUBJECT

> **Janek collects foreign coins. He sometimes acquires interesting medallions. He also collects old U.S. paper money.**

> **Janek collects foreign coins, interesting medallions, and old U.S. paper money.**
> COMPOUND DIRECT OBJECT

In the passage below, the author describes a whole series of events in just two sentences.

LITERARY MODEL

The large woman simply turned around and kicked him right square in his blue-jeaned sitter. Then she **reached down, picked the boy up by his shirt front, and shook him until his teeth rattled.**
COMPOUND VERB

—Langston Hughes, "Thank You, Ma'm"

Don't forget to use commas to separate words in a series!

PRACTICE A Paint a Word Picture

In your 📁 **Working Portfolio,** find your **Write Away** paragraph from page 325. Add words and phrases to describe the painting more precisely. You may want to combine related sentences to strengthen your writing.

② Adding Words that Change Form

Sometimes you must change the form of a word before adding it to another sentence. For example, you might need to add *-y* or *-ly* to some words, *-ed* or *-ing* to other words.

> **Ann produced the concert posters. She did** quick **work.**
>
> **Ann** quickly **produced the concert posters.**

> **The students cheered the football team. The team** had **returned.**
>
> **The students cheered the** returning **football team.**

PRACTICE B From One to the Other

Combine the sentences in each item below by adding a key word or phrase from one sentence to the other. If necessary, change the form of the word you add.

1. Clarice borrowed a jacket. The jacket had stripes.
2. Tamera had a burrito for dinner. She also had a taco.
3. You could bring some sunscreen to the beach. You could bring a volleyball. You could bring a towel, too.
4. The audience began to applaud. It was all very sudden.
5. Sara sighed. She stared into space. She wondered when the bus would arrive.

Building Sentences **333**

CUSTOMIZING TIP

Students Acquiring English/ESL
For visual practice with adding words, phrases, and appositives to sentences, see **Side by Side** p. 28.

Also suitable for:
Less Proficient Learners

Answers

PRACTICE B From One to the Other

1. Clarice borrowed a striped jacket.
2. Tamera had a burrito and a taco for dinner.
3. You could bring some sunscreen, a volleyball, and a towel to the beach.
4. Suddenly, the audience began to applaud.
5. Sara sighed, stared into space, and wondered when the bus would arrive.

MORE MODEL SENTENCES

Write the following pairs of sentences on the board. Ask students to combine each pair, changing the form of a word before adding it to the other sentence.

Reggie made a mistake. It cost a lot.

Reggie made a costly mistake.

You will hear from us. It will be in a short time.

You will hear from us shortly.

🏛 **Visual Grammar™**

Use **Visual Grammar™ Tiles Lesson 19** and **Sentence P** to show how to combine sentences by inserting words and phrases. Here is part of Lesson 19.

Inserting a word:

| THE | EXPLORER | CRAWLED OUT OF THE CAVE | . |

| SHE WAS | MUDDY | . |

Result:

| THE | MUDDY | EXPLORER | CRAWLED OUT OF THE CAVE | . |

LESSON OBJECTIVES

To recognize details in a sentence

To add details by combining sentences using *who, that,* or *which*

DAILY TEST PREPARATION

Error Correction: Sentence Fragments Write the following item on the board or use **Daily Test Preparation Transparency** p. DT41. Choose the <u>best</u> way to write the underlined part of the sentence.

<u>Kept me busy for years,</u> but my sponsor dropped me after the shark attack.

A. Kept me busy for years,

B. Surfing kept me busy for years,

C. Kept me busy for years.

D. No change

Teaching Point: Error identification questions often test your ability to recognize sentence fragments. In this case, the first clause is not a complete thought. The underlined part of the sentence is missing a subject: *what* kept me busy?

Answers

PRACTICE A ▶ **Who Is It?**

1. Dr. Carter, who was a pediatrician, hoped one of his children would study medicine.

2. The cheerleader who has a megaphone is the loudest.

3. The camp counselor who had the most experience led the hike.

4. I baby-sit for my neighbor, who has lived next door to us for several years.

5. Cyclists who follow traffic safety rules are rarely in accidents.

 LESSON 5 Using *Who, That,* and *Which*

Sometimes you will introduce a person, place, or thing in one sentence and give details about it in another sentence. You may be able to combine the sentences using *who, that,* or *which.*

❶ Adding Details About People

Use the word *who* when adding details about people. If the information you are adding is not essential to the meaning of the sentence, set it off with commas. If the information is essential, leave out the commas.

Essential detail

> One monster scares me most. That monster is Frankenstein.

> The monster **who scares me most** is Frankenstein.

Nonessential detail

> The writer of *Frankenstein* was born in London in 1797. Her name was Mary Wollstonecraft Shelley.

> The writer of *Frankenstein*, **Mary Wollstonecraft Shelley,** was born in London in 1797.

 Information is essential if you need it to understand the basic meaning of the sentence. Information is not essential if it adds extra information to a sentence in which the meaning is already clear.

PRACTICE A ▶ **Who Is It?**

Combine each pair of sentences below with the word *who.* Use commas if necessary.

1. Dr. Carter hoped one of his children would study medicine. He was a pediatrician.

2. The cheerleader has a megaphone. He is the loudest.

3. The camp counselor led the hike. That camp counselor had the most experience.

4. I baby-sit for my neighbor. She has lived next door to us for several years.

5. Cyclists follow traffic safety rules. Those cyclists are rarely in accidents.

334 Essential Writing Skills

TEACHING RESOURCES

 Time-Saver Transparencies Binder:
• Daily Test Preparation p. DT41
• Visual Grammar™ Tiles Lessons 20–21

SKILLS PRACTICE RESOURCES

 Writing and Communication Masters p. 9

② Adding Details About Places and Things

When combining sentences in which details about places or things are given, use *that* if the details are essential. Use *which* if the details are not essential. If the meaning of the sentence is complete without the detail, the detail is not essential.

Essential detail

We have a chameleon in our science classroom. That chameleon is the biggest one I have ever seen.

The chameleon that lives in our science classroom is the biggest one I have ever seen.

Nonessential detail

Rain forced cancellation of the three-legged sack race. Rain had been predicted yesterday.

Rain, which had been predicted yesterday, forced cancellation of the three-legged sack race.

HOT TIP

When you use *which* to add information, set off the information with commas. When you use *that*, no commas are needed.

PRACTICE B ▸ **Which Is It?**

Combine each pair of sentences below using either *that* or *which*.

1. Diamond fields were first discovered in South Africa in 1867. They have also been found in Australia, Botswana, and Russia. *(which)*
2. The rubies sold for a high price. They had no flaws. *(that)*
3. Emeralds are highly valuable gemstones. They were once thought to cure certain diseases. *(which)*
4. There were emerald mines in ancient Egypt. The mines provided gems for Egyptian rulers. *(that)*
5. Garnets are more common gemstones. They are less valuable than diamonds. *(which)*

Building Sentences **335**

SENTENCES

ELABORATION

Answers

PRACTICE B ▸ **Which Is It?**

1. Diamond fields, which were first discovered in South Africa in 1867, have also been found in Australia, Botswana, and Russia.

2. The rubies that had no flaws sold for a high price.

3. Emeralds, which are highly valuable gemstones, were once thought to cure certain diseases.

4. There were emerald mines in ancient Egypt that provided gems for Egyptian rulers.

5. Garnets, which are more common gemstones, are less valuable than diamonds.

ASSESSMENT

Teacher's Guide to Assessment and Portfolio Use

Visual Grammar™

Use **Visual Grammar™ Tiles Lessons 20–21** and **Sentences Q–R** to teach sentence combining and essential and nonessential details. Here is part of Lesson 21.

Essential detail:

THE PLAYER WHO SCORED THE MOST POINTS

IS MARIA .

Nonessential detail:

MARIA , WHO SCORED THE MOST POINTS ,

IS OUR BEST PLAYER .

Student Help Desk

Students can use the Student Help Desk as a quick review prior to testing or as a quick reference as they revise a piece of writing.

Teacher's Notes

WHAT WORKS:

CHAPTER 13

CHAPTER 13

Student Help Desk

Building Sentences at a Glance

Does It Make Sense? Be sure your sentence expresses a complete thought. Use precise words.

Is That All There Is? Decide whether you should add detail to the beginning, middle, or end of the sentence.

Can You Combine It? See if you can combine two sentences into one more sophisticated sentence.

Expanding Sentences — Cook up Something Interesting

Technique	Example
Adding a sentence opener	**Scratching her head,** Lucy wondered what she should have for lunch.
Adding to the middle	The cafeteria special, **lasagna,** was her favorite.
Adding a sentence closer	Lucy decided to have the lasagna, **even though she had brought her lunch.**

Add More Ingredients

Combining Sentences

Technique	Example
Combining complete sentences	Pizza is my favorite food. I don't eat it every day. Pizza is my favorite food, **but** I don't eat it every day.
Adding words and phrases	Joshua had cake for lunch. He had it for dinner, too. Joshua had cake for lunch **and for dinner.**
Adding words that change form	Dan gulped some soda. He was noisy. Dan **noisily** gulped some soda.
Adding details	The macaroni that my uncle makes is my friends' favorite. It is very cheesy. The macaroni that my uncle makes, **which is very cheesy,** is my friends' favorite.

Menu for Adding Details

	Rule	Example
Who	Use *who* when adding details about people.	The boy **who ate six hot dogs** feels ill.
	If the details are not essential, add commas.	His friends, **who can't believe how much he ate,** are taking him to the school nurse.
	If they are essential, don't use commas.	The girl **who dared him to eat that much** feels guilty.
That	Use *that* when adding essential details about places or things. Don't use commas.	The kind of carrot cake **that my mother bakes** is my favorite.
Which	Use *which* when adding nonessential details about places or things. Use commas.	Her carrot cake, **which has cream-cheese frosting,** always gets eaten quickly.

The Bottom Line

Checklist for Stronger Sentences

Have I . . .

____ made sure that each sentence expresses a complete thought?

____ given enough detail about my subject?

____ combined similar sentences to eliminate unneeded repetition?

____ added words and phrases to make my sentences stronger?

____ added details about people, places, or things to my sentences?

Building Sentences **337**

SENTENCES

ELABORATION

TEACHER'S LOUNGE

A Slice of Life

"Everything that can be said can be said clearly."

—Ludwig Wittgenstein

Brain Break

Can you name something that has to be broken before it is used?

Answer: An egg has to be broken before it is used.

TEACHING TIP

Using References If students are unable to determine the meanings of words from the context, have them use a dictionary or a thesaurus to look up words.

TEACHING TIP

Have students choose the appropriate form to use in writing the steps of one of their favorite recipes.

TEACHING TIP

Have students stage a cooking show in which a celebrity chef demonstrates the recipes students wrote for the **Your Turn** exercise. Encourage the "chef" to use the words from **One Step at a Time** to emphasize the importance of keeping an orderly kitchen.

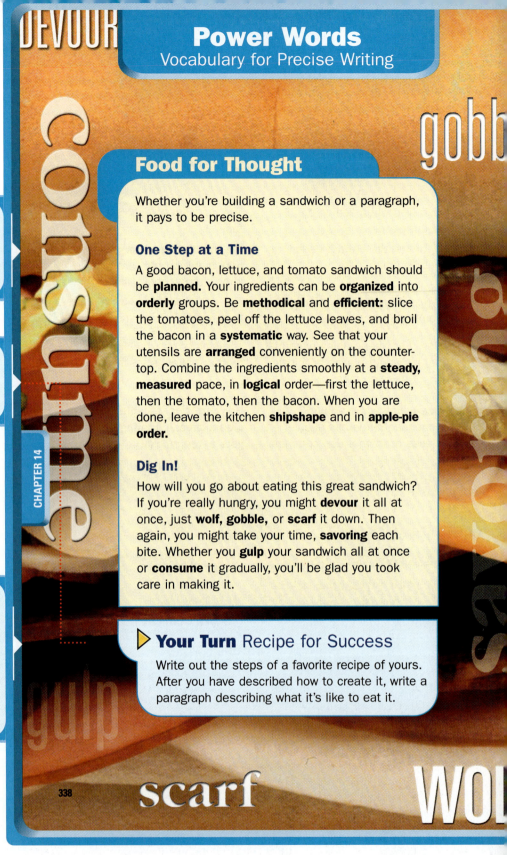

Power Words
Vocabulary for Precise Writing

Food for Thought

Whether you're building a sandwich or a paragraph, it pays to be precise.

One Step at a Time

A good bacon, lettuce, and tomato sandwich should be **planned.** Your ingredients can be **organized** into **orderly** groups. Be **methodical** and **efficient:** slice the tomatoes, peel off the lettuce leaves, and broil the bacon in a **systematic** way. See that your utensils are **arranged** conveniently on the countertop. Combine the ingredients smoothly at a **steady, measured** pace, in **logical** order—first the lettuce, then the tomato, then the bacon. When you are done, leave the kitchen **shipshape** and in **apple-pie order.**

Dig In!

How will you go about eating this great sandwich? If you're really hungry, you might **devour** it all at once, just **wolf, gobble,** or **scarf** it down. Then again, you might take your time, **savoring** each bite. Whether you **gulp** your sandwich all at once or **consume** it gradually, you'll be glad you took care in making it.

▶ **Your Turn** Recipe for Success

Write out the steps of a favorite recipe of yours. After you have described how to create it, write a paragraph describing what it's like to eat it.

Building Paragraphs

PARAGRAPHS 1

PARAGRAPHS

CHAPTER RESOURCES

Time-Saver Transparencies Binder:
- Critical Thinking Graphic Organizers pp. CT3, 11
- Daily Test Preparation pp. DT42–43
- Writing and Communication Skills p. WC4

Writing and Communication Masters pp. 10–12

Integrated Technology and Media

Electronic Teacher Tools CD-ROM

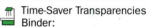mcdougallittell.com

Assessment

Teacher's Guide to Assessment and Portfolio Use

Students Acquiring English/ESL

Side by Side pp. 18–20

Putting It Together

Open up the average lunch bag and you'll find a sandwich—two pieces of bread with something in the middle. They're all built basically the same way, but you can use a seemingly endless number of ingredients to make your own unique sandwich.

Good paragraphs are also built with some basic "ingredients" and follow logical structural patterns. Once you master those elements and patterns, however, each paragraph can be as unique as the subject you're writing about.

Write Away: Starting from Scratch

Write a paragraph of five or six sentences about a time you put something together. Maybe you were doing a science project, building a model, or making a scrapbook. Save your paragraph in your 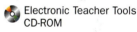 **Working Portfolios.**

Pressed for Time?

Use the introductory material in **Lesson 1, Qualities of a Good Paragraph,** to provide an overview of the elements in a well-constructed paragraph. Use **Lesson 2, Unity and Coherence,** to introduce the two basic qualities of a good paragraph.

Time for More?

After completing all the lessons in the chapter, divide students into four groups. Assign each group a paragraph type (descriptive, narrative, informative, or persuasive), and then have each one write a paragraph about ice cream.

DAILY TEST PREPARATION

Sentence Completion:
Vocabulary Write the following item on the board or use **Daily Test Preparation Transparency** p. DT42. Choose the word that *best* fits the meaning of the sentence.

Usually his advice is sound, but once in a while his ideas seem to _____ conventional wisdom.

A. disturbing

B. contradict

C. support

D. questionable

Teaching Point: For sentence completion questions, the correct answer will always

· fit the meaning of the sentence (*support* does not make sense with the transitional word *but*).

· fit grammatically within the sentence (*disturbing* and *questionable* do not fit with *seems to*).

CUSTOMIZING TIP

Students Acquiring English/ESL
For visual practice with organizing paragraphs, see **Side by Side** pp. 18–20.

Also suitable for:

Less Proficient Learners

LESSON 1

Qualities of a Good Paragraph

Because paragraphs are the building blocks of most writing assignments, you'll need to know what it takes to craft a good one. Two basic qualities appear in any well-written paragraph—unity and coherence. Understanding these qualities means you'll have the tools to put together any type of paragraph, including descriptive, narrative, informative, and persuasive paragraphs.

❶ What Makes a Good Paragraph?

Recipe for a Good Paragraph	
Unity	A **topic sentence** states the main idea of the paragraph. All sentences contain **related information** that supports the topic sentence.
Coherence	All sentences connect to one another smoothly and logically.

STUDENT MODEL

You may have seen a movie in which some unlucky character is slurped down into quicksand. But could that really happen? Quicksand exists, but it's not quite as scary as the movies make out. Quicksand is sand that has so much water in it that it acts like a fluid and cannot support as much weight as usual. If the trapped person tries to lift out one foot, the other foot sinks deeper. A person could even sink in to her waist. However, it's impossible to sink entirely below the surface. Thus, the main danger with quicksand is that it's hard to get out if someone isn't there to help.

Topic Sentence
Quicksand isn't what you might think.

Related Information
Each sentence tells more about quicksand.

Coherence
However and *thus* link ideas in sentences.

Unity
All sentences help support the topic sentence.

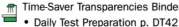

TEACHING RESOURCES

Time-Saver Transparencies Binder:
• Daily Test Preparation p. DT42

SKILLS PRACTICE RESOURCES

Side by Side pp. 18–20

Unity and Coherence

You'll know a paragraph has **unity** if all its sentences help explain the main idea. You'll know a paragraph has **coherence** if all the sentences flow smoothly and logically. Achieving both unity and coherence is easier if you start with a good topic sentence.

❶ Unity: What's the Big Idea?

Stating the "big idea" of your paragraph in a **topic sentence** can help keep you on track as you write, as well as introducing the subject of the paragraph. A good topic sentence also hooks the audience into wanting to know more.

James Armisted

STUDENT MODEL

No one suspected that James Armisted was a spy. During the American Revolution, the young African-American man was a waiter at the camp of the British commander general Cornwallis in Virginia. While he waited on the British officers, Armisted listened carefully for information that could help the American rebels. Then he smuggled information to the American commander general Lafayette. Armisted never was caught.

> **Topic sentence** introduces subject of the paragraph and captures the reader's attention.

Here's How Writing a Topic Sentence

1. Decide what your main point will be.

2. Write a sentence that states your main point and gives information about the subject.

3. Look for ways to make the topic sentence interesting and engaging.

   WEAK: I'm going to tell you about James Armisted.
   (doesn't tell who he was or what the paragraph will say)

   BETTER: No one suspected that James Armisted was a spy.
   (interests the reader and tells what the paragraph will be about)

Building Paragraphs **341**

PARAGRAPHS 1

PARAGRAPHS

 DAILY TEST PREPARATION

Error Correction: Capitalization
Write the following item on the board or use 🖥 **Daily Test Preparation Transparency** p. DT42.

> Cutting mr. James's grass is boring, but it does give me some extra cash.

How is this sentence best written?

A. Cutting mr. james's grass is boring, but it does give me some extra cash.

B. Cutting Mr. James's grass is boring, but it does give me some extra cash.

C. Cutting MR. James's grass is boring, but it does give me some extra cash.

D. As it is

Teaching Point: A common capitalization item in error correction questions is the use of capital letters in abbreviations. Remember to capitalize abbreviations that stand for titles, such as *Mr.* and *Mrs.*

CUSTOMIZING TIP

Students Acquiring English/ESL
Since some cultures feature diffuse and elaborate styles of writing, students from these cultures may think that addressing a topic concisely and directly would be too blunt or awkward. Encourage students to create and use clear, directly stated topic sentences.

TEACHING RESOURCES

 Time-Saver Transparencies Binder:
- Critical Thinking Graphic Organizers p. CT3
- Daily Test Preparation p. DT42
- Writing and Communication Skills p. WC4

SKILLS PRACTICE RESOURCES

 Writing and Communication Masters pp. 10–11

❷ Unity: Supporting the Big Idea

What if you found a salamander in your sandwich? The first thing you'd probably wonder is why this creature is in your lunch. You don't want odd things cluttering up your paragraphs either. **Unity** means that each sentence contains information that supports your topic sentence. As you write, try to stay focused on the topic sentence.

STUDENT MODEL

DRAFT

Early one morning, a bear came down out of the mountains into our yard. It was as big as a car. It snacked on food scraps from three cans of garbage in our shed. **Last week we had a raccoon in our shed. Dad built that shed himself.** Finally, it left.

Topic Sentence

Unrelated information distracts from topic sentence.

REVISION

Early one morning, a bear came down out of the mountains into our yard. The bear was as big as a car. It knocked our garbage shed over on its side. Then the bear sat down and rummaged for some breakfast. By the time the bear left about 30 minutes later, it had snacked on food scraps from all three of our garbage cans.

Related information supports the main idea and creates unity.

 HOT TIP When you write a paragraph, test for unity by looking at each sentence and asking: How does this sentence develop or support the idea stated in the topic sentence?

PRACTICE A ▶ **Room for Improvement?**

In your 🗂 **Working Portfolio,** find your **Write Away** paragraph from page 339. Check for a topic sentence, unity, and coherence. Revise the paragraph until there is no unrelated information, and the sentences connect in a way that is easy to understand.

Spice It Up!

Play a unity game with the class. Read aloud the following topic sentence: *My house on Mars is the envy of the neighborhood.* Then read each of the following details and ask students to decide whether the detail is related to the topic sentence.

1. The house is a beautiful red—just like my home planet. related

2. Mars is the fourth planet from the sun unrelated

③ Coherence: Making Connections

To give your paragraphs coherence, use words that connect sentences to one another so your readers easily can see how one idea leads to the next.

STUDENT MODEL

DRAFT

Don't buy a backpack unless it fits you and will last a long time. The seams shouldn't be single row stitches. They should be zig-zag stitches. They are better. The zippers should be covered by flaps. The pack should rest on your hips. Your homework shouldn't get wet when it rains.

> Sentences do not connect to one another or flow smoothly.

REVISION

Before you buy a backpack, you should make sure it fits you and will last a long time. **First,** check the seams to be sure they are zig-zag stitched and not single-row stitched. This is because zig-zag stitches hold together longer. **Next,** check that the zippers are covered by flaps so your homework doesn't get wet when it rains. **Finally,** make sure the pack fits you. The bottom of the pack should rest comfortably on your hips.

> Using **before, first, next,** and **finally** helps the reader follow the process.

For more on connecting words, see p. 349.

PRACTICE B Smooth It Out

Rewrite this paragraph, adding words that logically connect sentences to each other. Choose from the following: *also, in addition, finally, second, first, in the end.*

Three inventions helped settlers survive on the Great Plains in the 1800s. The steel plow made it possible for farmers to till prairie sod and plant crops. Fences stopped cattle from trampling farmers' fields. Portable windmills pumped water from deep in the earth for irrigating crops and for drinking. These things all contributed to successful life on the prairie.

Building Paragraphs **343**

PARAGRAPHS 1

PARAGRAPHS

TEACHING TIP

Speaking and Listening Read aloud the revised **Student Model** on the previous page. Have students listen for and identify the connecting words in the paragraph.

CUSTOMIZING TIP

Gifted and Talented Tell students that repeated keywords and pronouns also help make a paragraph coherent. As an example, read the first sentence of the revised **Student Model.** Point out that the pronoun *it* refers to the keyword *backpack*. Then ask students to read the rest of the paragraph and see if they can identify the repeated words and pronouns in the other sentences.

Answers

PRACTICE B **Smooth It Out**

Responses may vary. Possible response (connecting words are italicized):

Three inventions helped settlers survive on the Great Plains in the 1800s. *First*, the steel plow made it possible for farmers to till prairie sod and plant crops. *Second*, fences stopped cattle from trampling farmers' fields. *In addition*, portable windmills pumped water from deep in the earth for irrigating crops and for drinking. *In the end*, these things all contributed to successful life on the prairie.

Drive-Through Grammar

Commas Tell students that connecting words are often set off by commas. As an example, point out the connection words *first, next,* and *finally* in the revised **Student Model** on this page. Then write the following sentences on the board. Ask students to insert commas where needed.

Then my family traveled to Maine. no comma

However it rained during the entire trip. However,

Nevertheless we had a terrific vacation. Nevertheless,

LESSON 3 # Paragraphs: Descriptive and Narrative

Use **descriptive** paragraphs to describe a person, place, thing, or experience. Use **narrative** paragraphs to relate a story or event.

❶ Paragraphs That Describe

Have you ever read a description so good that you could almost see the subject? You can write good descriptive paragraphs that give the reader an opportunity to re-create a scene. They bring a character to life and create a picture in your reader's mind.

LITERARY MODEL

Henrietta even looked submissive. She was **thin** and **pale.** She had enormous **sky-blue** eyes surrounded by a long fringe of totally **colorless** eyelashes. Her hair was a **dim beige** color without gradations of light or dark, and it hung **straight and lifeless** from two barrettes. Her fingers were **long and bony,** and she kept them folded in her lap, **motionless,** like a tired old lady.

—Budge Wilson, "Waiting"

> **Carefully chosen adjectives and adverbs** appeal to the sense of sight

Here's How **Planning a Descriptive Paragraph**

- Use a cluster diagram to list sights, sounds, smells, tastes, and textures that describe the person, place, or thing.
- Choose specific and vivid nouns, verbs, adjectives, and adverbs.
- Arrange the details in an order that readers can follow, such as head to toe, side to side, front to back.

For more on sensory details, see p. 375.

 PRACTICE A **As You See It**

Using the model above as a guide, write a descriptive paragraph about a person you know well. Include vivid sensory details that you think will help this person spring to life for your reader.

344   Essential Writing Skills

❷ Paragraphs That Tell a Story

You can use narrative paragraphs to tell a story or report an event. Because most things you write about have a beginning, middle, and end, it's important that your paragraph does too. Add **connecting words** to help readers follow the narrative.

PROFESSIONAL MODEL

Showing off for the bridesmaids at my sister's wedding reception **years ago,** I caught and ate a large black cricket. **Later** I mentioned the incident in a book I wrote. At a talk I gave **recently,** someone who had read the book asked if the story was true. My sister happened to be present, **so** I pointed her out and told the questioner he should ask her himself. All heads swiveled to look at her where she was sitting by the aisle in the back row. "He eats bugs," she explained shortly, her lip curled in understated disgust.

— Ian Frazier, "It's Hard to Eat Just One"

Beginning

Middle

End

Here's How ▸ Planning a Narrative Paragraph

- Include details that will answer the questions *who, what, when, where, why,* and *how.*
- Use connecting words to help readers follow the sequence of events.
- Give your paragraph a clear beginning, middle, and end.

For more connecting words, see p. 349.

PRACTICE B ▸ What's Going On?

Write a narrative paragraph about the picture to the right. Use your imagination to invent details that help answer *who, what, when, where, why,* and *how.*

345

PARAGRAPHS 1

PARAGRAPHS

TEACHING TIP

Cross-Curricular Connection History Tell students that narrative writing is often used in history texts to tell the story of a particular place, group of people, or event. Encourage students to find a narrative paragraph in their history textbooks and to identify the connecting words that help readers follow the narrative.

CUSTOMIZING TIP

Less Proficient Learners Work with students to help them identify the details in the model that answer the question *who* (the narrator), *what* (ate a bug), *when* (years ago), *where* (at his sister's wedding reception), *why* (to show off), and *how* (he apparently liked to eat bugs).

Also suitable for:
Students Acquiring English/ESL

CUSTOMIZING TIP

Gifted and Talented It is sometimes beneficial to use a thesaurus for assistance in replacing common verbs and adjectives in descriptive and narrative paragraphs. Remind students, however, to be careful when using a thesaurus. Some words may have similar meanings but very different connotations. For example, *meek* and *unassuming* have similar meanings, but *meek* has a more negative connotation.

Also suitable for:
Linguistic Learners

Answers

PRACTICE B ▸ What's Going On?

Responses will vary. However, narrative paragraphs should include details that answer the following questions: Who are the people in the pictures? What are they doing? Where are they? When does the narrative take place? Why have the people come together? How do they get along?

LESSON OBJECTIVES

To recognize and write informative and persuasive paragraphs

DAILY TEST PREPARATION

Error Identification: Spelling
Write the following item on the board or use **Daily Test Preparation Transparency** p. DT43.
Look for mistakes in spelling. Decide which word, if any, contains a mistake.

A. slipery

B. territory

C. juvenile

D. grievous

E. No mistakes

Teaching Point: Error identification questions often test your knowledge of basic spelling rules. In this case, the item tests whether you know to add a *p* to *slip* before adding the suffix *-ery (slippery)*.

Answers

PRACTICE A ▶ **Explain This!**

Responses will vary. Students should write a topic sentence that introduces the subject in an interesting way, and then use facts, examples, and statistics to explain the subject.

TEACHING TIP

Have students use **Critical Thinking Graphic Organizer Vertical Category Chart** p. CT11, to plan an informative paragraph. They can use the chart to organize their facts, examples, and statistics.

LESSON 4 Paragraphs: Informative and Persuasive

If you need to explain something or provide information on a subject, you can choose to write an **informative**, or expository, paragraph. If you want to offer information about your own ideas to persuade someone to see things your way, a **persuasive** paragraph is a good tool.

❶ Paragraphs That Inform

Informative paragraphs are used when you need to present facts and examples to explain how something works, give directions, define a term, or provide the origin or history of a person, place, or thing.

PROFESSIONAL MODEL

Venus is the solar system's most devastating example of the greenhouse effect. The great amounts of carbon dioxide and other greenhouse gases trap so much heat under the clouds that the temperature is about 875 Fahrenheit on the venusian plains. An unprotected person would burn up almost instantly. . . .

—*Odyssey* science magazine

Topic sentence presents the main idea.

Facts and examples help define "greenhouse effect."

Here's How Planning a Persuasive Paragraph

- Write a topic sentence introducing the subject in an interesting way.
- Explain your subject with definitions and other specific information.
- Illustrate your ideas with examples, facts, statistics, and definitions.

PRACTICE A ▶ **Explain This!**

Choose one of the three terms below. Define and explain the term in an informative paragraph of five to six sentences. Use an encyclopedia, dictionary, or the Internet to find information.

Supernova	*What is it? How did it get its name?*
Great Wall of China	*Why was it built? How long is it?*
Giant squid	*How is it different from other squid?*

TEACHING RESOURCES

Time-Saver Transparencies Binder:
- Critical Thinking Graphic Organizers p. CT11
- Daily Test Preparation p. DT43

2 Paragraphs That Persuade

In a persuasive paragraph, you present your point of view and try to make readers agree with you, or follow your suggestions. This writer argues that dolphins that perform in shows, like the one pictured, should be set free.

PROFESSIONAL MODEL

Keeping dolphins in marine parks is harmful to the species. Those who run "dolphinariums" say the purpose of their shows is to educate the public. Ask someone who has been to a dolphin show what they learned, and you'll hear, "They jump really high!" and "They sure are cute!" How is that educational? In addition, dolphins in "petting pools" are touched by hundreds of people everyday, exposing them to human diseases. Dolphins in captivity live only 25 to 30 years, but in the wild they can live up to 50 years. Shouldn't they be given that chance?

—Becky Polivka

Topic Sentence

Writer presents an opposing argument, then responds to it.

Writer provides facts and examples.

Here's How Planning a Persuasive Paragraph

- Clearly state your opinion or idea in the topic sentence.
- Use clear reasoning to sway readers to your point of view.
- Offer specific facts, examples, and statistics to support your opinion.

PRACTICE B Be Convincing

Community leaders are voting on the following issues:

- Banning in-line skating in public places.
- Banning jeans and jewelry in school.

Could you sway the voters? Pick one issue, and state in a topic sentence whether you agree or disagree. Use the rest of your persuasive paragraph to support your opinion.

Building Paragraphs **347**

PARAGRAPHS 1

TEACHING TIP

Point out that the writer of the **Professional Model** responds to an opposing argument and reveals its flaws. Tell students that this is an effective way to persuade readers.

Answers

PRACTICE B **Be Convincing**

Responses will vary. Students should choose one of the issues, state their opinion in a topic sentence, and use facts, examples, and statistics to support their point of view.

PARAGRAPHS

TEACHING TIP

Cooperative Learning Before students complete the **Practice** exercise, have them work in groups of three to brainstorm arguments for and against the issues.

ASSESSMENT

Teacher's Guide to Assessment and Portfolio Use

Spice It Up!

Hold a five-minute class debate on the following issue: A singe admission price should be charged at movie theaters. Ask students who support the issue to provide specific facts and examples that strengthen their point of view. Then ask students who oppose the issue to present their reasons. Jot the reasons—pro and con—on the board, and ask the class to vote on which side presented the better argument.

Student Help Desk

Building Paragraphs at a Glance

Topic Sentence	Unity	Coherence
The "big idea"	All sentences support the "big idea."	All sentences are logically and smoothly connected.

Unity and Coherence — Pull it Together!

Take out what doesn't fit and connect what does.

Did you know that you don't actually have to touch poison ivy to be poisoned? *One time,* My cousins went camping. At night they built a campfire to roast marshmallows. ~~They also brought brownies for dessert.~~ A little later, they had an itching sensation in their lungs. They had accidentally pushed a dried poison ivy leaf into the fire. ~~Did you know pine cones pop when they burn?~~ The oil that contains the "poison" is called urushiol, and when it burns it goes airborne. *So* My cousins had inhaled urushiol! ~~They are my favorite cousins.~~ Next time you're camping, watch where you walk and what you throw onto the fire.

> Add connecting words and phrases between sentences.

> Delete unrelated information.

Calvin and Hobbes by Bill Watterson

Paragraph Types — Decisions, Decisions

Type	Uses
Descriptive	Presents colorful, exact picture of a person, place, thing, or experience by appealing to the five senses
Narrative	Tells a story and often answers the questions *who, what, where, when, why,* and *how*
Informative	Defines terms, gives directions, or tells how things work by presenting or explaining facts or ideas
Persuasive	Uses facts and reasons to support a point of view and tries to persuade reader to agree

Connecting Words and Phrases — A Few Coherence "Condiments"

on the other hand
although
because

besides
eventually
one time
for this reason

however
for example
but
in the same way

also
therefore
yet
in addition

PARAGRAPHS 1

The Bottom Line

Checklist for Building Paragraphs

Have I . . .

____ stated the main idea clearly in a topic sentence?

____ made sure all sentences support the topic sentence?

____ made a descriptive paragraph lively by using sensory details?

____ helped readers follow narrative events by using connecting words?

____ used facts and examples to explain my topic?

____ included logical reasoning in a way that is likely to persuade readers?

Building Paragraphs **349**

Just for Laughs

A tourist was visiting New Mexico. While gazing at the dinosaur bones that were everywhere, he met an old man who acted as an unofficial guide.

"How old are these bones?" asked the tourist.

"Exactly one hundred million and three years old," was the man's reply.

"How can you be so definite?" inquired the tourist.

"Oh, a geologist told me they were one hundred million years old," replied the man, "and that was exactly three years ago."

PARAGRAPHS

Teacher's Notes
WHAT DOESN'T WORK:

TEACHER'S LOUNGE

Brain Break

Can you decipher this famous nursery rhyme?

A geriatric human female proceeded to a storage compartment to procure a fragment of osseous tissue from a deceased specimen to transfer to an indigent carnivore. She found the storage compartment in denuded condition, with the consequence that the indigent carnivore was deprived of the intended donation.

Answer: "Old Mother Hubbard"

OBJECTIVES

To increase vocabulary through the recognition and understanding of words that describe ways to give directions.

To use words in speaking and in writing that describe directions

Power Words
Vocabulary for Precise Writing

guide   CONDUCT   pil

Getting from Here to There

It's especially important to be clear and precise when you are giving directions.

Giving Directions

The easiest way to get somewhere new—if you don't have access to the transporter room, that is—is if someone who knows the way **accompanies** you. He or she may **conduct** you to the exact spot and even **usher** you in the door. However, if you don't have a **navigator, pilot, guide,** or **shepherd,** use your map-reading skills and try to figure it out on your own.

Taking Control

Giving directions doesn't always mean going from one place to another. If you are the leader of a country, a photo safari, or a white-water rafting trip, you are the one in charge. You may have to **initiate** the planning, **marshal** the available resources, and **steer** things in the right direction. It's up to you to **assign, coordinate, supervise,** and **administer** to make sure that the project is a success.

▷ **Your Turn** I'm in Charge Here!

Write a description of your ideal job. List the job's duties, location, hours, and needed abilities.

supervise   ACCOMPANIES   navigator   steer   USHER   coordinate

▼ 350 ▼

Organizing Paragraphs

Alternate Routes

An adult is driving you to a party and you are giving him directions. Since he is famous for getting lost, you've got to be extra careful and clear. "Turn here," just won't do it. He'd probably respond, "What?" "Now?" "Left or right?" You've got to give him advance warning and be specific: "*After* you get to the *next* stoplight, *then* turn *left*."

You've probably noticed that it is also possible to get "lost" while you're reading. Good writers organize their paragraphs in logical patterns so readers can easily follow their ideas. In this chapter, you'll learn to recognize these patterns and use them yourself.

Write Away: **Pointing the Way**

A new student has to get to gym class on time. Write a set of detailed directions in paragraph form that will take her from your classroom to the girls' locker room. Save your paragraph in your **Working Portfolio.**

CHAPTER RESOURCES

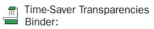 Time-Saver Transparencies Binder:
- Critical Thinking Graphic Organizers pp. CT7, 15
- Daily Test Preparation pp. DT44–45
- Writing and Communication Skills p. WC5

Writing and Communication Masters pp. 13–15

Integrated Technology and Media

 Electronic Teacher Tools CD-ROM

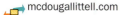 mcdougallittell.com

Assessment

Teacher's Guide to Assessment and Portfolio Use

Students Acquiring English/ESL

Side by Side pp. 18–20

PARAGRAPHS 2

PARAGRAPHS 2

BLOCK SCHEDULING

Pressed for Time?

Focus only on **Lesson 1, Sequential Order,** and **Lesson 2, Spatial Order,** which are less conceptual than the other lessons.

Time for More?

Use all lessons in this chapter to teach students about the various ways to organize paragraphs. Then have students work in pairs to write two paragraphs for the Practice in Lesson 4. In one paragraph they should use the subject-by-subject approach. In the other they should use the feature-by-feature approach.

LESSON 1 Sequential Order

All writing must to be organized to be understood. Choose a method of organizing that is most appropriate for the purpose of your paragraph. In this chapter, you'll see how sequential, spatial, cause-and-effect, and compare-and-contrast order can help you organize paragraphs.

Paragraphs That Show Time and Sequence

Writers use **sequential order** to show how events follow one another in a certain order. A term for showing how events unfold over a certain period of time is **chronological order.**

> **LITERARY MODEL**
>
> At one-hour intervals the night guards paced past every room. Each time I heard the approaching footsteps, I jumped into bed and feigned sleep. And as soon as the guard passed, I got back out of bed onto the floor area of that light-glow, where I would read for another fifty-eight minutes—until the guard approached again. That went on until three or four every morning.
>
> —Malcolm X with Alex Haley, *The Autobiography of Malcolm X*

FIRST EVENT

SECOND EVENT

THIRD EVENT

FOURTH EVENT

In the cartoon below notice how Calvin uses sequential order to explain to Susie the process of his great idea in action.

Calvin and Hobbes by Bill Watterson

352 Essential Writing Skills

Connecting words, or **transition words,** link sentences and help readers relate one event in time to another.

Between 1100 and 1300 in England, the goal of many boys was to become a knight. The **first** step began at age seven when a boy went to live with a knight or nobleman and work for him as a page. **Next,** when he had reached age 15 or 16, the page became a squire and served the knight in battle. The **last** stage occurred at age 21, when the squire took vows to uphold the code of knighthood.

> **Transition words** link one step to another, adding unity and coherence to the paragraph.

For more transition words, see p. 361.

PRACTICE ▶ **No Wrong Turns**

Your friend has given you the map below to help you find the way to his party. In a paragraph that you will read to the driver, write directions in sequential order based on this map. Use the landmarks and street names as well as transition words to help get you to the party on time.

Then, in your 📁 **Working Portfolio,** find your **Write Away** paragraph, and add transition words to those directions.

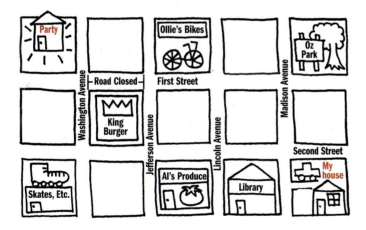

Speaking and Listening Read aloud the **Student Model** and have students listen for the transition words and write them down. Then have volunteers describe how they got ready for school that morning using these transition words.

Less Proficient Learners If students have difficulty organizing a paragraph with a sequence of events, they may find it helpful to draw a time line. Explain that a time line will help them order the events and serve as a reference.

Answers

PRACTICE ▶ **No Wrong Turns**

Answers will vary. Possible answer:

First, when we leave my driveway, we'll turn right onto Madison Avenue. The **next** street we'll come to is Second Street; here we turn left. **Then** keep driving down Second Street. On the left, we will pass the library and Al's Produce. **After** one more block, we'll come to Washington Avenue. **Finally,** we will turn right at the stoplight onto Washington Avenue and continue for two more blocks. My friend lives at the corner of Washington Avenue and First Street.

PARAGRAPHS 2

PARAGRAPHS 2

Spice It Up!

Play a variation of Simon Says in which players only do what they're told if the instructions are preceded by transitions. Have students stand up, and then begin giving them instructions. For example, you might use the following prompts:

First, raise your hand over your head. Then wave to me. Put your arm down— No. I didn't use a transition.

Students who follow instructions that aren't preceded by transitions should sit down. Play for five minutes or until only a handful of students remain standing.

DAILY TEST PREPARATION

Sentence Completion: Subject-Verb Agreement Write the following item on the board or use **Daily Test Preparation Transparency** p. DT44. Choose the word that belongs in the space.

> There ____ a variety of apples in the basket. Pick one.

A. are

B. some

C. will

D. is

Teaching Point: Sentence completion questions often test your knowledge of agreement in inverted sentences. When you see a sentence beginning with *Here* or *There*, look for the subject after the verb. In this case, the subject *variety* takes a singular verb (*is*).

CUSTOMIZING TIP

Addressing Learning Styles
Visual, Spatial Explain that a writer, like a painter, must make a decision to limit how much space to describe. Suggest that students "put a frame" around the part of the larger picture that they want their readers to focus on.

THE LANGUAGE OF
LITERATURE

The passage on the student page is from an excerpt of *The Serial Garden* in *The Language of Literature*, Level 7.

LESSON 2 # Spatial Order

Writers use **spatial** (space) **order** to show how people and objects appear. When you read a paragraph that uses spatial order, you might have the feeling of following a camera as it pans across a scene.

Paragraphs That Put Things in Their Place

You can use spatial order any time you want readers to picture a place as it really looks or as you imagine it. You can describe a space from top to bottom, left to right, front to back, faraway to close-up, or outside to inside.

> **LITERARY MODEL**
>
> Miss Pride's **shop window** was full of nasty, dingy old cardboard cartons with nothing inside them, and several empty display stands which had fallen down and never been propped up again. **Inside the shop** were a few small, tired-looking tins and jars, which had a worn and scratched appearance as if mice had tried them and given up.
>
> —Joan Aiken, *The Serial Garden*

The writer begins with the outside window of the store.

Then the writer describes the inside of the store.

Here's How Using Spatial Order

- Look at or picture in your mind the place you want to show and the people and objects within it.
- Decide how much of the space you will describe.
- Present the description from top to bottom, left to right, front to back, faraway to close up, or outside to inside.
- As you write, move from object to object and use transition words to describe the relationship of one object to another.

354 Essential Writing Skills

TEACHING RESOURCES

Time-Saver Transparencies Binder:
- Daily Test Preparation p. DT44
- Writing and Communication Skills p. WC5

SKILLS PRACTICE RESOURCES

Writing and Communication Masters p. 14

Direction or location words within a paragraph can help you show where objects and people are in relation to each other.

STUDENT MODEL

As I stepped into Jewel Cave, I noticed that the walls sparkled as if they were wallpapered with diamonds. When I walked up **close to** the wall, I realized that it was covered with a thick layer of crystals. **At the base of** the wall, I saw a massive stalagmite jutting up toward the ceiling. A huge stalactite directly **above** it dripped steadily down onto the giant stalagmite.

Close to lets us "zoom in" and see the wall's crystals.

At the base of and **above** help us locate the formations within the cave.

For more direction words, see p. 361.

Avoid writing sentences such as "There was a book." Was it on a desk, inside a backpack, on someone's head? Be sure the objects in your sentences don't just float in space.

PRACTICE ▶ **Picture This**

Using spatial order, describe what is happening in this picture so that your readers would be able to imagine the picture without seeing it. You may want to give the dog a name and tell a brief story using the objects you see. Use direction and location words to help define where things are in relation to each other.

Organizing Paragraphs **355**

PARAGRAPHS 2

For more direction words, see p. 361.

TEACHING TIP

Cooperative Learning/Paired Activity
To help students understand "zooming in," have them work in pairs and take turns describing what they see when they look closely at an object on their desks. What do they leave out of their descriptions?

Answers

PRACTICE ▶ **Picture This**

Answers will vary. Possible answer:

Our dog needed a bath. My brother and I placed a big bucket **in the middle** of the kitchen floor. I filled it with soapy water until the bubbles spilled **over** the sides. Then we put our dog, Jingles, **inside** the bucket. We were supposed to be folding laundry, but we left the basket on the counter **behind** and **to the right** of Jingles, and forgot about it. Before we started bathing him, we decided to stop and take a picture. We set the bar of soap on the floor **in front of** Jingles' bucket and next to the scrub brush. Jingles set his paw **on the edge** of the bucket almost like he was waving, and just then my brother snapped a picture.

PARAGRAPHS 2

Drive-Through Grammar

Prepositional Phrases Prepositions, such as *from, on,* and *to,* are the most common type of direction or location words. Prepositional phrases consist of a preposition, an object and any modifiers. Writers use prepositional phrases to add details that show where objects and people are located in relation to each other.

Write the following sentence on the board and ask students to identify the prepositional phrases and the preposition and object contained in each phrase.
He danced around the crowd and then ran up the stairs.

(*around* the *crowd*; *up* the *stairs*)

DAILY TEST PREPARATION

Sentence Completion:
Vocabulary Write the following item on the board or use
📖 **Daily Test Preparation Transparency** p. DT45. Choose the word that *best* fits the meaning of the sentence.

> With her bags packed, dogs fed, and sleigh mounted, Mel set out on her Antarctic ____.

A. racing

B. redemption

C. barbecue

D. expedition

Teaching Point: For sentence completion questions, the correct answer will always

- fit the meaning of the sentence (*barbecue* and *redemption* do not fit with *Antarctic*).

- fit grammatically within the sentence (*racing* does not fit with the phrase *on her Antarctic*).

CUSTOMIZING TIP

Students Acquiring English/ESL To help students write about causes and effects in English, teach them the following transition words as vocabulary: *therefore, so, as a result, because, since.*

LESSON 3

Cause-and-Effect Order

Just about any time you explain why or how something occurs, you'll find yourself presenting causes and effects. A **cause** is something that brings about a result. An **effect** is the result of the cause.

Paragraphs That Explain Why or How

You can use cause-and-effect to explain a process or an event. Sometimes there is more than one cause for a given effect. At other times, a single cause can lead to several effects.

> **PROFESSIONAL MODEL**
>
> During the medieval period, travel across Europe became difficult and dangerous as many kingdoms fought among themselves for land and wealth. As a result, trading activities diminished and towns . . . became depopulated. Many people had to move to the countryside to make their living as peasants on large estates called manors, owned by lords.
>
> *Across the Centuries,* Houghton Mifflin

This chart shows the cause-and-effect chain described above.

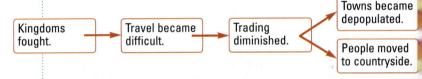

> **Here's How** **Using Cause-and-Effect Order**
>
> - Use your topic sentence to introduce the cause or the effect.
> - Explain each cause and each effect clearly.
> - Use transition words or phrases to link causes and effects.

Often, transitions, such as **because, as a result,** and **consequently,** signal cause and effect. Notice how transition words make these relationships clear in the student model.

TEACHING RESOURCES

 Time-Saver Transparencies Binder:
- Critical Thinking Graphic Organizers p. CT15
- Daily Test Preparation p. DT45
- Writing and Communication Skills p. WC5

SKILLS PRACTICE RESOURCES

 Writing and Communication Masters p. 15

Because Maria Mitchell's father was an amateur astronomer, she learned how to use a telescope at an early age. As a girl, she studied hard, especially astronomy and the sciences. As a result of her hard work, she discovered a new comet in 1847. Consequently, she became the first American woman to be recognized as an astronomer.

Notice how these causes and effects relate to one another.

Father was an astronomer. → Maria used his telescopes.

Years of hard work. → Discovered a comet. → Recognized as astronomer.

For more transition words, see p. 361.

Make sure that you have chosen a true cause-and-effect relationship. Ask yourself this: "Is it clear to me how one event led to the next? Could I make it clear to a reader?"

PRACTICE What's Happening?

Create a chart like those in this lesson showing the cause-and-effect relationships in the following paragraph.

"Dust Bowl" is the term used to describe the severe conditions of the early 1930s that caused a migration westward. Farmers in the Great Plains region of the Southwest dug up prairie grass and planted crops with roots too shallow to hold soil. Drought conditions, combined with severe winds, caused great clouds of dust to rise and blow through the air. As a result, farmers lost their crops. Many families moved west in search of more fertile soil.

TEACHING TIP

Use ▨ **Critical Thinking Graphic Organizer Cause-and-Effect Chart,** p. CT 15, to list the causes and effects in the **Student Model.** Point out that the chart shows how events are related. You might want to chart another series of causes and effects to reinforce the skill. For example, you could chart the series of events that may take place during a rainstorm. Heavy rains fall —> Large puddles form —> Children splash in puddles —> They get very wet

TEACHING TIP

Cross-Curricular Connection
Science Tell students to beware of using faulty cause-and-effect reasoning when they write about a scientific event. For example, "Many scientists believe that the greenhouse effect has resulted in higher worldwide temperatures" presents a true cause-and-effect relationship. However, "As temperatures continue to rise, more and more scientists support the theory" describes sequential events.

CUSTOMIZING TIP

Addressing Learning Styles
Auditory Before students create a chart for the **Practice** exercise, have them first read the passage aloud and identify the transition words that signal cause-and-effect relationships.

Especially suitable for:
Less Proficient Learners

PARAGRAPHS 2

Answers

PRACTICE What's Happening?

Farmers planted crops with shallow roots—> Roots couldn't hold soil—> Land stricken by drought and severe winds—> Clouds of dust rose and blew through the air—> Farmers lost crops—> Families moved west

LESSON OBJECTIVES

To recognize and use compare-and-contrast order in writing

CHAPTER 15

 LESSON 4 # Compare-and-Contrast Order

When you tell how two things are alike, you are **comparing** them. When you tell how two things are different, you are **contrasting** them.

Using Compare-and-Contrast Order

Use compare-and-contrast order to show similarities and differences. Scientific and historical writing often use this order. A subject-by-subject approach is used below. This means that one subject is discussed completely before the second is introduced.

PROFESSIONAL MODEL

Eskimo clothing was extremely efficient. It was lightweight, comfortable, warm, and allowed the wearer to move around easily. A complete winter outfit weighed only about ten pounds. **By contrast,** an average Minnesota businessman wears twenty to thirty pounds of clothing on his way to work in winter: if caught in a sudden blizzard, he would be in danger of freezing to death.

—Charlotte and David Yue, "The Igloo"

Subject 1:
Eskimo clothing

Linked by
transition

Subject 2:
modern clothing

In the model below, the two subjects are compared feature-by-feature.

STUDENT MODEL

Alligators and crocodiles look a lot alike. Both have long, thick bodies, strong tails, and powerful jaws with sharp teeth. **However,** crocodiles have snouts that come to a point. **In contrast,** alligators have round snouts. Crocodiles are lighter in weight than alligators and are more likely to attack humans than are alligators.

Similar features
of alligators and
crocodiles

Linked by
transitions

Different features
of alligators and
crocodiles

TEACHING RESOURCES

 Time-Saver Transparencies Binder:
- Critical Thinking Graphic Organizers p. CT7
- Daily Test Preparation p. DT45
- Writing and Communication Skills p. WC5

SKILLS PRACTICE RESOURCES

 Side by Side pp. 18–20

Here's How — Writing a Compare-and-Contrast Paragraph

1. Find similarities and differences between the subjects.
2. Use a Venn diagram to help organize your thoughts.

Features of Subject A — Shared Features — Features of Subject B

3. State the main idea in a topic sentence.
4. Choose subject-by-subject or feature-by-feature organization. Use transition words where they are helpful or needed.

For more transition words, see p. 361.

WATCH OUT

When choosing your own subjects to compare and contrast, be sure the subjects have plenty of similarities as well as differences. If not, you will run out of things to discuss.

PRACTICE — Jupiter Versus Saturn

Use the comparison made in the Venn diagram below to write a paragraph comparing and contrasting Jupiter and Saturn. You may use a subject-by-subject approach, in which you discuss the features of Jupiter first, then the features of Saturn. Or, you may choose a feature-by-feature approach, in which you compare and contrast features of Jupiter to features of Mars.

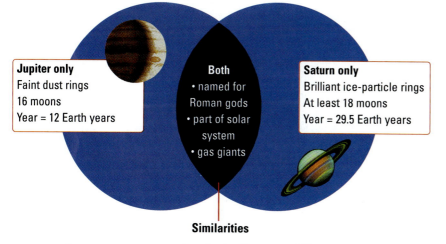

Jupiter only
Faint dust rings
16 moons
Year = 12 Earth years

Both
• named for Roman gods
• part of solar system
• gas giants

Saturn only
Brilliant ice-particle rings
At least 18 moons
Year = 29.5 Earth years

Similarities

For more on compare-and-contrast order, see pg. 446.

Organizing Paragraphs **359**

Spice It Up!

Have student pairs play a compare-contrast game. One student in the pair should select two subjects and name some of the features they share. The other student should use the clues to guess what the subjects are. If the student has trouble naming the subjects, the partner should identify some of the subjects' differences.

PARAGRAPHS 2

TEACHING TIP

Use Critical Thinking Graphic Organizer Venn Diagram p. CT7, to demonstrate how to list two subjects' similarities and differences. Have students reread the **Student Model** on the preceding page. Then ask them to identify features that are unique to alligators, features that are unique to crocodiles, and features that the two animals share. List the features on the diagram.

Answers

PRACTICE — Jupiter Versus Saturn

Answers will vary. Possible responses:

Subject-by-Subject

Jupiter and Saturn, the "gas giants" in our solar system, are both named for Roman gods. However, they are very different planets. For one thing, Jupiter is circled by faint dust rings and is orbited by 16 moons. Also, one year on Jupiter is equal to 12 years on Earth. By contrast, Saturn is encircled by brilliant ice-particle rings and is orbited by 18 moons. In addition, a year on Saturn is equal to 29.5 Earth years.

Feature-by-Feature

Jupiter and Saturn, the "gas giants" in our solar system, are both named for Roman gods. However, they are very different planets. For one thing, Jupiter is circled by faint dust rings and is orbited by 16 moons. By contrast, Saturn is encircled by brilliant ice-particle rings and is orbited by 18 moons. Also, while one year on Jupiter is equal to 12 years on Earth, a year on Saturn takes 29.5 Earth years.

ASSESSMENT

 Teacher's Guide to Assessment and Portfolio Use

PARAGRAPHS 2

Organizing Paragraphs **359**

Student Help Desk

Student Help Desk

Organizing Paragraphs at a Glance

Sequential Order

First
Event 1

↓

Next
Event 2

↓

Final
Event 3

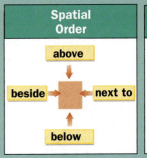

Spatial Order

above

beside → ■ ← next to

below

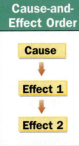

Cause-and-Effect Order

Cause

↓

Effect 1

↓

Effect 2

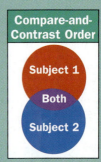

Compare-and-Contrast Order

Subject 1
Both
Subject 2

Organizing a Paragraph   Where to Find Order

Sequential

Used in how-to instructions and manuals, stories, science writing, directions
Example: First, we sprayed our dog Bubba with a hose. Next, we lathered him up until he was good and sudsy, rinsed, and repeated the process because he was still smelly.

Spatial

Used in eyewitness accounts, crime reports, stories
Example: To the left of the doghouse lay the hose. Next to it was a pile of soggy towels with an empty bottle of shampoo on top. To the right of the doghouse was Bubba, rolling in the mud.

Cause and Effect

Used in stories, science or history reports, news articles, editorials
Example: Giving a dog a bath frequently reduces the risk of the animal getting fleas or being infected by ticks. In a severe case, a dog could catch mange and end up losing all its fur.

Compare and Contrast

Used in consumer guides, reviews, descriptions
Example: Compared with giving a cat a bath, bathing a dog is easy. Dogs jump into ponds and run through puddles, but cats can't stand being wet.

Transition Tool Box

Sequential Order	Spatial Order (direction words)	Cause-and-Effect Order	Compare
during	around	caused by	also
eventually	center	as a result	by comparison
last	in front of	so	either . . . or
later	below	thus	neither . . . nor
meanwhile	outside	for this reason	the same as
now	inside	affected by	
once	to the left	owing to	**Contrast**
tomorrow	to the right	accordingly	instead
yesterday	underneath	in this way	nevertheless
	on top of	consequently	on the contrary
			unlike
			yet

The Bottom Line

Checklist for Organizing Paragraphs

Have I . . .

____ made sure the method of organization fits the purpose?

____ written steps and ideas in an order that is easy to follow?

____ used the correct transition words and phrases?

____ included a beginning, middle, and end when writing sequentially?

____ allowed the reader to see the space I am describing when using spatial descriptions?

____ made sure causes and effects are correct and clear?

____ shown similarities and differences when using compare-and-contrast order?

Organizing Paragraphs **361**

Teacher's Notes
WHAT DOESN'T WORK:

TEACHER'S LOUNGE

A Slice of Life

"It usually takes me more than three weeks to prepare a good impromptu speech."—Mark Twain

Just for Laughs

A colleague in North Dallas High School had finally discovered the student who had taken the teacher's edition textbook from his desk. "When I corrected a recent homework assignment, I knew I'd found the culprit by his answer to question six." "What did he write?" I asked. "Answers will vary."

OBJECTIVES

To increase vocabulary through the recognition and understanding of words that describe size and strength

To use words in speaking and writing that describe size and strength

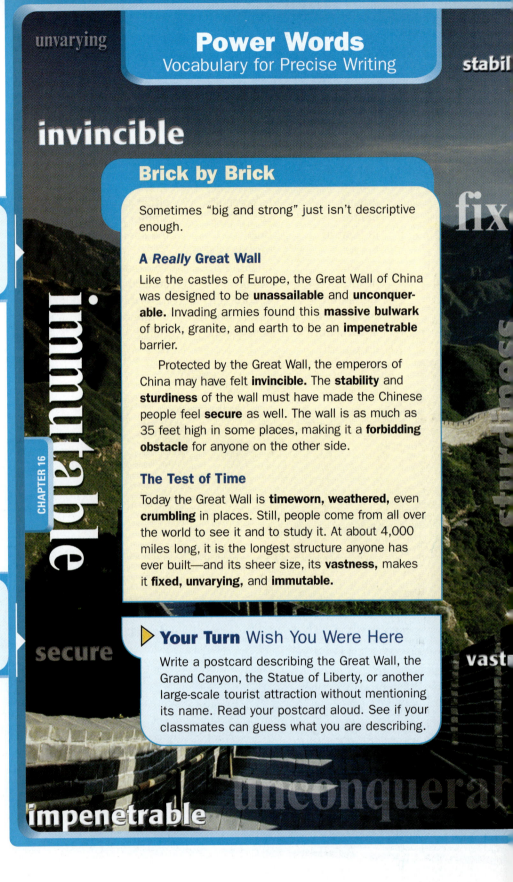

Power Words
Vocabulary for Precise Writing

Brick by Brick

Sometimes "big and strong" just isn't descriptive enough.

A *Really* Great Wall

Like the castles of Europe, the Great Wall of China was designed to be **unassailable** and **unconquerable**. Invading armies found this **massive bulwark** of brick, granite, and earth to be an **impenetrable** barrier.

Protected by the Great Wall, the emperors of China may have felt **invincible**. The **stability** and **sturdiness** of the wall must have made the Chinese people feel **secure** as well. The wall is as much as 35 feet high in some places, making it a **forbidding obstacle** for anyone on the other side.

The Test of Time

Today the Great Wall is **timeworn, weathered,** even **crumbling** in places. Still, people come from all over the world to see it and to study it. At about 4,000 miles long, it is the longest structure anyone has ever built—and its sheer size, its **vastness**, makes it **fixed, unvarying,** and **immutable**.

▶ **Your Turn** Wish You Were Here

Write a postcard describing the Great Wall, the Grand Canyon, the Statue of Liberty, or another large-scale tourist attraction without mentioning its name. Read your postcard aloud. See if your classmates can guess what you are describing.

Building Compositions

Chapter 16

Building Compositions

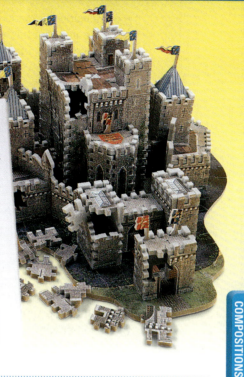

Medieval castles were enormous stone buildings built to protect a lord and lady, their family, and their servants. The ground level, also called the cellar, contained a granary, casks, and great boxes storing food and utensils.

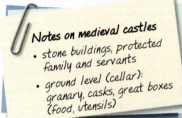

Notes on medieval castles
- stone buildings, protected family and servants
- ground level (cellar): granary, casks, great boxes (food, utensils)

COMPOSITIONS

Piece by Piece

Think about the last time you built a puzzle. What do you remember being the most challenging about it? Perhaps you couldn't find all the pieces. Maybe you couldn't fit the pieces together right away. Writing a composition can seem very similar to putting together a puzzle. However, when you build a composition, by focusing on one part at a time, you will often find the right way to fit your ideas together, and the final product will take shape before your eyes.

Write Away: Built to Last

Human beings have built some pretty amazing structures: medieval castles, Egyptian pyramids, the Eiffel Tower. Write a paragraph describing a structure you've seen that seems as if it must have been impossible to build. What about it impresses you the most? Save your paragraph in your **Working Portfolio.**

CHAPTER OVERVIEW

Introduction p. 363

1 Structuring a Composition pp. 364–365
2 Writing an Introduction pp. 366–367
3 Writing the Body pp. 368–370
4 Writing the Conclusion p. 371

CHAPTER RESOURCES

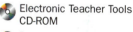 Time-Saver Transparencies Binder:
- Daily Test Preparation pp. DT46–47
- Quick-Fix Grammar and Style Charts pp. QF19–20
- Writing and Communication Skills pp. WC6–7

 Writing and Communication Masters pp. 16–18

Integrated Technology and Media

Electronic Teacher Tools CD-ROM

Power Presentations CD-ROM Lesson 5

mcdougallittell.com

Assessment

Teacher's Guide to Assessment and Portfolio Use

Students Acquiring English/ESL

Side by Side pp. 21–23

COMPOSITIONS

BLOCK SCHEDULING

Pressed for Time?

Focus on **Lesson 1, Structuring a Composition,** for an overview of the structure of a composition. Also work through **Lesson 3, Writing the Body,** to emphasize unity, organization, and coherence in a composition.

Time for More?

After working through all the lessons, have students look for articles in magazines, newspapers, and on the World Wide Web. Have groups of students analyze the articles, identifying the different parts of a composition.

LESSON OBJECTIVES

To recognize and structure a composition using its basic elements

DAILY TEST PREPARATION

Error Identification:

Capitalization Write the following item on the board or use **Daily Test Preparation Transparency** p. DT46. Decide which type of error, if any, appears in the underlined section.

> His <u>Father, however, periodically</u> jogs along the lake.

A. Spelling error

B. Capitalization error

C. Punctuation error

D. No error

Teaching Point: Error correction questions often test your knowledge of basic capitalization rules. In this case, *father* should not be capitalized because it is preceded by a modifier (*his*).

TEACHING RESOURCES

Time-Saver Transparencies Binder:

- Daily Test Preparation p. DT46
- Writing and Communication Skills p. WC6

LESSON 1 Structuring a Composition

❶ What Makes a Composition?

A **composition** is made up of paragraphs. Each paragraph is a separate unit that helps develop, or build on, the main idea of the composition. Your understanding of how paragraphs work can help you to write a strong composition. Notice the similarities and differences between them shown in the chart below.

Paragraphs and Compositions	
A paragraph has	**A composition has**
a topic sentence	an introductory paragraph that states the topic of the composition
sentences that support the topic	body paragraphs that develop the topic, or "main idea"
	a concluding paragraph

Unity and coherence are just as important in compositions as they are in paragraphs. **Unity** means that the information in each paragraph supports the thesis statement. A composition has **coherence** when paragraphs are connected smoothly to one another with transition words and phrases.

❷ What Does a Composition Look Like?

A composition has three parts:

The **introduction** begins the composition and tells what it is about. The introduction includes a sentence stating the main idea of the composition, called a **thesis statement.**

The **body** is the central part of a composition, usually made up of three or more paragraphs. Each paragraph builds on and explains the thesis statement.

The **conclusion** finishes a composition by restating the main idea, offering a summary, and giving a final comment or opinion.

As you read the model, notice how the parts build on one another to create a finished composition.

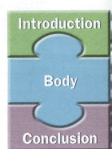

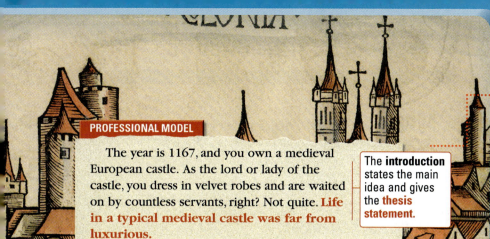

PROFESSIONAL MODEL

The year is 1167, and you own a medieval European castle. As the lord or lady of the castle, you dress in velvet robes and are waited on by countless servants, right? Not quite. **Life in a typical medieval castle was far from luxurious.**

At the first light of dawn, it's time to get up. After a quick sponge bath with icy cold water, you put on your woolen undergarments and hurry off to a short religious service. After church you eat breakfast, which is nothing more than a bland slice of bread.

After several hours of carrying out your morning duties, you must be hungry. On today's menu: stewed pigeon, boiled starling, and roasted sea gull. Sorry, there's no lark's tongue today—you only get that on special occasions. Be sure to wash your hands; you have to eat everything with your fingers.

Once your midday meal is over, afternoon activities begin. The lord of the castle goes hunting to make sure there is something on tomorrow's dinner table. The lady of the castle oversees household chores, including keeping the castle warm—there is no central heating!

As the sun sets, it's time for the last meal of the day and some entertainment. While you eat, a lady acrobat does a handstand while balancing on the tips of two swords. Then it's off to your bed—a hard rope mattress covered by feather pillows and animal fur.

Perhaps your day in a medieval castle wasn't as luxurious as you expected. Was one day enough? You probably want to race back to the hot showers and soft beds of the 21st century.

—Elizabeth Laskey

> The **introduction** states the main idea and gives the **thesis statement**.

> **Body** paragraphs support the thesis statement.

> The **conclusion** restates the thesis and offers an opinion.

COMPOSITIONS

LESSON OBJECTIVES

To identify and write an introduction that has a clear thesis statement and that captures the reader's attention

DAILY TEST PREPARATION

Error Correction: Subject-Verb Agreement Write the following item on the board or use **Daily Test Preparation Transparency** p. DT46. Choose the <u>best</u> way to write the underlined part of the sentence.

> One of the ants <u>guard the queen</u>.

A. guarding the queen

B. guards the queen

C. are guarding the queen

D. No change

Teaching Point: Error correction questions often test your knowledge of subject-verb agreement. In this case, the item tests whether you know that *guard* must be made singular to agree in number with the indefinite pronoun *one*. The word *ants* is part of a prepositional phrase and does not serve as the subject of the sentence.

TEACHING RESOURCES

 Time-Saver Transparencies Binder:
- Daily Test Preparation p. DT46
- Writing and Communication Skills p. WC6

SKILLS PRACTICE RESOURCES

 Side by Side pp. 21–23

 Writing and Communication Masters p. 16

LESSON 2 Writing an Introduction

An **introduction** tells readers what your topic is, lets them know how you plan to discuss that topic, and captures their attention so they'll want to read more of your composition.

❶ Thesis Statement

Your introduction should always include a **thesis statement,** a sentence that clearly presents your main idea and your purpose for writing.

Thesis Statement	
A thesis statement SHOULD	**A thesis statement SHOULD NOT**
tell the subject of your composition	be an incomplete thought: "Battles in the 1300s."
give your view on the subject and your purpose for writing	be a simple statement of fact: "Battles in the 1300s were bloody."
be a statement supported by fact	be merely an opinion: "Battles in the 1300s were cool!"
be stated in an interesting way	be an announcement: "In this paper I will write about . . ."

DRAFT

I'm going to tell you about how battles were fought in the 1300s.

(too general)

REVISION

Warfare in medieval times was fairly simple and included unusual strategies.

(more specific and effective)

❷ Types of Introductions

Capture your readers' imagination at the earliest opportunity—in the introduction. Use one or more of these attention-getting techniques in the first sentence to grab readers' attention.

- include an interesting fact
- use a vivid description
- ask a question
- use a quotation

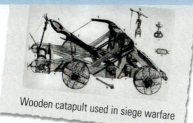
Wooden catapult used in siege warfare

STUDENT MODEL

Have you ever seen a flying horse? Many soldiers in medieval times did. Attackers would sometimes catapult the rotting corpse of a horse over the castle wall in hopes of spreading disease among the enemy. In the heat of battle, any available object would do—rocks, branches, and, of course, flaming arrows. Today, warfare is strategically planned and weapons are carefully crafted. **Warfare in medieval times, however, was fairly simple and included many unusual strategies.**

The writer addresses the reader with a question.

Thesis statement appears at the end of the paragraph.

Students Acquiring English/ESL
For visual practice with organizing a five-paragraph essay, including an introduction and conclusion, see **Side by Side** pp. 21–23.

STUDENT MODEL

Read the following paragraph aloud. Ask students to identify the thesis statement.

The lute is a stringed instrument that was popular in the 16th century. The lute's popularity inspired volumes of songs. These songs were often sung by a minstrel seated on a cushion below the queen's throne. Thesis statement: The lute's popularity inspired volumes of songs.

STUDENT MODEL

"Send to us forty of the fattest pigs of the sort least good for eating to bring fire beneath the tower," commanded. King Alfred while preparing to burn his way into an enemy castle. **As strange as this plan might seem, it was just one of the many unusual strategies used by warriors in medieval times.** Since medieval warfare was not sophisticated, attackers had to take advantage of any weakness in the enemy's fortress. The king who demanded the pigs knew that lard burned well and that the tower's foundation was weak. Believe it or not, burning pigs under castle walls wasn't even the most bizarre strategy used during that time.

Writer begins with a quotation to spark the reader's interest.

Thesis statement

Last line introduces the next paragraph.

COMPOSITIONS

COMPOSITIONS

TEACHING TIP

Cooperative Learning/Paired Activity Explain to students that an interesting or vivid title is another way to spark a reader's interest. Have students work in pairs to write titles for the **Student Models.**

HOT TIP

The thesis statement doesn't have to be the first sentence of your introduction. It can come anywhere within the opening paragraph.

Building Compositions **367**

Drive-Through Grammar

Kinds of Sentences Tell students that they can also grab readers' attention by beginning an introduction with an imperative or an exclamatory sentence.

Remind students that an **imperative sentence** is used to give a command, to make a request, or to give a direction. *Take the train to Union Station.* An **exclamatory sentence** expresses strong feeling or excitement. *What a beautiful day!*

Write the following sentence on the board: *Both drivers and passengers should always wear their seat belts.* Then have students recast the sentence as an imperative and exclamatory sentence.

Imperative: Wear your seat belts.

Exclamatory: Please, buckle up!

LESSON OBJECTIVES

To recognize that the body of a composition is unified, organized, and coherent, and to write a composition that exemplifies these qualities

 DAILY TEST PREPARATION

Sentence Completion: Subject-Verb Agreement Write the following item on the board or use 📺 **Daily Test Preparation Transparency** p. DT47. Choose the word that belongs in the space.

> Both her looks and her distinct style _____ an air of superiority.

A. conveying

B. conveys

C. conceal

D. convey

Teaching Point: For sentence completion questions, the correct answer will always

- fit the meaning of the sentence (*conceal* does not make sense with *looks* and *style*).

- fit grammatically within the sentence (*conveys* does not agree in number with the compound subject; *conveying* does not complete the sentence).

TEACHING RESOURCES

 Time-Saver Transparencies Binder:
- Daily Test Preparation p. DT47
- Quick-Fix Grammar and Style Charts pp. QF19–20
- Writing and Communication Skills p. WC7

SKILLS PRACTICE RESOURCES

 Writing and Communication Masters p. 17

 LESSON 3

Writing the Body

Introduction

Body

Conclusion

The **body** of a composition is made up of three or more paragraphs that support the thesis statement. Each paragraph in a composition should be organized logically and should have unity and coherence.

❶ Unity in a Composition

Unity in a composition means that all of the paragraphs relate to and support the thesis statement. Writing an informal outline is one way to see whether your plan for the composition has unity. First, jot down the main idea of each paragraph to be sure it relates to the thesis statement. Then develop each main idea into a topic sentence.

> **Informal Outline: Warfare in the Middle Ages**
>
> **Introduction, Thesis Statement:**
> Warfare in medieval times was unsophisticated and included unusual strategies.
>
> **Body:**
> **1st paragraph:** entering a fortress (ladders, trickery)
> **2nd paragraph:** hand-held weapons (crossbows, longbows)
> **3rd paragraph:** siege engines (catapults, mobile towers)
> **4th paragraph:** use of fire (flying "Greek fire")
> ~~**5th paragraph:** castle treasures (gold and jewelry)~~
>
> Unrelated topic is deleted.
>
> **Conclusion:**
> Today it is hard to imagine a battle in which things like ladders, bows, and catapults play a role.

Paragraphing also helps keep the body unified. Each paragraph should focus on one main idea—the idea presented in the topic sentence. You should start a new paragraph when:

- you present a new idea
- there is a change in time or place
- the dialogue shifts to a new speaker

The following model shows how one writer broke his composition into paragraphs and then rearranged his ideas as necessary.

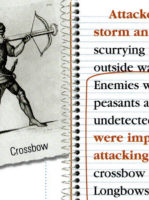

Crossbow

Attackers used several strategies to storm an enemy stronghold. One was scurrying up long ladders placed against the outside walls. A second strategy was trickery. Enemies would disguise themselves as peasants and walk right through a castle gate undetected. **Crossbows and longbows were important weapons used when attacking a castle.** Arrows shot from a crossbow could be fired long distances. Longbows had a shorter range and were good on the battlefield. However, castle soldiers would sometimes see attackers climbing the ladders and simply push them away from the wall.

> This is the **topic sentence** of the first paragraph.

> This becomes the **topic sentence** of the second paragraph.

> This sentence belongs in the first paragraph.

❷ Organization and Coherence

In addition to supporting the thesis statement, paragraphs should be organized logically. Your method of organization should be based on what your composition is trying to achieve.

Types of Organizations	
If you need to . . .	**Use this . . .**
explain events in chronological order or explain a process	sequential order
describe how something happens	cause-and-effect order
show likenesses or differences	compare-and-contrast order

A composition that has **coherence** flows logically from one paragraph to the next. **Transition words and phrases** helps connect ideas both within paragraphs and between paragraphs, as shown in the model on the next page.

Building Compositions **369**

Write the sentences below on the board and have students organize them into a unified, coherent paragraph.

Then in 1911, Frederick Maytag invented the electric washing machine. In the 1800s people washed their clothes once or twice a year. Finally, clothing could be washed more often. Clothes were washed in the spring and sometimes in the autumn.

In the 1800s people washed their clothes once or twice a year. Clothes were washed in the spring and sometimes in the autumn. Then, in 1911, Frederick Maytag invented the electric washing machine. Finally, clothing could be washed more often.

Spice It Up!

Tell students that a correctly assembled puzzle, like a composition, forms a unified, coherent whole. Combine the pieces from three or four simple puzzles. Divide students into groups, and give each group some of the mixed-up puzzle pieces. Then have groups work together to figure out which pieces go where. When the puzzles have been assembled correctly, have students compare the process to writing a composition. Ask them what each puzzle piece might represent.

Answers

PRACTICE → **Unity and Coherence**

Responses may vary.

The paragraph should be broken into two paragraphs. Paragraphs should be rewritten with transition words or phrases added between sentences. Unrelated sentences (Jesters seldom lived in castles. / My parents have a bathroom in their bedroom.) should be removed.

Possible response:

In the Middle Ages, a "bathtub" was a small wooden tub with a padded lining. **Often,** the wooden tub was placed in a chamber near the fireplace for warmth. **Sometimes,** in warm weather, the tub was moved to an outside garden for bathing.

However, members of royalty often had permanent bathrooms in their quarters. **For example,** Henry III had hot and cold running water for bathing and drinking. **In addition,** Edward II even had a tiled floor in his bathroom.

STUDENT MODEL

In contrast to hand-held weapons, "siege engines" like catapults and mobile towers did wide-scale damage. Soldiers loaded huge boulders onto catapults and flung them at foes. **In addition,** mobile towers could protect many archers while being wheeled toward an enemy castle.

However, one of the deadliest strategies was the use of fire. A certain explosive called "Greek fire" actually ignited when moistened. Attackers would load it onto catapults, ignite it, and fling it over fortress walls. It blazed fiercely, and the flame was difficult to put out.

PRACTICE ▶ **Unity and Coherence**

Rewrite the following and break it into two paragraphs. Add transitions where necessary. Delete unrelated sentences.

In the Middle Ages, a "bathtub" was a small wooden tub with a padded lining. The wooden tub was placed in a chamber near the fireplace for warmth. In warm weather the tub was moved to an outside garden for bathing. Jesters seldom lived in castles. Members of royalty often had permanent bathrooms in their quarters. My parents have a bathroom in their bedroom. Henry III had hot and cold running water for bathing and drinking. Edward II even had a tiled floor in his bathroom.

Writing the Conclusion

In the **conclusion**, you can end your composition by restating your thesis statement and leaving your reader with a final thought about your topic.

Introduction

Body

Conclusion

Types of Conclusions

A good conclusion is interesting as well as useful to a reader. The conclusion gives you an opportunity to sum up your message and leave the reader with your final thoughts.

> **Here's How** Writing the Conclusion
>
> - Restate your thesis statement.
> - Sum up your composition in an interesting way.
> - Offer your opinion on the subject, leaving readers with something to think about.

STUDENT MODEL

Today it is hard for us to imagine ladders, bows, and catapults being used in battle. Yet such "primitive" strategies accomplished the attackers' main goal—to get a castle's inhabitants to surrender. While these strategies seem strange and even funny to us, they were taken very seriously in medieval times. Warfare is serious and deadly business, no matter what century you are in!

> Writer sums up the composition.

> Writer offers a personal opinion on the subject.

Be careful not to introduce any new information in the conclusion. Stick to the topic of your composition.

COMPOSITIONS

COMPOSITIONS

Student Help Desk

Students can use the Student Help Desk as a quick review prior to testing or as a quick reference as they revise a piece of writing.

Teacher's Notes
WHAT WORKS:

Student Help Desk

Building Compositions at a Glance

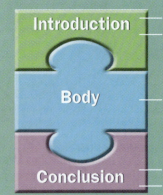

Introduction	— Catches readers' attention — Gives thesis statement
Body	— Develops and supports thesis statement
Conclusion	— Restates main idea — Gives readers something to think about

Getting a Reader's Attention   Reeling Them In

Types of Introductions	Examples
Use vivid or sensory descriptions	The marketplace echoed with the sounds of geese honking, cows mooing, pigs oinking, and shoppers arguing heatedly with merchants.
Include startling or interesting facts	Pepper was so expensive that a medieval housewife sometimes could afford only a single peppercorn. Even then she would have to inspect it to be sure it wasn't a fake made of clay, oil, and mustard.
Ask questions	How would you like to catch and roast a seagull over an open fire for dinner every night? That's what you would have had to do back in the 1300s.
Use quotations	Erasmus once said that on castle floors lay "an ancient collection of grease, fragments, bones, spittle, . . . and everything that is nasty."

372 Essential Writing Skills

Ways to Conclude — A Final Thought on the Subject . . .

Types of Endings	Examples
Restate the thesis statement	Most people today don't realize they live in the lap of luxury compared with people in the Middle Ages.
Make a recommendation	If you could choose to live in the 1300s or now, I'd suggest staying in the 21st century.
State an opinion	We should all be grateful we don't have to hunt for our food like the lord of a medieval castle did.

Coherence Connection — Putting Things in Order

Types of Order	Transitional Words and Phrases
Sequential	finally, during, while, last, soon, at the beginning, at the same time, before, after
Cause and effect	so, consequently, for this reason, because, resulting from, accordingly, thus, therefore
Comparison	either . . . or, neither . . . nor, by comparison, also, likewise, just as, in addition
Contrast	yet, still, unlike, instead, nevertheless, on the contrary, in spite of, regardless, although

The Bottom Line

Checklist for Building Compositions

Have I . . .

____ written a thesis statement that describes my subject and purpose for writing?

____ used an attention-getting technique in my introduction?

____ organized my composition logically and checked for unity?

____ made sure my topic sentences support my main idea?

____ used transitions to create coherence?

____ checked my paragraph breaks?

____ restated my main idea in the conclusion?

Building Compositions **373**

Teacher's Notes
WHAT DOESN'T WORK:

TEACHER'S LOUNGE

Brain Break

Take a word that means "ire" and place an *r* before it. The new word means a kind of park employee. (Answer: *anger, ranger*)

Take a word that means "friend" and place an *r* before it. The new word means a gathering with a purpose. (Answer: *ally, rally*)

A Slice of Life

Why are there no female characters in Robert Louis Stevenson's *Treasure Island*?

Answer: Stevenson was following the instructions of his stepson, Lloyd Osbourne for whom he wrote the book. "[It was to be] about a map, a treasure, a mutiny, and a derelict ship," Stevenson wrote. "No women in the story, Lloyd's orders."

OBJECTIVES

To increase vocabulary through the recognition and understanding of words that describe food

To use words in speaking and writing that describe food

Power Words
Vocabulary for Precise Writing

On the Menu

We cannot live without food. Perhaps that's why we have so many words for it.

Formal and Fancy

We have many fancy words for food: **nourishment, refreshment, edibles,** and **sustenance. Rations** are the food of a soldier at war, and people stock up on **provisions** when they are about to go camping. **Nutriment, aliment,** and **alimentation** are words that doctors and scientists use to describe digestion. **Comestibles, victuals,** and **viands** are very old-fashioned ways of describing food, but you'll want to recognize them when you read them.

Time for Some Grub!

Instead of saying, "Would you join me for a **meal?**" you might ask, "Want some **chow?**" Other informal or slang words for food are **eats, grub,** and **vittles.** For snacks we have the delicious words **munchies, tidbits,** and **treats.**

The **board** in "room and board," **keep** in "earn your keep," **chuck** in "chuck wagon," and **fare** in "hearty fare" are yet other ways to say *food.*

▷ **Your Turn** Eat Up and Chow Down

Create three dinner invitations: a formal one to someone you don't know very well, an informal one to some friends, and an old-fashioned one that might have been sent 200 years ago.

Elaboration

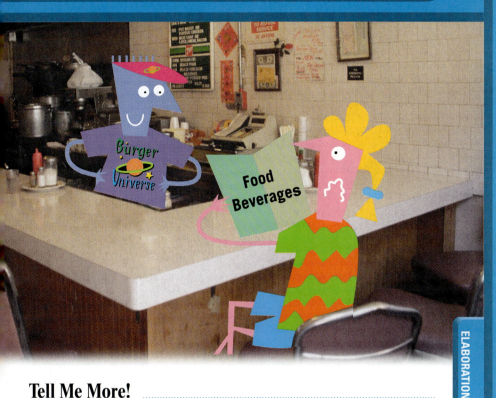

Tell Me More!

What's wrong with this customer's menu? If you were ordering lunch at this restaurant, wouldn't you want to know a few more details? For example, you'd probably be just a little curious about what kinds of food and drinks the restaurant had and how much each cost! This menu needs elaboration to answer all of those questions.

Elaboration means adding supporting details and explanations to your writing. Elaboration enriches descriptions, narrations, arguments, and just about any other kind of writing.

Write Away: **Food, Glorious Food**

Write a paragraph about the best or worst meal you have ever had. Make sure you add enough supporting details for your readers to understand why this meal was the best or the worst. Save your work in your ▸ **Working Portfolio.**

Elaboration **375**

CHAPTER OVERVIEW

CHAPTER RESOURCES

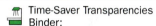 Time-Saver Transparencies Binder:
- Daily Test Preparation pp. DT48–49
- Quick-Fix Grammar and Style Charts p. QF15
- Writing and Communication Skills pp. WC8–9

Writing and Communication Masters pp. 19–20

Integrated Technology and Media

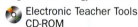 Electronic Teacher Tools CD-ROM

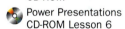 Power Presentations CD-ROM Lesson 6

↪ mcdougallittell.com

Assessment

Teacher's Guide to Assessment and Portfolio Use

Students Acquiring English/ESL

Side by Side pp. 24–26

ELABORATION

ELABORATION

BLOCK SCHEDULING

Pressed for Time?

Use the introductory material in **Lesson 1, Uses of Elaboration,** to provide an overview of elaboration. Use **Lesson 2, Sensory Details,** to provide examples of the most immediate and exciting kinds of elaboration.

Time for More?

Use all the lessons in the chapter to teach students about elaboration. To expand on elaboration, use

💿 **Power Presentations CD–ROM Lesson 6.**

LESSON OBJECTIVES

To recognize forms of elaboration and to use them to make writing clearer, stronger, and more effective

DAILY TEST PREPARATION

Sentence Completion:
Vocabulary Write the following item on the board or use **Daily Test Preparation Transparency** p. DT48. Choose the word that *best* fits the meaning of the sentence.

> Stepping on Angela's delicate toes while dancing made Edward feel _____.

A. truant

B. awkward

C. graceful

D. awkwardly

Teaching Point: For sentence completion questions, the correct answer will always

- fit the meaning of the sentence (*graceful* and *truant* do not make sense with *Stepping on Angela's . . . toes*).

- fit grammatically within the sentence (*awkwardly* confuses the adverb with the adjective *awkward*).

TEACHING RESOURCES

Time-Saver Transparencies Binder:

- Daily Test Preparation p. DT48
- Quick-Fix Grammar and Style Charts p. QF15

SKILLS PRACTICE RESOURCES

Side by Side pp. 24–26

LESSON 1 # Uses of Elaboration

❶ What Is Elaboration?

FoxTrot by Bill Amend

Elaboration provides details that help your reader fully understand your topic. It's a lot easier to picture a log ride with "three stomach-wrenching corkscrews" than just "the log ride." Use elaboration to make a story more exciting, strengthen a persuasive essay, or improve a report like the one below.

STUDENT MODEL

DRAFT

In 1892, George Ferris designed an observation wheel. The wheel was very big. It was expensive to build.

> Information on how the wheel was designed helps the reader "see" it.

> Details help the reader understand how big and expensive the wheel was.

REVISION

In 1892, George Ferris designed an observation wheel for the Columbian Exposition in Chicago. The wheel was made of steel, with two inner and two outer rings connected by steel spokes. The seats were attached to the outer rings. The two support towers were 140 feet high. Ferris's wheel was 250 feet in diameter and could carry 1,440 riders. It cost $300,000 to build.

Drive-Through Grammar

Elaborating with Modifiers To elaborate, writers often use the following modifiers:

Adjectives Write *horse* on the board and ask students to modify the noun with an adjective. For example, *old*

Adverbs Write the verb *moved* on the board and ask students to modify the verb with an adverb. For example, *stiffly*

Prepositional phrases Ask students to supply a prepositional phrase that modifies the adjective or adverb. Then put all the modifiers together to form a complete sentence. For example, *The old horse moved stiffly to the side of the road.*

② Why Use Elaboration?

Elaboration makes your writing clearer, stronger, and more effective. You can use elaboration for these purposes:

TO EXPLAIN Give your reader facts, statistics, and definitions.

TO DESCRIBE Use sensory details that show how the subject looks, sounds, tastes, feels, or smells.

TO ANSWER QUESTIONS Think about questions your reader might ask, and then answer them in your writing.

TO SUPPORT OPINIONS Give reasons for your opinions. You may need to do research to support them.

TO SHOW, NOT TELL Instead of just *telling* your reader that a roller coaster is scary, *show* how scary it is by describing its effects.

PRACTICE ➤ Let's Go!

You want to spend the day at a local amusement park, but your friend isn't sure about going. Write a paragraph persuading your friend. Use sensory details to describe the park. Answer questions your friend might have. Give reasons for any opinions you state.

Elaboration **377**

LESSON OBJECTIVES

To identify sensory details and to use them to enrich writing

 DAILY TEST PREPARATION

Error Identification: Punctuation
Write the following item on the board or use **Daily Test Preparation Transparency** p. DT48.

Look for mistakes in punctuation in the sentence. Decide which line, if any, contains a mistake.

A. Greta stuffed after winning

B. the pie-eating contest, rode

C. home with great difficulty.

D. No mistakes

Teaching Point: Error identification questions often test your knowledge of basic punctuation rules. In this case, the item tests whether you know to use commas to set off participial phrases, such as *stuffed after winning the pie-eating contest.* Such phrases are set off with commas because they interrupt the flow of the sentence.

CUSTOMIZING TIP

Less Proficient Learners Have students use sensory details to recall an encounter with a natural wonder, such as a sunset, a cave, an ocean, or a desert.

Sensory Details

Using the Senses

Sensory details are bits of information that you collect by using your five senses: sight, sound, touch, taste, and smell. When you elaborate with sensory details, you give the reader a much clearer idea of what you are describing. The models below show how sensory details can enrich both fiction and nonfiction.

LITERARY MODEL

At the first step upon the cold surface, Buck's feet sank into a white mushy something very much like mud. He sprang back with a snort. More of this white stuff was falling through the air. He shook himself, but more of it fell upon him. He sniffed it curiously, then licked some up on his tongue. It bit like fire, and the next instant was gone. This puzzled him. He tried it again, with the same result. The onlookers laughed uproariously and he felt ashamed, he knew not why, for it was his first snow.

—Jack London, *The Call of the Wild*

TOUCH

SIGHT

SOUND

TASTE

PROFESSIONAL MODEL

The [Arctic] air was filled with a thundering, grinding, rumbling roar, a very frightening sound, one we had not heard before.... What I saw amazed me. A wall of ice, 20 feet tall and as long as a football field, was moving our way as if being pushed by the blade of a giant bulldozer.

—Will Steger and Jon Bowermaster, *Over the Top of the World*

SOUND

SIGHT

TEACHING RESOURCES

 Time-Saver Transparencies Binder:
- Daily Test Preparation p. DT48
- Writing and Communication Skills pp. WC8–9

SKILLS PRACTICE RESOURCES

Writing and Communication Masters p. 19

You can use a word web to help you add sensory details to your writing.

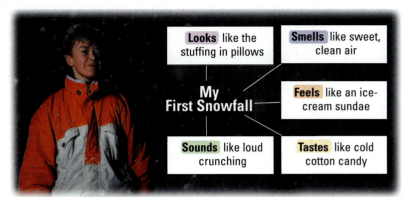

Looks like the stuffing in pillows

Smells like sweet, clean air

My First Snowfall

Feels like an ice-cream sundae

Sounds like loud crunching

Tastes like cold cotton candy

STUDENT MODEL

I saw snow for the first time when I was ten. I was visiting my grandparents in Wisconsin. When I looked out the window early one morning, it seemed like someone was shaking the stuffing out of pillows and letting it drift downward. I put on my new boots and ran outside. I was surprised by the noise of my boots crunching on the hard surface of the packed snow. It sounded the way hard pretzels sound in my head when I am chewing them. The air smelled clean and sweet. I grabbed a handful of snow. It felt like I was putting my hand into an ice-cream sundae! The snow tasted like cold cotton candy as it melted on my tongue.

 To gather details about a person or object, make careful observations. Keep a small notebook or journal with you and jot them down. If you are writing about something that has happened, close your eyes and try to visualize the event.

PRACTICE > **A Meal to Remember**

In your 📁 **Working Portfolio,** find your **Write Away** paragraph from page 375. Add sensory details to show your reader exactly what made this meal so delicious or so horrible. Then trade papers with a partner. Discuss whether your descriptions are clear enough to "taste" the meal.

Elaboration **379**

TEACHING TIP

Although description adds information, too many descriptive words may confuse the reader. Write the following sentence on the board: *It was a fierce, jittery, groovy, twitchy, swinging, wild beat.* Ask students which words might be deleted.

NEED MORE INFORMATION?
For a review of writing descriptions, see **Chapter 14, Building Paragraphs**

TEACHING TIP

Speaking and Listening Read aloud the **Student Model,** emphasizing the sensory details. Have students listen for the sensory information that makes the ideas clearer. Ask students how the sensory details help the selection "come to life."

CUSTOMIZING TIP

Students Acquiring English/ESL
Point out that descriptive phrases and idioms in one language often cannot be literally translated into English. For example, *¡Qué Padre!* means "That's great!" in Spanish, but literally means "How Father!" in English. Share some English idioms, such as "in a pickle" and "out on a limb."

ELABORATION

Spice It Up!

Have students work in pairs to create a detailed drawing of a picnic. Tell students to make sure their drawings include images of things they would see, hear, touch, smell, and taste at a picnic. Encourage students to choose unusual settings. Have students label each sense suggested by the drawing in some creative way (abbreviations, color-coding, symbols, etc.). Display the drawings in the classroom as a reminder to students to use sensory details in their writing.

DAILY TEST PREPARATION

Error Correction: *Who* and *Whom* Write the following item on the board or use 🗒 **Daily Test Preparation Transparency** p. DT49. Choose the best way to write the underlined section.

> <u>Who</u> knows about summer camp?

A. Whom

B. Who's

C. Whose

D. Correct as is

Teaching Point: Error correction questions often test your knowledge of commonly confused words, such as *who* (a subject pronoun) and *whom* (an object pronoun). In this case, *who* should be used to serve as the subject of the sentence.

TEACHING TIP

Cross-Curricular Connection

Science Explain to students that facts and statistics should be used in scientific essays and reports to make the writing more precise and interesting and to support statements and opinions. Have students study the graphic and then write a few sentences comparing the *Titanic* with the *Santa María* or the *Mayflower*.

THE LANGUAGE OF LITERATURE

The passage on the student page is from an excerpt from *Exploring the Titanic* in *The Language of Literature,* Level 7.

LESSON 3 Facts and Statistics

Using Proven Information

Facts are statements that can be proved. **Statistics** are facts expressed with one or more numbers. Statistics can be used to make comparisons between things or between a part of something and the whole. When you elaborate with facts and statistics, you help your readers understand your ideas.

Read the sentence below and then look at the literary model. In what ways does the literary model give you a better understanding of the size of the *Titanic*?

The *Titanic* was a large ship.

> **LITERARY MODEL**
>
> The final size and richness of this new ship was astounding. She was **882 feet long, almost the length of four city blocks.** With **nine decks, she was as high as an eleven-story building**....
>
> As her name boasted, the *Titanic* was indeed **the biggest ship in the world.**
>
> —Robert D. Ballard, *Exploring the Titanic*

HOT TIP Give your reader comparisons, not just numbers. Knowing that the *Titanic* was 882 feet long is interesting, but knowing that it was nearly the length of four city blocks gives the reader a much better understanding of its size. This bar graph compares the *Titanic* with other famous ships.

882 feet
length of the *Titanic*

117 feet length of the *Santa María*, one of Christopher Columbus's ships

90 feet length of the *Mayflower*, the ship that took the Pilgrims to Plymouth, Mass

380 Essential Writing Skills

TEACHING RESOURCES

 Time-Saver Transparencies Binder:
- Daily Test Preparation p. DT49
- Quick-Fix Grammar and Style Charts p. QF15
- Writing and Communication Skills p. WC8

SKILLS PRACTICE RESOURCES

 Writing and Communication Masters p. 20

Using facts and statistics can improve your essays, stories, lab reports, and research papers.

STUDENT MODEL

DRAFT

Wolverines are medium-sized animals. They are good hunters and can be very fierce.

REVISION

Adult wolverines are about three feet long and can weigh more than 55 pounds. They are known for their strength and will attack reindeer or even bears.

Here's How **Using Facts and Statistics**

1. Ask yourself: What does my reader need to know? Use facts and statistics to make your topic clearer, not just longer.

2. Look for facts and statistics in reference books, in newspapers, in magazines, and on the Internet. Gather them from your own interviews and observations.

3. Tell your reader exactly where the information is from and how old it is by citing the source and the date it was written.

For more on finding facts, see p. 502.

For more on finding facts, see p. 502.

PRACTICE **Prove It!**

Choose from the facts and statistics below to write a paragraph about a lost ship. Put the items in a logical order. Don't use items that are unrelated to the topic.

Topic Sentence

In 1865, a ship called *Sultana* sank in the Mississippi River.

- ship was rediscovered in 1982
- Civil War lasted from 1861 until 1865
- ship found two miles away from the river under 21 feet of earth
- Mississippi River is 2,350 miles long
- river changed its course over many decades
- between 1,800 and 2,100 people died when ship sank
- a farmer was growing crops on top of the buried ship

Elaboration **381**

ELABORATION

ELABORATION

Spice It Up!

Play a facts and statistics game. Read the following answers—assorted facts and statistics—and have students supply the appropriate questions.

His film, *Jurassic Park*, is the all-time top moneymaker at the box office. Who is Steven Spielberg?

There are 5,280 feet in this unit of measurement. What is a mile?

The Sears Tower, one of the tallest buildings in the world, is in this city. What is Chicago?

The number of innings in a regulation baseball game. What is nine?

Born into slavery, she was one of the most famous conductors on the Underground Railroad. Who was Harriet Tubman?

Elaboration **381**

LESSON OBJECTIVES

To recognize how visuals help readers understand information and to use visuals to show information

DAILY TEST PREPARATION

Sentence Completion:
Conjunctions Write the following item on the board or use **Daily Test Preparation Transparency** p. DT49. Choose the word that belongs in the space.

> _____ we were climbing up the face of the rock, it began to rain.

A. Because

B. Quickly

C. While

D. There

Teaching Point: For sentence completion questions, the correct answer will always

- fit the meaning of the sentence (*Because* does not fit; climbing did not cause the rain).

- fit grammatically within the sentence (*Quickly* and *There* create an incomplete sentence).

TEACHING RESOURCES

Time-Saver Transparencies Binder:
- Daily Test Preparation p. DT49
- Writing and Communication Skills p. WC8

LESSON 4 # Visuals

Using visuals to elaborate is a great way to show rather than tell. Your reader can see at a glance what information you are giving and how it all fits together.

❶ Making a Point with Diagrams

Diagrams are drawings that give information about an object or a process. Time lines, flow charts, and labeled drawings are all types of diagrams. You can make a definition clearer by adding a labeled drawing like the one below.

> A **volcano** is an opening in the crust of the earth where lava, ashes, and gases are released.
>
> **Inside a Volcano**
>
> **Ash cloud**
> full of bits of magma (hot, liquid rock) and rock
>
> **Magma chamber**
> volcanic eruption happens when magma travels upward and breaks through the earth's crust
>
> **Cone**
> layers of hardened, cooled lava and other materials ejected from the volcano
>
> **Central vent** and **side vent**
> magma flows from the chamber through here
>
> Sources: Jon Erickson, Volcanoes and Earthquakes, 1988; World Book Encyclopedia

❷ Showing Information with Other Visuals

Charts and **graphs** present facts and statistics in a visual format. They let your reader see and compare information easily. The writer of the student model on the next page added a bar graph, which she created with the graphing function of a word-processing program, to support her statements.

382 Essential Writing Skills

Spice It Up!

Have each student create a diagram that illustrates a familiar process, such as preparing for a test, doing homework, eating a meal, and so on. Then have students get together in small groups and use the diagrams to play a game. Each student in a group will take turns showing his or her diagram, while the other students try to identify the process.

Volcanoes have caused some of the worst natural disasters in history. Lava flows have destroyed whole towns, and people have starved to death because their farmland got covered with ashes and nothing could grow. Over the past 200 years, more than 250,000 people have died because of volcano eruptions. Four huge eruptions caused about 70 percent of those deaths.

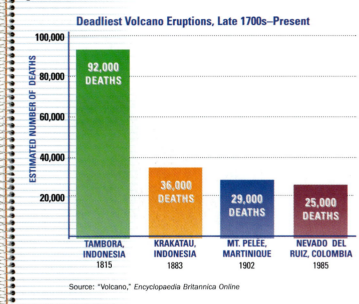

Deadliest Volcano Eruptions, Late 1700s–Present

ESTIMATED NUMBER OF DEATHS

100,000
80,000
60,000
40,000
20,000

92,000 DEATHS — TAMBORA, INDONESIA 1815

36,000 DEATHS — KRAKATAU, INDONESIA 1883

29,000 DEATHS — MT. PELÉE, MARTINIQUE 1902

25,000 DEATHS — NEVADO DEL RUIZ, COLOMBIA 1985

Source: "Volcano," *Encyclopaedia Britannica Online*

For more examples of visual displays of information, see pp. 510–511.

PRACTICE > **Be a Statistician**

Work with three or four classmates to take a survey of your class's preferences. Pick a topic to ask about, such as favorite foods, hobbies, sports, or video games. Combine your group's results and present them as a chart or graph. For example, you might find out that 12 of your classmates say that pizza is their favorite food, 10 prefer hamburgers, and 7 like hot dogs best.

ELABORATION

ELABORATION

Student Help Desk

Elaboration at a Glance

What is it?
Supporting details, reasons, and explanations that enrich your writing

Why should I use it?
To give your reader enough details to understand your topic

What kinds can I use?
- sensory details
- facts and statistics
- graphs, charts, and other visuals

Adding Sensory Details   Just the Right Word

These words may spark an idea for adding your own sensory details.

SIGHT
shiny, pale, furry, sparkling

SMELL
fishy, sweet-smelling, fragrant

TASTE
bitter, salty

SOUND
growling, gurgling, fluttering, crunching

TOUCH
slippery, smooth, bumpy, cold, wet, scaly

Finding Facts   Where to Go, Whom to Ask

Here are some good places to dig up facts and statistics.

Almanacs, atlases, encyclopedias, and other reference books

Online databases of newspaper and magazine articles

Interviews you conduct, either in person, by telephone, or by e-mail

Web sites of publishers, museums, or other reliable sources

Kinds of Visuals Get the Picture?

Maps, charts, and graphs give your reader information at a glance.

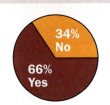

Pie Graph: shows how one or more parts relate to the whole

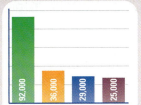

Bar Graph: compares numbers or sets of numbers

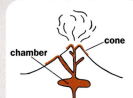

Diagram: shows information about an object or process

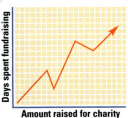

Line Graph: shows change over time

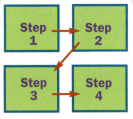

Flow Chart: shows steps in a process

Map: shows physical location

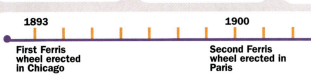

Time Line: shows order of events

The Bottom Line

Checklist for Elaboration

Have I . . .

____ told my reader enough about my topic?

____ explained, described, answered questions, and supported opinions where needed?

____ used sensory details to give my reader a clear picture?

____ used facts and statistics to give more information?

Elaboration **385**

ELABORATION

ELABORATION

TEACHER'S LOUNGE

A Slice of Life

"Words, when well chosen, have so great a force in them that a description gives us more lively ideas than the sight of things themselves."
—Joseph Addison

Brain Booster

"The brain is very poor at maintaining a continuous, sustained focus. It's better at short bursts. Sometimes your reading bursts might be 10 minutes, other times as long as 30 to 50 minutes, but rarely longer than that. Feel free to take breaks. They are normal and natural ways that the brain rides out the effects of nutrition, hormones, and environmental stimuli."—Eric Jensen

OBJECTIVES

To increase vocabulary through the recognition and understanding of words that describe strength

To use words in speaking and in writing that describe strength

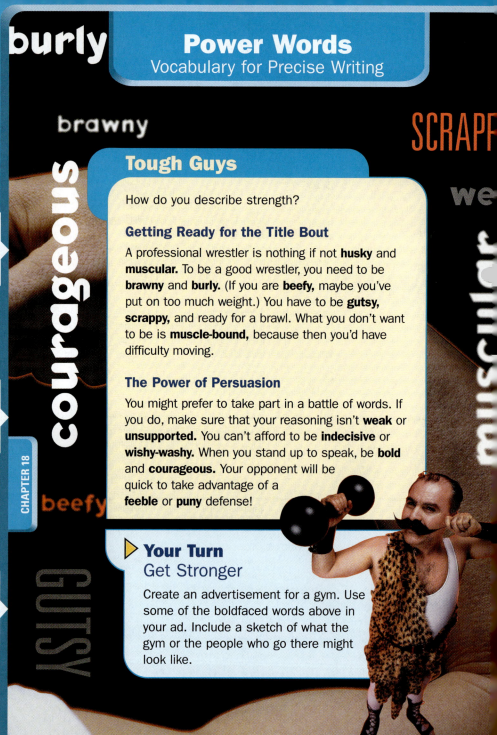

Power Words
Vocabulary for Precise Writing

Tough Guys

How do you describe strength?

Getting Ready for the Title Bout

A professional wrestler is nothing if not **husky** and **muscular.** To be a good wrestler, you need to be **brawny** and **burly.** (If you are **beefy,** maybe you've put on too much weight.) You have to be **gutsy, scrappy,** and ready for a brawl. What you don't want to be is **muscle-bound,** because then you'd have difficulty moving.

The Power of Persuasion

You might prefer to take part in a battle of words. If you do, make sure that your reasoning isn't **weak** or **unsupported.** You can't afford to be **indecisive** or **wishy-washy.** When you stand up to speak, be **bold** and **courageous.** Your opponent will be quick to take advantage of a **feeble** or **puny** defense!

▷ Your Turn
Get Stronger

Create an advertisement for a gym. Use some of the boldfaced words above in your ad. Include a sketch of what the gym or the people who go there might look like.

Revising Sentences

"I was a writing weakling. My sentences were boring. They were choppy. They were dull."

"Then I used the AMAZING SENTENCE DEVELOPER! Now my sentences have variety and structure. They thrill, they delight, and they sing, sing, *sing!*"

Making Sentences Stronger

The writer on the left knows he has a problem—he hasn't learned how to revise his sentences to make them more interesting and sophisticated. You can learn to be like the writer on the right. The techniques found in this chapter will help you make your sentences stronger and more energetic.

Write Away: How Strong Is He?
On a separate piece of paper, write the sentence *Charles is strong.* Add details, examples, descriptions, or other information, and write a sentence that is 10 to 12 words long. Save your work in your 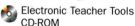 **Working Portfolio.**

Revising Sentences **387**

CHAPTER OVERVIEW

CHAPTER RESOURCES

Time-Saver Transparencies Binder:
- Daily Test Preparation pp. DT50–51
- Quick-Fix Grammar and Style Charts pp. QF11–14
- Visual Grammar™ Tiles Lesson 22

Writing and Communication Masters pp. 21–22

Integrated Technology and Media

 Electronic Teacher Tools CD-ROM

 Power Presentations CD-ROM Lesson 7

 mcdougallittell.com

Assessment

Teacher's Guide to Assessment and Portfolio Use

Students Acquiring English/ESL

Side by Side p. 27

REVISING

BLOCK SCHEDULING

Pressed for Time?
Focus on **Lesson 1, Padded and Empty Sentences,** and **Lesson 2, Stringy and Overloaded Sentences,** to help students identify two common weaknesses in sentence style.

Time for More?
Use all of the lessons to teach students about different ways to revise their sentences. Then use 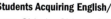 **Power Presentations CD-ROM Lesson 7** to give students more practice in identifying problem sentences and revising them.

LESSON OBJECTIVES

To recognize padded and empty sentences and to learn how to revise them

DAILY TEST PREPARATION

Error Correction: Conjunctions
Write the following item on the board or use 🖥 **Daily Test Preparation Transparency** p. DT50.
Choose the best way to write the underlined section.

> Alice began mowing lawns <u>and she needed money</u> for a backpack.

A. that she needed money

B. during she needed money

C. because she needed money

D. Correct as is

Teaching Point: Error correction questions often test your use of conjunctions. The conjunction *and* is often used inappropriately in compound sentences that express a specific type of relationship. In this case, the transition *because* best expresses the cause-and-effect relationship in the sentence.

CUSTOMIZING TIP

Gifted and Talented Some people think that padding their sentences makes them appear more intellectual. Point out to students that, in fact, padding usually muddles ideas and makes the speaker appear pretentious. Emphasize that effective writing is clear and concise and not dependent on the use of big words.

LESSON 1

Padded and Empty Sentences

❶ Refining Padded Sentences

A **padded sentence** has more words than are needed to communicate an idea. Sometimes padded sentences have long phrases that can be replaced with shorter ones. At other times, padded sentences bore your reader by needlessly repeating an idea.

STUDENT MODEL

DRAFT
I was upset because **of the fact that** my friend wouldn't ride the roller coasters with me. The reason is he **is of the opinion that** roller coasters look **like they could be full of danger.**

REVISION
I was upset because my friend wouldn't ride the roller coasters with me. He thinks they look dangerous.

> Does the writer really need all these words to make his point?

Here's How) Filling Empty Sentences

1. Think about what you really want to say.

2. Look for words and phrases that could be deleted and never missed.

3. Look for places where one or two words could replace many words.

Unnecessary Phrase	Replacement
on account of the fact that	because *or* since
is of the opinion that	thinks *or* believes
what I really want to say is	(Just say it!)

Peanuts by Charles M. Schulz

PEANUTS reprinted by permission of United Feature Syndicate, Inc.

TEACHING RESOURCES

 Time-Saver Transparencies Binder:
• Daily Test Preparation p. DT50
• Quick-Fix Grammar and Style Charts pp. QF11–12

SKILLS PRACTICE RESOURCES

 Writing and Communication Masters p. 21

❷ Improving Empty Sentences

Some sentences say nothing or repeat an idea that has already been stated. Other sentences make statements that are not supported by facts.

STUDENT MODEL

DRAFT

I like bike riding because **it is fun** and **enjoyable.** It is good transportation. Mountain bikes are **the best.** They are **my favorite** bikes because they are **the best ones.**

REVISION

I like bike riding. It's a **fun** way **to get somewhere quickly.** Mountain bikes are my favorite kind of bike **because you can ride them almost anywhere, even over hills and through mud.**

> This sentence says the same thing three times.

> Tell *why* they are the best.

> Here the writer supports her opinion and eliminates repetition.

Here's How Filling Empty Sentences

1. Eliminate words and phrases that needlessly repeat an idea.
2. Don't leave your reader asking, "Why?" Add reasons, examples, and facts to support your opinions.

PRACTICE   Tell More, Repeat Less

Follow the instructions in parentheses to revise these sentences.

1. A pickup truck is better than a car. (Add a reason or fact.)
2. What I really mean is that I hope your team wins. (Eliminate unnecessary words.)
3. Science fiction rules! (Add a reason or fact.)
4. I don't like scary movies because they are frightening. (Eliminate the repeated idea; then add a reason or fact.)

Revising Sentences   **389**

Answers

PRACTICE ▸ **Tell More, Repeat Less**

Answers will vary but should include at least one reason to support the stated opinion.

Possible responses:

1. A pickup truck is better than a car because a pickup can carry more cargo.
2. I hope your team wins.
3. Science fiction is the best form of writing because it gives readers a glimpse into the future.
4. I don't like scary movies because they give me nightmares.

REVISING

REVISING

Stringy and Overloaded Sentences

LESSON 2

Both stringy and overloaded sentences confuse the reader by forcing too many ideas into one sentence. Often, the reader can't tell how the ideas in the sentence are related.

Fixing Stringy and Overloaded Sentences

A **stringy sentence** contains too many ideas loosely connected by the word *and.* Stringy sentences seem to go on and on. To fix stringy sentences, make each complete thought a separate sentence. Write the sentences in a logical order.

You can use conjunctions such as *first, then, when, next, after that,* and *because* to show the relationship between ideas.

HOT TIP

STUDENT MODEL

DRAFT	**REVISION**
My class visited Washington, D.C., and we went to the National Air and Space Museum, and we saw the Wright 1903 Flyer, which was the first successful airplane, and we saw Viking 1, the first spacecraft to operate on the surface of Mars, and I thought seeing Viking 1 was the best part of the tour, and I would really like to go to Mars someday.	**When** my class visited Washington, D.C., we went to the National Air and Space Museum. **First,** we saw the Wright 1903 Flyer, which was the first successful airplane. **After that,** we saw Viking 1, the first spacecraft to operate on the surface of Mars. I thought seeing Viking 1 was the best part of the tour **because** I would really like to go to Mars someday.

PRACTICE A ▶ **Blast Off!**

Rewrite this stringy sentence.

Viking 1 landed on Mars on July 20, 1976, and it was designed to search for life on Mars, and scientists couldn't prove that there is life on that planet, but the information Viking 1 collected gave them a better understanding of Martian weather and the Martian landscape.

390 Revising Sentences

An overloaded sentence contains too much information about a single topic. You may know what you want to say, but your reader won't understand you.

STUDENT MODEL

DRAFT

    Even though most people think that pterodactyls, flying reptiles that lived more than 65 million years ago in Europe and East Africa, were huge animals, not all of them were, and some of them were about the same size as a sparrow.

There are too many facts and details here for one sentence.

REVISION

    Pterodactyls were flying reptiles that lived more than 65 million years ago in Europe and East Africa. Most people think that pterodactyls were huge animals, **but** not all of them were. **Some** pterodactyls were about the same size as a sparrow.

This version is easier to understand because it has been broken into three sentences.

REVISING

Write the following overloaded sentence on the board. Then have students rewrite the sentence, creating several sentences.

I stayed up all night finishing my homework, but my dog ate my paper and the vet took my chewed-up paper out of the dog's stomach, and I have to put it together like a puzzle.

REVISING

Here's How) **Revising Stringy and Overloaded Sentences**

1. Break down your sentence into separate ideas.

2. Combine related ideas, using conjunctions such as *and, but, or, so, then,* and *when.*

3. Rewrite your sentence as two or more sentences, making sure that you have not packed too many ideas into any one sentence.

PRACTICE B **Sentence Checkup**

In your 📁 **Working Portfolio,** find your **Write Away** sentence from page 387. Make sure it is not padded, empty, stringy, or overloaded. Revise your work to make it even stronger. If your revisions make your sentence longer, you may want to break it into two or more sentences.

Revising Sentences **391**

Drive-Through Grammar

Subordinating Conjunctions A clause that cannot stand alone as a sentence—called a subordinate clause—is joined to a clause that can stand alone—called an independent clause—by a subordinating conjunction. Subordinating conjunctions do not merely connect the thoughts; they establish a relationship between them.

Write the following sentences on the board. Ask students to describe the relationships created by the underlined words.

1. *We ran inside <u>when</u> it started to rain.* sequence

2. *We stayed inside <u>because</u> it was raining.* cause/effect

LESSON OBJECTIVES

To recognize and use different ways to vary sentence structure for added impact

CHAPTER 18

LESSON 3 # Varying Sentence Structure

❶ Rearranging Phrases

Try rearranging the phrases in your sentences for more impact. Words that give the most important information often have the greatest effect at the start or end of a sentence.

Minerva opened her front door, and fifteen of her friends spilled out, wishing her a happy birthday.

Fifteen of Minerva's friends spilled out her front door as she opened it, wishing her a happy birthday.

Wishing her a happy birthday, fifteen of Minerva's friends spilled out her front door as she opened it.

There are no precise rules about the "most important" words in a sentence. You can put interesting details up front to grab your reader's attention or at the end to go out with a bang.

PRACTICE A ▶ Order, Order!

Rewrite each sentence two ways, as shown in the examples above.

1. Matala checked the controls and gazed out the window as her rocket blasted off.
2. She switched on the rocket boosters and began planning her return while the ship gathered speed.

392 Essential Writing Skills

Answers
PRACTICE A ▶ Order, Order!

Answers may vary. Possible responses:

1. As her rocket blasted off, Matala checked the controls and gazed out the window; Matala gazed out the window and checked the controls as her rocket blasted off.

2. While the ship gathered speed, she switched on her rocket boosters and began planning her return; She began planning her return and switched on her rocket boosters while the ship gathered speed.

❷ Varying Sentence Types

You can make your writing livelier by including questions, exclamations, and commands.

PROFESSIONAL MODEL

What can kids do about pollution in their communities? Students at Bellamy Middle School in Chicopee, Massachusetts, found out. Chicopee had a problem storing sludge from factories and sewers. In winter the sludge froze before it could be taken to landfills. Some Bellamy students toured the sludge plant to see the problem for themselves—and smell it too! The town used the students' idea of building a greenhouse to keep the sludge from freezing. Look around your community for environmental problems you can help solve.

—Greg Hess

The writer uses a question to draw readers into the topic.

An exclamation adds emphasis.

A command urges readers to apply the example to their own lives.

 WATCH OUT Don't overuse exclamations. Too many can make your writing seem breathless or overexcited.

For more on questions, exclamations, and commands, see p. 16.

For more on questions, exclamations, and commands, see p. 16.

PRACTICE B ▷ **Question? Exclaim! Command.**

Add some variety to the letter below. Rewrite at least three sentences as questions, exclamations, or commands.

Dear Jennifer,

I'm not sure if you heard that I won first place in the science fair. I bet you can imagine how surprised I was to win. It was thrilling. The science-fair judges asked me lots of questions. I hope you will tell your aunt about it the next time she is in town. The information she gave me helped a lot. I wonder what I should do for next year's science project.

Write back soon!

Trish

 Visual Grammar™

Use **Visual Grammar™ Tiles Lesson 22** and **Sentence S** to show how to vary sentence structure. Here is part of Lesson 22.

Change the location of a word within a sentence. Four options:

THE SKATER	TWIRLED	GRACEFULLY	ON THE ICE	.
THE SKATER	TWIRLED	ON THE ICE	GRACEFULLY	.
THE SKATER	GRACEFULLY	TWIRLED	ON THE ICE	.
GRACEFULLY	,	THE SKATER	TWIRLED	ON THE ICE	.

TEACHING TIP

Cross-Curricular Connnection

Science Encourage students to revise a science report they have recently written by varying sentence structure. Suggest that they replace the first sentence of the report with a question or exclamation. Then have them look for other places to add questions, exclamations, and commands.

CUSTOMIZING TIP

Less Proficient Learners Some students may have trouble understanding that it is acceptable—or even *possible*—to transform one type of sentence into another.

Ask students to use the following prompt to create a statement, question, exclamation, and command:

barking dog

Possible responses:

A barking dog is alert.

Doesn't a barking dog drive you crazy?

I love a barking dog!

Shush your barking dog.

Also suitable for:
Students Acquiring English/ESL

Answers

PRACTICE B ▷ **Question? Exclaim! Command.**

Answers will vary. Possible response:

Did you hear that I won first place in the science fair? I bet you can imagine how surprised I was to win. It was thrilling! Will you tell your aunt about it the next time she is in town? The information she gave me helped a lot. What should I do for next year's science project?

REVISING

Varying Sentence Length

CHAPTER 18

❶ Changing Sentence Length and Rhythm

Professional writers know that using sentences of varying lengths is an important way to keep reader interest.

LITERARY MODEL

> People who live on hills sleep so close to the stars they forget those of us who live too much on earth. They don't look down at all except to be content to live on hills. They have nothing to do with last week's garbage or fear of rats. Night comes. Nothing wakes them but the wind.
>
> —Sandra Cisneros, *The House on Mango Street*

Cisneros's long sentences give information.

Her short sentences add drama.

As you write and revise, think about the length and rhythm of your sentences. Do they keep the reader interested?

Don't mistake short sentences for sentence fragments. "Night comes" is a complete sentence—the subject is *night* and the predicate is *comes*.

❷ Combining Choppy Sentences

Choppy sentences are a series of short sentences that often lack detail. When read in a group, choppy sentences seem boring and immature. Your writing falls into the same rhythm for sentence after sentence, and pretty soon . . . zzzzzzzzz. This writer fell asleep reading his own essay!

> I have many chores to do. My least favorite chore is mowing the lawn. It is hard work. It takes a long time. It is boring. I am tired when I finish.

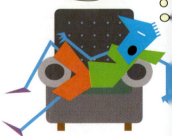

STUDENT MODEL

DRAFT

Guide dogs were first trained in Germany. They were trained to help blind veterans. Doberman pinschers have been trained as guide dogs. Golden retrievers have also been trained as guide dogs. German shepherds are the most commonly used breed of guide dog.

REVISION

Guide dogs were first trained in Germany **to help blind veterans.** Doberman pinschers **and** golden retrievers have been trained as guide dogs, **but** German shepherds are the most commonly used breed.

This version gives the same information with less repetition.

Here's How Smoothing Choppy Sentences

1. Use conjunctions such as *but, and,* and *or* to combine related sentences.

2. Get rid of repetitive sentences that add only one or two details about your subject. Insert those details into other sentences.

Don't create run-ons as you combine sentences.

My dog got loose , and **she ran all over the neighborhood.**

For more on sentence combining, see p. 26.

 PRACTICE Smooth It Out

Rewrite this choppy paragraph. Add conjunctions where they are needed. Vary the length and rhythm of the sentences.

> We took a field trip. We went to the aquarium. It was interesting. There were guides. One of them showed us around. There were tanks of fish. There was a huge shark tank. I thought the best part was the tank full of horseshoe crabs. We could touch them. Their shells felt bumpy.

Revising Sentences **395**

REVISING

REVISING

TEACHING TIP

Not every conjunction can be used to join two choppy sentences. Explain to students that if the sentences express similar ideas, join them with *and*. If the sentences express contrasting ideas, join them with *but* or *or*.

Answers

PRACTICE Smooth It Out

Answers may vary. Possible response:

We took an interesting field trip to the aquarium. One of the guides showed us around. There were tanks of fish, including a huge shark tank. I thought the best part was the tank full of horseshoe crabs. You could touch them, and their shells felt bumpy.

ASSESSMENT

Teacher's Guide to Assessment and Portfolio Use

Student Help Desk

Students can use the Student Help Desk as a quick review prior to testing or as a quick reference as they revise a piece of writing.

Teacher's Notes
WHAT WORKS:

Student Help Desk

Revising Sentences at a Glance

Trim excess words from padded and empty sentences.

Reorganize stringy and overloaded sentences to make your ideas clearer.

Vary the length and structure of your sentences to keep your reader interested.

Phrases to Avoid   Get to the Point!

These words and phrases bog down your writing. Get rid of them or replace them with shorter, simpler words or phrases.

Unnecessary Word or Phrase	Replacement
on account of the fact that being that	because *or* since
the reason is the reason why is that the reason is because	because
is of the opinion that	thinks *or* believes
at this point in time at the present time at the current time presently	now
in spite of the fact that	although
what I mean is the point is the fact is	(Just say it!)

Conjunctions — Connect Your Ideas.

Use these conjunctions to show how your ideas are related.

To connect ideas that are . . .	. . . try using these conjunctions:
similar	and, plus, also
different	not, but, however
related in time	first, then, next, later, finally
related in space	beside, over, under, between

Rephrasing Sentences — Say It a Different Way.

Strengthen your writing by changing some of your statements into questions, commands, and exclamations.

Type of sentence	Can be used to . . .	Example
Question	• draw your reader into your subject • help your reader think about how your topic relates to his or her life	Have you ever wanted to be stronger and faster?
Command	• ask your reader to consider a point you have made • urge your reader to take action	Think about adding more exercise to your routine.
Exclamation	• emphasize a point • add feeling to your writing	Being in shape is really fun!

The Bottom Line

Checklist for Revising Sentences

Can I improve my sentences by . . .

____ cutting unneeded words from padded sentences?

____ deleting empty sentences?

____ breaking up stringy sentences to make them clearer?

____ reworking overloaded sentences to make my ideas more understandable?

____ changing sentence structure and length to add variety?

TEACHER'S LOUNGE

Slice of Life

"There's always room for improvement, you know—it's the biggest room in the house."
—Louise Heath Leber

Brain Break

Read this sentence:
FINISHED FILES ARE THE RESULT OF YEARS OF SCIENTIFIC STUDY COMBINED WITH THE EXPERIENCE OF MANY YEARS OF EXPERTS.
Now count the F's in the sentence above. Count them *only once,* without going back to count them again. See if you can find all seven.

TEACHING TIP

Using References If students are unable to determine the meanings of words from the context, have them use a dictionary or a thesaurus to look up words.

CHAPTER 19

TEACHING TIP

Cooperative Learning/Paired Activity Using photographs from newspapers or magazines, have students work in pairs to compose a critique or review of a celebrity's personal style. Ask volunteers to read their reviews or critiques to the class.

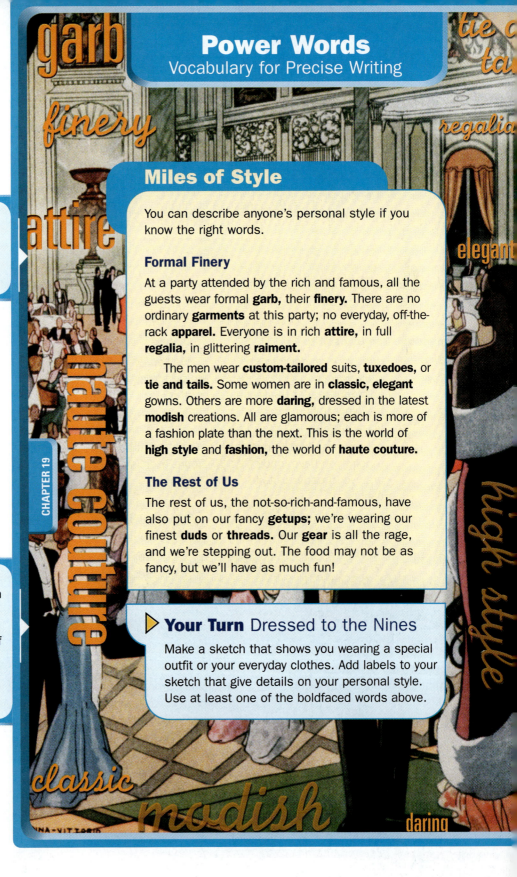

Power Words
Vocabulary for Precise Writing

CHAPTER 19

Miles of Style

You can describe anyone's personal style if you know the right words.

Formal Finery

At a party attended by the rich and famous, all the guests wear formal **garb,** their **finery.** There are no ordinary **garments** at this party; no everyday, off-the-rack **apparel.** Everyone is in rich **attire,** in full **regalia,** in glittering **raiment.**

The men wear **custom-tailored** suits, **tuxedoes,** or **tie and tails.** Some women are in **classic, elegant** gowns. Others are more **daring,** dressed in the latest **modish** creations. All are glamorous; each is more of a fashion plate than the next. This is the world of **high style** and **fashion,** the world of **haute couture.**

The Rest of Us

The rest of us, the not-so-rich-and-famous, have also put on our fancy **getups;** we're wearing our finest **duds** or **threads.** Our **gear** is all the rage, and we're stepping out. The food may not be as fancy, but we'll have as much fun!

▷ **Your Turn** Dressed to the Nines

Make a sketch that shows you wearing a special outfit or your everyday clothes. Add labels to your sketch that give details on your personal style. Use at least one of the boldfaced words above.

Style and Effective Language

Which hat might have an owner who would say . . .

"Them's fightin' words, pardner!"

"You have been most ungracious, sir."

"Say that again and I'll throw you in the brig!"

STYLE

Which Style Suits You Best?

Which of these hats would you like to wear? Would you rather wear a different kind altogether, or maybe no hat at all? Your choice was probably affected by your own personal style—the way you look, dress, talk . . . and write. Clothes help show your fashion style. Your choice of words, the length and complexity of your sentences, and the expressions you use combine to make up your **writing style.** Just about everything you write lets a little of your personality show through.

Write Away: Who's That in the Hat?
Choose one of the hats in the photograph. Imagine a person who might wear the hat, and write a paragraph about him or her. Save your work in your **Working Portfolio.**

CHAPTER OVERVIEW

CHAPTER RESOURCES

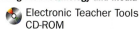 Time-Saver Transparencies Binder:
- Daily Test Preparation pp. DT52–54
- Quick-Fix Grammar and Style Charts pp. QF16–18

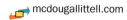 Writing and Communication Masters pp. 23–25

Integrated Technology and Media

 Electronic Teacher Tools CD-ROM

mcdougallittell.com

Assessment

Teacher's Guide to Assessment and Portfolio Use

STYLE

BLOCK SCHEDULING

Pressed for Time?
Use **Lesson 1, The Elements of Style,** to provide an overview of style and its various elements. Then focus on **Lesson 2, Choosing Language Levels,** and **Lesson 3, Choosing Precise Words,** to cover the essential elements of style covered in the chapter.

Time for More?
Work through all of the lessons. Then write the following paragraph on the board and have students revise it, using precise words and fresh figures of speech:

My sister got married. She looked pretty as a picture. The whole thing went by quick as a flash. Everyone had a good time.

LESSON OBJECTIVES

To recognize style and explore the elements that constitute style

Sentence Completion: Subject-Verb Agreement Write the following item on the board or use ⬚ **Daily Test Preparation Transparency** p. DT52. Choose the word that belongs in the space.

> One of the students _____ organizing a field trip to Peru.

A. are

B. volunteers

C. is

D. rose

Teaching Point: For sentence completion questions, the correct answer will always

- fit the meaning of the sentence (*rose* does not make sense with *organizing*).

- fit grammatically within the sentence (*are* does not agree in number with the subject *one*; *volunteers* would take the infinitive *to organize*).

TEACHING TIP

Engage students in a discussion about how the figures of speech in the **Literary Model** affect the tone of the story. Ask students, for example, how the tone would change if "his little eyes like hot coals" were changed to "his little eyes like twinkling stars."

THE LANGUAGE OF
LITERATURE

The passage on the student page is from "Rikki-tikki-tavi" in *The Language of Literature,* Level 7.

LESSON 1

The Elements of Style

Style means the way you express yourself in writing. The words you choose and the way you use them affect how your reader reacts to your writing.

❶ Exploring Style

Read the two passages below. The first model, from an encyclopedia article, is meant to inform. The second, from a story about a mongoose named Rikki-tikki-tavi and a snake named Nagaina, is intended to entertain.

PROFESSIONAL MODEL

The mongoose is best known for its ability to kill snakes. It is not immune to poison, but its swiftness allows it to seize and kill poisonous snakes such as the cobra. The mongoose also kills mice, rats, poultry, wild birds, and other small animals.

—*World Book Encyclopedia,* "Mongoose"

> Details are made up of facts and concrete words.

> Tone is very matter-of-fact.

LITERARY MODEL

Rikki-tikki was bounding all round Nagaina, keeping just out of reach of her stroke, his little eyes like hot coals. Nagaina gathered herself together and flung out at him. Rikki-tikki jumped up and backwards. Again and again and again she struck, and each time her head came with a whack on the matting of the veranda, and she gathered herself together like a watch spring.

—Rudyard Kipling, "Rikki-tikki-tavi"

> Writer uses strong images and figures of speech.

> Tone is one of excitement.

TEACHING RESOURCES

Time-Saver Transparencies Binder:
- Daily Test Preparation p. DT52

SKILLS PRACTICE RESOURCES

Writing and Communication Masters p. 23

❷ Recognizing Elements of Style

As you read, look for these elements of style. You will learn more about them in the rest of the chapter.

Levels of Language

Writers use formal or informal language, depending on their audience and purpose.

Formal The mongoose is a carnivorous creature.

Informal A mongoose eats just about anything it can catch.

Precise Words

Writers choose words carefully to create just the right effect.

Vague wording Rikki-tikki **moved** toward the **snake.**

Precise wording Rikki-tikki **leaped** toward the **hissing cobra.**

Connotation and Denotation

Denotation is the dictionary definition of a word. **Connotation** is all the thoughts and feelings the word brings into the reader's mind.

What's the best way to describe a mongoose?

Positive Connotation   **Negative Connotation**

brave   aggressive   vicious
hunter   meat-eater   killer

Other Elements of Style

- **Figures of speech** describe something by comparing it to something else, as in "Nagaina gathered herself together like a watch spring."

- **Imagery** refers to the "pictures" a writer creates for the reader.

- **Tone** is the writer's attitude toward the subject, as shown in the words and images he or she chooses.

Style and Effective Language **401**

LESSON OBJECTIVES

To identify the characteristics of formal and informal language and to choose the level of language appropriate for a particular audience

DAILY TEST PREPARATION

Revision-in-Context: Spelling
Write the following item on the board or use 🖥 **Daily Test Preparation Transparency** p. DT52.

> **1** Pike livers, pheasant
> **2** brains, and flamingo
> **3** tongues are delicacys
> **4** reserved for emperors.

What is the **BEST** change, if any, to make in the sentence in line 3?

A. Change *delicacys* to *delicacies*

B. Change *tongues* to *tonges*

C. Change *tongues* to *tungues*

D. Make no change

Teaching Point: A common item in revision-in-context questions is spelling. In this case, the item tests whether you know to change the *y* to *i* and add *es* when forming the plural of *delicacy*.

TEACHING TIP

Speaking and Listening Read aloud the letters in the **Student Model,** using volume, pitch, and tone that are appropriate for their audience. Ask students to listen for and identify the formal and informal elements in the letters.

 LESSON 2

Choosing Language Levels

Formal and Informal Language

You may not realize it, but you speak and write differently depending on the situation. Knowing when to use formal and informal language can make you a more confident and successful writer.

Formal language is serious and polite. It often uses sophisticated words and longer sentences. **Informal language** is more like conversation. It uses simpler words, shorter sentences, and more contractions.

For example, an informal E-mail to a friend is very different from a formal letter of complaint to a manufacturer.

STUDENT MODEL

INFORMAL

Hey Dani,

I am so **steamed!** You know that new **bike** I bought? Well, **it's** a **piece of junk.** Even my **bike shop guy can't** fix it. **I'm gonna** write to the manufacturer.

Meg

> Uses informal language, contractions, and slang

FORMAL

Dear Madam or Sir:

The Mountain Express **bicycle** I **purchased** last week has already broken down. Some of the plastic parts have cracked, and my local repair shop tells me that they **cannot** be repaired. I am enclosing a copy of the shop's diagnosis for your reference. **Please let me know how I can receive a refund or a new bicycle.**

Yours truly,
Megan Briggs

> Uses more sophisticated vocabulary and precise language

 HOT TIP

As you choose what level of language to use, think about your audience—the person or people who will read your writing. Also, think about why you are writing—your purpose.

TEACHING RESOURCES

 Time-Saver Transparencies Binder:
- Daily Test Preparation p. DT52
- Quick-Fix Grammar and Style Charts p. QF16

SKILLS PRACTICE RESOURCES

 Writing and Communication Masters p 23

Choosing Formal or Informal Language

Formal	Informal
Audience: teacher or someone you don't know well	**Audience:** friends or family
When to use: speeches, essays, reports, or formal letters	**When to use:** friendly letters and E-mails, casual conversation
Formal writing has . . . • few or no contractions (such as *you're* or *I'll*) • no slang (or very informal language, such as *goofing off* or *did a number on us*) • longer, more sophisticated sentences • exact words • a serious, impersonal tone (attitude toward the topic)	**Informal writing has . . .** • contractions where they are needed • slang (if the audience understands it) • shorter, simpler words and sentences • a friendly, personal tone

Some writers think that using difficult, impressive-sounding words makes their writing seem more important. However, using too many of these words can confuse your reader. Your goal is to communicate clearly, whether you're using formal or informal language.

Expressions such as *ain't got none* and *them things* are not considered Standard English. Nonstandard English often violates accepted rules of spelling and grammar. If you use nonstandard English in formal writing or speaking, people tend to focus not on *what* you are saying but on *how* you say it. Use Standard English in school and business situations.

PRACTICE **A Number-One Hit?**

With a partner, change these song titles into formal language.

1. "You Stomped on My Heart, You Nasty Toad"
2. "I Ain't Gonna Listen to You No More"
3. "I Am Such a Cool Dude"
4. "Why Are Ya Freaking Me Out Like This?"
5. "My Love for You Has Totally Croaked, Baby"

Style and Effective Language **403**

TEACHING TIP

Remind students that formal writing often uses long, sophisticated sentences. However, tell them that from time to time they should use short, simple sentences to create sentence variety.

Example:
Although the cave artists did occasionally paint people, most of the paintings are of animals, such as bison, bulls, mammoths, deer, and horses. The motives of the cave artists are unknown.

CUSTOMIZING TIP

Students Acquiring English/ESL
Students acquiring English may have difficulty distinguishing between levels of language in new words they acquire. When they come across a new word, have them record in a journal where and when they heard or read it. Have them guess what the word means and whether it is informal or formal language. Then have them verify their guesses with a dictionary.

Answers

PRACTICE **A Number-One Hit?**

Answers will vary. Possible responses:

1. "You Have Made Me Miserable, You Unlikable Person"

2. "I Refuse to Continue Listening to You"

3. "What a Remarkable Human Being I Am"

4. "Why Must You Cause Me to Feel So Uncomfortable?"

5. "My Love for You No Longer Exists, My Dear"

Spice It Up!
Divide students into small groups to play a game that is a take-off on the **Practice** exercise. Have students take turns selecting a line from a popular song and "translating" it into formal language. The other students in the group should try to identify the line and the song it is from.

LESSON OBJECTIVES

To recognize and use precise words to make writing stronger and clearer.

DAILY TEST PREPARATION

Definition: Vocabulary Write the following item on the board or use 📖 **Daily Test Preparation Transparency** p. DT53.

Choose the word that means the same, or about the same, as the underlined word.

> A bay that is <u>placid</u> is

A. temperate

B. disturbed

C. calm

D. silent

Teaching Point: For definitions, use context clues to decipher the meaning of the underlined word. In this case, answers A, B, and D are not usually associated with a body of water, such as a bay. *Calm* is closest in meaning.

TEACHING TIP

Explain to students that they need to consider their audience when choosing precise words. For example, the sentence "My computer has a 10-gigabyte hard drive" may be may be suitable for a computer-savvy audience. However, the sentence "My computer can store a lot of information" may be more effective for an audience that knows little about computers.

THE LANGUAGE OF
LITERATURE

The passage on the student page is from "Last Cover" in *The Language of Literature*, Level 7.

 LESSON 3

Choosing Precise Words

The Best Way to Say It

Precise words give your reader a better idea of your message. Notice how the second passage gives a clearer picture of the scene.

> I was **angry.** I remember the **sadness** of Colin's face in the **light.**

LITERARY MODEL

> I was **stricken** and **furious.** I remember the **misery** of Colin's face in the **lamplight.**
>
> —Paul Annixter, "Last Cover"

Many times, one very precise word can give your reader a more accurate picture than a long string of words.

Draft

The audience **made a lot of noise to show** its approval.

Revision

The audience **roared** its approval.

You can make your own writing stronger by using strong nouns and verbs instead of a series of weak modifiers.

STUDENT MODEL

DRAFT

The **small brown birds quickly ate** the crumbs and flew away. The **little child** who had been feeding them **said in a loud voice** that she wanted to keep them as pets.

REVISION

The **sparrows gobbled** the crumbs and flew away. The **toddler** who had been feeding them **screamed** that she wanted to keep them as pets.

 HOT TIP

Try using strong verbs instead of *is* or *was*. "The sun blazed in the sky" is stronger than "The sun was very bright in the sky."

TEACHING RESOURCES

 Time-Saver Transparencies Binder:
- Daily Test Preparation p. DT53
- Quick-Fix Grammar and Style Charts p. QF17

SKILLS PRACTICE RESOURCES

 Writing and Communication Masters p. 24

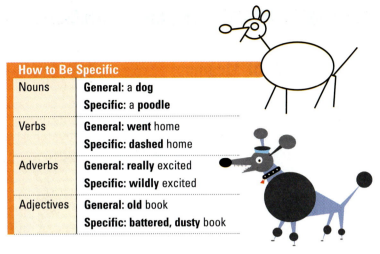

How to Be Specific	
Nouns	**General: a dog** **Specific: a poodle**
Verbs	**General: went** home **Specific: dashed** home
Adverbs	**General: really** excited **Specific: wildly** excited
Adjectives	**General: old** book **Specific: battered, dusty** book

As you write and revise, ask yourself whether the words you have chosen give an accurate picture of your topic. A friend, relative, or classmate can help you by asking questions about parts of your writing that seem unclear.

Revising with Exact Words

First Draft	Peer Reader's Comments	Revised Version
When I was young, I traveled by airplane for the first time. It was really scary. There was a lot of noise when the plane took off.	How old were you? Why was it scary? What were the noises like?	When I was **four and a half**, I traveled by airplane for the first time. I was **terrified** by the **whining, buzzing, and thumping** when the plane took off.

For more on powerful words, see p. 410.

For more on powerful words, see p. 410.

PRACTICE ▸ **As You See It**

Revise these boring sentences with precise words. Use the information in the picture to help you.

> The girl danced. Her costume was pretty. The audience cheered for all the dancers.

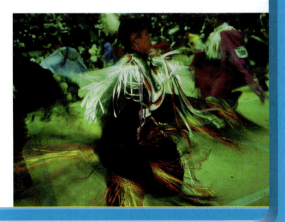

For additional information on using exact words to improve sentences, direct students to **Chapter 13, Building Sentences.**

NEED MORE INFORMATION?

For additional information on using exact words to improve sentences, direct students to **Chapter 13, Building Sentences.**

CUSTOMIZING TIP

Addressing Learning Styles

Visual Suggest to students that, while revising a draft, they try visualizing what they want to say. For example, if they want to write about a car, they should try to "see" the car in their mind. As a result, instead of writing about a generic car, they might write about a shiny, red convertible.

Answers

PRACTICE ▸ **As You See It**

Answers will vary. Possible response:

The Native American girl danced skillfully. Her beautiful costume was covered with delicate ribbons. Everyone in the audience cheered and stomped their feet for all the dancers.

STYLE

STYLE

Spice It Up!

Challenge students to use specific words. Read the following general words and phrases, and see how many specific ones students can come up with.

1. performer actor, blues singer, violinist

2. very happy deliriously delighted, overjoyed

3. bird robin, vulture, parrot

4. food macaroni and cheese, Spanish omelet

5. run race, speed, hasten

To recognize and use words based on their connotations

Error Identification: Capitalization Write the following item on the board or use **Daily Test Preparation Transparency** p. DT53. Look for mistakes in capitalization in the sentence. Decide which line, if any, contains a mistake.

A. We saw the Principal

B. speaking with Ms. Anne

C. at lunch.

D. *(No mistakes)*

Teaching Point: Error identification questions often test your knowledge of basic capitalization rules. In this case, the item tests whether you know not to capitalize titles, such as *principal*, that are used as common nouns. Capitalize titles only when they are used with a personal name, such as *Principal Frederick*.

Gifted and Talented Challenge students to analyze the two connotations of the word *unusual* in the **Hot Tip.** Ask students: What different connotations does the word suggest in each sentence?

 Time-Saver Transparencies Binder:
- Daily Test Preparation p. DT53

LESSON 4

Connotation and Denotation

Two Kinds of Meaning

Almost every word you use has two kinds of meanings. A word's **denotation** is the straightforward dictionary definition. The **connotation** of a word includes all the thoughts and feelings that word may bring to people's minds. When you choose a word, make sure that you have considered its possible connotations.

What's the Connotation?	
When you write . . .	**Your reader may think . . .**
Phil is **conceited**.	Phil has a very high opinion of himself and his abilities—probably too high. He thinks he can't do anything wrong. *(negative connotation)*
Phil is **confident**.	Phil is certain of himself and his abilities. *(positive connotation)*

Words can have positive, negative, or neutral connotations. Use words with neutral connotations when you don't want to show strong positive or negative feelings in your writing.

POSITIVE

Aunt Callie is always interested in what other people are doing.

NEUTRAL

Aunt Callie is always curious about others.

NEGATIVE

Aunt Callie is nosy. What a snoop!

HOT TIP

Connotations can depend on your audience. If you say, "Gee, Uncle Ted, what an unusual tie," your uncle may be pleased. However, if you tell your mother, "That dinner was, uh . . . unusual, Mom," she may be insulted. Ask someone else to review your writing to be sure that your message gets across.

Decoding Connotations

Positive	Neutral	Negative
That's a **glamorous** necklace.	That's an **attractive** necklace.	That necklace is **gaudy**.
The racehorse was **slender**.	The racehorse was **thin**.	The racehorse was **scrawny**.

If you're not sure what connotations a word may have, check a dictionary for the uses of the word. If you need to find a word with a similar meaning but a different connotation, use a thesaurus.

PRACTICE **Can You Picture It?**

For each phrase, write "positive" for positive connotations and "negative" for negative connotations. Use a dictionary if you are uncertain of a word's meaning. Then use each phrase in a sentence that reflects the connotation.

Example:
an **imaginative** sculpture—positive
a **crazy** sculpture—negative

The imaginative sculpture drew a crowd of admirers.

The crazy sculpture made the children giggle.

1. an unusual stench;
   an unusual fragrance
2. a brave explorer;
   a reckless explorer
3. an inexpensive present;
   a cheap present
4. a decisive camp counselor;
   a bossy camp counselor
5. hoarded the supplies;
   preserved the supplies

A garish shirt?
A colorful shirt?

How would you describe this shirt? Write two sentences, one with a positive connotation and one with a negative connotation.

Student sentences will vary. Possible responses:

1. The unusual stench made me wonder what kinds of foul meals were being cooked in the cafeteria.

   The unusual fragrance wafted on the air like perfume.

2. The brave explorer overcame many dangers on her trip across the desert.

   The reckless explorer didn't bother to take water or a compass on her trip across the desert.

3. Bob loved Arnetta's inexpensive, homemade present.

   Bob was insulted by the cheap present that Arnetta gave him.

4. The decisive camp counselor planned a challenging hike for us.

   The bossy camp counselor couldn't stop telling people what to do.

5. Trey hoarded the supplies, refusing to share with those who needed them.

   Trey preserved the supplies, making sure that everyone had enough for the week.

Answers will vary. Possible responses:

The garish shirt had so many glaring colors that it made my eyes water.

Jon's colorful Hawaiian shirt brightened everyone's mood.

STYLE

STYLE

LESSON OBJECTIVES

To recognize figures of speech and to use them in writing

DAILY TEST PREPARATION

Error Correction: Capitalization
Write the following item on the board or use 📖 **Daily Test Preparation Transparency** p. DT54. Choose the best way to write the underlined section.

> Ms. Blancher said that <u>she already returned the book to mother.</u>

A. she already returned the Book to mother.

B. she already returned the Book to Mother.

C. she already returned the book to Mother.

D. Correct as is

Teaching Point: Error correction questions often test your knowledge of basic capitalization rules. In this case, the item tests whether you know to capitalize *Mother* when it is used as a name.

CUSTOMIZING TIP

Students Acquiring English/ESL
Encourage students acquiring English to share with the class images and figures of speech from their own cultures. Have them use these devices in their own writing to develop a colorful personal style.

THE LANGUAGE OF LITERATURE

The passage on the student page is from "A Crush" in *The Language of Literature,* Level 7.

LESSON 5

Using Figurative Language

❶ Figures of Speech

Figures of speech are expressions that go beyond the dictionary definitions of the words being used. Figures of speech and other kinds of descriptive language are often easy to remember because they appeal to the senses. They have strong **imagery**—in other words, they bring clear pictures to your reader's mind.

One figure of speech, a **simile,** is a comparison using the word *like* or *as.*

Bizarro by Dan Piraro

LITERARY MODEL

Dolores was the assistant manager at Stan's and had worked there for twenty years, since high school. **She knew the store like a mother knows her baby.** . . .

—Cynthia Rylant, "A Crush"

A **metaphor,** which is a comparison that does not use the word *like* or *as,* can contribute even stronger imagery to your writing. Which of the following sentences paints a more vivid picture?

SIMILE

Mr. Patel knew so much sports trivia that he was like an encyclopedia.

METAPHOR

Mr. Patel was an encyclopedia of sports trivia.

TEACHING RESOURCES

 Time-Saver Transparencies Binder:
- Daily Test Preparation p. DT54
- Quick-Fix Grammar and Style Charts pp. QF16, 18

SKILLS PRACTICE RESOURCES

 Writing and Communication Masters p. 25

Another type of figurative language, **personification,** gives human qualities to animals or objects.

The light danced on the surface of the water.

As I stumbled around the forest carrying 40 pounds of camping equipment, I could hear an owl laughing at me.

❷ Avoiding Clichés

Many figures of speech have been overused. These tired phrases are called **clichés.** Instead of relying on clichés, try to think of fresher ways to say what you mean.

Cliché Alert!	
Stale Imagery	**Fresh Replacement**
free as a bird	free as a student on the first day of summer vacation
raining cats and dogs	thousands of stinging raindrops
big as a house	enormous, gigantic, *or* vast
stubborn as a mule	stubborn as a toddler who hasn't had his nap
quick as a flash	a human lightning bolt

DANGER Clichés Ahead

PRACTICE A **Away with Clichés**

Revise this dull paragraph. Replace the clichés with fresh figurative language of your own.

> My first week at camp was as dull as dishwater. I just sat around like a bump on a log. Then I made some friends, and the difference in my attitude was like night and day. Spending time with them made me as happy as a clam. I can't wait to go back next year!

PRACTICE B **Making It All Work**

In your **Working Portfolio,** locate your **Write Away** paragraph from page 399. Use what you have learned about style and effective language to revise your paragraph. Add some figurative language, but don't include any clichés!

Style and Effective Language **409**

STYLE

STYLE

Student Help Desk

Style and Effective Language at a Glance

Keep It on the Level	Precisely Right	Brave or Foolhardy?	Light as a *What?*
Select formal or informal language to match audience and purpose.	Get rid of vague words.	Weigh the connotations of your words.	Use fresh figurative language.

Language Levels

Dressing Up or Down

Extremely Formal	Somewhat Formal	Somewhat Informal	Extremely Informal
displeased	angry	mad	blowing a gasket
dine		eat	munch
funds	money	cash	dough

Powerful Words

Pack a *Genuine* Punch

Nifty Nouns	Vivid Verbs	Appealing Adjectives	Admirable Adverbs
redwood, cloak	sweep, flutter	plush, wrinkled	freshly, gloom
otter, rubbish	float, polish	cautious	recently, spe
toddler, mare	soothe, whisper	handsome	gracefully
chimes	demolish, shriek	scaly, hushed	suspiciously
quilt, desert	scrape, perspire	costly, crowded	violently, war

Spot the Connotation

What I *Mean* Is . . .

The words you choose can bring positive, negative, or neutral feelings to your reader's mind.

Positive	Marcia's new dog is **lively.**
Neutral	Marcia's new dog is **active.**
Negative	Marcia's new dog is **wild.**

Phrases to Avoid: Cliché Display

How many clichés can you find?

As quick as a wink, Trent rose to the occasion. With a mind like a steel trap, he saw that the sink was not clean as a whistle, the way Dad liked it. In the blink of an eye, he put a little elbow grease into his chore. Soon, Trent was working like a house afire. A man's home is his castle, he reasoned, and Dad should be home any minute. You could set your watch by him.

Trent was right as rain. When Dad saw the sparkling kitchen, he was pleased as punch.

"Let's eat at Pizza Heaven!" he said. "You've worked like a dog today, and this money is burning a hole in my pocket!"

The Bottom Line

Checklist for Style and Effective Language

Have I . . .

____ chosen the right language level?

____ used precise, effective words?

____ considered the connotation and denotation of my words?

____ enriched my writing with figurative language?

STYLE

STYLE

TEACHER'S LOUNGE

Just for Laughs

A synonym is the word you use when you can't spell the word you want to use.

A Slice of Life

"Avoid cliches like the plague."
—Anonymous

Writing Workshops

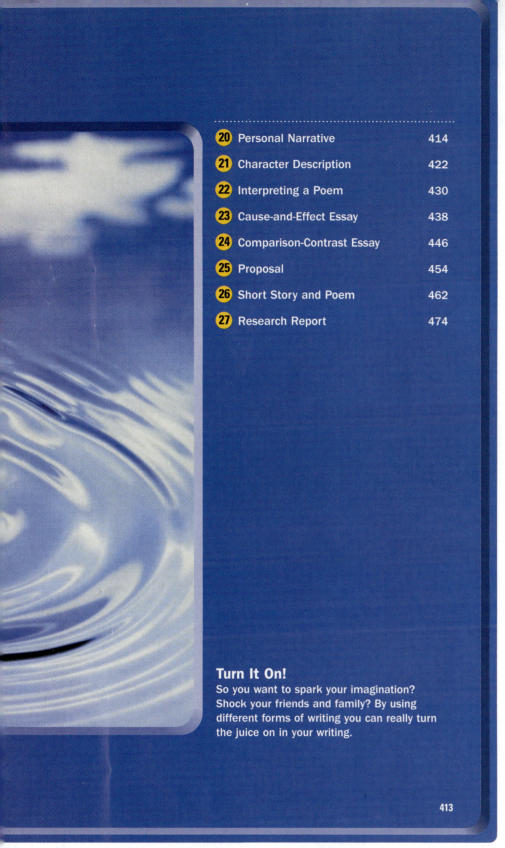

Turn It On!

So you want to spark your imagination? Shock your friends and family? By using different forms of writing you can really turn the juice on in your writing.

413

RESOURCE MANAGEMENT GUIDE

Chapters 20-23 Writing Workshops

Use the online lesson planner at **mcdougallittell.com** to customize instruction.

Pupil Edition

	Print Resources	Time-Saver Transparencies Binder						Integrated Technology and Media		Students Acquiring English/ESL
	Writing and Comm. Masters	Basics in a Box	Critical Thinking Graphic Organizers	Daily Test Preparation	Quick-Fix Grammar and Style Charts	Revising Editing, Proofreading Models	Writing and Communication Skills	Media Focus	Writing Coach	Side by Side
CHAPTER 20 Personal Narrative pp. 414-421	pp. 26-34	p. BB 1		p. DT 54		pp. RE 1-4		Program 4	Personal Narrative	pp. 31-42
CHAPTER 21 Character Description pp. 422-429	pp. 35-43	p. BB 2	p. CT 23	p. DT 55		pp. RE 5-8				pp. 25, 43-54
CHAPTER 22 Interpreting a Poem pp. 430-437	pp. 44-52	p. BB 3		p. DT 55		pp. RE 9-12	pp. WC 6-8		Writing about Literature: Interpretive Essay	pp. 55-66
CHAPTER 23 Cause-and-Effect Essay pp. 438-445	pp. 53-61	p. BB 4	pp. CT 15	p. DT 56	p. QF 1	pp. RE 13-16	pp. WC 5, 7		Cause-Effect Explanation	pp. 19, 67-78

ASSESSMENT

Assessment Masters	Writing Prompts	Rubrics	Student Models
Chapter 20	p. 126	p. 135	pp. 144-146
Chapter 21	p. 127	p. 136	pp. 147-149
Chapter 22	p. 128	p. 137	pp. 150-152
Chapter 23	p. 129	p. 138	pp. 153-155

Teacher's Guide to Assessment and Portfolio Use

 mcdougallittell.com

Visit our web site for:
- Student activities
- Links to related resources
- Teaching resources
- Professional articles

 **Electronic Teacher Tools**

Print-Out Option: Exercises in the following components may be printed from the Electronic Teacher Tools as worksheets.

- Writing and Communication Masters
- Test Preparation (Use for levels 6-10)
- College Test Preparation (Use for levels 11 and 12)
- Weekly Vocabulary and Spelling
- Assessment Masters
- Students Acquiring English/ESL
- English Grammar Survival Kit
- Side by Side
- Test Preparation

Chapters 24-27 Writing Workshops

Use the online lesson planner at mcdougallittell.com to customize instruction.

Pupil Edition	Print Resources — Writing and Comm. Masters	Time-Saver Transparencies Binder — Basics in a Box	Critical Thinking Graphic Organizers	Daily Test Preparation	Quick Fix Grammar and Style Charts	Revising Editing, Proofreading Models	Writing and Communication Skills	Integrated Technology and Media — Writing Coach	Students Acquiring English/ESL — Side by Side
CHAPTER 24 **Comparison-Contrast Essay** pp. 446-453	pp. 62-70	p. BB 5	p. CT 7	p. DT 56	p. QF 8, 13	pp. RE 17-20	pp. WC 7	Comparison-Contrast	pp. 20, 79-90,
CHAPTER 25 **Proposal** pp. 454-461	pp. 71-79	p. BB 6	pp. CT 19, 23	p. DT 57	p. QF 2	pp. RE 21-24		Explanation of an Idea	pp. 91-102
CHAPTER 26 **Short Story and Poem** pp. 462-473	pp. 80-97	p. BB 7	pp. CT 1, 9	p. DT 57	pp. QF 3-4	pp. RE 25-32		Short Story	pp. 103-114
CHAPTER 27 **Research Report** pp. 474-489	pp. 98-109	p. BB 8	p. CT 5	p. DT 58	p. QF 5	pp. RE 33-40	pp. WC 6, 7	Report	pp. 115-129

ASSESSMENT

Assessment Masters	Writing Prompts	Rubrics	Student Models
Chapter 24	p. 130	p. 139	pp. 156-158
Chapter 25	p. 131	p. 140	pp. 159-161
Chapter 26	p. 132-133	p. 141-140	pp. 162-167
Chapter 27	p. 134	p. 143	pp. 168-173

 Teacher's Guide to Assessment and Portfolio Use

CHAPTER OBJECTIVES

To analyze and write an effective personal narrative

Chapter 20 · Writing Workshop

CHAPTER 20

DAILY TEST PREPARATION

Revision Strategies: Parallel Structure Write the following item on the board or use 🖳 **Daily Test Preparation Transparency** p. DT54. Choose the *best* way to express the idea.

A. This summer, I want to swim, read, and watch movies.

B. This summer, I want to be a swimmer, reader, and watch movies.

C. This summer, I want to spend time swimming, reading, and watch some movies, too.

D. This summer, I want to swim, read, and I'll watch movies.

See 🖳 **Time-Saver Transparencies Binder** for the Teaching Point.

The **Basics in a Box** provides graphic and verbal guidelines for organizing a personal narrative. The graphic demonstrates that a personal narrative is divided into a beginning, middle, and end.

The **RUBRIC**, or Standards for Writing, describes a personal narrative that would merit the highest score. A complete rubric, describing several levels of proficiency, is on page 135 of the 📑 **Assessment Masters.**

Chapter 20 · Writing Workshop

Personal Narrative

Learn What It Is

Stories about events in people's lives fascinate us. They are the focus of many television programs and articles in newspapers and magazines. You may have an interesting story to tell about your own life. Writing your own **personal narrative** may help you understand better why certain events in your life are so important to you.

Basics in a Box

PERSONAL NARRATIVE AT A GLANCE

Beginning

Introduces the incident, including the people and place involved

Middle

- Describes the event using descriptive details and dialogue
- Makes the importance clear

End

- Tells the outcome or result of the event
- Presents the writer's feelings about the experience

RUBRIC

Standards for Writing

A successful personal narrative should

- focus on one well-defined experience
- begin with an image or idea that makes readers want to find out more
- make the importance of the event clear
- show clearly the order in which events occurred
- use details that appeal to the senses to describe characters and setting
- use dialogue to develop characters
- provide a strong conclusion

414 Writing Workshop

WORKSHOP RESOURCES

 Time-Saver Transparencies Binder:
- Basics in a Box p. BB1
- Daily Test Preparation p. DT54
- Revising, Editing, and Proofreading Models pp. RE1–4

 Writing and Communication Masters pp. 26–34

Integrated Technology and Media

 Electronic Teacher Tools CD-ROM

 Writing Coach CD-ROM Personal Narrative

 mcdougallittell.com Additional Writing Prompts

See How It's Done: *Personal Narrative*

RUBRIC IN ACTION

Tackle Football

On a warm Friday in early October my friend asked me if I wanted to play tackle football after school.

"Someone's really going to get hurt one of these days," I said in my usual cautious way. "I bet one of us is going to break an arm or a leg."

"No one's going to get hurt," said Tom. "How many times have we played tackle football without getting more than a scrape or a bruise?"

"About a million times," I said, sort of agreeing with him. "Fine," I said, "I'll go."

Later that day, after we had been playing football for no longer than 15 minutes, it happened. Larry was tackled. I heard a loud snap and then screaming and crying, and not only from Larry. About three kids who were huddling around him were saying, "Oh, man! Oh, man!" over and over. Larry was on the ground, but I thought he had just a cut or a scrape. Then I saw it. His arm was snapped to the side just below his elbow. You could see the bone sticking through his skin!

Tom and I started running to find help. I ran faster than I ever had or probably ever will. When I got to a house, I started banging and pressing the doorbell as hard as I could. Finally the door opened.

"There's a kid over there who's really badly hurt!" I said, panting. "I really need to use your phone!"

"Settle down, young fella," the old man said. "The phone's in back." After about 40 seconds I was able to dial 911. My hands were shaking so hard!

A policewoman answered the phone and I said, "There's a kid over here and he's really badly hurt! He's at Herrington Park, right near the baseball field."

❶ Begins with a scene that makes readers want to find out what will happen

❷ Uses details that appeal to the senses

❸ Clearly shows the order in which events occurred

NARRATIVE

ANALYZING THE MODEL

Use the numbered questions below to make sure that students understand how the model satisfies the rubric.

❶ How does the writer make the reader want to find out what will happen?

He foreshadows the fact that somebody is going to get hurt.

❷ What details does the writer use to appeal to the senses?

"I heard a loud snap and then screaming and crying . . ."

"Then I saw it . . . . You could see the bone sticking through the skin!"

❸ What transition words does the writer use to clearly show the order of events?

"When I got to the house . . .";
"Finally the door opened."

TEACHING TIP

Write the following sensory words on the board: *fuzzy, freezing, warm, gooey, melodious, blaring, delicious, perfumed, salty, sweet.* Ask students to identify the sense that each word appeals to and discuss how sensory words help bring personal narratives to life.

NARRATIVE

THE LANGUAGE OF
LITERATURE

See the Personal Narrative Writing Workshop in *The Language of Literature,* Level 7.

---

4 **Critical Thinking** What do the lines of dialogue reveal about the characters?

Larry's dialogue reveals his sense of drama and kindheartedness. The police officer's dialogue reveals that he is insensitive and controlling.

5 What details make the importance of the event clear?

The presence of the police officer and the paramedics impress readers with the gravity of the situation.

6 What sensory words does the writer use to make the writing more vivid?

"screamed," "screeched," "blasting"

7 **Critical Thinking** How does the writer let the reader know how the event affected him?

He shows the effect by describing his shivering and his nightmares.

CUSTOMIZING TIP

Gifted and Talented Point out to students that the writer could have ended his personal narrative at an earlier point. Ask students to identify this alternative ending the paragraph ending "without saying anything". Then ask them to discuss which ending they prefer. Encourage students to evaluate the conclusion of the **Student Model** using the criteria described in the Rubric on page 414.

ASSESSMENT

 Assessment Masters:
- Writing Prompts p. 126
- Rubrics p. 135
- Student Models pp. 144–146

 Teacher's Guide to Assessment and Portfolio Use

"An ambulance is on its way," she said.

Slam! I hung up the phone and ran all the way back to Larry. A bunch of my friends were sitting near him with wide eyes and teary faces. I lay down near Larry and told him that an ambulance was coming.

"I'm going to die!" said Larry. "It hurts so much! I want you to give all my money to my mom and dad when I die!" he said, panting for air.

By the time a police officer got there, Larry was beginning to curse. "What did I just hear you say?" asked the police officer. He was just like the ones in the movies, a little chubby, dark sunglasses, and it looked like he had just eaten a powdered donut.

"Sir," I said, "the kid just broke his arm. See it?"

"I'll ask for your opinion when I want it, young man."

The police officer then started to talk to Larry until the ambulance came. Larry said that the pain had stopped. When the paramedics got him onto the stretcher, Larry screamed again. "Oww! The pain started again!"

Then the ambulance screeched away with sirens blasting and everything. We could hear it for a long time, and all of us just stood or sat there without saying anything.

On my way home, I started running as fast as I could for no reason. I was really thirsty, but when I got there, I just went to bed and tried to stop shivering.

I had nightmares for about a week after that.

4 Uses dialogue to develop the characters

5 Uses details to make the importance of the event clear

6 Includes sensory words to show the drama of events

7 Provides a strong conclusion by telling the effect the event had on the writer

---

Spice It Up!

Quotable Quote "Persons attempting to find a motive in this narrative will be prosecuted; persons attempting to find a moral in it will be banished; persons attempting to find a plot in it will be shot."—Mark Twain, *The Adventures of Huckleberry Finn*

Have students discuss the meaning of this quote. Do they think that Mark Twain *really* doesn't want people to interpret his narrative? Or do they think he wants the readers to look for exactly the elements of narrative that he is warning them about?

Do It Yourself

Writing Prompt Select an event from your own experience, and write a personal narrative about it.

Purpose To entertain and inform

Audience Friends, classmates

1 Prewriting

Brainstorm topics. Think of subjects to write about by recalling what you remember most about a vacation, a school event, or a favorite place.

For more topic ideas, see the Idea Bank, p. 420.

Freewrite about one event. How did things look, smell, feel, taste, sound? Who was there? What was the most interesting part? Circle the idea that interests you the most. You may be able to use that idea as your focus.

Analyze why you care. Think about why this event sticks in your mind. Did you learn something important? Did it change your life in any way?

2 Drafting

Consider the organization. Every narrative must have a beginning, middle, and end. Can you fit the key elements of your narrative into the chart below?

Organization of a Personal Narrative

Beginning	Middle	End
• Who was involved? • What happened? • What will grab a reader's attention?	• How did the event progress? • What caused each part to happen?	• What changed after the event? • Why is this event meaningful to you?

Think about descriptive details. What words or images can you use to make readers see, hear, and feel what is happening?

Wrap it up. Make sure that by the end of your story, readers will understand what happened and why it was important to you.

For information about getting feedback from your peers, see p. 421.

TEACHING TIP

Cooperative Learning Divide students into small groups and ask them to share memories that they might write about. This brainstorming may help trigger ideas.

TEACHING TIP

Speaking and Listening/Paired Activity As an alternative to freewriting, encourage students to work in pairs and take turns describing the event. Partners should listen and ask questions that elicit more vivid descriptions of the event.

TEACHING TIP

Cross-Curricular Connection

History Encourage students who have witnessed or participated in a local newsmaking event to use the event as a writing topic. Students can supplement their narratives with research from the library or the Internet.

CUSTOMIZING TIP

Less Proficient Learners Some students may have difficulty organizing their narratives. You might suggest that these students organize the events in their narratives on a time line.

NARRATIVE

Cooperative Learning/Paired Activity Have students exchange copies of their personal narratives with peer readers. Emphasize the importance of "friendly feedback" by referring students to the questions in the Student Help Desk. In this activity, students are expected to respond in constructive ways to others' writing.

Students Acquiring English/ESL In some languages, dialogue is indicated by a dash or by special quotation marks, such as << and >>, " and „. Remind students to use standard American quotation marks to punctuate dialogue.

❸ Revising

TARGET SKIL ▸Using Dialogue Quoting people directly can make your essay lively and easy to read. For more help with revising, review the rubric on page 414.

> "Sir,"
> ^ I said, that the kid just broke his arm, ~~and I pointed to it.~~ see it?"
> ¶ The officer told me he would ask for my opinion when he "I'll   your   I
> wanted it. ^ young man."

❹ Editing and Proofreading

TARGET SKILL ▸Punctuating Dialogue Put quotation marks around the speaker's exact words. Put end punctuation inside the quotation marks.

> When the paramedics got him onto the stretcher, Larry
> screamed again. "Oww! The pain has started again "!
> ^

For more about quotation marks, see p. 248.

❺ Sharing and Reflecting

You can **share** your personal narrative with others by making copies for friends and classmates. You might want to put the work of several classmates together into booklets.

For Your Working Portfolio It can be helpful to read others' work to help you **reflect** on your own writing. Read published writers as well as peers and identify the strategies they used to write their personal narratives. How can these other writers help you learn to write better? Attach your reflections to your finished work. Save your narrative in your 📁 **Working Portfolio.**

Drive-Through Grammar

Punctuating Dialogue Tell students that question marks and exclamation points go inside the quotation marks only if they are part of the quotation. Question marks and exclamation points should be placed outside the quotation marks if they are not part of the quotation. Write the following sentences on the board and have students add quotation marks correctly.

He asked Sam, Do you want to be an astronaut?

He asked Sam, "Do you want to be an astronaut?"

I couldn't believe she said, You failed!

I couldn't believe she said, "You failed"!

Speak for Yourself: *Telling an Anecdote*

"I'll never forget the time Larry broke his arm when we were playing football. . . ."

When you share a story like this, recalling a funny or interesting incident, you are telling an anecdote. Turning your **personal narrative** into an anecdote is a way to present your story orally in an entertaining and informal way.

Here's How Creating an Anecdote

- Choose a specific part of your narrative to share. Pick the section that has the most action or the most interesting characters.

- Think about what you could add to the story, or places where you could condense what you wrote.

- Change your more formal written language to everyday, conversational language.

- Act out the parts. Use different voices for each character.

- Memorize your anecdote so you are free to add gestures and voices.

- Ask a friend to listen as you practice telling the story.

For more information on speaking skills, see p. 545–47.

see p. 545–47.

TEACHING TIP

Remind students that an anecdote is a very short narrative. Point out that an anecdotes, like other narratives, contains story elements such as characters, setting, and plot.

TEACHING TIP

Paired Activity Have students get together with a partner and take turns presenting their anecdotes. Tell the listener to help the speaker by giving feedback on the delivery of the anecdote. Have the listener focus on the speaker's voice, gestures, eye contact, and speed of delivery.

NARRATIVE

NARRATIVE

Personal Narrative   **419**

Student Help Desk

Students can use the Student Help Desk as a quick review or as a quick reference as they write their personal narratives.

Teacher's Notes
WHAT WORKS:

Student Help Desk

Personal Narrative at a Glance

Beginning	Middle	End
Introduces the incident, including the people and place involved	• Describes the event using descriptive details and dialogue • Makes the importance clear	• Tells the outcome or result of the event • Presents the writer's feelings about the experience

Idea Bank

Need a topic for a personal narrative?

Write about when a special pet did something funny.

Choose an event that helped you deal with anger or disappointment.

Think of someone who surprised you by being different from what you expected.

Remember a time when you were really scared.

Recall how you felt when you walked into a group of people and you didn't know any of them.

Read a personal narrative by someone else to give you ideas. Try a narrative such as Ernesto Galarza's *Barrio Boy* (*Language of Literature*, Grade 7).

Sensory Details

Add details like these to your personal narrative.

Sense	Details
Sight	*bright, green, dark*
Sound	*loud, buzzing*
Touch	*cold, rough*
Smell	*lemony, smoky*
Taste	*sour, sweet*

420 Writing Workshop

Friendly Feedback

Questions for Your Peer Reader

- What is the subject of my narrative?
- What did you like best about my narrative?
- How do I show that the subject is important to me?
- What details are most memorable?
- How could I make what happened more clear?
- What could I do to make either the beginning or the ending more interesting?

Publishing Options

Print	Begin a scrapbook that will contain essays about interesting events in your life.
Oral Communication	Form a circle of friends who will read or tell your personal narratives to one another. Practice using gestures and tone of voice to communicate actions and feelings. Ask your audience to give you feedback on the effectiveness of your presentation.
Online	Check out **mcdougallittell.com** for more publishing options.

The Bottom Line

Checklist for Personal Narrative

Have I . . .

- ____ focused on one particular experience?
- ____ used an interesting beginning?
- ____ made the importance of the event clear?
- ____ made the order of events clear?
- ____ included details that appeal to the senses?
- ____ used dialogue when appropriate?
- ____ written a strong ending?

A Slice of Life

Noah Webster—

An educator of the late eighteenth and nineteenth centuries, best known for his *American Dictionary of the English Language* and *Blue-Backed Speller,* Noah Webster worked to establish a distinctive American version of the English language. For example, he insisted on such spellings as *wagon, center,* and *honor,* in place of the standard British *waggon, centre,* and *honour.*

Teacher's Notes
WHAT DOESN'T WORK:

TEACHER'S LOUNGE

Brain Booster

"Once you begin to read, learn to pause, every half page, and write down key ideas, thoughts, and facts. You might add the information to a visual map. Keep the information useful to you. Add pictures, drawings, or illustrations to what you write down. The colors and doodles that you add to your mind map will help your brain understand and remember it better."

—Eric Jensen, M.A.

CHAPTER OBJECTIVES

To analyze and write an effective character description

 DAILY TEST PREPARATION

Error Identification: Capitalization
Write the following item on the board or use 📊 **Daily Test Preparation Transparency** p. DT55.
Decide which type of error, if any, appears in the underlined section.

> Recent <u>archaeological finds have turned up alternative versions of the koran.</u>

A. Spelling error
B. Capitalization error
C. Punctuation error
D. No error

Teaching Point: Error identification questions often test your knowledge of basic capitalization rules. This item tests whether you know to capitalize the names of religious scriptures, such as the *Koran*.

The **Basics in a Box** provides graphic and verbal guidelines for writing a character description. The cluster diagram indicates the types of details that the description should include.

The **RUBRIC**, or Standards for Writing, describes a character description that would merit the highest score. A complete rubric, describing several levels of proficiency, is on page 136 of the 📄 **Assessment Masters.**

Character Description

Learn What It Is

An artist draws a sketch to give a quick impression of a person. A writer can accomplish the same goal with words. Like a sketch, a **character description** includes details about how the person looks and feels and what the person does and says, for example, that give readers a quick impression.

Basics in a Box

CHARACTER DESCRIPTION AT A GLANCE

- physical description
- person's actions and speech
- mannerisms of person
- **Main Impression of Subject**
- writer's feelings about the person
- other people's reactions to the person
- surroundings

RUBRIC

Standards for Writing

A successful character description should

- describe the personality and physical appearance of the person
- give a main impression of the person
- include dialogue, descriptions, and other devices that show, rather than tell, what the character is like
- reveal the writer's response to the person
- place the person in surroundings that will help readers understand him or her
- have a clearly organized structure, an effective beginning, and a strong conclusion

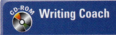 **Writing Coach**

WORKSHOP RESOURCES

 Time-Saver Transparencies Binder:
- Basics in a Box p. BB2
- Critical Thinking Graphic Organizers p. CT23
- Daily Test Preparation p. DT55
- Quick-Fix Grammar and Style Charts p. QF6
- Revising, Editing, and Proofreading Models pp. RE5–8

 Writing and Communication Masters pp. 35–43

Integrated Technology and Media

 Electronic Teacher Tools CD-ROM

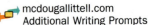 mcdougallittell.com
Additional Writing Prompts

See How It's Done: *Character Description*

RUBRIC
IN ACTION

Fallen Ballerina

Shannon's hands were like a baby's, so soft and pudgy. Her skin was fair and soft. Her hair was like black velvet. She smelled of medicine and flowers. Shannon's speech was mumbled and hard to understand because of the tubes that went down her nose and throat. At the time I thought that she was lucky to have an oxygen tank and I wanted one badly. Now, I realize that her oxygen tank was only prolonging her death. . . .

I remember carrying Shannon's oxygen tank around because she was so little that she couldn't support the weight. We met in first grade, and Shannon's oxygen tank was very small. At that time she could go outside and play like all of the other kids. As the year went on, her tank got bigger and bigger, and her playing time got smaller. It seemed as Shannon's tank grew, so did our friendship. Later in the year, Shannon missed more and more school, because she spent her time home sick, or in the hospital. When she was in school, she had to sit in a soft chair, and toward the end, she couldn't move very much at all. That is when I started to read to her. . . .

I can remember reading to her during recess, because she could not go outside for fear of getting holes in her oxygen tubes. When I read to Shannon, I would hold her soft, puffy hand. Every now and again, I would make a mistake, and Shannon would correct me. Some days, she would read to me. We would read books about princesses or ponies, because those were the things she loved most. . . .

❶ Presents details about the person's physical appearance

❷ Places the person in a setting that enables readers to understand more about her situation

❸ Describes the writer's interaction with the character

DESCRIPTION

Character Description **423**

ANALYZING THE MODEL
Use the numbered questions below to make sure that students understand how the model satisfies the rubric.

❶ What details does the writer use to describe her subject's appearance?

She describes her subject's soft and pudgy hands, her velvety hair, and the fact that she smelled of medicine and flowers.

❷ What does the setting tell us about Shannon's situation?

At school, she must sit in a soft chair, which is an indication of her declining health.

❸ **Critical Thinking** What does the writer's interaction with Shannon suggest about the writer?

She was loving and patient with Shannon.

DESCRIPTION

TEACHING TIP

Speaking and Listening Read aloud the opening paragraph of the **Student Model.** Have students listen for and then describe the mood that the writer establishes. Ask students to support their ideas with images and descriptions that convey the mood.

THE LANGUAGE OF
LITERATURE

See the Character Sketch Writing Workshop in *The Language of Literature,* Level 7.

Assessment

 Assessment Masters:
- Writing Prompts p. 127
- Rubrics p. 136
- Student Models pp. 147–149

 Teacher's Guide to Assessment and Portfolio Use

Students Acquiring English/ESL

Side by Side pp. 25, 43–54

4 What do the descriptions reveal about Shannon?

She was like other girls her age.

5 What impression does the writer give of Shannon in the funeral description?

That Shannon was very loving.

6 Critical Thinking What impact do you think Shannon had on the writer's life?

Shannon taught the writer about compassion and acceptance of death.

Other than her tubes and tanks, Shannon was just like all the other girls at school. She thought boys had cooties and Barbies were the best thing next to chocolate chip cookies. Shannon's black hair was always up in pretty braids or in a cute little bun. She wanted to be a ballerina when she grew up. She even used to bring a tutu to school. Shannon and I would dance and play dolls during free time.

Shannon will never get the chance to be a ballerina. I often wonder why Shannon, who wanted something so badly, can never have it and why I, who never really wanted to be a dancer, have a chance to be one. . . .

Shannon's funeral was beautiful. There were pink and white flowers everywhere. Pictures of her favorite items, stuffed animals and dolls, filled the room. Shannon was a very loving person, and many people came to her funeral.

When I saw Shannon lying in her casket, she looked like she was asleep, with her pretty blue dress and her favorite doll in her arms. With all the tubes and the oxygen bottle gone, I remember thinking that for the first time Shannon looked peaceful. She looked very beautiful. . . .

I live close to the cemetery where Shannon is buried. Every time I go there, I stop and talk to her. I only wish that she could be talking with me, but I know that she's listening. I believe that Shannon's short time with me has made me richer.

4 This writer includes descriptions that show, rather than tell, what the character is like.

Another option: Include dialogue that reveals the character's personality.

5 Gives a main impression of the character

6 Ends with a strong statement expressing the impact that the character had on the writer's life

Do It Yourself

Writing Prompt Write a character description of someone you find fascinating.

Purpose To show why the person is especially interesting

Audience Classmates or anyone else who might be interested

❶ Prewriting

First, choose a person. Make a list of people whom you really like, admire, or find interesting.

For more ideas, see the Idea Bank, p. 428.

Freewrite. Make a list of words and phrases that come to mind about the person—*grows the tallest sunflowers, has the silliest laugh, taught me to ride a bike.*

Focus on your strongest image of the person. When you think of your subject, what is the first thing you see that person doing? Where is the person? What is he or she wearing? Record your thoughts in a chart like the one below.

Observations of a Person	
Physical appearance	*dirty uniform, wispy hair*
Voice	*high, silly laugh*
Mannerisms	*pulls ear*
Personality	*friendly, laughs often*

Choose a main idea. Focus only on memories of your subject or select just one that will give your readers a strong impression of the person.

❷ Drafting

Use vivid details. Try to visualize your subject as you write. Refer to your lists of words and phrases and your chart of observations to help you choose details. For example, don't just say that your subject wore a dirty uniform. Help readers picture the stain: "Ice cream, catsup, and specks of sand formed an almost planned pattern on the front of her uniform."

For information about getting feedback from your peers, see p. 429.

Character Description **425**

TEACHING TIP

Tell students that additional writing prompts can be found at ↵⬚ **mcdougallittell.com.**

CUSTOMIZING TIP

Addressing Learning Styles

Visual Have students think like an artist. How would a painter effectively convey a subject's appearance, mannerisms, and personality? Suggest that students create rough drawings of their subjects before they start writing to discover which characteristics they should focus on in their essays.

Especially suitable for: Less Proficient Learners

DESCRIPTION

CUSTOMIZING TIP

Students Acquiring English/ESL For visual practice with adding sensory details to a paragraph, have students use **Side by Side** p. 25.

TEACHING TIP

Cooperative Learning Have students review each other's work in small groups. Have students identify the most vivid and powerful details in each draft. Then have the peers list aspects that might need improvement. Ask students to revise their drafts by adding, elaborating, deleting, combining, or rearranging text.

DESCRIPTION

Spice It Up!

Have students get together in pairs and take turns describing the physical appearance, voice, mannerisms, and personality of celebrity subjects—actors, singers, comedians, politicians, and so on. Partners should use the descriptions to guess each subject's identity.

MORE MODEL SENTENCES

Write the following sentences on the board. Ask students to choose more vivid and descriptive words.

Anna wore a nice dress with a pretty pattern. She stood in the bright sunshine.

Possible revision: Anna wore a red dress with pretty white flowers on it. She stood in the glaring sunshine.

TEACHING TIP

Gifted and Talented Remind students to avoid excessive descriptions in their character sketches. Explain that when they describe a character, too much information can distract or bore the reader. Encourage students to elaborate on one or two characteristics that are central to their subjects' identities.

ASSESSMENT

 Assessment Masters:
- Writing Prompts p. 127
- Rubrics p. 136
- Student Models pp. 147–149

 Teacher's Guide to Assessment and Portfolio Use

---

❸ Revising

TARGET SKILL ▶ **Making Effective Word Choices** Choosing the right words can make the difference between a description that is adequate and one that is fascinating. For instance, saying that someone is messy is not nearly as descriptive as saying that mounds of clothes covered almost every inch of the person's room. Effective words will give readers more to see. For more help with revising, review the rubric on page 422.

> Shannon's hands were like a baby's, so soft and ~~fat~~ *pudgy*. Her skin was ~~smooth~~ *fair and soft*. Her hair was like a black ~~crayon~~ *velvet*. She smelled ~~both strong~~ *of medicine* and ~~sweet~~ *flowers*.

❹ Editing and Proofreading

TARGET SKILL ▶ **Correcting Pronoun Case** If a pronoun is used as the subject of a sentence, use *I, she,* or *he.* If a pronoun is used as an object, use *me, her,* or *him.*

> Shannon and ~~me~~ *I* would dance and play dolls during free time.

For more help with pronoun case, see pp. 56–89.

❺ Sharing and Reflecting

After you have organized and edited your character description, **share** it with another person or a group, either by handing out copies or by reading it to them. Have them give you feedback on the effectiveness of your character description.

For Your Working Portfolio Use the readers' reactions and comments to **reflect** on how effective your description is. Can the audience picture the person clearly? Does the person's personality come through? Make notes on what you might do to make the character sketch even more effective. Save your notes and your description in your 📁 **Working Portfolio.**

426 Writing Workshop

Drive-Through Grammar

Subject and Object Case Pronouns

Students sometimes have difficulty selecting the correct pronoun form in a compound subject or compound object. To decide on the correct form, suggest that they try each pronoun separately with the verb. Write the following sentences on the board and have students use this technique to identify the correct pronoun form.

She gave Michael and (I, me) the letter.

Sarah and (he, him) will leave tomorrow.

Speak for Yourself: *Roleplaying a Character*

"I love books about princesses and ponies."

History lessons can be much more interesting when guest speakers assume the roles of historical figures. Sometimes comedians have great success in entertaining when they assume the role of another person. They speak to the audience as that person—the bus driver, the worried parent, the rebellious child. You can make your **character description** especially memorable by turning it into a roleplay in which you become the character you wrote about.

Give Women the VOTE

Here's How Creating a Character

- Decide what aspects of your character to focus on. What parts of your character's life would be most interesting to your audience?

- Create a script in which you present yourself as the character, telling the audience about yourself. Use the pronoun "I" when referring to the character.

- Use costumes, props, or anything else to make you look like your character.

- Include some dialogue so your character has a chance to speak rather than simply tell about an event or another person.

For more information on speaking skills, see p. 545–47.

For more information on speaking skills, see p. 545–47.

Character Description **427**

TEACHING TIP

Cross-Curricular Connection History Encourage students to research a historical figure that they could role-play for the class. For example, students could research and role-play Susan B. Anthony, Martin Luther King, Jr., or Harriet Tubman.

TEACHING TIP

Have students discuss and generate criteria to evaluate their own oral presentations and the presentations of others. Use the **Critical Thinking Graphic Organizer Rubric for Evaluation,** p. CT23, to demonstrate how students can organize their criteria.

TEACHING TIP

Encourage students to imitate their character's manner of speaking. For example, if their character speaks in a particular dialect (from another region or time), have students affect the same accent when they present their role-play. Doing so will help students understand how language use reflects regions or cultures.

DESCRIPTION

DESCRIPTION

Student Help Desk

Student Help Desk

Students can use the Student Help Desk as a quick review or as a quick reference as they write their character descriptions.

Teacher's Notes

WHAT WORKS:

Character Description at a Glance

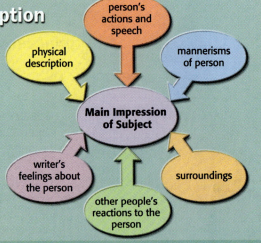

Idea Bank

Tips for finding a subject

Make a list of people who have been important in your life since your childhood.

Recall the most unusual person you ever knew.

Think of a person who is not famous but should be.

Look through a magazine or a newspaper for a well-known person you admire or one who puzzles you.

Choose a beloved pet or a neighbor's pet that has been terrorizing you.

Read literature featuring a character description to see the strategies a published author uses. Try "An Hour with Abuelo" by Judith Ortiz Cofer (*The Language of Literature*, Grade 7).

Adding Details

Don't Tell	Show
Her knee hurt.	She winced when she bent her knee to sit down.
He felt cold.	The wind whistled through his thin jacket and made him shiver.
She yelled at her younger brother.	"Stop it! Can't you do anything right?" she roared as the boy tried to look away from her.

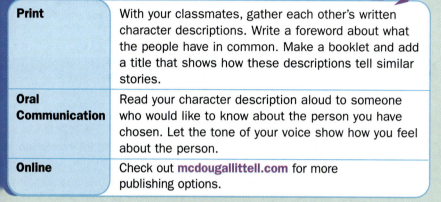

Friendly Feedback

Questions for Your Peer Reader

- How would you describe my character?
- How do you think I feel about this character?
- What was the most interesting part of the character description?
- How could I have done a better job of showing instead of telling?
- Where should I have added more details?

Publishing Options

Print	With your classmates, gather each other's written character descriptions. Write a foreword about what the people have in common. Make a booklet and add a title that shows how these descriptions tell similar stories.
Oral Communication	Read your character description aloud to someone who would like to know about the person you have chosen. Let the tone of your voice show how you feel about the person.
Online	Check out **mcdougallittell.com** for more publishing options.

The Bottom Line

Checklist for Character Description

Have I . . .

____ given vivid details about the physical appearance and the personality of the character?

____ given a main impression of the person?

____ included dialogue and mannerisms to show, rather than tell, what the character is like?

____ made the time and place obvious?

____ let readers know my reaction to the person?

____ used an effective beginning, a clearly organized middle, and a strong ending?

DESCRIPTION

DESCRIPTION

TEACHER'S LOUNGE

A Slice of Life

"Be kind, for everyone you meet is fighting a hard battle."—Plato

A Slice of Life

"See if you can think of something really thoughtful to do for someone, and don't expect anything in return—whether it's surprising your spouse with a clean garage or organized desk, mowing your neighbor's lawn, or coming home early from work to give your spouse a break from the kids. When you complete your favor, see if you can tap into the warm feeling of knowing you have done something really nice without expecting anything from the person you have just helped. If you practice, you will discover that the feelings themselves are reward enough."—Richard Carlson, Ph.D.

CHAPTER OBJECTIVES

To explore and write a personal response to a poem

DAILY TEST PREPARATION

**Sentence Completion:
Vocabulary** Write the following item on the board or use ⬛ **Daily Test Preparation Transparency** p. DT55.
Choose the word that *best* fits the meaning of the sentence.

John made only a _____ attempt to do his homework over the weekend.

A. sturdy

B. superficially

C. considerable

D. feeble

See ⬛ **Time-Saver Transparencies Binder** for the Teaching Point.

The ▮ Basics in a Box ▮ provides graphic and verbal guidelines for organizing a successful interpretation of a poem. The open book details the types of evidence that can be used to support a response.

The ▮ RUBRIC ▮ , or Standards for Writing, describes an interpretation of a poem that would merit the highest score.
A complete rubric, describing several levels of proficiency, is on page 137 of the ⬛ **Assessment Masters.**

Interpreting a Poem

Learn What It Is

You probably have had strong reactions to a poem, whether you liked or disliked it. You may have loved a poem that tells a story, or perhaps a poem helped you explore feelings that puzzled you. When you read a poem more than once, you often discover new meanings. Writing to **interpret a poem** means going below the surface to find the deeper meanings waiting for you.

Basics in a Box

INTERPRETING A POEM AT A GLANCE

Introduction
Introduces the title, author, and a clear statement of your response

Body
Supports the response with evidence from the work

Evidence

examples from the poem

quotations

specific reactions

Conclusion
Summarizes the response

RUBRIC

Standards for Writing

A successful interpretation of a poem should

- state the title and author of the poem
- give a clearly stated interpretation of the poem's message
- present examples from the poem to support the interpretation
- use transitions to guide the reader
- summarize the interpretation in the conclusion

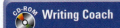

WORKSHOP RESOURCES

 Time-Saver Transparencies Binder:
- Basics in a Box p. BB3
- Daily Test Preparation p. DT55
- Revising, Editing, and Proofreading Models pp. RE9–12
- Writing and Communication Skills pp. WC6–8

 Writing and Communication Masters pp. 44–52

Integrated Technology and Media

 Electronic Teacher Tools CD-ROM

 Writing Coach CD-ROM
Writing About Literature: Interpretive Essay

See How It's Done: *Interpreting a Poem*

The Rider

A boy told me
if he rollerskated fast enough
his loneliness couldn't catch up to him,

the best reason I ever heard
for trying to be a champion.

What I wonder tonight
pedaling hard down King William Street
is if it translates to bicycles.

A victory! To leave your loneliness
panting behind you on some
   street corner
while you float free into a cloud
  of sudden azaleas,
luminous pink petals that have
   never felt loneliness,
no matter how slowly they fell.

             —Naomi Shihab Nye

Student Model
Elizabeth Albertson
Chute Middle School

Response to "The Rider"

When I read the poem "The Rider" by Naomi Shihab Nye, I noticed that there didn't seem to be a hidden message that required a lot of interpretation. However, that's not to say that the idea expressed in the poem is unimportant. I think the speaker of this poem is trying to describe how certain events or activities have the power to remove fears and worries.

A boy has told the speaker that "if he rollerskated fast enough his loneliness couldn't catch up to him." The speaker seems to be lonely when she thinks about this because she tries to apply it to herself. She wonders whether this idea will apply to bicycling, which is what she herself is doing. For

RUBRIC IN ACTION

1 Names the poem and author

2 Clearly states the interpretation of the poem

3 Tells enough about the poem so that readers who are not familiar with it can understand this response

POEM

Interpreting a Poem **431**

TEACHING TIP

Speaking and Listening Read the poem aloud and have students discuss their reactions to specific lines. Then ask: What mood does the poet create? What images in the poem contribute to this mood?

ANALYZING THE MODEL

Use the numbered questions below to make sure that students understand how the model satisfies the rubric.

1 Who wrote "The Rider"?
Author: Naomi Shihab Nye

2 What is the writer's interpretation of the poem's message?

She thinks the poem is describing how certain events or activities have the power to remove fear and worries.

3 How does the writer tell the reader about the poem?

The writer quotes specific lines from the poem and summarizes other lines.

THE LANGUAGE OF LITERATURE

See the Response to Literature Writing Workshop in *The Language of Literature*, Level 7.

POEM

 mcdougallittell.com
Additional Writing Prompts

Assessment

 Assessment Masters:
- Writing Prompts p. 128
- Rubrics p. 137
- Student Models pp. 150–152

 Teacher's Guide to Assessment and Portfolio Use

Students Acquiring English/ESL

Side by Side pp. 55–66.

④ Critical Thinking What feeling does the poet create with the quoted line about "a cloud of sudden azaleas"?

A feeling of freedom, beauty, and wonder

⑤ Critical Thinking How does the poem relate to the writer's own life?

The feelings evoked by the poem remind her of how her worries seem to disappear while taking part in sports and other activities.

⑥ How does the writer summarize her response?

She states that she believes Nye conveys an important message in a simple way—that loneliness can be forgotten when one engages in an enjoyable task.

her, to bike is to "float free into a cloud of sudden azaleas," which I have taken to mean that she is so focused on going faster that her mind forgets all worries and concentrates on that one goal.

I love the way the poet uses personification to describe the loneliness. When the speaker says, "A victory! To leave your loneliness panting behind you on some street corner," it almost seems that the loneliness is a person, trying to catch up with her as she rides and trying to take her focus away from the wonderful feeling of bicycling.

When I read this poem, I couldn't help thinking about my own experiences taking part in sports and different activities. During some activities my mind is incapable of thinking about anything other than doing my best, and all of my other thoughts and worries seem to disappear. However, I have found that this incredible feeling cannot happen unless I'm doing something that I love to do. For example, when I play softball, if I'm into the game, I don't worry about having to do something great. My worries leave me and I can think of nothing but having fun.

I think this poem is very well written. Naomi Shihab Nye's strength is her ability to convey an important message simply. She believes that loneliness can be left behind when you are doing something you enjoy and are "trying to be a champion."

④ Supports statements with quotations and details

⑤ This writer gives her personal reactions and responses to the poem.

Another option: Intersperse references to or quotations from the poem along with personal experiences.

⑥ Summarizes the interpretation of the poem in the conclusion

Do It Yourself

Writing Prompt   Write a personal response to a poem.

Purpose To share your reaction

Audience Classmates, teacher, others who would be interested

❶ Prewriting

Select a poem. You might choose a poem that you already know well and love. You can use your essay to share your enthusiasm. You might choose a poem that puzzles you and use your essay to either figure out why it puzzles you or to explain why you don't understand it.

For more topic ideas, see the Idea Bank, p. 436.

- **Read and reread.** Go through the poem line by line. Make notes as you read. Write down anything that comes to mind. Don't worry about whether your ideas are good or bad.
- **Think about your reactions.** Ask yourself how the poem relates to your own life, as well as your own thoughts and feelings.
- **Think about your audience.** What will readers need to know in order to understand your essay?

❷ Drafting

Start writing. Write down your thoughts in as much detail as possible. Keep in mind that there are no right or wrong ideas when you are responding to a poem. What is important is to express your own response as honestly and as clearly as you can. After you have written your ideas down, revise them, as needed, to make sure that you have an introduction, a body, and a conclusion.

- **Introduction:** Include the title, the author's name, and your response to the poem.
- **Body:** Support your response with quotations and details.
- **Conclusion:** Summarize your response.

For information on getting feedback from your peers, see p. 437.

Interpreting a Poem   **433**

POEM

POEM

Spice It Up!

Quotable Quote "Painting is silent poetry, and poetry painting that speaks." —Simonides
Have students write poems based on paintings. Suggest that they try to communicate to the reader of their poem what they think the painter wanted to communicate to the viewer of his or her painting. Ask volunteers to read their poems to the class.

TEACHING TIP

Paired Activity/Speaking and Listening Have student pairs take turns reading aloud their drafts. While one student reads, the other listens for and identifies areas where examples could be used to further elaborate statements made about the poem.

CUSTOMIZING TIP

Students Acquiring English/ESL If students would like to include quotations in their interpretation, remind them to use standard American quotation marks. Quotation marks vary across languages, and students might be tempted to use marks such as « and » or „ and „.

CUSTOMIZING TIP

Gifted and Talented Encourage students who are fond of a poem they have analyzed to research other works by the same poet in the library or on the Internet.

NEED MORE INFORMATION?

For additional information on proofreading marks, direct students to **Chapter 12, The Writing Process.**

ASSESSMENT

 Assessment Masters:
- Writing Prompts p. 128
- Rubrics p. 137
- Student Models pp. 150–152

Teacher's Guide to Assessment and Portfolio Use

❸ Revising

TARGET SKILL ▶ Elaborating with Examples When responding to a poem, you should give specific examples to help your readers understand your reactions. For more help with revising, review the rubric on page 430.

> For her, to bike is to "float free into a cloud of sudden az-aleas," which I have taken to mean
> ~~I think~~ that ~~when she bikes~~ she is so focused on going faster that her mind forgets all worries and concentrates on that one goal.

❹ Editing and Proofreading

TARGET SKILL ▶ Using Correct Punctuation and Spelling For your ideas to be clear to your reader, you must use correct punctuation and spelling. Use a dictionary or a word processing program to check your spelling.

> The speaker
> ~~She~~ seems to be ~~lonly~~ lonely when she thinks about this because she tries to apply it to herself. she wonders whether ~~or not~~ this idea will apply to bicycling. Which is what she herself is doing.

For more about punctuation and spelling, see pp. 250–69 and 628–35.

❺ Sharing and Reflecting

Share your response with others who wrote about the same poem. Hold a discussion about the varied interpretations.

For Your Working Portfolio After you have shared your response, reflect on the experience of writing it. Did it help you understand the poem better? Did it help you understand something about yourself? Attach your answers to your interpretation and save them both in your 📁 **Working Portfolio.**

Drive-Through Grammar

Using Commas When students write a personal interpretation of a poem, they often use more than one adjective to describe a particular image or mood. Tell students that they can determine whether the adjectives are of equal rank—and so should be separated by commas—by placing *and* between them. If *and* sounds natural and can be used to reverse the order of the adjectives, then a comma is needed. Write the following sentences on the board and have students add commas as needed.

The red rubber ball bounced into the street. no comma needed

On Friday, she wore baggy old blue jeans to school. comma after baggy

Speak for Yourself: *Oral Interpretation*

"A *victory!* To leave your loneliness . . . *panting* behind you. . . ."

A poem you have found difficult to understand may become clear when you hear it read aloud with expression and gestures. You can take the **interpretation of a poem** you wrote and express your ideas by interpreting the poem orally.

A boy told me *(slowly)*
if he rollerskated fast enough *(faster)*
(slow with emphasis)
his loneliness couldn't

catch up to him. *(pause)*

Here's How) Oral Interpretation

- Plan how you will communicate your interpretation. Where will you make your voice loud? soft? On what lines will you speed up or slow down? Where will you pause? What tone of voice will you use? angry? sad? amused? thoughtful?

- Practice reading the poem out loud. Make notes on the poem for pauses, gestures, tone of voice, and rhythm.

- Read the poem in front of an audience. Act it out enough so that the meaning of each word is communicated.

- You might follow your reading with a brief explanation of your interpretation.

- Invite questions and discussion from your audience.

For more information on speaking skills, see p. 545–49.

For more information on speaking skills, see p. 545–49.

POEM

POEM

Interpreting a Poem **435**

Student Help Desk

Students can use the Student Help Desk as a quick review or reference as they interpret poetry.

Teacher's Notes
WHAT WORKS:

Student Help Desk

Interpreting a Poem at a Glance

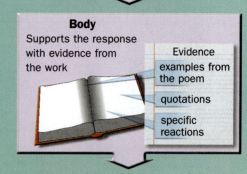

Introduction
Introduces the title, author, and a clear statement of your response

Body
Supports the response with evidence from the work

Evidence
- examples from the poem
- quotations
- specific reactions

Conclusion
Summarizes the response

Idea Bank

Tips for choosing a poem to interpret

Make a list of the poems you have studied in class to help you choose a poem.

Note your reactions. Make a list of things you might say about several poems: how each poem makes you feel, what you don't understand, what you find particularly interesting. Then choose the one that inspires you the most to talk about.

Ask other people to talk about their favorite poems.

Including Quotations

Quoting directly from the poem at key points will

- support your opinions
- help give your readers a feel for the work
- help give vigor to your own words

However, do not use too many quotes. After all, the interpretation is supposed to show your own ideas.

Friendly Feedback

Questions for Your Peer Reader

- What did I seem to feel most strongly about?
- What was my main point?
- What could have been stated more clearly?
- What seemed to be unnecessary?

Publishing Options

Print	Submit your response to a student literary magazine.
Oral Communication	Present the poem as an oral interpretation. Use your voice and gestures to convey the emotional content of your interpretation. Follow the presentation with a discussion about your presentation.
Online	Check out **mcdougallittell.com** for more publishing options.

The Bottom Line

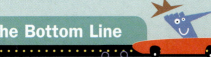

Checklist for Interpreting a Poem

Have I . . .

____ named the title and the author in the introduction?

____ clearly stated how I feel about the poem in the introduction?

____ told enough about the poem so that readers who are unfamiliar with it can understand my response?

____ given my specific reactions and responses to the work?

____ supported my statements with quotations and details from the poem?

____ summarized my response to the poem in the conclusion?

Interpreting a Poem **437**

POEM

POEM

Cause-and-Effect Essay

CHAPTER OBJECTIVES

To analyze and write an effective cause-and-effect essay

The **Basics in a Box** provides visual and verbal guidelines for writing a cause-and-effect essay. The graphic indicates ways to order causes and effects in the body.

The **RUBRIC**, or Standards for Writing, describes a cause-and-effect essay that would merit the highest score. A complete rubric, describing several levels of proficiency, is on page 138 of the **Assessment Masters.**

Learn What It Is

Why do athletes exercise and eat balanced diets? It's so that they can keep their bodies in tiptop shape. They see a relationship between diet and exercise and physical fitness. Writing a **cause-and-effect essay** can help you examine the causes leading up to an effect as well as the effects of an event or action.

Basics in a Box

CAUSE-AND-EFFECT ESSAY AT A GLANCE

Introduction
Introduces the subject

Body
Describes the cause and its effects*

cause

effect effect effect

Conclusion
Summary

*or presents an effect and then analyzes the causes

RUBRIC

Standards for Writing

A successful cause-and-effect essay should

- clearly identify the cause-and-effect relationship
- provide any necessary background information
- make clear the relationship between causes and effects
- arrange details logically and include transitions to show relationships between causes and effects
- summarize the cause-and-effect relationship in the conclusion

WORKSHOP RESOURCES

 Time-Saver Transparencies Binder:
- Basics in a Box p. BB4
- Critical Thinking Graphic Organizers p. CT15
- Daily Test Preparation p. DT56
- Quick-Fix Grammar and Style Charts p. QF1
- Revising, Editing, and Proofreading Models pp. RE13–16

- Writing and Communication Skills pp. WC5,7

 Writing and Communication Masters pp. 53–61

Integrated Technology and Media

 Electronic Teacher Tools CD-ROM

 Writing Coach CD-ROM Cause-Effect Explanation

See How It's Done: Cause-and-Effect Essay

RUBRIC
IN ACTION

Pinned Up over the Summer

On June 11, 1999, I was hit by a pick-up truck while I was riding my bike. I was thrown several feet and fractured my left femur, or thigh bone. I needed four pins to hold my broken bone in place. After ten days in the hospital, I was told I could go home. The doctor gave me some rules to follow. He told me not to put any weight on my leg, and that I would need therapy.

When I got home, I began to realize that because of the accident, I was going to have to change my lifestyle. I was going to have to slow down. I was also going to try not to concentrate on the pain in my leg.

Now that my leg is broken, I need help doing things that are ordinarily easy, like carrying a package and walking at the same time! I can't carry anything while walking with crutches. I can't even leave the house on my own. I can't play baseball or basketball or go swimming with my friends and family.

Because of the accident I can't go to camp. I have to go to therapy instead, to learn how to walk again. Sometimes therapy is okay. Sometimes it isn't, and it hurts.

One thing that has helped me, though, is the support that I received from friends and family. My mom used all her sick days at work so she could take care of me in the hospital. After that, I got to see my grandmas, who took care of me when my mom had to go back to work. I got many calls and visits from family and friends. I also got presents!

❶ Strong opening includes needed background information

❷ Clearly identifies the cause-and-effect relationship being discussed

❸ Arranges details logically by listing bad effects, and then listing good effects

CAUSE-EFFECT

Cause-and-Effect Essay **439**

ANALYZING THE MODEL
Use the numbered questions below to make sure that students understand how the model satisfies the rubric.

❶ How does the writer make his opening interesting and strong?

He begins with a detailed description of his accident.

❷ What is the cause-and-effect relationship being discussed in the essay?

Because of the writer's accident, he has to change his lifestyle.

❸ **Critical Thinking** Why does the writer list the good effects after the bad?

By listing the good effects after the bad, the writer leaves readers thinking more about the positive aspects of the experience.

TEACHING TIP

Cooperative Learning/Paired Activity
Have students work in pairs to read through the **Student Model** and identify the writer's cause-and-effect statements. Have students evaluate how these statements enable the writer to achieve his purpose.

CAUSE-EFFECT

---

 mcdougallittell.com
Additional Writing Prompts

Assessment

 Assessment Masters:
- Writing Prompts p. 129
- Rubrics p. 138
- Student Models pp. 153–155

 Teacher's Guide to Assessment and Portfolio Use

Students Acquiring English/ESL

Side by Side pp. 19, 67–78

4 Critical Thinking What is the purpose of repeating the key items of the essay?

To conclude the essay by summing up the key ideas.

CUSTOMIZING TIP

Students Acquiring English/ESL To help students discuss causes and effects more naturally in English, teach them the following sentence starters and transition words as vocabulary: *because, therefore, since, so.*

CUSTOMIZING TIP

Gifted and Talented Ask students how the tone of the essay would be affected if the writer listed only the bad effects of his accident. What different judgment might readers draw about the writer? The tone would be dark and depressing. Readers might assume that the writer feels defeated and sorry for himself.

It's strange that seeing so many people and having a good time with them is the result of being hit by a truck.

Some other good things that came out of the accident are not having to do my chores and not having to practice my viola. These can be overshadowed, though, by bad things like losing my summer job. Since I broke my leg, I had to give up my lawn-mowing job, and I may not get it back next year. I can always look on the bright side, though; I don't have to cut their lawns or mine!

So, all in all, getting hit by a truck doesn't make summer fun, but it doesn't ruin it, either. It has the effect of making the summer very different. Normally I would have gone to camp and gone on hikes and climbed mountains, but instead I get to watch really good movies I probably never would have seen. And instead of playing baseball with my team this year, I watched and got to keep score. I can now score better than ever before!

4 This writer summarizes the cause-and-effect relationship by first giving an overview, and then repeating key items.

Another option: Repeat key items, and then conclude with the overview statement.

Do It Yourself

Writing Prompt Write a cause-and-effect essay to show what caused an event to happen and what effects it had.

Purpose To explain and to inform

Audience Classmates or other interested readers

1 Prewriting

Choose a topic. Think about an important past event. What caused the event? What effects did it have? Think about the future. Do you need to make a decision about something? What effect will your decision have on others?

For more topic ideas, see the Idea Bank, p. 444.

Decide what you need. Can you draw on your own thoughts and observations for the necessary background information? Or will you need to do research?

Do a reality check. Did one event really cause another or did one event simply follow another? Use a map like the one below to organize your ideas.

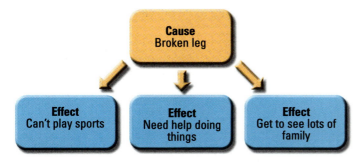

2 Drafting

State your cause-effect relationship. Try to sum up the cause-and-effect relationship in a sentence or two. Refer to this statement as you write to keep yourself on track. Be sure to include your statement in your draft.

Organize your ideas. Keeping your statement in mind, decide how to organize your ideas. Here are two possibilities:

• Describe how one cause can have many effects.

• Show how many causes can lead to one effect.

For information about getting feedback from your peers, see p. 445.

Cause-and-Effect Essay **441**

CAUSE-EFFECT

CAUSE-EFFECT

Spice It Up!

Have students play a game in which they construct a cause-and-effect chain. Begin the game by saying, "Because I got a dog" and ask students to complete the clause with an effect—"I had to feed it," for example. The next student would then continue the chain by saying (for example), "Because I had to feed it, I needed some money." See if students can add ten links to the chain.

ASSESSMENT

 Assessment Masters:
- Writing Prompts p. 129
- Rubrics p. 138
- Student Models pp. 153–155

Teacher's Guide to Assessment and Portfolio Use

❸ Revising

TARGET SKILL ▶**Transitions** Use transitions to show how your ideas are related. Some words and phrases that show cause-and-effect relationships are *because, since, as a result.* For more help with revising, review the rubric on page 438.

> When I got home, I began to realize that I was going to *because of the accident,* have to change my lifestyle.

❹ Editing and Proofreading

TARGET SKILL ▶**Fragments** If you don't use complete sentences, readers may have trouble following your ideas. Make sure every group of words you have put together as a sentence has a subject and predicate.

> Some other good things that came out of the accident, *are* Not having to do my chores and not having to practice my viola.

For more on sentence fragments, see pp. 25–27.

❺ Sharing and Reflecting

Did your cause-and-effect essay help you learn something about yourself that would be worth **sharing** with others? Did you make a scientific discovery that could be formally presented in science class or at a science fair?

For Your Working Portfolio After you have shared your essay, reflect on the way you wrote it. Did you leave out any good points you could have made or include material you didn't need? Were there parts that you particularly liked? Attach your answers to your essay and save them both in your **Working Portfolio.**

Drive-Through Grammar

Sentence Fragments A sentence fragment is a group of words that does not express a complete idea. A sentence fragment leaves out something important, such as the subject, the predicate, or sometimes both. Write the following fragments on the board. Have students identify what's missing and then rewrite the fragment as a complete sentence.

The bone that I broke last summer.

Missing complete predicate.

The bone that I broke last summer finally healed this fall.

Ran under the trees.

Missing subject.

The team ran under the trees.

Speak for Yourself: *Demonstration*

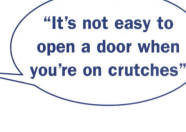

"It's not easy to open a door when you're on crutches"

When you say this, most people will understand what you mean. However, if you actually get a pair of crutches and try to open a door, everyone will see exactly what you mean. By giving a demonstration, you can show an audience your ideas in action. The ideas in your **cause-effect essay** may make a good basis for a demonstration. You can act out some of the causes or effects or stage a demonstration with objects.

Here's How | Creating a Demonstration

- Choose specific causes or effects from your essay that would be easy to demonstrate in a classroom. Is it something you could act out? If it's a more scientific cause-effect, can you perform an experiment before your audience?

- Get whatever props or materials you will need. What materials do you need to perform your experiment? What props do you need to act it out?

- Practice your demonstration and memorize the explanations you will give.

For more information on speaking skills, see p. 545–47.

Cause-and-Effect Essay   **443**

CAUSE-EFFECT

CAUSE-EFFECT

Student Help Desk

Student Help Desk

Students can use the Student Help Desk as a quick review or as a quick reference as they write their cause-and-effect essays.

Teacher's Notes

WHAT WORKS:

Student Help Desk

Cause-and-Effect Essay at a Glance

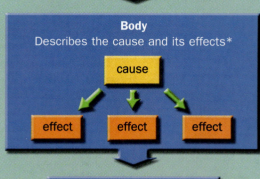

Introduction
Introduces the subject

Body
Describes the cause and its effects*

cause

effect   effect   effect

*or presents an effect and then analyzes the causes

Conclusion
Summary

Idea Bank

How do you find a topic?

Discuss how a recent change at school affected the students.

Consider what effects might result if you take up a new activity.

Write about how a change in your family's life has affected family members.

Research how a certain historical event affected your town or state.

Imagine what the effects would be if cars or television or computers were suddenly removed from our lives.

Read literature such as *The Autobiography of Malcolm X* by Malcolm X with Alex Haley to see how other writers handle causes and effects (*The Language of Literature*, Grade 7).

Friendly Feedback

Questions for Your Peer Reader

- What is the main cause that I named? What is the major overall effect?
- What flaws in my logic could you find?
- What parts did you have trouble understanding?
- What did you need to know more about?

Publishing Options

Print	Submit your essay to the school newspaper or literary magazine. Use a desktop publishing program to produce a booklet of essays from your class.
Oral Communication	Present your essay to your classmates, to an appropriate school club, or to a local speech club. Use charts to illustrate your points.
Online	Check out **mcdougallittell.com** for more publishing options.

The Bottom Line

Checklist for Cause-and-Effect Essay

Have I . . .

____ clearly identified the cause-and-effect relationship that I was discussing?

____ given any background information that was needed?

____ made the relationship between causes and effects clear?

____ arranged details logically?

____ used transitions to show relationships between causes and effects?

____ used language and details appropriate to my audience?

____ summarized the cause and effect relationship in the conclusion?

Teacher's Notes
WHAT DOESN'T WORK:

TEACHER'S LOUNGE

A Slice of Life

Meatballs

1 lb. lean ground beef
1 egg (2 for very lean beef)
3 tbsp milk
2 tsp fresh or frozen parsley
3 tbsp grated parmesan
1 tbsp grated romano
1/8 tsp garlic powder
1/2 tsp salt

Combine beef, egg(s), and milk in large bowl. Add dry ingredients and mix well. Form into balls (about 2") and bake in 350 degree oven for about 25 minutes.

Brain Break

The Biggest Department Store At 2.15 million square feet, the largest department store by area is Macy's. The shop's 11-story building occupies an entire block in Herald Square in New York City. Macy's also has a chain of department stores across the U.S. and was one of the first major retailers to place stores in shopping malls. The firm's red star trademark derives from a tattoo borne by its founder, Rowland Macy.

CHAPTER OBJECTIVES

To analyze and write an effective comparison-contrast essay

DAILY TEST PREPARATION

Error Correction: Punctuation
Write the following item on the board or use ▦ **Daily Test Preparation Transparency** p. DT56.
Choose the best way to write the underlined section.

> The talented young woman loved <u>to write verse direct plays and compose music.</u>

A. to: write verse, direct plays, and compose music.

B. to write verse, and direct plays, and compose music.

C. to write verse, direct plays, and compose music.

D. Correct as is

See ▦ **Time-Saver Transparencies Binder** for the Teaching Point.

The ▮ Basics in a Box ▮ provides graphic and verbal guidelines for organizing a comparison-contrast essay. The Venn diagram in the body presents one way to organize similarities and differences.

The ▮ RUBRIC ▮, or Standards for Writing, describes a comparison-contrast essay that would merit the highest score. A complete rubric, describing several levels of proficiency, is on page 139 of ▦ **Assessment Masters.**

Comparison-Contrast Essay

Learn What It Is

Maybe you need to decide between two brands of athletic shoes. Or, maybe you're considering whether to join the marching band or the chorus. One way to make decisions is to study the similarities and differences of two subjects. Writing a **comparison-contrast essay** can help you see the subjects clearly and make a decision if that is your purpose.

Basics in a Box

COMPARISON-CONTRAST ESSAY AT A GLANCE

Introduction
- introduces the **subjects** being compared
- tells the **reason** for the comparison

Body
explains similarities and differences

Subject A only | Both subjects | Subject B only

Conclusion
- summarizes the comparison
- explains new understanding

RUBRIC

Standards for Writing

A successful comparison-contrast essay should

- introduce the subjects being compared
- state a clear purpose for the comparison
- include transitional words and phrases to make similarities and differences clear

- follow a clear organizational pattern
- include both similarities and differences and support them with specific examples and details
- summarize the comparison in the conclusion

WORKSHOP RESOURCES

Time-Saver Transparencies Binder:
- Basics in a Box p. BB5
- Critical Thinking Graphic Organizers p. CT7
- Daily Test Preparation p. DT56
- Quick-Fix Grammar and Style Charts pp. QF8, 13
- Revising, Editing, and Proofreading Models pp. RE17–20

- Writing and Communication Skills p. WC7
- Writing and Communication Masters pp. 62–70

Integrated Technology and Media
- Electronic Teacher Tools CD-ROM
- Writing Coach CD-ROM Comparison-Contrast

See How It's Done: *Comparison-Contrast Essay*

Student Model
Caroline Watkins
Lake Forest Country Day
School

RUBRIC
IN ACTION

Culture Shock!

Culture shock! Before I moved to Japan, I never really knew what the meaning of those words was. Now I do. I thought that Japan and America couldn't be that different. But with 6,300 miles and the largest ocean in the world separating us, cultural differences really do exist. The biggest shock for me was how different the teenagers were.

One example of how Japanese and American teenagers differ is their school backgrounds. From kindergarten, Japanese are taught discipline and obedience. There are many more rules and regulations in Japanese schools than in American schools. Children have to follow these rules and they always do. Students in Japan never disobey their teachers. They have about three more hours of school every day than Americans do, and they have school every other Saturday. They also have less than a month of summer break.

Another difference is that they honor their elders much more than most American teenagers do. They don't ever question their parents. Obedience, instead of creativity and independence, is what's taught.

Many Japanese teenagers are very superstitious and are devoted to tradition. For example, a Japanese person would never stand in the doorway of a temple because the person would worry about that causing years and years of bad luck. If American teenagers break a mirror, they jokingly say that they will have bad luck for seven years. Japanese teenagers actually believe it.

<u>Another difference</u> between the teenagers is their views on fashion. While teens in America were wearing jeans, overalls, and pea coats, teens in

① Establishes the purpose for the comparison

② Identifies the subjects being compared

③ This writer uses a feature-by-feature organization, first discussing school backgrounds for both sets of teens.
Another option: Use a subject-by-subject organization, discussing all the characteristics of each group separately.

④ Lists differences and supports them with specific examples and details

⑤ Uses transitional phrases to make relationships between ideas clear

Comparison-Contrast Essay **447**

ANALYZING THE MODEL
Use the numbered questions below to make sure that students understand how the model satisfies the rubric.

① What is the purpose for the comparison?

To explain cultural differences

② What subjects does the writer compare?

Teenagers in America and teenagers in Japan

③ **Critical Thinking** What would a subject-by-subject organization be like in this essay?

The writer would discuss Japanese teens and American teens separately. The actual comparison would come at the end.

④ What specific example does the writer use to support her claim that Japanese teenagers are superstitious?

The Japanese don't stand in the doorway of a temple because they fear it will bring bad luck.

⑤ What signal does the underlined transitional phrase give?

It signals a change to the discussion of another difference.

THE LANGUAGE OF LITERATURE

See the Comparison-Contrast Writing Workshop in *The Language of Literature*, Level 7.

COMPARISON

COMPARISON

 mcdougallittell.com
Additional Writing Prompts

Assessment

Assessment Masters:
- Writing Prompts p. 130
- Rubrics p. 139
- Student Models pp. 156–158

 Teacher's Guide to Assessment and Portfolio Use

Students Acquiring English/ESL

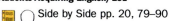 Side by Side pp. 20, 79–90

6 Critical Thinking Why do you think the writer summarizes the similarities last?

To leave readers with the impression that the similarities outweigh the differences.

7 Critical Thinking What new understanding of Japanese teens did the writer gain?

She learned that, in spite of their different upbringing, Japanese and American teens have many things in common.

Japan were wearing camouflage; really, really short skirts or incredibly baggy or flair jeans; and knee-high boots. Also, a lot of Japanese teens, once they get out of high school, think it is cool to dye their hair. Some of the colors they use are blond, red, brown, purple, silver, gold, pretty much anything.

There are also interesting similarities between Japanese and American teens, such as how Japanese teens like American "things" and American teens like Japanese "things" so much. Whenever I would go shopping in Tokyo, I would see countless teens with shirts that bore American writing. I always wondered if they knew what it said on their shirts because often there were pretty strange phrases that an American teenager would never wear. In Tokyo I saw a 15-year-old girl wearing a shirt that said, "The flowers in the garden of heaven smell tasty." Somehow, I don't think an American would wear that shirt. Back in the U.S., I have seen my friends wearing T-shirts that bear Japanese characters; my Japanese friends would never wear these shirts.

My Japanese friends loved my American items, such as movies, food, and magazines. I didn't think of them as anything special, but my Japanese friends thought they were the coolest things in the world. And my American friends loved my Japanese things like pens, pencils, and diaries.

I learned a lot in my four years in Japan. I learned that even though American and Japanese teens grow up differently and learn to like different things, it doesn't make them completely different.

6 Includes similarities and supports them with specific examples and details

7 Summarizes the comparison in the conclusion

Do It Yourself

Writing Prompt Choose two subjects and write a comparison-contrast essay to show how they are alike and how they are different

Purpose To explain or to clarify

Audience Anyone interested in your subjects

1 Prewriting

Choose a topic. You might start by making a list of decisions you've made recently that involved making a choice between two things.

For more topic ideas, see the Idea Bank, p. 452.

Make a list of the similarities and differences in your topics.

Decide on an organizational pattern. Use a chart like the one below to help you decide how to present the similarities and differences of your subjects.

Subject-by-Subject		Feature-by-Feature	
Subject A	*Japanese teens*	**Feature 1**	*Rules, obedience*
Feature 1	*Rules, obedience*	Subject A	*Japanese teens*
Feature 2	*Dress*	Subject B	*American teens*
Subject B	*American teens*	**Feature 2**	*Dress*
Feature 1	*Rules, obedience*	Subject A	*Japanese teens*
Feature 2	*Dress*	Subject B	*American teens*

2 Drafting

Get started. Start writing in the organizational pattern you choose, which you can always change when you revise. For either pattern, you will need an **introduction, body,** and **conclusion.**

- **Introduction.** Identify the subjects you are comparing and tell your purpose for making the comparison.

- **Body.** In the body, explore each subject or feature in turn. Use examples and details for support.

- **Conclusion.** Here is where you sum up the comparison and tell your decision if that was your purpose.

For information about getting feedback from your peers, see p. 453.

Comparison-Contrast Essay **449**

COMPARISON

COMPARISON

Spice It Up!

Draw a Venn diagram on the board and fill it with the following information. Ask students to guess the two topics.

Topic A (Soccer) players use their feet, score points by kicking the ball into a net

Topics A and B: played by teams, played with a ball, players wear shorts

Topic B (Basketball) players use their hands, score points by throwing the ball

❸ Revising

TARGET SKILL ▶**Varying Sentence Structure** To engage your readers' interest and to show the relationship between ideas, vary the structure of some of your sentences. Use a variety of simple, compound, and complex sentences. For more help with revising, review the rubric on page 446.

> I thought that Japan and America couldn't be that
> different. *But with* ~~There are~~ 6,300 miles ~~between Japan and America.~~ *and*
> ~~The Pacific Ocean~~ is the largest ocean in the world. ~~It~~
> *separating us,*
> ~~separates Japan and America.~~ Cultural differences really
> do exist.

❹ Editing and Proofreading

TARGET SKILL ▶**Making Comparisons** When you use adjectives and adverbs to make comparisons, use only one form of comparison at a time. Do not use *more* and *-er* together or *most* and *-est* together.

> I didn't think of them as anything special, but my
> Japanese friends thought they were the ~~most~~ coolest things
> in the world.

For more on comparisons, see pp. 351–361.

❺ Sharing and Reflecting

Share your essay with classmates who are interested in your subjects. After reading, ask what similarities and/or differences were more important to them.

For Your Working Portfolio As you **reflect** on your writing, think about how effective it was. Did your audience find it convincing? Were there other points you could have made? Attach your answers to your finished work. Save your essay in your 🗀 **Working Portfolio.**

Drive-Through Grammar

Complex Sentences Tell students that they can vary sentence structure by including complex sentences. A complex sentence contains one independent clause and one or more subordinate clauses. A clause that can stand on its own is an independent clause; a clause that cannot stand alone is a subordinate clause. Write the following sentence on the board and have students identify the independent clause (underlined once) and the subordinate clause (underlined twice):

Even though she had never been to China, she discovered how easy it was to get around.

Speak for Yourself: *Multimedia Presentation*

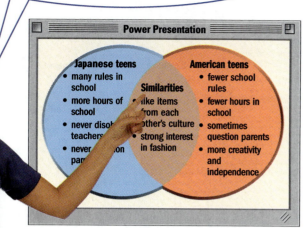

"In Japan, we love American things." "Really? In America, we love Japanese things!"

Power Presentation

Japanese teens
- many rules in school
- more hours of school
- never disobey teachers
- never question parents

Similarities
- like items from each other's culture
- strong interest in fashion

American teens
- fewer school rules
- fewer hours in school
- sometimes question parents
- more creativity and independence

The flowers in the garden of heaven smell tasty.

When you talk with a friend you often compare things. You might tell each other about your summer vacations and compare the experiences. Or you might discuss the advantages and disadvantages of playing certain sports. To make the ideas in your **comparison-contrast essay** clear to an audience, you might give a multimedia presentation to show clearly the similarities and differences in the two items.

Here's How **Creating a Multimedia Presentation**

- Choose items from your essay that you can show to an audience either through actual objects or through media like photographs, videos, or computer presentations.

- If you're comparing two products, bring them in. If you are comparing two cultures, use items from the cultures in your presentation.

- Don't forget low-tech media like overhead projectors and flip charts. Graphs, tables, and charts can effectively demonstrate the differences in two items.

- Practice with your visuals before you give your presentation.

For more information on speaking skills, see p.545–47.

Comparison-Contrast Essay **451**

TEACHING TIP

Cooperative Learning Have students work together in groups on a comparison-contrast multimedia presentation. Once students agree on a topic, encourage them to brainstorm ideas on presenting information using text, sound, graphics, and images. Tell them to follow these steps as they design and develop their presentations:

- create an outline of the content

- make a flow chart to organize the material

- design a storyboard that details how audio and visual elements will be combined

- rehearse the presentation before a group of peer reviewers

Finally, have students deliver their presentations to the class.

COMPARISON

COMPARISON

Student Help Desk

Students can use the Student Help Desk as a quick review or as a quick reference as they write their comparison-contrast essays.

Teacher's Notes
WHAT WORKS:

Student Help Desk

Comparison-Contrast Essay at a Glance

Introduction	Body	Conclusion
• introduces the **subjects** being compared • tells the **reason** for the comparison	explains similarities and differences Subject A only / Both subjects / Subject B only	• summarizes the comparison • explains new understanding

Idea Bank

Tips for finding a topic

- **Debate** who the greatest athlete of all time was.
- **Consider** the best computers for a computer lab.
- **Decide** how to spend the money in the science club treasury.
- **Recommend** a video to rent for a quiet night at home.
- **Pick** the most appropriate television program for the family to watch together.

Transition Words and Phrases   Glue It Together

Comparison Words	Contrast Words
Use these words to show similarities.	**Use these words to show differences.**
like also too the same as in the same way	instead unlike however on the other hand yet

452 Writing Workshop

Friendly Feedback

Questions for Your Peer Reader

- What was the purpose of my essay?
- What is the most important similarity?
- What is the most important difference?
- What other points could I have made to strengthen the comparison?
- What did I explain that you didn't already know?

Publishing Options

Print	Look for a publication that deals with the subject you have written about, and submit your essay for an article or guest editorial.
Oral Communication	As a class, choose two subjects to compare and contrast. Then form small groups to create a list of similarities and differences between the two subjects. Share and discuss your list with the other groups in class.
Online	Check out **mcdougallittell.com** for more publishing options.

The Bottom Line

Checklist for comparison-contrast essay

Have I . . .

____ identified the subjects being compared?

____ made the purpose for comparison clear?

____ included both similarities and differences?

____ provided support with specific examples and details?

____ followed a clear organizational pattern?

____ used transition words and phrases appropriately?

____ summarized the comparison in the conclusion?

Comparison-Contrast Essay **453**

Teacher's Notes
WHAT DOESN'T WORK:

CHAPTER OBJECTIVES

To analyze and write an effective proposal

Chapter 25 Writing Workshop

Proposal

Learn What It Is

Have you ever seen a problem or a situation that you would like to change? Perhaps you have some ideas for solutions or improvements. If so, you could write a **proposal,** a document or speech that offers solutions to a problem or ideas about how to change a situation.

Basics in a Box

PROPOSAL AT A GLANCE

Summary of Proposal

Briefly states the purpose of the proposal

Need
• Defines the problem or need
• States why addressing it is important

Proposed Solution
• Presents a detailed solution
• Explains its benefits
• Restates the problem or need and the benefits of the solution

RUBRIC

Standards for Writing

A successful proposal should

• target a specific audience
• clearly define a problem or state a need
• present a clear solution, using evidence to demonstrate that the plan is workable

• show how the plan will be implemented and what resources will be required
• show that the advantages of the plan outweigh possible objections to it

 **Writing Coach**

DAILY TEST PREPARATION

Sentence Completion: Vocabulary Write the following item on the board or use **Daily Test Preparation Transparency** p. DT57. Choose the word that *best* fits the meaning of the sentence.

It was pleasing to _____ the boy learning how to read.

A. observe

B. contemplating

C. learn

D. observed

See **Time-Saver Transparencies Binder** for the Teaching Point.

The Basics in a Box provides graphic and verbal guidelines for organizing a proposal. The diagram illustrates the points that a proposal should address.

The RUBRIC, or Standards for Writing, describes a proposal that would merit the highest score. A complete Rubric, describing several levels of proficiency, is on page 140 of the Assessment Masters.

WORKSHOP RESOURCES

 Time-Saver Transparencies Binder:
• Basics in a Box p. BB6
• Critical Thinking Graphic Organizers pp. CT19, 23
• Daily Test Preparation p. DT57
• Quick-Fix Grammar and Style Charts p. QF2
• Revising, Editing, and Proofreading Models pp. RE21–24

 Writing and Communication Masters pp. 71–79

Integrated Technology and Media

 Electronic Teacher Tools CD-ROM

 Writing Coach CD-ROM Explanation of an Idea

 mcdougallittell.com Additional Writing Prompts

See How It's Done: *Proposal*

Student Model
Andy Sturgeon
Thomas Middle School

Cheer on Thomas

You are at a Thomas Middle School home basketball game, and the score is tied at 32 with only five seconds left until the final buzzer will sound. The star player is hurt, and it looks like Thomas has no chance. The crowd is starting to doubt their own team. To boost the fans' excitement and team spirit, a newly introduced pep band plays a roaring rouser that gets the fans into it. That one rouser may give our Timber Wolves the edge they need to defeat their opponent.

Nothing creates school spirit like a winning team, and a team needs the energy of the crowd to keep winning. Therefore, I propose a Thomas pep band, which would give our musicians another outlet for their talents and would keep our school spirit high.

To begin with, Thomas has a lot of talent in music, and not everyone gets to show it off. For instance, a tuba or flute player may not want to play in a jazz or rock band in addition to the concert music they already play. There's not really any room for a tuba in a jazz band, but it's perfect for a pep band. The pep band would let musicians play the kind of music they want to, without making them change their instruments.

Also, having a pep band would increase school spirit. How many students know the Thomas school song? Almost no one does, and that shouldn't be. A pep band could learn the music for the school song and teach it to the basketball crowd with the help of the cheerleaders. At the pep rallies the school holds, the pep band would play some of their prepared songs. Having them

Proposal **455**

RUBRIC IN ACTION

❶ Targets a specific audience—fans of the Thomas basketball team

❷ Clearly states a need

❸ Presents a clear solution

❹ Uses evidence to demonstrate that the plan is workable

PROPOSAL

❶ How does the writer make clear who his specific audience is?

By setting the scene at a home game and observing from within the crowd

❷ What need does the writer define?

The team needs the energy of the crowd to keep winning.

❸ What solution does the writer propose?

To create a pep band

❹ What evidence does the writer use to support his plan?

The school has a lot of musical talent, and the pep band would let the musicians play the kind of music they want to without changing their instruments.

CUSTOMIZING TIP

Less Proficient Learners Remind students that it is important to support their proposals with verifiable facts and statistics. Have students discuss why these types of evidence are more effective than supporting proposals with opinions alone.

THE LANGUAGE OF LITERATURE

See the Problem-Solution Writing Workshop in *The Language of Literature,* Level 7.

PROPOSAL

Assessment

 Assessment Masters:
- Writing Prompts p. 131
- Rubrics p. 140
- Student Models pp. 159–161

 Teacher's Guide to Assessment and Portfolio Use

Students Acquiring English/ESL

Side by Side pp. 91–102

❺ Critical Thinking How do the transitions tie the paragraphs together?

They connect ideas and help readers follow the writer's argument.

❻ How does the writer propose to implement his plan?

By arranging rehearsal time for the band members who are interested in joining the pep band

❼ Critical Thinking After having read this essay, what do you think might be some objections to forming a pep band at Thomas Middle School, and how could the writer address them in his proposal?

The school principal might be concerned about additional supervisory time needed to organize and keep the pep band going. The writer could show that the band director supports the idea.

play would get the students into the team spirit and the school spirit.

<u>In addition</u>, a pep band would make games more interesting. At some games where there is no band, spectators may get restless and not watch or cheer their own team on. A band will cause the crowd to stay involved and actually participate. Cheering is what gives a team a home court advantage. A band would increase this advantage and give Thomas a better chance at winning home games.

<u>Finally</u>, to get a pep band organized would be simple. Talented musicians are already available in the concert band, waiting to get started on something like this. In fact, nine out of ten Thomas band performers said they would want to be in a pep band. All that would be required would be some rehearsal time for the band members.

As you can see, a Thomas pep band would be a great addition to the Thomas band program. It would let talented musical performers play music they enjoy. A pep band would keep school spirit high at Thomas and give the basketball team an edge over their opponents. Can't you just hear the band, with the crowd roaring in the stands and cheering the Thomas team to victory?

❺ Uses transitions to tie paragraphs together smoothly

❻ Shows how the plan can be implemented and what resources are available

❼ This writer shows the advantages of the plan.
Another option: Include possible objections and show how the advantages outweigh the objections.

456 Writing Workshop

Do It Yourself

Writing Prompt Write a proposal to change or improve a situation.

Purpose To inform and to convince others to follow your proposal

Audience People who can make the change you recommend

❶ Prewriting

Identify a problem or a need. Talk to friends and neighbors about issues that bother them. Or you may already know about a situation that could be improved. Jot down several ideas, and brainstorm possible solutions for each one.

For more topic ideas, see the Idea Bank, p. 460.

Explore your issue. One way to plan your proposal is to make a chart listing support for your proposal and answers to possible objections.

Need: Video yearbook	
Proposal: Video Yearbook Club	
Support	• collection of memories • hear students as well as see them • generate funds for the school
Possible Objections	• finding equipment and members—A/V room has both • cost to produce—less than print yearbook

❷ Drafting

State the need early. Start by writing a clear statement of what is needed and your proposal for meeting that need. Explain why the need or problem is important.

Support your proposal. Include facts, statistics, or examples that support your plan, and show how it will work. If you propose a solution that requires money, you'll need to figure out where the money will come from.

Answer the critics. Include what your opponents might say. Then tell how the advantages of your plan will outweigh their objections to it.

For information about getting feedback from your peers, see p. 461.

Proposal **457**

Spice It Up!

Quotable Quote "If you don't like the way the world is, you change it. You have an obligation to change it. You just do it one step at a time." —Marian Wright Edelman. Briefly discuss with the class how this quote is relevant to their proposals.

TEACHING TIP

Write the following questions on the board to help students identify their target audience. Who would benefit from my idea? Who shares my concern about a particular issue? How does my proposal fulfill a particular need?

TEACHING TIP

Cooperative Learning/Paired Activity Have pairs of students discuss their proposal topics with each other. Students can connect their insights and ideas with those of their partners. Encourage students to incorporate new insights into their proposals.

TEACHING TIP

Cross-Curricular Connection Civics Encourage students to identify a problem or need in their school and address their proposal to the school principal. For example, students may want to address a problem in the school cafeteria or a need in the sports department.

CUSTOMIZING TIP

Addressing Learning Styles Visual Use 📖 **Critical Thinking Graphic Organizer Problem-Solution Chart** p. CT19, to show students a visual way to identify a problem and list possible solutions.

CUSTOMIZING TIP

Students Acquiring English/ESL Skills such as directly stating an idea and using persuasive techniques may be considered rude or presumptuous in some cultures. Tell students that stating their opinions clearly and giving specific reasons in their essays will help their readers understand their proposal topics better.

PROPOSAL

PROPOSAL

Write the following sentences on the board. Ask students to reorder the sentences in a clear sequence.

1. In October 1492, Columbus landed on an island he named San Salvador.

2. Queen Isabella of Spain agreed to pay for Christopher Columbus's expedition because she hoped he would bring back riches from the New World.

3. Columbus embarked on his dangerous voyage across the Atlantic Ocean in August 1492.

Answer: 2-3-1

ASSESSMENT

 Assessment Masters:
  • Writing Prompts p. 131
  • Rubrics p. 140
  • Student Models pp. 159–161
Teacher's Guide to Assessment and Portfolio Use

❸ Revising

TARGET SKILL ▶Making Sequence Clear Your plan won't win any support if it's not easy to follow. Read the following sentences in the order indicated by the numbers. How does the new order improve the paragraph? For more help with revising, review the rubric on page 454.

④ All that would be required would be to schedule some rehearsal time for the band members. ③ In fact, nine out of ten Thomas band performers said they would want to be in a pep band. ② Talented musicians are already there in the concert band, waiting to get started on something like this. ① Finally, to get a pep band organized would be simple.

❹ Editing and Proofreading

TARGET SKILL ▶Correcting Run-ons A run-on sentence, two or more sentences written as a single sentence, can make your proposal confusing. One way to correct this error is to write the sentence as two separate sentences.

How many students know the Thomas school song ? almost no one does, and that shouldn't be.

For more on run-on sentences, see pp. 25-27.

❺ Sharing and Reflecting

Share your proposal with an audience. Ask both supporters and critics of your ideas if you made a convincing case.

For Your Working Portfolio As you talked with others about your proposal, what changes did you think of? Was the proposal still important to you? As you **reflect** on your work, think of how you might have made an even stronger case. Save your answers along with your finished proposal in your 🗂 **Working Portfolio.**

Drive-Through Grammar

Conjunctions Remind students that they can use conjunctions such as *and, but,* and *or* to correct run-on sentences. Write the following run-on sentence on the board and have students use a conjunction to correct it.

I shivered in the early evening air I didn't want to go home.

I shivered in the early evening air, but I didn't want to go home.

Speak for Yourself: *Persuasive Speech*

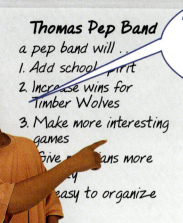

Thomas Pep Band
a pep band will . .
1. Add school spirit
2. Increase wins for Timber Wolves
3. Make more interesting games
   Give musicians more
   easy to organize

"Can't you hear it now? The Thomas Pep Band *roaring* in the stands!"

GO Timber Wolves

Persuading your family to set a later curfew time or persuading your friend to see the movie you like is a form of persuasive speech. On television you've seen politicians make formal speeches to persuade people to support their ideas and plans. Turning your proposal into a persuasive speech will give you the chance to look your audience in the eye, present your **proposal**, and convince them face-to-face that your ideas are good ones.

Here's How **Creating a Persuasive Speech**

- Choose specific parts of your proposal to emphasize. Don't simply plan to read your proposal aloud. A speech needs brief, clearly stated ideas, plenty of emphasis, and a clear call to action.

- Consider your audience. Do you need to define terms? give background explanations? Or can you get right to your proposed idea?

- Present yourself in a way that will make the audience pay attention. If you appear sloppy, for instance, you won't be taken as seriously as if you are dressed neatly.

- Use a flip chart as a point-by-point map of your proposal showing why your ideas are good and how they will work.

- Write out your speech. You may speak from notes, but you should write out the speech and practice your tone of voice, the pacing (how quickly or slowly you will speak), and gestures before you give the speech.

For more information on speaking skills, see pp. 545–547.

Proposal **459**

PROPOSAL

PROPOSAL

LESSON OBJECTIVES

To create and deliver a persuasive speech based on a proposal

TEACHING TIP

Discuss with the class different persuasive techniques they can use in their presentations. Then have students generate criteria to evaluate their own presentations and the presentations of others. Use **Critical Thinking Graphic Organizer Rubric for Evaluation** p. CT23, to show students how to organize their criteria.

TEACHING TIP

Speaking and Listening Have students present their speeches to a small group of peers. Tell the peer group to listen for and identify the proposed need and call to action. Peer listeners should also indicate whether they think more evidence is needed to support the proposal.

Students can use the Student Help Desk as a quick review or reference as they write their own proposals.

Teacher's Notes
WHAT WORKS:

_____

_____

_____

_____

_____

_____

_____

_____

_____

_____

_____

_____

_____

_____

Student Help Desk

Proposal at a Glance

Summary of Proposal	Need	Proposed Solution
Briefly states the purpose of the proposal	• Defines the problem or need • States why addressing it is important	• Presents a detailed solution • Explains its benefits • Restates the problem or need and the benefits of the solution

Idea Bank

Finding an Idea

Look in a newspaper for current concerns and issues.

Read about volunteer projects.

Think about how you might change one thing in the world. What would it be, and how would you do it?

Check out your school. Are there ways to reduce crowding in the halls or lunchroom? How could cafeteria food be improved? Should a particular sport be added to after-school activities?

Look at situations close to home. Maybe you want more responsibility at home to show that you can also handle a few more activities after school.

Make a list of things that bother you, like Calvin is doing in the cartoon below.

Calvin and Hobbes by Bill Watterson

Friendly Feedback

Questions for Your Peer Reader

- What problem or need did I address?
- What other points should I add to support my plan?
- How did I address possible objections to my plan?
- What problems do you see in carrying out my plan?

Publishing Options

Print	If your proposal is to correct a problem, you might print it as a leaflet and hand it out to support the change you recommend.
Oral Communication	Invite interested people to hear you present your proposal as a speech.
Online	Check out **mcdougallittell.com** for more publishing options.

The Bottom Line

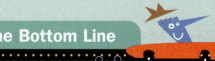

Checklist for Proposal

Have I . . .

- ____ written in an appropriate way for a specific audience?
- ____ clearly stated a need or defined a problem?
- ____ presented a clear solution?
- ____ used evidence to show that the plan will work?

- ____ shown how to implement the plan?
- ____ shown what resources will be required?
- ____ demonstrated clearly that the advantages of the plan outweigh possible objections to it?

Teacher's Notes
WHAT DOESN'T WORK:

_____

_____

_____

_____

_____

_____

_____

_____

_____

_____

_____

_____

_____

_____

TEACHER'S LOUNGE

Brain Break

Can you decipher this famous saying?

Individuals who perforce are constrained to be domiciled in vitreous structures of patent frangibility should on no account employ petrous formations as projectiles.

Answer: People in glass houses shouldn't throw stones.

Just for Laughs

"This exercise is great for your arms, shoulders, chest and back. Do four sets of 15 repetitions, then move on to the yarn ball for your aerobics."

©1997 Randy Glasbergen. www.glasbergen.com

CHAPTER OBJECTIVES

To recognize aspects of effective short stories and poems, and to write original fiction and poetry

DAILY TEST PREPARATION

Revision Strategies: Misplaced Phrases Write the following item on the board or use 📖 **Daily Test Preparation Transparency** p. DT57. Choose the *best* way to express the idea.

A. I watched a movie at home about the Soviet Union yesterday.

B. I watched at home a movie about the Soviet Union yesterday.

C. I watched a movie at home yesterday about the Soviet Union.

D. Yesterday, I watched a movie about the Soviet Union at home.

See 📖 **Time-Saver Transparencies Binder** for the Teaching Point.

The ▐ **Basics in a Box** ▌ provides graphic and verbal guidelines for organizing the elements of a successful story. The arrows indicate the order of the elements.

The ▐ **RUBRIC** ▌, or Standards for Writing, describes a short story that would merit the highest score. A complete rubric, describing several levels of proficiency, is on page 141 of 📖 **Assessment Masters.**

Short Story and Poem

Learn What It Is: *Short Story*

When you want to capture an event or a feeling in words, you can try your hand at writing a story or a poem. In this workshop, you will have the opportunity to try both.

Writing a **short story** is a way to share an experience or to explore an interesting idea. In writing a short story, you use the same elements you use in telling your friends about something amazing that just happened: the people, the event, and the place. Your story might be about a real event or an imagined one.

Basics in a Box

SHORT STORY AT A GLANCE

Introduction

Sets the stage by
• introducing the **characters**
• describing the **setting**

Body

Develops the plot by
• introducing the conflict
• telling a sequence of **events**
• developing **characters** through words and actions
• building towards a **climax**

Conclusion

Finishes the story by
• resolving the **conflict**
• telling the **last event**

RUBRIC

Standards for Writing

A successful short story should

• have a strong beginning and ending
• have a central conflict
• present a clear sequence of events
• maintain a consistent point of view
• use techniques such as vivid sensory language, concrete details, and dialogue to create believable characters and setting
• use the elements of character, setting, and plot to create a convincing world

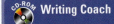 **Writing Coach**

CHAPTER 26

WORKSHOP RESOURCES

 Time-Saver Transparencies Binder:
• Basics in a Box p. BB7
• Critical Thinking Graphic Organizers pp. CT1, 9
• Daily Test Preparation p. DT57
• Quick-Fix Grammar and Style Charts pp. QF3–4
• Revising, Editing, and Proofreading Models pp. RE25–32

 Writing and Communication Masters pp. 80–97

Integrated Technology and Media

 Electronic Teacher Tools CD-ROM

 Writing Coach CD-ROM Short Story

 mcdougallittell.com Additional Writing Prompts

See How It's Done: *Short Story*

Student Model
Rachel Smith
King Philip Middle School

The Floodgates of the Sky

Flood. The word scared her—she tried to dismiss it, but it just kept repeating in her mind. Flood . . . flood . . . flood . . . No. It was impossible, impossible and ridiculous. Nothing like that could ever happen to her family, she was sure of that, and nothing ever would. But then what would you call the mountains of water swallowing everything in their path? . . .

She felt nauseous. The sickening smell of garbage mixed with water and dead fish choked her and seemed to hang limply in the air. There was a terrible knot in her stomach, tightening until she could hardly breathe. She looked over at her siblings, Peter, four years old, and baby Jane. If only she could be sleeping as peacefully as they. Her mother was white-faced and tense, and her father kept pacing back and forth across the tiny attic. Trying to distract herself from the pain and fright, she scrubbed at the dusty attic window with her fist. The clouds were still dark and the rain continued to beat down in a steady deluge. She could make out the shapes of familiar household items being swept away. Even the house across the street was gone. "Please don't let that happen to us!" she prayed. She looked away quickly. Better to hurt than to see others hurt.

Suddenly an ear-splitting *crack*! broke the silence. The family rushed to the window just in time to see the garage swept away by the great torrent of water.

"My car . . . Leo's wood business . . . gone!" her mother whispered in disbelief. . . .

"No warning. None." That was her father, sounding broken and far away. She had never heard

RUBRIC IN ACTION

❶ Has a strong, tense beginning

❷ Includes vivid, sensory language and concrete details

❸ Provides details that make the scene convincing and vivid

❹ Uses dialogue to increase the tension and make the characters believable

Short Story **463**

SHORT STORY

---

❶ How does the writer create tension in the beginning of the story?

She begins with the story's conflict: her family against the flood.

❷ What are some examples of vivid sensory language?

the smell of the garbage, the dead fish, the knot in her stomach

❸ What details make the scene convincing?

her mother's white face, her father's pacing, the dusty attic window, and the shapes of things being swept away

❹ **Critical Thinking** Suppose the writer had described the characters' reaction to the destruction of the garage rather than let them speak for themselves. How would the absence of dialogue affect readers' insight into the characters?

Readers wouldn't learn as much about them. The dialogue helps reveal the characters' personalities.

THE LANGUAGE OF
LITERATURE

See the Short Story Writing Workshop in *The Language of Literature,* Level 7.

SHORT STORY

Assessment

 Assessment Masters:
- Writing Prompts pp. 132–133
- Rubrics pp. 141–142
- Student Models pp. 162–167

 Teacher's Guide to Assessment and Portfolio Use

Students Acquiring English/ESL

Side by Side pp. 103–114

⑤ Critical Thinking What effect would a first-person point of view have on the story?

A first-person narrator would draw the reader in and make the action seem more immediate.

him cry before. Somehow that scared her more than a flood ever could. She pinched herself so hard she thought it might bleed. A nightmare. In a few minutes she would wake up, have some cornflakes, and tell her mom all about the horrible dream. Her mom would say "tsk-tsk" and it would all be over.

She woke up suddenly, shaking. It was a dream! she thought excitedly. It was! But if it was a dream, why wasn't she in her bed? Why were they in the attic? Why was it so damp and cold? Remembrance almost knocked her over. She'd fallen asleep, but in the middle of a flood, not in her bedroom.

"Oh, thank God!" her mother whispered unexpectedly. "Finally!" Variations of this comment moved throughout the room. She wondered why, until finally she glanced out the window and saw a rowboat heading toward them. Two men were in it, wearing bright red jackets saying Coast Guard. Relief flooded her like the water that had so quickly ruined her life on Scoville Street, Torrington, Connecticut. She was saved. She knew she would remember this day, August 18, 1955, forever.

"Come on, Elaine," said her father, standing up. "We're starting over."

This is a true story. The event happened to my mother's family in 1955. The story is written from the perspective of the oldest child in the family, my aunt.

⑤ This writer adds a paragraph to explain the point of view.

Another option: Tell the whole story in the first person from her aunt's point of view.

Do It Yourself

Writing Prompt   Write a short story about something that happened
to you or something that might have happened.

Purpose To entertain

Audience Family, friends, others who might be interested

❶ Prewriting

Find a story idea. Recall stories you have heard in your family,
or make up something that might have happened. Can you
create a story around something you saw at a shopping mall,
or a story you heard from a friend?

For more topic ideas, see the Idea Bank, p. 472.

Think about story elements. Your story will need characters, a
plot, and a setting.

Story Elements

Characters	Plot	Setting
• Who tells the story?	• What happens?	• Where does the story take place?
• Who is the main character?	• What is the central conflict?	• When does it happen?
• What are the other characters like?		

❷ Drafting

Make a plot outline. List all the events, and work out how
to develop the conflict. Decide how to begin and end your
story. Remember, you can change your plot at any time.

Begin writing. Start writing at any place in the story. As you
write, you can see where the story takes you. You can go
back later to make changes.

Use dialogue. Look for places to add dialogue so that your
characters can speak for themselves.

Use description. Use as many details as possible. For
example, a crack of lightning may show a person in danger,
or hurried footsteps may reveal fright.

For information about getting feedback from your peers, see p. 473.

SHORT STORY

SHORT STORY

Spice It Up!

Quotable Quote "When I write stories I am
like someone who is in her own country,
walking along streets that she has known
since she was a child, between walls and
trees that are hers" —Natalia Ginzberg

Ask students to describe how they feel
when they write stories. Do they re-create
worlds that are familiar to them, or do
they create worlds that become familiar
as they write?

For further practice with the concept of showing instead of telling, write the following sentences on the board. Have students revise them, supplying descriptive, vivid words that show the action rather than simply tell it.

My mother was excited as she set the dessert before me. When the people around me sang "Happy Birthday," I was glad.

My mother's eyes shone as bright as the candles on the cake she set before me. When my family and friends sang "Happy Birthday," I couldn't stop smiling.

CUSTOMIZING TIP

Students Acquiring English/ESL
Encourage students to share examples of stories and plot lines that are part of their own culture. You might ask them why the hero is important— because of his/her words, actions, honor, etc.—to better understand what is valued in your students' native cultures.

ASSESSMENT

Assessment Masters:
- Writing Prompts p. 132
- Rubrics p. 141
- Student Models pp. 162–164

Teacher's Guide to Assessment and Portfolio Use

❸ Revising

TARGET SKILL ▶Show, Don't Tell Using words that show action rather than telling about the action is the way to keep your story moving. For more help with revising, review the rubric on page 462.

> Her mother was ^white-faced and^ tense, and her father ~~was nervous.~~ ^kept pacing back and forth across the tiny at^
>
> Trying to distract herself from the pain and fright, she
> ~~dusted~~ ^dusty^ the attic window with her fist.
> ^scrubbed at^

❹ Editing and Proofreading

TARGET SKILL ▶Subject-verb Agreement If the subject of a sentence or clause is singular, the verb that goes with it must also be singular. If the subject is plural, the verb must also be plural. Check to see that you have correct subject-verb agreement throughout your story.

> The clouds ~~was~~ ^were^ still dark and the rain continued to beat
> down in a steady deluge.

❺ Sharing and Reflecting

To **share** your story with your family or with friends, give it a dramatic reading, or get some friends and act out the characters. Ask your audience to give you feedback on your presentation.

For Your Working Portfolio Make notes of how you developed your story. As you **reflect** on the process, recall what was the most enjoyable part and what was the most challenging. Save your comments and your completed story in your 📁 **Working Portfolio.**

Drive-Through Grammar

Subject-Verb Agreement Tell students to be sure to check subject-verb agreement in their stories when they use indefinite pronouns. Remind them that some indefinite pronouns are always singular: some are always plural; and some can be either singular or plural depending on how they are used. Write the following sentences on the board, and have students select the correct form of the verb.

Each of the girls (carries, carry) a rose.

Many of the boys (plays, play) soccer after school.

None of the children (wants, want) to go home.

Learn What It Is: *Poem*

Poems express ideas and feelings in a way that uses every word for a certain effect. Poems can be about anything and can take almost any form. Your poem can tell a story, express an emotion, or describe an experience. It can rhyme or not. Your poem will be most successful when it is about something that matters to you.

Basics in a Box

POETRY AT A GLANCE

rhythm

figurative language

rhyme

mood

sensory words

sound devices

stanzas

RUBRIC

Standards for Writing

A successful poem should

- focus on a single experience, idea, or feeling
- use precise, sensory words in a fresh, interesting way
- include figurative language such as similes and metaphors
- include sound devices such as alliteration and rhyme to support the meaning of the poem

The **Basics in a Box** uses graphic and verbal guidelines to describe the elements in a successful poem.

The **RUBRIC**, or Standards for Writing, describes a poem that would merit the highest score. A complete rubric, describing several levels of proficiency, is on page 142 of the **Assessment Masters**.

NEED MORE INFORMATION?
Refer students to **Chapter 19, Style and Effective Language**, for more instruction on figurative language.

TEACHING TIP

Explain to students that alliteration is the repetition of consonant sounds at the beginning of words.

POEM

SHORT STORY

POETRY RESOURCES

 Time-Saver Transparencies Binder:
- Critical Thinking Graphic Organizers p. CT1
- Revising, Editing, and Proofreading Models pp. 29–32

 Writing and Communication Masters pp. 89–97

Integrated Technology and Media

Electronic Teacher Tools CD-ROM

 mcdougallittell.com
Additional Writing Prompts

Assessment

 Assessment Masters:
- Writing Prompts p. 133
- Rubrics p. 142
- Student Models pp. 165–167

Teacher's Guide to Assessment and Portfolio Use

ANALYZING THE MODEL

Use the numbered questions below to make sure that students understand how the model satisfies the rubric.

1 What is the feeling expressed by the poet?

She hates school.

2 Critical Thinking In what other way in the first two stanzas does the poet create a rhythmic feel?

She repeats lines from the first stanza in the second stanza.

3 4 Critical Thinking Why does the poet try to convey a feeling of sameness?

She wants to reflect the numbing structure of school.

5 Critical Thinking Why does the writer mix school and personal topics?

To show that school and personal life are strongly intertwined

6 Critical Thinking What is the effect of the poem's ending?

It echoes the first line and creates the feeling that nothing has changed.

See How It's Done: *Poem*

Student Model
Kate Frasca
John Jay Middle School

RUBRIC
IN ACTION

Middle School Blues

I hate school.
Did I finish last night's math homework?
I forgot my lunch, again!
Act 1 scene 3 rehearsal today.

Did I finish last night's math homework?
Someone just spilled red punch on my Adidas.
Act 1 scene 3 rehearsal today.
What do you mean it's not block scheduling?

Someone just spilled red punch on my Adidas.
5 poems with a cover all due tomorrow.
What do you mean it's not block scheduling?
The health test is today?

5 poems with a cover all due tomorrow.
Morgan and Carrie are in another fight.
The health test is today?
I got called to Ms. Tormey's office.

Morgan and Carrie are in another fight.
My homework folder ripped in half.
I got called to Ms. Tormey's office.
Kelly tripped me right in front of that cute boy.

My homework folder ripped in half.
Have you seen my science text book?
Kelly tripped me right in front of that cute boy.
There are no seats left at my lunch table.

Have you seen my science text book?
My mother just kissed me in front of that cute boy.
There are no seats left at my lunch table.
Oh no! I didn't make honor roll.

My mother just kissed me in front of that cute boy.
I got lunch detention for talking during a fire drill.
Oh, no! I didn't make honor roll.
I hate school.

1 Focuses on a single feeling

2 Repeats the *s* sound to give a rhythmic feel to the lines

3 Repeats the second line of each stanza as the first line of the next stanza to create the feeling of sameness and boredom

4 Uses repetition of the fourth line of each stanza as the third line of the next stanza.

5 This writer mixes the topics of school work and personal interests throughout.
Other options: Stick to one topic.

6 Last line repeats the first line and ties the poem together

Do It Yourself

Writing Prompt   Write a poem about anything that matters to you.

Purpose To write expressively

Audience Friends, family members, classmates

1 Prewriting

Seeing again for the first time. Look at all the ordinary things around you—but try to see them for the first time. How would the rain taste? What is the most significant yellow thing you see? Make some notes.

For more topic ideas, see the Idea Bank, p. 472.

Make an observation chart. Begin with your topic, and think of all the ways your senses can give more details about the topic. Record your ideas in a chart like the one below.

Observation Chart: Cafeteria	
Sight	kids in line at the cafeteria, cafeteria staff in white uniforms, kids at tables eating lunches brought from home
Sound	the clank of silverware on metal trays, boys yelling at each other across the room
Touch	warm, wet dishes, cold milk carton
Taste	spicy pizza sauce, apple cobbler
Smell	soapy steam from the kitchen, garlic, fresh-baked peanut butter cookies

2 Drafting

Explore associations. Pick one or more of your most vivid observations, such as "fresh-baked peanut butter cookies," and list words, feelings, or ideas that come to mind when you think of it.

Put your observations together. Try various ways of stringing your observations together into a poem about a single moment, experience, or idea. As you experiment with different order and arrangements, think about whether you want to make your lines rhyme.

For information about getting feedback from your peers, see p. 473.

Short Story **469**

CUSTOMIZING TIP

Less Proficient Learners Help students come up with sensory details. Name an evocative topic, such as the beach, a park, or a street fair. Then use **Critical Thinking Graphic Organizer Observation Chart**, p. CT1, to record their ideas on the topic.

POEM

SHORT STORY

TEACHING TIP

A title can add additional meaning to the poem. Have students discuss what the title, "Middle School Blues," adds to their understanding of the poem. Encourage students to think of titles for their own poems that reveal something about their poems' subjects or themes.

Spice It Up!

Have groups of students play a guessing game. Have group members take turns describing an object in the classroom, using details that appeal to the senses. The other members of the group should use the details to guess what the object is.

❸ Revising

TARGET SKILL ▶ **Using Precise Words** Make every word in your poem say exactly what you mean. Substitute specific, colorful nouns, adjectives, and verbs for more general ones. For more help with revising, review the rubric on page 467.

> ~~just~~ that cute boy.
> My mother kissed me in front of ~~everyone~~
> lunch detention
> I got ~~punished~~ for talking *during a fire drill.*
> I didn't make the honor roll.
> *Oh, no!*

❹ Editing and Proofreading

TARGET SKILL ▶ **Punctuating Poetry** Punctuation in a poem helps readers put ideas together and also understand when to pause. Poets can make their own decisions about how to punctuate their poems, but in general it is best to use standard rules for punctuating your poetry. Use end marks after full sentences, and use commas in the correct way.

> The health test is today**?**
> I got called to Ms. Tormey's office**.**

❺ Sharing and Reflecting

After you have revised and edited your poem, **share** it with an audience. You might have a poetry reading in your class where you and your classmates read your poems aloud. Remember to read your poem with expression. Ask your classmates to provide feedback on your delivery.

For Your Working Portfolio As you **reflect** on your writing process, make some notes about what you enjoyed most and least about writing a poem. Keep your notes along with your finished poem in your 📁 **Working Portfolio.**

Drive-Through Grammar

Capitalizing Poetry In general, the first word of every line of poetry is capitalized. However poets often break sentences into shorter pieces. Then the usual capitalization rules apply. Write the following lines on the board. Have students capitalize words as necessary.

first, my child,
you must understand
the history of sweet potatoes.

Capitalize only First. The other lines finish the sentence.

Speak for Yourself: *Drama*

If you've ever seen a movie based on a book you've read, you know that books and movies tell stories very differently. When you adapt your **short story** into a drama, you will be able to show your story in action. You will also have to consider how things that work in a story will need to be done differently when they are acted out.

Student Model
Rachel Smith
King Philip Middle School

The family rushed to the window just in time to see the garage swept away by the great torrent of water. "My car . . . Leo's wood business . . . gone!" her mother whispered in disbelief. . . .

The family rushes to the window

ELAINE: The garage! It's being swept away!

Mother is stunned

MOTHER: My car . . . Leo's wood business . . . gone!

"I wish this were all just a nightmare!"

Here's How **Creating a Drama**

- Write the dialogue from your story on a separate page. Label all the dialogue with the names of the characters who say it.

- Add any background information, unspoken feelings, or thoughts from your story to your dialogue so the audience will understand everything. It could be as simple as a character saying, "I'm scared," or, "I haven't seen you since last summer."

- Write some stage directions so the actors will not only know what to say, but also what to do. Mention if a character is yelling, or whispering a line, or standing in a certain place.

- Bring in props, music and costumes to add some realism and mood to your drama.

- Assign roles to your friends and act out your drama in front of the class.

For more information on speaking skills, see p. 545–47.

Short Story **471**

SHORT STORY

SHORT STORY

Student Help Desk

Students can use the Student Help Desk as a quick review or as a quick reference as they write a short story or poem.

Teacher's Notes
WHAT WORKS:

Student Help Desk

Short Story and Poem at a Glance

SHORT STORY

Introduction
Sets the stage by
- introducing the **characters**
- describing the **setting**

Body
Develops the plot by
- introducing the conflict
- telling a sequence of **events**
- developing **characters** through words and actions
- building towards a **climax**

Conclusion
Finishes the story by
- resolving the **conflict**
- telling the **last event**

POEM

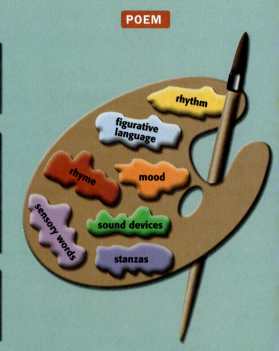

rhythm

figurative language

rhyme

mood

sensory words

sound devices

stanzas

Idea Bank

Finding a topic for a short story or poem

Talk with older family members about their experiences.

Play "remember when . . ." with other family members.

Imagine how your great-great-grandchild will see your life.

Recall an event or person that was especially important to you.

Make up a tall tale about something that might have happened years ago.

Look hard at the world around you. What sounds or textures do you like best?

Friendly Feedback

Questions for Your Peer Reader

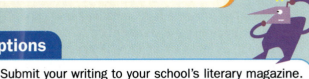

- What surprised you about my story or poem?
- What effect did my writing have on you?
- What was the part you liked best?
- How could I have improved my story or poem?
- What parts should I keep and make better?

Publishing Options

Print	Submit your writing to your school's literary magazine.
Oral Communication	Read your story or poem aloud to a small group, or turn it into a dramatic reading using props and music to enhance the mood.
Online	Check out **mcdougallittell.com** for more publishing options.

The Bottom Line

Checklist for Short Story

Have I . . .

____ provided a strong beginning and ending?

____ used story elements of character, setting, and plot to create a convincing world?

____ included sensory language and concrete details?

____ used dialogue effectively?

____ developed a main conflict?

____ made the sequence of events clear?

____ maintained a consistent point of view?

Checklist for Poem

Have I . . .

____ focused on one idea or feeling?

____ used precise words in an interesting way?

____ included fresh sensory words?

____ used figurative language, such as similes and metaphors?

____ included sound devices, such as alliteration and rhyme?

Short Story **473**

TEACHER'S LOUNGE

A Slice of Life

"It is not because things are difficult that we do not dare; it is because we do not dare that they are difficult."
—Seneca

A Slice of Life

What product did a Brooklyn kerosene dealer develop after seeing workers treat cuts and burns with grease that accumulated on drill rods in the Titusville, Pennsylvania, oil field?

Answer: Vaseline. Robert Chesebrough visited Titusville in 1859—the year the nation's first commercially productive oil well was discovered there—and soon afterward figured out how to produce the grease from raw crude oil. He began manufacturing and marketing it as a salve in 1870.

CHAPTER OBJECTIVES

To prepare and write a successful research report

DAILY TEST PREPARATION

Revision-in-Context: Combining Sentences Write the following item on the board or use **Daily Test Preparation Transparency** p. DT58.

1 The reporter wrote his
2 story. He investigated
3 reports of raw sewage
4 polluting local beaches.

What is the **best** way to combine the two sentences in line 2?

A. story until he investigated

B. story after he investigated

C. story, and he investigated

D. story unless he investigated

Teaching Point: A common item in revision-in-context questions is combining sentences. In this case, the conjunction *after* explains the sequential order of the two events.

The Basics in a Box provides graphic and verbal guidelines for organizing a research report. As the diagram indicates, the material gathered through research is presented in the report's body.

The RUBRIC, or Standards for Writing, describes a research report that would merit the highest score. A complete rubric, describing several levels of proficiency, is on page 143 of the Assessment Masters.

Learn What It Is

Did you ever hear about something and think, "I'd like to know more about this?" If you went on to talk to people about the subject, or to look it up in books or on the Internet, you were doing research. A **research report** is a formal written report on a given subject. Here is how you write such a report.

Basics in a Box

RESEARCH REPORT AT A GLANCE

Introduction — Body — Conclusion — Works Cited — Thesis

Research

RUBRIC

Standards for Writing

A successful research report should

- include a strong introduction with a clear thesis statement
- use evidence from several sources to develop and support ideas
- credit the sources of information

- follow a logical pattern of organization, using transitions between ideas
- summarize ideas in the conclusion
- include a Works Cited list at the end

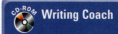 **Writing Coach**

WORKSHOP RESOURCES

 Time-Saver Transparencies Binder:
- Basics in a Box p. BB8
- Critical Thinking Graphic Organizers p. CT5
- Daily Test Preparation p. DT58
- Quick-Fix Grammar and Style Charts p. QF5
- Revising, Editing, and Proofreading Models pp. RE33–40

- Writing and Communication Skills pp. WC6–7

 Writing and Communication Masters pp. 98–109

Integrated Technology and Media

 Electronic Teacher Tools CD-ROM

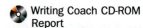 Writing Coach CD-ROM Report

See How It's Done: Research Report

Clark 1

Joe Clark
Mrs. Williams
English
16 April 2000

Tsunamis

You probably know something about tornadoes, hurricanes, earthquakes, floods, and forest fires. You may not know much about tsunamis, or giant ocean waves. However, the deadly waves of a tsunami can be a serious natural disaster, striking with almost no warning. As Kathy A. Svitil has written, "If you can see the wave coming, it's too late to escape."

According to Robert E. Wilson, tsunamis are started by landslides, earthquakes, or volcanoes. The Handy Science Answer Book says that the ocean floor must shift upward. A horizontal, or sideways, shift will not cause the waves ("What" 82). Such a wave travels very fast, but it gets dangerous when it gets close to shore. There the wave slows down in shallow water, and it gets higher ("Physics"). In fact, the name *tsunami* means "harbor wave." Frank I. González thinks that the name may come from the fact that you can't really see a tsunami until it gets close to shore. Yet the earthquake that causes the tsunami can occur thousands of miles away.

One of the worst tsunamis in this century hit Papua, New Guinea, on July 17, 1998. As described by Svitil, the first event was an earthquake, only about 15 miles offshore, that measured 7.1 on the Richter scale. Within ten minutes, a wall of water about 40 feet high slammed into four small villages. The villages of Arop and Warapu were wiped out.

RUBRIC IN ACTION

❶ This writer begins with a strong introduction that involves the reader.
Another option: Begin with a description of what happened when an actual tsunami struck land.

❷ Clear thesis statement

❸ Credits source of information. No page number is provided for an Internet source.

❹ This paragraph supports the thesis statement's claim that a tsunami is a serious natural disaster.

Research Report **475**

REPORT

ANALYZING THE MODEL
Use the numbered questions below to make sure that students understand how the model satisfies the rubric.

❶ Critical Thinking Why would the introduction be just as effective if the report began with a description of a tsunami strike?

Because the description would grab readers' attention and make them want to continue reading

❷ Critical Thinking Why is it important to state the thesis in the introduction?

So the reader will know precisely what points the writer is going to cover in the body of the report

❸ Why doesn't the writer provide a page number after the citation for "Physics"?

The information was obtained from an Internet source.

❹ How does the writer support the thesis statement in this paragraph?

The writer provides details of the size and devastating power of the tsunami.

NEED MORE INFORMATION?
Refer students back to **Chapter 17, Elaboration,** for a review of how to effectively use facts and statistics to support main ideas.

REPORT

THE LANGUAGE OF **LITERATURE**

See the Research Report Writing Workshop in *The Language of Literature,* Level 7.

---

 mcdougallittell.com
Additional Writing Prompts

Assessment

Assessment Masters:
• Writing Prompts p. 134
• Rubrics p. 143
• Student Models pp. 168–173

Teacher's Guide to Assessment and Portfolio Use

Students Acquiring English/ESL

Side by Side pp. 115–129

⑤ Use the Works Cited list to determine the author's full name, the article, and the publication that the writer credits.

"Tsunami!" by Frank I. Gonzalez, in Scientific American

Clark 2

Two-thirds of the village of Sissano and half of the village of Malol were also ruined. More than 2,100 people died.

Although records show that about 57 tsunamis happen every ten years (González), between 1990 and May 1999—slightly less than 10 years—82 had been reported. This "increase" is probably due to better communication. There may not be more killer waves, but we know about almost every one that happens.

Can anything be done to reduce the damage of tsunamis? Yes. The good news is that there would have been many more deaths in the last ten years if countries had not started warning systems and

⑤ Credits source of information

Clark 4

Works Cited

González, Frank I. "Tsunami!" <u>Scientific American</u> May 1999. 5 Jan. 2000 <http://www.scientificamerican.com/1999/0599issue/0599gonzalez.html>.

"Physics of Tsunamis." <u>West Coast and Alaska Tsunami Warning Center Home Page</u>. 6 Sept. 1999. West Coast and Alaska Tsunami Warning Center. 7 Mar. 2000 <http://wcatwc.gov/physics.htm>.

Svitil, Kathy A. "A Deadly Wave." <u>Discover</u> Jan. 1999: 68.

"What Is a Tsunami?" <u>The Handy Science Answer Book</u>. Detroit: Visible Ink, 1994.

Wilson, Robert E. "Tsunami." <u>Grolier Multimedia Encyclopedia</u>. CD-ROM. Deluxe ed. Danbury: Grolier, 1998.

Works Cited
- Identifies all sources credited in the report
- Presents entries in alphabetical order
- Gives complete publication information
- Contains correctly punctuated entries
- Is double-spaced throughout
- Follows an accepted style, such as MLA style

Drive-Through Grammar

Punctuating Titles When students use articles in their research reports, the title of the article—whether from a magazine or from an Internet source—should be in quotation marks. Titles of books, encyclopedias, and magazines are underlined. Write the following source citations on the board. Have students punctuate them correctly:

Bernstein, Ralph W. Run for Your Lives! Tornado Magazine. January 1998: 23–24.

Bernstein, Ralph W. "Run for Your Lives!" <u>Tornado Magazine</u>. January 1998: 23–24.

Hernandez, Sue. A Book of Disasters. New York: Big Apple, 1999.

Hernandez, Sue. <u>A Book of Disasters</u>. New York: Big Apple, 1999.

Do It Yourself

Writing Prompt Write a research report about a topic that interests you.
Purpose To share information about the topic
Audience Your teacher, your classmates, and anyone else interested in the topic

① Developing a Research Plan

When you write a research report, you need to gather information from several sources. At first, your topic will probably be too broad. Your first job will therefore be to use information to narrow your topic to a size you can manage.

Narrowing Your Topic

Use several sources to learn more about your broad topic. Look for one aspect that interests you and that you could cover in the number of pages you have been assigned to write. To narrow your topic you might

- browse the Internet
- skim books on your broad topic. Check each book's introduction, table of contents, and picture captions
- ask questions of other people

Developing Research Questions

Once you have narrowed your topic, develop a set of questions to direct further research. For example, the writer of the report on tsunamis was assigned the subject of natural disasters. He wanted to explore a kind of natural disaster that was not well-known to most of his classmates. His research questions included the following:

- Just what is a tsunami?
- What does the name *tsunami* mean?
- How big a danger are tsunamis?

As you discover ideas and information during your research, you may decide to change the direction of your topic.

REPORT

REPORT

❷ Finding Information

Locating Sources

It is important to use information from several sources in writing your report. Reading multiple sources will give you a deeper understanding of your subject and more ideas about

For in-depth information on finding useful sources, read Chapter 28, "Finding Information," on pages 493–505. Belo are some of the many sources you should consider.

Information Resources		
Books	Dictionaries	CD-ROM encyclopedias
Newspapers	Atlases	Statistical abstracts
Magazines	Thesauri	On-line databases
Encyclopedias	Almanacs	Internet sites

Evaluating Sources

Once you have located sources, you must make sure they are good ones. Ask yourself these questions for each source you consider.

- Is the author an expert? What qualifications does he or sh have?
- Is the author fair?
- Is the source up-to-date?

For more on choosing and evaluating sources, see p. 502.

Making Source Cards

When you find a good source, write down its author, title, an publication information on an index card. This becomes your **source card.** See the chart and sample cards on the next pa for guidelines on documenting each kind of source.

Number each of your source cards. Numbered source car can help you in two ways. First, when you take notes, you ca refer to the source by number instead of writing down the tit and author again and again. Second, your source cards will h you create your Works Cited list, an alphabetized list of the sources actually used in writing the report. You will learn more about the Works Cited list on page 485.

Here's How Making Source Cards

- **Book** Write the author's name, the title, the location and name of the publisher, the copyright date, and the library call number.
- **Magazine or newspaper article** Write the author's name if the name is given, the title of the article, the name and date of the publication, and page numbers of the article.
- **Encyclopedia Article** Write the author's name if given, the title of the article, and the name and copyright date of the encyclopedia.
- **Internet** Write the author's name if given, the title of the document, the publication name of any print version, the date you accessed the article, and the electronic address <in angle brackets>.

Sample Source Cards

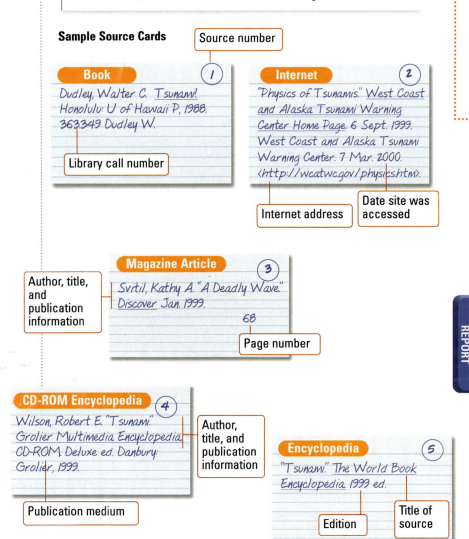

Source number

Book ①
Dudley, Walter C. *Tsunami!*
Honolulu: U of Hawaii P, 1988.
363.349 Dudley W.

Library call number

Internet ②
"Physics of Tsunamis." *West Coast and Alaska Tsunami Warning Center Home Page.* 6 Sept. 1999. West Coast and Alaska Tsunami Warning Center. 7 Mar. 2000. <http://wcatwc.gov/physics.htm>.

Internet address

Date site was accessed

Magazine Article ③
Svitil, Kathy A. "A Deadly Wave." *Discover* Jan. 1999.
                    68

Author, title, and publication information

Page number

CD-ROM Encyclopedia ④
Wilson, Robert E. "Tsunami." *Grolier Multimedia Encyclopedia* CD-ROM. Deluxe ed. Danbury: Grolier, 1999.

Author, title, and publication information

Publication medium

Encyclopedia ⑤
"Tsunami." *The World Book Encyclopedia.* 1999 ed.

Edition

Title of source

Research Report **479**

Taking Notes

Take notes on any information you find that will be useful in writing your paper. Write each note on a separate index card. Most of your notes will paraphrase the author's words.

Taking Notes

- **Use a separate index card** for each piece of information.
- **Give each card a heading** to show the subject of the note.
- **Write the number of the matching source card** on each note card.
- **Write the number of the page** where you found the information.
- **Put quotation marks around anything** you copy word for word from the source.

For more on taking notes, see pp. 512–514.

Paraphrasing

When you paraphrase, you rewrite what the text says in your own words. Your words will usually be simpler. Here is a paragraph from a magazine article, followed by a note card with a paraphrase of the same paragraph.

PROFESSIONAL MODEL

Five or ten minutes later a wall of water 40 feet high at some points slammed into the spit, engulfing the villages. Almost instantly, Arop and Warapu, each home to 2,500 people, were gone; half of Malol and two-thirds of Sissano were also destroyed.

—Kathy A. Svitil, "A Deadly Wave"

Note Card

> **Paraphrase**   3
> What tsunami did in Papua, New Guinea
> 40-foot-high wall of water hit 4 small vil-
> lages 5 or 10 minutes after quake. Arop
> and Warapu wiped out. Two-thirds of
> Sissano and half of Malol ruined.   68

Source number

Heading showing subject

Page number

TEACHING TIP

If students have difficulty paraphrasing text in their own words, suggest that they put the original material aside while they rewrite the ideas from memory. They may find this strategy helps them use more familiar words and focus on the main ideas.

CUSTOMIZING TIP

Students Acquiring English/ESL
Explain to students that, when they paraphrase, they should write in their own words. Encourage students to look up any unfamiliar words in the dictionary and to use simple vocabulary when paraphrasing.

Spice It Up!

Have students get together in groups and take turns paraphrasing lines from their favorite movies. Point out to students that they can use their movie-paraphrasing skills when they conduct research.

Quoting

Although most of your notes will paraphrase the source material, sometimes you will want to copy the author's words exactly. When you do, be sure to use quotation marks. You should save quotations for times like these:

- The author's words make the point in especially vivid language.
- The author's point is so important that it needs to be reported exactly.

Avoiding Plagiarism

If you use an author's words without giving credit, you are committing plagiarism. You are stealing words from the author and passing off his or her work as your own. Sometimes it is easy to let paraphrasing slip into plagiarism by accident.

ORIGINAL

In fact, the Japanese word *tsunami* translates literally as "harbor wave," perhaps because a tsunami can speed silently and undetected across the ocean, then unexpectedly arise as destructively high waves in shallow coastal waters.

—Frank I. González, "Tsunami!"

PLAGIARIZED VERSION

The Japanese word *tsunami* translates as "harbor wave," perhaps because a tsunami can speed unseen across the ocean, then unexpectedly arise as destructively high waves in coastal waters.

The writer did make changes. He left out some words ("literally," "shallow") and changed some words ("silently and undetected" became "unseen"), but that is not enough. The writer has plagiarized the source. Following is a version in which the source has been noted, and plagiarism is avoided.

STUDENT MODEL

In fact, the name *tsunami* means "harbor wave." Frank I. González thinks that the name may come from the fact that you can't really see a tsunami until it gets close to shore.

> Source is credited.

Research Report **481**

STUDENT MODEL

For additional practice with paraphrasing, write the following paragraph on the board. Ask students to avoid plagiarizing by rewriting the information in their own words.

A disastrous tsunami slammed into the coasts of Chile on May 22, 1960. It resulted from a mammoth Pacific Ocean earthquake, which carried a magnitude of 8.6. The tsunami arrived on Chilean shores only 10 to 15 minutes after the earthquake hit.

An earthquake originating in the Pacific Ocean caused a tsunami that devastated the Chilean coast on May 22, 1960. Moving quickly, the wall of water slammed the coast only about 10 to 15 minutes after the 8.6-magnitude earthquake struck.

REPORT

REPORT

CUSTOMIZING TIP

Gifted and Talented Encourage students to experiment with the introductions and conclusions of their research reports. Tell them that they can begin with an engaging question, a surprising fact, a vivid description, or a well-chosen quotation.

CUSTOMIZING TIP

Addressing Learning Styles
Visual Before creating an outline, some students might want to use a spider map to break up their topic into its parts. Use 🏛 **Critical Thinking Graphic Organizer Spider Map,** p. CT5, to show students how to list ideas for a report on tsunamis.

TEACHING TIP

Remind students that their outlines do not have to use complete or detailed sentences. Many people only list the topics or general ideas for the categories in their outlines, and organize these topics into complete ideas and sentences later.

❹ Organizing and Outlining

Planning Your Report

Your research report will have three parts: the **introduction,** the **body,** and the **conclusion.**

Introduction Here is where you tell what your report is about. The introduction should have a lively opening and should include your **thesis statement,** or your statement of the main idea. A good thesis statement

- tells the subject of the report
- can be supported with facts

Body The body of your research report gives the information that supports your thesis statement. Good body paragraphs have the following characteristics:

- The topic sentences support the thesis statement.
- The paragraphs are logically organized, so that ideas flow smoothly.

Conclusion The end of your research paper should sum up your ideas and restate your thesis statement in different words.

Making an Outline

To ensure that your report will be well organized, prepare an outline before you write. To make an outline, begin by grouping your note cards according to key ideas. Then you can put them into an order that supports your thesis statement and flows logically. Here is the beginning of the outline for the research report on tsunamis.

> Tsunamis
>
> **Thesis statement:** A tsunami can be a deadly natural disaster, striking with almost no warning.
>
> I Introduction
> II What a tsunami is
> III The kinds of damage it can cause
> IV How often tsunamis happen

For more about creating outlines, see p. 515.

❺ Drafting

Use your outline and notes to begin your draft. You don't have to begin at the beginning and work straight through to the end. If you want to, you can start with the section you have the strongest ideas about. As you work, follow these guidelines.

Follow your outline. Write one or more paragraphs for every major part of your outline. (If you don't have enough material to make a paragraph, either frame new questions and do further research or revise your plan.)

Put paragraphs in order. Make sure your paragraphs are in order before you begin your revision.

Support your thesis. Remember that everything in your paper should support your main idea.

Integrating Your Notes Into Your Report

The writer of the report on tsunamis found a lot of material in several sources, so he took a lot of notes. When it was time to write his report, he grouped note cards into sections. Here are two notes he took about early-warning systems. Following the notes is a paragraph from his report that uses the information from the notes. Note that the writer gives credit to his source.

Early-Warning Systems ⑥

Over a fourth of Pacific tsunamis reported since 1895 began near Japan. The Japanese have developed programs to reduce hazards, including warning systems, education, and coastal barriers.

Early-Warning Systems ⑥

Japan has done better with cutting deaths than other countries, such as Indonesia. There most people did not know that an earthquake could be followed by a tsunami. In Papua, New Guinea, some actually went to the beach to see what was going on.

STUDENT MODEL

The good news is that there would have been many more deaths in the last ten years if scientists had not started educational programs and warning systems. The bad news is that in many places warning systems are not in place, and people have not been trained to recognize warning signals (González).

Addressing Learning Styles
Visual Suggest that students experiment with "cutting and pasting" the old-fashioned way by using scissors and tape to cut their drafts into paragraphs that they can rearrange on their desktops, or even on the floor!

TEACHING TIP

Cross-Curricular Connection
Art Encourage students to create visuals for their research reports. Students can use art supplies to create diagrams, charts and other visual aids.

REPORT

REPORT

6 **Documenting Information**

You do not have to document, or give a source for, information that your readers could be expected to know. An example of such information is that the United States experiences tornadoes, hurricanes, floods, and forest fires.

For less well-known material, the most common way to document it is to refer to its source in parentheses within the report. This is called **parenthetical documentation.** The reference in parentheses directs your reader to the Works Cited list at the end of your report. You should supply parenthetical documentation for each quotation, paraphrase, or summary that you use.

Here's How **Guidelines for Parenthetical Documentation**

Work by One Author: Give the author's last name and the page number (unless it is a nonprint work) in parentheses.

> Records show that about 57 tsunamis happen every ten years (González).

If you mention the author's name in the sentence, give only the page number if the source is more than one page.

> As Dudley reports, tsunami waves in the open ocean are many hundreds of feet long but only a few feet high. In deep water, the wave usually passes unnoticed. In shallow water, however, the wave can become as high as a 10-story building (76).

Work with No Author Given Give the title (or a shortened version of the title) and the page number if it is a print work.

> A horizontal shift will not cause the waves ("What" 82).

Electronic Source Give the author's last name. If no author is given, list the title.

> Such a wave travels very fast, but it gets dangerous when it gets close to shore. There the wave slows down in shallow water, and it gets higher ("Physics").

TEACHING TIP

Remind students to insert parenthetical documentation as they develop their drafts to avoid mislabeling or plagiarizing quotations.

CUSTOMIZING TIP

Less Proficient Learners Tell students to use their source cards to help them insert parenthetical documentation in their reports. Encourage students to insert a note in parentheses in their drafts whenever they use information or a quote from a source. The notes do not have to be in proper form at first. The important thing is to identify the source and page number if there is one. The format can be corrected later.

Spice It Up!

Quotable Quote "I don't wait for moods. You accomplish nothing if you do that. Your mind must know it has got to get down to work." —Pearl S. Buck

Discuss why it is sometimes difficult to start an extensive research project. Ask students what strategies they can use to get their minds in a research "mood."

Preparing a Works Cited List

- First, gather your source cards.
- Next, read your report.
- Whenever you come to a reference, put a check on the card for that source.
- If when you finish reading you find that any source card remains unchecked, put it aside. Your Works Cited list will include only those sources you actually used in writing your paper.
- Place your checked source cards in alphabetical order by the last name of the author. If a card names more than one author, use the first author. If no author is named, use the first word of the title. Don't count *A, An,* or *The* as a title word. Use the format shown here.

Clark 4

Works Cited

González, Frank I. "Tsunami!" <u>Scientific American</u> May 1999. 5 Jan. 2000 <http://www.scientificamerican.com/1999/0599issue/0599gonzalez.html>.

"Physics of Tsunamis." <u>West Coast and Alaska Tsunami Warning Center Home Page</u>. 6 Sept. 1999. West Coast and Alaska Tsunami Warning Center. 7 Mar. 2000 <http://wcatwc.gov/physics.htm>.

Svitil, Kathy A. "A Deadly Wave." <u>Discover</u> Jan. 1999: 68.

"What Is a Tsunami?" <u>The Handy Science Answer Book</u>. Detroit: Visible Ink, 1994.

Wilson, Robert E. "Tsunami." <u>Grolier Multimedia Encyclopedia</u>. CD-ROM. Deluxe ed. Danbury: Grolier, 1999.

> **Indent the second and subsequent lines of each entry one-half inch or five spaces.**

> **Center the title, "Works Cited."**

> **Double-space the whole list.**

For more about documenting sources, see MLA Citation Guidelines pp. 640–647.

NEED MORE INFORMATION?
For additional information on pronouns and their antecedents, direct students to **Chapter 3, Pronouns.**

ASSESSMENT

 Assessment Masters:
- Writing Prompts p. 134
- Rubrics p. 143
- Student Models pp. 168–173

 Teacher's Guide to Assessment and Portfolio Use

---

❼ Revising

TARGET SKILL ▶Paragraphing Start a new paragraph every time you begin a new subject. For more help with revising review the rubric on page 474.

> As Kathy A. Svitil has written, "If you can see the wave coming, it's too late to escape.¶ According to Robert E. Wilson, tsunamis are started by landslides, earthquakes, or volcanoes.

❽ Editing and Proofreading

TARGET SKILL ▶Pronoun-Antecedent Agreement A pronoun needs to agree in number and person with its antecedent, the word it refers to.

> Such a wave travels very fast, but it gets dangerous
> *it gets*
> when ~~they get~~ close to shore, because the wave slows down in shallow water, and it gets higher.

For more on pronoun-antecedent agreement, see pp. 73–75.

❾ Sharing and Reflecting

When you are satisfied with your report, **share** it with others giving an oral presentation. You may want to use photos or possibly a videotape or an interactive Web site to add excitement to your presentation. Ask for feedback regarding the content, purpose, and message of your report.

For Your Working Portfolio After sharing, **reflect** on what you learned by writing your report. Did you learn more about your topic? Are there still things you would like to know about it? Evaluate your own research and frame new questions for further investigation. Attach your reflections to your finished report and save them in your 📁 **Working Portfolio.**

Drive-Through Grammar

Pronoun-Antecedent Agreement Tell students that when two singular antecedents are joined by *or* or *nor*, they should use a singular pronoun. When a singular and plural antecedent are joined by *or* or *nor*, they should use the noun nearer the verb to determine the pronoun. Write the following sentences on the board and have students select the correct pronoun.

Neither the father nor his children had finished (his, <u>their</u>) meal.

Either the cat or the dog will have to give up (<u>its</u>, their) bed.

Speak for Yourself: *Oral Report*

LESSON OBJECTIVES

To plan and present an oral report

"A wall of water 40-feet high and traveling at tremendous speed smashed into the villages."

What force could create such a wave? Because you have researched and written about tsunamis, often called tidal waves, you can tell others about them. Presenting your report to an audience offers many opportunities. You will have the chance to use charts, graphs, photographs, and multimedia to illustrate the information in your essay. Your report may get others so interested in your subject that they want to research another aspect of your topic.

Here's How Creating an Oral Report

- Use your written report to plan the points of your presentation, but don't read the report to your audience.
- Gather charts, graphs, photographs, and anything else that will help make the facts you are presenting clear.
- Make an outline of the information you will present. Note when and where you will introduce the visuals.
- Make sure the visuals can be seen clearly from the back of the room.
- Practice your presentation, including how you will handle the charts, photographs, and other visuals.

For more information on speaking skills, see p. 545–47.

Research Report   **487**

REPORT

REPORT

TEACHING TIP

Cooperative Learning Have students work in groups to generate ideas for visuals they can use in their oral reports. Encourage students to suggest specific photographs, videos, and charts that could visually clarify information.

TEACHING TIP

Speaking and Listening Have students practice presenting their oral reports to a small group of peers. Ask the peer audience to listen for and identify areas that need further information, areas that are unclear, and areas that would benefit from a visual representation.

TEACHING TIP

Have students discuss and generate criteria to evaluate their own presentations and the presentations of others.

Student Help Desk

Students can use the Student Help Desk as a quick review or as a quick reference as they write their research reports.

Teacher's Notes

WHAT WORKS:

Student Help Desk

Research Report at a Glance

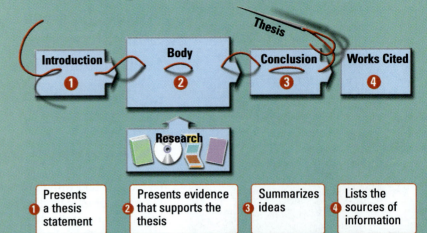

Thesis

| Introduction ❶ | Body ❷ | Conclusion ❸ | Works Cited ❹ |

Research

| ❶ Presents a thesis statement | ❷ Presents evidence that supports the thesis | ❸ Summarizes ideas | ❹ Lists the sources of information |

Idea Bank

Tips for Finding a Topic

Freewrite. List subjects like food or weather. Then list smaller parts of each subject. For example, you could begin with sports, then move to basketball, and then to women's college basketball. Finally, you might focus on the history of one women's college basketball team.

Listen to the news. As you listen, list any subject that appeals to you as a possible topic.

Think of people. Make a list of people you admire or wonder about. Review your list to see if one of them would make a good subject for a research report.

Think of places. Make a list of landmarks or historic places in your area. Include places that may be famous only in your area. Plan to write a research report about a place on your list.

Read literature. Think about authors you have been studying, such as Ray Bradbury and Virginia Hamilton. What topics did they write about that you might like to explore further? What more would you like to know about their lives?

488 Writing Workshop

Friendly Feedback

Questions for Your Peer Reader

- What did you like best about my report?
- What parts weren't clear?
- What did you learn from it?
- What further information should have been included?
- What information should have been left out?

Publishing Options

Print	Group your class's research reports by category, such as science, history, or popular culture. Make booklets compiling the reports in each category. Put the booklets in the classroom library.
Oral Communication	Work with another classmate to present your reports. One partner should tell the narrative of the report. The other partner should use visuals to illustrate key points, explaining what is being shown.
Online	Check out **mcdougallittell.com** for more publishing options.

The Bottom Line

Checklist for Research Report

Have I . . .

- ____ written a strong introduction?
- ____ stated my thesis clearly?
- ____ used evidence from reliable sources to support my ideas?
- ____ credited my sources of information?
- ____ used a logical pattern of organization?
- ____ used transitions?
- ____ written a strong summary for the conclusion?
- ____ included a correctly formatted Works Cited list at the end?

Teacher's Notes
WHAT DOESN'T WORK:

TEACHER'S LOUNGE

Just for Laughs

A man who can smile when things go wrong has probably just thought of someone he can blame it on.

A Slice of Life

Vegetable Roll-Ups

Lettuce, shredded carrots, chopped cucumber, red and green pepper strips, tomato slices, thin onion slices, grated cheese, humus, soft tortillas.

Spread each tortilla with a generous coating of humus. Place some of each of the remaining ingredients in the center of the bread. Fold up bottom of bread and roll.

Communicating in the Information Age

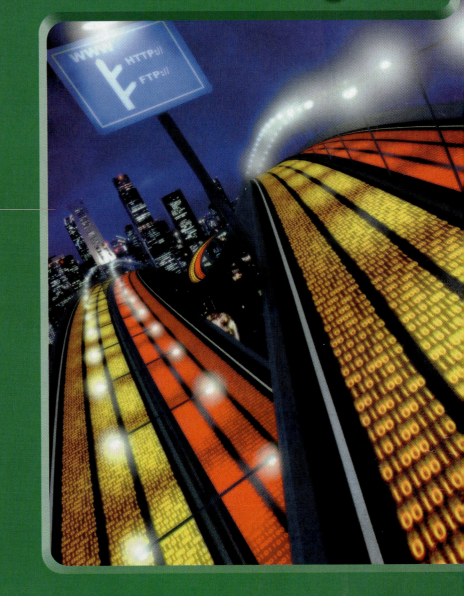

Reading the Signs

To travel the information highway, you're going to need some special skills. By learning how to find, analyze, and use information, you can make the trip a lot less stressful and more enjoyable. So get ready to take a trip to knowledge! Who knows where you'll end up?

491

Chapter 28 Finding Information

Use the online lesson planner at **mcdougallittell.com** to customize instruction.

Pupil Edition	Print Resources Writing and Communication Masters	Time-Saver Transparencies Binder Daily Test Preparation
LESSON 1 The Library and Media Center p. 494		p. DT 58
LESSON 2 Locating Sources pp. 495-497	p. 110	p. DT 59
LESSON 3 Reference Works pp. 498-499	p. 111	p. DT 59
LESSON 4 Using The Web pp. 500-501		p. DT 60
LESSON 5 Choosing and Evaluating Sources pp. 502-503		p. DT 60

ASSESSMENT

 Teacher's Guide to Assessment and Portfolio Use

 mcdougallittell.com

Visit our web site for:
· Student activities
· Links to related resources
· Teaching resources
· Professional articles

 Electronic Teacher Tools

Print-Out Option Exercises in the following components may be printed from the **Electronic Teacher Tools** as worksheets.

· Writing and Communication Masters
· Test Preparation (Use for levels 6-10)
· College Test Preparation (Use for levels 11 and 12)
· Weekly Vocabulary and Spelling
· Assessment Masters
· Students Acquiring English/ESL
   · English Grammar Survival Kit
   · Side by Side
   · Test Preparation

Chapter 29 Study and Test-Taking Skills

Use the online lesson planner at **mcdougallittell.com** to customize instruction.

Pupil Edition	Print Resources		Time-Saver Transparencies Binder	Students Acquiring English/ESL
	Writing and Communication Masters	Test Preparation	Daily Test Preparation	Test Preparation
LESSON 1 Reading for Information pp. 508-509		Lessons 1-2	p. DT 61	pp. 19-23, 25-53
LESSON 2 Understanding Graphic Aids pp. 510-511			p. DT 61	
LESSON 3 Taking Notes pp. 512-514	p. 112		p. DT 62	
LESSON 4 Creating Outlines p. 515	p. 113		p. DT 62	
LESSON 5 Taking Objective Tests pp. 516-517		Lesson 1	p. DT 63	pp. 1-8
LESSON 6 Answering Essay Questions p. 519		Lesson 6	p. DT 63	pp. 54-57

ASSESSMENT

Teacher's Guide to Assessment and Portfolio Use

Chapter 30 Using Thinking Skills

Use the online lesson planner at **mcdougallittell.com** to customize instruction.

Pupil Edition	Print Resources — Writing and Communication Masters	Time-Saver Transparencies Binder — Critical Thinking Graphic Organizers	Time-Saver Transparencies Binder — Daily Test Preparation	Integrated Technology and Media — Media Focus: Analyzing and Producing Media	Students Acquiring English/ESL — Side by Side
LESSON 1 How Ideas Are Related pp. 524-525		pp. CT 13-15	p. DT 64		pp. 19-20
LESSON 2 Separating Facts from Opinions pp. 526-527			p. DT 64		
LESSON 3 Going Beyond the Facts pp. 528-529			p. DT 65		
LESSON 4 Avoiding Errors in Reasoning pp. 530-531	p. 114		p. DT 65	Program 2	
LESSON 5 Recognizing Emotional Appeals pp. 532-533	p. 115		p. DT 66		

ASSESSMENT

 Teacher's Guide to Assessment and Portfolio Use

 mcdougallittell.com

Visit our web site for:
· Student activities
· Links to related resources
· Teaching resources
· Professional articles

 Electronic Teacher Tools

Print-Out Option Exercises in the following components may be printed from the **Electronic Teacher Tools** as worksheets.

· Writing and Communication Masters
· Test Preparation (Use for levels 6-10)
· College Test Preparation (Use for levels 11 and 12)
· Weekly Vocabulary and Spelling
· Assessment Masters
· Students Acquiring English/ESL
  · English Grammar Survival Kit
  · Side by Side
  · Test Preparation

RESOURCE MANAGEMENT GUIDE

Chapter 31 Listening and Speaking Skills

Use the online lesson planner at **mcdougallittell.com** to customize instruction.

Pupil Edition	Print Resources — Writing and Communication Masters	Time-Saver Transparencies Binder — Daily Test Preparation	Time-Saver Transparencies Binder — Writing and Communication Skills
LESSON 1 — Listening Actively pp. 538-540		p. DT 66	p. WC 10
LESSON 2 — Interviewing pp. 541-542	p. 116	p. DT 67	p. WC 11
LESSON 3 — Speaking Informally pp. 543-544		p. DT 67	p. WC 12
LESSON 4 — Preparing an Oral Report pp. 545-547	p. 117	p. DT 68	
LESSON 5 — Presenting an Oral Interpretation pp. 548-549		p. DT 68	

ASSESSMENT

Teacher's Guide to Assessment and Portfolio Use

RESOURCE MANAGEMENT GUIDE

Chapter 32 Examining the Media

 Use the online lesson planner at **mcdougallittell.com** to customize instruction.

Pupil Edition	Time-Saver Transparencies Binder	Integrated Technology and Media
	Daily Test Preparation	Media Focus: Analyzing and Producing Media
LESSON 1 Comparing Media pp. 554-556	p. DT 69	
LESSON 2 Media Influence pp. 557-558	p. DT 69	Program 3
LESSON 3 Analyzing Media Messages pp. 559-560	p. DT 70	Program 1
LESSON 4 Using Media in Your Presentations pp. 561-563	p. DT 70	Program 5

ASSESSMENT

 Teacher's Guide to Assessment and Portfolio Use

 mcdougallittell.com

Visit our web site for:
· Student activities
· Links to related resources
· Teaching resources
· Professional articles

 Electronic Teacher Tools

Print-Out Option Exercises in the following components may be printed from the **Electronic Teacher Tools** as worksheets.

· Writing and Communication Masters
· Test Preparation (Use for levels 6-10)
· College Test Preparation (Use for levels 11 and 12)
· Weekly Vocabulary and Spelling
· Assessment Masters
· Students Acquiring English/ESL
  · English Grammar Survival Kit
  · Side by Side
  · Test Preparation

Chapter 33 Developing Your Vocabulary

Pupil Edition	Print Resources	Time-Saver Transparencies Binder	
	Writing and Communication Masters	Daily Test Preparation	Vocabulary Transparencies
LESSON 1 Building Vocabulary p. 568-569		p. DT 71	
LESSON 2 Using Context Clues pp. 570-572	pp. 118-119	p. DT 71	pp. VS 1-3
LESSON 3 Analyzing Word Parts pp. 573-575	pp. 120-122	p. DT 72	pp. VS 4-6
LESSON 4 Understanding Related Words pp. 576-577		p. DT 72	pp. VS 7-8
LESSON 5 Using References pp. 578-579		p. DT 73	

Use the online lesson planner at **mcdougallittell.com** to customize instruction.

ASSESSMENT

Teacher's Guide to Assessment and Portfolio Use

To increase vocabulary through the recognition and understanding of words that describe different ways of seeking

To use words in speaking and in writing that describe different ways of seeking

CHAPTER 28

CHAPTER 28

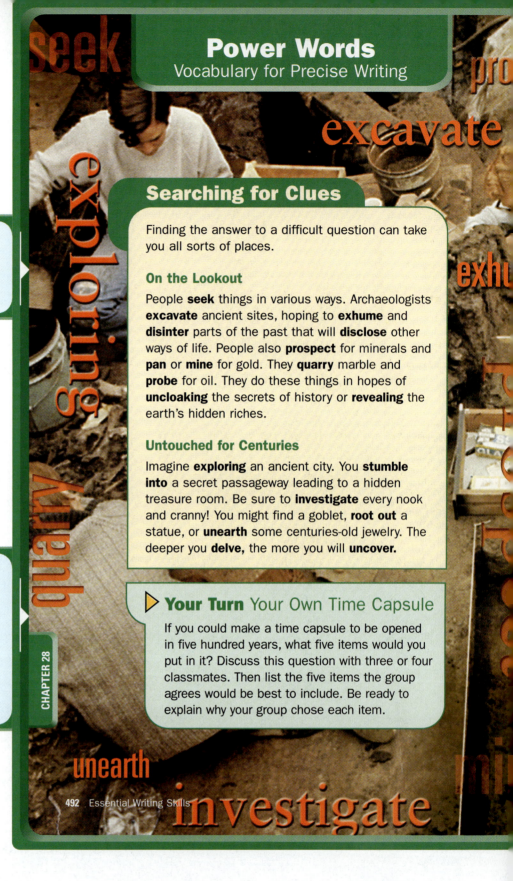

Power Words
Vocabulary for Precise Writing

Searching for Clues

Finding the answer to a difficult question can take you all sorts of places.

On the Lookout

People **seek** things in various ways. Archaeologists **excavate** ancient sites, hoping to **exhume** and **disinter** parts of the past that will **disclose** other ways of life. People also **prospect** for minerals and **pan** or **mine** for gold. They **quarry** marble and **probe** for oil. They do these things in hopes of **uncloaking** the secrets of history or **revealing** the earth's hidden riches.

Untouched for Centuries

Imagine **exploring** an ancient city. You **stumble into** a secret passageway leading to a hidden treasure room. Be sure to **investigate** every nook and cranny! You might find a goblet, **root out** a statue, or **unearth** some centuries-old jewelry. The deeper you **delve,** the more you will **uncover.**

▶ **Your Turn** Your Own Time Capsule

If you could make a time capsule to be opened in five hundred years, what five items would you put in it? Discuss this question with three or four classmates. Then list the five items the group agrees would be best to include. Be ready to explain why your group chose each item.

Finding Information

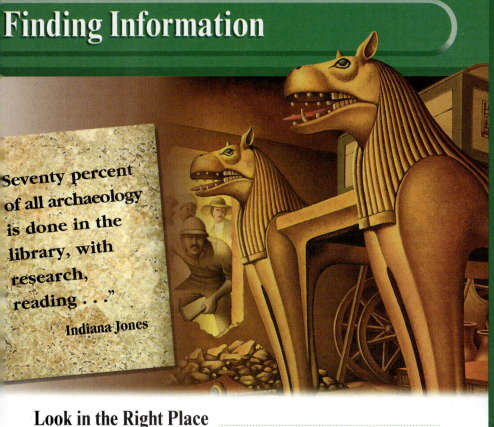

> "Seventy percent of all archaeology is done in the library, with research, reading . . ."
>
> **Indiana Jones**

Look in the Right Place

Can you imagine how much time archaeologists would waste if they simply wandered around looking for discoveries? Before they look for artifacts, scientists use books, journals, maps, and computers to figure out where rivers flowed and sediments were deposited millions of years ago. Then they dig.

Before you dig into a project, think about the research tools you can use—catalogs, indexes, reference books, periodicals, and on-line search engines. You may discover some new sources for the information you need.

Write Away: Finding a Place
Think of a topic that you know a lot about. How did you get your information? Write a brief paragraph about your source of knowledge on that topic. Then, as you work your way through this chapter, try using some of the resources suggested. See how much new knowledge you can dig up about your topic.

ClassZone at mcdougallittell.com

FINDING INFO.

CHAPTER OVERVIEW

CHAPTER RESOURCES

Time-Saver Transparencies Binder:
- Daily Test Preparation pp. DT58–60

Writing and Communication Masters pp. 110–111

Integrated Technology and Media

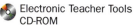 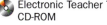 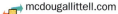 Electronic Teacher Tools CD-ROM

mcdougallittell.com

Assessment

Teacher's Guide to Assessment and Portfolio Use

FINDING INFO.

Pressed for Time?
Use **Lesson 2, Locating Sources,** and **Lesson 3, Reference Works,** for an overview on using the library and electronic resources. Then focus on **Lesson 5, Choosing and Evaluating Sources,** for general research strategies.

Time for More?
After working through all the lessons, have students select a topic, write a research question, and find three appropriate references using card or computer catalogs, reference books, CD-ROMs, databases, or the World Wide Web.

LESSON 1 The Library and Media Center

The library and media center is a great place to find information on many topics. A number of different research sources are available, and the methods for finding and using them are easier than ever before.

❶ Using the Library Collection

Find out how your library is organized so you can easily get the material that you need. This diagram shows one common method of organization.

Sections of the Library

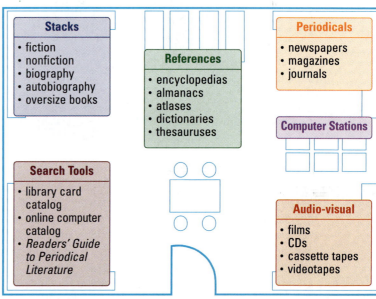

Stacks
- fiction
- nonfiction
- biography
- autobiography
- oversize books

References
- encyclopedias
- almanacs
- atlases
- dictionaries
- thesauruses

Periodicals
- newspapers
- magazines
- journals

Computer Stations

Search Tools
- library card catalog
- online computer catalog
- *Readers' Guide to Periodical Literature*

Audio-visual
- films
- CDs
- cassette tapes
- videotapes

❷ Using Special Services

Public libraries usually have special collections that might include rare books, public records, manuscripts, genealogical information, scrapbooks, maps, journals, and print or oral histories of a town, city or regions. Reference librarians, who are trained to find information about a wide variety of subjects, can help you to use these sources and others.

494 Communicating in the Information Age

TEACHING RESOURCES

 Time-Saver Transparencies Binder:
- Daily Test Preparation p. DT58

SKILLS PRACTICE RESOURCES

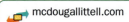 mcdougallittell.com

Locating Sources

Locating the right resources is an important step in preparing a report or completing an assignment that requires research.

❶ Using Catalogs

Head first to the library catalog. It lists all of the books, magazines, and other materials in the library.

Computer Catalog

Today, many libraries list all their materials in a computer catalog, which can be searched by author, title, subject, or keyword. A keyword search is unique to the computerized catalog. To develop a list of keywords, write down research questions and circle the most important words.

Example: How does (gravity) affect a (baseball) pitch?

Then, read the information on the computer screen to find out what commands to use for your keywords. The computer will search its index of the library's collection, and give you a list of all the materials that match your search request.

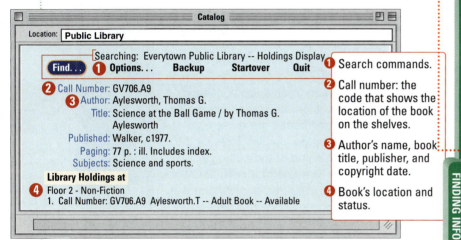

Catalog
Location: **Public Library**

Searching: Everytown Public Library -- Holdings Display

Find... ❶ **Options. . .   Backup   Startover   Quit**

❷ Call Number: GV706.A9
    ❸ Author: Aylesworth, Thomas G.
        Title: Science at the Ball Game / by Thomas G. Aylesworth
    Published: Walker, c1977.
        Paging: 77 p. : ill. Includes index.
    Subjects: Science and sports.

Library Holdings at
❹ Floor 2 - Non-Fiction
   1. Call Number: GV706.A9 Aylesworth.T -- Adult Book -- Available

❶ Search commands.

❷ Call number: the code that shows the location of the book on the shelves.

❸ Author's name, book title, publisher, and copyright date.

❹ Book's location and status.

FINDING INFO.

If your search turns up too many resources, you will need to narrow your topic. Try different research questions, or try different keywords.

To understand and use card catalogs, computer catalogs, and periodical indexes to locate reference sources

DAILY TEST PREPARATION

Error Identification: Spelling
Write the following item on the board or use 🖥 **Daily Test Preparation Transparency** p. DT59.
Decide which type of error, if any, appears in the underlined section.

> She heard a joiful noise coming from the auditorium.

A. Spelling error

B. Capitalization error

C. Punctuation error

D. No error

Teaching Point: Error identification questions often test your knowledge of basic spelling rules. Words that end in *y* preceded by a vowel, such as *joy*, usually do not change when a suffix is added (*joyful*).

TEACHING TIP

Explain to students that a *keyword* is an important word in a title or document that is used to index, or organize, content. Point out that the index of this textbook is an organized list of keywords.

FINDING INFO.

Gifted and Talented Ask students how knowing the copyright date might be helpful when conducting research for a report about the history of computers. (Possible response: The copyright date may indicate that the information in a book is either current or out-of-date.)

Explain that the Library of Congress holds a copy of every book copyrighted in the United States. The library houses more than 88 million items, including over 14 million books and 36 million manuscripts, as well as maps, music, art prints, photographs, motion pictures, videotapes, newspapers, pamphlets, recordings, and other materials.

CHAPTER 28

CHAPTER 28

Card Catalog

Card catalogs contain most of the same information that computer catalogs do. The information is listed on index cards in drawers, organized alphabetically. You can search by subject, author, or title, just as you could on the computer. Write down the title, call number, and author's last name to help you find the book. Here is a sample of a subject card.

❶ SPACE SHUTTLE

❷ TL795.5.J63 1982

❸ Joels, Kerry Mark, 1931--

❹ The space shuttle operator's manual/Kerry Mark Joels, Gregory P. Kennedy; designed by David Larkin. 1st ed. ❺--New York: Ballantine Books, ❻c1982.

❼ 154 p. : ❽ill. ; 28 cm.--(A Del Rey book)

❾ 1. Space shuttles. 2. Piloting. I. Title II. Author

❶ subject
❷ call number and year of publication
❸ author and date of birth
❹ title
❺ publisher
❻ copyright date
❼ number of pages
❽ illustrated
❾ all the ways the book is listed

Classification Systems

All libraries use the Dewey Decimal System and/or the Library of Congress classification system to organize nonfiction books on the library shelves. Fiction books are always organized alphabetically by the last name of the author.

The spine of a book lists the title, author(s), and **call number,** a location code that tells you the library shelf where you can find that particular book. The call number also is found on the card in the card catalog.

For more on Dewey Decimal System see p. 505.

Kerry Mark Joels, Gregory P. Kennedy

The Space Shuttle Operator's Manual

TL795.5. J63 1982

❶ author names
❷ title of book
❹ call number
❺ author's assigned number
❻ copyright date

Spice It Up!

Quotable Quote "Knowledge is of two kinds; we know a subject ourselves, or we know where we can find information upon it." —Samuel Johnson, lexicographer and author

Ask students to discuss the differences between these two types of knowledge. Is one type more important or useful than the other? Ask students to think of situations where they have needed information off the top of their head or times when they have had to do research.

❷ Using Periodical Indexes

Periodical indexes list, by subject, articles published in newspapers, magazines, and journals. Use periodical indexes to find information that is more up-to-date and focused than the information found in books.

The most widely used periodical index is the *Readers' Guide to Periodical Literature*, a monthly index. Here is a sample entry.

❶ **MUMMIES**
    ❷ *See also*
    ❸   Mummy portraits
❹ Children of the ice [mummified remains of Incan sacrifices found by J. Reinhard]
❺ D. Schrieberg and S. Begley. il por maps
❻ *Newsweek* v126 p72-5 N 6 '95
      ❼   ❽

❶ subject heading
❷ cross-reference to other subject headings
❸ article about the subject
❹ article title
❺ authors
❻ periodical title
❼ volume and page numbers
❽ date of publication

You can find periodical indexes on CD-ROMs in your library's reference section or online in some libraries. You may also want to consult newspaper indexes, such as the *New York Times Index*, or electronic indexes, such as *Infonet*.

❸ Gathering Resources

Now that you have collected information on a number of possible resources, begin tracking them down. Books will be arranged on shelves that are marked with numbers or letters matching the information you found in the card catalog. Periodicals may be found in bound volumes, on microfilm, or sometimes in **vertical files:** a set of cabinets that contain current information in the form of pamphlets, handbooks, booklets, and clippings. Print out any good electronic sources you found on the computer.

Your library may not carry all the periodicals indexed by the *Readers' Guide*. You may be able to order copies of articles through an interlibrary loan program.

Finding Information   **497**

FINDING INFO.

FINDING INFO.

To identify and use print and electronic reference sources

Error Correction: Sentence Fragments Write the following item on the board or use **Daily Test Preparation Transparency** p. DT59. Choose the best way to write the underlined section.

> While she ate her cheese-burger.

A. Although

B. After she ate

C. She ate

D. Correct as is

Teaching Point: Error correction questions often test your ability to recognize sentence fragments. Remember that any clause that begins with a subordinating conjunction, such as *while, although,* and *after,* cannot stand on its own. Answer C eliminates the subordinating conjunction in order to create an independent clause.

Explain to students that most multi-volume encyclopedias publish annual yearbooks with new information and updates of articles that appear in the regular volumes. Many encyclopedia publishers also have Web sites that provide up-to-date information.

LESSON 3 · Reference Works

All libraries have a reference collection of material shelved together in a separate area or room. Most reference works cannot be checked out, but they can be photocopied. Some are even available on CD-ROM.

❶ Reference Books

Reference books give background information that might steer your research in a new direction. The chart below will give you an idea of the kind of research material available.

Library Reference Books	
If You Need...	**Try...**
general articles about a topic	• general encyclopedias 　*World Book* 　*Encyclopædia Britannica* • specialized encyclopedias 　*Encyclopedia of Sports* 　*Baseball Encyclopedia*
information about specific people	• biographical indexes 　*Who's Who in America*
facts and statistics	• *Information Please Almanac* • *The World Almanac* • *Statistical Abstract of the United States*
maps	• *National Geographic Atlas*
word meanings, word origins, spellings, pronunciations, word choices	• dictionary • thesaurus
current information on a topic	• pamphlet files • periodical indexes • newspaper indexes

HOT TIP Your search for information should start, not end, with the encyclopedia. Use the encyclopedia to get background information and check facts, statistics, and dates. Then move on to other sources.

---

② Electronic Reference Sources

Electronic reference sources put a huge amount of information at your fingertips. Here are some types of electronic reference sources and tips for using them.

Reference Sources on CD-ROM

Many classrooms and libraries have encyclopedias on CD-ROM. Some news magazines also prepare CD-ROMs that contain summaries of the year's news.

Tips:
- Use these CD-ROMs to find general information and to check facts from other sources.
- These CDs often are updated only once a year or less frequently, so check the copyright date to judge if the source is out of date.
- Don't rely on just one CD-ROM for an entire report—try books, newspapers, magazines, or the World Wide Web as well.

Online Databases

Libraries often have online databases that contain tens of thousands of articles from magazines and newspapers. These databases include both general interest and specialized articles.

Tips:
- Check the dates of articles you find on these databases. Is this information months or years old?
- Use these databases after you have done some general background research. Reading dozens of news articles on a topic can be a confusing way to start your research.

World Wide Web Sites

If you have access to the Web in your library, classroom, or home, you have access to Web pages.

Tips:
- Web pages aren't always fact checked and can disappear without notice. Look for the Web pages created by museums, government agencies, libraries, and other institutions.
- Make sure the Web site is up to date.

Finding Information **499**

FINDING INFO.

FINDING INFO.

TEACHING TIP

Point out that most libraries provide pamphlets or information sheets that explain how to use the online databases.

TEACHING TIP

Web site listings for some World Wide Web search engines include the date the Web sites were "last modified." Suggest that students look for this date to confirm that the Web site is up-to-date. Have students visit **mcdougallittel.com** for more suggestions regarding online research.

Spice It Up!

Reference Race Which is a faster resource: reference books or electronic media? Have students form small groups and assign each group a state name. Have each group search for their state's official bird and flower. Groups can use encyclopedias, CD-ROM encyclopedias, or the World Wide Web. The first team to find the answers wins.

Sentence Completion: Subject-Verb Agreement Write the following item on the board or use ▦ **Daily Test Preparation Transparency** p. DT60. Choose the word that belongs in the space.

> _____ these exercises for homework also?

A. Is

B. Are

C. Does

D. There

Teaching Point: Sentence completion questions often test your knowledge of agreement in inverted sentences. For inverted sentences phrased as questions, look for the subject after the verb. In this case, the subject *exercises* takes a plural verb *(are)*.

TEACHING TIP

Paired Activity Some students may have more experience than others with using World Wide Web search engines. Pair experienced students with those who are relatively new to the Web. Have the experienced students show their partners how to use the search engines.

TEACHING TIP

Remind students of the benefits of taking notes when doing online searches.

LESSON 4 Using the Web

❶ Planning Your Search Strategy

The World Wide Web contains millions of pages of text as well as graphics, audio, and video. Here's a plan of attack for finding the information you need.

Step 1: Think ahead.
- Create research questions that summarize what you want to learn.
- Circle **keywords** in your questions—words that are likely to appear on pages that have the information you need.

Step 2: Try several search engines.
- No two search engines cover exactly the same pages. Use different search engines to expand your research.
- Most engines let you do advanced or expert searches. Use the "Help" buttons to learn about these searches.

Step 3: Choose sites wisely.
- Look for "best matches first"—that is, matches that include all your keywords early in the document.
- Many engines also tell you when each Web page was last updated and show the first few lines of text on the page.
- If you still have too many sites, narrow your search by adding more keywords.

Step 4: Explore and document.
- Open the site. Find the name of the person who created the page.
- Click on links that give other information.
- Print out useful pages or save them as text files. Note their Web addresses in case you need to go back to them.

500 Communicating in the Information Age

TEACHING RESOURCES

 Time-Saver Transparencies Binder:
- Daily Test Preparation p. DT60

SKILLS PRACTICE RESOURCES

 mcdougallittell.com

② Analyzing Your Search Results

Take a look at the sample search results page below. Use the tips to make your own selection of sites more useful.

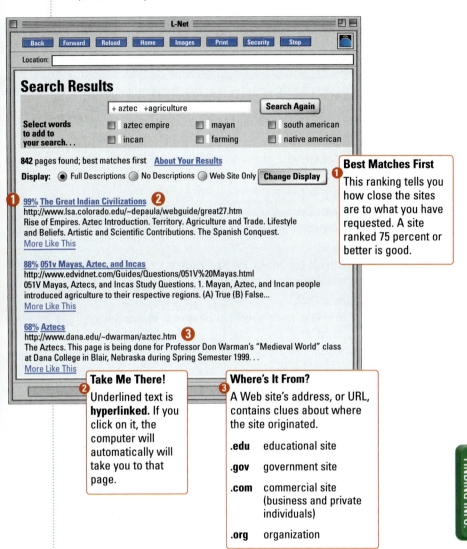

Best Matches First
This ranking tells you how close the sites are to what you have requested. A site ranked 75 percent or better is good.

Take Me There!
Underlined text is **hyperlinked.** If you click on it, the computer will automatically will take you to that page.

Where's It From?
A Web site's address, or URL, contains clues about where the site originated.

.edu   educational site

.gov   government site

.com   commercial site (business and private individuals)

.org   organization

Sentence Completion:
Vocabulary Write the following item on the board or use 🏛 **Daily Test Preparation Transparency** p. DT60. Choose the word that *best* fits the meaning of the sentence.

Sheila is _____, but not complacent, with the posi-tive results.

A. content

B. disgruntled

C. methodical

D. responsive

Teaching Point: For sentence completion questions, use context clues in the text. In this case, Sheila is *content* (meaning "satisfied") but not *complacent* (meaning "overly satisfied or unconcerned") with the grade.

TEACHING TIP

Explain to students that when they scan and skim, they are looking for keywords.

CHAPTER 28

CHAPTER 28

 LESSON 5 **Choosing and Evaluating Sources**

When you're doing research, too many sources can be a bigger problem than too few sources. To help narrow down your best sources, use the strategies in this lesson.

❶ Choosing Sources

After you have searched library catalogs, checked periodical indexes, and powered up World Wide Web search engines, you may feel as though you are swimming in information. Fortunately, not everything will be usable. Choose the sources that you think will be most helpful by using this five-step process.

Step 1:

Review your research questions. This will help remind you about the kind of information you really need.

Step 2:

Scan the table of contents to get an overview of a book or magazine. Identify chapters and articles that appear useful.

Step 3:

Check the index for key terms. Use the index to lead you to relevant information.

Step 4:

Preview each source's chapters or sections to see if they cover useful information.

• Skim titles, headlines, highlighted words or phrases, and topic sentences.

• Check maps, charts, and illustrations to see if the information applies to your topic.

• Read introductions, conclusions, and summaries.

• Scan for specific facts.

• If you need statistics, pay special attention to charts and graphs.

Step 5:

Return books that don't help you answer your research questions. Avoid books that oversimplify the subject, or that will be too difficult for you.

502 Communicating in the Information Age

TEACHING RESOURCES

🏛 Time-Saver Transparencies Binder:
• Daily Test Preparation p. DT60

SKILLS PRACTICE RESOURCES

↪ mcdougallittell.com

② Evaluating Sources

Now that you know which sources relate to your topic, evaluate each one for reliability. The questions and the scale below were used to judge sources for a research paper on immigration. The most reliable sources fell on the left side of the scale, and the least reliable fell on the right.

Most Reliable   **Least Reliable**

Topic: Immigration

1. Is the writer an expert on the subject?

a scholar who has studied immigration	a reporter writing a story on immigration	a tabloid story

Whether you need an expert depends on your topic. Sometimes a general interest book is the best source.

2. Does the source give a balanced point of view?

a scholarly paper that gives pros and cons	an autobiography telling one immigrant's experience	a political speech promoting changes to immigration laws

The best solution is to use more than one source.

3. Is the material current for the topic?

current immigration statistics	magazine article from 1950	immigration records from 1900

Information need not be current to be useful. But be sure to use current sources for information about science and technology.

4. Is the publisher trustworthy?

published by the Immigration and Naturalization Service	published by a national magazine	published on the Web by an unidentified person

Finding Information   **503**

Cooperative Learning/Paired Activity Have students work with partners to search the World Wide Web for two Web sites with biographical information about Woody Guthrie. Ask them to print out the information they find and evaluate which of the two sources is more informative. Have students evaluate their own research methods and frame new questions for further investigation.

ASSESSMENT

 Teacher's Guide to Assessment and Portfolio Use

Drive-Through Grammar

Sentence Fragments Point out to students that book titles and headlines are often written as sentence fragments to conserve space and make them more eye-catching. Remind students that a complete sentence must contain both a subject and predicate. Have students rewrite the following headlines, making them complete sentences. (Possible responses are shown below.)

Caught in the Act

The criminal was caught in the act.

A Destructive Plan

A destructive plan was approved.

Student Help Desk

Students can use the Student Help Desk as a quick review prior to testing or as a quick reference as they revise a piece of writing.

CHAPTER 28

CHAPTER 28

Student Help Desk

Finding Information at a Glance

AAA Information Interchange

Ask Questions
- Prepare research questions.
- Identify keywords.

Access Library
- Find print and technological resources.

Analyze Source
- Scan table of contents, index, Web search page.
- Evaluate reliability.

Evaluating Web Sites

Does the Web site . . .

. . . present material issued by a reliable organization or expert?

. . . have a current date?

. . . publish a bibliography?

. . . link to other Web sites?

. . . provide information based on facts, not opinions?

"On the Internet, nobody knows you're a dog."

© The New Yorker Collection 1993 Peter Steiner from cartoonbank.com.

Information Sources   Consider the Possibilities!

- Books
- Magazine articles
- Web sites
- Newspapers
- Reference sources
- Special collections

Dewey Decimal System   Find That Book!

Most libraries use the Dewey Decimal System to classify all nonfiction books by number in ten major subject categories.

Numbers	Subject Areas	Examples
000-099	General Works	encyclopedias, handbooks
100-199	Philosophy	psychology, ethics, personality
200-299	Religion	Bibles, mythology, theology
300-399	Social Sciences	government, law, economics
400-499	Languages	dictionaries, grammars
500-599	Science	general science, mathematics
600-699	Technology	engineering, inventions
700-799	The Arts	music, theater, recreation
800-899	Literature	poetry, dramas, essays
900-999	History	biography, geography, travel

The Bottom Line

Checklist for Evaluating Information

Have I found sources that . . .

____ answer my research questions?

____ are easy to understand?

____ are up to date?

____ present both sides of my topic?

____ are written by experts?

____ are published by reliable sources?

A Slice of Life

But whether it be dream or truth, to do well is what matters. If it be truth, for truth's sake. If not, then to gain friends for the time when we awaken.

—Pedro Calderón de la Barca

Teacher's Notes
WHAT DOESN'T WORK:

TEACHER'S LOUNGE

Brain Break

The partial last names of seven authors are listed below. Fill in the missing letters and say hello to some literary giants.

C _ _ E R _ D _ E

D _ _ K _ N S

W _ R _ S W _ _ T H

T H _ M _ S

K _ P _ _ N G

C H _ _ C _ R

J _ N S _ N

Answers: Coleridge, Dickens, Wordsworth, Thomas, Kipling, Chaucer, Jonson

TEACHING TIP

Using References If students are unable to determine the meanings of words from the context, have them use a dictionary or a thesaurus to look up words.

TEACHING TIP

Speaking and Listening Prepare students to be good partners. Remind them that a good listener:

- Keeps focused on the speaker
- Listens for words and phrases that support the main idea (in this case, the situation and the emotion the speaker is talking about)
- Doesn't interrupt the speaker

Encourage active participation by having students:

- Evaluate what they hear before they speak
- Ask questions to clarify information, if necessary
- Speak clearly, concisely, and to the point

CHAPTER 29

TEACHING TIP

Ask students if their partner's description effectively portrayed the emotion he or she was trying to describe and if they were able to interpret how the experience felt through their partner's delivery and the use of descriptive words.

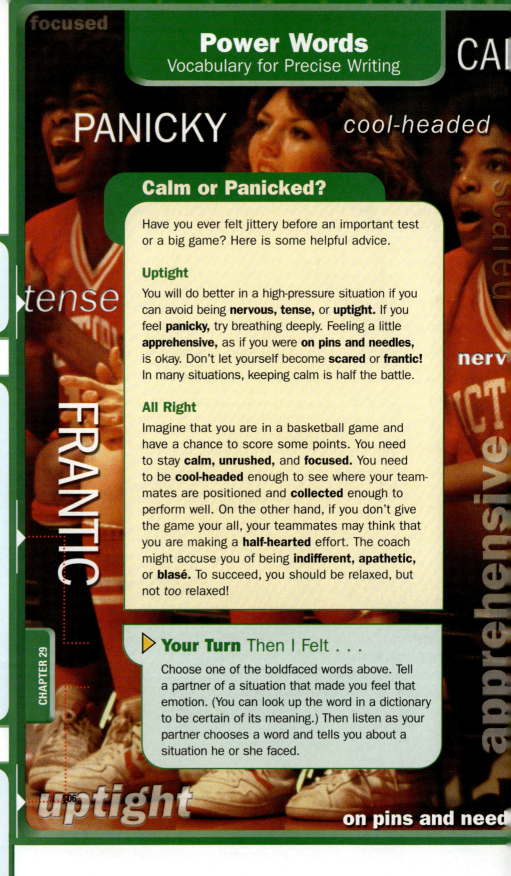

Power Words
Vocabulary for Precise Writing

focused   PANICKY   cool-headed   CALM

tense   FRANTIC

CHAPTER 29

Calm or Panicked?

Have you ever felt jittery before an important test or a big game? Here is some helpful advice.

Uptight

You will do better in a high-pressure situation if you can avoid being **nervous, tense,** or **uptight.** If you feel **panicky,** try breathing deeply. Feeling a little **apprehensive,** as if you were **on pins and needles,** is okay. Don't let yourself become **scared** or **frantic!** In many situations, keeping calm is half the battle.

All Right

Imagine that you are in a basketball game and have a chance to score some points. You need to stay **calm, unrushed,** and **focused.** You need to be **cool-headed** enough to see where your teammates are positioned and **collected** enough to perform well. On the other hand, if you don't give the game your all, your teammates may think that you are making a **half-hearted** effort. The coach might accuse you of being **indifferent, apathetic,** or **blasé.** To succeed, you should be relaxed, but not *too* relaxed!

▷ **Your Turn** Then I Felt . . .

Choose one of the boldfaced words above. Tell a partner of a situation that made you feel that emotion. (You can look up the word in a dictionary to be certain of its meaning.) Then listen as your partner chooses a word and tells you about a situation he or she faced.

uptight   506   on pins and need

nerv

apprehensive

Study and Test-Taking Skills

CHAPTER OVERVIEW

CHAPTER RESOURCES

Time-Saver Transparencies Binder:
- Daily Test Preparation pp. DT61–63

Test Preparation

Writing and Communication Masters pp. 112–113

Integrated Technology and Media

Electronic Teacher Tools CD-ROM

mcdougallittell.com Test Practice

Assessment

Teacher's Guide to Assessment and Portfolio Use

Students Acquiring English/ESL

Test Preparation

Perfect Papers and Terrific Tests

Do you panic when you open your assignment notebook? Are you feeling overloaded with papers and tests? Do you forget what you've read before you've even shut the book? Does writing an outline pose an overwhelming challenge?

Relax! There is a simple way to keep up with your schoolwork and handle almost any assignment or test: develop good study skills. Whether you're writing a paper or taking a test, it's important to focus on the task at hand and follow through on a plan.

Write Away: Scheduling Your Day

Are you an organized student? Make an outline of a typical school day. Remember to include meals, television viewing, and telephone conversations. Put your outline in your 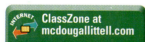 **Writing Portfolio.**

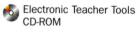 **ClassZone at** 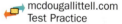 mcdougallittell.com

STUDY SKILLS

STUDY SKILLS

BLOCK SCHEDULING

Pressed for Time?
Review note-taking skills in **Lesson 3.** Then work through **Lesson 5, Taking Objective Tests,** and **Lesson 6, Answering Essay Questions,** to help students improve their test-taking skills.

Time for More?
After completing all of the lessons, have students visit mcdougallittell.com for additional test practice questions.

LESSON OBJECTIVES

To recognize and understand ways to read for information

Error Correction: Gerunds Write the following item on the board or use **Daily Test Preparation Transparency** p. DT61.

> We dislike to read at our desks.

How is this sentence best written?

A. Reading we dislike at our desks.

B. At our desks we dislike to read.

C. We dislike reading at our desks.

D. As it is

Teaching Point: Error correction questions often test your use of different verb forms, such as gerunds. In this case, a gerund (*reading*) is required to serve as the direct object of *dislike*.

TEACHING TIP

Ask students to skim the chapter on thunderstorms on the student page. What do they look at first? How does skimming help guide their reading?

LESSON 1 Reading for Information

Reading Tips

Reading for information requires different skills than reading for pleasure does. Use these active reading strategies to stay on top of your material.

Preview

- Skim the pages.
- Read chapter title, introduction, and conclusion for overview.
- Note subheads, key words, pronunciation guides, and margin information.
- Read questions at the end of the chapter to give you an idea of the information you'll need to learn.
- Note maps, diagrams, and other graphics.

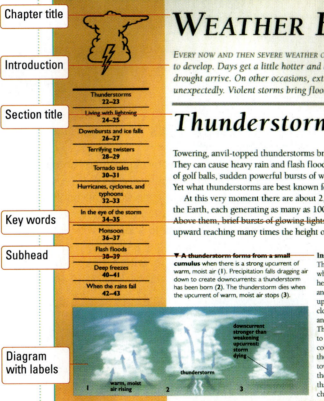

TEACHING RESOURCES

Time-Saver Transparencies Binder:
- Daily Test Preparation p. DT61

Test Preparation

SKILLS PRACTICE RESOURCES

mcdougallittell.com
Test Practice

Read actively
- Read the text thoroughly.
- Read the first sentence of every paragraph for main ideas.
- Examine and answer all questions posed by the text.

Interpret maps and graphics
- Read the labels, captions, and explanations of graphics.
- Look through the text for reference to the graphic aids.
- Compare text information with graphic aids.

Review and take notes
- Reread difficult sections.
- Jot down important words, phrases, and facts.

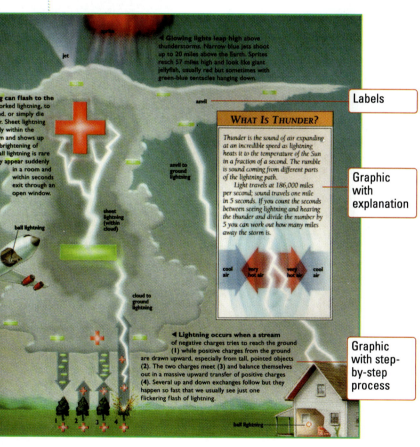

Labels

WHAT IS THUNDER?

Thunder is the sound of air expanding at an incredible speed as lightning heats it to the temperature of the Sun in a fraction of a second. The rumble is sound coming from different parts of the lightning path.

Light travels at 186,000 miles per second; sound travels one mile in 5 seconds. If you count the seconds between seeing lightning and hearing the thunder and divide the number by 5 you can work out how many miles away the storm is.

Graphic with explanation

◄ Lightning occurs when a stream of negative charges tries to reach the ground (1) while positive charges from the ground are drawn upward, especially from tall, pointed objects (2). The two charges meet (3) and balance themselves out in a massive upward transfer of positive charges (4). Several up and down exchanges follow but they happen so fast that we usually see just one flickering flash of lightning.

Graphic with step-by-step process

Study and Test-Taking Skills **509**

LESSON 2
Understanding Graphic Aids

When you read for information, let built-in visual aids guide you through the material and increase your understanding.

Common Types of Graphic Aids

Diagrams

Diagrams are drawings that show how something works. Use these strategies to interpret diagrams.

How a Thunderstorm Forms

Study the sequence of pictures.

Read the captions for an explanation of the subject.

Read the labels to understand each picture.

Maps

Maps are visual representations of an area. Consult the legend or key for help in understanding the symbols and colors on the map.

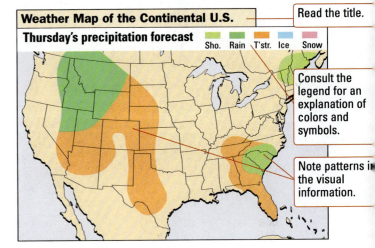

Read the title.

Consult the legend for an explanation of colors and symbols.

Note patterns in the visual information.

510 Communicating in the Information Age

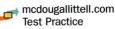

Tables and Scales

Tables allow you to compare facts. They are usually in column form. Tables often show numerical information. Read titles and column heads. A **scale** is a particular kind of table that shows information in order by size, degree, amount, or other ranking. The scale below shows one method of judging wind speed from the wind's effects.

Read the title.

Read the column heads.

The Beaufort Scale of Wind Strength		
Wind	**Wind Speed**	**Effect of Wind**
Calm (0)	Less than 1 mph	Smoke rises straight up.
Light air (1)	1 to 5 mph	Smoke drifts.
Light breeze (2)	6 to 11 mph	Wind felt on face.
Gentle breeze (3)	12 to 19 mph	Leaves and twigs move.
Moderate breeze (4)	20 to 28 mph	Flags flap.
Fresh breeze (5)	29 to 38 mph	Small trees sway.
Strong breeze (6)	39 to 49 mph	Large branches move.
Moderate gale (7)	50 to 61 mph	Whole trees sway.
Fresh gale (8)	62 to 74 mph	Twigs break off trees.
Strong gale (9)	75 to 88 mph	Branches break off trees.
Whole gale (10)	89 to 102 mph	Trees uprooted.
Storm (11)	103 to 117 mph	Widespread damage.
Hurricane (12)	More than 117 mph	Destruction.

PRACTICE ▶ **Understanding Graphic Aids**

Use the three graphics to answer the following questions.

1. Look at the diagram.
   • Does warm air rise or descend?
2. Look at the weather-map legend.
   • What color is used to show rain?
   • What is the forecast for Thursday on the Southeast coast?
3. Look at the Beaufort Scale.
   • When the wind is described as a fresh breeze, what effect does it have on trees?
   • How fast is a strong gale?

Study and Test-Taking Skills **511**

Answers

PRACTICE ▶ Understanding Graphic Aids

1. Warm air rises.
2. Green is used to show rain. The forecast for Thursday on the Southeast coast predicts rain and thunderstorms.
3. A fresh breeze causes small trees to sway. Wind speeds of 75 to 88 mph are classified as strong gales.

STUDY SKILLS

STUDY SKILLS

To recognize and use various methods for taking notes

DAILY TEST PREPARATION

Error Identification:

Capitalization Write the following item on the board or use **Daily Test Preparation Transparency** p. DT62. Look for mistakes in capitalization in the sentence. Decide which line, if any, contains a mistake.

A. Leaves underfoot and bright

B. blue skies make Autumn

C. his favorite season.

D. No mistakes

Teaching Point: Error identification questions often test your knowledge of basic capitalization rules. In this case, the item tests whether you know that the names of the seasons (*autumn, winter, spring,* and *summer*) are not capitalized.

TEACHING TIP

Cooperative Learning/Paired Activity Have students work in pairs to identify the title, the four subtitles, and the topic sentences of each section in this lesson. Encourage students to paraphrase each topic sentence.

CHAPTER 29

CHAPTER 29

LESSON 3 # Taking Notes

Taking notes helps you to remember what you read. You can take notes by paraphrasing or summarizing on note cards.

❶ Recognizing Key Information

When taking notes, focus on only the most important information. Pay attention to material presented in titles, topic sentences, and boldface type.

PROFESSIONAL MODEL

❶ **Inside a Thunderstorm**

❷ Thunderstorms can form on hot days when moist air close to the ground is heated and rises quickly. Strong upward and downward rushes of air (called ❸ **upcurrents** and **downcurrents**) within the cloud sweep ice crystals, water droplets, and ice pellets past and into one another. This creates static electricity, which begins to build up. Negative electrical charges collect in the middle and lower parts of the cloud and positive charges gather toward the top. The difference between the charges builds up ❹ until it is so great that a massive spark is released as the charges even themselves out again.

❹ —Derek Elsom, *Weather Explained*

❶ The subtitle gives a clue to the content.

❷ The topic sentence tells the main idea.

❸ Boldface type calls attention to key words and phrases.

❹ The source line tells where the information was found.

Formation of a Thunderstorm

- *occurs on hot days*
- *upcurrents, downcurrents cause water and ice particles to collide*
- *static electricity builds*
- *energy releases in a massive spark*

The page lists the main idea and supporting details.

TEACHING RESOURCES

 Time-Saver Transparencies Binder:
• Daily Test Preparation p. DT62

 Test Preparation

SKILLS PRACTICE RESOURCES

 Writing and Communication Masters p. 112

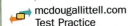 mcdougallittell.com
Test Practice

❷ Paraphrasing

Paraphrasing is rewriting the text in your own words. A good paraphrase is about the same length as the original. It includes the main ideas and supporting details. It is often written in simpler language than the author used. If you use the author's exact words, put them in quotation marks. Using another person's words without giving credit to him or her is called **plagiarism** and is unlawful. Compare the two versions of the student model, each written from the following example.

Thunderstorms can form on hot days when moist air close to the ground is heated and rises quickly.

STUDENT MODEL

PLAGIARIZED VERSION

Thunderstorms form on hot days when moist air heats up and rises quickly.

PARAPHRASED VERSION

Hot, sticky days provide perfect conditions for thunderstorms. Thunderstorms form when moist air gets hot and rises fast.

❸ Summarizing

A summary is similar to a paraphrase, but it is shorter. In **summarizing** you make your own connections between ideas and details, and rewrite the main points in simple language. A summary is usually about one-third as long as the original. The following paragraph summarizes the model on page 512.

STUDENT MODEL

Thunderstorms happen on hot days when moist, hot air quickly rises. Upcurrents and downcurrents cause ice particles and raindrops to collide. This creates static electricity. As the charges build, negative ones sink to the bottoms of clouds, and positive ones rise to the tops. Finally, the difference between the charges becomes so great that it produces a giant spark.

TEACHING TIP

Speaking and Listening Read the following sentence. Ask students to listen carefully and then paraphrase the spoken message, seeking clarification as needed.

The storm's gale-force winds uprooted trees and downed power lines, making driving dangerous. Trees and power lines felled by the storm created hazardous driving conditions.

TEACHING TIP

Ask students to analyze the **Student Model** and explain the differences between plagiarizing and paraphrasing. Point out that paraphrasing—putting a text into their own words—will ensure that they understand what they are reading.

Drive-Through Grammar

Punctuating Quotations Tell students that, when they take notes, they should jot down the direct quotations they may want to use. Remind students that direct quotations require quotation marks, whereas paraphrased information consisting of indirect quotations does not. Have students rewrite the following sentences, inserting quotation marks where needed.

The book states that increased recycling is essential. Correct

Most cities are expanding their recycling efforts, said Alderman Alvarez.

"Most cities are expanding their recycling efforts," said Alderman Alvarez.

4 Using Note Cards

Using note cards is a practical way to take notes when you are doing research. When your information is on cards, you can sort and re-sort your material until you find an order that works well. Use a different card for each idea, quotation, or statistic. Be sure to give each card a heading that describes the note. Also remember to write the source of the information on the card.

Heading

How Thunderstorms Are Formed   2

air rushes up, upcurrent air rushes down, downcurrent ice, pellets, drops crash together static electricity builds up negative charges in middles and bottoms of clouds positive charges in upper clouds

Elsom, Derek, Weather Explained p. 99

Source

Thunderstorm Effect: Area   6

Most of the time, thunderstorms cover an area of ten square miles.

"Storm." World Book Encyclopedia, 1999 ed. p. 912

Page number from source

Thunderstorm Formation: Squall Lines   4

"They are an unbroken line of black, ominous clouds, towering 40,000 feet or more into the sky, including thunderstorms of almost incredible violence."

Lehr, Paul, Weather p. 84

Quotation

Here's How Using Note Cards to Organize

1. Sort your cards by topic.
2. Stack the cards into piles. This will help to identify the main ideas and bring together information from different sources.
3. Look for patterns of information in each stack and between stacks.
4. Reorder the piles until you are satisfied.

HOT TIP

To avoid having to write source information on every note card, create source cards.

For more on source cards, see p. 474.

LESSON 4 — Creating Outlines

Creating a Formal Outline

You can outline a chapter of your textbook to identify main ideas. In addition, you can use an outline to prepare a research paper. Use groups of note cards as the basis for this second kind of outline. Below is an outline for a research paper on thunderstorms using the note cards on page 514.

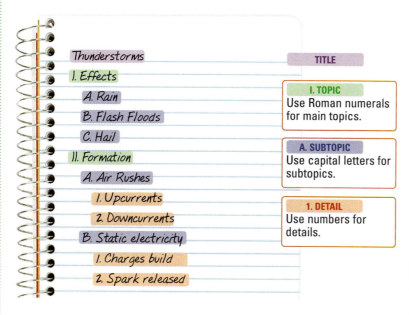

Thunderstorms — **TITLE**

I. Effects — **I. TOPIC** Use Roman numerals for main topics.
　A. Rain
　B. Flash Floods
　C. Hail
II. Formation
　A. Air Rushes — **A. SUBTOPIC** Use capital letters for subtopics.
　　1. Upcurrents
　　2. Downcurrents
　B. Static electricity
　　1. Charges build — **1. DETAIL** Use numbers for details.
　　2. Spark released

When outlining, remember to keep all items of the same rank in parallel form. If subtopic *A* is expressed as a noun, then *B* and *C* should also be expressed as nouns. Also remember that when subtopics follow a topic or details follow a subtopic, there must be two or more of them: for every *I* there must be a *II*, for every *A* a *B*, and for every *1* a *2*. Finally, begin each item with a capital letter, and do not use end punctuation.

PRACTICE ▸ Revising Your Schedule

Take a second look at the outline you made for the **Write Away** on page 507. Add or subtract details where necessary, then develop the outline into a paragraph.

LESSON OBJECTIVES

To understand and use outlines to prepare research reports

DAILY TEST PREPARATION

Error Correction: Spelling Write the following item on the board or use 📖 **Daily Test Preparation Transparency** p. DT62.
Look for mistakes in spelling. Decide which word, if any, contains a mistake.

A. loving

B. hopeful

C. baking

D. management

E. (No mistakes)

Teaching Point: Error correction questions often test your knowledge of basic spelling rules. In this case, the item tests whether you know to drop the silent e in *love* when adding the suffix *-ing*.

STUDY SKILLS

STUDY SKILLS

TEACHING RESOURCES

  Time-Saver Transparencies Binder:
　• Daily Test Preparation p. DT62
Test Preparation

SKILLS PRACTICE RESOURCES

 mcdougallittell.com
Test Practice

To recognize and use strategies for answering different types of questions on objective tests

Reading Comprehension:
Vocabulary Write the following item on the board or use
📗 **Daily Test Preparation Transparency** p. DT63.

As a means of reinforcing their troops during the Revolutionary War, the British hired German mercenaries. The majority of these hired soldiers came from a region in Germany known as Hesse-Kassel, hence they were known as Hessians.

Based on the above passage, who are *mercenaries?*

A. disloyal Hessians

B. hired soldiers

C. British soldiers

D. Germans

Teaching Point: A common item in reading comprehension questions is vocabulary. In this case, the definition of *mercenaries* is given in the second sentence: *hired soldiers.*

MORE MODEL SENTENCES

Write the following sentences on the board. Ask students to determine whether they are true or false:

1. A hurricane *always* causes many deaths. false

2. *Sometimes* people have to evacuate their communities because of dangerous weather. true

3. Weather forecasters can often predict the weather, and they are *never* wrong. false

CHAPTER 29

LESSON 5 Taking Objective Tests

Objective tests are designed to see how well you recall important facts and details. The key to success with such tests is to make sure you understand the test questions and what you are being asked to do. Objective questions come in several different forms: true-false, matching, multiple-choice, and short-answer. Before answering a question, be sure you know exactly what it is asking.

❶ True-False

A true-false question tests your ability to recognize what you've learned when that material is presented as a statement of fact.

> **Directions:** Indicate whether each statement is true or false.
>
> **1.** Sandra Day O'Connor, appointed to the Supreme Court by President Ronald Reagan in 1981, was the first woman to sit on the court.
> ❏ **True**   ❏ **False**

Answer: **True.** (All parts of the statement—including the date, and the name of the president—are correct)

> **2.** Thurgood Marshall was the first African-American member of the Senate.
> ❏ **True**   ❏ **False**

Answer: **False.** Thurgood Marshall was the first African-American member of the Supreme Court.

⭐ Tips for Success

• Remember that for a statement to be true, every part of it must be true. If any part of it is false, the whole statement is false.

• Look for words like *all, always, never, only,* and *every.* Such words often signal a false statement.

• Look for words like *may, most, few, probably, usually, typically,* and *sometimes,* which often signal a true statement.

CHAPTER 29

TEACHING RESOURCES

 Time-Saver Transparencies Binder:
• Daily Test Preparation p. DT63

 Test Preparation

SKILLS PRACTICE RESOURCES

 Writing and Communication Masters p. 113

 mcdougallittell.com
Test Practice

❷ Matching

Matching questions test your ability to recognize relationships between items in two columns and to pair items accordingly.

> **Directions:** Match each item in the left-hand column with one item in the right-hand column.
>
> Match the invention with the inventors. Use each answer only once.
>
> _____ **1.** Thomas Edison   **a.** airplane
> _____ **2.** Henry Ford   **b.** phonograph
> _____ **3.** Orville and Wilbur Wright **c.** assembly line
> _____ **4.** Eli Whitney   **d.** cotton gin

Answers: **1-b, 2-c, 3-a, 4-d**

Tips for Success

- Determine from the directions whether you can use an item more than once.
- Check to see if there are extra items in the answer column.
- Match the items you are sure of first.

❸ Multiple-Choice

Multiple-choice questions test your ability to choose the correct answer from among several choices. In a well-written test, each of the wrong answers represents an error in thinking.

> **Directions:** Write the letter of the correct answer.
>
> **1.** What was the name of the Wright brothers' plane?
>
> **a.** *Spirit of St. Louis*
> **b.** *Concorde*
> **c.** *Enola Gay*
> **d.** *Flyer*
>
> **2.** What did Thomas Edison invent?
>
> **a.** the electric light
> **b.** the telegraph
> **c.** the movie projector
> **d.** all of the above

Answer: **d**   *Answer:* **d**

CUSTOMIZING TIP

Students Acquiring English/ESL
If students were penalized for guessing on tests in their native country, they might hesitate to resort to guessing on classroom and standardized tests. If the test does not penalize for guessing, tell students that it is best to cross out the two answers that are probably wrong and select one of the remaining answers. For instruction and practice with the elimination process and pacing on tests, have students use **Test Preparation** for students acquiring English, pp. 55–57.

CUSTOMIZING TIP

Less Proficient Learners Tell students that question #2 on the student page asks for more than just identification of the inventor of the assembly line. Ask students whether the following answers the question:

Henry Ford invented the assembly line. It was used in factories.

Point out that the answer is incomplete because it simply rewords the question. It does not address how the assembly line *changed* factories.

⭐ Tips for Success

- Read the question and try to answer it before you read the answer choices.
- Consider all the choices before selecting one.
- Cross out incorrect answers first.
- Look for words like *always, never,* and *only.* They often signal incorrect answers.

❹ Short-Answer

There are two kinds of short-answer questions. For one you supply missing information to fill in a blank. The other requires you to answer with one or two sentences.

> **Directions:** Supply the missing word or phrase.
>
> 1. _____ invented the telephone.

Answer: Alexander Graham Bell

> **Directions:** Write a brief response.
>
> 2. Name the inventor of the assembly line. Describe how this invention changed American factories.
>
> _____
> _____
> _____

Answer: Henry Ford invented the assembly line. It allowed factories to produce more goods in less time.

The question above requires exactly two answers. Do not include unnecessary information.

⭐ Tips for Success

- Make sure your answer to a fill-in-the-blank question fits grammatically into the sentence.
- If the question asks for more than one answer, be sure you provide all of them.
- When you are asked to reply in a sentence, make sure to avoid fragments. Also include phrases from the question in your answer.

Answering Essay Questions

LESSON OBJECTIVES
To understand and use strategies for answering essay questions

Essay questions test your ability to reason, write persuasively, and communicate your ideas in a logical order. They require you to support your statements with appropriate facts.

① Understanding the Task

Before you start your essay, read the question carefully. Underline key words, and circle words that signal how to organize your answer.

> **Directions:** Write an **essay** to answer the following question.
>
> 1. **Discuss three** key factors that motivated early pioneers to settle the American West.

- Asks for essay.
- Asks you to **discuss,** or look at a topic from all sides.
- Asks for three reasons.

For more on essay questions, see the Student Help Desk, page 520.

② Writing the Response

Once you're sure you understand the question, you can draft your response. Organize your information into an informal outline before you begin to write.

> *Settling the American West*
> *Motivating Factors*
> *- Cheap, available land*
> *- Get-rich-quick mentality*
> *- Better climate for farming*

 Tips for Success

- Read the question carefully.
- Underline key words.
- Make a quick outline.
- Jot down examples and details under each outline heading.
- State your main point clearly in the first sentence of the essay.
- Write and proofread your essay.

Study and Test-Taking Skills **519**

 DAILY TEST PREPARATION
Sentence Completion: Vocabulary
Write the following item on the board or use 🖥 **Daily Test Preparation Transparency** p. DT63.

Choose the word that *best* fits the meaning of the sentence.

> The two roads _____ into a single path.

A. diverged
B. converged
C. destination
D. dislodged

Teaching Point: For sentence completion questions, the correct answer will always

- fit grammatically within the sentence (*destination* does not).
- fit the meaning of the sentence (*diverged* and *dislodged* do not make sense with two roads becoming *a single path*).

TEACHING RESOURCES

 Time-Saver Transparencies Binder:
- Daily Test Preparation p. DT63
 Test Preparation

SKILLS PRACTICE RESOURCES

 mcdougallittell.com Test Practice

ASSESSMENT

 Teacher's Guide to Assessment and Portfolio Use

STUDY SKILLS

STUDY SKILLS

Drive-Through Grammar

Run-ons and Fragments Remind students to use complete sentences when answering essay questions. Point out that they should avoid run-on sentences and fragments. Write the following on the board and have students identify the complete sentence and eliminate the run-on and fragment.

Rain is formed by a constantly repeating cycle it begins when water evaporates.

Rain is formed by a constantly repeated cycle. It begins swhen water evaporates.

The water rises into the atmosphere.

Complete sentence

Forming a cloud above.

The water turns to gas, forming a cloud above.

Student Help Desk

Students can use the Student Help Desk as a quick review prior to testing or as a quick reference as they revise a piece of writing.

Teacher's Notes
WHAT WORKS:

Student Help Desk

Study and Test-Taking Skills at a Glance

Read Carefully

There is a simple way to keep up with your school work and handle almost any assignment or test: develop good study skills.

Use Assessment Skills

Take Notes

A+ Study Tips

- Take notes by listing, paraphrasing, summarizing, or outlining.
- List key terms, names, dates, and statistics.
- Briefly define or identify each term, name, or date.
- Review your notes regularly.
- Form a study group and split the work load among members.

Types of Essay Questions

If the question asks you to . . .	You should . . .
Compare/contrast	show similarities and differences between two or more topics
Describe	explain the most important aspects of a topic
Define	explain the basic meaning of a term
Discuss	look at a topic from all sides
Explain	tell how or why something happened or how something works
Analyze	examine the parts of a whole
Evaluate	examine and judge a topic carefully
Summarize/outline	give a brief overview of a topic

Before the Test

- Find out what the test will cover.
- Make a study plan.
- Allow yourself time to go over the material several times.
- Review your notes.
- Memorize key facts.
- Review sample tests or create your own.
- Give yourself a timed mock test.

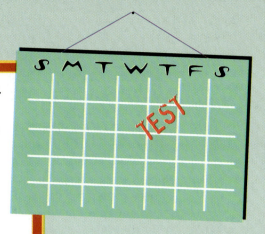

During the Test

- Skim the test.
- Read all of the instructions.
- Read each question carefully.
- If you don't know the answer to a question, skip it.
- Return to the hard questions after you've finished the others.
- Note the time limit and keep track of the time remaining.

The Bottom Line

Checklist for Developing Study and Test-Taking Skills

Have I . . .

____ read to obtain information?

____ created a formal outline?

____ taken and reviewed notes?

____ practiced my test skills?

STUDY SKILLS

TEACHER'S LOUNGE

STUDY SKILLS

A Slice of Life

"The questions which one asks oneself begin, at last, to illuminate the world, and become one's key to the experience of others."

—James Baldwin

Brain Break

What two words, formed from different arrangements of the same six letters, can be used to complete the sentence below?

After growing up in the country, the son of a _____ went to the big city, became interested in art and started working as a picture _____.

Answer: farmer, framer

Power Words
Vocabulary for Precise Writing

Brains Behind the Operation

What do you think of these words about thinking?

Train Your Brain

To be a great scientist or philosopher, you have to **think clearly** and **use your head** in the best possible way. A scientist will **reflect** on a problem and **mull over** a possible solution. A philosopher spends hours **meditating** and **cogitating**. Both like to **ruminate** on an interesting thought, and a difficult matter may cause them to **brood** unhappily. So as you **muse** about your future, if you **contemplate** being a scientist or philosopher, be prepared to **put on your thinking cap.**

Take a Brain Break

Spending hours **pondering** an idea can make you tired and irritable. Take a moment to gaze at some passing clouds and **imagine** what their shapes look like. Perhaps you can **visualize** an elephant or a herd of camels up there. At night, looking up at the sky, maybe you can **envision** yourself in a spaceship, speeding among the stars. It's fun to **daydream** and **woolgather** like this—to **build castles in the air.**

▶ **Your Turn** A Place to Think

Where and when do you think best? Do you prefer to do your homework alone or with friends, in silence or with music playing? Are you at your best in the morning, afternoon, or at night? Discuss these questions in a small group.

daydream

ruminate

CHAPTER 30

mull o

BROOD 522 visualize

TEACHING TIP

Using References If students are unable to determine the meanings of words from the context, have them use a dictionary or a thesaurus to look up words.

TEACHING TIP

Allow time for students to have a discussion with their classmates regarding whether they agree or disagree on the best setting and time to do homework based on their own experiences.

CHAPTER 30

Using Thinking Skills

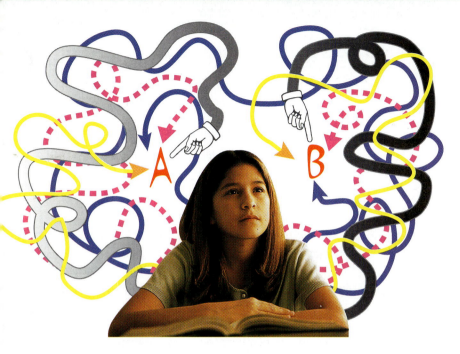

CHAPTER RESOURCES

Time-Saver Transparencies Binder:
- Critical Thinking Graphic Organizers pp. CT13, 15
- Daily Test Preparation pp. DT64–66

Writing and Communication Masters pp. 144–115

Integrated Technology and Media

Electronic Teacher Tools CD-ROM

mcdougallittell.com

Media Focus: Analyzing and Producing Media Program 2

Assessment

Teacher's Guide to Assessment and Portfolio Use

Students Acquiring English/ESL

Side by Side pp. 19–20

What a Thought!

There's so much information coming at you from all directions these days that it's easy to get confused. How do you sort out facts from opinions? How do you know which opinions are reliable? How do you keep from thinking in circles? The good news is that learning some simple skills can help you answer these questions and think in a straight line from point A to point B. Read on in this chapter to find out how.

Write Away: Huh?

With a partner, discuss something you heard, saw, or read that didn't make sense to you. Then write a paragraph describing what you didn't understand and how talking with your partner helped—or didn't help—you understand it. Save your paragraph in your 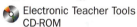 **Writing Portfolio.**

THINKING SKILLS

THINKING SKILLS

BLOCK SCHEDULING

Pressed for Time?

Focus on **Lesson 2, Separating Facts from Opinions,** and **Lesson 3, Going Beyond the Facts,** to familiarize students with some basic critical thinking skills. Encourage interested students to read **Lessons 1, 4,** and **5** independently.

Time for More?

After completing all of the chapter lessons, have pairs of students identify facts and opinions in newspaper or magazine editorials. Using colored pencils or markers, have students underline facts with one color, opinions with another.

CHAPTER 30

How Ideas Are Related

How do you make sense of the information you hear, read, and see every day? You can start by deciding which ideas are important and which are not, and by figuring out how ideas are related.

❶ Main Ideas and Supporting Details

The first thing to do to make sense of new information is to find the **main idea,** or the important point expressed.

Here's How **Identifying Main Ideas**

Pay special attention to ideas

- at the beginning or the end of a selection
- at the beginning of paragraphs or following pauses in a speech
- that are repeated several times
- that follow statements such as "The point is" and "This is about"
- that are underlined, bold-faced, or italicized in print, or that are spoken with emphasis or accompanied by forceful gestures

After you identify the main idea—or ideas—look for **supporting details.** These details often follow statements such as "For example" and "To illustrate the point."

PROFESSIONAL MODEL

What amazing device is spelled the same backwards and forwards? You guessed it—radar. Radar uses radio waves to determine how far away something is and how fast it's going. Our lives wouldn't be the same without it. Air traffic controllers, police officers, weather forecasters, and military personnel use it to guide planes, monitor car speeds, track tornadoes, and detect missiles.

—Annette Ford

Main idea— Radar is an amazing device.

Supporting details.

If an idea has weak—or no—supporting details, ask yourself, Why should I believe this? Where's the proof?

524 Communicating in the Information Age

2 Cause and Effect

One common way that ideas are related is by **cause and effect,** a relationship that shows why something happens. Information handouts and news reports often deal with causes and effects.

STUDENT MODEL

Due to budget cuts, the school band may have to go without uniforms this year. **However, band members are hoping that a car wash next weekend will help them raise the money they need. Strong support by both the faculty and student body could guarantee their success.**

> **Cause**—budget cuts→
> **Effect**—no band uniforms
>
> **Cause**—car wash→
> **Effect**—money to buy uniforms
>
> **Cause**—faculty and student support→
> **Effect**—success

In thinking about past events, look for solid evidence that connects them. The fact that one event happened after another does not necessarily mean the first event caused the second.

3 Similarities and Differences

Another way that ideas are connected is by **similarities and differences.** Science articles and movie reviews often compare and contrast the similarities and differences among ideas.

PROFESSIONAL MODEL

[A Utah fossil bed]... held the bones of two types of dinosaurs.... Both belonged to a group called ankylosaurs. They were plant eaters who were covered in thick, armorlike plates. They could grow to more than 30 feet long. [However] one... had a long tail with a heavy club at the end.... The other... had spikes on its shoulders.

—*Time for Kids*

Dinosaur 1
long tail with heavy club

Both Dinosaurs
ankylosaur, plant eater, thick, armor-like plates, more than 30 feet long

Dinosaur 2
spiky shoulders

Using Thinking Skills **525**

CUSTOMIZING TIP

Students Acquiring English/ESL
For visual practice with organizing cause-and-effect and comparison-contrast paragraphs, see **Side by Side** pp. 19–20.

Also suitable for:
Visual Learners

TEACHING TIP

Point out that a single effect may have several causes. Moreover, a single cause may result in a chain of several effects. Write this sentence on the board: *I overslept this morning.* Have students brainstorm possible causes and effects. Use **Critical Thinking Graphic Organizer Cause and Effect Chart** p. CT15, to organize their ideas.

CUSTOMIZING TIP

Less Proficient Learners Remind students that when they compare items, they tell how the items are alike. When they contrast items, they tell how the items differ. Some words that signal a comparison are *both, same, like, also, neither/nor, too,* and *just as.* Some words that signal a contrast are *different, but, unlike, although,* and *instead of.*

Also suitable for:
Students Acquiring English/ESL

THINKING SKILLS

TEACHING TIP

Cross-Curricular Connection Science Tell students that when they write about a science topic, they often address causes and effects or similarities and differences. For example, an essay on earthquakes would probably discuss its causes (two plates colliding) and its effects (collapsed buildings). An essay on whales might compare the sizes and behavior of different types of whale.

LESSON 2 Separating Facts from Opinions

After you understand ideas and how they're related, you still need to figure out how reliable they are. To do this, you have to be able to separate facts from opinions.

❶ Identifying Facts

A **fact** is a statement that can be proved. Solid information is well supported by facts.

> **Here's How** **Identifying and Proving Facts**
>
> • Make a personal observation.
> The weather report says the temperature is 80°.
> **To prove:** Check an outdoor thermometer.
>
> • **Consult an authoritative source.**
> A friend tells you the fastest animal is the cheetah.
> **To prove:** Look up the information in an encyclopedia.
>
> • **Ask an expert.**
> A cereal ad says that eating oatmeal can lower cholesterol.
> **To prove:** Ask your doctor or the school nutritionist.

A statement is not necessarily a fact just because you agree with it. Be sure to check it out by one of the methods listed above.

❷ Identifying Opinions

An **opinion** is a statement of personal belief that cannot be proved. Words and phrases like those listed below signal opinions.

Signals of Opinion			
believe	feel	think	would argue
doubt	don't see why	agree	don't agree
the best	excellent	the worst	useless

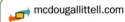

An opinion can be a good source of information, depending on whose opinion it is. Ask yourself, How much does this person know about the topic? and How reliable is he or she?

Not All Opinions Are Created Equal

—	+	Why
"Lulu's is the best ice cream ever." **Jenny Landers** Seventh grader	*"Lulu's ice cream is better for you than other popular ice creams."* **Inez Molino** Nutritionist	The nutritionist has scientific knowledge about foods. The seventh grader just likes ice cream.
"Grass courts are the worst courts to play on." **Dr. Mark Cattel** Mathematician	*"Tennis matches are more challenging on clay than on grass courts."* **Nikita Pinsky** Eighth-grade tennis champion	The tennis champ plays hours of tennis every day. The mathematician probably plays tennis only on weekends.
"Terriers are not very friendly dogs." **Alvin Brown** College sophomore	*"Most terriers are easy to train."* **Leslie Chin** Dog trainer	The dog trainer has worked with many dogs. The college student probably hasn't.

PRACTICE Identifying Facts and Opinions

Identify each of the following statements as a fact or an opinion. Write F for fact and O for opinion.

1. Mercury is the planet closest to the sun.
2. New York is the most exciting city in the United States.
3. Golf is a boring sport.
4. Rhode Island is the smallest state.
5. A vegetarian diet is the most healthy diet.

Explain what method you would use to prove each of the facts above.

Using Thinking Skills **527**

THINKING SKILLS

THINKING SKILLS

Spice It Up!

Quotable Quote "Never be afraid to sit awhile and think." —Lorraine Hansberry, American playwright

Ask students when they have time to just sit and think. Where does this usually take place? Ask students if they have ever sat in a room in silence, without a radio, television, or CD player on. What was the experience like? Did the silence help them think?

LESSON OBJECTIVES

To recognize the need to "go beyond the facts" and to make inferences, draw conclusions, and make generalizations

LESSON 3

Going Beyond the Facts

Understanding and evaluating what you read or hear are important first steps in thinking. But you can't stop there. You have to go beyond the facts and think about how the new information affects what you already know. You can do this in three ways—by making inferences, drawing conclusions, and making generalizations.

❶ Making Inferences

An **inference** is a logical guess you make by "reading between the lines" of new information. You do this by combining what you learn with your prior knowledge. You make many inferences every day, probably without even knowing it. For example, if you walk into your classroom and see an answer sheet on each desk, you might infer that you're going to have a test.

New Information + **Prior Knowledge** = **Inference**

My sister came home from a date with a diamond ring on her finger.

My sister has been dating her boyfriend for three years.

Women often get diamond rings when they get engaged.

My sister's engage

❷ Drawing Conclusions

A **conclusion** is a judgment or decision you arrive at by going "beyond the lines" of what you read or hear. A conclusion is based on a number of facts, inferences, and pieces of prior knowledge. It carries more weight than just a guess or inference

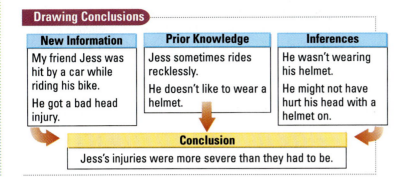

Drawing Conclusions

New Information	Prior Knowledge	Inferences
My friend Jess was hit by a car while riding his bike.	Jess sometimes rides recklessly.	He wasn't wearing his helmet.
He got a bad head injury.	He doesn't like to wear a helmet.	He might not have hurt his head with a helmet on.

Conclusion

Jess's injuries were more severe than they had to be.

❸ Making Generalizations

A **generalization** is a broad idea or statement based on several specific examples. Generalizations help you group information which makes it both easier to understand and to remember.

Specific Examples

Food prices increased by 10%.
+
Housing costs have doubled.
+
Clothing is more expensive.
↓
Generalization

The cost of living has gone up.

Don't make generalizations that are too broad; for example, it would be wrong to conclude from the examples above that all girls like sports.

PRACTICE ▶ **Making Inferences and Drawing Conclusions**

List the inferences you can make and the conclusions you can draw about the person who lives in this room.

Using Thinking Skills **529**

DAILY TEST PREPARATION

Error Correction: Subject-Verb Agreement Write the following item on the board or use **Daily Test Preparation Transparency** p. DT65. Choose the best way to write the underlined section.

> Torquing his rider this way and that, the great steed at last <u>wrench itself free</u>.

A. wrenches itself free.

B. wrench themselves free.

C. wrench free.

D. Correct as is

Teaching Point: A common item in error correction questions is subject-verb agreement. In this case, the subject *steed* takes a singular verb *(wrenches)*.

CUSTOMIZING TIPS

Addressing Learning Styles

Logical Unlike overgeneralizations, which are statements too broad to be accurate, oversimplifications are too narrow to be accurate. For example, the statement "Doing homework makes Tom sleepy" is probably not accurate because it omits relevant information that might explain why he is sleepy: he eats a large meal before doing homework; he puts off his homework until the end of the day; he devotes too much time and energy to other activities, etc. Discuss with students how overgeneralizations and oversimplifications tempt us with neat, tidy, and simple answers to complex problems that deserve complex answers.

Especially suitable for: Gifted and Talented

Avoiding Errors in Reasoning

LESSON 4

Much of what you see, read, and hear is meant to persuade you to buy, believe, or do something. Before you make decisions or take action, use your thinking skills to look for reasoning errors. Becoming aware of these errors will help you avoid them in your own speaking and writing too.

❶ Overgeneralization

An **overgeneralization** is a statement that is too broad to be true. All it takes is one exception to make a statement false. Overgeneralizations often include words such as *always, never, all, none, everybody,* and *nobody.*

Overgeneralization

All tall people are good basketball players.

True Statement

Some tall people are good basketball players.

> That's not true. My science teacher's really tall, and he's a terrible basketball player.

An overgeneralization about a group of people, such as this one about tall people, is called a **stereotype**.

❷ Circular Reasoning

Circular reasoning is merely repeating an idea in different words instead of giving good reasons to support it.

I'm tired because I don't have any energy.

Miss Peach by Mell Lazarus

530 Communicating in the Information Age

TEACHING RESOURCES

Time-Saver Transparencies Binder:
• Daily Test Preparation p. DT65

SKILLS PRACTICE RESOURCES

Writing and Communication Masters p. 114

mcdougallittell.com

In the cartoon, the statement "There's stuff in it that I don't know" is an example of circular reasoning because it's just another way of saying that the textbook is confusing. Here are some statements the boy could have made that would give readers more information.

- "The book is written in Japanese."
- "It doesn't have any punctuation."
- "I'm reading it upside down."

❸ False Cause and Effect

False cause and effect is the mistaken idea that one event caused another. Be careful not to assume that Event A caused Event B just because Event A happened first. Consider other facts as well.

False Cause and Effect

I ate cold pizza this morning. That's why I got sick this afternoon.

Correct Reasoning

The pizza probably had nothing to do with my getting sick. I just caught the flu that was going around.

> That's not true. I've eaten cold pizza before with no problem. Also, two of my friends got sick, and neither of them ate any pizza.

PRACTICE **Identifying Errors in Reasoning**

For each sentence below, identify the error in reasoning. Then rewrite the statement to correct the error.

1. Mt. Everest is the supreme challenge for every mountain climber.
2. Because we were running late, we got a flat tire.
3. No one wants to be alone.
4. Sara is smart because she is so intelligent.
5. If I had bought those new running shoes, I would have won the race.

Using Thinking Skills **531**

THINKING SKILLS

LESSON OBJECTIVES

To recognize emotional appeals and to use critical thinking skills to evaluate them

DAILY TEST PREPARATION

Sentence Completion: Subject Pronouns Write the following item on the board or use **Daily Test Preparation Transparency** p. DT66. Choose the word that belongs in the space.

> ____ students are the cream of the crop.

A. Them

B. Us

C. We

D. Delirious

Teaching Point: For sentence completion questions, the correct answer will always

- fit the meaning of the sentence (*delirious* does not make sense with *cream of the crop*).

- fit grammatically within the sentence (neither *them* nor *us* fits as the subject of the sentence).

TEACHING RESOURCES

 Time-Saver Transparencies Binder:

- Daily Test Preparation p. DT66

 Media Focus: Analyzing and Producing Media, Program 2

SKILLS PRACTICE RESOURCES

 Writing and Communication Masters p. 115

mcdougallittell.com

LESSON 5

Recognizing Emotional Appeals

Emotional appeals are statements directed at people's emotions rather than at their sense of reason. There's nothing wrong with these kinds of appeals. But make sure you don't reach decisions without thinking about the information logically too.

❶ Loaded Language

Loaded language uses words that have strong positive or negative associations. The positive associations of words like *fresh, forceful,* and *fantastic* in this poster make you want to support Barbara. But remember who wrote the poster—people who want her to be elected. So before voting—or acting on any information that includes loaded language—think carefully about the issue and about the source of the information.

For more information on loaded language, see pp. 406–407.

Choose the best answ

A student council president ne

a) fresh ideas   c) fantastic pe
b) forceful   skills
   leadership   d) all of the ab

If you
answe
is d, v
for me

#1

Barbara Larson's the choic
student council preside

 If reading or hearing something makes you angry, enthusiastic, afraid, or sad, the message probably includes loaded language.

❷ Name Calling

Name calling is a way of getting people to reject someone's ideas by attacking the person rather than the ideas themselves. Even if the charges against a person aren't true, name calling can make you doubt the person. Politicians sometimes use this technique against their opponents.

③ Bandwagon and Snob Appeal

Some people want to be just like everybody else. Others want to stand out from the crowd. Writers and speakers often appeal to these desires to help get their ideas across or sell a product. Be aware of these appeals and examine the ideas or products carefully and logically before taking action.

Bandwagon appeal is aimed at people's desire to be like everyone else.

> **Don't be left behind! Hop on the bike everyone's riding!**

Snob appeal is aimed at people's opposite desire—to be seen as individuals.

> **Safari Tours—only for the wild at heart!**

PRACTICE ▶ **Recognizing Emotional Appeals**

Identify the different types of emotional appeals in this advertisement.

What are you waiting for?

Only the coolest people wear **Ray-Ons** – and that could be you! Don't hide your face behind those other boring brands. Put on a pair and have your day in the sun!

Using Thinking Skills **533**

THINKING SKILLS

THINKING SKILLS

Student Help Desk

Students can use the Student Help Desk as a quick review prior to testing or as a quick reference as they revise a piece of writing.

Teacher's Notes

WHAT WORKS:

Student Help Desk

Using Thinking Skills at a Glance

Use your thinking skills to. . .

- identify main points
- discover relationships among ideas
- look for supporting evidence
- separate facts from opinions
- make inferences and generalizations
- draw conclusions
- find errors in reasoning
- recognize emotional appeals

Fact or Opinion — Can You Prove It?

Statement	Fact	Opinion	Check It Out!
It's a rainy day today.	✓		**See for yourself.** Look outside.
The rafflesia is the world's largest flower.	✓		**Go to a reliable source.** Check an encyclopedia or guide to plants.
Too much vitamin A can be harmful.	✓		**Ask an expert.** Talk to a doctor or a nutritionist.
This is the best grammar book I've ever seen.		✓	**Consider all the options.** Ask, What grammar books has the person seen?
Talking to my father is useless.		✓	**Define terms.** Ask, What does *useless* mean?
That was an excellent meal.		✓	**Get the details.** Ask, What made the meal excellent?

CHAPTER 30

Thinking Skills at Work

Give Me One Good Reason

Please, can I have a dog? All my friends have one.

I don't fall for that bandwagon appeal.

You never get me anything I want.

Now that's an overgeneralization, isn't it?

I'm the saddest and loneliest kid in the world.

If you're using emotional appeals to make me feel guilty, it's not working.

But a dog will keep me company and protect the house.

Ok, that sounds reasonable. What kind of dog should we get?

The Bottom Line

Checklist for Thinking Skills

Have I . . .

____ located main ideas and supporting details?

____ identified relationships among ideas?

____ separated facts from opinions?

____ gone beyond the facts to make inferences, drawn conclusions, and made generalizations?

____ recognized and avoided errors in reasoning?

____ recognized and evaluated emotional appeals?

TEACHER'S LOUNGE

Just for Laughs

The entering freshman was asked to fill in a form when she arrived at teacher's college. At the top was the question: Give two reasons for becoming a teacher. She wrote, 'July and August.'

A Slice of Life

"My mother drew a distinction between achievement and success. She said that achievement is the knowledge that you have studied and worked hard and done the best that is in you. Success is being praised by others, and that's nice, too, but not as important or satisfying. Always aim for achievement and forget about success."

—Helen Hayes

OBJECTIVES

To increase vocabulary through the recognition and understanding of words that communicate praise and criticism

To use words in speaking and writing that convey praise and criticism

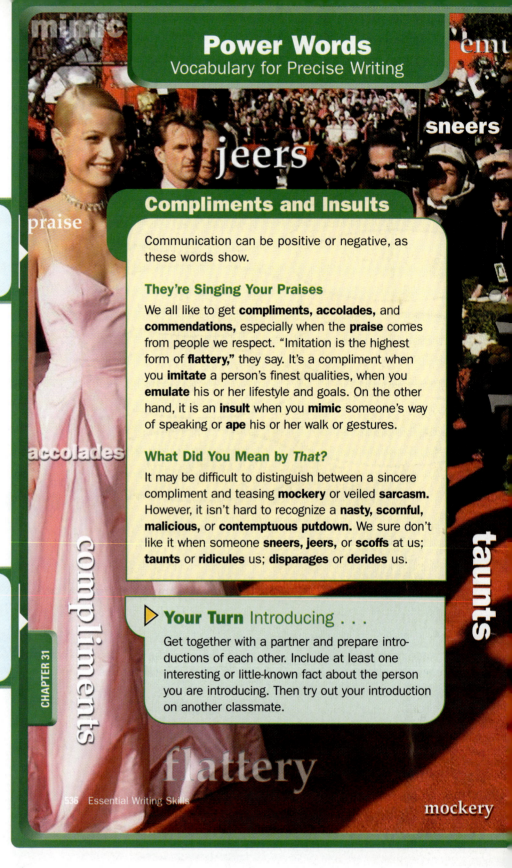

Power Words
Vocabulary for Precise Writing

Compliments and Insults

Communication can be positive or negative, as these words show.

They're Singing Your Praises

We all like to get **compliments, accolades,** and **commendations,** especially when the **praise** comes from people we respect. "Imitation is the highest form of **flattery,**" they say. It's a compliment when you **imitate** a person's finest qualities, when you **emulate** his or her lifestyle and goals. On the other hand, it is an **insult** when you **mimic** someone's way of speaking or **ape** his or her walk or gestures.

What Did You Mean by *That*?

It may be difficult to distinguish between a sincere compliment and teasing **mockery** or veiled **sarcasm.** However, it isn't hard to recognize a **nasty, scornful, malicious,** or **contemptuous putdown.** We sure don't like it when someone **sneers, jeers,** or **scoffs** at us; **taunts** or **ridicules** us; **disparages** or **derides** us.

▷ **Your Turn** Introducing . . .

Get together with a partner and prepare introductions of each other. Include at least one interesting or little-known fact about the person you are introducing. Then try out your introduction on another classmate.

536 Essential Writing Skills

Listening and Speaking Skills

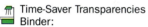

Did I hear you say . . . ?

Huh?

You're kidding!

Pardon me?

Say what?

Read My Lips

How many times a day do you think you use the phrases shown in the picture above? How many times do you hear others say them? The problem might be as simple as a noisy room or clogged ears. However, it's more likely that you or your friends suffer from an acute case of poor listening skills!

Write Away: What's That Again?
Write about a time when poor listening led to a problem. The situation you write about can be real or imagined, serious or humorous. For example, what would happen if everybody were always plugged into an audiocassette player? Save your paragraph in your 📁 **Working Portfolio.**

CHAPTER OVERVIEW

CHAPTER RESOURCES

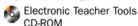 Time-Saver Transparencies
Binder:
  • Daily Test Preparation
    pp. DT66–68
  • Writing and
    Communication Skills
    pp. WC10–12
 Writing and Communication
Masters pp. 116–117

Integrated Technology and Media

🔘 Electronic Teacher Tools
CD-ROM

↩ mcdougallittell.com

Assessment

📋 Teacher's Guide to
Assessment and
Portfolio Use

LISTEN/SPEAK

LISTEN/SPEAK

BLOCK SCHEDULING

Pressed for Time?
Cover **Lesson 1, Listening Actively,** for an overview of listening strategies and evaluation techniques. Then focus on **Lesson 4, Preparing an Oral Report,** and **Lesson 5, Performing an Oral Interpretation,** to help students prepare and practice oral presentations.

Time for More?
After working through all the lessons, have students find famous speeches using such resources as history textbooks, biographical CD-ROMs, and politically related Web sites. Have students practice delivering and listening to the speeches.

To identify different purposes for listening and to use strategies for active listening

LESSON 1 Listening Actively

When you have something important to say, you want to make sure that people are listening. But are *you* a good listener?

The fact that you hear sounds and words doesn't mean that you are really listening. To be a good listener, you must think about what you hear and actively try to remember it.

❶ Listening with a Purpose

People who listen effectively know why they're listening and what they're listening for. Whenever you're in a situation that requires you to listen to someone, try to match *how* you listen to *why* you're listening.

Reasons for Listening		
Situation	**Reason for Listening**	**How to Listen**
Your friend tells a funny story about her pet iguana.	For enjoyment, to provide your friend with an audience	Maintain eye contact, nod to show you understand what he or she is saying, and make appropriate comments.
You're watching a TV show called "Wolves of the Tundra."	For enjoyment, to learn something new	Think about what you already know about the subject; listen for ideas that interest you or add to your own knowledge.
Your mother explains why you can't have an alligator as a pet.	To understand her point of view, to find opportunities to share your own ideas	Listen carefully to what she's saying, respond positively to the good points she makes, and listen for opportunities to state your own reasons.
You and your friends are trying to figure out how to arrange a trip to a concert.	To solve a problem	Identify goals and potential problems; listen closely to each other's ideas and build on them.

538 Communicating in the Information Age

② Strategies for Active Listening

No matter what your purpose for listening is, using techniques like these can help you understand the speaker's message:

Look for signals indicating main ideas.

- Listen for ideas presented first or last or repeated several times.
- Note statements such as "My point is . . . ." Then listen carefully to what follows.
- Pay attention to ideas that the speaker says loudly or with forceful gestures.
- During a multimedia presentation, note the points the speaker has presented visually.

Block out distractions and focus on the speaker.

- Keep your eyes on the speaker.
- Rein in your mind if it starts to wander.

Look for relationships between ideas.

- Look for comparisons and contrasts.
  Signals: *similarly, but,* and *on the other hand.*
- Pay attention to causes and effects.
  Signals: *because, if . . . then,* and *as a result.*

Take notes, if appropriate.

- Don't worry about writing complete sentences.
- List questions that occur to you as you listen.
- Think about points you want to pursue.
- Read over your notes to help you remember what you heard.

Summarize and paraphrase.

- Identify the main ideas and the details that support them.
- Put information in your own words.

Ask questions for clarification.

- Ask for explanations of points that confuse you.
- Indicate if you don't agree with something or if you need more information.

Listening and Speaking Skills **539**

SKILLS

LISTEN/SPEAK

CUSTOMIZING TIP

Addressing Learning Styles
Auditory Some students may find it helpful to record lectures and speeches on audiotape so that they can listen to them more closely at a later date.

TEACHING TIP

Remind students to eliminate barriers to effective listening. Tell them to turn off the radio, CD player, and TV when they listen to anyone. These distractions can keep them from hearing what is being said and prevent them from being understood.

CUSTOMIZING TIP

Students Acquiring English/ESL
Speaking and listening styles vary across cultures. For example, in some cultures, it is acceptable to interrupt while another speaker is talking. In others, it is considered disrespectful to make eye contact while listening to an adult. As you teach your students new speaking and listening techniques, ask them about their own cultures and present this style as an addition to, not a replacement for, what they already know.

Drive-Through Grammar

Compound and Complex Sentences
Relationships between ideas are often expressed in compound and complex sentences. Subordinating conjunctions such as *when, because, after, since,* and *then,* establish the relationship between clauses. Write the following sentences on the board. Ask students to describe the relationship created by the underlined words.

1. *They could not play ball <u>because</u> not enough players showed up.* cause/effect

2. *Our team was fast, <u>but</u> their team was faster.* compare/contrast

❸ Evaluating What You Hear

Understanding a person's message is important, but good listening does not stop there. You also have to evaluate the information. This means deciding whether the information makes sense and is well supported by details, facts, and examples.

When evaluating what you hear, you should think about the **content,** or the information presented. Ask yourself questions like those in the box below.

Evaluating Content

- Does the information make sense?
- Does it contradict anything I already know?
- Are ideas presented in an interesting and logical way?
- Are points supported with facts and details?
- What is the purpose of the talk, and does the speaker achieve it?
- Do I still have any questions after hearing the talk?

Negative answers to several of these questions should alert you to think very carefully about the information you hear before believing it or acting on it.

The speaker's **delivery**—the way the information is presented—is also important. Thinking about the following points can help you evaluate the delivery of a message.

Evaluating Delivery

Does the speaker . . .
- speak clearly and understandably?
- seem confident about his or her knowledge of the topic?
- use helpful gestures and body language?
- make eye contact with the audience?
- stand up straight and not fidget?
- use appropriate presentation aids, such as charts and slides?

For more information on evaluating what you hear, see pp. 527–533.

Interviewing

A special situation that will put your listening skills to good use is conducting an interview. An **interview** is a formal question-and-answer session in which you tap into someone's special in-depth knowledge.

1 Planning an Interview

Good planning can help to make an interview run smoothly. The important steps to consider are (1) identifying an appropriate, knowledgeable person to interview, (2) setting up the interview, and (3) preparing for the interview.

Identifying a Person to Interview

The quality of the information you get from an interview depends a great deal on the person you talk with, so pick that person carefully. Here are some steps to follow.

- **Identify** several people who are experts in your subject and who might be willing to speak with you. You also could contact an organization in that field and ask to be connected with an appropriate person.
- **Research** each person's background and experience to be sure the person actually has the kind of knowledge you are looking for.
- **Rank** the people whom you have researched and contact your first choice first. If that person is unavailable, try the next person on your list.

Setting Up an Interview

Telephone the first person on your list and ask for an interview. Be sure to cover the following points:

- identify who you are and why you want to interview the person
- arrange a time, date, and place that would be convenient for both of you to meet
- determine whether audiotaping or videotaping the interview is acceptable
- state where you can be contacted for a change of plans

Listening and Speaking Skills **541**

Preparing for an Interview

Be sure to prepare yourself carefully for an interview.

- Do background reading about the subject and make a list of questions to ask the interviewee.

- Create open-ended questions that can't be answered by a simple yes or no. Questions that begin with *How* or *Why,* for example, are particularly useful.

- Call the interviewee a day or two before the interview to remind him or her of your interview appointment.

❷ Conducting and Following Up on an Interview

To get the most useful information from the person you are interviewing, follow the tips and techniques listed below. Be sure to be punctual and polite and to bring all the supplies you'll need, such as a notebook, pens, and audio tape or video tape recorder.

> **Here's How** **Interviewing**
>
> **During the interview**
> - Ask your questions clearly and listen carefully. Give the person plenty of time to answer.
> - Be flexible with your plan and ask follow-up questions about anything that is especially interesting or confusing.
> - Even if you're recording the interview, take notes. Jot down the main ideas or interesting statements that can be used as quotes.
> - At the end of the interview, thank the person and offer to send him or her a copy of the final material.
>
> **After the interview**
> - While the interview is still fresh in your mind, review your notes and write a brief summary of the conversation.
> - If you recorded the interview, you may want to transcribe it or make a written version for your records.
> - Send a thank-you note to the person you interviewed.

Remember that your role as an interviewer is to ask questions and to listen. Show your interest in the person rather than in talking about yourself.

542 Communicating in the Information Age

Speaking Informally

To speak informally means to speak "on the spot" without time to prepare beforehand. Most of the speaking you do every day—both inside and outside the classroom—is informal.

❶ Everyday Speaking

You speak informally many times a day. Here are some tips for clear communication:

- Speak clearly and don't mumble.
- Get to the point and don't ramble.
- Avoid using slang such as "like" and "you know."
- Make eye contact with the person you're speaking to.
- Let the other person speak without interrupting them.

It's always important that you listen carefully, think about what you're going to say *before* you say it, and speak confidently. Also, always be sure to use language and ideas that suit your audience.

❷ Participating in a Group Discussion

You also have to speak with others in school and elsewhere. Participating in a discussion requires all of your listening, speaking, and interpersonal skills.

The key to a successful group discussion is consideration for others. The best way to get your ideas across is to listen and think about others' ideas and feelings before speaking.

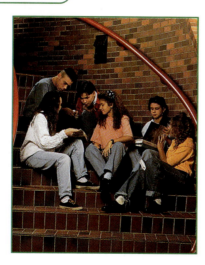

DAILY TEST PREPARATION

Error Identification: Spelling
Write the following item on the board or use 📖 **Daily Test Preparation Transparency** p. DT67.
Look for mistakes in spelling. Decide which word, if any, contains a mistake.

A. interrelated

B. irreplaceable

C. misspell

D. unerving

E. *(No mistakes)*

Teaching Point: Error identification questions often test your knowledge of basic spelling rules. In this case, the item tests whether you know not to drop a letter from a base word *(nerving)* when adding a prefix *(un-)*.

CUSTOMIZING TIP

Less Proficient Learners Explain to students that "on the spot" is an idiom (an expression that cannot be understood from its literal meaning). Discuss the meaning of other speaking-related idioms: "off the cuff" (not prepared in advance, spontaneous), "on/off the record" (spoken in confidence and not for publication).

LISTEN/SPEAK

LISTEN/SPEAK

Listening and Speaking Skills **543**

TEACHING RESOURCES

 Time-Saver Transparencies Binder:
- Daily Test Preparation p. DT67
- Writing and Communication Skills p. WC12

SKILLS PRACTICE RESOURCES

 mcdougallittell.com

Teaching Tips (left margin)

Group Skills

There are many reasons to have a group discussion—from just sharing ideas to solving problems. Following these simple rules can help you participate effectively in any group.

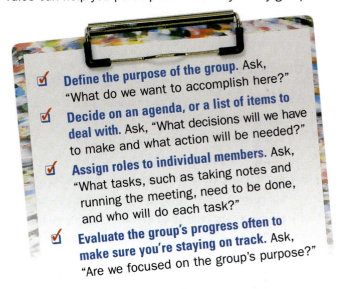

☑ **Define the purpose of the group.** Ask, "What do we want to accomplish here?"

☑ **Decide on an agenda, or a list of items to deal with.** Ask, "What decisions will we have to make and what action will be needed?"

☑ **Assign roles to individual members.** Ask, "What tasks, such as taking notes and running the meeting, need to be done, and who will do each task?"

☑ **Evaluate the group's progress often to make sure you're staying on track.** Ask, "Are we focused on the group's purpose?"

Discussion Skills

Good discussion participants both speak *and* listen effectively.

Here's How **Taking Part in a Discussion**

DO . . .
- Take turns speaking.
- Listen attentively to each speaker and take notes.
- Ask questions or comment on others' ideas.
- Speak clearly and confidently.

DON'T . . .
- Interrupt someone who is speaking.
- Think only about what you're going to say next.
- Use disrespectful language.
- Dismiss others' ideas without evaluating them.

HOT TIP Before you respond to a person in a group, ask yourself, "How would I feel if someone said that to me?"

Preparing an Oral Report

An oral report or a speech is probably the most formal oral presentation you will have to make as a student. Making an oral presentation involves careful research, preparation, and practice. It can be based on a report you've already written or can be prepared originally as a speech.

❶ From Writing to Speaking

When preparing an oral report, you will often be working with material you have already written. You shouldn't just get up and read your report aloud, though. You have to think about your listeners, so that might mean making changes like these:

- creating an attention-grabbing opener
- shortening the material
- simplifying the language
- adding audio or visual aids or both
- using facial and hand gestures
- including humor

For information on writing reports see pp. 478–493.

Adapting Different Types of Writing

The specific changes you must make to adapt a written report to an oral one can depend on the type of writing.

Adapting Different Types of Writing	
	Strategies to Consider
Informative	Using photographs, diagrams, and props to illustrate ideas
Persuasive	Using graphs and charts, body language, and differing tones of voice to emphasize your opinions and reasons
Interpretive	Using distinct voices and body language to portray individual characters
Research	Cutting unnecessary information, simplifying language, using visual aids whenever possible to make the important points clear

Listening and Speaking Skills **545**

To understand how to adapt a written report for oral presentation and to present an oral report

 DAILY TEST PREPARATION

Error Correction: Subject Pronouns Write the following item on the board or use **Daily Test Preparation Transparency** p. DT68.

> Peter and me are doing our homework together.

How is this sentence best written?

A. Peter and I are doing our homework together.

B. Peter and me do our homework together.

C. Peter and I does our homework together.

D. As it is

Teaching Point: Error correction questions often test your use of pronouns. In this case, the subject pronoun *I* is required because it is part of a compound subject. The object pronoun *me* cannot serve as the subject of a sentence.

LISTEN/SPEAK

TEACHING TIP

Tell students that they should also adapt their report to their audience. An oral report on whales presented to second graders, for example, may include more visuals than a similar report presented to seventh graders.

LISTEN/SPEAK

TEACHING RESOURCES

 Time-Saver Transparencies Binder:
- Daily Test Preparation p. DT68

SKILLS PRACTICE RESOURCES

 Writing and Communication Masters p. 117

 mcdougallittell.com

Choosing Presentation Aids

Think of an oral report as an opportunity to demonstrate, as well as talk about, your ideas. Using appropriate presentation aids can not only keep your audience awake but also can help to inform and entertain them. Here are some presentation aids you can use to turn a good report into a great one.

Presentation Aids

	Advantages	Special Considerations
Slides	Show real people, places, and things	Require special projection equipment
Maps	Show specific locations and relations of events	Must be large, simple, and well-labeled
Drawings	Illustrate real or imaginary ideas or things	Need to be large, simple, and well-labeled
Photos	Show real people, places, and things	Probably should be passed around the room
CDs	Provide sound effects and music that help create an atmosphere or illustrate a point	Require special sound equipment
Web sites	Provide additional sources of information on your topic	A computer and a special projector may be too small to be seen if not projected on a large screen

HOT TIP Mark your note cards or report notes to remind you where and when to use your presentation aids. Make sure that all the equipment you need is available and working before you make plans to use it.

For more information on using presentation aids, see pp. 561–563.

❷ Presentation Skills

When preparing to present an oral report, you have to consider not only the words you're going to say but also how you're going to say them and how you can best incorporate your presentation aids. Getting all of these elements to work together effectively requires practice, practice, and more practice.

Using Your Voice and Gestures

The success of an oral presentation often depends on how well you deliver it. Pay attention to the following points.

Delivering an Oral Presentation

Body Language

- Make eye contact with the audience.
- Use your hands and body to emphasize ideas.
- Use facial expressions to help express emotions.

Posture

- Stand straight and tall, but maintain a relaxed posture.
- Act naturally.
- Don't fidget.

Voice

- Speak loudly and clearly.
- Vary your tone and pitch.
- Pause for emphasis.

Dealing with Fear

Even the most experienced performers get stage fright. So if you feel butterflies in your stomach before giving an oral report, don't worry—you're in good company. Here are some symptoms many people experience and some ways to overcome them.

- **Dry mouth:** Drink plenty of water before speaking, or suck on a piece of hard candy or a mint. Stay away from milk—it can make your mouth sticky.
- **Shaky hands or voice:** Relax your muscles and breathe deeply. Speak slowly and pause or drink some water if you have to.
- **Queasy stomach:** Eat lightly before giving your report. Once you're on stage, relax and focus on a friendly face in the audience.

Listening and Speaking Skills **547**

LISTEN/SPEAK

LISTEN/SPEAK

TEACHING TIP

Have each student prepare a persuasive speech for the class. Make sure that students adapt their word choice, diction, and usage to their audience, purpose, and occasion. For example, students may try to persuade their audience to endorse a candidate for student council, accept their opinion of a particular movie, or take action to improve the food in their school cafeteria. Have classmates evaluate the presentations.

TEACHING TIP

Remind students that they should speak slowly to an audience. Their pace may sound too slow to them, but it will probably be just right for listeners.

TEACHING TIP

Tell students that some people find that visualization helps calm their nerves before making an oral presentation. Suggest that students sit quietly by themselves, close their eyes, and visualize reading to an appreciative audience.

DAILY TEST PREPARATION

Sentence Completion: Subject-Verb Agreement Write the following item on the board or use ☐ **Daily Test Preparation Transparency** p. DT68. Choose the word that belongs in the space.

The boy's books _____ in his locker.

A. sitting

B. lost

C. is

D. are

Teaching Point: For sentence completion questions, the correct answer will always

- fit the meaning of the sentence (*lost* does not).
- fit grammatically within the sentence (*sitting* does not complete the sentence; *is* does not agree in number with *books*).

Performing an Oral Interpretation

LESSON 5

An oral interpretation is a way to show listeners what a story or a poem—whether it's yours or someone else's—means to you. By using appropriate vocal or facial expressions and gestures, you can create a special world for your audience.

❶ Choosing a Selection

When choosing a poem or a story for an oral interpretation, you should think about factors such as the assignment, your interests, your audience, and how much time you will have to make the presentation. The key, however, is to choose a selection that you enjoy and feel strongly about.

Once you have chosen a story or a poem, you may have to adapt or adjust it to fit your audience or the available time.

Here's How) **Adapting a Selection for Oral Interpretation**

- Select your favorite part of the piece.
- Identify a good place to begin and end your selection.
- Make sure that the selection is complete in itself and that it allows you to express a number of emotions.
- Cut out parts that are boring or are unrelated to the selection.
- Cut out speakers' tags, such as *he said angrily* or *she sighed sadly.* You will express these emotions in your voice.

 Avoid selections that include only description or only dialogue. Also avoid selections that have so many characters that listeners will be confused.

TEACHING RESOURCES

 Time-Saver Transparencies Binder:
- Daily Test Preparation p. DT68

SKILLS PRACTICE RESOURCES

 mcdougallittell.com

❷ Practicing Your Delivery

Once you have chosen and adapted your selection, prepare a reading script. A **reading script** is a typed or neatly handwritten copy of your selection, marked with cues that remind you when to express an emotion, emphasize something, pause, or use a visual aid.

As you practice, try out different voices and gestures. Also, think about sound effects, costumes, props, or other presentation aids that will make the characters and situations come alive. When you're comfortable with your delivery, present your interpretation with your friends and family as an audience. Ask them for their reactions and suggestions.

STUDENT MODEL

Use low and scary voice and spread hands and arms wide.

Play owl's cry on CD.

Emphasize with a pause and louder voice.

Use a high, frightened voice.

Pause dramatically.

Turn lights out.

It was dark and gloomy as they entered the forest. An owl's cry shattered the eery silence. They had felt pretty brave starting out on their hike that morning. Now, they were beginning to wish they had stayed at home. Fear—true fear—descended on them in waves. Suddenly, Sara stumbled. She gripped Rachel's arm and cried out, "What's that?" Before Rachel could reply, a fierce gust of wind tore the flashlight from her hand. As she stooped down to pick it up, she and Sara became separated. They were then alone, each totally alone . . . in total darkness.

Listening and Speaking Skills **549**

LISTEN/SPEAK

TEACHING TIP

Speaking and Listening Have students present a dramatic interpretation to the class. Make sure they use an effective rate, volume, pitch, and tone of voice. Have the class assess how the actual presentation contributes to the message.

TEACHING TIP

Suggest that students conduct informal interviews with family members, neighbors, and friends to find out what kinds of oral traditions are prevalent in their regions and cultures. Encourage students to discuss the traditions they or their friends/family grew up with, and/or still maintain.

STUDENT MODEL

Write the following reading script on the board. Have students suggest cues for its performance. Suggested cues are in parentheses.

As Aaron leaned over the water fountain, he unknowingly dropped the dog leash. He cupped his hands and filled them with water. "Here you go, boy," Aaron said, turning. (happy, upbeat tone) *His dog was gone. "Roger?"* (voice rises for a question) *Aaron looked around. He called, "Roger, come here, boy!"* (loud, panicky) *Nothing. Aaron whistled.* (whistling sound) *Still nothing. Roger had totally disappeared.* (whisper)

LISTEN/SPEAK

ASSESSMENT

Teacher's Guide to Assessment and Portfolio Use

Student Help Desk

Students can use the Student Help Desk as a quick review prior to testing or as a quick reference as they revise a piece of writing.

Teacher's Notes
WHAT WORKS:

Student Help Desk

Listening and Speaking Skills at a Glance

Think about what you're going to say.

Speak clearly and confidently.

Consider your listeners.

Use active listening strategies.

Evaluate what you hear.

Speaking Tips   You Don't Say?

Believe in yourself and in what you're saying.
If you don't, your audience won't.

Stand straight and tall.
Show your confidence and pride.

Act naturally.
If you're uncomfortable, your audience will be too.

Speak loudly and clearly.
Make sure the people at the back of the room can hear you.

Make eye contact with people in the audience.
Pick several people in different parts of the room to focus on.

Use your voice, hands, and face for emphasis.
Vary your pacing and gestures to express emotion and create interest.

Evaluating What You Hear — Ears the Deal

Is it . . .	Ask Yourself
factual?	What are the facts? How easy is it to tell facts from opinions?
well-supported?	Which details and examples are provided? How strong and convincing are they?
believable?	How much does the speaker know about the subject? Which experts are quoted?
persuasive?	Which techniques are being used to convince me? Are they directed at my emotions or at my mind?

Group Participation — Join the Club

- Define the purpose of the group.
- Assign roles.
- Stay on track.
- Be considerate and polite.

- Listen before you speak.
- Respond to others' ideas.
- Ask questions.
- Compromise to reach the group's goal.

The Bottom Line

Checklist for Listening and Speaking Skills

Have I . . .

____ paid careful attention to the speaker?

____ looked for main ideas and supporting details?

____ identified relationships between ideas?

____ asked questions if necessary?

____ evaluated the information?

____ waited for my turn to speak in a group?

____ spoken confidently and clearly?

____ varied my voice for emphasis and effect?

____ used appropriate gestures and facial expressions?

____ included presentation aids when possible?

LISTEN/SPEAK

LISTEN/SPEAK

TEACHER'S LOUNGE

A Slice of Life

"Time cools, time clarifies; no mood can be maintained quite unaltered through the course of hours."
—Thomas Mann

Just for Laughs

Concerned about the maintenance of his school's newly painted walls, the custodian had this sign posted: "This is a partition, not a petition. No signatures required."

OBJECTIVES

To increase vocabulary through the recognition and understanding of words that are used in advertisements

To use words in speaking and in writing that describe items that are for sale

Power Words
Vocabulary for Precise Writing

Ours Is the Best!

You may see some of these words in advertising—and you may want to use them if you are selling something.

You Won't Believe This Offer!

"Don't do a thing until you see our **stupendous** offer," says the advertisement you are reading. "We have the **finest, all-new** product on the market, with **breakthrough** advances in technology and **cutting-edge** design. On the **deluxe** model, **peak** performance is achieved through **superlative** engineering and **maximum** power output. Our sales force is **unmatched** in customer service and our company's reputation is **second to none**. This is a **once-in-a-lifetime** opportunity. Act now!"

Nothing But the Best

"Quality is the **hallmark** of our programming," you hear the announcer on the TV commercial say. "Our news programs have been a **benchmark** in responsible broadcasting, and every year our sports coverage reaches a new **high-water mark**. We represent the **gold standard**, the **acme** and **zenith** in the business, even if we do say so ourselves."

▶ Your Turn For Sale

Suppose you had to sell something of yours, such as a skateboard, an article of clothing, or a video game. Create an ad that convinces people of its worth. Be sure to include at least one of the boldfaced words above.

Examining the Media

Media Circus

Just about everywhere you go these days, you're bombarded by the media—advertisements, newspapers, magazines, radio, and television. Different kinds of media are all competing for your attention, telling you, "Buy this product. Listen to this music. Read this story. Look at this image. Think about this opinion."

How can you make your way through this media circus? You need to know what media products are, who creates them, and what they mean. Then, you may just want to create some media products of your own.

Write Away: Life Without Media

How would your life be different if you had no access to media of any kind? That means no TV, no video games, no magazines, no books, and definitely no recorded music. What might be better in your life? What might be worse? Write a few sentences describing your thoughts and save them in your 📁 **Working Portfolio.**

**Media Wise
Media Literacy**

Examining the Media **553**

CHAPTER OVERVIEW

Introduction p. 553

1 Comparing Media pp. 554–556

2 Media Influence pp. 557–558

3 Analyzing Media Messages pp. 559–560

4 Using Media in Your Presentations pp. 561–563

CHAPTER RESOURCES

🖥 Time-Saver Transparencies Binder:
- Daily Test Preparation pp. DT69–70

Integrated Technology and Media

💿 Electronic Teacher Tools CD-ROM

🔲 mcdougallittell.com

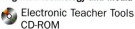 Media Focus: Analyzing and Producing Media Programs 1, 3, 5

Assessment

📋 Teacher's Guide to Assessment and Portfolio Use

BLOCK SCHEDULING

Pressed for Time?
Focus on **Lesson 1, Comparing Media,** and **Lesson 2, Media Influence,** to review the different types of media and understand ways to evaluate media messages.

Time for More?
Supplement the instruction of the chapter with  **Media Focus: Analyzing and Producing Media** Programs 1, 3, 5.

To recognize and compare the different forms of electronic and print media

CHAPTER 32

CHAPTER 32

Comparing Media

LESSON 1

A **medium** is a system of communication. Forms of media that are designed to communicate with a large audience are called **mass media.** Newspapers, magazines, TV, and radio are considered mass media. So are books, movies, advertisements, billboards, junk mail, cartoons, and the Internet. Many media products get their message across using **verbal elements** (written or spoken words) plus **nonverbal elements** such as

- images (photos, art, and video or film footage)
- graphics (maps, charts, icons, and logos)
- design (use of color and placement of items)
- sound effects and music

You need to be able to understand these nonverbal elements of the media just as you understand the words you read or hear. The examples in this lesson have to do with tornadoes. As you look at the examples, think about how the coverage is similar and how it is different.

1 Electronic and Film Media

The term **electronic media** refers to television, film, radio, and the Internet. This lesson concentrates on TV, Web sites, and documentaries.

Television Newscast

Television newscasts often show dramatic footage of news events. Nightly news programs include many close-ups of the news anchor. The program's producers want viewers to be comfortable with the anchor and to feel loyal to that person.

The anchor's facial expression and voice affect how viewers react to information.

On-screen graphics, such as this map, help viewers pinpoint the location.

Video footage from the scene gives a "you are there" feel.

Twister of Terror
Iowa · Moline · Illinois

Web Site

Like TV news, Web sites can provide a broad range of up-to-the-minute information. Sites can contain text, pictures, video and audio clips, and interactive features such as surveys.

Headlines identify written text, video, and audio that users can get to by clicking on <u>underlined words,</u> or links.

Information is presented in short summaries that are easy to scan.

This site is updated as new information becomes available.

Documentary

Documentaries often provide more in-depth coverage of a subject than TV newscasts or Web sites, but the information they contain is often less current and more general. This documentary follows "stormchasers," people who observe tornadoes.

Dramatic footage shows what being close to a tornado is like.

Viewers receive detailed information on storms and the people who follow them.

Music and sound effects create a dramatic mood.

Examining the Media **555**

Answers

PRACTICE → Choose Your Coverage

Answers will vary.

A student who chooses to compare coverage of an oil spill in a newsmagazine and on a television news program, for example, might mention that the newsmagazine included detailed information on the spill, photographs of oil-soaked animals, and a diagram of how and where the oil spilled. The TV news coverage might include information that is less detailed but more up-to-date, showing oil-soaked animals while sad music plays in the background. Both sources might include interviews with experts and information on how people can donate to cleanup foundations.

❷ Print Media

Print media include newspapers, magazines, newsletters, brochures, and junk mail. Print media are usually not as up to date as electronic media. However, print sources can provide a wealth of information in a format that is easy to understand. This article gives in-depth information and analysis.

Magazine Article

The design gives more space to the powerful photo than to the written text.

This big, sensational headline grabs readers' attention.

FUNNEL OF DEATH

In Oklahoma the wind came sweeping down the plains with record-breaking fury. And the tornado season has just begun

The brief summary of the article makes the reader want to read further.

A caption not only explains the photo but also gives interesting details.

PRACTICE → **Choose Your Coverage**

Choose a current news item and compare the coverage of the same item in two different media, one electronic and one print. Then, create a chart or a Venn diagram highlighting the major differences between the two media. (For an example of a Venn diagram, see p. 359.)

Media Influence

Anyone who creates a media product has a message that he or she wants heard. As you become more media savvy, you will notice how different media messages try to **influence** you, or affect how you think about something.

❶ Identifying Purposes

All media programs and products—from news reports to video games—are created by specific people for specific purposes. Whenever you read, watch, or listen to a form of media, ask yourself: "Why was this created? Who developed it? What is it trying to accomplish?" This chart can help you think about these questions.

Purposes of Media Products

Purpose	Examples
Inform: to present information or to analyze an issue	news reports and articles; public service announcements; certain Web sites
Persuade: to sway the feelings, beliefs, or actions of an audience	advertisements; "infomercials" (program-length commercials); editorials; reviews; political cartoons
Entertain: to amuse or delight	most TV shows; recorded music; video and computer games; cartoons; most talk shows

Most types of media have more than one purpose. For example, TV commercials are often entertaining, but their main purpose is to persuade you to buy something.

❷ Determining the Audience

Target audiences are portions of the population that have certain things in common. You are a member of several target audiences based on your age, whether you are male or female, your likes and dislikes, and many other factors.

LESSON OBJECTIVES

To identify and evaluate a media product's purpose, it's target audience, and its message

📑 DAILY TEST PREPARATION

Definition: Vocabulary Write the following item on the board or use 📕 **Daily Test Transparency** p. DT69. Choose the word that means the same, or about the same, as the underlined word.

> Someone who is <u>pretentious</u> is

A. humble

B. deserving

C. arrogant

D. timid

Teaching Point: For definitions, rule out any answer options that are opposite in meaning to the underlined word (*humble* and *timid*). Answer C is closest in meaning.

CUSTOMIZING TIP

Less Proficient Learners Some students may have a difficult time remembering the vocabulary in this lesson. You might want to create a poster listing some of the terms used and display the poster in the classroom. The list might include: *media, target audience, sponsor, bias,* and *loaded language.*

Also suitable for:
Students Acquiring English/ESL

MEDIA

MEDIA

TEACHING RESOURCES

 Time-Saver Transparencies Binder:
 • Daily Test Preparation p. DT69
 Media Focus: Analyzing
 and Producing Media, Program 3

SKILLS PRACTICE RESOURCES

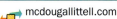 mcdougallittell.com

CHAPTER 32

Some companies spend millions of dollars to target a particular audience and get its support. For example, a cereal company targeting young children might advertise on Saturday-morning cartoon shows.

❸ Evaluating What You See and Hear

Most likely, you tune out media messages that don't target you. You probably grab the remote during commercials for minivans and life insurance, for instance. However, are you critical of media messages that do target you? To be a smart consumer of media, keep these questions in mind.

- **What sponsors are targeting you?** Pay attention to the products advertised on your favorite TV and radio shows and in your favorite magazines. The companies that make those products **sponsor,** or pay for, the programs and articles.

    Sponsors can affect what gets on the airwaves and in print. For example, if a TV show offends people, it may not attract many sponsors and will probably be canceled.

- **What messages are you getting?** A sponsor that is targeting you will try to tap into your hopes, fears, and desires. The sponsor may show people who look and sound like you. Think about whether the message is designed to inform, entertain, or persuade you.

- **Are the messages based on fact or opinion?** Some media messages are **biased,** or unfairly weighted toward one point of view. Others use **loaded language**—words that have strong positive or negative feelings attached to them. Watch out for messages that try to change your mind about something without giving you all the facts.

LESSON 3 — Analyzing Media Messages

① What's Behind the Message?

You need to be able to analyze a media message so that you can develop a thoughtful opinion about it. On these two pages are messages about a band called the Gopher Brains. Notice what's behind the sometimes conflicting messages.

TV Commercial

This commercial tells viewers that *Gopher Broke,* the Gopher Brains' new album, is available now.

- **Purpose:** The recording company that sponsored Gopher Broke wants to inform viewers about the new album. It also wants to persuade them to buy it!
- **Target audience:** Teenagers with money to spend.
- **Methods:** The commercial uses footage of the band, graphics, music, and sound effects to attract viewers. It also uses loaded language, describing the album as "hot" and urging viewers not to miss it.

Evaluate: Do you think the claim in the commercial is an exaggeration? What do you think about when deciding whether to buy a product you see advertised?

Documentary

In a documentary, the Gopher Brains play four new songs and talk about the band's early years.

- **Purpose:** The music video network that created the documentary wants to inform viewers about the band's music. It also wants to entertain viewers and create interest in the band.
- **Target audience:** Fans of music and of the group.
- **Methods:** The documentary holds viewers' attention by combining footage, music, and sound effects.

Evaluate: The documentary might be interesting and informative, but it might also be a thinly disguised advertisement for the new album. Have you ever been persuaded to buy something without even realizing that you were being persuaded?

Examining the Media **559**

LESSON OBJECTIVES

To identify and analyze different types of media messages

DAILY TEST PREPARATION

Error Identification: Punctuation
Write the following item on the board or use **Daily Test Preparation Transparency** p. DT70. Decide which type of error, if any, appears in the underlined section.

> The Smith's were character-istically late to the dinner party.

A. Spelling error

B. Capitalization error

C. Punctuation error

D. No error

Teaching Point: Error identification questions often test your knowledge of basic punctuation rules. In this case, the plural noun *Smiths* should be used, not the possessive *Smith's.*

TEACHING TIP

Tell students that companies use methods other than commercials to try to persuade people to buy their products. For example, many companies pay to have their products appear in movies.

MEDIA

MEDIA

TEACHING RESOURCES

 Time-Saver Transparencies Binder:
- Daily Test Preparation p. DT70

Media Focus: Analyzing and Producing Media, Program 1

SKILLS PRACTICE RESOURCES

 mcdougallittell.com

CUSTOMIZING TIP

Students Acquiring English/ESL

Some students might think a critic is someone who always criticizes, or expresses negative opinions. Explain that a critic is someone who analyzes, interprets, and/or evaluates artistic works without necessarily finding faults in them.

Answers

PRACTICE ▸ You Be the Judge

Answers will vary. Possible responses:

The purpose of the advertisement is to persuade readers to buy jeans. The ad is sponsored by Total Denim. Because the person shown in the ad is a teenage girl, teenage girls are most likely the ad's target audience. The ad uses persuasive language—"choose the jeans that fit your attitude"—as well as attractive, colorful photographs and an eye-catching design to achieve its purpose. The ad is effective because it makes the jeans look attractive and lets readers know where to find them (or, the ad is not effective because it doesn't tell the reader anything important about the jeans, such as how much they cost or what sizes they are available in).

CHAPTER 32

Music Review

This newspaper's music critic believes that *Gopher Broke* is a disappointment.

- **Purpose:** The newspaper that pays the critic wants its readers to be well-informed about new music. It wants readers to trust and depend on its critics.

- **Target audience:** Readers who buy albums regularly.

- **Methods:** An eye-catching image and clever headline draw readers in.

Evaluate: Does this critic support her opinion? When you are thinking about buying a product, whose opinions do you seek?

Arts & Entertainment

Music

Gopher Broke Goes Nowhere

The new Gopher Brains CD is getting a great deal of attention, though it's hard to see why. This bland collection of songs is the Gophers' lamest effort in years.

PRACTICE ▸ **You Be the Judge**

Now it's your turn. Analyze and evaluate this magazine ad.

- What is the purpose?
- Who is the sponsor?
- Who is the target audience?
- What methods are used to achieve the purpose?
- Do you think this ad is effective? Why or why not? Does it matter that the ad gives very little information?

CHOOSE THE JEANS THAT FIT YOUR ATTITUDE

Shop at TOTAL DENIM

CHAPTER 32

Spice It Up!

Give students some more experience analyzing ads. Collect a variety of ads and then distribute them, one apiece, to small groups of students. Have students use the questions in **Practice** to guide their analysis.

Using Media in Your Presentations

LESSON 4

1 Exploring Multimedia

You've already learned to be a smarter consumer of media. What about becoming a creator of media as well?

The next time you have a report or a project to do, consider doing a multimedia presentation. A **multimedia presentation** is a computer-enhanced report. It presents several kinds of media combined on a computer. Software programs such as PowerPoint and HyperStudio make multimedia presentations easier than ever to create.

You can combine some or all of the following media elements into an interesting, informative presentation.

Possible Components for Your Presentation	
Video	Video clips can add a "you are there" feel to your presentation. Use just a few, though—they can take a long time for your computer to load and play.
Sound	Recorded words, music, or sound effects can give your audience information or set a mood.
Graphs and charts	Visual aids give your audience lots of factual information at a glance.
Graphics and animation	These can make your presentation more attractive and lively. Many software programs provide graphics and animation for you to use.
Photographs and illustrations	Adding photographs and illustrations makes your presentation more informative and attractive.
Text	Don't forget the most important part of your presentation: writing the text that ties everything together!

You can create a great presentation even if you don't have access to a computer. The next time you are assigned an oral report, consider creating posters and playing recorded words or music to go with your report.

Examining the Media **561**

MEDIA

MEDIA

② Planning Your Presentation

The planning stage of your multimedia presentation is essential. In fact, planning ahead for multimedia is just as important as for a written report because you have so many parts to track. Here are some steps that can help.

Here's How **Planning a Multimedia Presentation**

1. Choose a topic that will work well in a multimedia format. Are there photos, illustrations, video clips, and audio clips available? Can you create them yourself?
2. Identify your audience and purpose.
3. Look for information as you would for a traditional report.
4. Create a flow chart or outline that shows what visuals, sounds, and information you will use.
5. Write a script of what you will say when each screen is displayed.

③ Organizing Your Presentation

Organize your research in an outline, in a flow chart, or on note cards. Know exactly what kind of information you want to appear on each screen.

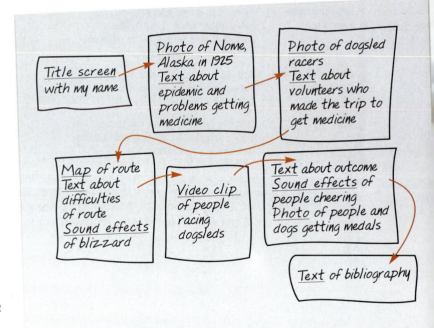

562

Creating a Script

It's a good idea to create a script to go with your presentation, so you'll know what you will talk about at each point. Here's how one student did it. Notice that the onscreen text gives only the main ideas.

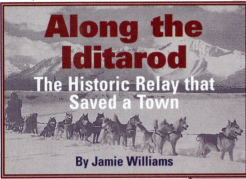

Along the Iditarod
The Historic Relay that Saved a Town
By Jamie Williams

Diphtheria, a deadly infection, broke out in Nome, Alaska, in January of 1925. Most of its victims were children. There was a serum that would prevent more children from getting sick, but it was more than 1,000 miles away. Planes could not carry the serum to Nome because the weather there was so severe.

Script
Have you ever faced a problem that seemed impossible to solve? Here's how the people of one town saved their children from an outbreak of a deadly disease.

The Problem
· Diphtheria outbreak in Nome
· Serum over 1,000 miles away
· Planes unable to get through

Rehearse your presentation several times. Make sure all the parts are in the right order, the presentation flows smoothly, and all equipment works.

For more on giving presentations, see pp. 545–547

PRACTICE **Multimedia About Media**

Go back to your **Write Away** exercise from page 553. Using what you wrote then, plan a multimedia presentation on how media affect your life. How do TV, magazines, radios, and other forms of media make your life better? In what ways do they make your life worse? In your plan, explain what images and sounds you might use for each screen and make notes about the kind of text you would write.

MEDIA

MEDIA

Drive-Through Grammar

Commas with Interrupters As students write the text for their presentations, remind them to use commas with interrupters. Interrupters are words or phrases that interrupt, or break, the flow of thought in a sentence. Commas used with interrupters mark pauses before and after the interruption. Write the following sentences on the board and ask students to add commas where necessary.

It could however clear up tomorrow.

It could, however, clear up tomorrow.

My aunt who is never wrong says it will rain.

My aunt, who is never wrong, says it will rain.

Student Help Desk

Students can use the Student Help Desk as a quick review prior to testing or as a quick reference as they revise a piece of writing.

Teacher's Notes

WHAT WORKS:

_____

_____

_____

_____

_____

_____

_____

_____

_____

_____

_____

_____

_____

_____

_____

_____

_____

_____

_____

_____

_____

CHAPTER 32

Student Help Desk

Examining Media at a Glance

IDENTIFY
- What is the purpose: to inform, persuade, or entertain? Is there more than one purpose?
- Who is the target audience?

UNDERSTAND
- What is the written or spoken message?
- What does the overall design of images, colors, and/or sounds tell you?

ANALYZE
- Who sponsored the message?
- Why is the audience being targeted?
- Does the message use bias or loaded language?

Targeting Audiences   Out to Get Your Attention

Media creators choose target audiences—groups of people who have certain things in common. These magazines target very different audiences.

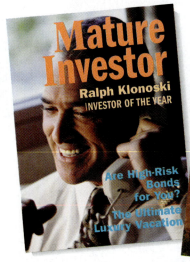

Ask yourself:
- Who is the target audience?
- What messages are being sent to that audience?
- Do the messages include bias or loaded language?
- Are the messages effective? Why or why not?

CHAPTER 32

Persuasive Pitfalls

Bias **means unfair preference.**

"All our store owners agree—our products are the best!"

Loaded language **is designed to give you strong positive or negative feelings.**

"Vote for the brightest star in our school. Tran will take us to the top!"

Multimedia Presentations

Six Quick Tips

- Don't use too many multimedia elements.
- Keep video and audio clips short.
- Make sure your text ties together all the multimedia elements.

- Rehearse your presentation several times.
- Speak clearly and in a loud voice.
- Make eye contact with your audience.

FOXTROT by Bill Amend

The Bottom Line

Checklist for Examining the Media

Have I . . .

____ been aware of how media messages try to influence me?

____ identified the purpose and target audience?

____ thought about who sponsored the message and why?

____ planned and created a multimedia presentation?

MEDIA

TEACHER'S LOUNGE

MEDIA

Just for Laughs

I really wish I was young enough to know everything.

A Slice of Life

"A good book is a garden carried in the pocket." — Africa

To increase vocabulary through the recognition and understanding of words that describe kinds of trips

To use words in speaking and writing that describe kinds of trips

CHAPTER 33

CHAPTER 33

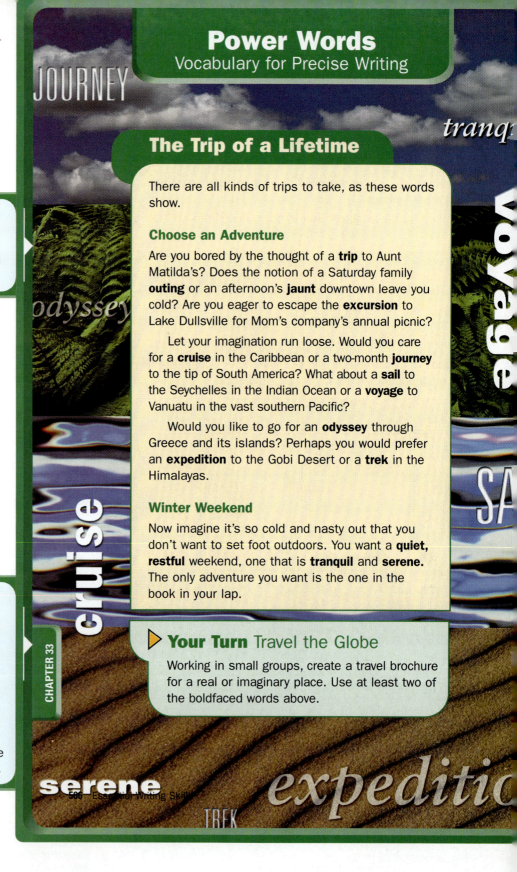

Power Words
Vocabulary for Precise Writing

The Trip of a Lifetime

There are all kinds of trips to take, as these words show.

Choose an Adventure

Are you bored by the thought of a **trip** to Aunt Matilda's? Does the notion of a Saturday family **outing** or an afternoon's **jaunt** downtown leave you cold? Are you eager to escape the **excursion** to Lake Dullsville for Mom's company's annual picnic?

Let your imagination run loose. Would you care for a **cruise** in the Caribbean or a two-month **journey** to the tip of South America? What about a **sail** to the Seychelles in the Indian Ocean or a **voyage** to Vanuatu in the vast southern Pacific?

Would you like to go for an **odyssey** through Greece and its islands? Perhaps you would prefer an **expedition** to the Gobi Desert or a **trek** in the Himalayas.

Winter Weekend

Now imagine it's so cold and nasty out that you don't want to set foot outdoors. You want a **quiet, restful** weekend, one that is **tranquil** and **serene**. The only adventure you want is the one in the book in your lap.

▷ **Your Turn** Travel the Globe

Working in small groups, create a travel brochure for a real or imaginary place. Use at least two of the boldfaced words above.

JOURNEY   tranqu   voyage   odyssey   cruise   SA   serene   expediti   TREK

566 Essential Writing Skills

Developing Your Vocabulary

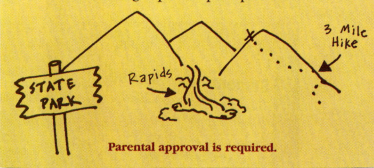

Weekend Adventure Trip
For Kids Ages 12 to 14

Do you have the endurance needed to hike an arduous trail and raft the state's most formidable river? If you've got the right stuff, this adventure will really test your mettle. Sign up in the principal's office.

3 Mile Hike

STATE PARK

Rapids

Parental approval is required.

Is This Trip for You?

How can you tell if you've got "the right stuff" for this adventure if you don't know the meanings of key words in the poster? You'll have to figure out what *arduous, formidable,* and *mettle* mean. Expanding your vocabulary will improve your communication skills and help you to understand new concepts, like the ones in the poster above. When you build word power, you also build brain power!

Write Away: Figuring Out Meanings
Try rewriting the poster above using words that you think have the same meanings as *arduous, formidable,* and *mettle.* Then check the dictionary! Save your work in your 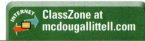 **Working Portfolio.**

ClassZone at mcdougallittell.com

Developing Vocabulary **567**

CHAPTER RESOURCES

Time-Saver Transparencies Binder:
- Daily Test Preparation pp. DT71–73
- Vocabulary pp. VS1–8

Writing and Communication Masters pp. 118–122

Integrated Technology and Media

Electronic Teacher Tools CD-ROM

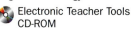 mcdougallittell.com

Assessment

Teacher's Guide to Assessment and Portfolio Use

VOCABULARY

VOCABULARY

BLOCK SCHEDULING

Pressed for Time?
Focus only on **Lesson 2, Using Context Clues**, and **Lesson 3, Analyzing Word Parts**, to introduce two important methods for determining the meaning of unfamiliar words.

Time for More?
After covering all of the material in the chapter, have students explore the World Wide Web for online dictionaries and thesauruses. Ask students to compile a list of online vocabulary resources.

To identify and use strategies for understanding unfamiliar words

Sentence Completion:

Vocabulary Write the following item on the board or use **Daily Test Preparation Transparency** p. DT71. Choose the word that *best* fits the meaning of the sentence.

It's very difficult to _____ venom from an eastern diamondback timber snake.

A. extract

B. insert

C. extracts

D. collected

Teaching Point: For sentence completion questions, the correct answer will always

- fit the meaning of the sentence (*insert* does not make sense with *venom from*).

- fit grammatically within the sentence (*extracts* and *collected* cannot serve as part of an infinitive verb).

TEACHING TIP

Engage students in a discussion about strategies they already use for determining the meaning of unfamiliar words. Some students may say that they skip unfamiliar words, while others may say that they ask a friend or family member what a word means.

CHAPTER 33

 LESSON 1 # Building Vocabulary

❶ Strategies for Understanding New Words
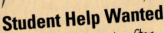

Using a dictionary to learn the meaning of a new word is a good strategy for building your vocabulary. However, looking up a word means interrupting your reading. Three strategies—using context clues, analyzing word parts, and learning from related words—can help you guess the meanings of new words *while* you read. You can look up the definitions later if you still need help.

This poster contains words that you may not know. Use the clues given to figure out the meanings. You will learn more about each kind of clue later in the chapter.

CHAPTER 33

Student Help Wanted

The main office needs after-school help with **collating** (assembling pages) of the Student Handbook and **screenprinting** of P.E. activity posters. If you are a reliable and **conscientious** worker, we need your energy! Pick up a work release form and an application from Mrs. Greene, fill them out with a parent's signature on each, and **resubmit** them to the main office. You will be called for an interview if you can work at least ten hours per week

Collating is defined in parentheses.

Notice the two words that make up **screenprinting**.

You may recognize a part of the word **resubmit**.

Conscientious may be understood from the sentence in which it appears.

TEACHING RESOURCES

 Time-Saver Transparencies Binder:
- Daily Test Preparation p. DT71

SKILLS PRACTICE RESOURCES

mcdougallittell.com

② Strategies for Remembering New Words

As you learn new words, you won't want to forget them. Use these strategies to help you remember.

> **Here's How** Remembering New Words
>
> - Keep a personal word list and add a new word to it right away. Review the list often to refresh your memory.
> - Begin to use the new word in conversations and in your writing as soon as possible.
> - Make up a memory cue, such as "a conscientious judge" or "collate, crease, and staple." Notice how rhyming can also be a helpful memory trick in the examples that follow.
>
> **evade** (to escape or avoid):   "**Evade** the raid!"
>
> **elude** (to hide from or lose):   "**Elude** the dude; he's too crude."
>
> **avert** (to ward off or prevent):   "**Avert** the hurt."
>
> **entice** (to attract or lure):   "**Entice** the mice with a little rice."

Add to your personal word list as you read textbooks, scan a newspaper or magazine, or hear an interesting word in conversation.

One new word a day adds up to 365 new words a year!

Jan.1
evade

FoxTrot by Bill Amend

TEACHING TIP

Cooperative Learning/Paired Activity Have students work in pairs to create new rhymes for the words in the **Here's How.** Ask volunteers to read their rhymes to the class. This activity will give students practice in collaborating with other writers to compose different types of text.

CUSTOMIZING TIP

Less Proficient Learners Direct students to 🔲 **mcdougallit-tell.com** for extra practice with new vocabulary words.

Also suitable for:
Students Acquiring English/ESL

VOCABULARY

VOCABULARY

Developing Vocabulary **569**

Spice It Up!

Play a game that is a take-off on the *Fox Trot* cartoon. Write the following four words on the board, and challenge students to use four in a single sentence. Encourage students to be creative, but to use the words correctly.

computer	avalanche
misfortune	tremendous

LESSON OBJECTIVES

LESSON OBJECTIVES

To recognize and use context clues to determine the meanings of unfamiliar words

DAILY TEST PREPARATION

Error Correction: Object Pronouns Write the following item on the board or use **Daily Test Preparation Transparency** p. DT71.

> Tom sent a letter to she.

How is this sentence best written?

A. Tom sent a letter to hers.

B. Tom sent a letter to her.

C. Tom sent a letter to herself.

D. As it is

Teaching Point: Error correction questions often test your use of pronouns. In this case, the object pronoun *her* should be used to serve as the object of the preposition *to*.

THE LANGUAGE OF LITERATURE

The passage on the student page is from *Boy: Tales of Childhood* in *The Language of Literature,* Level 7.

LESSON 2

Using Context Clues

One way to understand an unfamiliar word is to look at its **context,** the words and sentences surrounding it. Context often provides clues to help you infer, or figure out, the general meaning of the word.

❶ General Context

General context refers to the several sentences or the whole paragraph surrounding an unfamiliar word. Photos, charts, and drawings can also be part of the general context. Notice how the details in this paragraph help you understand the meaning of the word *loathsome.*

> **LITERARY MODEL**
>
> But by far the most **loathsome** thing about Mrs. Pratchett was the **filth** that clung around her. Her apron was **grey** and **greasy.** Her blouse had **bits of breakfast** all over it, **toast crumbs and tea stains** and **splotches of dried egg yolk.** It was her hands, however, that disturbed us most. They were **disgusting.** They were **black with dirt and grime.**
>
> —Roald Dahl, *Boy: Tales of Childhood*

Clues to the meaning of *loathsome.* How would you define this word?

❷ Definition and Restatement

Some texts define new words or restate their meanings in another way. Certain words and special punctuation (commas, dashes, and parentheses) may signal that a definition or restatement follows a new word.

Signal Words: Definition or Restatement

which	that is	where	is called
in other words	or	this means	

TEACHING RESOURCES

 Time-Saver Transparencies Binder:
- Daily Test Preparation p. DT71
- Vocabulary pp. VS1–3

SKILLS PRACTICE RESOURCES

 Writing and Communication Masters pp. 118–119

 mcdougallittell.com

VOCABULARY

VOCABULARY

1. *Integrity* means "strict honesty." The word is defined within the dashes.

2. *Lagged* means "moved slowly." The word "unlike" signals that *lagged* is the opposite of *hurried*.

3. *Turmoil* means "unrest" or "extreme confusion." The second sentence gives examples of turmoil.

4. *Sabotaged* means "destroyed" or "interfered with normal operations." The word can be understood from the phrase "keep us from voting."

5. *Conundrum* means "difficult problem." The word can be understood through general context and clues such as *solved*.

6. *Prerogative* means "right" or "privilege." The term is defined within the commas.

7. *Ardent* means "passionate." The words "in contrast to" signal a contrast with "did not seem to care."

8. *Predicament* means "very difficult problem." The term is defined within the dashes.

9. *Proposition* means "plan." The words "in contrast to" signal that the sentence gives a contrasting example.

10. *Partaking* means "taking part in" or "participating." The word can be understood through general context.

CHAPTER 33

❹ Comparison and Contrast

Sometimes a sentence compares or contrasts a familiar word or phrase with a less familiar one. If you know one word, you can often figure out the other.

Signal Words: Comparison or Contrast			
like	as	instead of	but
unlike	in contrast to	on the other hand	

STUDENT MODEL

Like the rest of my **frugal** family, I always save part of the money I earn. I wish I had more **ingenuity** in making money instead of simply relying on the same old baby-sitting jobs.

Clue words signal a comparison and a contrast. What do the words in red mean?

PRACTICE ▸ **Use Those Clues!**

Use context clues to define the following underlined words. Be ready to tell what clues you used.

1. Jane's underlined integrity—the strict honesty with which she lived—made her the best candidate for class president.

2. We all hurried to vote, unlike Joe, who lagged behind.

3. At the gym, there was turmoil. Lemonade pitchers had been overturned, and we had to search for clean ballots.

4. Had someone sabotaged the election to keep us from voting?

5. The conundrum was solved when Joe discovered a squirrel's nest nearby with scraps of lemonade-stained ballots in it!

6. The election gave us an opportunity to exercise our prerogative, or right, to select our class leaders.

7. In contrast to the lower school, where students did not seem to care, the middle school showed an ardent enthusiasm.

8. The biggest predicament facing the new president—a very difficult problem—was how to unite the seventh grade.

9. Jane's proposition included regular open meetings, in contrast to her opponents, who proposed no plans at all.

10. No naughty squirrels could prevent us from partaking in the exciting election process!

CHAPTER 33

Analyzing Word Parts

LESSON OBJECTIVES

To identify the different parts of words—prefixes, base words, word roots, and suffixes—and to use these parts to determine the meaning of unfamiliar words

Breaking an unfamiliar word into its parts can often help you figure out its meaning. Words can be composed of prefixes, base words, word roots, and suffixes.

❶ Base Words

A **base word** can stand on its own or be combined with other words or word parts to form new words. The examples below show how adding word parts to a base word (shown in orange) can change its meaning.

violin + ist = violinist
inter + planet + ary = interplanetary

Two base words can be connected to make a **compound word**, which has a meaning that is different from but sometimes related to the original words.

BASE	+	BASE	=	COMPOUND WORD
grass	+	hopper	=	grasshopper
motor	+	cycle	=	motorcycle
quarter	+	master	=	quartermaster

❷ Prefixes and Suffixes

A **prefix** is a word part added to the beginning of a base word or root. Prefixes are powerful. They can turn a base word into its opposite or make the meaning more specific. Notice how the prefixes in this chart change the meanings of base words.

Common Prefixes

Prefix	Meaning	Examples
auto-	self	autopilot, automobile
mal-, mis-	bad *or* wrong	malfunction, misplace
micro-	small *or* short	microphone, microscope
pre-	before	predawn, preschool
semi-	half	semicircle, semicolon

Developing Vocabulary **573**

 DAILY TEST PREPARATION

Definition: Vocabulary Write the following item on the board or use 🏛 **Daily Test Preparation Transparency** p. DT72.
Decide which of the four answers has most nearly the same meaning as the underlined word.

> An <u>anonymous</u> caller

A. well-known

B. strange

C. confused

D. unknown

Teaching Point: For definitions, use the parts of an an unfamiliar word to decipher its meaning. In this case, the prefix *a-* in *anonymous* means "not." The prefix *un-* in *unknown* also means "not." An *anonymous* caller is someone who is not known or identified.

TEACHING TIP

Point out that there are three types of compound words. The first type is joined together, like the words on this page. The second type is hyphenated, like *grown-ups*, *hide-and-seek*, and *merry-go-round*. The third type is open, like *high school*, *hot dog*, and *all right*.

TEACHING RESOURCES

 Time-Saver Transparencies Binder:
• Daily Test Preparation p. DT72
• Vocabulary pp. VS4–6

SKILLS PRACTICE RESOURCES

 Writing and Communication Masters pp. 120–122
 mcdougallittell.com

A **suffix** is a word part added to the end of a base word. Suffixes usually suggest a word's part of speech. For example, add suffixes to the adjective *popular* to get *popularly* (adverb), *popularity* (noun), and *popularize* (verb).

Prefixes and suffixes make it possible to expand one base word into several words. How many different words can be made by combining the following prefixes and suffixes with the base word?

Notice how the base words in the following chart change meanings as prefixes and suffixes are added to them.

PREFIX	+	BASE	+	SUFFIX	=	NEW WORD
re-	+	charge	+	-able	=	rechargeable
en-	+	courage	+	-ment	=	encouragement
pre-	+	history	+	-ic	=	prehistoric
semi-	+	week	+	-ly	=	semiweekly

Notice that you may have to change the spelling of the base word when adding a suffix: **cycle + ist = cyclist.**
For more about spelling changes, see pages 000–000.

❸ Word Roots

A **word root** is the part of a word that contains its basic meaning. A word root cannot stand on its own like a base word, but it may be combined with other word parts.

Related English words: cyclist, cyclone, tricycle

Greek root: cycl

The ancient Greek and Latin languages give English its most common roots. Knowing just some of these word roots can help you decode many complex English words.

Common Roots		
Root	**Meaning**	**Examples**
bio	life	biology, biography
gram	something written	diagram, grammar
graph	write	autograph, photograph
phon	sound	symphony, telephone
photo	light	photography, photosynthesis
scop	see	microscope, telescope
therm	heat	thermal, thermometer
Root	**Meaning**	**Examples**
aud	hear	auditorium, audience
cred	believe	credit, incredible
dict	speak	predict, diction
man	hand	manual, manufacture
mob, mot	move	mobile, motion, promote
rupt	break	rupture, bankrupt, interrupt
spec	see	inspect, suspect, respect

(GREEK for rows bio–therm; LATIN for rows aud–spec)

Word roots are frequently combined with prefixes and suffixes in the same way that base words are.

re + **cycl** + able = recyclable

PRACTICE **What Does It Say?**

Analyze the following words to figure out their meanings.

1. photosensitive
2. semifinal
3. microcomputer
4. misstatement
5. autotimer
6. audition
7. spectacle
8. malformed
9. presuppose
10. mobilize

Developing Vocabulary **575**

VOCABULARY

Answers

PRACTICE A **What Does It Say?**

Answers may vary.
Possible responses:

1. *Photosensitive* means "affected by light."
2. *Semifinal* means a "match or competition one round before the finals."
3. A *microcomputer* is a very small computer.
4. A *misstatement* is a false or incorrect declaration.
5. An *autotimer* is a device that keeps track of time without need of a human programmer.
6. An *audition* is a trial performance in which a potential performer is heard.
7. A *spectacle* is a performance or display seen by the public.
8. *Malformed* means "badly formed."
9. To *presuppose* means "to suppose beforehand" or "believe in advance."
10. *Mobilize* means "assemble" or "put into motion."

VOCABULARY

LESSON OBJECTIVES

To identify and use word families and synonyms to understand the meaning of related words

DAILY TEST PREPARATION

Error Identification: Punctuation
Write the following item on the board or use **Daily Test Preparation Transparency** p. DT72.
Decide which type of error, if any, appears in the underlined section.

> The buses, that were late, are parked across the street.

A. Spelling error

B. Capitalization error

C. Punctuation error

D. No error

Teaching Point: Error identification questions often test your knowledge of basic punctuation rules. In this case, the item tests whether you know that essential clauses (usually introduced with *that*) are not set off with commas.

TEACHING RESOURCES

 Time-Saver Transparencies Binder:
- Daily Test Preparation p. DT72
- Vocabulary pp. VS7–8

SKILLS PRACTICE RESOURCES

 mcdougallittell.com

Understanding Related Words

① Word Families

A **word family** is a group of words with a common root. Look for similarities in both meaning and spelling in the following words, whose roots come from the Latin words *viviere*, meaning "to live," and *vita*, meaning "life."

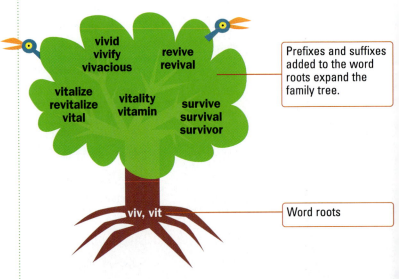

vivid
vivify
vivacious

revive
revival

vitalize
revitalize
vital

vitality
vitamin

survive
survival
survivor

viv, vit

Prefixes and suffixes added to the word roots expand the family tree.

Word roots

When you recognize the family resemblance between a word you know and one you don't know, you are on your way to learning the one you don't know.

Here's How · Using Word Families

- To figure out the meaning of *vivacious,* first look for the root: *viv.*
- Think of other words that have the same root, such as *survive, vivid,* and *revive.* Decide what common meaning they share.
- Consider prefixes and suffixes that may change meaning: the suffix *–ous* makes *vivacious* an adjective.
- From these clues, you can make a reasonable guess that *vivacious* means "full of life or lively."

 Grouping words into families when studying them makes them easier to remember.

② Synonyms

Synonyms are words that have similar meanings. Building your vocabulary involves learning synonyms. Since synonyms do not always have identical meanings, learning to distinguish slight differences in meaning is important.

SYNONYMS

Slow → Sluggish
Slow → Unhurried
Slow → Leisurely

Fast → Hasty
Fast → Swift
Fast → Rapid

The words *unhurried* and *leisurely* generate more positive feelings than *sluggish*. *Leisurely* and *sluggish* have different **connotations**—in other words, they bring different emotions to the reader's mind. Of the three synonyms for *fast,* which one implies that fast is not always good?

For more on connotation, see pg. 406.

Think of a synonym as meaning "similar to," not "the same as." Watch for shades of meaning among synonyms for a word.

PRACTICE ▷ **Finding Synonyms**

Think of one synonym for each of the following words. Then use each in a different sentence. Try to make each sentence reflect the exact shade of meaning of the word you use.

1. **finish** the assignment
2. **bother** your brother
3. the **last** day
4. **under** the porch
5. washed the **cars**
6. **ruined** the drawing
7. bought his **food**
8. a **book** of biographies
9. a **short** answer
10. **stuff** from the store

Developing Vocabulary **577**

Answers

PRACTICE → Finding Synonyms

Answers will vary. In possible responses, synonyms are underlined.

1. It took me half an hour to <u>complete</u> the assignment.
2. I wish you wouldn't <u>pester</u> your brother.
3. On the <u>final</u> day of camp, we had a fantastic cookout.
4. My cat likes to hide <u>below</u> the porch.
5. Have you washed the <u>automobiles</u>?
6. The rain <u>destroyed</u> the drawing I made!
7. Shane bought his <u>meal</u> with the four dollars he had left.
8. A <u>volume</u> of an encyclopedia does not make a good fly swatter.
9. All I want is a <u>brief</u> answer from you.
10. Can you get me some <u>materials</u> from the store?

VOCABULARY

VOCABULARY

Spice It Up!

Divide the class into teams of partners. Prepare a set of cards with "mystery words"—such as *fearful, cold, attractive,* etc.—written on them. Then give three or four cards to two sets of teams. Have team members take turns providing their partners with synonym clues to help them guess the mystery words. The first team in each set to guess all of the words correctly wins.

LESSON OBJECTIVES

To understand the applications of dictionaries and thesauruses and to use them to build vocabulary

DAILY TEST PREPARATION

Sentence Completion: Imperatives Write the following item on the board or use
🏛 **Daily Test Preparation Transparency** p. DT73.
Choose the word that belongs in the space.

_____ me today's newspaper.

A. Brought

B. Bringing

C. Bring

D. Brings

Teaching Point: Error correction questions often test your knowledge of different verb forms. In imperative sentences, the verb must agree with the implied subject *you*. Answer C is the only verb that agrees with the imperative.

CUSTOMIZING TIP

Students Acquiring English/ESL
Have students collaborate to create their own dictionary of American terms, expressions, and slang. Discuss with students how language use, such as sayings, reflects different cultures.

 Using References

❶ Dictionaries

Sometimes context clues and word parts aren't enough to help you figure out a word. Then it's time to turn to the dictionary. Dictionaries do more than just furnish the definition for a word. They also provide the pronunciation of a word, its **etymology** (origin), and connotations that might concern the reader.

offense / ogle

of • fense (ə-fĕns´) *n.* **1.** The act of offending. **2.** A violation of a moral or social code. **3.** A crime. **4.** (ŏf´ĕns´). *Sports.* A team in possession of the ball or puck. [< Lat. *offendere,* offend.]

of • fen • sive (ə-fĕn´siv) *adj.* **1.** Disagreeable to the senses. **2.** Causing anger, resentment, or affront. **3.** Making an attack. **4.** (ŏf´ĕns-. *Sports.* Relating to the offense. –**of • fen´sive • ly** *adv.* –**of • fen´sive • ness** *n.* **Syns:** *offensive, disgusting, loathsome, nasty, repellent, repulsive, revolting* **adj.**

of • fer (ô´fər, ŏf´ər) **v.** **1.** To present for acceptance or rejection. **2.** To present for sale. **3.** To present as payment; bid. **4.** To present as an act of worship. **5.** To put up; mount. **6.** To produce or introduce on the stage. [< Lat. *offerre : ob-,* to + *ferre,* bring.] –**of´fer** *n.* –**of´fer • er, of´fer • or** *n.*

of • fi • ci • ate (ə-fĭsh´ē-āt´) *v.* –**at • ed,** –**at • ing.** **1.** To perform the functions of an office or position of authority, esp. at a religious service. **2.** *Sports.* To serve as a referee or umpire. –**of • fi´ci • a´tor** *n.*

of fense (ə-fĕns´) *n.* **1.** The act of offending. **2.** A violation of a moral or social code. **3.** A crime. **4.** (ŏf´ĕns´). *Sports.* A team in possession of the to

578

Guide words, or first and last words on page

Entry word divided into syllables

Different pronunciations for different definitions

Label identifying special usage

Synonyms

Part of speech being defined

Definitions

Etymology, or history of word

Other forms of entry word

Endings for irregular verbs and for verbs that change their spelling

TEACHING RESOURCES

🏛 Time-Saver Transparencies Binder:
• Daily Test Preparation p. DT73

SKILLS PRACTICE RESOURCES

 mcdougallittell.com

Dictionaries frequently list several definitions for the same word. How do you know which definition is the right one for you?

> **Here's How** **Choosing the Right Definition**
>
> • Read through all the definitions in the dictionary entry.
> • Decide which definition best fits the meaning of the sentence in which you found the word. For example, "an offensive smell" probably matches the first definition listed on the left; "an offensive play in football" probably refers to the fourth definition.

Many textbooks have a **glossary**—a type of mini-dictionary—at the end to help you learn new words in that subject.

② Thesauruses

A **thesaurus** is a dictionary of synonyms. Some thesauruses also include definitions, sample sentences, antonyms, and other related words. Notice the difference between the thesaurus entry below and the dictionary entry for the same word, to the left. The thesaurus entry has no definitions to help you understand the differences between synonyms.

offensive *adj.* utterly unpleasant or distasteful to the senses or sensibilities
syn atrocious, disgusting, evil, foul, hideous, horrible, horrid, icky, loathsome, nasty, nauseating, noisome, obscene, repellent, repugnant, repulsive, revolting, sickening, ungrateful, unwholesome, vile
ant inoffensive, unoffensive

| Part of speech |
| Definition |
| Synonyms |
| Antonyms |

Don't pick just any synonym or antonym from a thesaurus. Be sure you know the dictionary definition and the positive or negative feelings the word brings to your audience's minds.

Students Acquiring English/ESL
You might suggest that, after students look up a word in an English dictionary, they also check the word's meaning in a dictionary that translates words into their first language.

CUSTOMIZING TIP

Students Acquiring English/ESL
Tell students to double check their word choice from the thesaurus by looking it up in a dictionary of their first language to be sure they've selected a synonym with the proper connotation and level of language.

TEACHING TIP

Have students revise a **Write Away** paragraph and use a thesaurus to replace words using different connotations.

ASSESSMENT

Teacher's Guide to Assessment and Portfolio Use

VOCABULARY

VOCABULARY

Student Help Desk

Students can use the Student Help Desk as a quick review prior to testing or as a quick reference as they revise a piece of writing.

Teacher's Notes
WHAT WORKS:

Student Help Desk

Developing Vocabulary at a Glance

Look for context clues.	Analyze the parts of a word.	Look for related words.	Use a dictionary.
Calm and collected, she **dispassionately** argued her case.	**dis passion ate ly** **dis** = not **ate** = to make **ly** = in what manner	dis**passion**ate **passion**ate com**passion**	**dis pas sion ate** (dĭs-păsh'ə-nĭt) *adj.* Not influenced by emotion or bias.

Building Blocks

semiautobiographical: relating to a work that falls between fiction and autobiography, as in partly true and partly made up.

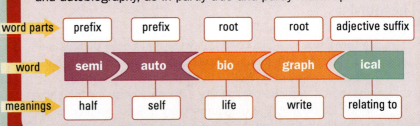

word parts	prefix	prefix	root	root	adjective suffix
word	semi	auto	bio	graph	ical
meanings	half	self	life	write	relating to

Suffixes and Parts of Speech

	Suffix	Meaning	Examples
Nouns	-er, -ist, -or	one who does	teacher, cyclist, governor
	-ation, -ism, -ment	action or process	narration, heroism, development
Verbs	-ate, -en, -fy, -ize	to make	activate, darken, satisfy, terrorize
Adjectives	-able, -ible	capable of	readable, gullible
	-ate	state or quality of	fortunate, passionate
Adverbs	-ily, -ly	in what manner	speedily, slowly

Some Word Origins in English

Many English words came from other languages. Knowing a word's origin can help you figure out its meaning.

Old English (Anglo-Saxon)

Words in our daily life: man, woman, child, eat, drink, sleep, house, love, life, death

Hunting/gathering/farming terms: meat, cow, sheep, pig, farmer, fisherman, hunter, shepherd

Old French (Norman)

Words related to government, culture, and society: president, congress, mayor, constitution, city, state, nation, religion, art, poetry, court, army, navy, dance, fashion, physician, attorney

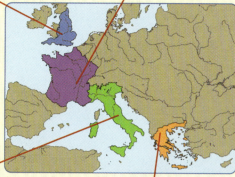

Latin

Abstract ideas: independence, loyalty, honor, unity

Technical terms: data, quarter, century, criteria, annual, gradual

Greek

Words related to science: architect, astronaut, hydrophobia, microscope, photograph, telescope, thermometer, psychology

The Bottom Line

Checklist for Developing Vocabulary

Have I . . .

____ looked at the context in which a word appears to figure out its meaning?

____ analyzed all the parts of a word?

____ tried to think of other words in the same word family?

____ thought of synonyms to replace overused words?

____ used a dictionary or a thesaurus to help me understand a word?

____ begun to use new words in my conversation and writing?

Developing Vocabulary **581**

Teacher's Notes
WHAT DOESN'T WORK:

TEACHER'S LOUNGE

Brain Break

A friend comes to you and says, "I have hidden a hundred-dollar bill in one of my books in the library. The hundred-dollar bill is located between pages 75 and 76 of the book. If you can locate the book, you may keep the money." Would you look for the $100 bill?

Answer: Don't waste your energy. It's impossible to hide anything between pages 75 and 76 of a book because they are on the front and back of the same page.

Just for Laughs

© 1996 Randy Glasbergen

"The red blobs are your red blood cells. The white blobs are your white blood cells. The brown blobs are coffee. We need to talk."

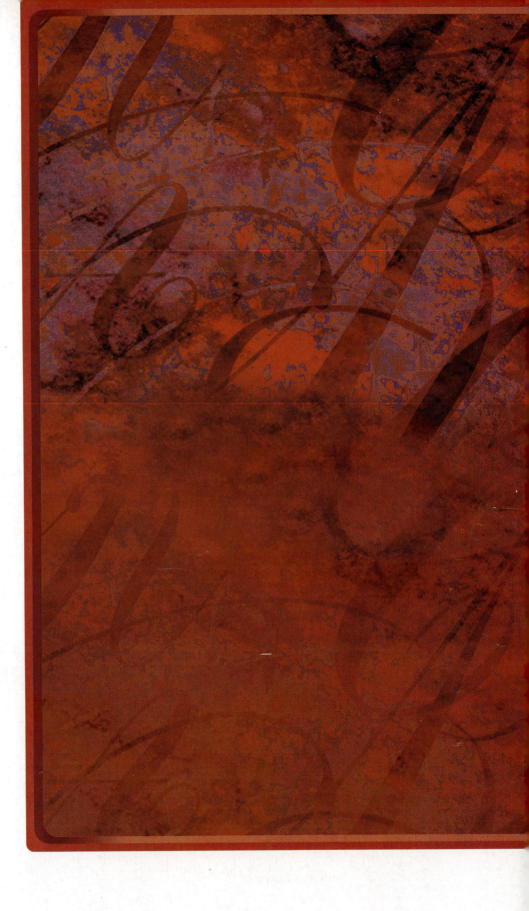

Student Resources

Answer Key

Print-Out Option You may create worksheets of the exercises in the Exercise Bank for your students by using the 💿 **Electronic Teacher Tools CD-ROM.**

Chapter 1
The Sentence and Its Parts

Lesson 1 Complete Subjects and Predicates

Answers shown on page. Complete subjects are underlined once. Complete predicates are underlined twice.

Lesson 2 Simple Subjects

Answers shown on page. Simple subjects are underlined.

Exercise Bank

Boost your grammar fitness! Use the circled arrows ➡ to find the answers to the Self-Check items. In addition, you can complete exercises in this section to get extra practice in a skill you've just learned.

1 The Sentence and Its Parts

1. Complete Subjects and Predicates (links to exercise on p. 7)

➡ **1.** Complete subject: *Frank Lloyd Wright;* complete predicate: *designed an unusual home in the Pennsylvania woods*
2. Complete subject: *The owners;* complete predicate: *called the house Fallingwater*

In separate columns on a sheet of paper, write the complete subjects and complete predicates of these sentences.

1. Albert Frey was a world-famous architect.
2. The talented Mr. Frey was 94 years old in 1998.
3. He lived modestly in a 16-by-32-foot house on a mountain in southern California.
4. The architect built his desert house in 1965.
5. This amazing house is a rectangular glass-walled shed with a corrugated aluminum roof.
6. A large boulder is in the center of the house!
7. The unusual house has a single room for dining, living, and sleeping.
8. Mr. Frey deliberately built his house with low-maintenance materials.
9. Aluminum was one of the materials he used.
10. This durable material does not need to be repainted or repaired.

2. Simple Subjects (links to exercise A, p. 9)

➡ **2.** Lodges   **5.** rodents

Write the simple subject of each sentence.

1. Arctic seals spend most of their lives in water.
2. In the winter, they live under the ice.
3. The female digs out a lair, or den, in a snowbank.
4. The lair is on top of the ice but under the snow.
5. The seal creates a hole down to the ocean below.
6. First she breathes on the ice from underneath.

7. Next, the <u>female</u> nibbles on the softened ice.
8. Then, with her flippers, <u>she</u> scoops out the ice.
9. <u>She</u> also makes air holes through the ice.
10. Her "<u>igloo</u>" will have a wide floor for her and her cub.

3. Simple Predicates, or Verbs (links to exercise A, p. 11)

➡️ **1.** lived   **2.** traveled

Write the simple predicate, or verb, in each sentence.

1. In the 1800s four sisters <u>claimed</u> 1,920 acres of land on the Great Plains.
2. Settlers <u>dug</u> wells as soon as possible.
3. Many families <u>built</u> windmills.
4. These windmills <u>pumped</u> water from the wells.
5. Some families <u>had</u> no wells.
6. Women <u>carried</u> water several miles to their sod houses.
7. Farmers often <u>used</u> dried buffalo droppings for fuel!
8. Many homesteaders <u>came</u> from Europe.
9. Hundreds of African-American families <u>settled</u> on the plains.
10. These "exodusters" <u>were</u> former slaves.

4. Verb Phrases (links to exercise A, p. 13)

➡️ **1.** was developed   **2.** could communicate

Write the verb or verb phrase in each sentence below.

1. Using a kit, you <u>can build</u> a house like the graceful Japanese country houses of the 16th century.
2. Large-diameter poles <u>support</u> your finished house.
3. Each house <u>is surrounded</u> by a large veranda.
4. The veranda <u>should provide</u> a pleasing view of nature.
5. Glazed tiles from Japan <u>are supplied</u> for the roof.
6. Only wood from replaceable trees <u>has been chosen</u> for the kits.
7. These graceful houses <u>can be built</u> in all climates.
8. They <u>have been constructed</u> in the United States, the Caribbean, Europe, and Southeast Asia.
9. Such houses <u>have</u> recently <u>survived</u> hurricanes in the West Indies.
10. They <u>have</u> also <u>been winning</u> architectural awards.

Lesson 3 Simple Predicates, or Verbs

Answers shown on page. Simple predicates, or verbs, are underlined.

Lesson 4 Verb Phrases

Answers shown on page. Verbs and verb phrases are underlined.

EXERCISE BANK

EXERCISE BANK

RESOURCES

Lesson 5 Compound Sentence Parts

Answers shown on page. Compound subjects are underlined once. Compound verbs are underlined twice. They are identified using these codes:

CS = compound subject

CV = compound verb

Lesson 6 Kinds of Sentences

Answers shown on page using these codes.

D = declarative voice

INT = interrogative sentence

EXC = exclamatory sentence

IMP = imperative sentence

Lesson 7 Subjects in Unusual Order

Answers shown on page. Subjects are underlined once. Verbs and verb phrases are underlined twice. If the subject is the understood you, it is written in parentheses in the margin.

5. Compound Sentence Parts (links to exercise A, p. 15)

➡ **1.** *Space stations* and *platforms*
   2. *may design* and *build*

Write and identify the compound subject (CS) or compound verb (CV) in each sentence.

1. Since the 1950s, pesticides and pollution have almost wiped out the peregrine falcon. **CS**
2. Peregrines and some other birds of prey live high up in cliffs. **CS**
3. They swoop down and eat smaller birds and rodents. **CV**
4. In the 1980s scientists and researchers introduced falcon pairs to skyscrapers. **CS**
5. The birds now nest and breed on ledges of tall buildings. **CV**
6. There they have no natural predators and can see lots of prey on the ground below. **CV**
7. City falcons hunt and eat pigeons and starlings. **CV**
8. They kill and consume mice as well. **CV**
9. Some peregrines have been attacked by other falcons or even eaten by them. **CV**
10. Office workers and apartment dwellers can now watch the birds from their high-rise windows. **CS**

6. Kinds of Sentences (links to exercise A, p. 17)

➡ **1.** INT   **2.** D

Identify each of the following sentences as declarative (D), interrogative (INT), exclamatory (EXC), or imperative (IMP).

1. Look at that big yellow and black bee. **IMP**
2. That's a bumblebee! **EXC**
3. Did you know they can live as far north as the Arctic Circle? **INT**
4. The buzzing sound is a bumblebee fanning its wings. **D**
5. Tell me how they build their nests. **IMP**
6. The queen constructs a pot of wax and fills it with honey. **D**
7. She lays her eggs in another pot of wax. **D**
8. What happens to the eggs? **INT**
9. They hatch and become worker bees. **D**
10. Some hives are a foot wide and have up to 700 workers! **EXC**

7. Subjects in Unusual Order (links to exercise A, p. 20)

➡ **1.** Subject: *benefits;* verb: *are*
   2. Subject: *fans;* verb: *sit*

In separate columns on a sheet of paper, write the subjects and the verbs or verb phrases in these sentences.

1. There <u>are</u> the two <u>skiers</u> in the starting gates.
2. <u>Give</u> the signal for the giant slalom race to begin. **(You)**
3. Down the steep slope <u>race</u> the <u>athletes</u>.
4. From their skis <u>sprays</u> <u>snow</u>.
5. <u>Watch</u> the next one jump off the top of that ridge. **(You)**
6. <u>Did</u> the <u>one</u> on the right <u>miss</u> a gate?
7. Across the hill <u>tumbles</u> the first <u>skier</u>.
8. There <u>is</u> the <u>winner</u> of the giant slalom.
9. <u>Are</u> <u>you</u> <u>skiing</u> in this event?
10. <u>Avoid</u> that icy turn near the third gate. **(You)**

8. Complements: Subject Complements (links to exercise A, p. 22)

➡ **1.** highways, PN   **2.** difficult, PA

Write the underlined word in each sentence, and identify it as a predicate noun (PN) or a predicate adjective (PA).

1. The Arctic National Wildlife Refuge is an <u>area</u> in northeastern Alaska. **PN**
2. It is the largest <u>refuge</u> in the United States. **PN**
3. Half of the Arctic National Wildlife Refuge is a <u>tundra</u>, or treeless plain. **PN**
4. The tundra is so <u>cold</u> that the ground never thaws completely. **PA**
5. The refuge is <u>home</u> to many animals, including caribou, polar bears, snowy owls, and lemmings. **PN**
6. Lemmings are mouselike <u>creatures</u> that live on the tundra. **PN**
7. The arctic fox is a <u>predator</u> that hunts lemmings. **PN**
8. Caribou are <u>migratory</u>, traveling more than 1,000 miles each spring to the coastal plain in the refuge. **PA**
9. The snowy owl is a large <u>bird</u> that lives in the Arctic during the entire year. **PN**
10. Environmentalists are <u>protective</u> of the land and creatures of the Arctic National Wildlife Refuge. **PA**

Lesson 8 Complements: Subject Complements

Answers shown on page using these codes:

PN = predicate nominative

PA = predicate adjective

9. Complements: Objects of Verbs (links to exercise on p. 24)

➡ **1.** house, DO   **2.** inhabitants, IO; level, DO

Write the objects in these sentences, identifying each as a direct object (DO) or an indirect object (IO).

1. The United States, Russia, and 14 other nations are building a <u>space station</u>. **DO**

Lesson 9 Complements: Objects of Verbs

Answers shown on page. Direct objects are underlined once. Indirect objects are underlined twice. They are identified using these codes:

DO = direct object

IO = indirect object

2. This space station will orbit the <u>earth</u> at 17,500 miles per hour. **D**
3. It will give <u>astronauts</u> a <u>place</u> to live and work in space. **IO/DO**
4. Scientific and medical experiments aboard the space station will offer <u>people</u> new <u>insights</u> into life in space. **IO/DO**
5. Engineers are constructing the <u>modules</u> of the space station. **D**
6. Rockets and space shuttles are giving these <u>modules</u> a <u>lift</u> into space. **IO/DO**
7. During space walks, astronauts will connect the various <u>parts</u> of the space station. **DO**
8. A Russian rocket lifted the first <u>section</u>, Zarya, into orbit in November 1998. **DO**
9. In December 1998 the crew of the U.S. space shuttle *Endeavour* connected the Unity <u>module</u> to Zarya. **DO**
10. Solar panels will give <u>astronauts</u> <u>power</u> for the space station. **IO**

10. Fragments and Run-Ons (links to exercise A, p. 27)

➡ **1.** CS   **2.** F

Identify each of the following groups of words as a fragment (F), a run-on (RO), or a complete sentence (CS).

1. The Anasazi, a Native American people. **F**
2. Represented by present-day Pueblo people. **F**
3. *Anasazi* is a Navajo word. **CS**
4. It may mean "ancient ones" it may also mean "enemy ancestors." **RO**
5. Anasazi groups have lived in the Southwest for at least 1,800 years. **CS**
6. Built huge dwellings in sandstone cliffs. **F**
7. These dwellings are impressive, you can still see them today. **R**
8. One cliff palace has 150 rooms! **CS**
9. Around 1300 A.D. these dwellings were abandoned, nobody knows why. **RO**
10. Mysterious but true. **F**

② Nouns

1. Kinds of Nouns (links to exercise A, p. 38)

➡ **1.** *things*, C; *planet*, C; *sequoias*, C
   2. *Sequoya*, P; *scholar*, C; *leader*, C

Write the nouns in these sentences, identifying each as common or proper. Then identify three collective nouns in your list.

Lesson 10 Fragments and Run-Ons

Answers shown on page using these codes:

F = fragment

RO = run-on

CS = complete sentence

Chapter 2
Nouns

Lesson 1 Kinds of Nouns

Answers shown on page. Nouns are underlined. Proper nouns are underlined twice. The three collective nouns are also circled. Nouns are identified using these codes:

C = common noun

P = proper noun

CL = collective noun

1. The <u>Gateway Arch</u> soars high above <u>St. Louis</u>, <u>Missouri</u>. **P/P/P**
2. It is made of <u>stainless steel</u>. **C**
3. A <u>competition</u> was held, and the <u>architect Eero Saarinen</u> was chosen to build the <u>landmark</u>. **C/C/P/C**
4. His <u>idea</u> was to construct a giant <u>arch</u> like those built in ancient <u>Rome</u>. **C/C/P**
5. The <u>span</u> was constructed by raising <u>sections</u> with <u>cranes</u>. **C/C/C**
6. The two <u>sides</u> of the curving <u>arch</u> rose beside the <u>Mississippi River</u>. **C/C/P**
7. <u>Safety</u> was an important <u>concern</u>, and no one in the (crew) was injured during the <u>construction</u>. **C/C/CL/C**
8. Unfortunately, the <u>steel</u> expanded in the <u>sun</u>, and the two <u>sides</u> did not meet at the <u>top</u>. **C/C/C/C**
9. A (team) sprayed cool <u>water</u> on the <u>structure</u> until it shrank to the right <u>size</u>. **CL/C/C/C**
10. The (population) of <u>St. Louis</u> watched on <u>television</u> as the Gateway Arch was completed. **CL/P/C/P**

2. Singular and Plural Nouns (links to exercise A, p. 40)

➡️ **1.** engineers **4.** rays

Write the plural forms of the underlined nouns.

1. The Statue of Liberty was a gift from the <u>citizen</u> of France. **citizens**
2. France wanted to symbolize the similar <u>belief</u> of the two <u>country</u>. **beliefs/countries**
3. The statue was designed to be 151 <u>foot</u> (15 <u>story</u>) high. **feet/stories**
4. The iron frame was covered with <u>sheet</u> of copper. **sheets**
5. Different <u>part</u> were made in design <u>studio</u> throughout Paris. **parts/studios**
6. The statue was loaded into a ship in <u>section</u>. **sections**
7. Many <u>New Yorker</u>—<u>man</u> and <u>woman</u>, <u>boy</u> and <u>girl</u>—had raised money to build a base for the statue to stand on. **New Yorkers men/women/boys/girls**
8. Seventy-five <u>worker</u> took six <u>month</u> to put Liberty together. **workers/months**
9. Many workers hung from <u>rope</u> to fit the frame and the copper <u>plate</u> together. **ropes/plates**
10. <u>Visitor</u> were able to climb <u>step</u> into Liberty's torch. **Visitors/steps**

3. Possessive Nouns (links to exercise A, p. 43)

➡️ **1.** *Missouri's*, singular **3.** *country's*, singular

Write the possessive form of each underlined noun. Label it as singular or plural.

1. Stonehenge is a circular stone monument on <u>England</u> Salisbury Plain. **England's, Sing.**

Lesson 2 Singular and Plural Nouns

Answers shown on page.

Lesson 3 Possessive Nouns

**Answers shown on page.
Possessive nouns are labeled using these codes:**

Sing. = singular

Pl. = plural

EXERCISE BANK

EXERCISE BANK

2. This monument of an unknown <u>people</u> religion is believed to be more than 3,500 years old. **people's, Sing.**

America's, Sing.   3. <u>America</u> Stonehenge copies are younger and smaller.

4. <u>Sam Hill</u> Stonehenge sits overlooking <u>Washington</u> Columbia River. **Sam Hill's, Sing./Washington's, Sing.**

5. Hill built the monument in World War I <u>soldiers</u> honor. **soldiers', P**

6. <u>Georgia</u> Stonehenge copy, called the Georgia Guidestones, has six granite slabs. **Georgia's, Sing.**

slabs', Pl.   7. The <u>slabs</u> carvings are in 12 languages and suggest that
readers', Pl.   <u>readers</u> lives will be better if they "avoid useless officials."

8. Carhenge, an arrangement of cars in Alliance, Nebraska, forms that <u>town</u> tribute to Stonehenge. **town's, Sing.**

9. With some standing upright and others lying across them, the
stones', Pl.   cars reproduce the <u>stones</u> arrangement in the real Stonehenge.

residents', Pl.   10. In Alliance, <u>residents</u> pride in Carhenge is suggested by their gift <u>shop</u> sign: "We sell Carhenge souvenirs." **shop's, Sing.**

4. Compound Nouns (links to exercise A, p. 46)

➡ 1. *foodstuffs,* plural; *South Dakota,* singular
2. *cornstalks,* plural

Write the compound nouns in the sentences below. Identify each compound as singular or plural.

1. In 1968 the <u>Lorraine Motel</u> in Memphis, Tennessee, became the <u>backdrop</u> of a tragedy. **Sing./Sing.**

2. <u>Dr. Martin Luther King, Jr.</u>, a gifted <u>public speaker</u>, was killed on the motel's balcony. **Sing./Sing.**

3. The site is now a <u>landmark</u>, a museum of the struggle for <u>civil rights</u>. **Sing./Pl.**

4. In one exhibit <u>schoolchildren</u> can view a burned-out bus. **Pl.**

5. <u>Rosa Parks</u> rode such a bus in the Montgomery bus boycott. **Si**

6. Another exhibit celebrates college students who participated in a <u>sit-in</u>. **Sing.**

7. They quietly demanded their rights at a <u>lunchroom</u> in a <u>department store</u> and were arrested and locked up in the <u>jailhouse</u>. **Sing./Sing./Sing.**

8. Similar displays honor those who fought segregation at <u>public schools</u>, <u>swimming pools</u>, and <u>drinking fountains</u>. **Pl./Pl./Pl.**

9. <u>Sightseers</u> hear stories of courageous acts that helped to change <u>public policy</u> across the United States. **Pl./Sing.**

10. They leave with vivid mental <u>snapshots</u> of those who struggled for freedom. **Pl.**

Lesson 4 Compound Nouns

Answers shown on page. Compound nouns are underlined. They are labeled using these codes:

Sing. = singular

Pl. = plural

Sentences with no compound nouns are labeled *None*.

5. Nouns and Their Jobs (links to exercise A, p. 48)

➡ **1.** *Vietnam War,* subject; *country,* complement; *sorrow,* complement
3. *Veterans,* subject; *war,* object of a preposition

Identify each underlined noun as a subject, a complement, or an object of a preposition.

1. <u>Francis Johnson</u> began wrapping a twine <u>ball</u> in 1950. **S/Comp.**
2. <u>Johnson</u> added <u>twine</u> for four <u>hours</u> each day until his death in 1989. **S/Comp./OP**
3. A <u>crane</u> lifted the huge <u>ball</u> off the <u>ground</u> as it grew larger. **S/Comp./OP**
4. The finished <u>object</u> is roughly 38 <u>feet</u> around. **S/Comp.**
5. The huge <u>sphere</u> brought <u>Darwin</u>, Minnesota, <u>fame</u>. **S/Comp./Comp.**
6. Johnson's <u>ball</u> of twine was a <u>challenge</u> to <u>Frank Stoeber</u>. **S/Comp./OP**
7. He rolled his own <u>creation</u> of over 1.6 million feet of material. **Comp.**
8. Stoeber's huge <u>ball</u> grew to be only slightly smaller than Johnson's. **S**
9. But <u>death</u> brought an <u>end</u> to Stoeber's <u>project</u>. **S/Comp./OP**
10. Stoeber's Kansas <u>neighbors</u> set up the huge <u>object</u> as a roadside <u>attraction</u>, anyway. **S/Comp./OP**

③ Pronouns

1. What Is a Pronoun? (links to exercise A, p. 59)

➡ **1.** its   **3.** their, them

Write the personal pronouns used in these sentences. Identify each as a subject, an object, or a possessive form.

1. The discovery of King Tutankamen's tomb and <u>its</u> treasures was a great event in the history of archaeology. **Poss.**
2. The archaeologist Howard Carter discovered the tomb. At the time, <u>he</u> was searching Egypt's Valley of the Kings. **S**
3. The ancient Egyptians built fabulous tombs for <u>their</u> dead kings and queens. **Poss.**
4. Carter knew that many sites had been robbed, but <u>he</u> was not discouraged. **S**
5. <u>We</u> know that in 1922 Carter's crew uncovered a set of stairs in the sand. **S**
6. The stairs led <u>them</u> to King Tut's treasure rooms. **Obj.**
7. <u>They</u> found more than 5,000 objects, many made of solid gold. **S**
8. <u>You</u> may have seen pictures of the magnificent gold mask that covered the mummy's head and shoulders. **S**

Exercise Bank   **591**

Chapter 3
Pronouns

Lesson 1 What Is a Pronoun?

Answers shown on page. Personal pronouns are underlined. They are identified using these codes:

S = subject pronoun

Obj. = object pronoun

Poss. = possessive pronoun

9. King Tut's tomb is unique because <u>its</u> treasures were undisturbed by robbers. **Poss.**

Obj. **10.** Carter's discovery gave <u>us</u> new knowledge about ancient Egypt.

2. Subject Pronouns (links to exercise on p. 62)

➡ **1.** I   **2.** they

Write the correct pronoun form to complete each sentence.

1. When Howard Carter's workers uncovered King Tut's tomb, (<u>they</u>, them) also uncovered a mystery.

2. The first in my family to read about Carter was (<u>I</u>, me).

3. Carter began working in Egypt when (him, <u>he</u>) was only 17.

4. (Him, <u>He</u>) met a British lord, the earl of Carnarvon, who gave him money to explore Egypt's past.

5. Medical researchers found that Tut had died at the age of 18, and (<u>they</u>, them) suggested that he may have been murdered.

6. (Him, <u>He</u>) had many powerful enemies who may have wanted a new king.

7. The circumstances of King Tut's death are suspicious, but (us, <u>we</u>) will may never know the truth.

8. If people want to find out more about King Tut's life and death, (<u>they</u>, them) can read several good books.

9. (Me, <u>I</u>) have read an especially good one, called *Gods, Graves, and Scholars,* by C. W. Ceram.

10. My friend Kyra wants to explore too. (Her, <u>She</u>) and I plan to go to Egypt someday.

3. Object Pronouns (links to exercise on p. 64)

➡ **1.** *him,* object   **2.** *He,* subject

Write the correct pronoun form to complete each sentence. Identify each as a subject pronoun (SP) or an object pronoun (OP).

1. The mystery surrounding the disappearance of Amelia Earhart makes (I, <u>me</u>) wonder if her fate will ever be known. **OP**

2. In 1932 (<u>she</u>, her) became the first woman to fly alone across the Atlantic Ocean. **SP**

3. Because of her daring adventures, newspapers gave (she, <u>her</u>) the name First Lady of the Air. **OP**

4. It was (<u>she</u>, her) who wanted to be first woman to fly around the world. **SP**

5. Earhart would take with (she, <u>her</u>) a navigator, Fred Noonan. **OP**

6. The one who would plan the route was (him, <u>he</u>). **SP**

Lesson 2 Subject Pronouns

Answers shown on page. Correct pronouns are underlined.

Lesson 3 Object Pronouns

Answers shown on page. Correct pronouns are underlined. They are labeled using these codes:

SP = subject pronoun

OP = object pronoun

RESOURCES

RESOURCES

7. In 1937 Earhart and (<u>he</u>, him) set out on the historic round-the-world flight. **SP**
8. Earhart's plane disappeared in the Pacific Ocean. Time has given (<u>us</u>, we) few clues about what happened. **OP**
9. The disappearance of Amelia Earhart has mystified (<u>us</u>, we) ever since. **OP**
10. Earhart's husband, the publisher G. P. Putnam, wrote a biography of (she, <u>her</u>), called *Soaring Wings.* **OP**

4. Possessive Pronouns (links to exercise A, p. 67)

➡ **1.** you're   **2.** their

Write the correct pronoun or contraction for each sentence.

1. Why would anybody want to study (<u>your</u>, you're) garbage?
2. (<u>It's</u>, Its) an odd fact, but archaeologists are able to learn a lot about a society from the rubbish it leaves behind.
3. In fact, (<u>you're</u>, your) probably not aware that some scientists make a career of analyzing ancient refuse.
4. Recently, however, some scholars have turned (they're, <u>their</u>) attention to modern garbage.
5. (<u>They're</u>, Their) working in a new field called garbage archaeology, or garbology for short.
6. This new field had (it's, <u>its</u>) beginning in 1973, when William Rathje began the Garbage Project at the University of Arizona.
7. Rathje has used the garbage of some households in Tucson to study what (<u>they're</u>, their) buying and eating.
8. Since then the project has expanded (<u>its</u>, it's) scope to include dozens of other cities as well.
9. Scientists have learned a lot about how (<u>you're</u>, your) spending your money.
10. They know about (<u>your</u>, you're) eating and buying habits, and, of course, about the amount of garbage you throw out!

5. Reflexive and Intensive Pronouns (links to exercise on p. 69)

➡ **1.** *himself,* reflexive   **2.** *itself,* intensive

Write the reflexive or intensive pronoun in each sentence, labeling it *reflexive* or *intensive*.

1. We like to entertain <u>ourselves</u> by doing yo-yo tricks. **Rflx.**
2. Have you <u>yourself</u> ever tried tricks like "walk the dog," "around the world," and "lunar loops"? **Int.**
3. I <u>myself</u> did not know much about the history of the yo-yo until Beth told me about it. **Int.**

Exercise Bank   **593**

Lesson 4 Possessive Pronouns

Answers shown on page.

Lesson 5 Reflexive and Intensive Pronouns

Answers shown on page. Reflexive and intensive pronouns are underlined. They are labeled using these codes:

Reflx. = reflexive pronouns

Int. = intensive pronouns

4. The word <u>itself</u> may come from a Philippine word meaning "to return." **Int.**
5. Beth likes to keep <u>herself</u> informed on all kinds of subjects. **Rfl**
6. She told me that the toy <u>itself</u> was developed in prehistoric times in the jungles of the Philippines. **Int.**
7. People taught <u>themselves</u> how to make a type of weapon by tying a piece of cord around a grooved rock. **Rflx.**
8. They used these early yo-yos to hunt animals and to protect <u>themselves</u>. **Rflx.**
9. I taught <u>myself</u> how to do yo-yo tricks. **Rflx.**
10. Beth <u>herself</u> practices yo-yo tricks a little every day. **Int.**

6. Interrogatives and Demonstratives (links to exercise A, p. 72)

➡️ **1.** what   **4.** Who

Write the correct demonstrative or interrogative pronoun to complete each sentence.

1. From (who, <u>whom</u>) did you get this book, *The Atlas of Mysterious Places?*
2. (This, <u>These</u>) are the most amazing pictures I've seen!
3. One photograph shows stone statues on Easter Island in the Pacific Ocean. (That, <u>Those</u>) look like ancient guardians of the land.
4. (That, <u>Those</u>) are the cylinder-shaped stones that rest on the some of the statues' heads like hats.
5. (<u>Who</u>, Whom) carved these 15-foot-tall human busts?
6. (<u>Who</u>, Whom) would spend the time and energy needed to create them?
7. (<u>Whose</u>, Who's) was the face depicted on the giant figures?
8. (Who, <u>Whom</u>) do the statues honor?
9. (Whom, <u>What</u>) caused the sculptors to abandon their work and leave many statues unfinished?
10. (This, <u>These</u>) are some of the questions that have yet to be answered about the mysterious statues.

7. Pronoun Agreement (links to exercise on p. 75)

➡️ **1.** She, Agatha Christie; them, mysteries
    3. them, trips

Write the pronouns in these sentences, along with their antecedents.

1. Imagine over a hundred <u>people</u> completely vanishing from <u>their</u> village.

Lesson 6 Interrogatives and Demonstratives

Answers shown on page. Correct pronouns are underlined.

Lesson 7 Pronoun-Antecedent Agreement

Answers shown on page. Pronouns are underlined once. Their antecedents are underlined twice.

RESOURCES

RESOURCES

2. Such a <u>disappearance</u> occurred in Virginia in the late 1500s. <u>It</u> still has not been explained.

3. In 1587 <u>John White</u> sailed for Virginia with <u>his</u> fellow passengers—116 men, women, and children.

4. White's <u>daughter</u> and <u>her</u> husband were among the people aboard the ship.

5. A baby <u>girl</u> named Virginia Dare was born in Virginia. <u>She</u> was the first English child to be born in North America.

6. The child was born on Roanoke Island, the place where <u>White</u> and <u>his</u> group landed.

7. <u>White</u> sailed back to England for supplies, but <u>he</u> didn't return until three years later.

8. White searched for the English <u>colonists</u> but did not find <u>them</u>.

9. The <u>colonists</u> may have died, or <u>they</u> may have decided to live among a group of Native Americans.

10. The <u>mystery</u> has baffled many researchers. <u>It</u> remains unsolved.

8. Indefinite-Pronoun Agreement (links to exercise on p. 78)

➡ **1.** their **2.** their

Choose the pronouns that agree with the indefinite-pronoun antecedents.

1. Do you know anyone who has made (their, <u>his or her</u>) own Möbius strip?

2. Many have created this amazing object by first cutting a narrow strip of paper. (He or she, <u>They</u>) then gave one end a half twist before taping the two ends together.

3. Most who experiment with a Möbius strip will be astonished by (his or her, <u>their</u>) experience.

4. Few will fail to notice that the strip's behavior does not meet (his or her, <u>their</u>) expectations.

5. Ask someone to draw a pencil line around the "outside" of the strip. (<u>He or she</u>, They) will discover that the line also goes around the "inside" of the strip.

6. Nobody who cuts a Möbius strip in two lengthwise will end up with two rings. (<u>He or she</u>, They) will have only one ring!

7. Anyone who tries to color one edge of the strip will discover to (<u>his or her</u>, their) surprise that both edges wind up being colored.

8. Many find the Möbius strip mysterious. However, (his or her, <u>their</u>) questions could easily be answered by a topologist.

9. That is the name for someone who studies the properties of shapes. Using (<u>his or her</u>, their) mathematical skills, a

Lesson 8 Indefinite Pronoun Agreement

Answers shown on page. Correct pronouns are underlined.

topologist can explain why a Möbius strip has only one side.

10. Everyone has seen a Möbius strip, whether (he or she, <u>they</u>) knows it or not. It is a symbol that appears on many recyclable products.

9. Pronoun Problems (links to exercise A, p. 80)

 1. us

Write the correct pronoun form to complete each sentence.

1. (<u>We</u>, Us) mystery fans have started a club at our school.
2. The name Rue Morgue Society appealed to (we, <u>us</u>) club members, since the first American detective story was *The Murders in the Rue Morgue* by Edgar Allan Poe.
3. If anyone loves solving crime puzzles, it is (<u>we</u>, us) amateur detectives.
4. Sometimes, (<u>we</u>, us) students even talk about trying to help the local police solve real crimes.
5. People who listen to (we, <u>us</u>) mystery fans sometimes wonder if we're talking about real or fictional crimes.

Correct the unclear pronoun reference in the following sentences by replacing each underlined pronoun with a noun.

6. Luis and Rob saw a movie version of Poe's *The Murders in the Rue Morgue.* <u>He</u> thought the ending was disappointing. **Luis *or* R**
7. Poe and his hero C. Auguste Dupin shared a love of mystery. <u>He</u> had a brilliantly logical mind. **Dupin *or* Poe**
8. In the bedroom, the window and door are both closed. Yet <u>it</u> must have been opened by the murderer. **the window *or* the door**
9. The police and family members are baffled by the murders. <u>They</u> arrest a tradesman for the crime. **The police**
10. In the end, an orangutan, not the tradesman, turns out to be the killer. <u>He</u> lived in an East Indian forest and was brought to France by a sailor. **The orangutan**

10. More Pronoun Problems (links to exercise A, p. 82)

 1. I **2.** me

Write the correct pronoun to complete each sentence.

1. My friends and (<u>I</u>, me) were talking about alien life.
2. We wondered whether life on earth, in all its many forms, had (<u>its</u>, their) origin in space.
3. Miguel and Jake, friends of my brother's, said that (he, <u>they</u>) think alien life is a joke.

Lesson 9 Pronoun Problems

Answers shown on page. In the first five items, correct pronouns are underlined. In the second set of five items, the pronouns with unclear reference are underlined. Corrections appear in the margin.

Lesson 10 More Pronoun Problems

Answers shown on page. Correct pronouns are underlined.

4. They laughed at Denise and (I, <u>me</u>) when we disagreed.
5. (<u>She</u>, Her) and I have read about projects that search for alien life in space.
6. Some scientific projects, such as SETI, are clear about (its, <u>their</u>) goal—finding and contacting extraterrestrials.
7. I believe that the SETI program, which uses radio telescopes to detect signals from space, interests (<u>me</u>, I) the most.
8. SETI stands for "Search for Extraterrestrial Intelligence," Denise and (<u>I</u>, me) explained to Jake.
9. Scientists at NASA have (its, <u>their</u>) own organization to explore questions about extraterrestrial life.
10. This group is called the Astrobiology Institute, the librarian told Denise and (I, <u>me</u>).

4 Verbs

1. What Is a Verb? (links to exercise A, p. 84)

➡ **1.** may be   **3.** sail

Write the verb in each of the following sentences.

1. *Antz* <u>is</u> an example of feature-length animation.
2. The filmmakers <u>created</u> the graphics on computers.
3. The ants in the movie <u>behave</u> a lot like people.
4. Real ants, of course, <u>are</u> nothing like the ones in this film.
5. In the movie, a worker ant <u>falls</u> in love with a princess ant.
6. The worker and the princess <u>escape</u> to the outside world.
7. However, their home colony <u>faces</u> a serious threat.
8. The whole ant population <u>appears</u> in danger of destruction.
9. The worker and the princess <u>return</u> to the colony just in time!
10. The humble worker <u>becomes</u> a hero to the other ants.

2. Action Verbs and Objects (links to exercise A, p. 97)

➡ **1.** *people,* direct object
    2. *members,* indirect object; *assignments,* direct object

Write the 15 complements in these sentences, identifying each as a direct object or an indirect object.

1. Steven Spielberg has given <u>us</u> many hit <u>movies</u>, including *Jaws, Raiders of the Lost Ark*, and *E.T. the Extra-Terrestrial.* **IO/DO**
2. Spielberg made his first <u>film</u> at the age of 12. **DO**
3. He staged the <u>wreck</u> of two toy trains. **DO**
4. That experience gave <u>him</u> a <u>taste</u> for spectacular stunts. **IO/DO**

Lesson 1 What Is a Verb?

Answers shown on page. Verbs and verb phrases are underlined.

Lesson 2 Action Verbs and Objects

Answers shown on page. Complements are underlined. They are identified using these codes:

DO = direct object

IO = indirect object

EXERCISE BANK

EXERCISE BANK

5. He used <u>everyone</u> around him in his movies. **DO**
6. He gave his <u>mother</u> starring <u>roles</u> in many home movies. **IO/DO**
7. When he was 13, Spielberg joined a Boy Scout photography <u>program</u>. **DO**
8. He made the scout <u>troop</u> a three-minute <u>movie</u> about a stagecoach robbery. **IO/DO**
9. The movie won <u>Spielberg</u> his first filmmaking <u>award</u>—a merit badge. **IO/DO**
10. At the age of 16, Spielberg wrote *Firelight*, his first science fiction movie. **DO**

3. Linking Verbs and Predicate Words (links to exercise on p. 99)

➡ **1.** *are,* linking verb; *scary,* predicate adjective
   3. *was,* linking verb; *hit,* predicate noun

Identify each linking verb, predicate noun, and predicate adjective in the sentences below.

1. The job title "continuity clerk" <u>may seem</u> <u>unimpressive</u>. **PA**
2. But a continuity clerk <u>is</u> an important (person) on a movie set. **P**
3. The order in which scenes are shot <u>is</u> not the (order) in which they will appear in the film. **PN**
4. Footage from different days <u>can be</u> (part) of the same scene. **PN**
5. Such footage must <u>appear</u> <u>continuous</u>. **PA**
6. The continuity clerk's tasks <u>are</u> very <u>tedious</u>. **PA**
7. Most people <u>would grow</u> <u>bored</u> by all the details. **PA**
8. Good continuity clerks, however, <u>are</u> (perfectionists). **PN**
9. They <u>remain</u> <u>attentive</u> to the tasks. **PA**
10. Some continuity clerks even <u>become</u> (directors). **PN**

4. Principal Parts of Verbs (links to exercise on p. 101)

➡ **1.** present   **2.** past participle

Identify each underlined principal part as the present, the present participle, the past, or the past participle.

1. Photography has <u>existed</u> for only about 150 years. **PA**
2. Eadweard Muybridge <u>created</u> some of the first stop-action photographs. **Past**
3. In 1877 he <u>arranged</u> 12 cameras in a row. **Past**
4. Then he <u>snapped</u> photos, in sequence, of a galloping horse. **Pa**
5. Some people had <u>claimed</u> that a running horse always has two feet on the ground. **PA**
6. Muybridge's photos <u>proved</u> that all four feet are off the ground at some points. **Past**

Lesson 3 Linking Verbs and Predicate Words

Answers shown on page. Linking verbs are underlined once. Predicate adjectives are underlined twice. Predicate nouns are circled. Answers are also shown using these codes.

PA = predicate adjective

PN = predicate noun

Lesson 4 Principal Parts of Verbs

Answers shown on page using these codes.

Pres. = present

PR = present participle

Past = past

PA = past participle

7. A real horse never <u>assumes</u> a rocking-horse position, with two legs stretched forward and two back. **Pres.**

8. By 1900 Muybridge had <u>mastered</u> the art of stop-action photography. **PA**

9. He had <u>produced</u> many series of photos of people running and jumping. **PA**

10. Readers are still <u>enjoying</u> these photos in books and magazines today. **PR**

5. Irregular Verbs (links to exercise on p. 104)

➡ **1.** seen   **4.** made

In the sentences below, choose the correct forms of the verbs in parentheses.

1. The popular musical *Annie Get Your Gun* was (wrote, <u>written</u>) about a real person, Annie Oakley.
2. Annie Oakley had (<u>grown</u>, growed) up on a farm in Ohio.
3. She (beginned, <u>began</u>) teaching herself to hunt at an early age.
4. She (<u>brought</u>, bringed) home game to feed her family.
5. At the age of 15, she (winned, <u>won</u>) a shooting contest against Frank E. Butler, a well-known target shooter.
6. Before long, she had (<u>given</u>, gave) Butler her hand in marriage.
7. The two (<u>shot</u>, shooted) targets together in circuses and shows.
8. Oakley was so accurate with a rifle that she (<u>hit</u>, hitted) dimes thrown into the air.
9. If someone tossed a playing card into the air, she could riddle it with holes before it (<u>fell</u>, fallen) to the ground.
10. When Oakley performed with Buffalo Bill's Wild West Show, audiences (<u>knew</u>, knowed) her as Little Sure Shot.

6. Simple Tenses (links to exercise A, p. 107)

➡ **1.** future   **3.** present

Identify each underlined verb form as present, past, future, present progressive, past progressive, or future progressive.

1. Gwilym Hughes <u>watched</u> his first movie at the age of seven. **Past**
2. After that, he <u>was viewing</u> movies on a regular basis. **Past Prog.**
3. In the next 46 years he <u>watched</u> more than 24,000 feature films. **Past**
4. That <u>is</u> a record. **Pres.**
5. It <u>represents</u> more than one-tenth of all the feature films ever made. **Pres.**
6. Hughes <u>lives</u> in a remote corner of Wales. **Pres.**

Exercise Bank **599**

Lesson 5 Irregular Verbs

Answers shown on page.

Lesson 6 Simple Tenses

Answers shown on page using these codes:

Pres. = present

Past = past

Past Prog. = past progressive

Fut. = future

7. The nearest theater <u>is</u> 20 miles away. **Pres.**

7. The nearest theater <u>is</u> 20 miles away. **Pres.**
8. Yet Hughes <u>sees</u> nearly 20 movies every week. **Pres.**
9. He says he <u>will keep</u> up that pace. **Fut.**
10. He <u>will hold</u> the record for many years. **Fut.**

7. Perfect Tenses (links to exercise A, p. 110)

➡ 1. *had looked,* past perfect
  2. *have found,* present perfect

Identify the verb in each sentence, and indicate whether its tense is present perfect, past perfect, or future perfect.

1. Audiences <u>have watched</u> motion pictures for more than a century. **Pres. Perf.**
2. Before 1900, movies <u>had lasted</u> little as a minute or two. **Past Perf.**
3. These brief films <u>had showed</u> simple scenes, such as ocean waves. **Past Perf.**
4. Since the 1903 film *The Great Train Robbery,* movies <u>have featured</u> complete stories. **Pres. Perf.**
5. Westerns and thrillers <u>have attracted</u> audiences ever since that time. **Pres. Perf.**
6. Even a century from now, thrillers <u>will</u> surely <u>have lost</u> none of their appeal. **Fut. Perf.**
7. Before the maturation of the film industry, most producers <u>had filmed</u> movies in New York and New Jersey. **Past Perf.**
8. Because of its year-round good weather, southern California <u>has become</u> the biggest movie-making center in the United States. **Pres. Perf.**
9. By the year 2050, however, several other parts of the country <u>will</u> probably <u>have developed</u> into important centers of film production. **Fut. Perf.**
10. The movie business <u>has come</u> a long way since *The Great Train Robbery.* **Pres. Perf.**

8. Using Verb Tenses (links to exercise A, p. 114)

➡ 1. were using   2. lacked

In each sentence, choose the correct verb form in parentheses.

1. Television (had been, <u>has been</u>) around for less than 70 years.
2. Experiments with television broadcasting (begin, <u>began</u>) in the early 1930s.

Lesson 7 Perfect Tenses

Answers shown on page. Verbs are underlined. Their tenses are indicated using these codes:

Pres. Perf. = present perfect

Past Perf. = past perfect

Fut. Perf. = future perfect

Lesson 8 Using Verb Tenses

Answers shown on page. Correct verb forms are underlined.

---

3. Before TV sets became available commercially, scientists (will have demonstrated, <u>had demonstrated</u>) television at the 1939 New York world's fair.

4. Color television (<u>made</u>, will make) its first appearance in 1954.

5. Now virtually all television programs (<u>air</u>, aired) in color.

6. Early home TV sets (have, <u>had</u>) large cabinets but very small screens, never larger than 12 inches.

7. Some of today's televisions (<u>feature</u>, will feature) screens more than 60 inches in width.

8. In the near future, thin, flat TVs (<u>will become</u>, became) common.

9. Since the 1960s communications satellites (will enable, <u>have enabled</u>) television broadcasts from anywhere in the world.

10. In 1969 viewers (see, <u>saw</u>) one of the greatest thrills of the television era: astronauts on the moon.

9. Troublesome Verb Pairs (links to exercise A, p. 117)

➡ **1.** can   **5.** sat

Choose the correct word or words in parentheses in each of the following sentences.

1. Do the most talented artists (raise, <u>rise</u>) to the top?

2. In Hollywood, they (<u>may not</u>, cannot).

3. Most studio heads don't want to (<u>sit</u>, set) down with anyone who hasn't made a successful commercial movie.

4. But film festivals give young filmmakers a chance to (lie, <u>lay</u>) their reputations on the line.

5. They (<u>raise</u>, rise) the hopes of artists who might otherwise not have a chance.

6. They (sit, <u>set</u>) their sights on quality instead of money.

7. Winning at a festival can help a filmmaker (<u>raise</u>, rise) money for distributing his or her film.

8. Success (<u>lies</u>, lays) ahead for some of these artists.

9. They (sit, <u>set</u>) a festival's tone with movies about important themes.

10. Festival participation might not help, but it (may not, <u>cannot</u>) hurt.

Lesson 9 Troublesome Verb Pairs

Answers shown on page. Correct answers are underlined.

Lesson 1 What Is an Adjective?

Answers shown on page. Adjectives are underlined once. The nouns they modify are underlined twice.

5 Adjectives and Adverbs

1. What Is an Adjective? (links to exercise on p. 128)

 1. some, inventors; successful, inventors; mature, scientists

3. cold, ears; red, ears; harsh, winters; Northeastern, winters

Write each adjective and the noun it modifies. Do not include articles.

1. Alison DeSmyter is an inventive teenager from Texas.
2. Alison has a muscular disability and uses a wheelchair.
3. She invented a portable ramp that helps disabled people move over curbs.
4. She had only a few weeks to create an original design for a local contest.
5. She first considered and rejected an awkward ramp made of rubber.
6. Then she imagined an inflatable ramp, but who would blow it up?
7. Finally Alison created a lightweight metallic ramp and named it the Rampanion (ramp companion).
8. Alison made the exact measurements herself, and her father helped her build the ramp of aluminum.
9. The Rampanion weighs four pounds and comes in a handy bag.
10. Her invention won the grand prize for the fifth grade in a statewide contest.

Lesson 2 Predicate Adjectives

Answers shown on page. Predicate adjectives are underlined once. The nouns or pronouns they modify are underlined twice.

2. Predicate Adjectives (links to exercise A, p. 130)

1. common, wipers **2.** dangerous, trolleys

Write each predicate adjective and the noun or pronoun it modifies.

1. Many inventions have been useful to the food industry.
2. In a refrigerator, an apple remains tasty for a long time.
3. Thanks to canning, foods do not become spoiled.
4. But if they smell moldy, they should not be canned!
5. Dried foods stay edible for a long time.
6. Dried fruits are tasty even after long storage.
7. Dried eggs become usable when water is added.
8. Freeze-dried meals are expensive in comparison with other forms of dried food.
9. But they also taste better.
10. Of course, fresh food always seems best of all.

3. Other Words Used as Adjectives (links to exercise A, p. 132)

➜ **1.** Most; human   **3.** Our

Write each noun or pronoun that is used as an adjective.

1. What if you did not have <u>clothing</u> fasteners or <u>book-bag</u> snaps?
2. <u>All</u> zippers, buttons, clasps, and laces on <u>your</u> belongings are important.
3. But a more recent invention is replacing <u>these</u> fasteners.
4. Velcro was invented in 1957, long before <u>its</u> widespread use.
5. One of George de Mestral's <u>nature</u> walks led to a startling idea.
6. He found <u>many</u> burs with their tiny hooks clinging to <u>his</u> pants.
7. Burs carry seeds from <u>their</u> <u>parent</u> plants.
8. De Mestral spent <u>some</u> years creating Velcro, which makes <u>our</u> lives more comfortable.
9. A <u>Velcro</u> fastener consists of a <u>hook</u> strip and a <u>loop</u> strip.
10. Perhaps someday <u>most</u> fasteners will be made of Velcro.

4. What Is an Adverb? (links to exercise A, p. 136)

➜ **1.** experimentally, were flying (verb)
   2. yet, had flown (verb); successfully, had flown (verb)

Write each adverb and the word it modifies. Then label each modified word as a verb, an adjective, or an adverb. There may be more than one adverb in a sentence.

1. If you (have) ever <u>failed</u> at inventing something, join the club. **V**
2. The history of invention is full of <u>extremely</u> (embarrassing) events. **Adj.**
3. Robert Goddard <u>eventually</u> (invented) the liquid-fueled rocket. **V**
4. But Goddard's first rocket (rose) <u>rapidly</u> <u>upward</u> and <u>then</u> (crashed) into his aunt's garden! **V/V/V**
5. John Baird made <u>highly</u> (important) contributions to the invention of television. **Adj.**
6. He <u>also</u> (tried) to make self-warming socks, a device that (failed) <u>quite</u> (miserably.) **V/Adv./V**
7. In 1882 Henry Seeley invented a <u>very</u> (early) version of the electric iron. **Adj.**
8. But <u>hardly</u> (any) homes had electricity, so Seeley sold few irons! **Adj.**
9. Hubert Booth <u>cleverly</u> (invented) an early vacuum cleaner. **V**
10. Because it was <u>too</u> (large) to move by hand, horses pulled it from house to house! **Adj.**

Lesson 5 Making Comparisons

Answers shown on page. Correct comparative and superlative forms are underlined.

5. Making Comparisons (links to exercise A, p. 139)

➡ **2.** more important   **4.** newest

Choose the correct comparative or superlative form to complete each sentence.

1. The traffic signal is one of the (more important, <u>most important</u>) of all safety inventions.
2. The three-way traffic signal was not the (earlier, <u>earliest</u>) form of traffic control.
3. However, it was (<u>more practical</u>, most practical) than the previous model.
4. Garrett Morgan, who was granted a patent for the traffic signal in 1923, was one of the (more inventive, <u>most inventive</u>) minds of this century.
5. Because Morgan was black, however, his inventions were received (<u>less enthusiastically</u>, least enthusiastically) than those of white inventors.
6. For example, Morgan invented a gas mask that allowed rescue workers to enter gas-filled tunnels (<u>more safely</u>, most safely) than before.
7. In 1916 Morgan and some volunteers who were (<u>braver</u>, bravest) than average wore his masks to rescue 32 men after an underground explosion.
8. Two men with Morgan gas masks were (<u>more effective</u>, most effective) in the first 15 minutes of fighting a fire than a whole company without the masks.
9. Yet when Morgan brought his (later, <u>latest</u>) gas mask to the South, a white companion had to demonstrate it.
10. In World War I, soldiers used Morgan's gas masks to protect themselves from the (deadlier, <u>deadliest</u>) battlefield poison—chlorine gas.

Lesson 6 Adjective or Adverb?

Answers shown on page. Correct modifiers are underlined. They are labeled using these codes:

Adj. = adjective

Adv. = adverb

6. Adjective or Adverb? (links to exercise on p. 141)

➡ **1.** really (adverb)

For each sentence, choose the correct modifier from those given in parentheses. Identify each word you choose as an adjective or an adverb.

1. What makes an invention (<u>good</u>, well)? **Adj.**
2. Is a new device (real, <u>really</u>) good if people use it (bad, <u>badly</u>)?   Adv./Adv.
3. The writer Jared Diamond describes the history of some (<u>really</u>, real) helpful inventions that were not used (good, <u>well</u>) at first.   Adv./Adv.

RESOURCES

4. For example, the wheel was not a (<u>real</u>, really) advantage for the people of ancient Mexico. **Adj.**

5. Without animals to pull vehicles, they (real, <u>really</u>) couldn't use wheels. **Adv.**

6. An inventor may create something unique without knowing what it is (<u>good</u>, well) for. **Adj.**

7. This happened to Thomas Edison, who did very (good, <u>well</u>) as an inventor. **Adv.**

8. But his plans for the phonograph give us a (<u>good</u>, well) laugh today. **Adj.**

9. Some (<u>bad</u>, badly) ones included using it to teach speech or to record the words of dying people. **Adj.**

10. When businesspeople began playing music on the phonograph, Edison thought this was a (<u>real</u>, really) mistake! **Adj.**

7. Avoiding Double Negatives (links to exercise A, p. 143)

➡ **1.** can   **3.** are

Write the word in parentheses that correctly completes each sentence.

1. No one (<u>can</u>, can't) expect all new inventions to be successful.
2. Consider the poor inventor of the "parachute hat," who (<u>had</u>, hadn't) no luck.
3. The invention didn't (<u>ever</u>, never) work, and the inventor broke his neck trying it out!
4. In 1912 Mr. S. I. Russell (couldn't, <u>could</u>) give no reason why his electric heating pad burned.
5. The reason was that the wiring in the device (wasn't, <u>was</u>) no good.
6. Charles Adams (<u>had</u>, hadn't) no luck in turning chicle into a substitute for rubber.
7. He tried to use chicle for toys and boots, but he (<u>could</u>, couldn't) hardly succeed.
8. Chewing chicle one day, Adams regretted that it barely (<u>had</u>, hadn't) any flavor.
9. He added flavor and invented chewing gum, but doctors warned that it wouldn't be (no, <u>any</u>) good for people.
10. Today chewing gum is very popular, but you (<u>should</u>, shouldn't) never chew too much.

Lesson 7 Avoiding Double Negatives

Answers shown on page. Correct answers are underlined.

Chapter 6
Prepositions, Conjunctions, Interjections

Lesson 1 What Is a Preposition?

Answers shown on page. Prepositions are underlined once. Their objects are underlined twice.

Lesson 2 Using Prepositional Phrases

Answers shown on page. Prepositional phrases are underlined once. The words they modify are underlined twice. Types of phrases are indicated using these codes.

Adj. = adjective phrase

Adv. = adverb phrase

Lesson 3 Conjunctions

Answers shown on page. Conjunctions are underlined once. The words and groups of words they join are underlined twice.

---

6 Prepositions, Conjunctions, Interjections

1. What Is a Preposition? (links to exercise on p. 154)

➡ **1.** to, fires   **2.** from, miles

Write the preposition in each sentence, along with its object.

1. Many people are afraid of bugs.
2. They run from anything "creepy."
3. True, some types of insects are deadly.
4. But very few insects are actually harmful to people.
5. Ant tunnels let air into the soil.
6. Without insect predators, pests would devour farm crops.
7. Bees and butterflies carry pollen between plants.
8. Plants cannot produce fruits or vegetables without pollination.
9. Spiders destroy thousands of flies and other insects.
10. Bugs are a vital link in our ecosystem.

2. Using Prepositional Phrases (links to exercise A, p. 157)

➡ **1.** of spiders, kinds (adj. phrase)
    2. to people, dangerous (adv. phrase)

Write the prepositional phrase in each sentence, along with the word it modifies. Then indicate whether the phrase is an adjective phrase or an adverb phrase.

1. Most people are afraid of tarantulas.   **Adv.**
Adv. 2. They are actually less harmful to people than wasps or bees.
3. They would probably run from you and not attack. **Adv.**
4. Many people keep them as pets. **Adv.**
5. The goliath tarantula is the largest spider in the world. **Adv.**
6. It can grow to be a foot in length. **Adj.**
Adv. 7. However, this spider tips the scales at only about two ounces.
8. If you meet a goliath tarantula, beware the sharp barbs on its abdomen. **Adj.**
9. It can flick the barbs at attackers, causing an itchy rash. **Adv.**
Adv. 10. Luckily for us, South America is the goliath tarantula's home.

3. Conjunctions (links to exercise A, p. 160)

➡ **1.** and (lenses, light waves)
    2. but (Light waves show the details of ordinary objects, the waves are too long to reveal the smallest structures)

Write the conjunction in each sentence, along with the words or groups of words that it joins.

1. The <u>firefly</u> <u>and</u> the <u>lightning bug</u> are the same insect.
2. <u>Females lay eggs in soil</u>, <u>and</u> <u>four weeks later the eggs hatch into larvae</u>.
3. <u>These larvae</u>, <u>or</u> <u>glowworms</u>, are carnivorous.
4. Despite their small size, they can eat <u>slugs</u> <u>and</u> <u>snails</u>.
5. Not <u>only</u> <u>adults</u> <u>but also</u> <u>some larvae</u> glow.
6. The larvae <u>spend the winter in small tunnels</u> <u>and</u> <u>come out again in spring</u>.
7. Adult fireflies feed on <u>pollen</u> <u>and</u> <u>nectar</u>.
8. <u>Both</u> <u>male</u> <u>and</u> <u>female</u> fireflies light up.
9. On summer days fireflies rest <u>on plants</u> <u>or</u> <u>in trees</u>.
10. <u>Fireflies produce light</u>, <u>yet</u> <u>they don't produce heat</u>.

7 Verbals and Verbal Phrases

1. Gerunds (links to exercise A, p. 171)

➡ **1.** riding   **4.** Waiting

Write the gerunds in these sentences.

1. <u>Helping</u> people in wheelchairs is one job of service dogs.
2. People who are dedicated and good with animals are needed for <u>educating</u> the dogs.
3. <u>Loving</u> the animals is the first requirement for trainers.
4. <u>Training</u> a dog in obedience takes two to three months.
5. The next few months are devoted to <u>teaching</u> special skills.
6. The dog focuses on <u>learning</u> exactly the tasks it will need to perform for its new owner.
7. Retrievers are especially good at <u>fetching</u> things for disabled people.
8. Their favorite activity is <u>helping</u> people.
9. <u>Matching</u> each dog with a particular person is important.
10. New owners learn about <u>feeding</u> and <u>exercising</u> their dogs.

2. Participles (links to exercise A, p. 173)

➡ **1.** *acting,* participle
   3. *Training,* gerund

Write the participles in these sentences, identifying each as a present participle or a past participle. Also write the noun or pronoun that each participle modifies.

Lesson 2 Participles

Answers shown on page.
Participles are underlined
once. The nouns they modify
are underlined twice.
Participles are identified
using these codes:

PR = present participle

PA = past participle

EXERCISE BANK

EXERCISE BANK

1. Indian Red was a <u>horse</u> <u>living</u> in Ontario. **PR**
2. <u>Walking</u> along a road one night, <u>he</u> stopped suddenly. **PR**
3. <u>Chilled</u> and <u>fatigued</u>, <u>he</u> should have been seeking shelter. **PA/PA**
4. Instead <u>he</u> neighed and whinnied, <u>trying</u> to get cars to stop. **PR**
5. Only a few <u>speeding</u> <u>drivers</u> were out on that cold night. **PR**
6. <u>Those</u> who came by ignored the horse, <u>driving</u> right past him. **PR**
7. Finally, one driver, his <u>curiosity</u> <u>aroused</u>, stopped to see what was wrong. **PA**
8. <u>Searching</u> a snow-covered ditch near the horse, the <u>man</u> discovered an old woman. **PR**
9. The <u>woman</u>, now <u>numbed</u> by the cold, had fallen into the ditch. **P**
10. Not even <u>knowing</u> her, <u>Indian Red</u> wanted to get help for her. **PR**

3. Infinitives (links to exercise A, p. 175)

➡ **2.** To play   **4.** to let

Write the infinitives in these sentences. Identify whether each is used as a noun, an adjective, or an adverb.

1. Jackie Geyer liked <u>to feed</u> raccoons in her yard. **N**
2. One day a badly injured raccoon came <u>to eat</u>. **Adv.**
3. The raccoon needed <u>to limp</u> to the feeding station because its right hind leg was injured. **N**
4. "Chloe" seemed a good name <u>to give</u> the raccoon. **Adj.**
5. One day Chloe was missing, and Jackie began <u>to worry</u>. **N**
6. Finally Chloe appeared, using only her front legs <u>to walk</u> to the food bowl. **Adv.**
7. Jackie was surprised <u>to see</u> that Chloe's other hind leg was now injured. **Adv.**
8. Luckily, <u>to walk</u> on her "hands" was not very hard for a talented raccoon like Chloe. **N**
9. Chloe had decided that Jackie's was the only place in town <u>to eat</u>. **Adv.**
10. Chloe's injured legs were quick <u>to heal</u>, and she has now been dining at Jackie's place for eight years. **Adv.**

4. Verbal Phrases (links to exercise A, p. 177)

➡ **1.** *Strolling around the neighborhood,* gerund phrase
2. *slightly spoiled,* participial phrase

Write the verbal phrases in these sentences, identifying each as a gerund phrase, a participial phrase, or an infinitive phrase.

1. Many animals, <u>including chimpanzees and elephants</u>, have learned <u>to draw or paint</u>. **PP/IP**

2. A chimp <u>named Alpha</u> preferred <u>drawing pictures</u> to <u>eating meals</u>. **PP/GP/GP**

3. She would beg visitors, <u>fascinated by her behavior,</u> <u>to give her paper and a pencil</u>. **PP/IP**

4. Researchers asked a chimp <u>named Moja</u> <u>to draw various things,</u> <u>including a basketball</u>. **PP/IP/PP**

5. <u>Seeing vertical zigzags on the paper,</u> they thought that she had just scribbled. **PP**

6. Then they realized that the zigzags might represent <u>the ball's up-and-down bouncing</u>. **GP**

7. An elephant <u>named Ruby</u> loves <u>to paint abstract pictures</u>. **PP/IP**

8. <u>Choosing colors</u> is a creative act for her. **GP**

9. A visitor who enjoyed <u>watching Ruby paint</u> fell ill, and paramedics in blue uniforms came <u>to help him</u>. **GP/IP**

10. After they left, Ruby expressed herself by <u>painting a blue blob surrounded by a swirl of red</u>. **GP/PP**

8 Sentence Structure

1. What Is a Clause? (links to exercise A, p. 187)

➜ **1.** dependent clause   **5.** independent clause

Identify each underlined group of words as an independent clause or a dependent clause.

1. <u>Dalié Jiménez was concerned</u> that disadvantaged children were not getting books read to them often enough. **IC**

2. She had learned in her psychology class <u>that reading to young children was very important</u>. **DC**

3. Children need this experience <u>so that their brains can develop properly.</u> **DC**

4. <u>When she was 14 years old</u>, Dalié began volunteering at a Head Start program in her hometown of Miami, Florida. **DC**

5. She liked this work <u>because she was interested in children</u>. **DC**

6. When she told her friends about her work, <u>they wanted to volunteer too</u>. **IC**

7. Dalié and about 30 of her friends started a children's library <u>that consisted of donated books</u>. **DC**

8. They used puppets to act out stories <u>while they read</u>. **DC**

9. When Dalié heard that Head Start's funding was going to be cut by one-third, <u>she lobbied lawmakers</u>. **IC**

10. <u>Because they worked so hard</u>, she and her friends were able to help save the Head Start program. **DC**

Lesson 1 What Is a Clause?

Answers shown on page. Groups of words are identified using these codes:

IC = independent clause

DC = dependent clause

Lesson 2 Simple and Compound Sentences

Answers shown on page. Sentences are identified using these codes:

SS = simple sentence

CD = compound sentence

Lesson 3 Complex Sentences

Answers shown on page. Independent clauses are underlined once. Dependent clauses are underlined twice.

2. Simple and Compound Sentences (links to exercise A, p. 190)

➡ **1.** simple   **2.** compound

Identify each sentence as simple or compound.

1. Justin Lebo of Saddle Brook, New Jersey, loved bikes. **SS**
2. He and his dad shared an interest in bicycle racing. **SS**
3. They had their garage set up like a bike shop; they worked there on their bikes all the time. **CS**

CS 4. Justin bought a couple of rundown bikes, and he fixed them up.

5. The bikes looked as good as new, but Justin didn't need any more bikes himself. **CS**
6. He decided to donate them to the Kilbarchan Home for Boys. **SS**
7. Justin liked the idea of people fixing up bikes for less-fortunate so he continued to do so in his spare time. **CS**
8. Many people offered him their old bikes for free. **SS**
9. The donations were helpful for a time, but soon Justin ran out of space in his small garage. **CS**
10. Justin fixed and gave away 250 bikes before he was done. **CS**

3. Complex Sentences (links to exercise A, p. 193)

➡ **1.** Independent clause: *many people do not know about it;* dependent clause: *Although the Foster Grandparent Program is more than 30 years old*

2. Independent clause: *This program was established;* dependent clause: *so that hospitalized and institutionalized children could get special attention*

Write these sentences on a sheet of paper. Underline each independent clause once and each dependent clause twice.

1. National Youth Service Day is not well-known, although it has been celebrated for more than ten years.
2. This national event was founded so that young people's volunteer work would be recognized.
3. National Youth Service Day is a two-day event that brings together student volunteers working on community projects.
4. After they work on a project, the volunteers have a deep sense of satisfaction.
5. In Washington, D.C., an old building was turned into a community center so that children would have a safe place to go.
6. Because they wanted to help beautify their city, some volunteers in Atlanta, Georgia, painted a playground.
7. Although adult volunteers helped, most of the work was done by elementary-school and middle-school students.

8. <u>Since they were interested in identifying major problems in their neighborhood</u>, about 90 high school students in San Francisco conducted a community survey.
9. <u>Because they wanted to improve the environment</u>, volunteers in Troutdale, Oregon, planted new vegetation at a state park.
10. Nearly 3 million volunteers worked on one recent National Youth Service Day, <u>so that many communities benefited</u>.

4. Kinds of Dependent Clauses (links to exercise A, p. 197)

➡ 1. *who are visually challenged,* adjective clause
2. *because they help the people get around in daily life,* adverb clause

Write these sentences on a sheet of paper. Underline each dependent clause, identifying it as an adjective clause, an adverb clause, or a noun clause.

1. Christian Miller, <u>who is a young animal lover</u>, cared for sea turtles on a beach near his home in Palm Beach, Florida. **Adj. C**
2. You may know <u>that sea turtles are endangered</u>. **NC**
3. <u>Until he received training from the Florida Department of Natural Resources</u>, Christian could not work with the turtles. **Adv. C**
4. During the turtles' resting season, <u>which lasts from May to October</u>, Christian help the turtles for two to three hours a day. **Adj. C**
5. <u>After the turtles hatch in the sand</u>, they head for the ocean. **Adv. C**
6. Baby turtles <u>that have a hard time digging themselves out of the sand</u> may need extra help. **Adj. C**
7. Those <u>that were in need of help</u> were lucky to have Christian to assist them. **Adj. C**
8. Christian knows <u>where most of the 400 to 600 nests on his beach are</u>. **NC**
9. He keeps careful records of his beach patrols <u>so that he can send his findings to the U.S. Department of Natural Resources</u>. **Adv. C**
10. <u>Although the job of monitoring sea turtles is hard</u>, Christian finds it very rewarding. **Adv. C**

5. Compound-Complex Sentences (links to exercise A, p. 199)

➡ 1. complex   2. compound

Identify each sentence as compound, complex, or compound-complex.

1. When she was four, Mandy Van Benthuysen learned that she had muscular dystrophy. **CX**
2. Later she volunteered for the Muscular Dystrophy Association, which works to find treatments for neuromuscular diseases. **CX**

Lesson 4 Kinds of Dependent Clauses

Answers shown on page. Dependent clauses are underlined. They are identified using these codes:

Adj. C = adjective clause

Adv. C = adverb clause

NC = noun clause

Lesson 5 Compound-Complex Sentences

Answers shown on page. Sentences are identified using these codes:

CD = compound sentence

CX = complex sentence

CC = compound-complex sentence

EXERCISE BANK

EXERCISE BANK

3. Neuromuscular diseases are diseases that affect both the nerves and the muscles. **CX**
4. Mandy, who was a college student, traveled around the country, and she urged other young people to volunteer. **CC**
5. She said that volunteering helps those in need; it also "makes you a better person all around." **CC**
6. For more than 30 years, the comedian Jerry Lewis has hosted a telethon that raises money for the Muscular Dystrophy Association. **CX**
7. Celebrities who want to help volunteer to be on the show. **CX**
8. Among the stars who have volunteered are Mariah Carey, Jason Alexander, Judge Judy, and Cher. **CX**
9. Television viewers call in with pledges while they watch the show. **CX**
10. Millions of dollars have been raised, and this money has helped many Americans with neuromuscular diseases. **CD**

9 Subject-Verb Agreement

1. Agreement in Number (links to exercise A, p. 210)

➡️ 1. have   2. create

Rewrite these sentences so that verbs agree in number with their subjects. If a sentence contains no error, write *Correct.*

1. According to legend, the model for *kente* cloth <u>were</u> a spider's web. **was**
2. The word *kente* <u>come</u> from *kenten,* which means "basket." **come**
3. *Kente* cloth resembles the woven pattern of a basket. **Correct**
4. This finely woven cloth <u>are made</u> on homemade looms. **is made**
5. Weavers <u>moves</u> the looms with strings tied to their big toes. **mo**
6. Traditionally, *kente* cloth is made from silk. **Correct**
7. These days the cloth <u>don't</u> always <u>contain</u> silk. **doesn't contain**
8. Rayon threads <u>serves</u> as an inexpensive substitute. **serve**
9. Weavers <u>creates</u> four-inch strips of cloth and then <u>weaves</u> the strips together to make larger garments. **create,/weave**
10. Every design has a name, such as "crocodile tears." **Correct**

Lesson 1 Agreement in Number

Answers shown on page. Verbs are underlined. For sentences in which subjects and verbs do not agree, correct verbs appear in the margin. Correct sentences are labeled *Correct.*

RESOURCES

RESOURCES

2. Compound Subjects (links to exercise A, p. 212)

➡ **1.** Correct **2.** A basket or pot serves a practical function, such as food storage.

Write the verb form that agrees with the subject of each sentence.

1. Written reports and speeches (has, <u>have</u>) their limitations.

2. Many politicians and business executives (prefers, <u>prefer</u>) using multimedia presentations.

3. CDs and other technology (provides, <u>provide</u>) new ways of reaching audiences.

4. Text, images, and sound (combines, <u>combine</u>) to convey messages effectively.

5. A photograph, art reproduction, or video clip (<u>grabs</u>, grab) the audience's attention.

6. Recorded speech or music (<u>enlivens</u>, enliven) a presentation.

7. Charts and graphs (allows, <u>allow</u>) people to absorb information quickly.

8. Skill and imagination (contributes, <u>contribute</u>) to a presentation's success.

9. Either fuzzy images or poor sound quality (<u>makes</u>, make) a presentation less effective.

10. Poor organization and dull ideas also (displeases, <u>displease</u>) audiences.

3. Agreement Problems in Sentences (links to exercise A, p. 215)

➡ **1.** Do your classmates collect posters?
2. Correct

Rewrite these sentences so that verbs agree with their subjects. If a sentence contains no error, write *Correct*.

1. Posters <u>is</u> an effective way to sell goods and services. **are**

2. <u>Has</u> you ever seen a poster that sells war? **Have**

ve performed **3.** Propaganda posters during wartime <u>has performed</u> this function.

Correct **4.** Such posters are sometimes an important part of a war effort.

5. There <u>is</u> many examples from the two world wars. **are**

6. The slogan on one of the World War I posters <u>are</u> "Food *is* ammunition—Don't waste it." **is**

7. There <u>is</u> wartime posters designed to promote patriotism. **are**

8. Hatred and fear are other emotions that can be stirred up by propaganda posters. **Correct**

are recruited **9.** Through posters <u>is recruited</u> many volunteers for the military.

10. Advertising specialists and artists hired by the government are the creative force behind wartime posters. **Correct**

Lesson 3 Indefinite Pronouns as Subjects

Answers shown on page. Verbs are underlined. For sentences in which subjects and verbs do not agree, correct verbs appear in the margin. Correct sentences are labeled *Correct.*

EXERCISE BANK

EXERCISE BANK

Lesson 4 Problem Subjects

Answers shown on page.
Verbs are underlined.

4. Indefinite Pronouns as Subjects (links to exercise A, p. 218)

➡ **1.** Many know the saying "A picture's worth a thousand words." **2.** Correct

Rewrite these sentences so that verbs agree with their subjects. If a sentence contains no error, write *Correct*.

1. One glimpses 19th-century slum life in Jacob Riis's *How the Other Half Lives*. **Correct**
2. Another of his influential books <u>are</u> *Children of the Poor*. **is**
3. Each of these books <u>contain</u> photographs that convey the problems of immigrants. **contains**
4. Many of the photographs document conditions in New York City tenements. **Correct**
5. All of Riis's photographs <u>exposes</u> the horrors of overcrowding and malnutrition. **expose**
6. Both of these problems <u>was</u> common in 19th-century cities. **wer**
7. Few <u>has captured</u> urban poverty as vividly as Riis did. **have captured**
8. None of the written accounts so dramatically demonstrate the plight of the urban poor. **Correct**
9. Most of Riis's photographs <u>illustrates</u> problems caused by rapid growth. **illustrate**
10. Nearly everyone <u>credit</u> Riis with helping to improve conditions. **credits**

5. Problem Subjects (links to exercise A, p. 221)

➡ **1.** describes **2.** travels

Write the form of the verb that agrees with the subject of each sentence.

Lesson 5 Agreement Problems in Sentences

Answers shown on page. The correct verb forms are underlined.

1. Three and a half years (<u>seems</u>, seem) a short amount of time for planning and finishing the Vietnam Veterans Memorial.
2. Economics (<u>is</u>, are) always a concern in designing a large project.
3. About eight months (<u>is</u>, are) how long it actually took to construct the memorial.
4. The public (<u>lines</u>, line) up to view the wall and nearby statues at this popular site.
5. "Heroes in Black Stone" (<u>is</u>, are) a song about Vietnam veterans and the people who visit the memorial.
6. Politics (<u>is</u>, are) not the point of the wall.
7. A committee of distinguished sculptors and architects (<u>is</u>, are) to be congratulated for choosing such an effective tribute.
8. Only 600 feet (<u>separates</u>, separate) the wall from the Lincoln Memorial.

RESOURCES

RESOURCES

9. *Offerings at the Wall,* a book by Thomas Allen, (<u>contains</u>, contain) pictures of items left at the wall by visitors.

10. The National Park Service staff (<u>collects</u>, collect) personal items left at the wall.

🔟 Capitalization

1. People and Cultures (links to exercise A, p. 232)

➡️ **2**. Mr. Jones, Knight, Glubok, Tamarin

Write the words and abbreviations that should be capitalized but are not in these sentences. Capitalize each correctly.

1. Last week coach jackett told us a story about one of the most interesting tennis matches of the 20th century.
2. It all started with a man by the name of robert larimore riggs.
3. bobby riggs, as he was known in the tennis world, won the Wimbledon title in 1939.
4. Our coach said that mr. riggs won three U.S. Open championships but became famous for his weird tennis matches.
5. My friend roberta said that her aunt a.j. once played a match against riggs while he sat on a chair.
6. The one event that i found most interesting occurred when riggs challenged the australian margaret court to a tennis match.
7. Most people—including my aunt, who was a tennis fan— expected court to beat riggs because she was 25 years younger than he.
8. Riggs won that tennis match but later met another female challenger, billie jean king, who defeated him easily.
9. The match became one of the most publicized events in american sports, attracting 50 million viewers.
10. Years later, in another gender battle, riggs and vitas gerulaitis lost a doubles match to martina navratilova and pam shriver.

2. First Words and Titles (links to exercise A, p. 235)

➡️ **1**. How, Equipment, Baseball, Bat   **2**. Whoever

Write the words that should be capitalized but are not in these sentences, capitalizing them correctly. If there are no errors in a sentence, write *Correct*.

1. on July 20, 1998, the Special Olympics celebrated its 30th anniversary.

Exercise Bank **615**

Lesson 1 People and Cultures

Answers shown on page. using standard proofreading marks.

Lesson 2 First Words and Titles

Answers shown on page. using standard proofreading marks. Correct sentences labeled Correct.

EXERCISE BANK

EXERCISE BANK

2. *the today show* and *parade magazine* have featured inspiring stories about the courage of athletes in the Special Olympics.

3. The Special Olympics oath is "let me win. but if I cannot win, let me be brave in the attempt."

4. In 1997 a Christmas album benefiting the Special Olympics was produced, with songs like "blue christmas" and "the christmas song."

5. The Special Olympics has its own magazine, entitled *spirit*.

6. On February 11, 1990, the television drama *life goes on* devoted an hour-long episode to the Special Olympics.

7. In 1987 more than 4,700 athletes participated in the Special Olympics, the year's largest amateur sports event. **Correct**

8. The event was covered in *sports illustrated* and *time*.

9. For information on how to get involved, write a letter to Special Olympics headquarters, beginning "dear Sir or Madam."

10. If you would like to research the Special Olympics, you may want to make an outline that begins like this:

   I. general information
      a. athletes
      b. families
      c. volunteers
      d. national and worldwide chapters

Lesson 3 Places and Transportation

Answers shown on page. using standard proofreading marks. Correct sentences labeled *Correct*.

3. Places and Transportation (links to exercise A, p. 239)

➡ **1.** North America   **3.** Appalachian Mountains

Write the words that should be capitalized but are not in these sentences, capitalizing them correctly. If there are no errors in a sentence, write *Correct*.

Correct **1.** Have you ever wondered where the word *marathon* originated?

2. The first marathon was held during the first modern Olympics in athens, greece, in 1896.

3. The race was named for an ancient battle near the Greek town of marathon.

4. According to legend, the soldier Pheidippides raced from marathon to athens (about 25 miles) with news of the Greeks' victory over the Persians and then immediately died.

5. Today, marathons are held all over the world, in places like london, england; sydney, australia; and dublin, ireland.

6. Whether in the northern or the southern part of the country, on the east coast or the west coast, you'll find marathons.

7. For example, the one in new york city begins on staten island, at the verrazano-narrows bridge, and ends in central park.

8. There's even a marathon called Grandma's Marathon in duluth, minnesota, with a scenic course along lake superior.
9. Perhaps you'd be more interested in the Rock 'n' Roll Marathon, with a course that travels through the san diego zoo and along highway 163.
10. Known for its difficult course, the Boston Marathon begins in hopkinton and ends in copely square.

4. Organizations and Other Subjects (links to exercise A, p. 241)

→ **1.** North Side Junior High

Lesson 4 Organizations and Other Subjects

Answers shown on page using standard proofreading marks. Correct sentences labeled *Correct.*

Write the words that should be capitalized but are not in these sentences, capitalizing them correctly. If there are no errors write *Correct.*

1. Records show that as early as 400 b.c. the Chinese were playing a game similar to soccer.
2. Some early footballs were stuffed with hair or rags.   **Correct**
3. The term *soccer* was first used at oxford university.
4. James Richardson Spensley, founder of the genoa cricket and football club, introduced game of soccer to Italy in 1893.
5. On may 21, 1904, an international soccer federation was formed in paris, France.
6. The first world cup finals were held in Uruguay, but the teams could not agree on the size of the ball; therefore, different-sized balls were used in the two halves.
7. During world war II (1939–1945), the world cup was canceled.
8. The oneidas of boston, the first organized soccer club in America, were undefeated from 1862 to 1865.
9. The first series of games known as the women's world cup was played in China in 1991.
10. On saturday, july 10, 1999, the U.S. women's team won its second world cup title in Pasadena's rose bowl stadium.

11 Punctuation

**Chapter 11
Punctuation**

1. Periods and Other End Marks (links to exercise A, p. 252)

→ **1.** ?   **2.** !

Lesson 1 Periods and Other End Marks

Answers shown on page.

Write the punctuation end mark that should replace each numbered blank.

You don't have to use a code to keep a message secret_1_ You can use invisible ink. What substance should you use_2_ Well, lemon juice works well_3_ No kidding_4_ Dip a toothpick or brush into the juice and use it to write your message. Let the juice dry_5_ Your message will be invisible. Now, hold the paper so that it touches a hot light bulb. Be careful_6_ Don't burn yourself. The words of your message will appear. Amazing_7_ Do you want to try a different kind of ink_8_ Write your message in milk and let it dry. Now, empty pencil-sharpener shavings over the flat paper_9_ The shavings will stick to the invisible words and make the message appear_10_

Lesson 2 Commas in Sentences

Answers shown on page. Carets in the text show where commas should be inserted.

2. Commas in Sentences (links to exercise A, p. 255)

➡ Think of this, readers,

Rewrite this paragraph, adding commas where they are needed.

Some cultures lived in America for many centuries but then they disappeared. They left tools pottery and other artifacts behind. They also left carvings and paintings on rocks called rock art. Petroglyphs (rock carvings) show human figures animals and some designs that are not easily explained. Artists made petroglyphs with small pointed rocks or flat stones. They used these as knives picks and chisels to carve shapes on large stones. Pictographs (rock paintings) on the other hand were made with paint from berries or vegetables. Native American artists may have painted for pleasure or they may have painted to communicate with one another. In any case the pictures are like a form of code to us.

Lesson 3 Dates, Addresses, and Letters

Answers shown on page. Carets in the text show where commas should be inserted.

3. Commas: Dates, Addresses, and Letters (links to exercise A, p. 257)

➡ New York, NY   February 20, 2000

Rewrite the following letter, adding missing commas.

April 27 2000

Manuel Rojas
123 Maple Ave.
Los Angeles California

Dear Manny

Today I learned another interesting fact about secret codes. I found out how spies sent secret messages through the mail during World War II. It worked like this. A spy in London England might write a normal letter that contained no secret information. The spy would then address the envelope to his or superior in Paris France. In the upper right-hand corner of the envelope, the spy would write a tiny message in code. When the spy placed a stamp over the message, no one could detect the message. When the letter arrived, the recipient would steam off the stamp and decode the message. Even if enemy agents opened the letter, it would not arouse suspicion.

By the way, I read in the newspaper that a speaker will give a presentation at our local library about how information is coded in computers. The presentation is on May 18 2000. Would you like to go with me when you visit?

Your friend who loves codes

Jack

4. Quotation Marks (links to exercise A, p. 261)

➡ "Are you nuts?"   "I do," said Jay," and

Rewrite the following passage, correcting errors in the use of quotation marks.

"Some codes are spoken rather than written, Julia said. A whole town once used a secret language called Boontling."
"Why was it called that? asked Paul.
"The town was Boonville, California," Julia explained, "and the word *Boontling* stood for *Boonville lingo*".
Paul asked, "Is lingo the same as slang?"
"That's right! Julia exclaimed. "From the 1880s to the 1930s, nearly everyone who lived in Boonville could speak the lingo." She went on to say that "a few people still know it today."
"Give me some examples," Paul said, of Boontling words."
"Some combine parts of English words," said Julia. "For example, a schoolteacher is a schoolch." A rail fence is a relf."
Paul pointed out that "those words weren't too hard to decipher."
"No," said Julia, but other words are less obvious. A storyteller is called a bearman because the best storyteller in town hunted bears."

5. Semicolons and Colons (links to exercise A, p. 263)

➡ messages: a folk song;

Rewrite this paragraph, correcting errors in the use of semicolons and colons.

Lesson 4 Punctuating Quotations

Answers shown on page using standard proofreading marks.

Lesson 5 Semicolons and Colons

Answers shown on page. Punctuation that should be deleted is marked. Carets in the text show corrections.

EXERCISE BANK

EXERCISE BANK

The ancient Celts used a form of written communication called the ogham alphabet. This alphabet can still be seen in inscriptions on stones in fact, more than 350 such stones have survived. They are found in Ireland, Wales, Scotland, southern England, and the Isle of Man. During the time of ogham's use (about 600 B.C. to 700 A.D.), few people could read and write. To write a message in ogham, a person would draw or chisel a long, straight line. Each letter would be represented by one to five short lines, which might extend to the left of, to the right of, or completely through the long line. A message could also be written on a stick the letters were cut into its edge. The ogham alphabet had 20 letters, each named for a tree; a shrub or other plant or a natural element, like lightning or the sea. Among the trees represented were the following the birch, the oak, and the hawthorn. Nose ogham and shin ogham were variations in which people used their fingers to form the cross-strokes of the letters against the straight line of their nose or shinbone.

6. Hyphens, Dashes, and Parentheses (links to exercise on p. 265)

➡ **1.** — **2.** -

Indicate what punctuation mark—hyphen, dash, or parenthesis—should replace each numbered blank in this paragraph. If no mark is needed, write *None*.

— Imagine living in the Victorian era __1__ a time when messages had to be carried hundreds of miles on horseback or sent on ships

None that traveled across the ocean __2__ . It may have taken days, weeks, or even months for a message to reach its destination. This was how people communicated over long distances in the 1800s. What a

—/— tremendous improvement __3__ a leap in technology __4__ the invention of the telegraph was to the people of the Victorian era. Samuel Morse was one of the inventors of the telegraph. In 1844, at

- the age of fifty __5__ three, Morse demonstrated that messages could be sent quickly from Washington, D.C., to Baltimore, Maryland,

None __6__ by using his electric telegraph. Morse also invented his own

(/) code __7__ the Morse code __8__ , which is a system of long and short clicks used to transmit messages by means of the telegraph. When Morse code is written out, the letters of the alphabet appear as groups of dots and dashes. The most famous message in Morse code is (· · · — — — · · ·), or SOS, the widely recognized distress call.

7. Apostrophes (links to exercise A, p. 267)

➡ another's, Cryptoanalysts

Lesson 6 Hyphens, Dashes, and Parentheses

Answers shown on page. Correct punctuation marks appear in the margin.

Lesson 7 Apostrophes

Answers shown on page using standard proofreading marks.

RESOURCES

Rewrite this paragraph, correcting errors in the use of apostrophes and possessive pronouns.

It's easy to make a simple cipher called a scytale, which was invented by the Spartans in ancient Greece. To make you're own scytale, you'll need a long strip of plain paper and a cylinder, such as a pencil or the cardboard tube from a paper-towel roll. Wrap the strip of paper in a spiral around the cylinder. Then begin writing your message along the length of the cylinder. Write each letter on a different part of the paper spiral. Dont use punctuation. When you reach the end of a line, continue writing on the next line until your message is complete. Now unroll the paper from the cylinder. It'll look like a long strip of letters in a single column. To read your message, the recipient must wrap the strip of paper around a cylinder of the same size that you used in writing the message. Whose going to read your message? Lysander, an ancient Greek military leader, once received a scytale and used the information in it to win an important battle for the Greek's.

8. Punctuating Titles (links to exercise A, p. 269)

➡ Polygraphia   The Journal of Cryptology

Read this paragraph and rewrite the titles in it, using either quotation marks or underlining as appropriate.

Countries have spied on each other for centuries. In China 2,500 years ago, Sun Zi described how to organize military intelligence in his book The Art of War. In his epic poem the Iliad, Homer discussed spying during the Trojan War. Spying helped the Allies win World War II, as William Stevenson explains in his book A Man Called Intrepid. Codebreaking helped the Allies sink the German battleship Bismarck. Broadcast over the BBC, the first lines of Paul Verlaine's poem "Chanson d'Automne" warned the French Resistance that the Normandy invasion was imminent. Shortly after the war, an American engineer developed information theory in an article called "A Mathematical Theory of Communication." Even works of entertainment, like the 1960s TV show Secret Agent, have depicted the pressures of being a spy who can trust no one. Johnny Rivers sang about this dangerous life in the show's theme song, "Secret Agent Man." Contemporary movies, such as Mission Impossible and Tomorrow Never Dies, still thrill audiences with their tales of espionage.

Lesson 8 Punctuating Titles

Answers shown on page. Titles that should be italicized are underlined. Quotation marks are shown using standard proofreading marks.

Model Bank

Book Review

I enjoyed reading *Roll of Thunder, Hear My Cry* by Mildred D. Taylor even though a lot of it is very sad and some parts of it made me angry. The story is about a black family during the Great Depression. The kids and adults in the family suffer different kinds of discrimination through the course of the book. Sometimes they just have to deal with insulting things like having to wait in stores until the white people have been helped. At other times, the discrimination happens in much more violent ways, like people being burned or lynched.

There is some justice for the characters, though. My favorite scene is when the kids get sick of the school bus driver constantly speeding too close to them and running them off the road as they walk to school. They skip lunch and dig a huge hole on the road that wrecks the bus.

For me, the book is so effective because it is told by Cassie, who is in the first grade and is experiencing most of this racism for the first time. She is just discovering that by being black she is considered to be very different from white people. She gets angry when white people treat her as though she doesn't matter just because she's black. She doesn't know why that should make any difference.

Since I have not experienced racism firsthand, my point of view is similar to Cassie's. I hear a lot about racism on the news and in school, but reading this book from Cassie's point of view made it all very clear and made it feel personal. I felt like Cassie, seeing for the first time the way the world is, and not being able to do anything about it.

RUBRIC IN ACTION

❶ Clearly identifies the book and author and tells something about the story

❷ Gives specific examples to support a point

❸ Explains why the book was effective

❹ Sums up this writer's feeling about the book

Editorial

The Board of Education announced this week that starting next September, this school would be in session year-round. As expected, the moan of the student body could be heard throughout the building. Kids argued that having school all year, especially in the summer, was inhuman.

This reaction is understandable, but it's probably based more on gut feeling than on the facts. The problem is that when most students hear the words "school all year," the first idea they get is that it means no summer vacation. This simply isn't true.

The new schedule calls for three solid months of school at a time, followed by a one-month break. There are really many advantages to this schedule over the traditional one, if students will stop and think about it.

If students were to be completely honest with themselves, they would have to admit that a three-month summer break can get very long and very boring after awhile. With the new schedule, the three-month summer break will be broken up so that there will be one month-long break in March, one in July, and another in November. These breaks will be long enough to allow for trips as well as relaxation at home, but won't be so long that kids will start to get antsy and bored.

There also won't be the endless tunnel of school. When kids get back to school they can say, "Just three months of this and then another month off!"

So, kids don't need to worry about there being no summer vacation. This new schedule could make the year go a lot faster and strike a nice balance between school and vacation. Students should give it a chance and consider the possibilities the new schedule has to offer. Who knows? They may just love it.

RUBRIC IN ACTION

❶ Clearly identifies the topic of the editorial

❷ Answers a major objection to the new schedule

❸ Provides information and examples to support this writer's position

❹ Summarizes her position and uses examples to argue her ideas

Business Letter

180 Nemic Street
Boston, MA 02118

April 7, 2001

Joe Naglar
PBG Music Club
1 Beach Place
Stamford, CT 06904

Dear Mr. Naglar:

I'm writing to ask you about five CDs I ordered but never received. I ordered these selections over four months ago. My parents' credit card has been charged for them, but they still have not arrived.

If there is some problem with the availability of these selections, or some other problem with my order, please let me know. As it is now, it looks like I've been charged for things I never received and then I've been forgotten about.

I hope that whatever the problem was it has been cleared up and that I will soon receive my CDs, or that my parents' card will be credited.

Sincerely,

Charles Terhune

Charles Terhune

RUBRIC
IN ACTION

❶ Sender's address and date

❷ Addresses a specific person

❸ Explains the complaint

❹ Asks for specific action

❺ Signature above the typed name

RESOURCES

RESOURCES

Problem-Solution Essay

RUBRIC
IN ACTION

The talk around school lately has been the problem students are having with their lockers. They are so narrow that most students find them much too small to hold their coats along with their binders and books. Also, they are so close together that kids almost have to wait in line to get to their lockers. This causes many kids to be late for class.

Principal Sayre has been aware of this problem and is trying to solve it. She says that the main difficulty is obvious: If the school installed wider lockers, they would take up more room and there wouldn't be enough space to have a locker for each student.

My solution to this problem is just as obvious. Currently there are only lockers in the halls of the main building. The music building, however, has no lockers in its halls. The belief is that kids wouldn't want to go outside and walk all the way over to the music building just to get their things. This aspect of the problem could be made easier by assigning the music building lockers to kids who have regular music or drama classes. They would be spending a good part of the day over there anyway, so it wouldn't be such a hassle for them.

Since solving the problem is not a matter of money, but of space, we students should work hard to make this compromise. True, it seems like a hassle for some kids to have to walk to the music building to get their things, but other schools in the area have similar setups and their students don't even seem to notice a problem. And really which is worse, having to walk an extra fifty yards to get to your big, roomy, accessible locker, or being late for class because you couldn't get to your narrow, cramped, and crowded locker?

❶ This writer clearly identifies the problem.

❷ Gives an answer to the problem that reveals another problem

❸ Provides a solution and explains why it would work

❹ Offers more support for his solution and appeals to the readers' desire for bigger lockers

Process Description

In our science lab this week, we performed an experiment to discover the mechanical advantages of an inclined plane. The materials we used were a wooden board with a pulley at one end, seven textbooks, a spring scale, three feet of string, and a ruler.

We began by setting up our materials for the experiment.

First, we made a stack of six books. Then we rested one end of the board, the end with the pulley, on the stack. We let the other end rest on the table, making a ramp. The first illustration on the right shows these steps.

Then we tied one end of the string around another book and tied the other end to the spring scale. Suspending the book from the spring scale we found the weight of the book. We recorded the weight on a chart as the resistance force.

Next, we measured the height of the stack of books and recorded this as the resistance distance. We then measured the length of the board to find the effort distance.

Now that our materials were set up, we were ready to perform the experiment.

First, we rested the book at the bottom of the inclined board and ran the string over the pulley at the top of the board.

Next, we held the spring scale and slowly pulled the book up the board. As we did, we noted the measurement on the spring scale and recorded that as the effort force.

Next, we removed three of the books from the stack to lower the incline. We measured this new height and recorded this new resistance distance down in our chart. The second illustration shows this setup.

❶ Identifies the purpose of the experiment and names the materials needed

❷ Gives a step-by-step sequence to prepare for the experiment and indicates an illustration

❸ Uses a transition sentence to move to the next part of the sequence

❹ Identifies each step in the experiment, using transition words and phrases

We pulled the book up the incline again and recorded the new effort force from the spring scale.

When both of these experiments were complete, we compared all our data. We learned that the mechanical advantage increased as the height of the incline decreased.

5 Ends by giving the results of the experiment

Illustration 1

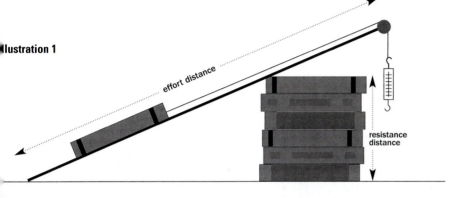

Illustration 2

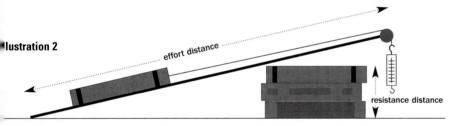

Quick-Fix Spelling Machine

QUICK–FIX SPELLING MACHINE: PLURALS OF NOUNS

SINGULAR	RULE	PLURAL
skateboard painting ticket	Add -s to most nouns.	skateboards paintings tickets
	WATCH OUT The exception to this rule are nouns whose plurals are formed in a special way, such as *man (men), woman (women),* and *child (children).*	
hiss dish ditch box buzz	Add -es to nouns that end in *s, sh, ch, x,* or *z.*	hisses dishes ditches boxes buzzes
auto igloo radio	Add -s to most nouns that end in *o.*	autos igloos radios
potato tomato mosquito	Add -es to a few nouns that end in *o.*	potatoes tomatoes mosquitoes
flurry deputy battery dairy	Change the *y* to *i* and add -es to most nouns that end in *y.*	flurries deputies batteries dairies
alley play turkey	Add -s when a vowel comes before the *y.*	alleys plays turkeys
calf thief wife leaf knife	Change the *f* to a *v* and add -es to most nouns ending in *f* or *fe.*	calves thieves wives leaves knives
belief muff safe	Add -s to a few nouns that end in *f* or *fe.*	beliefs muffs safes
data sheep e-mail software	Keep the spelling of some nouns.	data sheep e-mail software

QUICK–FIX SPELLING MACHINE: POSSESSIVES

NOUN	RULE	POSSESSIVE
moon	**Add an apostrophe and -*s* to singular nouns.**	moon's light
student		student's locker
club		club's president
restaurant		restaurant's menus
school		school's teachers
bank		bank's assets
college		college's facilities
dog		dog's fur
garden		garden's scents
catalog		catalog's merchandise
museum		museum's exhibit
flower		flower's fragrance
book		book's cover
holiday		holiday's traditions
turkey		turkey's drumstick

The exception to this rule is that the *s* after the apostrophe is dropped after *Jesus'*, *Moses'*, and certain names in classical mythology. Dropping the -*s* makes these possessive forms easier to pronounce.

NOUN	RULE	POSSESSIVE
x-rays	**Add an apostrophe to plural nouns that end in -*s*.**	x-rays' envelopes
organizations		organizations' budgets
teams		teams' coaches
buildings		buildings' windows
cities		cities' mayors
airports		airports' schedules
babies		babies' toys
groceries		groceries' prices
violets		violets' buds
necklaces		necklaces' clasps
butterflies		butterflies' wings

NOUN	RULE	POSSESSIVE
deer	**Add an apostrophe and -*s* to plural nouns not ending in -*s*.**	deer's hooves
oxen		oxen's load
salmon		salmon's gills
stepchildren		stepchildren's names
herd		herd's cattle
sheep		sheep's wool
mice		mice's nests
people		people's languages

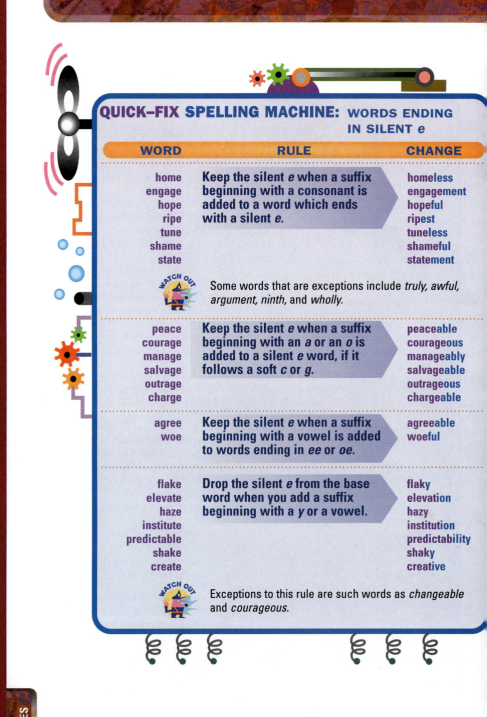

QUICK-FIX SPELLING MACHINE: WORDS ENDING IN SILENT e

WORD	RULE	CHANGE
home	**Keep the silent *e* when a suffix beginning with a consonant is added to a word which ends with a silent *e*.**	homeless
engage		engagement
hope		hopeful
ripe		ripest
tune		tuneless
shame		shameful
state		statement

WATCH OUT Some words that are exceptions include *truly, awful, argument, ninth,* and *wholly.*

WORD	RULE	CHANGE
peace	**Keep the silent *e* when a suffix beginning with an *a* or an *o* is added to a silent *e* word, if it follows a soft *c* or *g*.**	peaceable
courage		courageous
manage		manageably
salvage		salvageable
outrage		outrageous
charge		chargeable

WORD	RULE	CHANGE
agree	**Keep the silent *e* when a suffix beginning with a vowel is added to words ending in *ee* or *oe*.**	agreeable
woe		woeful

WORD	RULE	CHANGE
flake	**Drop the silent *e* from the base word when you add a suffix beginning with a *y* or a vowel.**	flaky
elevate		elevation
haze		hazy
institute		institution
predictable		predictability
shake		shaky
create		creative

WATCH OUT Exceptions to this rule are such words as *changeable* and *courageous.*

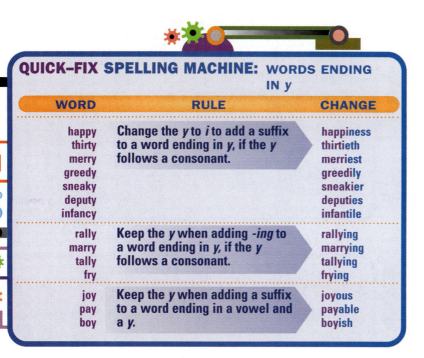

QUICK–FIX SPELLING MACHINE: WORDS ENDING IN y

WORD	RULE	CHANGE
happy thirty merry greedy sneaky deputy infancy	Change the *y* to *i* to add a suffix to a word ending in *y*, if the *y* follows a consonant.	happiness thirtieth merriest greedily sneakier deputies infantile
rally marry tally fry	Keep the *y* when adding *-ing* to a word ending in *y*, if the *y* follows a consonant.	rallying marrying tallying frying
joy pay boy	Keep the *y* when adding a suffix to a word ending in a vowel and a *y*.	joyous payable boyish

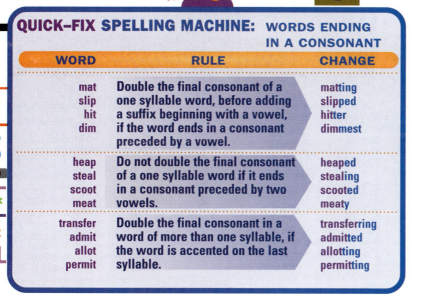

QUICK–FIX SPELLING MACHINE: WORDS ENDING IN A CONSONANT

WORD	RULE	CHANGE
mat slip hit dim	Double the final consonant of a one syllable word, before adding a suffix beginning with a vowel, if the word ends in a consonant preceded by a vowel.	matting slipped hitter dimmest
heap steal scoot meat	Do not double the final consonant of a one syllable word if it ends in a consonant preceded by two vowels.	heaped stealing scooted meaty
transfer admit allot permit	Double the final consonant in a word of more than one syllable, if the word is accented on the last syllable.	transferring admitted allotting permitting

Quick–Fix Spelling Machine **631**

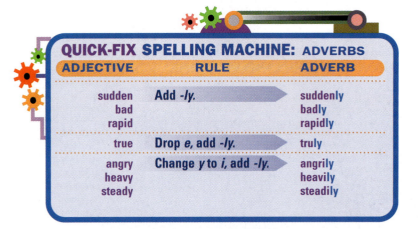

QUICK-FIX SPELLING MACHINE: ADVERBS

ADJECTIVE	RULE	ADVERB
sudden bad rapid	Add *-ly*.	suddenly badly rapidly
true	Drop *e*, add *-ly*.	truly
angry heavy steady	Change *y* to *i*, add *-ly*.	angrily heavily steadily

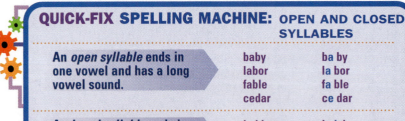

QUICK–FIX SPELLING MACHINE: COMPOUNDS

	SINGULAR	RULE	PLURAL
One word	dishcloth supermarket airport	Add *-s* to most words.	dishcloths supermarkets airports
Two or more words	bongo drum atomic bomb brussel sprout	Make the main noun plural. The main noun is the noun that is modified.	bongo drums atomic bombs brussel sprout
Hyphenated words	son-in-law attorney-general vice-president	Make the main noun plural.	sons-in-law attorneys-gen vice-president

QUICK-FIX SPELLING MACHINE: OPEN AND CLOSED SYLLABLES

An *open syllable* ends in one vowel and has a long vowel sound.	baby labor fable cedar	ba by la bor fa ble ce dar
A *closed syllable* ends in a consonant and has a short vowel sound.	ladder mischief problem plunder	lad der mis chief prob lem plun der

RESOURCES

RESOURCES

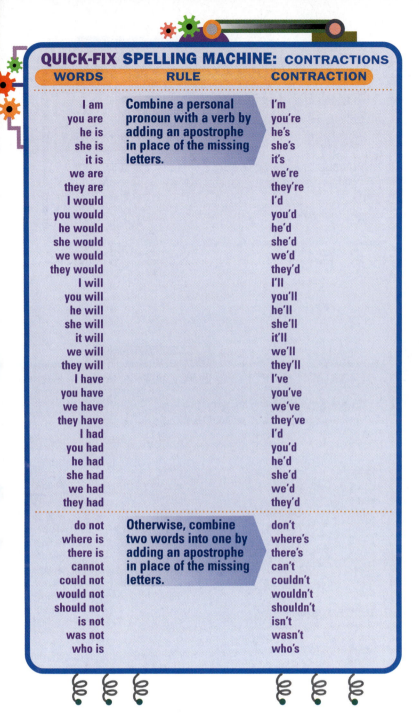

QUICK-FIX SPELLING MACHINE: CONTRACTIONS

WORDS	RULE	CONTRACTION
I am	Combine a personal pronoun with a verb by adding an apostrophe in place of the missing letters.	I'm
you are		you're
he is		he's
she is		she's
it is		it's
we are		we're
they are		they're
I would		I'd
you would		you'd
he would		he'd
she would		she'd
we would		we'd
they would		they'd
I will		I'll
you will		you'll
he will		he'll
she will		she'll
it will		it'll
we will		we'll
they will		they'll
I have		I've
you have		you've
we have		we've
they have		they've
I had		I'd
you had		you'd
he had		he'd
she had		she'd
we had		we'd
they had		they'd
do not	Otherwise, combine two words into one by adding an apostrophe in place of the missing letters.	don't
where is		where's
there is		there's
cannot		can't
could not		couldn't
would not		wouldn't
should not		shouldn't
is not		isn't
was not		wasn't
who is		who's

QUICK-FIX SPELLING MACHINE: SEED SORTER

Only one English word ends in *sede*.	supersede
Only three words end in *ceed*.	exceed proceed succeed
All other "seed" sound words end in *cede*.	accede concede precede recede secede

QUICK–FIX SPELLING MACHINE: *ie* AND *ei* ENGINES

In words with *ie* and *ei*, spell the long *e* sound with *ie*, unless it follows a *c*, or sounds like an *a*.

i BEFORE *e*	EXCEPT AFTER *c*	SOUNDS LIKE *a*	EXCEPTION
field	receipt	eight	their
chief	deceive	weight	height
piece	deceit	sleigh	counterfeit
grief	conceit	neigh	heir
belief	receive	feign	sheik
niece	perceive	vein	neither
priest	ceiling	skein	leisure
thief		rein	seize
relief		reign	either
brief		neighbor	weird
achieve			species
shield			financier
shriek			
believe			

QUICK-FIX SPELLING MACHINE: BORROWED WORDS

Over the centuries, as English speakers increased their contact with people from other lands, English speakers "borrowed" words from other languages. The English language began to grow in new directions, and became the colorful tapestry we know today.

Spelling follows certain patterns in every language. For example, some letter patterns in French, Spanish, and Italian appear in words commonly used in English.

PATTERN	WORD

Some borrowed words keep their original spellings and pronunciations.

In many words taken from the French, the final *t* is silent.	ballet beret buffet
In both English and French, the soft *g* is usually followed by *e, i,* or *y.*	mirage region energy
The hard *g* is followed by *a, o,* or *u.*	vague
Many words taken from the Dutch language have *oo* in their spellings.	cookie snoop hook caboose
Many words borrowed from Spanish end in *o.*	taco tornado rodeo bronco
Italian words that commonly appear in English often end in *i.*	spaghetti macaroni ravioli

Some words from other languages were changed to fit English rules in pronunciation, grammar, and spelling.

The original spellings of words in a few Native American and Eskimo languages have unusual letter combinations. Since English speakers found these words to be useful but difficult to pronounce, they changed their spellings.	topaghan = toboggan tamahaac = tomahawk pakani = pecan squa = squaw wampumpeag = wampum qajaq = kayak

SPELLING

Quick–Fix Spelling Machine **635**

Commonly Misspelled Words

A

abbreviate
accidentally
achievement
analyze
anonymous
answer
apologize
appearance
appreciate
appropriate
argument
awkward

B

beautiful
beginning
because
believe
bicycle
brief
bulletin
business

C

calendar
campaign
candidate
caught
certain
changeable
characteristic
clothes
column

committee
courageous
courteous
criticize
curiosity

D

decision
definitely
dependent
description
desirable
despair
desperate
development
dictionary
different
disappear
disappoint
discipline
dissatisfied

E

eighth
eligible
eliminate
embarrass
enthusiastic
especially
essay
exaggerate
exceed
existence
experience

F

familiar
fascinating
favorite
February
foreign
fourth
fragile

G

generally
government
grammar
guarantee
guard

H

height
humorous

I

immediately
independent
irritable

J, K, L

judgment
knowledge
laboratory
library
license
lightning

literature
loneliness

M

mathematics
minimum
mischievous

N

necessary
nickel
ninety
noticeable
nuclear
nuisance

O

obstacle
occasionally
once
opinion
opportunity
outrageous

P

parallel
particularly
people
permanent
persuade
pleasant
pneumonia

possess
possibility
prejudice
principal
privilege
probably
pursue
psychology

R

realize
receipt
receive
recognize
recommend
reference
rehearse
repetition
restaurant
rhythm
ridiculous

S

sandwich
schedule
scissors
separate
sergeant
similar
sincerely
souvenir
specifically
strategy
success
surprise
syllable
sympathy
symptom

T

temperature
thorough
throughout
tomorrow
traffic
tragedy
transferred
truly
Tuesday
twelfth

U

unnecessary
usable

V

vacuum
vicinity
village

W

weird

Commonly Confused Words

Good writers master words that are easy to misuse and misspell. Study the following words, noting how their meanings differ.

accept, except
Accept means "to agree to something" or "to receive something willingly." *Except* usually means "not including."
Did the teacher *accept* **your report?**
Everyone smiled for the photographer *except* **Jody.**

advice, advise
Advice is a noun that means "counsel given to someone." *Advise* is a verb that means "to give counsel."
Jim should take some of his own *advice.*
The mechanic *advised* **me to get new brakes for my car.**

affect, effect
Affect means "to move or influence" or "to wear or to pretend to have." *Effect* as a verb means "to bring about." As a noun, *effect* means "the result of an action."
The news from South Africa *affected* **him deeply.**
The band's singer *affects* **a British accent.**
The students tried to *effect* **a change in school policy.**
What *effect* **did the acidic soil produce in the plants?**

all ready, already
All ready means "all are ready" or "completely prepared." *Already* means "previously."
The students were *all ready* **for the field trip.**
We had *already* **pitched our tent before it started raining.**

all right
All right is the correct spelling. *Alright* is nonstandard and should not be used.

a lot
A lot may be used in informal writing. *Alot* is incorrect.

borrow, lend
Borrow means "to receive something on loan." *Lend* means "to give out temporarily."
Please *lend* **me your book.**
He *borrowed* **five dollars from his sister.**

bring, take
Bring refers to movement toward or with. *Take* refers to movement away from.
I'll *bring* **you a glass of water.**
Would you please *take* **these apples to Pam and John?**

can, may
Can means "to be able; to have the power to do something." *May* means "to have permission to do something." *May* can also mean "possibly will."

We *may* not use pesticides on our community garden.
Pesticides *may* not be necessary, anyway.
Vegetables *can* grow nicely without pesticides.

capital, capitol, the Capitol
Capital means "excellent," "most serious," or "most important." It also means "seat of government." *Capitol* is a "building in which a state legislature meets." The *Capitol* is "the building in Washington, D.C., in which the U.S. Congress meets."
Proper nouns begin with *capital* letters.
Is Madison the *capital* of Wisconsin?
Protesters rallied at the state *capitol.*
A subway connects the Senate and the House in *the Capitol.*

desert, dessert
Desert (des´ ert) means "a dry, sandy, barren region." *Desert* (de sert´) means "to abandon." *Dessert* (des sert´) is a sweet, such as cake.
The Sahara in North Africa is the world's largest *desert.*
The night guard did not *desert* his post.
Alison's favorite *dessert* is chocolate cake.

fewer, less
Fewer refers to numbers of things that can be counted. *Less* refers to amount, degree, or value.
Fewer than ten students camped out.
We made *less* money this year on the walkathon than last year.

good, well
Good is always an adjective. *Well* is usually an adverb that modifies an action verb. *Well* can also be an adjective meaning "in good health."
Dana felt *good* when she finished painting her room.
Angela ran *well* in yesterday's race.
I felt *well* when I left my house.

its, it's
Its is a possessive pronoun. *It's* is a contraction for *it is* or *it has.*
Sanibel Island is known for *its* beautiful beaches.
It's great weather for a picnic.

lay, lie
Lay is a verb that means "to place." It takes a direct object. *Lie* is a verb that means "to be in a certain place." *Lie,* or its past form *lay,* never takes a direct object.
The carpenter will *lay* the planks on the bench.
My cat likes to *lie* under the bed.

CONFUSED WORDS

CONFUSED WORDS

lead, led	*Lead* can be a noun that means "a heavy metal" or a verb that means "to show the way." *Led* is the past tense form of the verb. ***Lead* is used in nuclear reactors.** **Raul always *leads* his team onto the field.** **She *led* the class as president of the student council.**
learn, teach	*Learn* means "to gain knowledge." *Teach* means "to instruct." **Enrique is *learning* about black holes in space.** **Marva *teaches* astronomy at a college in the city.**
leave, let	*Leave* means "to go away from." *Leave* can be transitive or intransitive. *Let* is usually used with another verb. It means "to allow to." **Don't *leave* the refrigerator open.** **She *leaves* for Scotland tomorrow.** **Cyclops wouldn't *let* Odysseus' men *leave* the cave.**
like	*Like* used as a conjunction before a clause is incorrect. Use *as* or *as if*. **Ramon talked *as if* he had a cold.**
lose, loose	*Lose* means "to mislay or suffer the loss of something." *Loose* means "free" or "not fastened." **That tire will *lose* air unless you patch it.** **My little brother has three *loose* teeth.**
passed, past	*Passed* is the past tense of *pass* and means "went by." *Past* is an adjective that means "of a former time." *Past* is also a noun that means "the time gone by." **We *passed* through the Florida Keys during our vacation.** **My *past* experiences have taught me to set my alarm.** **Ebenezer Scrooge is a character who relives his *past*.**
peace, piece	*Peace* means "calm or quiet." *Piece* means a "section or part of something." **Sitting still can bring a sense of *peace*.** **Here's another *piece* of the puzzle.**
principal, principle	*Principal* means "of chief or central importance" and refers to the head of a school. *Principle* is a "basic truth, standard, or rule of behavior." **Lack of customers is the *principal* reason for closing the store.** **The *principal* of our school awarded the trophy.** **One of my *principles* is to be honest with others.**

raise, rise	*Raise* means "to lift" or "to make something go up." It takes a direct object. *Rise* means "to go upward." It does not take a direct object. **The maintenance workers *raise* the flag each morning.** **The city's population is expected to *rise* steadily.**
set, sit	*Set* means "to place" and takes a direct object. *Sit* means "to occupy a seat or a place" and does not take a direct object. **He *set* the box down outside the shed.** **We *sit* in the last row of the upper balcony.**
stationary, stationery	*Stationary* means "fixed or unmoving." *Stationery* means "fine paper for writing letters." **The wheel pivots, but the seat is *stationary.*** **Rex wrote on special *stationery* imprinted with his name.**
than, then	*Than* is used to introduce the second part of a comparison. *Then* means "next in order." **Ramon is stronger *than* Mark.** **Cut the grass and *then* trim the hedges.**
their, there, they're	*Their* means "belonging to them." *There* means "in that place." *They're* is the contraction for *they are.* **All the campers returned to *their* cabins.** **I keep my card collection *there* in those folders.** **Lisa and Beth run daily; *they're* on the track team.**
to, too, two	*To* means "toward" or "in the direction of." *Too* means a "also" or "very." *Two* is the number 2. **We went *to* the mall.** **It's *too* risky riding without a helmet.** **Two amusement parks are offering reduced rates for admission.**
whose, who's	*Whose* is the possessive form of *who*. *Who's* is a contraction for *who is* or *who has.* **Whose parents will drive us to the movies?** **Who's going to the recycling center?**
your, you're	*Your* is the possessive form of *you*. *You're* is a contraction for *you are.* **What was *your* record in the fifty-yard dash?** **You're one of the winners of the essay contest.**

MLA Citation Guidelines

Forms for Source Cards and Works Cited Entries

The following examples show some basic forms for bibliographic entries of your research tools. Use these forms on the source cards for your working bibliography and in the list of works cited at the end of your paper.

Whole Books

The following models can also be used for citing reports and pamphlets.

A. One author

Blackwood, Gary. The Shakespeare Stealer. New York: Dutton Children's Books, 1998.

B. Two authors

Cummings, Pat, and Linda Cummings. Talking with Adventurers. Washington: National Geographic Society, 1998.

C. Three authors

Silverstein, Alvin, Virginia Silverstein, and Laura Silverstein Nunn. The California Condor. Brookfield: Millbrook, 1998.

D. Four or more authors

The abbreviation *et al.* means "and others." Use *et al.* instead of listing all the authors.

Brown, Richard G., et al. Algebra 1: Explorations and Applications. Evanston: McDougal, 1998.

E. No author given

Webster's Word Histories. Springfield: Merriam-Webster, 1989.

F. An editor but no single author

Silverberg, Robert, ed. The Science Fiction Hall of Fame. Garden City: Doubleday, 1970.

G. Two or three editors

Colbert, Jan, and Ann McMillan Harms, eds. Dear Dr. King: Letters from Today's Children to Dr. Martin Luther King, Jr. New York: Hyperion, 1998.

H. An author and a translator

Pressler, Mirjam. Halinka. Trans. Elizabeth D. Crawford. New York: Holt, 1998.

I. An author, a translator, and an editor

Hugo, Victor. <u>The Hunchback of Notre-Dame</u>. Trans. Walter J.
Cobb. Ed. Robin Waterfield. London: Penguin, 1996.

J. An edition other than the first

Gibaldi, Joseph. <u>MLA Handbook for Writers of Research Papers</u>.
5th ed. New York: Modern Language Association of America,
1999.

K. A book or a monograph that is part of a series

Latta, Sara L. <u>Allergies</u>. Diseases and People. Springfield: Enslow,
1998.

L. A multivolume work

If you have used only one volume of a multivolume work, cite only
that volume.

Gonen, Amiram, ed. <u>Peoples of the World: Customs and Cultures</u>.
Vol. 3. Danbury: Grolier, 1998. 10 vols.

If you have used more than one volume of a multivolume work,
cite the entire work.

Gonen, Amiram, ed. <u>Peoples of the World: Customs and Cultures</u>.
10 vols. Danbury: Grolier, 1998.

M. A volume with its own title that is part of a multivolume work with a different title

Dué, Andrea, ed. <u>The Modern World</u>. Danbury: Grolier, 1999. Vol.
6 of <u>People and the Earth: An Environmental Atlas</u>. 6 vols.

N. A republished book or a literary work available in several editions

Give the date of the original publication after the title. Then give
complete publication information, including the date, for the
edition that you have used.

Lewis, C.S. <u>The Voyage of the</u> Dawn Treader. 1952. New York:
Harper, 1994.

O. A government publication

Give the name of the government (country or state). Then give the department if applicable, followed by the agency if applicable. Next give the title, followed by the author if known. Then give the publication information. The publisher of U.S. government documents is usually the Government Printing Office, or GPO.

United States. Dept. of Health and Human Services. National Center for Health Statistics. <u>Health, United States, 1996–1997 and Injury Chartbook</u>. Washington: GPO, 1997.

Parts of Books

A. A poem, a short story, an essay, or a chapter in a collection of works by one author

Wilder, Laura Ingalls. "Whom Will You Marry?" <u>A Little House Reader: A Collection of Writings by Laura Ingalls Wilder</u>. Ed. William Anderson. New York: Harper, 1998. 130–143.

B. A poem, a short story, an essay, or a chapter in a collection of works by several authors

Angelou, Maya. "Still I Rise." <u>I, Too, Sing America: Three Centuries of African American Poetry</u>. Ed. Catherine Clinton. Boston: Houghton, 1998. 107–108.

C. A novel or a play in an anthology

Stone, Peter. <u>Titanic</u>. <u>The Best Plays of 1996–1997</u>. Ed. Otis L. Guernsey, Jr. New York: Limelight-Proscenium, 1997. 157–189.

D. An introduction, a preface, a foreword, or an afterword written by the author(s) of a work

Bradbury, Ray. Afterword. <u>Fahrenheit 451</u>. Ed. Ray Bradbury. New York: Ballantine, 1982. 167–173.

E. An introduction, a preface, a foreword, or an afterword written by someone other than the author(s) of a work

Allende, Isabel. Foreword. <u>Where Angels Glide at Dawn: New Stories from Latin America</u>. Ed. Lori M. Carlson and Cynthia L. Ventura. New York: Lippincott, 1990. ix–xii.

Magazines, Journals, Newspapers, and Encyclopedias

A. An article in a magazine, a journal, or a newspaper

Allen, Jodie. "Working Out Welfare." <u>Time</u> 29 July 1996: 53–54.

Abelson, Philip H. "Preparing Children for the Future." <u>Science</u> 13 December 1996: 1819.

Voedisch, Lynn. "Have You Done Your Homework Yet?" <u>Chicago Tribune</u> 9 October 1997, sec. 5:5.

Fintor, Lou. "Cancer Control Efforts Reach Out to 'Culturally Isolated.'" <u>Journal of the National Cancer Institute</u> 90 (1998): 1424–1427.

B. An article in an encyclopedia or other alphabetically organized reference work

Give the title of the article, the name of the reference work, and the year of the edition.

"Sioux Indians," <u>The World Book Encyclopedia</u>. 1999 ed.

C. A review

Crain, Caleb. "There but for Fortune." Rev. of <u>Hearts in Atlantis</u> by Stephen King. <u>New York Times Book Review</u> 12 Sept. 1999: 10.

Miscellaneous Print and Nonprint Sources

A. An interview you have conducted or a letter you have received

Sosa, Sammy. Letter to the author [or, Personal interview]. 20 October 1998.

B. A film

<u>Ever After.</u> Screenplay by Susannah Grant and Andy Tennant. Dir. Andy Tennant. Perf. Drew Barrymore, Anjelica Huston, and Dougray Scott. 20th Century Fox, 1998.

C. A work of art (painting, photograph, sculpture)

Escher, M.C. <u>Sky and Water I</u>. National Gallery of Art, Washington.

D. A television or a radio program

Give the episode name (if applicable) and the series or the program name. Include any information that you have about the program's writer and director. Then give the network, the local station, the city, and the date of the airing of the program.

"The Idol Maker." Corr. Vicki Mabrey. 60 Minutes II. Prod. Aaron Wertheim. CBS. WBBM, Chicago. 29 Sept. 1999.

E. A musical composition

Mendelssohn, Felix. Symphony no. 4: 4th movement.

F. A recording (compact disc, LP, or audiocassette)

If the recording is not a compact disc, include *LP* or *Audiocassette* before the manufacturer's name.

Kraftwerk. "The Robots." The Man-Machine. LP. Capitol, 1978.

Prado, Perez. "Mambo #8." Que Rico Mambo. Audiocassette. Rhino, 1989.

Moby. "Run On." Play. V2 Records, 1999.

G. A lecture, a speech, or an address

Give the name of the speaker, followed by the name of the speech or the kind of speech (*Lecture, Introduction, Address*). Then give the event, the place, and the date.

Lowry, Lois. Speech. Newbery Award Acceptance, Miami, 26 June 1994.

Electronic Publications

The number of electronic information sources is great and increasing rapidly, so please refer to the most current edition of the MLA Handbook for Writers of Research Papers *if you need more guidance. You can also refer to the page on "MLA Style" on the Modern Language Association Web site <http://www.mla.org/>.*

Portable databases (CD-ROMs, DVDs, laserdiscs, diskettes, and videocassettes)

These products contain fixed information (information that cannot be changed unless a new version is produced and released). Citing them in a research paper is similar to citing printed sources. You should include the following information:

• Name of the author (if applicable)

- Title of the part of the work used (underlined or in quotation marks)
- Title of the product or the database (underlined)
- Edition, release, or version if applicable
- Publication medium (CD-ROM, DVD, videodisc, diskette, or videocassette)
- City of publication
- Name of publisher
- Year of publication

If you cannot find some of this information, cite what is available.

Burke, James. "Yesterday, Tomorrow and You." <u>Connections</u>. Prod. BBC. Ambrose Video, 1978.

<u>Antarctica</u>. Dir. John Weiley. 1991. DVD. Slingshot, 1999.

"Boston Tea Party." <u>Encarta 98 Encyclopedia</u>. 1998 ed. CD-ROM. Redmond: Microsoft, 1998.

<u>Nerds 2.0.1: A Brief History of the Internet</u>. Prod. Oregon. 3 videocassettes. PBS Video, 1998.

Online Sources

Sources on the World Wide Web are numerous and include scholarly projects, reference databases, articles in periodicals, and professional and personal sites. Not all sites are equally reliable, and therefore material cited from the World Wide Web should be evaluated carefully. Entries for online sources in the Works Cited list should contain as much of the information listed below as is available.

- Name of the author, editor, compiler, or translator, followed by an abbreviation such as *ed., comp.,* or *trans.* if appropriate
- Title of the material accessed. Use quotation marks for poems, short stories, articles, and similar short works. Underline the title of a book.
- Publication information for any print version of the source
- Title (underlined) of the scholarly project, database, periodical, or professional or personal site. For a professional or personal site with no title, add a description such as *Home page* (neither underlined nor in quotation marks).
- Name of the editor of the scholarly project or database.

- For a journal, the volume number, issue number, or other identifying number
- Date of electronic publication or of the latest update, or date of posting
- For a work from a subscription service, list the name of the service and—if a library is the subscriber—the name of the library and the town or state where it is located.
- Range or total number of pages, paragraphs, or other sections if they are numbered
- Name of any institution or organization that sponsors or is associated with the Web site
- Date the source was accessed
- Electronic address, or URL, of the source. For a subscription service, use the URL of the service's main page (if known) or the keyword assigned by the service.

Scholarly project

Donan, Leni, and Kathleen Ferenz, eds. America Dreams Through the Decades. Feb. 1999. The Library of Congress American Memory Fellows Program. 6 Oct. 1999 <http://www.internet-catalyst.org/projects/amproject/student.html>.

Professional site

United Nations Children's Fund. 10 Oct. 1999 <http://www.unicef.org>.

Personal site

Tomarkin, Craig. Web Tour: World Series History. 6 Feb. 1998. The Baseball Guru. 10 Oct. 1999 <http://members.aol.com/thebbguru/baseball/bbws1.html>.

Book

Twain, Mark. The Adventures of Tom Sawyer. New York: Harper, 1903. Tom Sawyer Home Page. August 1993. Electronic Text Center, University of Virginia Library. 10 Oct. 1999 <http://etext.virginia.edu/railton/tomsawye/tomhompg.html>.

Article in reference database

"Aztec." Encyclopedia.com. 1999. Infonautics Corp. 10 Oct. 1999 <http://www.encyclopedia.com>.

Article in journal

Kientzler, Alesha Lynne. "Fifth- and Seventh-Grade Girls' Decisions about Participation in Physical Activity." <u>Elementary School Journal</u> 99.5 (1999): 391-414. 15 Oct. 1999 <http://www.journals.uchicago.edu/ESJ>.

Article in magazine

Warrick, Joby. "Death in the Gulf of Mexico." <u>National Wildlife</u>. June/July 1999. 11 Oct. 1999. <http://www.nwf.org/nwf/natlwild/1999/mexico.html>.

Work from a subscription service

"Glasnost." <u>Merriam-Webster Collegiate Dictionary</u>. 1996. America Online. 7 Oct. 1999. Keyword: Collegiate.

Waserman, Ed. "Calories to Burn: Energy and Chemical Reactions." <u>The Chemistry Place</u>. 1999. Peregrine Pub. 13 Oct. 1999 <http://www.chemplace.com>.

Glossary for Writers

Alliteration	the repetition of beginning sounds of words in poetry or prose; for example, the "c" sound in "creeping cat"
Allusion	a reference to a historical or literary person, place, event, or aspect of culture
Analogy	a comparison used to explain an idea or support an argument. For example, an analogy for how a government works might be a family.
Analysis	a way of thinking that involves taking apart, examining, and explaining a subject or an idea
Anecdote	a brief story told as an example to illustrate a point
Argument	speaking or writing that expresses a position or states an opinion with supporting evidence. An argument often takes into account other points of view.
Audience	one's readers or listeners
Autobiography	a biography (life story) told by the person whose life it is
Bias	a preference to lean toward one side in an argument; to be unbiased is to be neutral
Bibliography	a list of sources (articles, books, encyclopedias) in a paper or report used to document research or to recommend further study
Body	the main part of a composition, in which its ideas are developed
Brainstorming	a way of generating ideas that involves quickly listing ideas as they occur without stopping to judge them
Cause and Effect	a strategy of analysis that examines the reasons for actions or events, and the consequences or results of those actions
Characterization	the way people (characters) are portrayed by an author
Chronological	organized according to time sequence
Clarity	the quality of being clear and easy to understand

Classification	a way of organizing information by grouping or categorizing items according to some system or principle
Cliché	an overused expression, such as "quiet as a mouse"
Clustering	a brainstorming technique that involves creating an idea or topic map made up of circled groupings of related details
Coherence	connectedness; a sense that parts hold together. A paragraph has coherence when its sentences flow logically from one to the next. A composition has coherence when its paragraphs are connected logically and linked by transitional words and phrases.
Collaboration	the act of working with other people on projects or to problem solve
Comparison and Contrast	a pattern of organization in which two or more things are related on the basis of similarities and differences
Conclusion	a judgment or a decision that is reached based on evidence, experience, and logical reasoning; also, the final section of a composition that summarizes an argument or main idea, and points the reader toward action or further reflection
Connotation	the meaning of a word that carries ideas and feelings, as opposed to the word's dictionary definition (denotation)
Context	the setting or situation in which something happens; the parts of a statement that occur just before and just after a specific word and help determine its meaning
Controversy	a disagreement, often one that has attracted public interest
Criticism	an analysis (usually an essay) of something (usually a literary or artistic work) that evaluates how it does or does not succeed in communicating its meaning
Critical Thinking	what a writer *does* with information; thinking that goes beyond the facts to organize, analyze, evaluate, or draw conclusions about them

Deductive Reasoning	the process of arriving at a specific conclusion by reasoning from a general premise or statement
Denotation	the dictionary definition of a word, as opposed to the ideas and feelings the word carries (connotation)
Descriptive Writing	an account of what it is like to experience some object, scene, or person; writing that usually gives one basic impression and emphasizes sensory detail
Dialect	a form of a language (usually regional) that has a distinctive pronunciation, vocabulary, and word order
Dialogue	spoken conversation of fictional characters or actual persons; the conversation in novels, stories, plays, poems, or essays
Documentation	the identification of documents or other sources used to support the information reported in an essay or other types of analysis; usually cited in footnotes or in parentheses
Editorial	an article in a publication or a commentary on radio or television expressing an opinion about a public issue
Elaboration	the support or development of a main idea with facts, statistics, sensory details, incidents, examples, quotations, or visual representations
Evaluation	writing that purposefully judges the worth, quality, or success of something
Expository Writing	writing that explains an idea or teaches a process; also called informative writing
Expressive	characterized by expression; refers to descriptive communication of ideas that are full of meaning or feeling, often used by writers in personal writing to explore ideas
Fiction	made-up or imaginary happenings as opposed to statements of fact or nonfiction. Short stories and novels are fiction, even though they may be based on real events; essays, scientific articles, biographies, news stories are nonfiction.

Figurative Language	language that displays the imaginative and poetic use of words; writing that contains figures of speech such as simile, metaphor, and personification
Formal Language	language in which rules of grammar and vocabulary standards are carefully observed; used in textbooks, reports, and other formal communications
Freewriting	a way of exploring ideas, thoughts, or feelings that involves writing freely—without stopping or otherwise limiting the flow of ideas—for a specific length of time
Gender Free	refers to language that includes both men and women when making reference to a role or a group that consists of people of both sexes. "A medic uses his or her skills to save lives" and "Medics use their skills to save lives" are two gender-free ways of expressing the same idea.
Generalization	a statement expressing a principle or drawing a conclusion based on examples or instances
Graphic Device	a visual way of organizing information. Graphic devices include charts, graphs, outlines, clusters, and diagrams.
Idea Tree	a graphic device in which main ideas are written on "branches" and related details are noted on "twigs"
Imagery	figurative language and descriptions used to produce mental images
Inductive Reasoning	a method of thinking or organizing so that pieces of evidence lead to a conclusion or generalization
Inference	a logical guess that is made based on observed facts and one's own knowledge and experience
Informative Writing	writing that explains an idea or teaches a process; also called expository writing
Interpretation	an explanation of the meaning of any text, set of facts, object, gesture, or event. To interpret something is to try to make sense of it.
Introduction	the opening section of a composition, which presents the main idea, grabs the reader's attention, and sets the tone

Invisible Writing	writing done with a dimmed computer screen or with an empty ballpoint pen on two sheets of paper with carbon paper between them
Irony	a figure of speech in which the intended meaning is the opposite of the stated meaning—saying one thing and meaning another
Jargon	the special language and terminology used by people in the same profession or with specialized interests
Journal	a record of thoughts and impressions, mainly for personal use
Learning Log	a kind of journal used for recording and reflecting on what one has learned and for noting problems and questions
Literary Analysis	critical thinking and writing about literature that presents a personal perspective
Looping	a repetitive process for discovering ideas on a topic through freewriting, stopping to find promising ideas, then producing another freewrite on that subject, and repeating the loop several times
Media	various forms of mass communication, such as newspapers, magazines, radio, television, and the Internet; the editorial voice and influence of all of these
Memoir	an account of true events told by a narrator who witnessed or participated in the events; usually focuses on the personalities and actions of persons other than the writer
Metaphor	a figure of speech that makes a comparison without using the word *like* or *as.* "All the world's a stage" is a metaphor.
Monologue	a speech by one person without interruption by other voices. A dramatic monologue reveals the personality and experience of a person through a long speech.
Mood	the feeling about a scene or a subject created for a reader by a writer's selection of words and details. The mood of a piece of writing may be suspenseful, mysterious, peaceful, fearful, and so on.

Narrative Writing	writing that tells a story—either made up or true. Some common types of narrative writing are biographies, short stories, and novels.
Onomatopoeia	the use of words (usually in poetry) to suggest sounds; examples are "the clinking of knives and forks," and "the hissing of the fans of the losing team."
Order of Degree	a pattern of organization in which ideas, people, places, or things are presented in rank order on the basis of quantity or extent. An example is listing items in order from most important to least important.
Paraphrase	a restatement in one's own words that stays true to the ideas, tone, and general length of the original passage
Parenthetical Documentation	the placement of citations or other documentation in parentheses within the text
Peer Response	suggestions and comments on a piece of writing provided by peers or classmates
Personal Writing	writing that focuses on expressing the writer's own thoughts, experiences, and feelings
Personification	a figure of speech in which objects, events, abstract ideas, or animals are given human characteristics
Persuasive Writing	writing that is intended to convince the reader of a particular point of view or course of action
Plagiarism	the act of dishonestly presenting someone else's words or ideas as one's own
Point of View	the angle from which a story is told, such as first-, second-, or third-person point of view
Portfolio	a container (usually a folder) for notes on work in progress, drafts and revisions, finished pieces, and peer responses
Proofreading	the act of checking work to discover typographical and other errors; usually the last stage of the revising or editing process
Propaganda	any form of communication aimed at persuading an audience, often containing false or misleading information; usually refers to manipulative political material

Prose	the usual language of speech and writing, lacking the characteristics of poetry; any language that is not poetry
Sensory Details	words that express attributes of the five senses—the way something looks, sounds, smells, tastes, or feels
Sequential Order	a pattern of organization in which information is presented in the order in which it occurs, as in telling a story chronologically or describing the sequence of steps in a process
Simile	a figure of speech that uses the word *like* or *as* to make a comparison. "Trees like pencil strokes" is a simile.
Spatial Order	a pattern of organization in which details are arranged in the order that they appear in space, such as from left to right
Style	the distinctive features of a literary or artistic work that collectively characterize a particular individual, group, period, or school
Summary	a brief restatement of the main idea of a passage
Symbol	something (word, object, or action) that stands for or suggests something else. For example, a flag can stand for or symbolize a nation; a withered plant may suggest or symbolize a failing relationship.
Theme	the central idea or message of a work of literature
Thesis Statement	a statement in one or two sentences of the main idea or purpose of a piece of writing
Tone	the writer's attitude or manner of expression—detached, ironic, serious, angry, and so on
Topic Sentence	a sentence that expresses the main idea of a paragraph
Transition	a connecting word or phrase that clarifies relationships between details, sentences, or paragraphs
Tree Diagram	a graphic way of showing the relationships among ideas; particularly useful in generating ideas; also known as an idea tree or spider map
Trite Phrase	a phrase overused so much that it loses meaning and suggests a lack of imagination on the part of the user

Unity a quality of oneness. A paragraph has unity if all its sentences support the same main idea or purpose; a composition has unity if all its paragraphs support the thesis statement.

Venn Diagram a way of visually representing the relationship between two items that are distinct but that have common or overlapping elements

Voice the personality of the writer communicated indirectly by such stylistic choices as word choice and tone

Index

A

A, 127, 485
Abbreviations
   capitalization in titles, 230
   capitalization of time, 240
   periods with, 251
Abstract nouns, 37
Action verbs, 10
   complements required by, 23–24,
      95–98
   transitive and intransitive, 96
Active listening, 538–540
   evaluating content and delivery,
      540
   for information, 539
   reasons for, 538
Active reading strategies, 508–509
A.D.
   capitalization of, 240
   periods with, 240
Addresses
   commas in, 56
   periods with abbreviations in, 251
Adjective clauses, 196, 198, 205
Adjective phrases, as prepositional
   phrases, 167
Adjectives, 126–132, 137–141,
   144, 145, 148, 149
   adverbs confused with, 140–141,
      149
   adverbs formed from, 135, 632
   adverbs modifying, 134
   articles, 127
   commas between two or more,
      254
   comparatives and superlatives,
      137–139, 145, 148, 293
   demonstrative pronouns as, 131,
      148

   in description, 144–145
   for expressing feeling and adding
      detail, 126, 128, 144–145
   indefinite pronouns used as, 131
   nouns used as, 132, 148
   other parts of speech used as,
      131–133, 148
   possessive pronouns used as,
      131, 132, 148
   predicate, 28, 129–130
   pronouns used as, 131, 132, 148
   proper, 127
Adverb clauses, 196–197
   function of, 205
Adverb phrases, as prepositional
   phrases, 167
Adverbs, 134–136, 137–139,
   140–141, 144–145, 148, 149
   adjectives confused with,
      140–141, 149
   adverbs modifying, 134
   comparatives and superlatives,
      137–139, 145, 148, 293
   comparisons, irregular, 138
   comparisons, regular, 137–138
   forming from adjectives, 135, 632
   intensifiers, 134–135
   -ly ending of, 135, 632
   position of, 134
   prepositions used as, 153
Advertisements, 532–533, 558,
   559–560
Agreement. See Pronoun-antecedent
   agreement; Subject-verb
   agreement.
Airplane names, capitalization of,
   238
Alphabetic order, for works cited list,
   485
A.M.

RESOURCES

RESOURCES

M

RESOURCES

RESOURCES

Person
  personal pronouns, 58–59,
    73–74, 89
  pronoun-antecedent agreement in,
    73–74, 89
Personal names
  capitalization of, 36, 51, 230,
    232, 246
  commas with, 254
Personal narrative, writing workshop
    for, 414–421
Personal pronouns, 58–60, 88
  agreement in number with
    indefinite pronouns, 76–78
  in case, number, and person, 58,
    88
  nominative case, 58–59, 88
  objective case, 58–59, 88
  possessive case, 58–59, 88
Personification, 409
Persuasive writing, 545
  paragraphs in, 347
Phrases, 176–177. *See also*
    Adjective phrases, as
    prepositional phrases; Adverb
    phrases, as prepositional
    phrases; Prepositional phrases;
    Verb phrases
  appositive, 255
  commas with, 254–255
  for description, 176
  gerund, 176
  infinitive, 176
  interrupters, 254
  participial, 176
  placement of, 392–393
  rearranging for sentence variety,
    392–393
  subject-verb agreement when
    inserting between subject and
    verb, 81, 220, 226
  unnecessary, 390
  verbal, 176
Place names
  capitalization of, 237, 246
  commas in, 256
Plagiarism, avoiding, 481, 513

Planets, capitalization of, 237
Planning
  drafting from a plan, 315
  of an interview, 541–542
  of a multimedia presentation, 562
  of a research report, 477, 482
  of a speech, 545–546
Plays
  capitalization of titles, 234
  italics for titles, 268
Plural nouns, 39, 42, 44, 45
  subject-verb agreement for, 208,
    211, 216–217
Plural pronouns
  indefinite, 76–78
  personal, 58–59
  pronoun-antecedent agreement
    with, 73, 76–78, 89
  reflexive and intensive, 68–69
Plurals. *See also* Plural nouns; Plural
    pronouns
  apostrophes for forming, 267
P.M.
  capitalization of, 240
  periods with, 251
Poetry
  capitalization of first words of
    lines, 233, 246–247
  capitalization of titles, 234
  italics for titles of epics, 268
  punctuation in, 470
  quotation marks for titles, 268
  writing workshop for, 467–472
Poetry interpretation, writing
    workshop for, 430–437
Portfolios, 321
  presentation portfolio, 321
  working portfolio. *See* Working
    portfolio
Possessive case. *See also*
    Possessive nouns; Possessive
    pronouns
  apostrophes for forming, 42–43,
    266, 629
Possessive nouns, 42–44, 51, 266,
    629
  apostrophes for forming, 42–43,
    266

RESOURCES

RESOURCES

RESOURCES

RESOURCES

Acknowledgments

For Literature and Text

Atheneum Books for Young Readers: Excerpt from "Eleanor Roosevelt," from *Great Lives: Human Rights* by William Jay Jacobs. Copyright © 1990 by William Jay Jacobs. Reprinted by permission of Atheneum Books for Young Readers, an imprint of Simon & Schuster, Inc.

Susan Bergholz Literary Services: Excerpt from *The House on Mango Street* by Sandra Cisneros. Copyright © 1984 by Sandra Cisneros. Published by Vintage Books, a division of Random House, Inc., and in hardcover by Alfred A. Knopf. Reprinted by permission of Susan Bergholz Literary Services, New York. All rights reserved.

Brandt & Brandt Literary Agents and A. M. Heath: "The Serial Garden," from *Armitage, Armitage, Fly Away Home* by Joan Aiken. Copyright © 1966 by Macmillan & Co., Ltd. Copyright © 1969 by Joan Aiken Enterprises, Ltd. Copyright renewed © 1994 by Joan Aiken Enterprises, Ltd. Reprinted by permission of Brandt & Brandt Literary Agents, Inc., and A. M. Heath & Co., Ltd., on behalf of the author.

Candlewick Press: "What Do Fish Have to Do with Anything?" from *What Do Fish Have to Do with Anything?, and Other Stories* by Avi. Copyright © 1997 by Avi Wortis. Reprinted by permission of Candlewick Press, Cambridge, MA.

Britney L. Chilcote: "Fallen Ballerina" by Britney L. Chilcote. First printed in *Statement, Journal of the Colorado Language Arts Society,* Vol. 33, No. 2, Spring 1997. Reprinted by permission of Britney L. Chilcote.

Cobblestone Publishing: Excerpt from "Ask Uly" by Lawrence Krumenaker, from *Odyssey*'s November 1992 issue, *Handshakes in Space.* Copyright © 1992 by Cobblestone Publishing Company, 30 Grove Street, Suite C, Peterborough, NH 03458. Reprinted by permission of the publisher.

Farrar, Straus & Giroux: Excerpt from "Thank You, M'am," from *The Langston Hughes Reader,* by Langston Hughes. Copyright © 1958 by Langston Hughes, renewed 1986 by George Houston Bass. Reprinted by permission of Farrar, Straus & Giroux, Inc.

Farrar, Straus & Giroux and David Higham Associates: Excerpt from *Boy: Tales of Childhood* by Roald Dahl. Copyright © 1984 by Roald Dahl. Reprinted by permission of Farrar, Straus & Giroux, Inc., and David Higham Associates.

Ian Frazier: Excerpt from "It's Hard to Eat Just One" by Ian Frazier, from *Outside,* April 1997. Copyright © 1997 by Ian Frazier. Used by permission of the author.

Golden Books Family Entertainment: Excerpt from *Weather* by Paul E. Lehr, R. Wil Burnett, and Herbert S. Zim. Copyright © 1987 by Western Publishing Company, Inc. Reprinted by permission of Golden Books Family Entertainment.

Grove/Atlantic: Excerpt from "The Turtle," from *Dream Work* by Mary Oliver. Copyright © 1986 by Mary Oliver. Reprinted with permission of Grove/Atlantic, Inc.

Table of Contents

Illustrations by Todd Graveline

6, 8, 16, 17 *top right,* 27, 32, 33 *top, center,* 38 *center left,* 39, 43, 44, 52, 55, 71, 76–77, 88, 89, 105, 113, 116, 123, 130, 143, 148, 152, 156 *top,* 167, 177, 182, 183, 189, 204, 205, 227, 235, 236, 246, 247, 272 *bottom right,* 274, 276, 284, 316, 322, 323, 328 *top,* 330 *top left,* 331, 333, 335, 336, 337, 342, 349 *top, center,* 360, 361, 372, 384 *bottom,* 389, 391, 392, 394, 396, 401, 403, 405 *top,* 406, 410, 411, 420, 421, 520 *center right,* 521, 528, 532, 533, 534, 535, 550 *top left, top right,* 551, 560 *top,* 565, 569 *center right,* 574.

Art Credits

COVER *top right* Copyright © David O'Connor/Graphistock; *center* Tabletop photo by Sharon Hoogstraten; *bottom left* Copyright © 1997 Stephen Simpson/FPG International.

CHAPTER 1 **2–3** Copyright © William Swartz/Index Stock Imagery/PNI; **4** Copyright © Reporters/Verpoorten/Leo de Wys, Inc.; **6** Photo by Sharon Hoogstraten; **7** Richard A. Cooke/Corbis; **8** Copyright © 1999 Harry Walker/AlaskaStock.com; **15** Corbis; **17** *bottom, FoxTrot* copyright © 1988 Bill Amend. Reprinted with permission of Universal Press Syndicate. All rights reserved; **25** Copyright © Pacific Pictures/John Penisten/Liaison Agency; **28** Photo by Sharon Hoogstraten; **29** Copyright © SuperStock.

CHAPTER 2 **34** Illustration by John Roman; **36** Copyright © Art Wolfe/AllStock/PNI; **38** *bottom right, Farcus®* is reprinted with permission from LaughingStock Licensing Inc., Ottawa, Canada. All rights reserved; **40** American Jewish Joint Distribution Committee Photo Archives; **41** The Purcell Team/Corbis; **48** Copyright © David Burnett/Contact/Camp; **50** *top* Copyright © Rob Boudreau/Tony Stone Images; **50–51** Illustration by John Roman; **51** *bottom right* Copyright © Donovan Reese/Tony Stone Images.

CHAPTER 3 **56** Copyright © Photofest; **59** Copyright © Paul Chesley/NGS Image Collection; **60** Copyright © Michael Melford, Inc./The Image Bank/PNI; **61** Copyright © National Museum of Natural History, Smithsonian Institution; **63** Copyright © Owen Franken/Stock Boston/PNI; **66** Copyright © Victor H. Mair; **69** Corbis; **72** Roman Soumar/Corbis; **74** Corbis-Bettmann; **78** AP/Wide World Photos; **79, 80** Copyright © 1999 PhotoDisc, Inc.; **83** *top* Corbis.

CHAPTER 4 **90, 93, 99** Copyright © Photofest; **101** AP/Wide World Photos; **108** Copyright © Photofest; **111, 112** Copyright © Photofest; **118** Photos by Sharon Hoogstraten; **120** Copyright © Time-Life Films/The Museum of Modern Art/Film Stills Archive.

CHAPTER 5 **124** *left, center* Corbis-Bettmann; *top right* Copyright © George Hall/Check Six/PNI; **126, 131** Copyright © 1999 PhotoDisc, Inc.; **139** *left* David G. Houser/Corbis; *center* Galen Rowell/Corbis; *right* Lowell Georgia/Corbis.

CHAPTER 6 **150** Copyright © Dr. Morley Read/Science Photo Library/Photo Researchers, Inc.; **153** Corbis; **154** The Granger Collection, New York; **156** *bottom* Copyright © 1994 Kim Taylor/PNI; **157** Copyright © 1999 PhotoDisc, Inc.; **158** *left* Copyright © K. G. Vock/OKAPIA 1989/Photo Researchers, Inc.; *right* Copyright © Andrew Syred/Science Photo Library/Photo Researchers, Inc.; **161** Copyright © 1983 FarWorks, Inc. All rights reserved. Reprinted with permission; **162** *back-*

RESOURCES

ground Photo by Sharon Hoogstraten; **163** Copyright © Des & Jen Bartlett/NGS Image Collection; **164** Copyright © Mervyn Rees/Tony Stone Images.

CHAPTER 7   168 Copyright © 1996 Robert Allison/Contact Press Images; **170** W. Perry Conway/Corbis; **171, 178, 179** *background* Photo by Sharon Hoogstraten; **179** *foreground* Copyright © Norman Myers/Bruce Coleman, Inc.; **180** Copyright © 1992 FarWorks, Inc. All rights reserved. Reprinted with permission.

CHAPTER 8   184 *background* Copyright © D. Young-Wolff/PhotoEdit; **186** Copyright © Myrleen Ferguson/PhotoEdit; **188** Copyright © 1999 Vickie Lewis. All rights reserved; **194** Copyright © Mary Kate Denny/PhotoEdit/PNI; **195** Copyright © PhotoDisc, Inc.; **197** Copyright © Charles Gupton/Stock Boston/PNI; **200** *background* Photo by Sharon Hoogstraten; *foreground* UPI/Bettmann.

CHAPTER 9   206 Courtesy of Boston Youth Fund; **216** *Model for East Building Mobile* (1972), Alexander Calder. Painted aluminum and steel wire, .289 x .692 (11 3/8 x 27 1/4). National Gallery of Art, Washington, D.C. Gift of the Collectors Committee; **218** Photo by Dorothea Lange. Courtesy of the Library of Congress; **222** Courtesy of The Historical Scenic Collection, School of Theatre and Dance, Northern Illinois University, DeKalb, Illinois, Alexander Adducci, curator; **224** Copyright © 1999 PhotoDisc, Inc.

CHAPTER 10   228 *background* David Lees/Corbis; *foreground* Copyright © 1999 PhotoDisc, Inc.; **231** The Granger Collection, New York; **233** Detail of *Baseball Scene of Batter, Catcher, and Umpire* (1915), Joseph Christian Leyendecker. Photo courtesy of the Archives of the American Illustrators Gallery, New York. Copyright © 1995 ARTShows and Products of Holderness 03245; **237** Copyright © 1999 PhotoDisc, Inc.; **242–243** *background* Copyright © Sovfoto/Eastfoto/PNI; **242** *foreground*, **244** *background, foreground* Copyright © 1999 PhotoDisc, Inc.

CHAPTER 11   248 *foreground* Photo by Sharon Hoogstraten; **265** Mark Gibson/Corbis; **269** Barnes Foundation, Merion, Pennsylvania/SuperStock; **270** *background* Photo by Sharon Hoogstraten; **271** Copyright © 1999 PhotoDisc, Inc.; **272** *top* Corbis.

CHAPTER 12   306–307 Copyright © Daryl Solomon/Photonica; **308** Copyright © Ken Fisher/Tony Stone Images; **309** Copyright © Bill Bachmann/PhotoNetwork/PNI; **310** Copyright © 1997 Lisa Rose/Globe Photos, Inc.; **314** *Calvin and Hobbes* copyright © 1989 Watterson. Dist. by Universal Press Syndicate. Reprinted with permission. All rights reserved; **315** Eliot Holtzman Photography; **320** *center* Copyright © Richard Shock/Tony Stone Images, Inc.; *bottom* Copyright © William Hart/PhotoEdit.

CHAPTER 13   324 Copyright © 1999 PhotoDisc, Inc.; **325** *background* Photo by Sharon Hoogstraten; *right* Copyright © Musée du Louvre, Paris/SuperStock; *frame* Copyright © Image Farm; **326** Copyright © 1998 James Frank/PNI; **328** *bottom* Copyright © Dick Young/Unicorn Stock Photos; **330** *bottom*, *Peanuts* reprinted by permission of United Feature Syndicate, Inc.

CHAPTER 14   338 Copyright © 1999 PhotoDisc, Inc.; **339** Craig Lovell/Corbis; **341** The Granger Collection, New York; **345** Copyright © 1994 Lawrence Migdale/PNI; **347** Copyright © Jim Sugar Photography/Corbis; **348** *Calvin and Hobbes* copyright © 1986 Watterson. Dist. by Universal Press Syndicate. Reprinted with permission. All rights reserved.

Acknowledgments   **685**

CHAPTER 15   **350** *top left* Copyright © Ronnie Kaufman/The Stock Market; *top right* Copyright © Paul Cherfils/Tony Stone Images; *bottom left* Copyright © Chris Shinn/Tony Stone Images; *bottom right* Copyright © Christopher Bissell/Tony Stone Images; **351** *background* Copyright © 1999 Gregg Mancuso/PNI; *foreground* Illustration by Todd Graveline; **352** *Calvin and Hobbes* copyright © 1991 Watterson. Dist. by Universal Press Syndicate. Reprinted with permission. All rights reserved; **355** Copyright © 1998 First Light/Zephyr Images; **357** Photo by Arthur Rothstein. Courtesy of the Library of Congress; **359** *left* Copyright © Finley Holiday Film; *right* Corbis.

CHAPTER 16   **362** Copyright © 1999 PhotoDisc, Inc.; **363** Photo by Sharon Hoogstraten; **365** Historical Picture Archive/Corbis; **367** Christel Gerstenberg/Corbis; **369** Corbis; **370** Illustration by the studio of Wood Ronsaville Harlin, Inc.

CHAPTER 17   **374** Copyright © 1999 PhotoDisc, Inc.; **375** *background* Robert Holmes/Corbis; *foreground* Illustration by Todd Graveline; **376** *FoxTrot* copyright © 1991 Bill Amend. Reprinted with permission of Universal Press Syndicate. All rights reserved; **377** Copyright © Will & Deni McIntyre/Tony Stone Images; **379** Paul A. Souders/Corbis; **384** *center* Copyright © 1999 Johnny Johnson/AlaskaStock.com.

CHAPTER 18   **386** *background* Copyright © 1999 PhotoDisc, Inc.; *foreground* Copyright © Simon Battensby/Tony Stone Images; **387** *background* Copyright © A. Bolesta/H. Armstrong Roberts; *foreground* Illustration by Todd Graveline; **388** *Peanuts* reprinted by permission of United Feature Syndicate, Inc.; **390** Copyright © National Air and Space Museum, Smithsonian Institution, Washington, D.C.

CHAPTER 19   **398** Corbis; **399** *bottom* Copyright © 1999 PhotoDisc, Inc.; *top* Photo by Sharon Hoogstraten; **400** Copyright © Daniel Heuclin-Bios/Peter Arnold, Inc.; **405** *bottom* Copyright © Jim Cammack/Black Star/PNI; **407** Copyright © 1999 PhotoDisc, Inc.; **408** *Bizarro* copyright © 1994 by Dan Piraro. Reprinted with permission of Universal Press Syndicate. All rights reserved.

CHAPTER 20   **412–413** Tecmap Corporation/Corbis; **419** Photos by Sharon Hoogstraten.

CHAPTER 21   **427** Photos by Sharon Hoogstraten.

CHAPTER 22   **435** Photos by Sharon Hoogstraten.

CHAPTER 23   **443** Photos by Sharon Hoogstraten.

CHAPTER 24   **451** Photos by Sharon Hoogstraten.

CHAPTER 25   **459** Photos by Sharon Hoogstraten; **460** *Calvin and Hobbes* copyright © 1993 Watterson. Dist. by Universal Press Syndicate. Reprinted with permission. All rights reserved.

CHAPTER 26   **471** Photo by Sharon Hoogstraten.

CHAPTER 27   **487** *background* Corbis; *foreground* Photo by Sharon Hoogstraten.

CHAPTER 28 **490–491** Copyright © Doug Armand/Tony Stone Images; **492** Copyright © 1997 Georg Gerster/Comstock, Inc.; **493** *right* Illustration Copyright © 1999 by Gary Overacre; **496** *bottom* Copyright © 1999 PhotoDisc, Inc.; **498** Photo by Sharon Hoogstraten; **504** Copyright © The New Yorker Collection 1993 Peter Steiner from cartoonbank.com. All rights reserved; **505** *top* Copyright © 1999 PhotoDisc, Inc.

CHAPTER 29 **506** Copyright © Bob Daemmrich/Stock Boston/PNI; **507, 520** *top center* Copyright © 1999 PhotoDisc, Inc.

CHAPTER 30 **522** Copyright © 1999 PhotoDisc, Inc.; **523** *background* Illustration by Todd Graveline; *foreground* Copyright © Bob Daemmrich/Stock Boston/PNI; **525** Illustration by Siena Artworks/London. Copyright © 1994 Michael Friedman Publishing Group; **529** Copyright © Rhoda Sidney/Stock Boston/PNI; **530** *bottom* Creators Syndicate, Inc. Copyright © 1999 Mell Lazarus; **532** *top* Photo by Sharon Hoogstraten.

CHAPTER 31 **536** Corbis; **537** Copyright © Andrew Errington/Tony Stone Images; **539** Copyright © 1999 PhotoDisc, Inc.; **541** Copyright © Allen Landau/Industry; **543** Copyright © H. Armstrong Roberts; **546, 547** Photos by Sharon Hoogstraten; **548** Photography by Gordon Lewis; **550** *bottom right* Photo by Sharon Hoogstraten.

CHAPTER 32 **552** Copyright © 1999 PhotoDisc, Inc.; **553** *background* Copyright © Andrea Pistolesi/The Image Bank/PNI; **554** *bottom left inset* Ed Eckstein/Corbis; *bottom right* Copyright © 1993 Steve Fenn/Capital Cities/ABC, Inc.; **555** *top left* Courtesy of Online NewsHour, MacNeil/Lehrer Productions; *bottom* Copyright © 1999 PhotoDisc, Inc.; **556** Copyright © 1999 Time Inc. Reprinted by permission. Photo courtesy of AP/Wide World Photos; **557** Copyright © Bob Daemmrich/Stock Boston/PNI; **558** Copyright © Stockbyte; **559** Copyright © 1999 PhotoDisc, Inc.; *inset* Copyright © Jim Whitmer; **560** *bottom background* Photo by Sharon Hoogstraten; *bottom foreground* Copyright © Frank Orel/Tony Stone Images; **563** *top left* Copyright © 1998 Anchorage Museum/AlaskaStock.com; *center right* F. H. Nowell/Corbis; **564** *left* Copyright © Adamsmith/FPG International/PNI; *right* Copyright © Rhoda Sidney/Stock Boston/PNI; **565** *FoxTrot* copyright © 1988 Bill Amend. Reprinted with permission of Universal Press Syndicate. All rights reserved.

CHAPTER 33 **566** Copyright © 1999 PhotoDisc., Inc.; **567** *background,* **568** Photos by Sharon Hoogstraten; **569** *bottom, FoxTrot* copyright © 1992 Bill Amend. Reprinted with permission of Universal Press Syndicate. All rights reserved; **578** Photo by Sharon Hoogstraten.

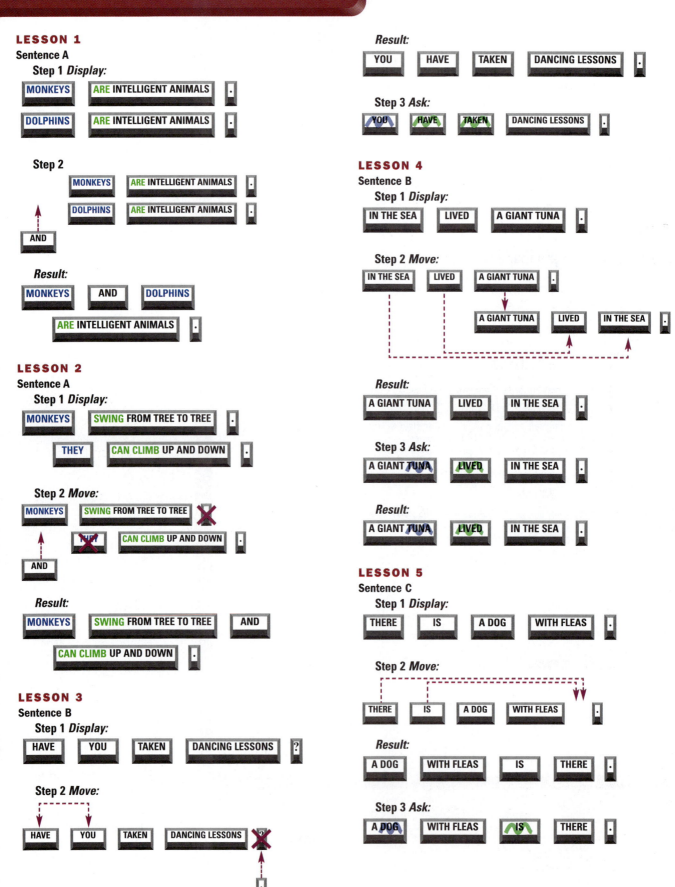

LESSON 1
Sentence A
Step 1 *Display:*

| MONKEYS | ARE INTELLIGENT ANIMALS | . |

| DOLPHINS | ARE INTELLIGENT ANIMALS | . |

Step 2

| MONKEYS | ARE INTELLIGENT ANIMALS | . |
| DOLPHINS | ARE INTELLIGENT ANIMALS | . |

AND

Result:

| MONKEYS | AND | DOLPHINS |

| ARE INTELLIGENT ANIMALS | . |

LESSON 2
Sentence A
Step 1 *Display:*

| MONKEYS | SWING FROM TREE TO TREE | . |

| THEY | CAN CLIMB UP AND DOWN | . |

Step 2 *Move:*

| MONKEYS | SWING FROM TREE TO TREE | ✗ |

| ~~THEY~~ | CAN CLIMB UP AND DOWN | . |

AND

Result:

| MONKEYS | SWING FROM TREE TO TREE | AND |

| CAN CLIMB UP AND DOWN | . |

LESSON 3
Sentence B
Step 1 *Display:*

| HAVE | YOU | TAKEN | DANCING LESSONS | ? |

Step 2 *Move:*

| HAVE | YOU | TAKEN | DANCING LESSONS | ✗ |

.

Result:

| YOU | HAVE | TAKEN | DANCING LESSONS | . |

Step 3 *Ask:*

| YOU | HAVE | TAKEN | DANCING LESSONS | . |

LESSON 4
Sentence B
Step 1 *Display:*

| IN THE SEA | LIVED | A GIANT TUNA | . |

Step 2 *Move:*

| IN THE SEA | LIVED | A GIANT TUNA | . |

| A GIANT TUNA | LIVED | IN THE SEA | . |

Result:

| A GIANT TUNA | LIVED | IN THE SEA | . |

Step 3 *Ask:*

| A GIANT TUNA | LIVED | IN THE SEA | . |

Result:

| A GIANT TUNA | LIVED | IN THE SEA | . |

LESSON 5
Sentence C
Step 1 *Display:*

| THERE | IS | A DOG | WITH FLEAS | . |

Step 2 *Move:*

| THERE | IS | A DOG | WITH FLEAS | . |

Result:

| A DOG | WITH FLEAS | IS | THERE | . |

Step 3 *Ask:*

| A DOG | WITH FLEAS | IS | THERE | . |

GRAMMAR TILES

LESSON 6
Sentence D
Step 1 Display:

MUSIC | IS | THE HOBBY FOR HIM | .

Step 2 Move:

MUSIC | IS | THE HOBBY FOR HIM ✕ | .

EASY FOR HIM

Result:

MUSIC | IS | EASY FOR HIM | .

Step 3 Ask:

MUSIC | IS | THE HOBBY FOR HIM | .

(PREDICATE ADJECTIVE) | VERY ENJOYABLE

(PREDICATE NOUN) | AN ART OF GREAT SKILL

(PREDICATE ADJECTIVE) | VERY SOOTHING

(PREDICATE ADJECTIVE) | INTERESTING

(PREDICATE NOUN) | A WONDER

LESSON 7
Sentence E
Step 1 Display:

WHO

SAW | THE MAN | ?

WHOM

Step 2 Ask:

WHO

SAW | THE MAN | ?

WHOM ✕

Result:

WHO | SAW | THE MAN | ?

Step 3 Move:

WHO | SAW ✕ | THE MAN | ?

WHOM | DID | SEE

Result:

WHO

DID | THE MAN | SEE | ?

WHOM

Step 4 Move:

WHO ✕

DID | THE MAN | SEE | ?

WHOM

Result:

WHOM | DID | THE MAN | SEE | ?

Step 5 Move:

WHO

DID | THE MAN | SEE | ?

WHOM

Result:

WHO

THE MAN | DID | SEE | ?

WHOM

Step 6 Ask:

WHO ✕

THE MAN | DID | SEE | ?

WHOM

Result:

THE MAN | DID | SEE | WHOM | ?

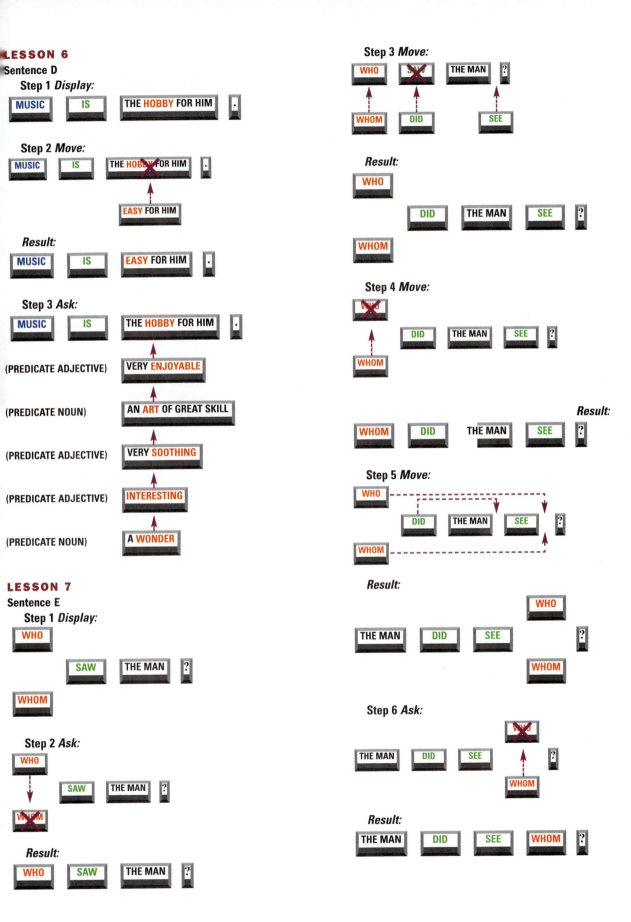

LESSON 8

Sentence F

Step 1 *Display:*

PARKED

HAD PARKED

WAS PARKING

IS PARKING

Step 2 *Ask:*

A MAN | PARKS | THE CAR | .

Step 3 *Move:*

A MAN | ~~PARKS~~ | THE CAR | .

IS PARKING

Result:

A MAN | IS PARKING | THE CAR | .

Step 4 *Ask:*

A MAN | ~~IS PARKING~~ | ~~THE CAR~~ | .

IN THE DRIVEWAY

Result:

A MAN | IN THE DRIVEWAY | .

Step 5 *Move:*

A MAN | IN THE DRIVEWAY | .

PARKED

Result:

A MAN | PARKED | IN THE DRIVEWAY | .

Step 6 *Move:*

A MAN | ~~PARKED~~ | ~~IN THE DRIVEWAY~~ | .

WHEN | THE GIRL SAW HIM

Result:

A MAN | WHEN | THE GIRL SAW HIM | .

Step 7 *Add:*

A MAN | WHEN | THE GIRL SAW HIM | .

WAS PARKING

Result:

A MAN | WAS PARKING | WHEN | THE GIRL SAW HIM | .

Step 8 *Move:*

A MAN | WAS PARKING | ~~WHEN~~ | THE GIRL SAW HIM | .

BEFORE

Result:

A MAN | BEFORE | THE GIRL SAW HIM | .

Step 9 *Move:*

A MAN | BEFORE | THE GIRL SAW HIM | .

HAD PARKED

Result:

A MAN | HAD PARKED | BEFORE | THE GIRL SAW HIM | .

LESSON 9

Sentence G

Step 1 *Display:*

CHRISTY | WROTE A STORY | AT SCHOOL | .

Step 2 Ask:

CHRISTY | WROTE A STORY | AT SCHOOL | .

Step 3 *Move:*

CHRISTY | ~~WROTE A STORY~~ | AT SCHOOL | .

USED THE COMPUTER

Result:

CHRISTY | USED THE COMPUTER | AT SCHOOL | .

Step 4 *Ask:*

CHRISTY | USED THE COMPUTER | AT SCHOOL | .

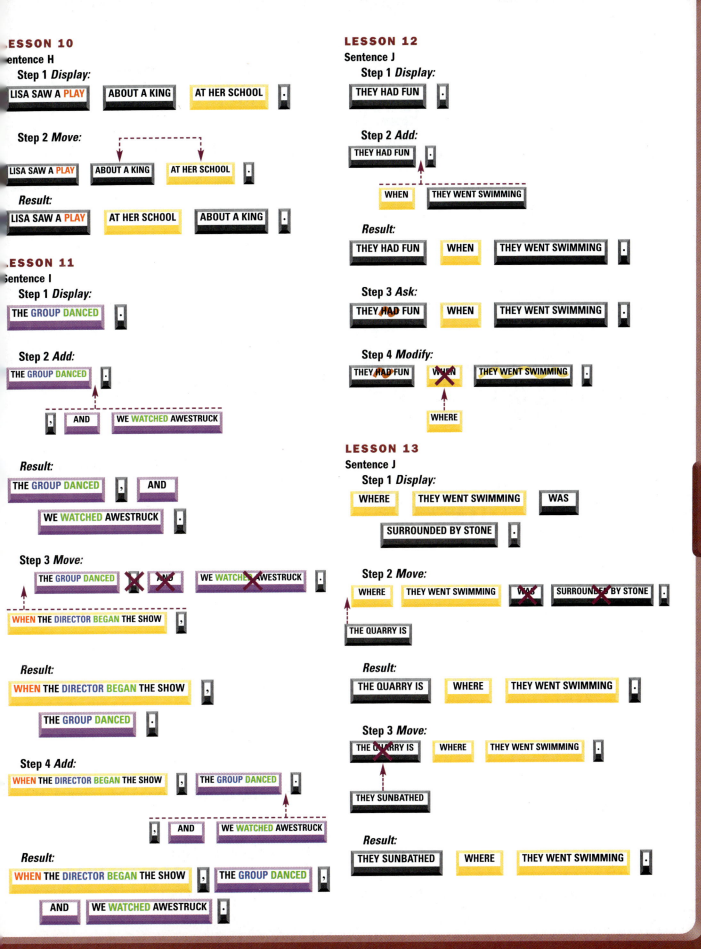

LESSON 10
Sentence H
Step 1 *Display:*

LISA SAW A PLAY   ABOUT A KING   AT HER SCHOOL   .

Step 2 *Move:*

LISA SAW A PLAY   ABOUT A KING   AT HER SCHOOL   .

Result:

LISA SAW A PLAY   AT HER SCHOOL   ABOUT A KING   .

LESSON 11
Sentence I
Step 1 *Display:*

THE GROUP DANCED   .

Step 2 *Add:*

THE GROUP DANCED   .

,   AND   WE WATCHED AWESTRUCK

Result:

THE GROUP DANCED   ,   AND

WE WATCHED AWESTRUCK   .

Step 3 *Move:*

THE GROUP DANCED   ✗   AND   WE WATCHED AWESTRUCK   .

WHEN THE DIRECTOR BEGAN THE SHOW   ,

Result:

WHEN THE DIRECTOR BEGAN THE SHOW   ,

THE GROUP DANCED   .

Step 4 *Add:*

WHEN THE DIRECTOR BEGAN THE SHOW   .   THE GROUP DANCED   .

,   AND   WE WATCHED AWESTRUCK

Result:

WHEN THE DIRECTOR BEGAN THE SHOW   ,   THE GROUP DANCED   ,

AND   WE WATCHED AWESTRUCK   .

LESSON 12
Sentence J
Step 1 *Display:*

THEY HAD FUN   .

Step 2 *Add:*

THEY HAD FUN   .

WHEN   THEY WENT SWIMMING

Result:

THEY HAD FUN   WHEN   THEY WENT SWIMMING   .

Step 3 *Ask:*

THEY HAD FUN   WHEN   THEY WENT SWIMMING   .

Step 4 *Modify:*

THEY HAD FUN   ✗WHEN   THEY WENT SWIMMING   .

WHERE

LESSON 13
Sentence J
Step 1 *Display:*

WHERE   THEY WENT SWIMMING   WAS

SURROUNDED BY STONE   .

Step 2 *Move:*

WHERE   THEY WENT SWIMMING   ✗WAS   ✗SURROUNDED BY STONE   .

THE QUARRY IS

Result:

THE QUARRY IS   WHERE   THEY WENT SWIMMING   .

Step 3 *Move:*

THE ✗QUARRY IS   WHERE   THEY WENT SWIMMING   .

THEY SUNBATHED

Result:

THEY SUNBATHED   WHERE   THEY WENT SWIMMING   .

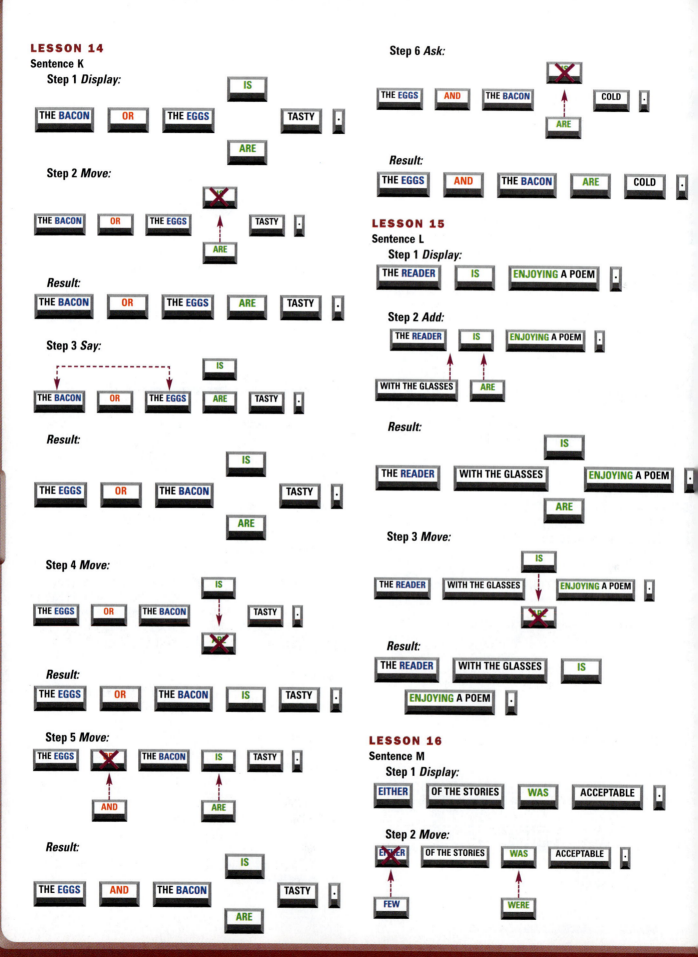

LESSON 14

Sentence K

Step 1 *Display:*

IS

THE BACON   OR   THE EGGS   TASTY .

ARE

Step 2 *Move:*

~~IS~~

THE BACON   OR   THE EGGS   TASTY .

ARE

Result:

THE BACON   OR   THE EGGS   ARE   TASTY .

Step 3 *Say:*

IS

THE BACON   OR   THE EGGS   ARE   TASTY .

Result:

IS

THE EGGS   OR   THE BACON   TASTY .

ARE

Step 4 *Move:*

IS

THE EGGS   OR   THE BACON   TASTY .

~~ARE~~

Result:

THE EGGS   OR   THE BACON   IS   TASTY .

Step 5 *Move:*

THE EGGS   ~~OR~~   THE BACON   IS   TASTY .

AND   ARE

Result:

IS

THE EGGS   AND   THE BACON   TASTY .

ARE

Step 6 *Ask:*

~~IS~~

THE EGGS   AND   THE BACON   COLD .

ARE

Result:

THE EGGS   AND   THE BACON   ARE   COLD .

LESSON 15

Sentence L

Step 1 *Display:*

THE READER   IS   ENJOYING A POEM .

Step 2 *Add:*

THE READER   IS   ENJOYING A POEM .

WITH THE GLASSES   ARE

Result:

IS

THE READER   WITH THE GLASSES   ENJOYING A POEM .

ARE

Step 3 *Move:*

IS

THE READER   WITH THE GLASSES   ENJOYING A POEM .

~~ARE~~

Result:

THE READER   WITH THE GLASSES   IS

ENJOYING A POEM .

LESSON 16

Sentence M

Step 1 *Display:*

EITHER   OF THE STORIES   WAS   ACCEPTABLE .

Step 2 *Move:*

~~EITHER~~   OF THE STORIES   WAS   ACCEPTABLE .

FEW   WERE

Result:

WAS

FEW | OF THE STORIES | ACCEPTABLE | .

WERE

Step 3 Move:

~~WAS~~

FEW | OF THE STORIES | ACCEPTABLE | .

WERE

Result:

FEW | OF THE STORIES | WERE | ACCEPTABLE | .

Step 4 Move:

WAS

~~FEW~~ | OF THE STORIES | WERE | ACCEPTABLE | .

SOME

Result:

WAS

SOME | OF THE STORIES | ACCEPTABLE | .

WERE

Step 5 Move:

~~WAS~~

SOME | OF THE STORIES | ACCEPTABLE | .

WERE

Result:

SOME | OF THE STORIES | WERE | ACCEPTABLE | .

Step 6 Move:

WAS

SOME | ~~OF THE STORIES~~ | WERE | ACCEPTABLE | .

OF THE STORY

Result:

WAS

SOME | OF THE STORY | ACCEPTABLE | .

WERE

Step 7 Move:

WAS

SOME | OF THE STORY | ACCEPTABLE | .

~~WERE~~

Result:

SOME | OF THE STORY | WAS | ACCEPTABLE | .

LESSON 17
Sentence N

Step 1 Display:

OLIVER PAINTS PICTURES | . | HE FRAMES THEM TOO | .

Step 2 Move:

OLIVER PAINTS PICTURES | ~~.~~ | HE FRAMES THEM TOO | .

, | AND

Result:

OLIVER PAINTS PICTURES | , | AND | HE FRAMES THEM TOO | .

Step 3 Display:

OLIVER PAINTS PICTURES | . | HE DOESN'T SELL MANY | .

Step 4 Move:

OLIVER PAINTS PICTURES | ~~.~~ | HE DOESN'T SELL MANY | .

, | BUT

Result:

OLIVER PAINTS PICTURES | , | BUT

HE DOESN'T SELL MANY | .

GRAMMAR TILES

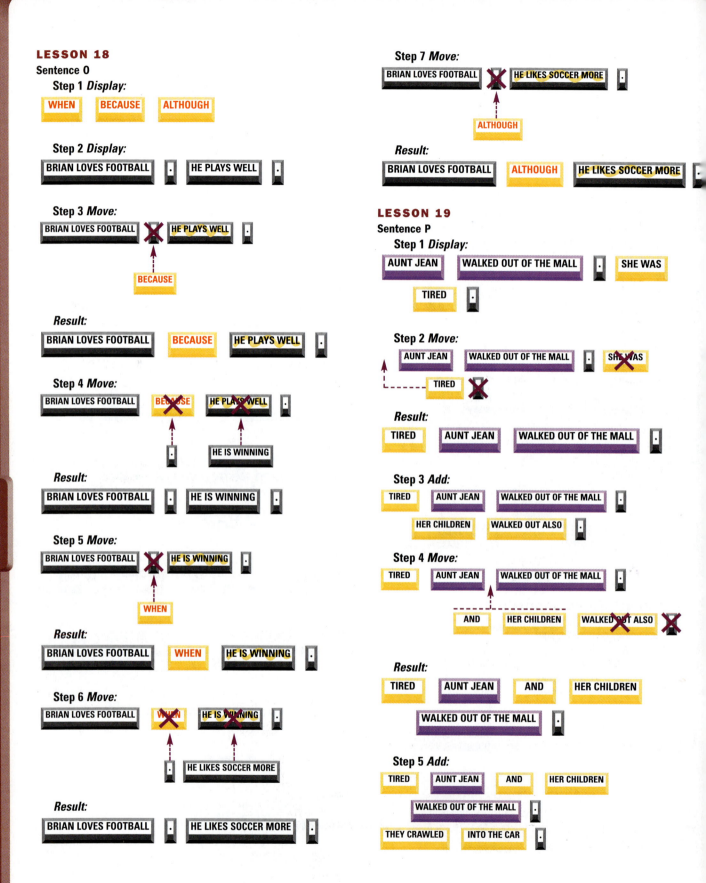

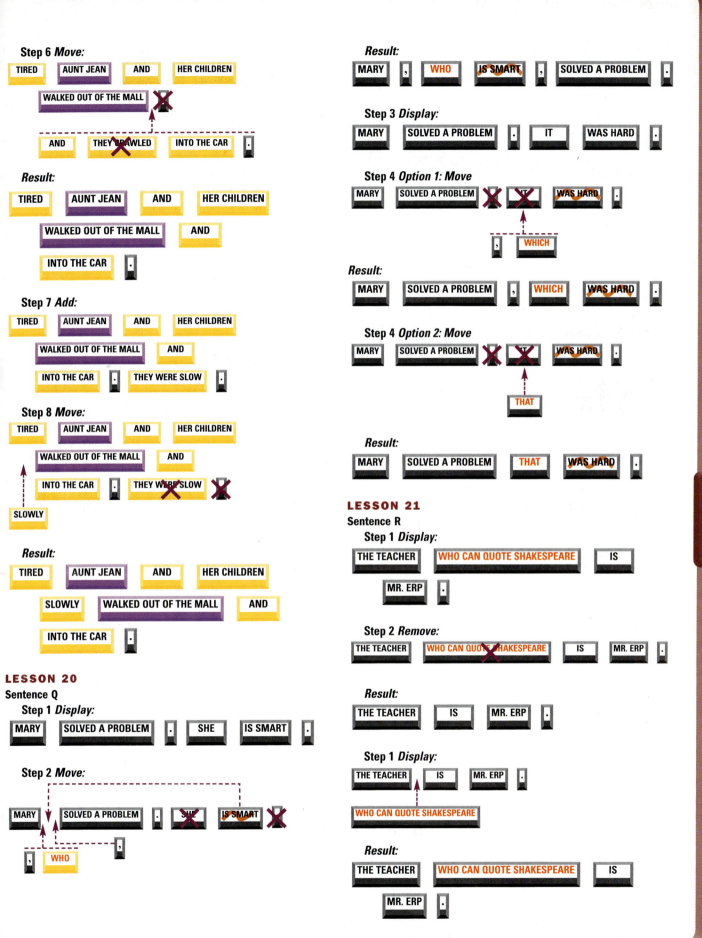

Step 6 *Move:*

TIRED AUNT JEAN AND HER CHILDREN

WALKED OUT OF THE MALL ✗

AND THEY CRAWLED INTO THE CAR .

Result:

TIRED AUNT JEAN AND HER CHILDREN

WALKED OUT OF THE MALL AND

INTO THE CAR .

Step 7 *Add:*

TIRED AUNT JEAN AND HER CHILDREN

WALKED OUT OF THE MALL AND

INTO THE CAR . THEY WERE SLOW .

Step 8 *Move:*

TIRED AUNT JEAN AND HER CHILDREN

WALKED OUT OF THE MALL AND

INTO THE CAR . THEY WERE SLOW ✗

SLOWLY

Result:

TIRED AUNT JEAN AND HER CHILDREN

SLOWLY WALKED OUT OF THE MALL AND

INTO THE CAR .

LESSON 20

Sentence Q

Step 1 *Display:*

MARY SOLVED A PROBLEM . SHE IS SMART .

Step 2 *Move:*

MARY SOLVED A PROBLEM . SHE IS SMART ✗

. WHO .

Result:

MARY , WHO IS SMART , SOLVED A PROBLEM .

Step 3 *Display:*

MARY SOLVED A PROBLEM . IT WAS HARD .

Step 4 *Option 1: Move*

MARY SOLVED A PROBLEM ✗ ✗ WAS HARD .

. WHICH

Result:

MARY SOLVED A PROBLEM , WHICH WAS HARD .

Step 4 *Option 2: Move*

MARY SOLVED A PROBLEM ✗ ✗ WAS HARD .

THAT

Result:

MARY SOLVED A PROBLEM THAT WAS HARD .

LESSON 21

Sentence R

Step 1 *Display:*

THE TEACHER WHO CAN QUOTE SHAKESPEARE IS

MR. ERP .

Step 2 *Remove:*

THE TEACHER WHO CAN QUOTE ✗ SHAKESPEARE IS MR. ERP .

Result:

THE TEACHER IS MR. ERP .

Step 1 *Display:*

THE TEACHER IS MR. ERP .

WHO CAN QUOTE SHAKESPEARE

Result:

THE TEACHER WHO CAN QUOTE SHAKESPEARE IS

MR. ERP .

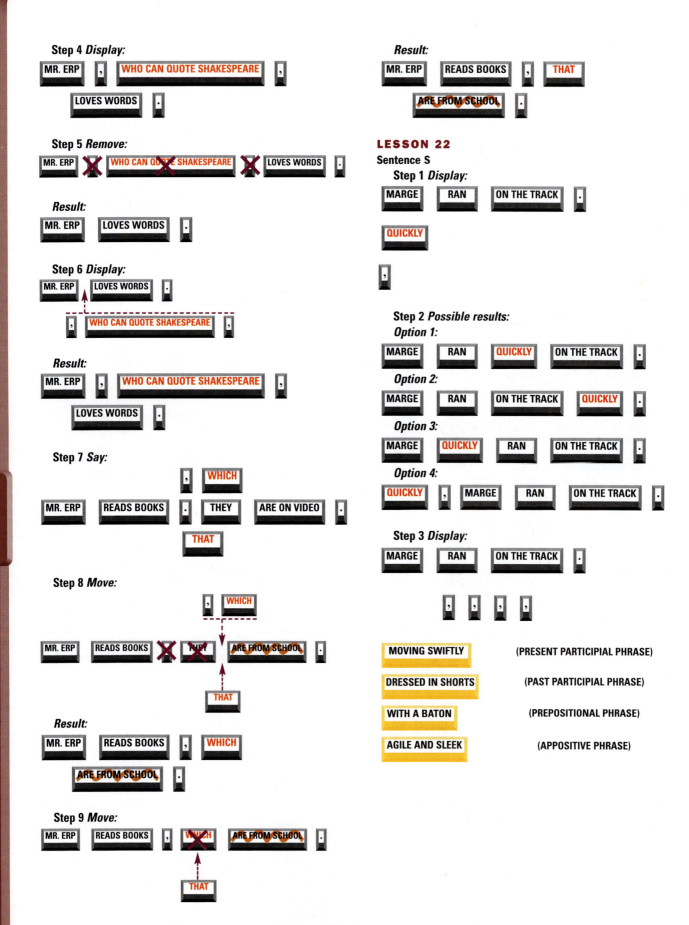

GRAMMAR TILES

Step 4 *Display:*

MR. ERP | , | WHO CAN QUOTE SHAKESPEARE | , | LOVES WORDS | .

Step 5 *Remove:*

MR. ERP ✗ WHO CAN QUOTE SHAKESPEARE ✗ LOVES WORDS | .

Result:

MR. ERP | LOVES WORDS | .

Step 6 *Display:*

MR. ERP | LOVES WORDS | .
, | WHO CAN QUOTE SHAKESPEARE | ,

Result:

MR. ERP | , | WHO CAN QUOTE SHAKESPEARE | ,
LOVES WORDS | .

Step 7 *Say:*

, | WHICH
MR. ERP | READS BOOKS | . | THEY | ARE ON VIDEO | .
THAT

Step 8 *Move:*

, | WHICH
MR. ERP | READS BOOKS | ✗ | THAT | ARE FROM SCHOOL | .
THAT

Result:

MR. ERP | READS BOOKS | , | WHICH
ARE FROM SCHOOL | .

Step 9 *Move:*

MR. ERP | READS BOOKS | , | WHICH✗ | ARE FROM SCHOOL | .
THAT

Result:

MR. ERP | READS BOOKS | , | THAT
ARE FROM SCHOOL | .

LESSON 22
Sentence S

Step 1 *Display:*

MARGE | RAN | ON THE TRACK | .
QUICKLY
,

Step 2 *Possible results:*

Option 1:

MARGE | RAN | QUICKLY | ON THE TRACK | .

Option 2:

MARGE | RAN | ON THE TRACK | QUICKLY | .

Option 3:

MARGE | QUICKLY | RAN | ON THE TRACK | .

Option 4:

QUICKLY | , | MARGE | RAN | ON THE TRACK | .

Step 3 *Display:*

MARGE | RAN | ON THE TRACK | .
, | , | , | ,

MOVING SWIFTLY — (PRESENT PARTICIPIAL PHRASE)

DRESSED IN SHORTS — (PAST PARTICIPIAL PHRASE)

WITH A BATON — (PREPOSITIONAL PHRASE)

AGILE AND SLEEK — (APPOSITIVE PHRASE)

Possible results:

`MOVING SWIFTLY` `,` `MARGE` `RAN` `ON THE TRACK` `.`

`MARGE` `RAN` `,` `MOVING SWIFTLY` `,` `ON THE TRACK` `.`

`DRESSED IN SHORTS` `,` `MARGE` `RAN` `ON THE TRACK` `.`

`DRESSED IN SHORTS` `,` `MARGE` `RAN` `ON THE TRACK` `WITH A BATON` `.`

`AGILE AND SLEEK` `,` `MARGE` `RAN` `ON THE TRACK` `.`

`AGILE AND SLEEK` `,` `MARGE` `RAN` `,` `MOVING SWIFTLY` `,` `ON THE TRACK` `.`

Diagramming Answer Key

Diagramming:

SENTENCE PARTS

D. MIXED REVIEW p. 279

1.

Jewel Cave | is \ gigantic

2.

It | is \ world
(an / unusual / underground)

3.

crystals | line | walls
(Shiny / calcite) (the)

4.

formations | fill | rooms
(Strange / colorful) (the / underground)

5.

temperature | is \ cool
(The / underground)

6.

Visitors | wear < shoes (sturdy) / jackets (light) [and]

7.

guides | give | tour
(Knowledgeable) (visitors) (the / a / lengthy)

8.

Tourists / guides [and] | see | crystals (shiny) / pools (dark) [and]

9.

visitors | can take | tour
(Brave) (a / candlelight)

10.

They | may encounter | bats
(many)

E. MIXED REVIEW, p. 283

1.

campers | planned | trip
(The) (a / canoe)
[and]
they | packed | duffels
(their)

2.

They | drove
(before) (for hours / three)
they | put | canoes
(in water / the) (their)

3.

they | were \ tired
(When) (very)
they | reached | destination
(their)

4.

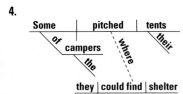

5.

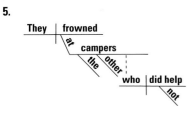

6.

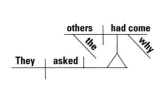

7.

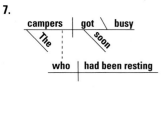

8.

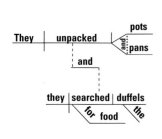

9.

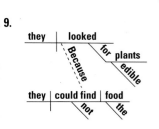

10.

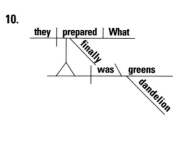

Acknowledgments

Barron's Educational Series: Excerpts from *B's and A's in 30 Days: Strategies for Better Grades in College* by Eric Jensen, M.A. Copyright © 1997 by Eric Jensen. Reprinted by permission of Barron's Educational Series, Inc.

Carol Publishing Group: Excerpt from *Dictionary of Word Origins: A History of the Words, Expressions, and Clichés We Use* by Jordan Almond. Copyright © 1985 by Book Sales, Inc. Reprinted by permission of Carol Publishing Group.

Guinness World Records: Excerpt from *The Guinness Book of Records 1999.* Copyright © 1999 by Guinness World Records Ltd. Reprinted by permission of Guinness World Records Ltd. Guinness® is a trade mark of Guinness World Records Ltd.

Houghton Mifflin Company: Excerpt from *The Dictionary of Cultural Literacy* by E. D. Hirsch, Jr., Joseph F. Kett, and James Trefil. Copyright © 1998 by Houghton Mifflin Company. Reprinted by permission of Houghton Mifflin Company. All rights reserved.

Hyperion: Excerpt from *Don't Sweat the Small Stuff . . . and It's All Small Stuff* by Dr. Richard Carlson. Copyright © 1997 by Richard Carlson, Ph.D. Reprinted by permission of Hyperion.

Penguin Books: Excerpts from *The Penguin Dictionary of Jokes, Wisecracks, Quips and Quotes,* compiled by Fred Metcalf. Copyright © 1993 by Fred Metcalf. Reprinted by permission of Penguin Books, Ltd.

Penguin Putnam: Excerpt from *Winnie-the-Pooh* by A. A. Milne. Copyright 1926 by E. P. Dutton, renewed © 1954 by A. A. Milne. Reprinted by permission of Penguin Putnam, Inc.

Prentice Hall: Excerpt from *Braude's Treasury of Wit and Humor* by Jacob M. Braude. Copyright © 1964 by Prentice-Hall, Inc. Reprinted by permission of Prentice Hall, Inc.

Reader's Digest Association: Anecdote contributed by Christine Nicolette Gonzalez to "Tales Out of School," *Reader's Digest,* May 1995. Copyright © 1995 by The Reader's Digest Association, Inc. Used by permission of Reader's Digest, Pleasantville, N.Y. (www.readersdigest.com).

Sterling Publishing Company: Excerpt from *Brain Bafflers* by Robert Steinwachs. Copyright © 1993 by Robert Steinwachs. Used by permission of Sterling Publishing Co., Inc., New York, N.Y.

Workman Publishing Company: Excerpts from *365 Brain Puzzlers: The Mensa 1999 Calendar* by Dr. Abbie F. Salny. Copyright © 1998 by Dr. Abbie F. Salny. / Excerpts from *365 Amazing Trivia Facts: 2000 Calendar* by Marsha Kranes. Copyright © 1999 by Workman Publishing Company, Inc. / Reprinted by permission of Workman Publishing Company, Inc.